Perspectives in Recreational Therapy

PERSPECTIVES IN RECREATIONAL THERAPY

ISSUES OF A DYNAMIC PROFESSION

Frank Brasile
Thomas K. Skalko
joan burlingame

Published by

Idyll Arbor, Inc.

PO Box 720, Ravensdale, WA 98051 (425) 432-3231

A portion of the revenue from *Perspectives in Recreational Therapy* will be donated to the American Therapeutic Recreation Foundation.

 Idyll Arbor, Inc. supports wise use of our natural resources. This book is printed on recycled paper.

Printed in the United States of America.

ISBN 1-882883-26-8

Contents

Section I

Introduction

Chapter 1

Overview

joan burlingame

Recreational therapy is a profession of practice — and our practice includes more than the hands-on application of knowledge and skills. It is unrealistic, and even ignorant, to assume that we can help our patients toward a more holistic lifestyle without also understanding the environment in which we practice. This book, then, is meant to be a tool to help the therapist fit into the professional environment of his/her choice. To be able to fit into this environment, the professional must be able to understand the issues and the trends along with the implications of both. To this end the editors and authors of this book hope to stimulate discussion and thoughtful dialog to allow readers to be critical thinkers.

Recreational therapy is also an exciting profession, one well placed to meet the challenges of the changing health care environment while remaining true to our primary purpose: to facilitate the movement of our patients toward more normalized experiences of their choice. While the therapist (and recreational therapy student) reads, learns and critically considers the information in this book, we hope that s/he will always hold dear to the belief that the patient is an individual first, with inherent rights and value. For recreational therapy, maybe more than any other health care profession, holds a unique position within a treatment environment. It is usually the recreational therapist who translates the skills and knowledge which the patient has learned during treatment into applications of living, as defined by what the patient chooses. The recreational therapist uses activity (both within and outside the context of "recreation") and the attitudes of leisure (perceived choice) to bring about change.

This book is divided into seven sections, organized in a micro to macro progression. Starting out, the authors address concepts and issues which are at the heart of our field including the conceptual development of the field, managing the quality of our practice to meet standards and the ethics which guide our practice by defining the things we value. Enlarging the circle of issues, the authors address issues of service delivery, of where we work and who we serve. From there we go to issues of education, training and credentialing, outside agencies and the role of information technologies. We end by exploring the impacts of global trends and look toward the future of our field.

A few comments are due about the nomenclature used within this book. Three words used throughout this book have multiple meanings within the field: "recreational therapy," "therapeutic recreation" and "patient." To help facilitate discussion of the topics, the editors, for the purpose of consistency of meaning, have chosen to use specific definitions of these terms. This was done to encourage the material to be used as a springboard for intense and critical discussions without having unclear meaning impeding the process. The editors have employed the following definitions for "recreational therapy" and "therapeutic recreation" throughout the book (with the exception of the chapter on Health Care Credentialing and NCTRC Certification, in which the author's own terms were used):

Recreational Therapy: The use of purposeful, prescribed activity to facilitate change in a patient's status using specific skills and techniques learned during the course of professional preparation and guided by the patient's own choices and definition of what s/he perceives as desired and normalized existence. This definition does not limit the location of the delivery of these services but does imply that an assessment of need, an agreement with the patient on desired directions and a commitment to adhering to standards of health care delivery are inherent in this work. "Recreational therapy," historically, is the original term used to describe this field of study, appearing during World War I when specialized training was developed, separate from the fields of recreation, social service and nursing (Menninger Clinic, 1995; James, 1998). The editors are assuming that recreational therapy services are provided by individuals who are certified by the National Council for Therapeutic Recreation Certification (NCTRC) at the Certified Therapeutic Recreation Specialist (CTRS) level or hold the equivalent professional credential at the state level.

Therapeutic Recreation: Historically this term is a newer term than "recreational therapy" and appeared during the 1940's as a compromise between two fields of practice which may or may not be two separate fields of professional study (Cox & Dobbins, 1970). This term was coined as an effort to try to bring together into one national organization three organizations whose members worked with individuals with illness and disability (James, 1998). Part of the group used the term "recreational therapy" as defined above and part of the group espoused the provision of recreation activities for special populations (Romney, 1945). The editors are choosing to use the term "therapeutic recreation" in two situations: (1) To signify a situation in which either a professionally trained CTRS *or* an individual trained to provide recreation activities for individuals with disabilities is providing a service. This service does not necessarily require an assessment of needs or adherence to health care standards but does require attention to the individual's preferences. (2) The editors use the term "therapeutic recreation" when discussing a historical event in which the term was used.

Patient: The term used to identify the individual receiving the services provided by a recreational therapist. Depending on the location where the services are being received, the individual may be referred to using a variety of terms, including client, patient or resident (burlingame & Skalko, 1997). With the increased emphasis on continuity of care it is becoming even harder to decide which term to use. In this book we have tried to use the term appropriate for the setting. In some places the terms "consumer" and "customer" are used to remind the reader that recreational therapists are providing a service.

We hope that the content of this book helps new therapists become critical thinkers as well as a skilled technicians. Take what we give you, digest it, and then act using your best ability to bring about change. For it is the actions of each and every one of you which will determine where our field goes in the future.

> Few will have the greatness to bend history itself; but each of us can work to change a small portion of events, and in the total of all those acts will be written the history of this generation — Robert F. Kennedy. (1966, p. 12430)

References

Cox, C. L. & Dobbins, V. (1970). Before the merger. *Therapeutic Recreation Journal, 4*(1), 3-8.

James, A. (1998). The conceptual development of recreational therapy. In F. Brasile, T. Skalko & j. burlingame (Eds.) *Perspectives in recreational therapy: Issues of a dynamic profession.* Ravensdale, WA: Idyll Arbor, Inc.

Kennedy, R. (1966, June 6). "Day of Affirmation" address delivered at the University of Capetown, South Africa, June 6, 1966. *Congressional Record, 112*, 12430.

Menninger Clinic. (1995). *A national resource.* Topeka, KS: Menninger Clinic.

Romney, G. O. (1945). *Off the job living.* Washington, DC: McGrath Publishing Co. & National Recreation and Park Association.

Chapter 2

The Conceptual Development of Recreational Therapy

Ann James

Tracing the development of recreational therapy from idea to idea leads one on a journey first traversed by men and women who shared a common conviction that experiences yielding perceptions of peacefulness, well-being, mastery, joy, discovery, concentration, belonging, support and delight had positive impacts on the physical and mental health of human beings and aided their recovery from illness or injury. They found that experiences could be constructed to teach skills enabling people to live more effectively, independently and happily. These concepts and the practices to enact them were developed over a long and crooked path with segments of backtracking. This chapter traces the development of recreational therapy from 1855 to the present.

Emerson declared that all history is biography and so it appears with much of the history of recreational therapy. It is largely a story about people, people whose observations brought them to acknowledge the great impact that certain experiences imbue on the learning, functioning and health of individuals. Further, these people were able to interact with the circumstances of their places and times to advance the provision of these experiences to increasing numbers of beneficiaries.

Origins

Ancient teachings are replete with assertions on the benefits of some recreation experiences: "A merry heart doeth good like a medicine (Proverbs);" "You can learn more about a man in an hour of play than in a lifetime of conversation (Plato)." But it is not until the 19th century that we see these principles applied in health care settings in a purposeful, organized manner. And the initial effort focused around one person, Florence Nightingale.

Nightingale descended upon the British military hospital scene in eastern Europe, in the midst of the Crimean War, to organize and reform the profession of nursing. But once she had largely accomplished this task, she expanded her vision to changing medicine's entire approach to treating patients. Nightingale arrived in the area to find a system in which the physician's administration of drugs or performance of surgery was largely the beginning and end of the treatment process. Following surgery the patient was deposited onto his cot in a drab ward and left to lie there, receiving minimal custodial care, until the treatment succeeded or failed (Woodham-Smith, 1951).

Nightingale protested to all who would listen that the dreary conditions of the hospital were counterproductive and that the monotony endured by the patients adversely affected their recoveries.

People say the effect [of a pleasing environment] is only on the mind. It is no such thing. The effect is on the body too. Little as we know about the way in which we are affected by form, by color and light, we do know this, that they have an actual physical effect. (Nightingale, 1859, p. 34)

Nightingale's observations also led her to conclude:

It is a matter of painful wonder to the sick themselves how much painful ideas predominate over pleasurable ones in their impressions; they reason with themselves; they think themselves ungrateful; it is all of no use. The fact is that these painful impressions are far better dismissed by a real laugh, if you can excite one by books or conversation, than by any direct reasoning; or if the patient is too weak to laugh, some impression from nature is what he wants. (Nightingale, 1859, p. 34)

Nightingale wrote of the benefits that accrued to patients from caring for pets, listening to and performing music, doing needle-work and writing. She chastised health care administrators to be more inclusive in their provision of services to patients: "Bearing in mind that you have all these varieties of employment which the sick cannot have, bear also in mind to obtain them all the varieties which they can enjoy" (Nightingale, 1859, p. 36).

In September of 1855 many of Nightingale's theories were manifested in the establishment of the Inkerman Cafe. This wooden hut, situated at the center of the hospital complex, served as a large recreation room and coffee house. Nightingale wrote that "Football and other games for the healthy, dominoes and chess for the sick, were in great request." She helped patients to organize sing-ing classes and urged friends in England to send costumes and materials for the theatrical group that the patients formed. She also received books, games, music scores, maps and "magic lanterns" to stock "the Inkerman" (Andrews, 1929, p. 157).

One of the main reasons that Nightingale established the recreation center was to give some competition to the bars that surrounded the hospital and the military installation. With nothing else to do, the common practice for patients receiving evening passes was to head straight for the bars. A large portion of the convalescents were carried back to the hospital drunk. "Dead drunk," com-plained Nightingale, "for they die of it and the officers look on with composure. Give them books and games and amusements and they will leave off drinking" (Woodham-Smith, 1951, p. 166).

Morally Based Recreation

In the United States, the physician Benjamin Rush had voiced convictions similar to Nightingale's and had made opportunities and equipment for recrea-tion available to convalescing patients (Morton, 1973). A few caregivers in mental health facilities, mostly Quakers, had imported the principles of "Moral Treatment" developed in France by Phillipe Pinel. Pinel had protested the harsh conditions and brutal treatments that were too often the fate of persons receiving care for psychiatric disorders. He had replaced dungeon-like warehouses with more pleasant, home-like environments that had included ample gardens. He had trained his staff to model healthy behaviors and to treat clients with patience and kindness, "fettering strong madness with a silken thread" (Guthrie, 1946, p. 233).

Unfortunately the Civil War and booming immigration of the 1800's made for large, crowded, understaffed hospitals. Widespread fear and ignorance re-garding the nature of illness, particularly mental illness, made humane treat-ments that included opportunities for recreation the rare exception to the rule.

During the latter part of the 19th and beginning of the 20th centuries, the in-dustrial revolution peaked, leaving America transformed from a land of self-sufficient farmers to one of interdependent factory workers. The urban envi-ronment during the last quarter of the 19th century had degenerated in several aspects. Factory jobs left many human needs unmet and, besides the ever-present bars, the cities offered few opportunities for involvement in meaningful activity. Immigration soared and outpaced the availability of housing and sup-portive resources to assimilate foreigners into a new culture. The industrial revolution stabilized allowing reformers to succeed with legislative efforts re-stricting the employment of children in manufacturing. Factories spewed surplus children into the growing crowd milling in the city streets. The stress from battling to succeed or to just survive in this environment was considerable. Rampant alcoholism further impaired the social health of the cities and the occupancy rates of "insane asylums" and prisons soared. Voices for reform began to emerge. The accepted thesis that heredity and nature were the primary determinants of a person's fate was being replaced by theories that favored the roles of environment and nurturance in developing human capacity. Municipal reformers of the 1890's felt that society could be improved if only people were given a favorable environment in which to develop.

By 1894 there were eighty citizen-led municipal reform groups, sixty of them founded after 1890. Recreation was seized upon by many of these groups as one of the vehicles through which reform could be achieved. The profession of social work emerged as paid workers replaced volunteers in organizing specific services to ameliorate the ills of urban society. By 1903 the New York School of Philanthropy offered a full year's course in social work. Social workers addressed education, housing, child welfare, health and crime. They expanded upon Nightingale's thesis that recreation experiences could be drawn upon to improve the human condition (Knapp & Hartsoe, 1979).

Leaders in social work, education and municipal reform were experimenting with the uses of recreation activities to transform the raw material of youth into vigorous adults who embraced high moral and democratic values and who were eager and able to uplift their fellow citizens as well as themselves. These interests were drawn together and for several years worked synergistically to propel play and recreation from its disdained status as a frivolous pastime to a tool for the social transformation of America. This period of joint activity to build the "play and recreation movement" could largely be attributed to the work of Joseph Lee. Lee was born to a wealthy Boston family and took to heart the admonishment of *noblesse oblige*, that with fortune comes responsibility. After completing law school at Harvard he set upon a lifetime of philanthropy. Lee viewed the problems of the time as the results of limited access to an environment in which people could develop into happy, responsible citizens. He saw overpopulation as one of the primary forces that limited people's access to the resources of this environment and thus he directed a portion of his efforts to the support of birth control, sterilization and restricted immigration. He devoted the rest of his attention to expanding people's access to the experiences that would enable them to develop their potentials as human beings. He saw recreation activities as major structures for delivering these nurturing, educational and character-building experiences (Knapp & Hartsoe, 1979).

Borrowing from a practice initiated in the crowded housing areas in Berlin, Germany, a Boston charity established a series of sand-pile play areas among the Boston tenements. In the early 1890's, Joseph Lee became very interested in this development, so much so, that he established his own playground for research and demonstration purposes. Lee hired and trained leaders to supervise his playground and for several years he studiously observed and recorded the outcomes of this project. Lee's observations along with his study of the sociological, educational and philosophical ideas of the period led him to acknowledge Aristotle's conclusion that play was indeed the "architect of man" (Rainwater, 1922).

Lee's speeches and articles in support of the playground movement spread his thesis across the continent. When the American Civic Association sponsored a "model street" for the 1904 World's Fair in St. Louis, Lee designed and financed the street's model playground. Lee became the director of the Association's Department of Public Recreation and drew together an advisory committee of leaders in recreation from the fields of social work and education (Knapp & Hartsoe, 1979).

Luther Gulick, an educator on that team, earned an MD degree at New York University before taking a faculty position at the YMCA college at Springfield, Massachusetts. There he transformed the physical education program from one of calisthenics to one based on games and sports. His creed on the interdependence of a healthy body, mind and spirit formed the familiar triangular logo of the YMCA. Gulick also taught that recreation activities had great formative power but he stressed that this power could have either positive or negative effects on the development of character. Skilled leadership was needed, he insisted, to insure that participants were enriched by the experience rather than degraded by it. (Knapp & Hartsoe, 1979).

Gulick proposed that a national playground association be formed to advance and unite the various recreation efforts emerging across the country. Several other leaders added their organizational skills to Gulick's vision and energy and in April of 1906 the founding meeting of the Playground Association of America (PAA) was held in Washington, DC. The eighteen educators, social workers and settlement workers present, eight of whom were women, were feted to a reception at the White House by Theodore Roosevelt and then set about the business of establishing this new association. Luther Gulick was elected president and Jane Addams and Joseph Lee, both absent, were elected vice-presidents. Gulick led the Association until 1910 and then passed the presidency to Lee who continued in that capacity for the next 30 years (Knapp & Hartsoe, 1979).

In April 1907 the group published its first issue of *Playgrounds* (later to become *Recreation*) and in June, held its second annual meeting in Chicago. The 200 delegates from 30 cities heard presentations on the relation of play to democracy, health, citizenship and social morality. The PAA established about a dozen national study and advisory committees, one of which focused on "play in institutions" (Knapp & Hartsoe, 1979). These social reformers not only further developed the ideas of Nightingale on the potentials of recreation experiences but added a new dimension that emphasized the need for trained recreation specialists to ensure that those potentials were achieved.

One of the most zestful participants in the playground and recreation movement was a diminutive social worker named Neva Leona Boyd. "She was a multifaceted, charismatic personality who swept you into her confidence, and in spite of being a short woman, could literally swing you into a mean turn during a folk dance pattern" (Katz, 1975, p. 1). Neva Boyd was born in Iowa in 1876 to parents whom she characterized as having independent and pioneering spirit. Having some of that spirit herself, she left her small town after graduating from high school and enrolled in the Chicago Kindergarten Institute in pursuit of one of the few career areas open to women. In Chicago, Boyd discovered Hull House, the famous settlement house established by Jane Addams that became the model for community centers providing social services to inner city immigrant populations. Prior to that time recreation activities for youth were recognized chiefly as stimuli to proper physical growth and development. In working with the youth at Hull House, Boyd became determined that society had missed many of the contributions that recreation experiences could give to the social and behavioral development of youth. Given an insightful leader with the skills to play an activity, releasing its opportunities for learning effective behaviors, Boyd felt certain that recreation could be an important tool in social education (Simon, 1971).

After finishing her study in Chicago, Boyd accepted a position with a kindergarten program at a settlement house in Buffalo. She returned to the Midwest in 1908 and enrolled in the University of Chicago. She again volunteered her services at Hull House and her work attracted the attention of the Chicago Women's Club, a local supporter of the playground movement. The club persuaded the park commission to employ Boyd to direct "informal social activities" at Eckhart Park. "She was officially titled 'social worker' and her duties included organization of social clubs, direction of dramatics, supervision of social dances and play activities quite different from those usually directed by physical education teachers. The experiment was so successful that the commission voted to hire such a person for each playground and to adopt a policy of developing social work in the parks" (Simon, 1971, p. 10).

"The utilization of games and play as media for producing change in the participants was always the central core of her philosophy" (Simon, 1971, p. 13). To help others successfully guide this process, Boyd developed her own training program. In 1911 she established the Chicago Training School for Playground Workers. Over time the curriculum evolved with Boyd's developing theory and practice to become a course of study in the emerging field of group work. Defined by Simon (1971, p. 13) as "the deliberate and purposeful use of activities in work with groups," group work's kinship to recreational therapy is easily recognizable. Most of Boyd's students had completed at least two years of college before enrolling in this one-year program. Besides offering extensive technical training in group games, gymnastics, dancing and dramatic arts, the school provided course work in the theory and psychology of play, social behavior problems and "preventive and remedial social efforts" (Simon, 1971, p. 14). The school was located at Hull House and the settlement house was a ready lab for class demonstrations and served as one of the sites for the field work that was required of all students (Simon, 1971).

In 1927 Boyd accepted an invitation from Northwestern University to place her program under its auspices. In a letter to former students, Boyd voiced mixed sentiments, which elicit empathy from recreational therapy educators today: "I am sure you all feel as I do, that we shall miss the freedom we enjoyed at Hull House...but let us dry our tears with the comforting picture of a monthly check...I hope you all realize that my latch string will still respond to your gentle pull for always and always, Neva L. Boyd" (Simon, 1971, p. 15).

Unfortunately, Boyd devoted little time to writing, but she responded to voluminous requests for lectures throughout Europe and the US and many of these manuscripts remain (Simon, 1971). Paul Simon of the University of Chicago cited Boyd's work as contributing to the development of game theory, problem solving methodology, play theory and to our knowledge of small group development, leadership principles, early childhood development, socialization patterns, psychodrama and administration. "She found application for these not only in settlement houses, community centers and recreational programs, but also in hospitals, institutions, community organizations, and rural settings" (p. 4).

World War I

In 1917 the United States entered World War I and Boyd and others soon had many more clients for their services. Military hospitals sprang up all over the country as the wounded returned from Europe. In the largest single project yet undertaken to aid the country's servicemen, the American Red Cross spent over a million dollars in donations to build 52 recreation centers, called convalescent houses, at military hospitals.

All of the centers were built from the same plans and completed in 1918. The Red Cross director at Quantico, VA described the facility as follows:

> The center of the building is entirely taken up by a general lounging and reading room. Great windows all around...flood the room with light and sunshine, and in spite of its size the room has an atmosphere of cheer and restfulness and even coziness. Immense fireplaces occupy the center of each side of the room, with big easy chairs all about. Four sides have well-stocked bookshelves. A piano and a phonograph

supply music, and already the boys have formed an orchestra. At one end of the Convalescent House is a stage...and at the other, a gallery housing a moving-picture machine. (Convalescent House at Quantico, 1919, p. 3)

The Red Cross hired the chairman of the Department of Recreational Leadership, Teachers College, Columbia University to hire and supervise several hundred "highly specialized and technically trained recreation and entertainment personnel" (Convalescent House at Quantico, 1919, p. 6). The Red Cross also hired a corps of recreation consultants to visit and advise the hospital staff. The philosophy of the program was reflected in this description:

Actual participation is necessary if the patient is to encourage his own initiative and develop the spirit of cooperation. Various games and contests have been devised to meet the limited physical possibilities of the disabled patients...Such play does wonders to restore self-confidence and banish self-consciousness. (Convalescent House at Quantico, 1919, p. 3)

The programs took different approaches at acute and chronic care hospitals. At the former "the program is not prepared with an idea of attempting even preliminary preparation of the patients for the vocational or semi-educational activities incident to the reconstruction work" (Manual of Red Cross Camp Service, 1919, p. 46).

The program drew from activity areas consistent with those used by group work services at the time. Among those were music, dance, gardening, community trips, drama, games and social recreation. The military was assigned supervision of physical education. Following the precedents established by the terms social work and group work, the Red Cross titled this new service: Hospital Recreation Work (Program of Recreation, 1919).

In 1919 the Red Cross newsletter informed hospital recreation workers of a new resource to help them in their planning: *Hospital and Bedside Games* by Neva L. Boyd. In the foreword to the booklet, Boyd said that she compiled the activities at the request of workers in civilian as well as military hospitals. "The work that they have done has convinced them that such games have curative value." Boyd quoted a hospital officer who reported, "Sluggish wounds that failed to heal after months of ordinary treatment are now showing remarkable improvement wholly due to increased circulation through pleasurable exercise and to quickened interest in the normal things of life." Boyd further supported these efforts by citing the Swiss scholar, Karl Groos, whose "experiments show that pleasure is accompanied by strengthened muscular activity, quickened pulse-beat and respiration, increased peripheral circulation and a heightened excitation of the sensor and motor centers of the cerebrum." Boyd also underlined the importance of the role of the recreation worker: "Any attempt at classification of these games relative to treatment has been studiously avoided because the use of games should be under the supervision of the person responsible for the treatment of the case" (1919, p. 3).

Between the World Wars

The war ended in November 1918 and by November of the following year the Red Cross staffed only 26 of the original 52 hospitals. The flurry of exploratory activity into the possible applications of experiential therapy in physical rehabilitation decreased as more workers were withdrawn from hospitals with dwindling patient loads. The Veterans' Bureau (later to become the Veterans' Administration and then Department of Veterans Affairs) assumed control of many of the former military hospitals in 1921. At the request of the government, the Red Cross continued services in those hospitals until 1931 when the Veterans' Bureau hired 49 Red Cross hospital recreation workers and established oversight of their own program (Becker, 1950).

Although development slowed in one area of the profession, interest in using recreational therapy with other populations was growing. In 1918 a two-year experiment to explore the efficacy of recreational therapy (the term used by Boyd) was undertaken by the state mental health system of Illinois. According to Boyd, an observer of the project reported that "the selection of recreational activities was placed not on entertainment,...nor on mere physical exercise, but rather on group activity in the form of games" (Boyd, 1935, p. 56). Dancing, marching and gymnastics were included for patients unable to function at the level required of game structures and strategies.

A report of the project noted that, "some of the results of this early experiment were so obvious that many of the medical doctors who had offered opposition in the beginning became ardent supporters of the work...A leading psychiatrist closely associated with the experiment said, when speaking before the managing officers of state institutions, that in his opinion neither medicine nor physiotherapy nor occupational therapy had anything to offer in the treatment of mental patients, but that effective treatment could be found in recreation" (Boyd, 1935, p. 56).

In 1919 Karl Menninger also referred to the contribution of "recreational therapy" in the treatment of persons with psychiatric disorders. In 1925 he joined his father, C.F., and his brother, William, to found the Menninger Clinic in Topeka, Kansas. Modeled on the Mayo Clinic, which united many specialists in one practice to collaborate in their fight against disease, the Menninger Clinic gathered a group of mental health professionals to create the same team effort to assist persons with mental health problems (Menninger Clinic, 1995).

The Menninger brothers experimented with various uses of recreational therapy and became enthusiastic advocates of its inclusion in the treatment of persons with mental health disorders. William Menninger believed that activities could be structured to simulate most of the demands and conditions that patients would confront in their daily living. The pliability of recreation activities allowed skilled therapists to increase the intensity of a situation or reduce threatening aspects. Social demands, task demands and other elements could be controlled, thereby creating a laboratory for assessing and improving patient functioning (Menninger & McColl, 1937).

Both Karl and William Menninger became respected authors in the area of mental health. Not only did they advocate the inclusion of recreational therapy (their term) in mental health treatment programs, but they also disseminated their firm beliefs in the significant contributions that active leisure lifestyles made to everyone's mental health. One of the issues of the Menninger Clinic's newsletter was devoted solely to staff analyses, including those by the Menninger brothers, of their hobbies and leisure preferences (Menninger, 1942).

Recreation had also been incorporated into the education of persons with developmental disabilities during the reform zeal of the latter 1800's. Unfortunately, unrealistic expectations of "cures" resulted in the termination of many of these programs. In the 1920's, more realistic efforts were reestablished. Bertha Schlotter recorded many of the efforts instituted by recreational therapy staff at the Lincoln (IL) State School and Colony for the Mentally Retarded. Schlotter was among the pioneers in this area who studiously tried to find the best contribution that recreational therapy could make to the lives of people with mental retardation. In 1929 she documented the results of a three-year project to uncover the potentials of recreational therapy with clients of Illinois' state institutions. Sponsors of the study concluded "that by selecting those activities which hold the greatest possibilities for growth and directing them in such a way that the potentialities of the individual, however limited, are called into action, a fuller utilization of the individual's powers may be accomplished and a more harmonious, constructive social life achieved" (Boyd, 1935, p. 59).

Recreational therapy was also introduced in correctional settings. Boyd (1935) reported on a program begun in 1932 at a training school for girls. Under the guidance of group workers, the students not only selected their recreation activities but set group objectives and standards of behavior. "As group activity developed, the girls began to have more self-confidence and to show more self-control. Their feeling of group responsibility was evidenced in their desire to improve the personal appearance of the whole group" (p. 58).

While recreational therapy was developing in a variety of settings, the public recreation movement in the US had changed considerably since its inception in 1906. The triad of professions (education, social work and recreation) that had envisioned community and school-sponsored, small group recreation opportunities under the direction of leaders trained in youth development and group dynamics, as well as in recreation leadership, had pulled apart, and with it the vision. The public recreation movement soon changed its focus from the leadership level to the management level, from guiding developmental experiences to providing systems that offered facilities and opportunities for recreation. Leaders, volunteers where possible, were selected for their knowledge of activity skills, not of conflict-resolution skills. Most public youth programs lost the diversity of the playground movement and became team sports programs (Knapp & Hartsoe, 1979).

In 1929 a Dutch historian diverged from his usual discourse on medieval Europe to publish his thoughts on leisure. In so doing, Johan Huizinga carved a fond niche in the hearts of current and future recreation managers. Huizinga (1944) defined play as voluntary activity characterized by freedom. Boyd agreed with this view and found in Huizinga's treatise confirmation of her previous assertions that play was a universal form of behavior indulged in for its own satisfaction (Simon, 1971). The public recreation movement, however, found in Huizinga's pronouncements liberation from the need to benefit their consumers in any way other than in the provision of the recreation experience. Huizinga's assertion that play was an end unto itself and was not required to produce other benefits to justify its existence was seized upon by leaders of the recreation movement to lend theoretical credence to the direction that public recreation had set upon long before the publication of Huizinga's treatise.

With a few exceptions, as in Milwaukee where in-depth city-school recreation programs were developed, municipal recreation and school programs went their separate ways (Knapp & Hartsoe, 1979). As the social work profession grew, it pulled further away from the changing mission of public recreation. As group work methodology developed, the area became recognized as a part of social work. In 1935 the National Conference of Social Work established a section on social group work. To the frustration of many group workers, however, the medium never attained parity with counseling skills in the social work profession. Some attributed this to the influence of Freudian psychology that had swept the country by the 1920's and firmly set treatment on an individual basis and in a talking mode (Simon, 1971). It would be many decades before mainstream psychology would "discover" the effectiveness of working in groups or the potentials of action therapies. As group work grew closer to social work, it grew further from its recreation roots. And, not withstanding the work of Neva Boyd and her students, the field largely targeted its services to "normal" populations (Simon, 1971).

World War II

When the US became involved in World War II, the Red Cross needed a great number of hospital recreation workers in a hurry. Recruits, women with college degrees in any area of study, were given four weeks of training in recreation leadership and three more weeks of orientation to working with patients in military hospitals. At their assigned hospitals they received additional help from a contingent of regional consultants, most of whom had degrees in group work. By 1945, the number of hospital recreation workers reached 1,808. Although the training program was a heroic effort to compensate for the lack of education programs available in recreational therapy, the knowledge imparted through it was minuscule in comparison to what was learned on the job throughout the war years. Never before had so many hospital recreation workers extended services to so many patients. New adaptations of equipment and activities were developed for patients with physical disabilities. Special techniques and programs were devised to serve patients in various diagnostic groups. For the first time, many physicians and psychologists were exposed to the applications of recreation in the treatment process (James, 1979).

Not among those initiates was Col. William Menninger who was appointed Consultant to the Neuropsychiatric Division of the Medical Corps. Throughout World War II he promoted the expansion of recreational therapy services in mental health treatment units. Menninger prepared a technical bulletin on the "Treatment Program for Psychiatric Patients in Station and General Hospitals" in which he stated that recreation was a very definite part of treatment. He felt that recreation services should be broad, varied and "definitely prescribed by the doctor" (Schuyler, 1944, p. 1).

Although the Red Cross provided extensive pre-service and in-service training, it never considered these programs to be a substitute for professional education. Wanting to establish a continuing education scholarship program for hospital recreation workers but not knowing where to send them, the Red Cross called for a curriculum conference in 1945. The organization invited the presidents of the American Recreation Society and the American Association of Group Workers and "educators and recognized leaders in the field of recreation" (Scholarship program, 1947, p. 40). After three days of deliberations the conferees emerged from the meeting with the first proposed graduate curriculum in the area of recreational therapy. Five universities, all meeting the stipulation of having medical and psychiatric social work programs, agreed to provide 21 Red Cross employees with the elements of the designated curriculum through their majors in group work. Unfortunately, Red Cross revenues plummeted before the students could begin their second year of study and the program was discontinued (Summers, 1962).

As the war ended and physicians returned to civilian practice, the demand for recreational therapy programs grew across the country. As they had since the beginning of the century, recreational therapists continued their efforts to increase their effectiveness in drawing growth and health enhancing experiences from recreation activities. Up until this time, this quest had proceeded unchallenged. But the compass arrow that had held so steady up until now was about to vacillate.

Recreation as Freedom of Choice

Anticipating the end of World War II and subsequent expansion of public recreation services in the United States, G. Ott Romney, one of the national leaders in the recreation movement, put forth a rationale to undergird and encourage this postwar development. In his book, *Off the Job Living*, co-published in 1945 by the American Recreation Association, Romney developed a position that sought to (1) place the provision of leisure services under the auspices of the recreation profession, (2) circumscribe the recreator's responsibilities to the provision of recreation opportunities and facilities and (3) make the receipt of these services an individual right and a public obligation.

To expand the market, Romney needed to democratize leisure, to erase the earlier notion that leisure was the realm of a privileged, wealthy few. Addressing a population that had worked hard and long throughout the war years, Romney managed this transformation the old-fashioned way, he told Americans that they had earned it: "Leisure is the time-off-the-job. It is earned choosing time. It belongs to all" (1945, p. 5).

> If the individual's own choosing-time, rich in self-respect because he has earned it in honorable, useful work, his time to feel life's warm breath on his heart and to call his soul his own — if this, his leisure, is barren because society has failed to show him how to use it, and provide him opportunity, democracy is a promise not entirely fulfilled. Man must work at democracy to make it live and democracy, in turn, must help man live — and live fully. (Romney, 1945, p. 10)

To reserve the provision of recreation services to its rightful providers, Romney had to denigrate former allies:

> Time was when recreation as a social concern was led by the hand of her dignified elders, Character-building, Physical Education, Delinquency Prevention, Citizenship Education and their ilk, into the living room of social welfare...Now she should be easily distinguished from physical education, occupational therapy, regimented character-

building services, and group work...All of which intends to say that
recreation is an end unto itself...It does not hide behind the skirts of
therapy nor find only group work reflected in its mirror. (Romney,
1945, p. 35)

To justify his opposition to the therapeutic use of recreation activities,
Romney coupled recreation and free choice, and refused to combine the terms
recreation and therapy. "If the patient is required for curative purposes to weave
a basket at a scheduled hour, whether he likes it or not, he is receiving occupational therapy. If he may exercise freedom of choice,...he is indulging in
recreation" (Romney, 1945, p. 42).

Few recreational therapists would argue with Romney's distinction between
group work (or recreational therapy) and recreation.

Group work is a method. Recreation is a function. Recreation is the
what; group work is sometimes its how. The fundamentals of the group
work method include voluntary participation, common interest,
purpose, skilled leadership, interaction of group members, program
development keyed to the ability and needs of the group and evaluation
in terms of group and individual growth. Group work is a democratic
process which provides needed group experiences for social
adjustment. The group work method is widely used in hospitals and
institutions for the physically handicapped and the socially ill.
(Romney, 1945, p. 49)

It is unfortunate that, in establishing the parameters of municipal recreation,
Romney felt it necessary to ridicule the role that activities served to enable other
professions to help people in need.

Surely it is not a prerequisite to a selection of recreation that the
individual catechize himself as to whether he has had his group work
vitamins for the week...Must the seeker of creative expression ask,
"Does this activity offer an adequate supply of character calories?" To
subject the emotionally under-nourished seeking balance, relaxation,
expression or adjustment to a lot of strictures, and a painfully conscious
self-analysis, is to squeeze out of recreation its very essence. (Romney,
1945, p. 51)

Romney was irritated by the existence of professions in which recreation
services formed only a portion of the discipline's efforts as they did in social
work (Romney, 1945). Professions that used recreation activity to help people
achieve treatment, educational or developmental goals posed a threat to the uni-

versal application of Romney's recreation-must-be-an-end-in-itself thesis. Not only did he criticize these professions but he challenged the capacity of recreation activity to alter behavior (Romney, 1945). Romney supported recreation programs in institutional settings as long as they were conducted for recreation purposes. Any incidental benefits that accrued were to be referred to as "by-products" (1945, p. 42).

By 1948 the Red Cross had eliminated more than four fifths of its hospital recreation positions. The reduction, due to a drastic drop in donations, far outstripped the postwar reduction in the military patient load. The skeleton staffs that remained could not possibly continue to provide the depth of service previously extended without greatly restricting the number of patients eligible to receive these services. The directors of the non-profit organization decided that the mission of the Red Cross would be better served by providing recreation to all military patients rather than by extending recreational therapy services to a vastly restricted number (James, 1979). Reversing the direction of a thirty-year heritage, Carolyn Nice, the national supervisor of the hospital recreation program wrote:

> The purpose of the recreation program in the hospital is the same as that of any recreation program in any setting, namely to provide opportunities for individuals to do the things of their choice, in their leisure time, for the satisfaction derived from the doing... Hospital recreation leaders are not therapists whose primary purpose is treatment, and they should not be asked to participate in providing treatment. (Nice, 1948, p. 642)

Philosophical Concerns

Affirming this decision, Red Cross recreation supervisors from the national and regional offices, turned away from group work and realigned with the recreation movement. In September of 1948, thirty-seven people in attendance at the annual conference of the American Recreation Society, established a committee to pursue the formation of an affiliation with the ARS. The committee was composed of six management level staff from the Red Cross and Veterans Administration (VA) and four people from private and public psychiatric hospitals (Committee at work, 1949). In October 1949, at the 31st National Recreation Congress in New Orleans, the Hospital Section became the first "special interest group" to form within the American Recreation Society (History, 1964).

Among the founding members of the Hospital Section of the ARS was Harold D. Meyer, chairman of the recreation curriculum at the University of North Carolina. As chairman of the education advisory committee, Meyer was instrumental in the development of hospital recreation curricula that began to appear in 1951 (History, 1964). An enthusiastic, animated speaker, Meyer championed the transfer of recreational therapy from group work to recreation and led his students in the often repeated exclamation, "I AM A REC-RE-A-TOR FIRST!"

Curricula diverged from the original plan-of-studies drawn in 1945, with its emphasis on content related to medicine and psychiatry, and came to more closely resemble the studies existing in the sponsoring departments of recreation or physical education. Some curricula were only one course and a fieldwork site away from being identical to their departments' majors in community recreation. Practitioner's complaints of being unprepared to deliver the knowledge and skills demanded of their positions were frequently dismissed with the response that students were being educated to make intelligent decisions and that "technical matters" could be mastered on the job. Students, and the recreational therapy profession as a whole, undoubtedly benefited from access to knowledge on leisure theory, philosophy and behavior. But individual and professional progress was also undoubtedly stalled by the hours spent in park planning classes instead of in treatment planning courses.

In the meantime, officers of the Hospital Section of ARS were at work developing the group's position statement on the purpose and nature of hospital recreation. As it became increasingly evident that the Hospital Section was going to declare its allegiance to the precepts of Ott Romney, dissenting recreational therapists began to pull away from the organization.

B. E. Phillips and several of his colleagues from the VA drew like-minded associates to the Recreation Division of the American Association for Health, Physical Education and Recreation and, in 1952, formed the Recreational Therapy section (Phillips, 1952b). Phillips described the VA program as providing for the leisure of hospitalized veterans but "its primary purpose is to assist physicians in their treatment of patients" (p. 2). Contrary to the dominant thesis of the Hospital Recreation Section, Phillips viewed recreational therapy as a "means toward patient recovery rather than as an end in itself. This concept dictates the selection of activities primarily on the basis of needs and capabilities, and secondarily on the basis of interests" (Phillips, 1952a, p. 29). In time, however, the Recreational Therapy section drew its membership from professionals associated with its parent group, recreation educators with ties to physical education, rather than from practitioners attracted by a particular philosophical position.

Charles Cottle, Director of Recreation and Education at Mississippi State Hospital, shared Phillip's position but perceived little relationship between the provision of recreational therapy in mental health treatment centers and physical education. In February of 1953, Cottle gathered 23 recreational therapists from 19 state mental health facilities and two state schools for persons with developmental disabilities and formed the National Association of Recreational Therapists (NART). Thus, in less than five years, the profession traversed from having no organizational affiliation to having three. Members from each group recognized the need for communication among the organizations to deal with matters of mutual interest. Within the year, representatives from each group formed the Council for the Advancement of Hospital Recreation. The Council was successful in establishing qualifying standards for hospital recreation personnel and the national registration program became the forerunner of today's certification program. By 1959 members of the Council examined the possibility of merging the three organizations. Several compromises were proposed, including the term therapeutic recreation, but the Council was not able to budge the groups from their disparate positions (Cox & Dobbins, 1970).

Throughout the fifties and into the sixties, few meetings of hospital recreators or of recreational therapists adjourned without one or more orations on the true nature of the art. Each school of thought trotted out physicians who championed the perspectives of its position.

In the hospital recreation corner was George S. Stevenson, medical director of the National Association for Mental Health. In 1951, Stevenson wrote that,

> recreation affects the individual deeply, somewhat akin to therapy, but is more positive than therapy. Recreation is pointed less toward the correction of a disorder than toward the elevation of the quality of living... The distinctive quality of recreation is its permissiveness. It can not be forced... Recreation may be therapeutic, but that is a byproduct. Its goal is not therapy and its therapeutic value is apt to be greatest when the person is least conscious of its therapeutic influences. (p. 1)

Stevenson did not perceive of hospital recreation as an altered process but only as recreation in a different setting.

Another psychiatrist, Paul Haun, held views very similar to Stevenson's:

> The very fact that [the hospital recreator's] work is not narrowly clinical, that it is fun, that it is spontaneous, is the quality that makes it important... He asks nothing of the patient but that he enjoy himself... Here is relief for the patient from the stare of clinical appraisal, from lips pursed over a thermometer reading, from laden glances and pregnant silences. (Haun, 1952, p. 7)

Haun's somewhat romanticized view of hospital recreation praised the creation of a hospital atmosphere that facilitated the treatment extended by physicians. Haun embraced the concept espoused by Alan Gregg, whom Haun called "the greatest physician of his generation," that the hospital was a temple of healing, not an institution devoted solely to the elimination of disease (Haun,

1965, p. 23). "A major improvement can be confidently expected in the ambiance of the institution where budgets permit the establishment of a recreation program" (Haun, 1969, p. 16).

Unfortunately, few hospital budgets today have major line items for "ambiance." Haun, however, became quite voluble in extolling the benefits of recreation while degrading the value of recreational therapy. He produced more than 20 speeches and articles on the subject, excerpts of which were reprinted by the National Therapeutic Recreation Society in "The Wisdom of Paul Haun" as recently as 1987 (Sylvester, 1987).

Haun expressed concern for recreation's lack of specificity as a treatment agent. He scoffed at suggestions that recreation could be prescribed.

A true prescription for recreation would have to be something like this:
Rx John Doe, Ward 18
32 quanta of moderate pleasure
Sig. 10:00 a.m. and 4:00 a.m. q.d. for one week.
Richard Doe, MD (Haun, 1965, p. 23)

Some have pointed out that Haun did not apply this test to his own work in psychotherapy which, like recreational therapy, is experientially based rather than chemically based.

But while some physicians ridiculed the efforts of recreational therapists, other physicians joined them in research activities to test their hypotheses. Cardiologist Joseph B. Wolffe was one such physician. In 1962 he reported one of the first scientific studies in the young field. Patients on one of his cardiac units received focused recreation activities each evening while patients on a second unit received none. At the conclusion of the study, it was found that members of the treatment group had made far fewer requests for sleep medications than had patients who had not received the recreational therapy services.

Wolffe's direct work with recreational therapists brought him to the following conclusion:

They are professionals...the men and women skilled in the arts of recreational therapy are capable of making clinical observations that are on a par with those produced by the best of physicians.

There is an area of diagnostic acumen and treatment know-how which, under the supervision of medical authority, can make the recreational therapist an invaluable member of the broad team involving the cardiologist, the neuropsychiatrist, the surgeon, and other specialists. (Wolffe, 1962, p. 18)

Contrary to Haun and Stevenson, Wolffe asserted that "cooperative planning by the physician, the recreational therapist and the patient, or group of patients, is essential. The patient must be made aware that this is an important form of therapy and not entertainment" (Wolffe, 1962, p. 18).

In a discussion chaired by Paul Haun, psychiatrist F. A. S. Jensen countered Haun's contention that hospital recreation's lack of precise measurability excluded it from the list of therapies. "[Prescribing] is knowing where you are going through conscious effort. This is a purposive action. This is therapy... Is there any scientific approach to the situation other than by a conscious knowledge of what we're doing? I don't think there's any question but that we have to indulge in the prescription of recreation. We have to go on the idea that we are interposing in the process of illness — we are interposing some measures which in some way, are going to complete a retrogression of that illness" (Haun, 1962, p. 28).

By 1962 the Hospital Recreation Section's publication *Recreation in Treatment Centers* had begun to reflect some diversity of opinion within the organization. The September issue was prefaced with the following remarks by Robert Felix, Director of the National Institute of Mental Health: "The greatest value of recreation is that it can be prescribed as a definitive therapeutic treatment" (Felix, 1962, p. 3). That same issue carried an article by Martin Meyer, "The Rationale of Recreation as Therapy." Noting that "no other issue has been so provocative and disuniting to the profession," Meyer gently proceeded to build a rationale that drew from both positions (Meyer, 1962, p. 23).

A movement began in the early 1960's to bring all organizations with interests in leisure services together into one loosely connected organization. Member organizations were to maintain autonomy over their operations while delegating daily business tasks to the central structure. When issues of common concern arose, the member organizations could rise to the occasion with one voice. Thus, five organizations aligned in 1965 to form the National Recreation and Park Association (NRPA).

The underlying principles supporting such an alliance were so attractive to members of NART and of the Hospital Section of ARS that they put aside their philosophical differences, voted to merge, agreed to a charter and bylaws and elected officers, all within a year. On Sunday, October 9, 1966, the Board of Trustees of NRPA approved the Charter of the National Therapeutic Recreation Society. The first official meeting was convened in January 1967 (O'Morrow, 1986).

At that meeting, President Ira Hutchison assured the Board of Directors that "there has not been a single instance whereby the officers and staff of the Association have made any attempt to usurp the autonomy of our Society. I have every intention of protecting our right to plot our own course within the framework of the NTRS and NRPA constitutions" (Hutchison, 1967, p. 2). The treasurer's report from the same meeting indicated that members' dues went to NTRS with a portion being designated to NRPA (Hutchison, 1967).

Within the next ten years, however, the Association changed significantly. All dues went to NRPA with budgetary authority placed in the hands of the Board of Trustees and the executive director. With no funds to command for its activities, NTRS was forced to discontinue two of its serial publications (O'Morrow, 1986).

In 1977 NRPA moved to complete the centralization of the Association by encouraging the dissolution of all branch organizations. NTRS was required to petition the Board of Trustees to be allowed to continue as a "special interest group" (Goals report, 1976, p. 5). The title of the executive secretary for NTRS was changed to branch liaison and the duties of the position were expanded to include other NRPA assignments.

During the first decade of NTRS's existence, efforts were focused internally on the development and refinement of professional structures. The membership, catalyzed by a dedicated leadership, worked earnestly to establish curriculum standards and field training guidelines, to develop a quality research journal, to prepare ethics and standards-of-practice documents, to sponsor an annual continuing education institute of high quality and diverse offerings, to develop a communication network with state therapeutic recreation groups and to refine the certification program, which became an independent entity, the National Council for Therapeutic Recreation Certification, in the early 1980's. Thus, in spite of fiscal and staff limitations, progress in developing the structures of the young profession remained steady (O'Morrow, 1986).

One area that did not receive significant attention was the adoption of a statement setting forth the nature, purpose and scope of therapeutic recreation. By and large, the unity of the Society had been maintained by avoiding deliberations of this divisive subject. In 1969, a group of participants at the Southern Regional Therapeutic Recreation Institute sponsored by the University of North Carolina at Chapel Hill drafted a position paper defining therapeutic recreation as "a process which utilized recreation services for purposive intervention in some physical, emotional and/or social behavior to bring about a desired change in the behavior and to promote the growth and development of the individual" (O'Morrow, 1980, p. 122). The statement was never adopted by NTRS, however, and the only people who cited it were the individuals who embraced its concepts.

By the mid-seventies it was becoming increasingly awkward for NTRS to present itself without a statement of basic tenants. With the passage of time, NTRS had gained more and more young members who were naive as to the divisive history of the philosophical issue and who were growing in impatience that the matter be finalized. Past president Lee Meyer was asked to lay out the various positions that could reflect the organization's interests. These positions were to be discussed during the next year at state and regional conferences and then voted upon by the membership.

> The first position, often referred to as the "special recreation" position, stated that therapeutic recreation was "the provision of recreation services and opportunities to persons with disabling conditions." The role of the special recreator was chiefly to adapt recreation opportunities and facilities to enable persons with disabilities to reap the same benefits from recreation as could their nondisabled counterparts. (Park, 1981, p. 6)

A second position, the therapy position, posited that the primary purpose of therapeutic recreation was to provide "experiences and opportunities to help treat, change, or otherwise ameliorate effects of illness and disability... The goal would be to provide services which would contribute to the achievement of optimal functioning and independence" (Park, 1981, p. 9).

A third position, sometimes referred to as the umbrella or therapeutic recreation position, stated that therapeutic recreation was both special recreation and therapy. This position acknowledged these services as separate specializations but held that the two specializations combined to constitute the therapeutic recreation profession (Park, 1981, p. 16).

The final option that was put forward was frequently associated with its authors, Carol Peterson and Scout Lee Gunn, as the Peterson/Gunn model. This position stated "that the uniqueness of therapeutic recreation is that it utilizes three specific types of services as part of a comprehensive approach toward enabling leisure ability" (Park, 1981, p. 12). (Thus, it was also dubbed the "leisure ability" position.) The three types of services were identified as therapy, leisure education and recreation facilitation. The decision as to which service was to be employed was to be based on the assessment of client need. Regardless of the service, the ultimate goal of this model was to assist individuals in the establishment and expression of an "independent leisure lifestyle" (Park, 1981, p. 12).

The continuum of services featured in this model was very appealing to members and Peterson, a past president of NTRS, defended the position very articulately at discussions held during the year. At one of these discussions, Fred Humphrey, a proponent of the special recreation position, put forth his contention that the continuum was of a procedural rather than a philosophical nature and that similar continuums could be practiced within the other models. Proponents of the therapy position, perhaps because they were represented on one end of the continuum of services, were uncharacteristically reserved in voicing their criticism. For some therapists who had sought to help their clients according to their assessed needs, it was difficult to replace the goal of optimum functioning with "leisure ability." Proponents of the leisure ability position responded that the therapy services in this model were justified because improvement of a functional behavior was prerequisite to achieving meaningful leisure experiences. To the therapists, these cognitive gyrations were unnecessary, it was perfectly appropriate to assist a person to attain better functioning so that the person could apply it in any way they wished, not just in their leisure realm. Recreational therapists felt that they were wholly justified in joining other treatment professionals in seeking optimum health and functioning for their clients. The uniqueness of their contribution lay in the resources and skills that they commanded on behalf of the client. The leisure ability proponents felt that in order for the profession to make a distinct contribution in the health care field it was necessary to seek a goal separate from other therapies. In addition, Peterson leaned toward the Haun definition of therapy that required specific measurability and reliability of treatment protocols such as those expected in drug therapies. Advocates of the therapy position were comfortable using a definition that placed its emphases on the goals and procedural distinctions between recreational therapy and special recreation, which was the accepted usage by other counseling and experiential modalities.

The leisure ability position received a majority of the votes cast for the four positions as shown in Table 2.1. In May 1982, it was adopted by NTRS as its official philosophical position.

In the meantime, if the expanded presence of therapeutic recreators among the players from the public recreation and park movement had any effect on the

Table 2.1: **NTRS 1982 Vote on the Philosophical Positions**

Position	Special Recreation	Therapy	Leisure Ability	Umbrella	Totals
Community	4 (9.5%)	2 (4.8%)	31 (73.6%)	5 (11.9%)	42 (12.0%)
Clinical Rehab	4 (1.9%)	61 (28.5%)	125 (58.4%)	24 (11.2%)	214 (61.1%)
Public School	0	2 (22.2%)	6 (66.7%)	1 (11.1%)	9 (2.6%)
Corrections	0	0	0	0	0
Higher Education	4 (8.3%)	13 (27.1%)	29 (60.4%)	2 (4.2%)	48 (13.7%)
Other	1 (2.8)	2 (5.6%)	28 (77.8%)	5 (13.9%)	36 (10.3%)
Total	13 (3.7%)	80 (22.9%)	220 (62.9%)	37 (10.6%)	350 (100%)

Used with permission from the National Therapeutic Recreation Society from *National Therapeutic Recreation Society Philosophical Issues Survey, Summary Report*, 1982, p. 9

ways in which the latter viewed their mission, it was not immediately discernible. In an address presented at the 1970 National Recreation and Park Association's annual conference in Philadelphia, Fred Humphrey, former president of NTRS, introduced his version of concepts earlier asserted by Luther Gulick. He said that contrary to the prose set forth in most introductory recreation texts, recreation was not an inherently good entity. He affirmed that recreation activity formed a neutral structure that could yield either positive or negative experiences for participants. He maintained that effective leadership was the primary factor that was needed to fulfill recreation's potential to benefit participants. In exercising that influence on the experience, Humphrey said to the recreation profession, "we are all therapeutic recreation specialists" (Humphrey, 1970). Humphrey's vision did not divert the movement from its focus on providing facilities and programs to one that emphasized leadership in releasing the benefits of recreation. In fact his words drew some irritation of the "who-do-these-people-think-they-are" variety. Even the challenges to "the establishment" and the social turmoil of the latter 1960's and early 1970's had little effect in budging the recreation movement from its adherence to the postwar principles of Ott Romney. Although the profession received more than one challenge to make its recreation centers and programs more involved in addressing the social ills of the day, the majority held that that was not the business of recreation.

One area in which NTRS did appear to effect some positive outcomes by working with NRPA was in increasing the opportunities for citizens with disabilities to join other beneficiaries of community, state and federal park and recreation services. In fact, this is what many members of NRPA thought that recreational therapists did: enabled people with disabilities to participate in recreation. It was one area in which therapists and general recreators could work without encountering philosophical differences.

In the latter 1970's and early 1980's, however, the parent organization had little interest in health care issues. As NRPA became more centralized, NTRS lost any influence it may have once had on the goals and resources of the association. NRPA was not directly involved in the arenas in which health care issues were being resolved. For example, while the American Occupational Therapy Association and the American Physical Therapy Association were involved in writing the home health care legislation, NRPA legislative staff were preoccupied with the Land and Water Conservation Fund and the Bureau of Outdoor Recreation. As fiscal management issues and changes became of critical importance to recreational therapists working in the health care industry, their frustration and impatience with NRPA's lack of leadership in confronting these issues grew. In October 1982, NTRS President Viki Annand asked the Council of Past Presidents to advise the Board of Directors. Specifically, a motion was laid before the Council that advised the Board to study alternative organizational structures, both within NRPA and apart from NRPA, through which NTRS might more effectively serve the needs of the profession. Nine former presidents of the society attended the meeting. "The consensus, from the opinions proffered, was that the Society was not where it ought to be and that the existing organizational structure was impeding rather than enhancing progress" (NTRS Council of Past Presidents, 1982, p. 1). There was much less agreement, however, on measures that should be taken to rectify the situation, but, after much discussion, the motion passed with six members voting for the exploration of other structures and three dissenting (NTRS Council, 1982).

After eight months of investigating structural options and many conversations with NRPA authorities, Ann James, the director of the study, called Ray West, chairman of the committee investigating external structures, and reported that NRPA officials had made it clear that they wanted no alterations in the NTRS/NRPA relationship that might set a precedent for the return to a decentralized organization. She concluded that modification of the relationship with NRPA was not a realistic option and advised West that he and like-minded colleagues should earnestly pursue the feasibility of establishing an independent organization (author's notes, 1983).

West solicited the help of Dave Park, former executive secretary and past president of NTRS, to establish the legal and organizational ground work. After surveying 25 colleagues to establish a proposal, Park summoned all interested persons to meet in his hotel room at the 1983 NRPA convention in Kansas City. At the appointed hour, every square foot of floor space and every piece of furniture appeared to be occupied by recreational therapists. People strained to hear from the doorway and the hallway. The temperature increased with the mixture of excitement and apprehension emanating from the crowded room. Park reiterated that there were respected leaders who said that an organization could not thrive apart from NRPA. "There are also some individuals who are opposed to this move, and that also is to be expected. It is my firm conviction that this move is necessary for the future of the therapeutic recreation profession and that we should press forward with vigor" (Park, 1983).

Park cautioned founding members to be focused in defining the new association's purpose and goals: "Another organization with an 'umbrella' orientation will not be any more successful than the present one" (Park, 1983). He also noted that since many of the people expressing an interest in the new organization were employed in the health care industry, some had characterized the organizational separation as the clinical proponents versus the community practitioners. Park contended that the distinction had nothing to do with setting and everything to do with process. He affirmed that using recreation experiences as an intervention to achieve a predetermined goal was the essence of therapeutic recreation and that this could "occur in a community recreation department, in a school, or in a clinical setting" (Park, 1983, p. 1). When asked whether the term for that concept might be more appropriately denoted as recreational therapy,

Park responded pragmatically that the term therapeutic recreation had burrowed its way into common usage and that a change at this time would only further confuse the public and other health care professionals.

Despite Park's urging, the statement-of-purpose committee composed of Carol Peterson, Dave Austin, Ray West, Dick Beckley and Melinda Conway proposed a definition with recreational therapy at the core but with enough added to the fringes to provide something for everyone:

> Therapeutic Recreation is the application, by qualified professionals, of appropriate intervention strategies utilizing recreation services to promote independent functioning and to enhance optimal health and well-being of individuals with illnesses and/or disabling conditions. Therapeutic Recreation places a special emphasis on the development of an appropriate leisure lifestyle as an integral part of that independent functioning. The underlying philosophy of Therapeutic Recreation is that all human beings have the right to and need for leisure involvement as a necessary aspect of optimal health and, as such, Therapeutic Recreation can be used as an important tool in becoming and remaining well. (Park, 1983, p. 1)

Needless to say, it did not flow readily off the tongue and was later replaced with the slightly more succinct:

> Therapeutic Recreation is the provision of treatment services and the provision of recreation services to persons with illnesses or disabling conditions. The primary purposes of treatment services, which are often referred to as recreational therapy, are to restore, remediate or rehabilitate in order to improve functioning and independence as well as reduce or eliminate the effects of illness or disability. The primary purposes of recreation services are to provide recreation resources and opportunities in order to improve health and well-being. Therapeutic recreation is provided by professionals who are trained and certified, registered and/or licensed to provide therapeutic recreation. (American Therapeutic Recreation Association, undated)

Clinician's who were responsible for facilitating leisure participation for their clients during evenings and weekends, which constituted most recreational therapists, felt that role needed to be reflected in the statement along with the therapy functions. Thus, the statement specifies two functions: treatment services and recreation services. Denoting them both as therapeutic recreation, however, reverted the statement to the umbrella dilemma.

By February 1984, fifty "founding members" had contributed one hundred dollars each to the establishment of the new association. These members elected an Interim Board of Directors, with Peg Connolly as the president, to complete the Articles of Incorporation. On June 12, 1984, the American Therapeutic Recreation Association was officially incorporated in Washington, DC (Connolly, 1984; Park, 1984a).

In the meantime, the officers of NTRS brought a list of the society's "most urgent needs" to the attention of the executive committee of NRPA (James, 1984). The NRPA officers responded with the provision of additional legislative assistance and a member of the Board of Trustees donated funding for additional staff assistance. For a while, the relationship grew more productive and tensions eased. Then in the summer of 1984, the executive director of NRPA pulled a manuscript from imminent publication in the *Therapeutic Recreation Journal*. Although the executive director objected to passages critical of NRPA, the article had passed review of the established editorial processes. This act of censorship again strained relations between NTRS and the parent organization (James, 1984). By July 1985, the membership of ATRA had grown to 300 (Membership Directory, 1985).

Evolving Concepts Based on Efficacy

Concepts of recreational therapy in the eighties and nineties were impacted by two elements: (1) increased research demonstrating the efficacy of recreational therapy and (2) the unsettling transition in the structure of American medicine.

More than a century after Florence Nightingale voiced her contention that laughter contributed to the recovery process, scientists confirmed that laughter altered the body chemistry in humans, increasing the presence of immune factors in the blood (Berk et al., 1988). This finding by immunologists was joined by the research of physiologists, physicians and psychologists, as well as by the research of recreational therapists. Evidence mounted indicating the contributions of recreational therapy interventions to achieving desired physical, cognitive, psychological and social outcomes (Coyle, Kinney, Riley & Shank, 1991). Increasing empirical evidence replaced the intuitive contentions of the sixties and earlier, contributed to the refinement and modification of some interventions and reinforced the confidence with which recreational therapy interventions were applied.

Thorough assessment and evaluation procedures became universally applied by professionals further adding to the documentation of treatment outcomes. Although the experiential nature of recreational therapy still does not allow the medium to approach the specificity usually expected of medications, the practice has come a long way since the tenuously-based activity of Paul Haun's era.

The changing structure of medical care in the United States has had a major effect on recreational therapy. During the first half of this century, the free enterprise basis of American medicine motivated the development of new information, technologies and medications until it offered the most advanced treatment opportunities in the world. However, by the mid-seventies, it was becoming increasingly difficult for individuals and their health insurers to pay for the more expensive care that these advances made possible. The assortment of measures instituted to contain costs have had considerable effects on recreational therapy as they have had on all components of health care. Most notably, the limitations of insurance covering mental health treatment costs have caused drastic reductions in hospital stays with concomitant reductions in services and personnel. Whereas twenty years ago the profession was heavily concentrated in mental health treatment settings, there has been a major shift of personnel to physical rehabilitation centers. Although many of the cost containment measures have brought constricting forces to the profession, some have propelled growth or at least reinforced stability. The new willingness and, in some cases, eagerness of medicine to look beyond technology and drugs for effective interventions places recreational therapy in an advantageous position. The cost-effectiveness of recreational therapy in comparison to many other treatments has also been noted by clinical directors, as well as by hospital administrators. Lastly, the marketing advantage afforded to institutions with leisure opportunities and recreational therapy programs has affirmed the value of recreational therapy services in increasingly competitive health care venues.

Recreational therapy has not been the only profession to undergo changes due to fiscal pressures. Increasing costs of government have led to tax protests and funding cutbacks in states and cities across the United States. Increased competition for remaining tax dollars have motivated public recreation professionals to become more persuasive in advocating for their shares of the budgets. At a press conference convened in 1994 in Washington, DC, the National Recreation and Park Association announced the results of a new study suggesting that many serious social issues, including juvenile crime, could be ameliorated through participation in recreation programs such as those found in many park and recreation departments. "The study, *Beyond Fun and Games: Emerging Roles of Public Recreation*, illustrates recreation-based programs that are successful at reducing crime, improving health and quality of life, and creating safer communities" (Kraus, 1997, p. 270).

Almost a century after Joseph Lee, Luther Gulick and Jane Addams brought together their respective fields of recreation, education and social work to provide recreation experiences for youth-at-risk in America, the National Recreation and Park Association was reaffirming the potential of recreation to yield personal and community benefits. The pendulum had swung from one extreme in 1890 when recreation was sanctioned only for its auxiliary benefits to the opposite extreme in mid-century when it was blasphemous to propose that recreation activities be conducted to produce anything other than inherent enjoyment. Perhaps this pendulum would now hold near the center where professionals could delight in recreation as being totally justified by its own reward while at the same time recognizing the tremendous potential of recreation experiences to achieve additional benefits. Recent NRPA sponsored continuing education programs have featured a Benefits-Based Management (BBM) system for program design. With its emphasis on (1) identifying benefits to be achieved by participants, (2) implementing program elements in ways needed to achieve the desired benefits and (3) evaluating results in terms of benefits achieved (Kraus, 1997), it is easy to see parallels to recreational therapy. In fact, developers of BBM seminars admit to drawing freely upon the body of knowledge established by recreational therapy (Allen, 1997). It is heartening to again see recreation professionals point with pride to the benefits their programs have generated for their communities. It is certainly a much more hospitable climate for recreational therapists than was the Romney era.

As the twentieth century draws to a close, many of the struggles experienced by the field because of the existence of two national organizations seem to be resolving. Both ATRA and NTRS have been working on creating a foundation for future collaboration between the two organizations for the past three years. In the summer of 1996 they joined together to form a joint committee on credentialing and in the summer of 1998 both organizations mutually developed a resolution and a letter of agreement which acknowledge that recreational therapists are represented by two national organizations, each making its own unique and valuable contribution to the continued growth of the field (Wenzel, 1998). The primary purpose of both the resolution and letter of agreement is to allow both the professional and the consumer to benefit from an effective and efficient use of opportunities and resources available. The resolution signed by both organizations is shown below:

ATRA and NTRS Joint Resolution

WHEREAS, professional involvement at the local, state and national level is imperative to enhance and promote the therapeutic recreation profession, and

WHEREAS, it is the responsibility of professional organizations to guide the growth and development of a professional body of knowledge, codes of ethical conduct, standards of professional practice, credentialing standards, professional preparation programs, and public recognition and support, and

WHEREAS, the profession of therapeutic recreation is served by two national organizations, each with a unique identity and each making valuable contributions, and

WHEREAS, both the American Therapeutic Recreation Association (ATRA) and the National Therapeutic Recreation Society (NTRS) recognize that the therapeutic recreation process is fundamental to service provision and endorse its implantation across all service settings, and

WHEREAS, communication, cooperation and collaboration are consistent with both origination's mission and professional codes of ethics, and are therefore integral to professional behavior and relationships,

NOW, THEREFORE, IT IS RESOLVED that the American Therapeutic Recreation Association (ATRA) and the National Therapeutic Recreation Society (NTRS) will communicate, cooperate and collaborate in the best interest of consumers and the therapeutic recreation profession, and will enter into a letter of agreement to operationalize the above stated intentions. (ATRA, NTRS Resolution, June, 1998)

Summary

Recreational therapy traces its roots to ancient teachings and more directly to the principles espoused by Florence Nightingale. In the United States, it was born with the reform movement at the turn of the twentieth century. Its early identification with the social work profession was transferred to the leisure service professions after World War II as part of several other larger organizations in recreation, most significantly NTRS. In the mid-eighties an independent professional association (ATRA) was established. Both organizations assisted the advancement of the field at a very critical time in its historical development but the existence of two national organizations representing the field of recreational therapy led to much energy being spent defining differences, similarities and rightful areas of jurisdiction. With the development of a more open atmosphere between the two professional associations, it appears that the field of recreational therapy is taking a purposeful step forward in providing the field with a stronger professional basis on which to develop practice and professional commitment for the benefit of the consumers whom we serve.

Learning Activities

1. Write a paper describing your own position on the nature of recreational therapy. Why do you agree or disagree with individuals such as Haun, Humphrey, Meyer, Menninger and Park?
2. Discuss the proper nomenclature for the field of recreational therapy/therapeutic recreation. What are the roots of each term? What is the original interpretation for recreational therapy? For therapeutic recreation?
3. Describe whether you, as a professional, could write or follow a prescription for a recreation activity. What form would the prescription take?
4. Which option would you have chosen in the 1982 vote for the philosophy of the profession? Debate the options in class and see if you can come up with a consensus. Search for other options which may be more acceptable.

Study Questions

1. What were the historical events which led to the first organized use of recreation as a component of treatment?
2. How are the birth of social work and the origins of recreational therapy linked? Explain why.
3. What benefits of recreation as part of treatment were already documented prior to 1920? List the benefits and group(s) who reported the benefits.
4. The end of World War II brought a period of division to the field. Discuss the beliefs and historic events which brought about this division.
5. What was the primary issue which motivated the NTRS Council of Past Presidents to study alternative organization structures?

References

Allen, L. (1997). Benefits-based management. Address delivered at the SC Park and Recreation Management Conference, February 24.

American Therapeutic Recreation Association. (undated). Membership information. Hattiesburg, MS: American Therapeutic Recreation Association.

Andrews, M. (1929). *A lost commander: Florence Nightingale*. Garden City, NY: Double Day.

Becker, S. (1950). *The history of hospital service, 1918-1947*. Washington, DC: The American National Red Cross.

Berk, L., Tan, S., Nehlsen-Cannarella, S., Napier, B., Lee, J., Lewis, J., Hubbard, R. & Eby, W. (1988). Humor associated laughter decreases cortisol and increases spontaneous lymphocyte blastogenesis. *Clinical Research, 36,* 435.

Boyd, N. L. (1919). *Hospital and bedside games*. Chicago: N. L. Boyd.

Boyd, N. L. (1935). Group work experiments in state institutions in Illinois. *Proceedings of the National Conference on Social Work*. Chicago: The University of Chicago Press.

Committee at work on Hospital Section of American Recreation Society. (1949, July). *American Recreation Society Quarterly Bulletin, 2*(21), 8.

Connolly, P. (1984). Letter to founding members. July 27.

Convalescent House at Quantico. (1919, March 31). *The Red Cross Bulletin.*

Cox, C. L. & Dobbins, V. (1970). Before the merger. *Therapeutic Recreation Journal, 4*(1), 3-8.

Coyle, C. P., Kinney, W. B., Riley, B. & Shank, J. W. (Eds.). (1991). *Benefits of Therapeutic Recreation.* Ravensdale, WA: Idyll Arbor.

Felix, R. H. (1962). Preface. *Recreation in Treatment Centers, 1,* 3.

Guthrie, D. (1946). *A history of medicine.* Philadelphia: J. B. Lippincott Co.

Haun, P. (1952). Recreation in the mental hospital: A philosophy. *Journal of the American Association for Health, Physical Education and Recreation, 7,* 55.

Haun, P. (1962). Mental and emotional ills: A discussion. *North Carolina Recreation Commission Bulletin,* No. 30, p. 51.

Haun, P. (1965). Prescribed recreation. *Recreation in Treatment Centers, 5,* 7.

Haun, P. (1969). The psychiatrist looks at recreation. *Proceedings, Mental Health Institute,* Independence, IA.

History of the American Recreation Society. (1964). *American Recreation Journal, 5*(3), 70-72.

Hospital Service. (1919, June 30). *The Red Cross Bulletin, 3*(27), 2-3.

Huizinga, J. (1944). *Homo ludens: A study of play elements in culture.* Boston: Beacon Press.

Humphrey, F. (1970). NTRS Institute Address. Author's notes.

Hutchison, I. (1967, January 28). Report to the board of directors. *Minutes of the National Therapeutic Recreation Society.*

James, A. (1979). *Therapeutic recreation in military hospitals.* Unpublished doctoral dissertation, University of New Mexico, Albuquerque.

James, A. (1984). Editorial control of Therapeutic Recreation Journal. Letter to Executive Committee, NRPA Board of Trustees, August 13.

Katz, H. F. (1974-1975, Winter). [Review of the book *Play and game theory in group work: A collection of papers by Neva Leona Boyd.*] *Program Aids.* New York: National Jewish Welfare Board.

Knapp, R. & Hartsoe, C. (1979). *Play for America: The National Recreation Association 1906-1965.* Ashburn, VA: National Recreation and Park Association.

Kraus, R. (1997). *Recreation and leisure in modern society.* New York: Addison-Wesley.

Manual of Red Cross Camp Service. (1919). Washington, DC: American Red Cross.

Membership directory. (1985). The American Therapeutic Recreation Association.

Menninger Clinic. (1995). A national resource. Topeka, KS: Menninger Clinic.

Menninger, K. & Jeanetta, L. (1942). Recreation for morale: Some tentative conclusions. *Bulletin of the Menninger Clinic, 6,* 96-102.

Menninger, W. C. (1942). Psychological aspects of hobbies. *American Journal of Psychiatry, 99,* 122-129.

Menninger, W. C. & McColl, I. (1937). Recreational therapy as applied in a modern psychiatric hospital. *Occupational Therapy and Rehabilitation, 16,* 296-302.

Meyer, M. W. (1962). The rationale of recreation as therapy. *Recreation in Treatment Centers, 1*, 23-26.

Morton, T. G. (1973). *History of Pennsylvania hospitals, 1751-1895*. New York: Arno Press.

Nice, C. J. (1948). Recreation is not therapy. *The Journal of Health and Physical Education, 19*, 642-643.

Nightingale, F. (1859/1946). *Notes on nursing: What it is, and what it is not*. Philadelphia: J. B. Lippincott Co. (Facsimile of the first edition that was printed in London by Harrison & Sons, 1859.)

NTRS Council of Past Presidents. (1982, October 26). Minutes of the meeting.

O'Morrow, G. S. (1980). *Therapeutic recreation: A helping profession*. Reston, VA: Reston.

O'Morrow, G. S. (1986). *National Therapeutic Recreation Society: The first twenty years: 1966-1986*. Ashburn, VA: National Recreation and Park Association.

Park, D. (1981). Philosophical Issues Report. NTRS document.

Park, D. (1983). Memo to founding members. September 30.

Park, D. (1984a). Memo to founding members. March 2.

Park, D. (1984b). Memo to all founding members. May 22.

Phillips, B. E. (1952a). Hospital recreation is unique. *Journal of the American Association for Health, Physical Education and Recreation, 23*(5), 29-30, 35.

Phillips, B. E. (1952b). Recreation therapy. *Journal of the American Association for Health, Physical Education, and Recreation, 23*(6), 23-24.

Program of recreation. (1919, January 27). *The Red Cross Bulletin*.

Rainwater, C. E. (1992). (See Knapp & Hartsoe, p. 4) *The play movement in the United States*. Chicago.

Romney, G. O. (1945). *Off the job living*. Washington, DC: McGrath Publishing Co. and National Recreation and Park Association.

Scholarship program. (1947). Washington, DC: The American National Red Cross.

Schuyler, D. (1944, March 8). Conference with Col. Menninger. *American Red Cross Archival File, 616.22*.

Simon, P. (1971). *Play and game theory in group work: A collection of papers by Neva Leona Boyd*. Chicago: University of Illinois at Chicago Circle.

Stevenson, G. S. (1951). Mental hygiene concept of recreation in the national emergency. *Recreation Service Exchange Bulletin*. (American Red Cross), June, 1.

Summers, L. (1962). The American Red Cross program of recreation in military hospitals: A retrospective view. *Recreation in Treatment Centers, 1*, 18-21.

Sylvester, C. (Ed.) (1987). *Philosophy of therapeutic recreation*. Ashburn, VA: National Recreation and Parks Association.

Wenzel, K. (1998, May, June, July). President's message. *NTRS Report, 23*(3), 1-5.

Wolffe, J. B. (1962). Recreation, medicine and the humanities. *North Carolina Recreation Commission Bulletin*, No. 30, 18-21.

Woodham-Smith, C. (1951). *Florence Nightingale: 1820-1910*. New York: McGraw-Hill.

Chapter 3

Managing Quality to Meet and Exceed Standards

joan burlingame
Thomas K. Skalko

For the recreational therapist, there are many types of standards which s/he must know about and adhere to in order to meet the quality of service expected of a health care professional. The chapter will begin by examining what a standard is, who develops standards and how benchmarking is a part of standards. Quality of service does not happen automatically. There are specific procedures that must be taken to be sure that standards of practice are being met. The second part of the chapter will give an overview of managing quality. Finally, the concept of best practices, how to identify them and develop them, will finish the discussion.

Standards

A standard is a defined level of expected performance (Ozeki & Asaka, 1990). Performance which meets or exceeds that level is considered to be acceptable, performance which falls short of the level is unacceptable. The consequences of exceeding, meeting or failing to meet any given standard varies, usually depending on what kind of standard it is and who is responsible for enforcing the standard.

Often when the recreational therapy student hears professionals discuss standards, s/he envisions the standards of practice developed by our two national organizations (which can be found Appendix B). These standards of practice are important to the professional, but they account for less than 5% of the written standards which apply to the practice of recreational therapy. There are also governmental agency standards, voluntary accreditation standards and facility standards which impact the practice of recreational therapy (Loeffler & Henley, 1997; Toppel, Beach & Hutchinson-Troyer, 1991). The three types of standards discussed in this chapter are regulatory standards (laws enacted by governments), organizational standards (voluntary standards set by the peer group) and facility standards (frequently referred to as standards of care).

Regulations

Standards which are written into law are called regulations. There are many sets of regulations which apply to health care settings, including Medicare/Medicaid regulations, public health regulations and worker safety regulations (Occupational Safety and Health Administration or OSHA). Because regulations are the law, if you don't comply with the law, you are, by definition, breaking the law. The consequences of breaking the law include problems with your boss, being fired, being fined and/or going to jail. Ignorance of the law is no excuse.

Regulations are written so that each measurable element (called a "Tag") is separate from others and has its own number assigned to it. (See the discussion in burlingame & Skalko, 1997 under "CFR" for an explanation of how the government numbers regulations.) One of the major areas of knowledge for the recreational therapist is knowing all of the applicable federal, state and local laws (tags) which apply to practice. Knowing does not mean memorizing them word-for-word, but understanding and remembering concepts including relevant indicators and benchmarks.

Regulations under Health Care Financing Administration (HCFA) tend to be facility-type or service-type specific. There are over fifteen specific sets of regulations, including regulations for hospitals, Intermediate Care Facilities for the Mentally Retarded (ICF-MRs), nursing homes (OBRA) and Comprehensive Outpatient Rehabilitation Facilities (CORFs). Some of the specific sets of regulations refer more to service types than facility types including Portable X-ray Service, Hospice and Mammography Suppliers. The recreational therapist working in any one of the listed facility types or with one of the listed service types needs to know the tags associated with that set of regulations.

There are also two sets of federal regulations which apply to all settings and services. These are the *Life Safety Code* regulations and the *Immediate and Serious Threat to Patient Health and Safety* regulations. *Life Safety Codes* generally address safety issues in the environment of care. An example is the regulation concerning the maximum temperature of tap water in the room used by the recreational therapist for cooking activities. Some states require that the tap water used by patients not exceed 120° F. However, the federal law states that the tap water used by patients may not exceed 110° F. Because there are so many overlapping standards, the rule of thumb is that the therapist must always comply with the most stringent of the standards. In this case, the recreational therapist will need to insure that the tap water does not exceed 110° F.

The other umbrella set of federal regulations is called *Immediate and Serious Threat to Patient Health and Safety*. This set of regulations contains basic standards, called core statements, which are meant to identify the most important standards which must be met to assure patient safety. The five core statements which speak to failing to meet standards are

1. Failure to protect patients from disease and infection.
2. Failure to provide care or services essential to maintaining or improving patient health.
3. Failure to maintain equipment and supplies at an acceptable level to ensure health.
4. Failure to prevent situations/conditions in environment or physical plant which would present a hazard and would jeopardize patient health and safety.
5. Failure to uphold patient rights whereby violations can result in harm or injury.

A serious violation of any regulation found in either the *Life Safety Codes* or *Immediate and Serious Threat to Patient Health and Safety* could cause the facility to be shut down within 24 hours. Needless to say, these two codes are good ones for the student intern and new therapist to be familiar with. It would be very uncomfortable if actions taken by the recreational therapist or recreational therapy intern were to cause HCFA to discuss potential closure with the administration of the facility. (An example of an immediate jeopardy citation for a nursing home in Alaska can be found on page 251.) When a facility is being surveyed by a deemed organization in place of HCFA, the term *sentinel event* is used instead of immediate jeopardy (JCAHO, 1998a).

The number of "tags" a therapist needs to know, in many cases, will exceed 500. Having to be able to demonstrate a clear understanding of the regulations can be overwhelming, especially when you consider that there are also standards from organizations (such as the CARF: The Rehabilitation Accreditation Commission and the Joint Commission on Accreditation of Healthcare Organizations), professional groups (American Therapeutic Recreation Association and National Therapeutic Recreation Society) in addition to the facility's own standards of care. It can be difficult but, perhaps, it is not quite as bad as it seems. Bonifazi (1998) states

Insiders often complain that long term care is the second most heavily regulated industry in the country, surpassed only by the nuclear power industry, but former HCFA Administrator Bruce Vladeck says that's not so. Long term care, he says, is less regulated than drug manufacturers, banks and all sorts of environmentally-related businesses. (pp. 56-57)

There are other governmental agencies who also have oversight for standards in health care (and beyond). The other primary governmental agency is OSHA which is responsible for the health and safety of employees. Included within the OSHA laws are bloodborne pathogen rules; sight, back and hearing safety; and protection from violence in the workplace. OSHA is one of the government agencies which has far more regulations to comply with than HCFA. The new regulations proposed for preventing the transmission of TB in the workplace totals more than 145 pages (Newsfronts, 1997b) which makes it longer than HCFA's regulations for inpatient hospitalization.

Fortunately, most groups, whether they are governmental bodies, organizations or facility practice groups, try to develop standards which contain similar (if not the same) standards. A therapist who meets expectations will be able to identify and implement the minimum standards for practice at his/her location of employment. The outstanding therapist will additionally be able to understand the differences between all of the standards which apply.

Organizational Standards

There are currently three primary accreditation organizations in the United States for health care services. These are the Joint Commission on Accreditation of Healthcare Organizations (JCAHO), CARF: The Rehabilitation Accreditation Commission and the National Committee for Quality Assurance (NCQA; for managed care organizations). The standards developed by all of these groups tend to be process specific (e.g., assessment, discharge planning) instead of occupation specific (e.g., recreational therapy, occupational therapy, physical therapy).

The *Joint Commission on Accreditation of Healthcare Organizations*, originally founded as the American College of Surgeons in 1913, is a standard setting group and credentialing organization for many areas of health care delivery including:

general, psychiatric, children's and rehabilitation hospitals; health care networks, including health plans, integrated delivery networks and preferred provider organizations; home care organizations, including those that provide home health services, personal care and support services, home infusion and other pharmacy services, durable medical equipment services and hospice services; nursing homes and other long term care facilities, including subacute care programs, dementia programs and long term care pharmacies; behavioral health care organizations, including those that provide mental health, chemical dependency and mental retardation/developmental disabilities services for patients of various ages in various organized service settings; and managed behavioral health care organizations; ambulatory care providers, including outpatient surgery facilities, rehabilitation centers, infusion centers, group practice and others, and clinical laboratories. (JCAHO, 1998b)

JCAHO considers the development of standards to be a dynamic process which is forever evolving as health care changes. It also considers standard setting one of its central tasks (JCAHO, 1998c). Further information about JCAHO can be obtained through its web site at http://www.jcaho.org.

CARF: The Rehabilitation Accreditation Commission helps develop standards for and provides accreditation to organizations providing rehabilitation services. CARF says its mission is "to serve as the preeminent standards-setting and accrediting body, promoting and advocating for the delivery of quality rehabilitation services" (CARF, 1998, p. 1). Evaluating a facility's ability to measure its outcomes is a major focus of the CARF survey (Frey, 1992). Further information about CARF: The Rehabilitation Accreditation Commission can be obtained through its web site at http://www.carf.org.

The *National Committee for Quality Assurance* (NCQA) is an accrediting body for managed care organizations. This standard setting and accrediting body strives to effectively evaluate organizations in the following areas: quality improvement, utilization management, physician credentialing, members' rights and responsibilities, preventative health services and medical records (NCQA, 1998). Further information about NCQA can be obtained through its web sit at http://www.ncqa.org.

While it may seem that all providers of health care are surveyed for accreditation by one of the three primary accreditation organizations, this is far from true. In 1996, Dennis O'Leary, President of the JCAHO, made the following observation:

Suddenly, we are sensitized to the fact there are hundreds of thousands of practitioner offices out there about which we know virtually nothing. And fewer than 20% of all provider organizations are accredited by anyone. Further, the tools that we have to measure performance in this new environment are, at best, incomplete, and many of the new performance measures that do exist have undergone no testing whatsoever. (O'Leary, 1996, p. 2)

Different terminology is used when discussing which type of standard has been passed as a result of an outside survey. Facilities which pass governmental surveys are considered to be *licensed*. Facilities which pass a survey by an organization are considered to be *accredited*. Just because a facility is not accredited does not mean that they also are not licensed. The providers need to hold some kind of license to function as a health care provider. It is important for a recreational therapist working at a facility to know the status of its licensure and accreditation.

Professional Standards

The recreational therapist also has two sets of professional standards of practice, one from the American Therapeutic Recreation Association (ATRA) and one from the National Therapeutic Recreation Society (NTRS).

NTRS developed their first set of standards in 1980. These standards were developed for two different settings: clinical and community (special populations). The development of two different sets of standards recognized the split in NTRS between the two types of service delivery. Developed for clinical settings, *Standards of Practice for Therapeutic Recreation Service* addressed standards for both the administration and treatment aspects of hospital-based practice. *Guidelines for Community-Based Recreation Programs for Special Populations* was the companion document which addressed standards for therapists working with special populations in the community. NTRS published a revised set of standards in 1995 which combined all standards for the practice of therapeutic recreation (regardless of setting or orientation) into one document titled *Standards of Practice for Therapeutic Recreation Services and Annotated Bibliography* (NTRS, 1995). Following NTRS's position of therapeutic recreation encompassing three levels (therapy, leisure education and recreation service), each standard contains criteria for each level of service.

The American Therapeutic Recreation Association published its *Standards for the Practice of Therapeutic Recreation* in 1991 and released its *Standards for the Practice of Therapeutic Recreation and Self Assessment Guide* in 1993 (ATRA, 1993). The *Self Assessment Guide* was the end product of a three year project undertaken by ATRA's Standards of Practice Committee. This guide is divided into two distinct areas, the Direct Practice of Therapeutic Recreation with seven standards and the Management of the Practice of Therapeutic Recreation with five standards. Following ATRA's position of therapeutic recreation being primarily clinical in nature, its standards of practice contains criteria for clinically based practice. A summary of both NTRS's and ATRA's Standards of Practice can be found in Appendix B of this book.

As treatment teams are becoming more transdisciplinary, the recreational therapist will also have the opportunity to qualify for and receive other credentials such as Certified Alcohol and Drug Counselor, Long Term Care Fitness Leader Certificate and American Board of Disability Analyst Fellow. These groups are likely to develop their own standards of practice which the therapist must also meet.

Professional Competency and Standards for Practice

When we consider the consumer and standards for the practice of a profession, competence in practice cannot be underestimated or ignored. The issue of quality education as it relates to competent practice has been discussed for decades (Austin, 1989; Brasile, 1992; Skalko & Goldenberg, 1995). The common thread is the belief that the quality of education cannot be minimized and the competence for professional practice is of utmost importance. Although most of these authors have focused on pre-professional education, ultimately the focus must change to the full spectrum of educational development including pre-professional education, specialized training and continuing professional development. The professional service provider, however, will increasingly be required to validate the acquisition of these skills through formal education and continuing development. This validation is currently being required by health care accrediting bodies.

The requirement for professional competence is coming from a number of sources. Today's consumer is expecting quality services that are value-filled and provided by competent professionals. In addition, the health care environment/industry itself is demanding high quality, outcome focused, cost-efficient services delivered by multi-skilled professionals. The professional must meet these challenges.

Customer satisfaction with health care is and will continue to be among the driving elements of quality care (Pew Health Professions Commission, 1995). The health care consumers of today expect quality, economical care that generates meaningful outcomes and is delivered by competent professionals. Unless the recreational therapy professional can deliver such services, the long term viability of the professional and the profession is in jeopardy. Consumer satisfaction with the quality of care and the competence of their health care provider both in skills and in caring will drive the market-place of the future.

The environment is changing more rapidly than the professional preparation programs are able to manage. Although the health care and educational systems have been slow to change their focus from a treatment orientation to a prevention, education and management approach, there is a shift in that direction. This means that health care providers will be required to work across the continuum of services from treatment through health promotion and disease prevention. This rapidly changing environment will demand professionals who are well prepared to both deliver services and to be able to adjust and adapt to new delivery systems.

The Pew Health Professions Commission (1995) emphasized that the health care provider of the future must be multi-skilled and competent. The competencies of this new breed of professionals will be broad-based and will encompass a broad spectrum of skills and knowledge. In addition, more functional skills and outcomes will be the target. Providers will be expected to assist the consumer in developing skills for life to the greatest extent they are capable.

> All allied health practitioners will be expected to have a strong foundation in the sciences, increased critical thinking and problem solving skills and excellent communication abilities. The emerging integrated delivery system will expect practitioners to work competently in acute care, ambulatory, managed care and home health environments. (PEW Health Professions Commission, 1995, p. 24)

The key for recreational therapy professionals is in their ability to develop such skills and competencies or to develop new competencies as they are needed. This continuing focus on competence for practice will demand life-long learning on the part of the health care provider and education and training that produces distinct skills for the service environment. It is only through competent practice that recreational therapists will be able to meet the intent of the evolving standards of care and best practice.

Standards and Professional Credentialing

In the past, health care standards were more prescriptive in nature — they stated how something was to be accomplished. Today, the trend is more outcome oriented in nature — fewer statements are given concerning how the facility is to reach an outcome. An example of this trend can be seen in OBRA, the federal law pertaining to nursing homes. Nursing homes are required to provide an activity program for their residents which achieves certain outcomes for quality and comprehensiveness. However, the law is less prescriptive about who must run the program. The activity professional is allowed to come from many types of academic backgrounds. The activity professional may also exchange experience for academic preparation to qualify for the job. Tag #249 of OBRA states

> that the qualification of an activity professional is defined as someone who is a qualified therapeutic recreation specialist or an activities professional who is licensed or registered, if applicable, in the state in which practicing; and is eligible for certification as a therapeutic

recreation specialist; as an activities professional by a recognized accrediting body on or after October 1, 1990; or has two years experience in a social or recreation program within the last five years, one of which was full-time in a patient activities program in a health care setting; or is a qualified occupational therapist or occupational therapy assistant; or has completed a training course approved by the state. (Best-Martini, Weeks & Wirth, 1996, p. 320)

Note that the provisions concerning the amount of formal academic preparation is not consistent for the individuals who may fill the position of an activity professional in a nursing home. However, the activity professional is not the only position in the nursing home which does not require a college degree. Twelve states still do not require that the administrator of the nursing home have a college degree (Brunk, 1998).

Many health care fields are struggling with issues of professional competency and standards. It is interesting to look at how well recreational therapy is doing compared to some of the other health care professions. Recreational therapy organized its first registration system in the early 1950's and incorporated the National Council for Therapeutic Recreation Certification (NCTRC) in 1981 (Connolly, 1998). Both of these actions (and the steps taken in between) helped articulate the standards for recreational therapy. There were nationally recognized standards in 1980 when NTRS published its first set of professional standards (Loeffler & Henley, 1997). By comparison, the administrators of nursing homes did not launch their first professional credentialing program until the late 1970's through the American College of Health Care Administrators (ACHCA) (Brunk, 1998). ACHCA published their first set of standards of practice in 1986. Directors of Nursing Service (DON) initiated their voluntary certification program in 1989 with their first standards of professional practice published in 1997 (Brunk, 1998). The National Council for Therapeutic Recreation Certification (NCTRC) adheres to the competency assurance standards outlined by the National Council for Certifying Agencies (NCCA) and has been recognized by NCCA as having met these standards. The national registration program for occupational therapists has not achieved this level of recognition yet.

Standards of Care

Standards of care refer to the minimum acceptable levels of patient care and staff performance based on all applicable standards (i.e., regulatory, voluntary, professional). Standards of care are generally facility specific but may be corporation specific. They help the professional by clearly defining what types of services/interventions the therapist will be expected to provide (thus implying authorization to do so) along with listed constraints of practice within the setting of that facility. Some facilities refer to standards of care as clinical practice guidelines. Standards of care are developed to help make compliance with government, organizational and facility standards easier. Care is taken to ensure that all applicable standards are translated into performance expectations for staff, including what types of services will be offered and what types of services will be considered outside the scope of practice for therapists working at that facility.

An example of a standard of care is assessing a patient on a psychiatric unit. When the occupational therapist shares an intake assessment with the recreational therapist (a very common occurrence with either one or the other therapist conducting the assessment), the standard of care might say that the patient will be assessed at a level necessary to provide good health care. The recreational therapist may ask the basic questions related to function on the test (expected service) and then determine that further information is needed about cognitive functioning related to supported employment (constraint of practice). The recreational therapist would then have the occupational therapist administer the *Allen Cognitive Level Test* (Hopkins & Smith, 1983) to complete the intake assessment. The opposite happens if the occupational therapist, in the process of conducting an intake assessment (expected service), determines that it is necessary to evaluate the patient's bus riding skills (constraint of practice) prior to the patient engaging in supported employment. In this situation the occupational therapist refers the patient to the recreational therapist so that the intake assessment can be completed using the *Community Integration Program, Second Edition* Module 4E: City Bus (Armstrong & Lauzen, 1994).

The Survey Process

Every agency, and it doesn't have to be a health care agency, will be surveyed by one group or another. In the United States, workplaces are surveyed by the Occupational Safety and Health Agency (OSHA). Health care agencies also have surveys from the Health Care Financing Administration (HCFA) or the state agency which represents HCFA. It is becoming more common for an organization like the Joint Commission on Accreditation of Health Care Organizations (JCAHO) to negotiate "deemed status" with HCFA to allow the survey done by JCAHO to also count as a survey done for HCFA (therefore having two surveys rolled into one survey process). This is allowed when the standards of the deemed organization meet or exceed the standards required by HCFA for Medicare/Medicaid programs (burlingame & Skalko, 1997).

Typically, the surveyors show up at the facility and stay for two days to two weeks, or even longer. The surveyors evaluate the facility's performance by sampling the work done by the facility's staff and contractors. Interviews are conducted with staff and patients, policy and procedure manuals are reviewed

Table 3.1: **How to Answer a Surveyor's Question**

Step 1. Restate the intent

Make sure that you understood what the surveyor asked. Restate the questions which you heard the surveyor ask.

Example:

How does our department ensure that we are providing a good environment of care?

Step 2. Identify the structures that support the intent of the question

The structures which support the intent of a question (e.g., environment of care) include any policies and procedures the department follows, any committee (and committee minutes) which the staff attend or support, any forms used to help meet the intent, specific orientation and ongoing education provided for staff, aspects of the department's quality assurance program which address the intent of the question and any questionnaires used to identify patient degree of satisfaction.

Example:

Our department enhances the environment of care for our patients through compliance with our policies and procedures. Some examples include our policies concerning staff preparedness for a disaster situation, marking and handling of hazardous materials and waste, life safety, security management and other aspects of environment of care.

Two of our staff are members of the Therapeutic Environment Committee and I sit on the Medical Equipment Utilization Committee as well as the Patient Care Quality Assurance Committee.

We have a manual of forms which we use in our department, including employee orientation and continuing education forms and material safety data sheets. They are located right next to our policy and procedure manual. All staff are required to review this manual at least annually.

Our last two patient satisfaction surveys included questions about the environment of care. The results have been summarized and changes implemented. That information is in the Quality Assurance Manual in the main staff office.

and medical charts analyzed. The facility's performance is measured against the appropriate standards and a survey document is written.

Many of the areas a therapist needs to know about for survey can be found in other parts of this book (outcome measurement, customer service, ethics, etc.). However, one very perplexing element of survey is when the therapist must actually speak to a surveyor to answer the surveyor's question. When the surveyor asks a question, s/he is not necessarily asking for the direct answer, but the *process* by which the facility reaches the answer (West, 1997). Being asked questions by a surveyor can be very stressful. The therapist will find that s/he can reduce his/her stress level by following a standard format for answering a surveyor's question. This technique should be practiced many times, until the therapist feels comfortable with the process. The two basic steps in answering a surveyor's question are shown in the Table 3.1.

When a survey is completed by a governmental agency, the facility generally receives a summary of its survey which lists only the standards which have not been met. For a variety of reasons, governmental agencies do not indicate the degree to which a facility passed or failed each tag; it only lists the ones which it did not pass. This type of survey summary can be emotionally devastating, as the facility and its staff are only told about their failures. Private organizations such as JCAHO, CARF and NCQA use a different system which shows the degree of compliance. Table 3.2 shows the one used by NCQA (NCQA, 1996).

Benchmarking

Benchmarking is the action of measuring your performance compared to someone else's performance in a pre-identified set of measurements. JCAHO defines benchmarking as:

> Continuous measurement of a process, product or service compared to those of the toughest competitor, to those considered industry leaders, or to similar activities in the organization in order to find and implement ways to improve it. This is one of the foundations of both total quality management and continuous quality improvement.

Table 3.2: **Compliance Designations**

Full Compliance	The organization consistently meets all the provisions of the Standard.
Significant Compliance	The organization meets most provisions of the Standard.
Partial Compliance	The organization meets some provisions of the Standard.
Minimal Compliance	The organization meets few provisions of the Standard.
Noncompliance	The organization fails to meet the provisions of the Standard.
Not Applicable	The Standard does not apply to the organization.

Internal benchmarking occurs when similar processes within the same organization are compared. *Competitive benchmarking* occurs when an organization's processes are compared with best practices within the industry. *Functional benchmarking* refers to benchmarking a similar function or process, such as scheduling, in another industry. (JCAHO, 1998a)

This type of measurement for performance is usually achieved through an audit done internally or an audit done by individuals outside of the facility (a survey). External audits are usually measurements against standards. Internal audits may include comparisons against much higher standards such as statistics from facilities who have been defined as sites working in best practice.

Managing Quality

Every accrediting organization and the federal government now require that health care providers have an ongoing program to measure the quality of the services provided. In almost every case a facility is now also required to report outcomes of treatment. The health care industry has done fairly well adjusting to these requirements considering it lacks a unified definition of *quality* (Frey, 1992). Even without a unified definition, most facilities, government agencies, organizations and payers would agree that quality is "the production of improved health and satisfaction of a population within the constraints of existing technology, resources and consumer circumstances" (Frey, 1992, p. 2).

There are two other words which are frequently brought up when discussing quality — value and outcome. Value refers to the perceived worth of a treatment or process. This perception may be described in terms of dollars and cents; described by its usefulness or importance; or it may be described in a more symbolic term, such as quality of life. Increased ability to become an active member of the community and use services in the community such as the parks department or library would be considered of value. Outcome refers to a change which is a result of actions taken. An example of an outcome would be that for each dollar spent on rehabilitation, as much as 30 additional dollars may be saved (Schlossman, 1992).

If the customer is who we serve, then the customer is the one who should receive value as a result of our actions. Increasingly, over the last twenty years, emphasis has been placed on an organization's ability to manage the quality of services and interventions provided to the consumer. The basic concept of value for the customer has not changed although the nomenclature has. Moore (1997) has this to say:

Management buzzwords such as "management by objectives" and "total quality management" come and go. Often perceived as vague, complex or confusing, they fade into the past before most of us understand or appreciate their true application or potential benefit to our operations. (p. 33)

Many words have been developed to denote the concept of managing quality including quality assurance (ensuring quality, QA), continuous quality improvement (ongoing programs, CQI), total quality management (system wide programs, TQM) and performance measurement, PM. The evolution of these concepts and their impact on providing recreational therapy are important and beyond the scope of this chapter. Below is a general overview of the necessary organizational behaviors to achieve value and a brief summary of the process to manage quality.

Organizational Behavior

An organization in which each and every employee believes deeply that s/he is *the one* who will make the difference is an organization likely to achieve value for the customer. Providing quality and value to the customer requires that ownership and pride in one's work is pervasive throughout the organization. In addition to ownership, the ability to be flexible is vital. The ability to accept change (and adapt to it) in the organizational culture is key to keeping up with the metamorphosis in health care.

Health care is changing, and each change impacts the entire integrated system of delivery. New approaches in treatment are implemented to improve the outcome and value for the patient. New approaches are being developed in many health care fields and, as each new innovation is implemented, it may change multiple elements of the patient's well-being, schedule and attitude. A change in what the recreational therapist does is likely to impact the job of the rest of the team and change the situation of the patient as well. An example is when recreational therapy increases its emphasis on hands-on community integration. Now, instead of taking inpatients out of the hospital two times a week, the therapist is taking one to two short outings a day. Just some of the changes include the physical absence of the recreational therapist from the building, the physical absence of patients, the patient having increased integration skills prior to discharge and more data for the team on how the patient can function. Multiply the impacts of these changes to account for the innovations made by each member of the team and major change is inevitable. When one member of the team makes a change, it causes changes throughout the treatment team.

This fast change is one of the primary reasons the recreational therapist must actively manage quality. The environment in which the therapist practices will never be static, so s/he needs to know how his/her process is being impacted by change. Managing quality means that the therapist is purposely controlling the process of delivering services so that the desired outcome is achieved, even when some other aspect of care is changed.

To empower every employee to embrace change while still striving to enhance value, the organizational behavior needs to encourage the following:

- The administration of the organization must believe that every employee is vital to managing quality and must have both the responsibility and authority to take action.
- The employees must be self-motivated, self-evaluative and hungry to facilitate the patient's move toward normalization and wholeness.
- The employees need to have the resources available to them to allow data collection. The data collection resources should be standardized to allow the use of integrated or interactive software to compare quality and outcomes with outside organizations.
- The delivery of quality services must go hand-in-hand with the conservative management of resources. Departments should not "pad" their budgets to get what they feel they need. Money and other resources should be allocated to service units based on their outcomes and perceived value.
- The health care organization must be willing to treat the customers' perceptions as paramount. The health care industry has been remiss by omitting the consumers' perception of value and utility as the primary outcome which drives planning (Malkmus & Evans, 1992).

Malkmus and Evans (1992) state:

Valid quality measures proven useful in other industries have been obscured by traditional medical, educational and vocational models perpetuated in rehabilitation service delivery. Consequently, the evolution and current state of rehabilitation services for persons with acquired brain injury have been primarily provider driven rather than consumer driven. (p. vii)

Improving Quality

When a performance or outcome does not match the intended result, locating the problem is the first step toward solving it. To be able to resolve a problem, it is best to identify the root of the problem. Without addressing the root of the problem, a reoccurrence is likely to take place. Most problems related to quality fall into one of five categories (Ozeki & Asaka, 1990). These categories are presented in Table 3.3.

Table 3.3: **Root Causes for Most Problems Related to Quality**

Problem	Root Cause
Problems related to worker skills or attitudes	• Pure mistake • Not following policies and procedures • Skills not yet adequate • Concern for quality not strong enough
Problems related to the workplace quality assurance system	• The quality characteristic is not well defined • Performance and operating standards incomplete • Management points and expectations unclear • Casual about quality assurance methods • Quality assurance process chart/plan not yet complete
Lack of motivation to solve the problem	• No desire to delve deeply into the problem and solve it • Management's leadership in setting improvement goals and in making improvement is inadequate
Problems in the workplace culture	• Never delving deeply into problems • Blaming the workplace custom
Problems originating in another department	• Design error • Error in understanding what the customer desires or holds valuable

Once the root of the problem has been identified the team can begin to develop the steps necessary to correct it. Any plan to improve quality contains some basic steps. These steps are presented in Table 3.4.

Table 3.4: **Steps of Quality Assurance Program**

Step 1 *Identifying Issues and Selecting Study Topics*	Obviously it is essential to begin with a determination of what needs to be improved to provide quality service. This first step has you look closely at the problem to specifically identify what is not right. Unfortunately, many quality assurance programs concern themselves with issues that are not important, or with procedural items that can be easily remedied, rather than those that justify being part of long-range planning.
Step 2a *Establishing Indicators*	Identifying elements that can be monitored to measure changes made. The elements or characteristics of the service you select to measure should be a general statement about what the service would look like if there was not a problem.

Table 3.4: Steps of Quality Assurance Program, *continued*

Step 2b *Developing Criteria*	Developing criteria for each indicator. Writing a plan that spells out exactly what should be found and ideally in what quantity and in what time frame.
Step 3a *Determining Methodology*	Establishing the exact method to be used to collect information: from which sources, by whom, how often, how long and how the results are going to be used.
Step 3b *Collecting Data*	Implementing the chosen methods of data collection.
Step 4a *Understanding the Problem*	Reviewing and assessing collected data to see what, where and how serious the problems are. Deciding which problem areas should be the focus of further study.
Step 4b *Setting Standards*	Standards are set to describe the desired outcomes in a measurable way.
Step 4c *Finding Solutions*	Searching for possible ways to reach the standards set.
Step 4d *Writing an Action Plan*	The methodology for implementing a change is determined along with decisions about who is to have the responsibility and what the time frames will be.
Step 4e *Implementing the Plan*	Putting into action the strategies that have been developed.
Step 5a *Assessing the Outcomes*	Did the plan work? Do the problems still remain? Has there been some improvement? This procedure often entails a repeat of steps 3 and 4: going back and re-collecting the data and then analyzing the results to see if the standards have been reached.
Step 5b *Identifying New Issues or Continuing to Work on the Old*	If the problems are not solved, new strategies must be planned. If, however, the process has been successful, a new plan should be developed for the next area of focus. As stated earlier, quality assurance is an ongoing process and does not stop once a particular problem is corrected. It is also necessary to periodically go back and monitor earlier plans and see if the goals are continuing to be met. Two or three past issues may be chosen at random for an ongoing audit in addition to the main topic of study. These could be changed periodically on a rotating basis to assure that new problems have not arisen in any of these areas.

Used with permission from R. N. Cunninghis & E. Best-Martini, *Quality Assurance for Activity Programs*, 2nd Edition, 1996.

The plan should answer some key questions, including what is going to be done, what process(es) will be followed to accomplish what is to be done, who will be responsible for making change happen and how will the process and outcome be measured and evaluated?

Quality Assurance Privileges

Improving the quality of a facility's performance through continuous quality monitoring has led to significant improvements in the delivery of health care. However, it did not take lawyers or state and federal surveyors long to figure out the documentation and reports generated by a facility's quality assurance program were ripe for the taking. Facility's which documented substandard care through their performance measurements were being penalized because court after court ordered the facility's own investigations to be turned over to "the other side." This potential that facility's own work to improve the situation could be used against the facility led many facilities to attend to performance improvement as an act of paper compliance only. To address this problem the United States Congress enacted the *Health Care Quality Improvement Act of 1986*. This act provided facilities with "limited immunity from damages and litigation as a result of peer reviews done to help improve the quality of services" (burlingame & Skalko, 1997). The federal government also built into its 1990 revision of OBRA (nursing home regulations) a provision which prohibits the state or federal surveyors from insisting on disclosure of a nursing home's quality assurance documents. A facility is only required to show enough of its quality assurance documents to prove that it has a functioning quality assurance program. These laws have been challenged by two recent court cases in which the mixed rulings helped better define a facility's actual rights. The first case was *Boone Retirement Center v. Hamilton*. The court ruled that lawyers were barred from compelling a nursing home to turn over its documentation produced by the facility's quality assurance committee on problems identified and actions taken. However, in *Department of Health v. Briarcliff Nursing Center*, another court ruled that incident reports and accident reports which were not produced as documentation by the quality assurance committee but by employees in the normal course of business were not protected (Infante, 1997). The sum results of these two court rulings demonstrate the value of self- and peer review and the need to fully investigate, document and then plan for improvement in areas of identified need. This process, worked through the facility's quality assurance committee, should be considered privileged information, allowing full disclosure only to the appropriate individuals within the facility.

Best Practices

A best practice is simply the best way to perform a business or therapy process (Hiebeler, Kelly & Ketteman, 1998). The recreational therapist can help determine a best practice for any process by exploring what others have done.

Best practice principles generally encourage people to look outside their own industry to see best practice for the process they want to improve (functional benchmarking). This allows break-through thinking. If you look only within your own industry, all you are doing is working to keep up with your competition. This does not qualify as a best practice. "Identifying and matching a best practice in your own field is nothing more than a catch-up game. What was really needed was some way of identifying and capturing best practices, not just in terms of a particular industry, but for all industries everywhere" (Hiebeler, Kelly & Ketteman, 1998, p. 20). Some examples of best practices throughout many industries are shown below. While two of the three examples are from outside the health care industry, the recreational therapist can still learn about the processes taken to make a best practice.

- Nike increased their total sales to women from 15% to 65% in just over two years by using a provocative marketing message which challenged long held stereotypes of women. There are many stereotypes held about individuals with disabilities which can be challenged.
- The Ritz-Carlton is the only hotel chain to win the prestigious Malcolm Baldrige National Quality Award. It has all of its staff who have direct contact with customers carry a notebook to write down customer preferences and complaints. These are entered into a database and analyzed.
- Holy Cross Hospital, Chicago in 1991 was ranked in the bottom 5% of hospitals in the United States. In 1994 it was ranked in the top 5% of hospitals in the United States. Holy Cross Hospital, in response to its poor rating in 1991 developed "commando teams" with specific goals (e.g., identifying barriers to prompt customer service) (Hiebeler, Kelly & Ketteman, 1998). It was through their commitment to increase the value of their service — value as defined by the consumer — that their position improved so much.

In each case, these companies saw that their ability to provide the customer with the best practice possible hinged on their ability to improve processes. To identify a best practice the therapist doesn't ask "what is the best practice in recreational therapy for physical medicine and rehabilitation?" Instead a series of questions would be asked, such as:

- What fundamental process do we want to improve?
- Who are we trying to better serve?

Table 3.5: **Sharing Innovations In Quality Topics List**

Topic	Subjects Included in Topic
How to care for the following special populations	Residents who have dementia/Alzheimer's disease, behavioral symptoms, depression/anxiety/other DSM-IV Axis I disorders. Note: This includes the provision of medical, nursing and psychosocial care, activities, drug regimens, enhancement of resident choices, nutrition, environmental manipulation, staff/resident interactions, etc.
Implementation of Clinical Practice	Infection control, pressure sores, incontinence, restorative care, nutrition/hydration, other.
New advances in knowledge	Knowledge related to the process of aging applied to the care of nursing home residents.
Fall prevention	Innovations in fall prevention.
Best practices associated with the dying process	Providing quality of care and life for residents throughout the dying process. This includes issues concerning the dying resident, other residents who are affected, family and staff.
Pain relief, control	Assessment and intervention for pain relief and control.
Optimizing use of all staff to meet quality of care and quality of life needs	Cross utilization, scheduling staff to maximize resident choices, use of volunteers (within the nursing home and community), recruitment, training, retention, facility pride, volunteers, other.
Creating a culture of trust and problem solving for residents and families	Resident rights and choices; privacy, dignity and autonomy; ethics, decision making.
Environmental enhancements	Layout (new facilities and those being remodeled), noise reduction, adaptation of space for multiple uses (enhancing residents' privacy), social aspects and quality of life in dining room, enhancing quality of life in ADL routines, other.
Resident's personal belongings	Prevention of loss/damage/theft, personalizing individual rooms, other.

- What are the best ways for us to respond to customer service issues?
- How can we team up with customers to design, market and deliver better services and interventions?
- How do other companies find and train employees to serve customers better?

In the spring of 1998 HCFA initiated a new program called *Sharing Innovations in Quality*, or SIQ. The Congress of the United States directed HCFA to develop a non-regulatory, collaborative project to develop and promote training materials concerning best practices in long term care. The SIQ collaborative council is made up of representatives from government, businesses and professional organizations. It is their responsibility to help identify best practices throughout the field in ten areas (see Table 3.5).

HCFA's web site (http://www.hcfa.gov.medicaid/qualhmpg.htm) lists practices which the SIQ collaborative council consider to be the best practices in the field. While this is not as sweeping as a list of practices in all industries, as described above, it does allow all long term care facilities to catch up with the best practices in the field.

The bottom line for providing your customer with a best practice is to have an unwavering focus on the customer; "understanding markets and customers; designing, marketing, selling, producing and delivering products and services; as well as providing customer service" (Hiebeler, Kelly & Ketteman, 1998, p. 228). By maintaining this focus, the recreational therapist will be able to know that s/he is providing a best practice.

Summary

Standards are a level of expected performance which are defined by governments, organizations and facilities. It is important for each health care professional to know all of the standards which apply to his/her practice. This chapter provided an overview of the types of standards that recreational therapists must understand. Learning the particular standards for a particular position is the responsibility of the professional.

Standards are enforced in a variety of ways, but the most common is through survey by a governmental agency or a private accrediting agency. Sometimes a survey by an accrediting agency serves both purposes.

The final topic of the chapter was improving the quality of services. This is an ongoing process. Because aspects of health care service and intervention are continually changing, the therapist needs to monitor not only the quality of his/her product, but also to know how the change others are producing affects his/her product. Facilities must embrace an organizational behavior and belief that meeting the consumers' needs takes the actions of each and every staff. The best value usually comes from groups of people who have developed a good process to discover and implement the best practices available.

Learning Activities

1. Search JCAHO's web site. What issues and trends concerning standards can you find? How might these affect the practice of recreational therapy?
2. Search CARF's web site. What issues and trends concerning standards can you find? How might these affect the practice of recreational therapy?
3. Search NCQA's web site. What issues and trends concerning standards can you find? How might these affect the practice of recreational therapy?
4. Pretend you are working at a health care facility. With another student practice answering questions from a "surveyor," drawing the questions from any of the standards of practice found in Appendix B.
5. Visit HCFA's web site for best practices. Find a practice concept which can be applied to recreational therapy and write up a program using that best practice.

Study Questions

1. Compare and contrast the different groups which develop standards. Which are the most basic, important standards to meet?
2. What are the primary differences and similarities of the professional standards set by NTRS and ATRA? Compare and contrast.
3. Based on health care trends and summarized by the PEW Commission, what type of skills will be required of professionals?
4. List the typical root causes for a lack of quality.
5. What is a "best practice" and why is it important to look outside the arena of health care for best practices?

References

American Therapeutic Recreation Association. (1993). *Standards for the practice of therapeutic recreation & self assessment guide*. Hattiesburg, MS: ATRA.

Armstrong, M. & Lauzen, S. (1994). *Community integration program* (2nd ed.). Ravensdale, WA: Idyll Arbor, Inc.

Austin, D. M. (1989). Therapeutic recreation education: A call for reform. In D. Compton (Ed.). *Issues in therapeutic recreation: A profession in transition* (pp. 145-156). Champaign, IL: Sagamore Publishing.

Best-Martini, E., Weeks, M. A. & Wirth, P. (1996). *Long term care for activity and social service professionals* (2nd ed.). Ravensdale, WA: Idyll Arbor, Inc.

Bonifazi, W. L. (1998). The federal factor: How government rules and regulations have shaped long term care. *Contemporary Long Term Care, 21*(2), 56-60.

Brasile, F. M. (1992). Professional preparation: Reported needs for a profession in transition. *Annual in Therapeutic Recreation, 3*, 58-71.

Brunk, D. (1998). Going pro. *Contemporary Long Term Care, 21*(5), 62-67.

burlingame, j. & Skalko, T. (1997). *Idyll Arbor's glossary for therapists.* Ravensdale, WA: Idyll Arbor, Inc.

CARF: The Rehabilitation Accreditation Commission. (1998). *CARF: A hallmark of quality.* http://www.carf.org/hallmark.html. 7/12/98.

Clifton, D. W. (1996). Utilization management: Whose job is it? *Rehab Management, 9*(4), 38-44.

Connolly, P. (1998). Health care credentialing. In F. Brasile, T. Skalko & j. burlingame (Eds.). *Perspective in recreational therapy: Issues of a dynamic profession.* Ravensdale, WA: Idyll Arbor, Inc.

Cunninghis, R. N. & Best-Martini, E. (1996). *Quality assurance for activity programs* (2nd ed.). Ravensdale, WA: Idyll Arbor, Inc.

Foltz-Gray, D. (1997). The golden state learns the golden rule. *Contemporary Long Term Care, 20*(10), 47.

Frey, W. R. (1992). Quality management: Protecting and enhancing quality in brain injury rehabilitation. *Journal of Head Trauma Rehabilitation, 7*(4), 1-23.

Hiebeler, R., Kelly, T. B. & Ketteman, C. (1998). *Best practices: Building your business with customer-focused solutions.* New York: Simon & Schuster.

Hopkins, H. L. & Smith, H. D. (1983). *Willard and Spackman's occupational therapy* (6th ed.). New York: J. B. Lippincott Company.

Huebler, D. (1994). Education for allied health professionals. *Rehab Management, 7*(4), 62-67.

Infante, M. C. (1997). Some assurance on quality assurance privilege. *Contemporary Long Term Care, 20*(8), 71.

Joint Commission on Accreditation of Healthcare Organizations. (1998a). Sentinel events — Glossary of terms. http://www.jcaho.org/sentinel/se_glsry.htm. 7/11/98 5:30 p.m.

Joint Commission on Accreditation of Healthcare Organizations. (1998b). Facts about the Joint Commission on Accreditation of Healthcare Organizations. http://www.jcaho.org/about_jc/mh_missn.htm. 7/12/98 7:46 p.m.

Joint Commission on Accreditation of Healthcare Organizations. (1998c). Joint Commission Standards. http://www.jcaho.org/perfmeas/stds.htm. 7/11/98 5:25 p.m.

Loeffler, M. A. & Henley, S. (1997). Standards of practice: Are they relevant? In D. M. Compton (Ed.) *Issues in therapeutic recreation: Toward the new millennium* (2nd ed.) (pp. 419-443). Champaign, IL: Sagamore Publishing.

Malkmus, D. D. & Evans, R. W. (1992). Preface to quality, outcome and value. *The Journal of Head Trauma Rehabilitation, 7*(4), vii-viii.

Moore, J. (1997). Benchmarking deserves a change. *Contemporary Long Term Care, 20*(12), 33-34.

National Committee for Quality Assurance. (1996). *Standards for the accreditation of managed care organizations, 1996 edition.* Washington, DC: National Committee for Quality Assurance.

National Committee for Quality Assurance. (1998). *HAP quality of care.* http://www.hapcorp.org.docs/HEALTHY/Ncqa.htm.

National Therapeutic Recreation Society. (1995). *Standards of practice for therapeutic recreation services and annotated bibliography.* Ashburn, VA: NRPA/NTRS.

Newsfronts. (1997a). Tools from the trades: Long term care groups develop new clinical practice guidelines. *Contemporary Long Term Care, 20*(8), 19.

Newsfronts. (1997b). OSHA's TB tome: Hefty proposed guidelines will be regulatory in nature. *Contemporary Long Term Care, 20*(12), 24.

O'Leary, D. S. (1996). President's column. *Joint Commission Perspectives.* January/February 1996.

Ozeki, K. & Asaka, T. (1990). *Handbook of quality tools: The Japanese approach.* Portland, OR: Productivity Press.

Pew Health Professions Commission. (1995). *Critical challenges: Revitalizing the health professions for the twenty-first century.* Pew Health Commission.

Riley, B. (Ed.). (1987). *Evaluation of therapeutic recreation through quality assurance.* State College, PA: Venture Publishing, Inc.

Schlossman, S. (1992). Lack of awareness is "formative obstacle" for rehabilitation providers. *AHA News, 28*, 4.

Skalko, T. K. & Goldenberg, R. (1995). Recreational therapy/therapeutic recreation education: A call for reform. *ATRA Newsletter, 11*(2), 11.

Toppel, A. H., Beach, B. A. & Hutchinson-Troyer, L. (1991). Standards: A tool for accountability the CARF process. *Annual in Therapeutic Recreation, 2*, 96-99.

Walton, M. (1986). *The Deming management method.* New York: Perigee Books.

West, R. E. (1997). Recreational therapy in managed care: Competency assessment and critical pathway development. Presentation at Overlake Hospital and Medical Center on November 21-22, 1997, Bellevue, WA.

Chapter 4

Ethics: To Do the Right Thing

Melany Bailey Spielman

The study of ethics has been around for thousands of years dating back to Plato, Aristotle, Socrates, Cicero and other great philosophers. Philosophical, legal and religious considerations belong to the ethos or mores of the greater society. To ignore, deny or be insensitive to their existence is unethical (Primeaux & Stieber, 1995). People live in relationships with others and have many arenas where values are learned. Family, church, school, friends and work all contribute to the assimilation of values.

Ethics or moral philosophy is the attempt to understand the nature of human values, how people ought to live and what constitutes right conduct. Ethics is a branch of philosophy whose object is an inquiry into what is good for people and what is bad for people. Ethics involves moral thought and reflection, as well as moral judgments. Ethics is the study of what rules ought to govern choices between possible behaviors. In essence, ethics is concerned with clarifying what constitutes human welfare and describing the kind of conduct necessary to promote it. Clark and Lattal (1992) point out that "Ethical behavior requires that in one way or another the interest of all affected human beings be taken into consideration, including oneself" (p. 11).

The study of ethics is properly categorized into three approaches: descriptive, analytical and prescriptive (normative). The descriptive approach comprises scientific studies or factual descriptions that describe or explain the similar or different moral behaviors and beliefs of different persons or societies.

The descriptive approach is interested in the phenomenon of morality in a non-philosophic context and seeks a deliberate neutrality concerning the validity, superiority, inferiority or justifiability of the values, norms and moral values or beliefs. People exploring this category are interested in what is and are not concerned for right or wrong. They want to explore what is and how it developed. A clinical psychologist is interested in his/her patient and is especially careful not to pass judgment on this patient's problems or behavior.

Analytical ethics studies the underlying suppositions upon which a philosophy is built. It looks systematically at the foundations of what societies or people believe to be right or wrong. Metaethics (another name for analytical ethics) "involves clarifying and evaluating presuppositions and investigating questions of meaning and justification...in an attempt to transcend existing ethical theories and principles, which may lead to conflicting courses of action, and judge them in light of ultimate values of human well-being and welfare to resolve such conflicts" (Bucholz, 1989, p. 10).

Prescriptive ethics is concerned with addressing the question of what is a valid or defensible principle of good and bad character or right and wrong conduct. It is concerned with the formulation and defense of basic moral norms governing moral life. "Prescriptivists present a particular group of principles and standards that would be best for people to use as guides in all aspects of their lives. Consequently, prescriptive ethics is not morally neutral" (Manley, 1990, p. 3).

Customary Actions

The student will hear the word "ethics" throughout his/her career. But what is "ethics" and is it something that s/he will need to deal with on a daily basis? Probably. Ethics is a term which originates from the Greek word "ethos" which means "customary." What is "customary" may vary depending on whether values are being applied to an individual, a member of a professional group or a business. Individuals learn to act in a right, or moral, manner as defined by their family, close social group and community. Customary implies the context and attitude in which an individual or group acts. While ethics are moral judgments related to the perceived correctness of an action, the context of who is taking the action also applies. Fain (1989) points out that stealing food from someone would normally be considered to be morally wrong. However, if the individual stealing is a two year old taking food off of a grandparent's plate, the ethical concerns fade. A soldier killing an enemy during war is generally viewed differently than a teenager shooting his/her classmates.

In therapy, ethics is "a system of values held by a group of people which outline acceptable and non-acceptable behavior" (burlingame & Skalko, 1997, p. 108). These values help professionals in the decision-making process to make choices between actions that could be taken.

Ethics also implies a reasonable quality and quantity to the actions. The ethical implementation of quality technical skills includes the use of modalities which are known to be beneficial and not harmful to the patient, the appropriate training and skill level of the practitioner to use the modalities, the maintenance of an honest and respectful communication with the patient throughout the treatment and the ongoing maintenance of confidentiality after the treatment has occurred (burlingame & Skalko, 1997). An example would be the therapist's ensuring the best positioning to maximize the patient's ability to perform a task while at the same time reducing skin integrity problems. Quantity related to ethical practice addresses the question, "Is the service provided in a cost-effective manner, with adequate duration and frequency, to justify the service based on the outcome achieved?" If the rest of the treatment team customarily takes a 20 minute break instead of the 15 minute break they are scheduled to take, does it mean that it is ethical for the therapist to also take a 20 minute break? Ethical behaviors are based on virtuous actions.

This is different than, but not separate from, the skills and knowledge you will use throughout your career. Technical knowledge and skills allow a professional to provide an intervention (e.g., teach anger management skills) but ethics guide the professional in providing treatment and the therapeutic environment to implement his/her technical knowledge.

Ethics, the morality of aspiration, is different from the law (regulations), the morality of duty. Recreational therapists are expected to follow the laws set by the government concerning boundaries of acceptable behavior. If the therapist violates these boundaries of acceptable behavior set by society, s/he risks incarceration or other legal consequences. Recreational therapists are also expected to follow the ethical ideals embodied within their field.

Personal Ethics

Your personal ethics is one of the core ingredients of who you are. Others can tell much about you by analyzing your value structure, personal integrity and personal standards of conduct. Your personal integrity is vital in the pursuit of a good life. We all have personal integrity but the quality of that integrity differs greatly from person to person and may fluctuate over a lifetime. Personal integrity is manifested through behaviors, attitudes and words. It incorporates being honest, consistent and it is ever present. You cannot have integrity in only one aspect of your life. It must be present in all decisions and be evident at all times (Edginton, Jordan, DeGraaf & Edginton, 1995). Having integrity means you have positive values and you act on them consistently. See Table 4.1. for a list of the five principles of personal ethics.

Professional Ethics

The use of moral judgment within one's profession and within the work place builds upon the personal moral judgment used by the individual. The individuals within a profession agree to adhere to an expanded set of moral behav-

Table 4.1: **The Five Principles of Ethical Power for Individuals**

Purpose	I see myself as being an ethically sound person. I let my conscience be my guide. No matter what happens, I am always able to face the mirror, look myself straight in the eye, and feel good about myself.
Pride	I feel good about myself. I don't need the acceptance of other people to feel important. A balanced self-esteem keeps my ego and my desire to be accepted from influencing my decisions.
Patience	I believe that things will eventually work out well. I don't need everything to happen right now. I am at peace with what comes my way!
Persistence	I stick to my purpose, especially when it seems inconvenient to do so! My behavior is consistent with my intentions. As Churchill said, "Never! Never! Never! Never! Give up!"
Perspective	I take time to enter each day quietly in a mood of reflection. This helps me to get myself focused and allows me to listen to my inner self and to see things more clearly.

Used with permission from Blanchard & Peale, 1988, p. 80, *The Power of Ethical Management.* William Morrow and Company, Inc.

iors beyond what each might normally display in other aspects of his/her life. Each professional group has its own set of morals or values, called codes of ethics (Fain, 1989).

Values are specific desires for objects or beliefs perceived as important, whereas ethics is a more general term that refers to the conception of human welfare and the promulgation of principles to enhance human welfare. Morality, further, usually refers to traditional beliefs of proper and improper conduct that have a historical context of years or centuries (Bucholz, 1989). But what, specifically, a group of people pursuing a united focus believes to be right is professional ethics.

In furthering the discussion of ethics and the role they play in the practice of our profession a few strategic definitions are needed. What do we mean when we talk about values, norms, laws and science and how do they contribute to the discussion of ethics? In the discussion that follows the definitions in Table 4.2 will be the operational descriptions of terms.

How are these terms different and how are they similar? Often they are in used in conversations interchangeably. The theoretical and practical differences that are conceived in varied approaches of ethics suggest five distinct, yet not mutually exclusive constructs. These are values, norms, science, laws and ethics. Figure 4.1 graphically shows the role these constructs play in specifying the domain of professional ethics (White & Wooten, 1986). The diagram shows how the five factors interact and how ethics is the intersection of the other four constructs.

White and Wooten (1986) believe that professional ethics must begin with values, beliefs or ideals held by the individuals or groups in a specific discipline. Professional norms are then established and lead to concerns of what ought to be done, what is expected and levels of performance. The next step in the evolution of professional ethics is the formal pursuit of knowledge based on the scientific method to investigate the substance of the discipline. Then based on its values, norms and body of knowledge, the discipline devises social rules and standards of behavior concerning the rights and wrongs of professional conduct. Some means of enforcement must then be established. A Code of Ethics can only emerge after a discipline can articulate these other things.

Our discipline has Codes of Ethics from both the American Therapeutic Recreation Association (ATRA) and National Therapeutic Recreation Society (NTRS). A copy of each is included in Appendix C. Read them and know they will be the documents outlining your obligations as a professional.

Table 4.2: **Definition of Terms Related to Professional Ethics**

Values	Beliefs or ideals held by individuals or groups concerning what is good, right, desirable or important in an idea, object or action.
Norms	An idea, conceptualization, belief or a statement enforced by the sanctions of members of a group concerning their behavioral rules, patterns and conduct, which is referenced in the form of what should be done, what ought to be done, what is expected and the level of action or expectation under specific circumstances.
Science	A body of knowledge that is characterized by the use of the scientific method which seeks out goal oriented information through systematic, unified, and self-correcting processes.
Laws	A system of social rules, norms or standards of behavior, concerning the right and wrong of human conduct that is put in codes enforced by sanctions imposed through recognized authority.
Ethics	Concepts and standards held by individuals or groups concerning the values surrounding the rightness and wrongness of models of conduct in human behavior and the result of human behavior actions.

From: White and Wooten (1986). *Professional Ethics and Practice of Organizational Development*, NY: Praeger Publishers.

Figure 4.1: The Domain of Professional Ethics

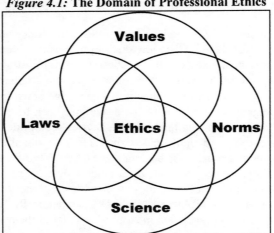

Corporate Ethics

As each professional group sets its code of ethics to guide the moral judg-ment of its members, so does a company set its own code of ethics to guide the moral judgment of its employees. There will be similarities between the code of ethics of the various professional groups which work within the structure of a company, especially in health care, where each professional is working toward addressing a patient's health status. A health care facility, as both a healer and a business, will have moral judgments related to both healing and business. Blanchard and Peale (1988) suggest three basic moral questions which address the scope of business ethics. They are

Is it legal? No employee will undertake any activity while on company premises, or while engaging in company business, that is (or gives the appearance of being) improper, illegal or immoral, or that could in any way harm or embarrass our company or our customers. (p. 21)

Is it balanced? Will the decision be fair or will it heavily favor one party over another in the short term or long term? If any individual in our company makes a decisions that benefits that person or our company at someone else's real expense — be it another employer, a supplier, a customer, or even a competitor — it will eventually come back to haunt the individual or the company. (p. 22)

How will it make me feel about myself? How would I feel if what I'm considering doing was published in the newspaper? (p. 24)

What would happen if the codes of ethics of a company were significantly different than the norms of a profession? Or what if there was a conflict in values? Dissonance would occur and people would become uncomfortable. While many areas of dissonance may be identified, one very prevalent one today is the conflict of values which arise because of managed care.

In managed care those things we value most highly, autonomy of physicians and decisions based on what is best for the patient, are being challenged. Daily, the news informs us of legislative actions on both the state and national level which forbid insurance carriers from carrying out their "gag rules." On December 9, 1996, Herb Denenberg from NBC News in Philadelphia reported on gag rules. Gag rules say a doctor is forbidden from explaining all the treatment options to the patient and must only outline those low cost options covered by the carrier policy. Mr. Denenberg pointed out the unethical position of the physicians in this matter. Medicine has a code of ethics that specifically outlines a physician's responsibility to his/her patient. However, in pursuit of a larger reimbursement from the HMOs, the physicians agreed to these stipulations. A dissonance exists between the physician's professional code of ethics and the businesses actions. The American Medical Association (AMA) examined 200 contracts between doctors and HMOs and found gag rules in virtually all of them. The Federal government recently announced gag rules were illegal under Medicare law and said it would be announcing it illegal under Medicaid law, too. Legislation mandating at least 48 hours of hospitalization for specific procedures has been enacted on the Federal level. Ten measures were recently introduced in the California legislature which would put constraints on how managed care is run. Physicians do not want someone telling them what they can do for their patients but they are also wary of the government micro-managing health care (CBS Nightly News, Feb. 26, 1997).

If corporations hold to the business ethic propounded by Milton Friedman in his celebrated 1970 article, the individual therapist might come into a situation of conflicting ethics. Friedman wrote that "there is one and only one social responsibility of business — to use its resources and engage in activities designed to increase its profits so long as it stays within the rules of the game, which is to say, engages in open and free competition without deception or fraud" (Friedman, 1970, p 126). We are often confronted today with the reality that patients will not be getting all the treatment they need because of their insurance coverage or limits on the hospital's total allowable payment for this patient. The purpose of therapy is to increase patients' quality of life and the therapist has decided the best way to assist the patient in accomplishing that goal. Conflict potentially occurs with the organizational goal of turning a profit.

When personal and professional ethics conflict with the organizational ethics of the employer, difficult decisions need to be made. If it seems realistic to change the organizational ethic which seems out of line with a personal or professional ethic, the choice may be made to stay and work through that process. If it is unrealistic to change the problematic organizational ethic, professionals will need to make the choice to stay and ignore internal conflict (professionals need to eat and provide for family) or to leave. Prolonged exposure to conflict of ethics and values has great emotional and physical costs. Being forced to act in a way believed to be fundamentally unethical can cause great stress. Dissonance can lead to subversion and rebellion.

Cialdini (1996) believes "ethics" doesn't have enough motivational power to cause someone concerned with profit making to do the right thing if other more motivational factors (e.g., sales quotas, corporate financial health and survival, career advancement) are pressing. Real problems occur when the employer is making decisions based on maximizing profits and ignoring the ethical issues of providing good service to its customers or patients. Any company that operates without ethics will lose money whether its employees' ethics match the organization or they are mismatched. If the employee is unethical and the organization is unethical, the organization must continually suspect employees of stealing and pilfering. Safety measures and punitive structures are costly. If on the other hand, the employee is ethical and the corporation is not, the employee will potentially experience higher stress and higher absences eventually leading to turnover. This resulting conflict of values is detailed in the Figure 4.2 which Cialdini calls the Triple Tumor Structure of Organizational Dishonestly.

In Figure 4.2 the company would potentially be unaware of the costs of not being honest. Recently when the Ethics Resource Center surveyed 100,000 American workers, they found that 33% of them had witnessed behavior on the job that either violated their company's code of conduct or broke the law. They reported that 56% of the employees say their supervisors lie, 41% saw records being falsified and 35% observed stealing. Occupational fraud costs US firms $400 billion a year (Khalfani/*Dow Jones News Service* on GT Online 1995-1996). It is important to note that dishonesty on the part of the organization can be disguised as "business as usual."

Health care providers or HMOs sell their products as being the "best" or most comprehensive but know, even while they are selling their products, they do not cover what many consider to be necessary services. They decline to make the agreements with physicians about compensation public. In some cases doctors profit more from not referring to specialists or alternative care. Keeping these unethical and now illegal provisions secret allowed the HMOs to sell more policies and make more money (Denenberg, Dec. 9, 1996).

Figure 4.2: **The Triple Tumor Structure of Organizational Dishonesty**

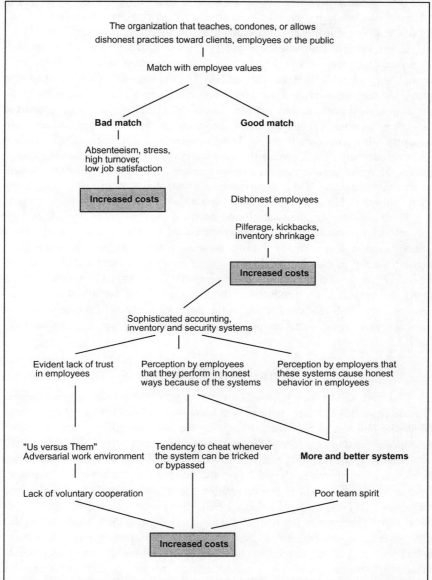

From Robert Cialdini (1996) Social Influence and the Triple Tumor Structure of Organizational Dishonesty in *Codes of Conduct: Behavioral Research into Business Ethics*, Russell Sage Foundation, NY.

If employees are required to operate outside their own personal values, they tend to rationalize behavior. Cialdini states, "Employees who have remained in a firm in part because they have been able to rationalize or excuse the immorality of cheating are prime candidates to cheat the organization as well" (p. 55).

Often for profit organizations are very concerned with short term profits. This focus on short term profit can cause the corporation trouble over the long term. Using a health care example, an HMO customer, part of a large corporate group, is diagnosed with acute lymphocytic leukemia (ALL) and after traditional treatment needs a bone marrow transplant. The HMO doesn't approve the procedure because it is too expensive and they are not convinced that this will be a profitable procedure to cover. The customer does not receive the transplant and subsequently dies. Because this customer was a member of this very large group, the word spreads about the circumstances of this man's treatment or lack of treatment and the HMO experiences a substantial loss of customers. Long term damage and financial loss results from a short term concern about profits.

If all business decisions are based on the pursuit of profit, then it is conceivable that many recreational therapists would have ethical dilemmas. How can a therapist deal with the conflict between wanting to give the patient the highest quality of care but at the same time needing to meet a daily quota of treatments while also having constraints on what the therapist may offer? When there are pressures for production, the therapist might be asked to "assist" someone else with his/her charting. If the therapist is asked to do the work and someone else signs his/her name, the therapist is being put in an ethical dilemma.

What's the Solution

The first step to the solution is something you probably have heard before, "Know Thyself." The therapist needs to know what s/he believes to be right and what s/he believes to be wrong. Following the *five principles of ethical power for individuals* will help identify individual beliefs about what is valuable.

Secondly, the therapist needs to know what his/her profession believes and holds true. The therapist should know and believe that "All people, therefore, have an inalienable right to leisure and the opportunities it affords for play and recreation" (NTRS, Code of Ethics, 1990). The therapist is called upon to believe that "Therapeutic Recreation personnel shall treat persons in an ethical manner not only by respecting their decisions and protecting them from harm but also by actively making efforts to secure their well-being. Personnel strive to maximize possible benefits and minimize possible harms. This serves as the guiding principle for the profession. The term 'persons' includes not only persons served but colleagues, agencies and the profession" *(ATRA Code of Ethics, Principle 1)*.

Thirdly, the therapist needs to know what structures in the organization deal with ethical issues and how each works. Many health care entities have ethics committees which help the facility deal with difficult issues. There are mechanisms for patients and caregivers to access and address ethical concerns. Ethics has been in the news recently more than ever before. Cloning has moved from the realm of science fiction to reality and this makes people nervous. The distribution system for organ transplants does not always provide organs to the most needy or the most logical. And, as mentioned before, ethical decisions may depend on the situation.

The effect of culture can have a big influence on a person's values and beliefs. In Japan, for instance, organ transplants are very rare because of the Shinto beliefs about death. Chinese people in San Francisco's Chinatown expect chickens to be killed when they are bought, not before reaching the store, so they are fresh. Animal rights activists believe that is cruelty to animals. Two groups of people with two diametrically opposed views and values need to have a resolution. The clash of cultural views and values will be more of an issue in our increasingly multicultural society.

And for those issues larger than your facility, you need to have a strategy to help you decide how to address big issues with ethical implications. As we move further into managed care and rationing of health care, where will you stand on the rights of the disabled or seniors to receive care? Who should be given a hip replacement, a thirty year old or a seventy year old? Banja (1997) offers an excellent presentation of the current and future ethical issues facing our medical establishment. If the value of human life is held to be the amount this life contributes financially to society, we, who believe in the intrinsic value of human life, have a serious problem. Because the United States of America is an ethically pluralistic population, there is no consensus on core values except to our cherished liberty, freedom and self-determination. People talk about the "good ole days" when you knew what your neighbor believed and we all held similar core values. Today with a vastly disparate population we have moved to what Daniel Callahan (1980) calls ethical minimalism. Because we cannot reach consensus on what it means to be, or do, good, we are reduced to agree on what is harmful. And the minimalist ethic states you have the right to express your own beliefs and only those things which prevent someone else from being able to express their beliefs is wrong.

As participants in this complex world we need tools to facilitate our successful journey through these yet to be explored territories. A starting point might be trying to determine what exactly is the question. What is the problem and how might you approach it? The five approaches listed in Table 4.3 are a way for you to analyze your particular dilemma and see where it might fall. They might assist you in asking the right questions. The tools that are presented below come from the Markkula Center for Applied Ethics at Santa Clara University in California. There are several different approaches you can take to address a problem. If you take your dilemma through all five approaches you will probably find that one of them makes more sense than the others by understanding what principle is at work in the particular approach.

Once you've decided on the approach, you then need to ask the right questions. How do you know what are the right questions? How do you arrive at deciding a problem and subsequent treatment plan for a patient? You complete an assessment. There are many ways to approach your problem. In Table 4.4 you will find some structures you might find useful.

Table 4.3: **Approaches To Ethics**

Approach	Examples	Principle States
The Virtue Approach	Honesty, courage, faithfulness, trustworthiness	"What is ethical is what develops moral virtues in ourselves and our communities."
The Utilitarian Approach	Focus on consequences that actions or policies have on the well-being ("utility") of all persons directly or indirectly affected	"Of any two actions, the most ethical one will produce the greatest balance of benefits over harms."
The Rights Approach	Each person has a fundamental right to be respected and treated as a free and equal rational person capable of making his or her own decisions	"An action or policy is morally right only if those persons affected by the decision are not used merely as instruments for advancing some goal, but are fully informed and treated only as they have freely and knowingly consented to be treated."
The Fairness Approach	Fairness requires consistency in the way people are treated	"Treat people the same unless there are morally relevant differences between them."
The Common Good Approach	Presents a vision of society as a community whose members are joined in a shared pursuit of values and goals they hold in common.	"What is ethical is what advances the common good."

In *Profit Maximization*, Primeaux and Stieber (1995) tell of a conversation with the Chairman and CEO of a Fortune 500 company. The authors asked him whether he would consider a seminar in business ethics for his company. His immediate response was negative because he thought if he allowed a discussion of ethics, the public and his stockholders would think the company was unethical and so were the employees. But the business climate is generating concern

Table 4.4: **Ethical Decision Making Process**

Process Steps	Possible Questions
Recognize a moral issue	Is this conflict at the personal, interpersonal, institutional or societal level? What about it makes you uncomfortable?
Begin your decision making	What are the relevant acts of the case? Who is involved (list all the players and potential players)? What are you obligations? To whom? Who has ultimate control over this situation? Who is affected by this action and how?
Brainstorm alternatives	What are all the potential alternatives and what are their consequences?
Look at each from various points of view	Take each one through the various perspectives listed in the approaches listed in Table 4.3.
Look at each suggested alternative in view of obligations, ideals and greatest good	Who will benefit most from this alternative? What obligation will be reneged on if this alternative action is completed? Could you live with that? How well does this hold up to the ideal? Identify all the possible effects this decision might have. Which alternative treats all parties in a fair manner? Which alternative is best for all concerned? Which alternative would make a good rule for people to live by in similar situations? Which alternative would lead to the best overall consequences?
Make your own decision	Considering everything which discussion is best? Would other people you respect approve of your choice? In retrospect, was that a good choice?

Adapted from two sources: *An Approach to Ethical Decision Making*, Markkula Center for Applied Ethics, Cases and Comments www.scu.edu/Ethics and Ethical Decision Making In Edginton's *Leisure and Life Satisfaction*, 1995, pp. 379-380.

both inside businesses and in the public. US companies are establishing codes of conduct at a frantic pace. Initiatives have more than doubled in the past 5 years. But are they real or just "window dressing" as Barbara Ley Toffler suggests? As the director of ethics at the consulting firm of Arthur Anderson LLP, she was quoted as saying "Ethics has now become a mindless focus on compliance without any focus on why things go wrong and why people engage in misconduct" (Khalfani, 1996). You can canonize the should and should nots but it is highly unlikely that employees will consistently follow them if the company continues to participate in unfair or unethical practices. If employees see unethical actions, either aimed at them (working people part-time at 38 hours a week to avoid paying benefits) or at the public (untruth in action), they will have more difficulty in being ethical. As illustrated in Figure 4.2, the end result, for both employees that match the lack of ethics of the company (unethical) and those that don't match (ethical), will be increased costs.

Ethical Concerns Related to Internships

There are five ethical issues which are somewhat unique to the internship experience required of recreational therapy students prior to their sitting for the national examination. All five revolve around the relationships between the university supervisor, the clinical supervisor, the student and the patient. The five issues are

- the requirement to avoid dual relationships,
- the competence of the clinical supervisor,
- the right of the patient to know the student's status,
- the right of future patients to be safeguarded and
- the limitations of confidentially between the student and supervisors

The first ethical issue related to the internship is dual relationships — when the student takes on more than one role with a supervisor or patient. The period of time that a student is in his/her internship placement is a stressful time of role changes. The student is needing to transition from the role of student to that of a therapist. The individuals at the university whom the student has worked with for the last few years are now replaced by a new set of peers and authority figures. Looming ahead is a question of finding employment in the field, which may also bring about a change in living situation. Students frequently look to their university supervisor for moral and emotional support. Students may also develop a close relationship with their clinical supervisor at their internship site. The closeness of both relationships is normal. However, at times a student may cross over the fine line between desiring support and needing counseling. Even though it is likely that both the university supervisor and the clinical supervisor are certified therapists, to avoid the unethical situation of a dual role (supervisor/counselor) it is the responsibility of the supervisors to avoid taking on the second role — the role of the counselor. Another dual role which is unethical is the mixing of a romantic or sexually intimate relationship with a supervisor/student role. Supervisors and students should not expand their relationship beyond the role of supervisor/student until after the internship is over, all grades are final and graduation has occurred. The same prohibition applies to a student developing a relationship with a patient which is more than a therapist/patient role.

The second ethical issue related to the internship is the expectation that the clinical supervisor (internship supervisor) be competent to supervise the student. Not only must the clinical supervisor be able to demonstrate competency in all aspects of clinical practice, s/he must be "well-trained, knowledgeable and skilled in the practice of clinical supervision" (Pope & Vasquez, 1991, p. 171). This goes beyond the requirement that the clinical supervisor be NCTRC certified. The requirement that the clinical supervisor be certified is a norm; being well-trained, knowledgeable and skilled in clinical supervision is a ethical expectation.

The third ethical issue related to the internship is the expectation that the student will ensure that all patients to whom s/he provides treatment clearly understand his/her status as a student and consent to receiving treatment from a student. This entails more than having the student's identification badge say "student intern." A job title on a name badge is not providing informed consent for treatment by a student. If the student is doing his/her internship at a teaching facility, it is likely that the informed consent signed by the patient upon admission notified the patient that s/he will be seen by both professionals and students. However, ethically the student must also ensure that the patient understands that *s/he* is one of those students mentioned in the informed consent signed. If the facility does not have such a statement on its informed consent document, ethically the clinical supervisor and student are compelled to inform each patient that s/he will be receiving treatment from a non-credentialed professional who will be supervised by a credentialed professional.

The fourth ethical issue related to the internship is the necessity for both the university supervisor and the clinical supervisor to safeguard future patients. If the student is not able to demonstrate adequate skills or judgment during his/her internship, *the student should not be allowed to graduate*. Due process should be taken to advise the student early on in the internship that concerns exist as to the readiness of the student to assume the role of professional. The student may need some extra coursework or may not be suited for practice. It is the ethical responsibility of both supervisors to ensure that students who are not ready to safely provide therapy do not graduate.

The fifth ethical issue related to the internship is the need for the student to understand the limitation of his/her supervisors to retain confidential information about the student. The student/supervisor role does not have the same requirements for confidentiality that is found in the patient/therapist role. In fact, the supervisor is compelled to share any confidential information about the student with appropriate others when issues of potential professional competency are involved.

Summary

Hopefully you found some of the ideas in this chapter thought-provoking. Challenge yourself to read, react and examine what you believe for several critical reasons. You will continually be confronted with "ethical" dilemmas throughout your career and chances are you have not had much exposure to the subject. Sometimes the question of "rightness" is relative and you need to be prepared to critically work through ethical solutions to dilemmas.

Given the rapid changes in the health care environment today, it is imperative for professionals to know what is the *right* thing to do. Your ethical background contributes to who you are today. Your values, your culture's mores, your religion's morals, your family's values all play a role in your professional ethics. Be aware of the ethical dilemmas around you. When ignored, the problems don't go away; they get bigger and become more pervasive. Take a stand. Make a difference. There are several reasons to do this noble action. First for your own health. When you must work where you are continually confronted with dissonance between your values and those of your employer, it will take a physical and emotional toll on your body. Secondly, you are a member of the world and, if your desire is for the world to be a better place, your inaction is actually an unethical decision. Inaction is a decision. Ethics are not neutral. They are either good or bad. Explore what you believe and make your workplace more ethical by being ethical.

Internet Resources on Ethics:

http://www.scuacc.scu.edu (Santa Clara University, Markkula Center for Applied Ethics)

http://www.wppost.depaul.edu (The Institute for Business and Professional Ethics, DePaul University)

http://www.acusd.edu/ethics/index.html (Incredible site at California State University, San Diego)

http://www.pitt.edu/^ca13/4/title.html

Learning Activities

1. Your supervisor is really busy and has asked you to see three of his patients when he goes to a special meeting. You agree but then he asks you to complete the documentation for those patients in his name so he can meet his productivity for the day. What would you do and what are the ethical principles surrounding this issue?

2. A patient with paraplegia has been seen by the entire treatment team following a automobile accident. During a community integration session the patient shares with you his feelings of despondency and his thoughts of suicide. He begs you not to tell anyone else. What should you do and what ethical precept is most important in this decision?

3. You are a therapist in a mental health facility and a colleague from a sister institution calls you and says she is a recreational therapist but wants your help to supervise interns. In talking with this person you find out she does not have a BS degree in anything. You find out she is filling a position that requires the therapist to be certified. What would you do? What would be the best way to handle this situation? Why?

4. What is your personal code of ethics? What are your core values that are unimpeachable? How do you think you will do in a for-profit health care organization?

5. As a class do a mini-study of core beliefs and values and see how much agreement or disagreement you have. Now have half the students take a position opposite the core values of the group and have a discussion and see what issues arise.

Study Questions

1. Compare and contrast descriptive, analytical and prescriptive ethics. Give examples of each.

2. Name and explain the ethical questions that are especially relevant to internships.

3. Where do personal ethics come from?

4. How are professional ethics statements created? What needs to be in place before the ethics statement can be written?

5. How does an unethical company lose money by unethical practices. Name ways it loses customers and ways it is hurt by employees.

References

Banja, J. (1997). Values, function and managed care: An ethical analysis. *Journal of Head Trauma Rehabilitation, 12*(1), 60-70.

Bayles, M. (1988). The professions. In J. Callahan (Ed.). *Ethical issues in professional life.* New York: Oxford University Press.

Blanchard, K. & Peale, N. V. (1988). *The power of ethical management.* New York: William Morrow and Company.

Bucholz, R. (1989). *Fundamental concepts and problems in business ethics.* Englewood Cliffs, NJ: Prentice-Hall, Inc.

burlingame, j. & Skalko, T. (1997). *Idyll Arbor's glossary for therapists.* Ravensdale, WA: Idyll Arbor, Inc.

Callahan, D. (1980). *Ethics teaching in higher education.* New York: Plenum Publishing.

Callahan, J. (Ed.). (1988). *Ethical issues in professional life.* New York: Oxford University Press.

Camenisch, P. (1983). *Grounding professional ethics in a pluralistic society.* New York: Haven.

Cialdini, R. (1996). Social influence and the triple tumor structure of organizational dishonesty. In D. Messick & A. Tenbrunsel (Eds.). *Codes of conduct: Behavioral research into business ethics.* New York: Russell Sage Foundation.

Clark, R. & Lattal, A. (1992). *Workplace ethics: Winning the integrity revolution.* Lanham, MD: Rowan & Littlefield.

DeGeorge, R. T. (1986). *Business ethics* (2nd ed.). New York: Macmillan.

Denenberg, H. (1996, December 9). NBC Nightly News.

Edginton, C., Jordan, D., DeGraaf, D. & Edginton, S. (1995). *Leisure and life satisfaction — foundational perspectives,* Dubuque, IA: Brown and Benchmark.

Fain, G. (1989). Ethics in the therapeutic recreation profession. In D. M. Compton (Ed.). *Issues in therapeutic recreation: A profession in transition.* Champaign, IL: Sagamore Publishing.

Friedman, M. (1970, September 13). The social responsibility of business is to increase its profits. *New York Times Magazine, 33,* 122-126.

Goodpaster, K. (1980). *Ethics: An overview.* Harvard Business School Public p. 381-050.

Khalfani, L. (1996). Ethics moves up among priorities for US businesses. In GT Online Business News, WWW.

Manley, W. (1990). *Critical issues in business conduct: Legal, ethical and social challenges for the 1990s.* Westport, CT: Quorum Books.

Markkula Center for Applied Ethics, Santa Clara University's site on WWW.

Messick, D. & Tenbrunsel, A. (Eds.). (1996). *Codes of conduct: Behavioral research into business ethics.* New York: Russell Sage Foundation Press.

National Therapeutic Recreation Society. (1990). *National Therapeutic Recreation Society code of ethics.* Ashburn, VA: National Recreation and Parks Association.

Primeaux, P. & Stieber, J. (1995). *Profit maximization: The ethical mandate of business.* San Francisco: Austin & Winfield.

Pope, K. S. & Vasquez, M. J. (1991). *A practical guide for psychologists.* San Francisco, CA: Jossey-Bass, Inc.

White, L. & Wooten, K. (1986). *Professional ethics and practice in organizational development: A systematic analysis of issues, alternative and approaches.* New York: Praeger Publishers.

Issues of the Field

Chapter 5

Clinical Practice Models

joan burlingame

The field of recreational therapy has had a variety of models proposed on which to base clinical practice. Many of these models are well thought out, and some, like the Therapeutic Recreation Service Model by Peterson and Gunn (1984) developed during the late 1970's, proved substantial enough to be adopted on a national basis. However, even the Therapeutic Recreation Service Model was felt to be lacking by many (Bullock, 1987; Gruver, 1994; Smith, Austin & Kennedy, 1996). This chapter will review the need for the field of recreational therapy to have a model on which to base practice and propose a modification of the Therapeutic Recreation Service Model which helps address one of the greatest problems with that model. The modification of the Therapeutic Recreation Service Model includes material from the World Health Organization and is called the Recreation Service Model.

Overview of Practice Models

The Therapeutic Recreation Service Model (Peterson & Gunn, 1984) defined the role of the recreational therapist and the purpose of treatment using a three level model. The first level, "treatment," defined the therapist's role as improving the patient's functional ability. It said that this treatment was a necessary antecedent to meaningful participation in activity. The second level, "leisure education," defined the therapist's role as instructing, advising or counseling the patient so that the patient could acquire knowledge and skills related to leisure activity. The third level, "recreation participation," defined the therapist's role as leading, facilitating and supervising the patient, allowing the patient to engage in organized leisure activities. In this model, as the patient moved from therapy to recreation participation, the patient gained a greater degree of freedom and the therapist decreased his/her degree of control.

On many levels, this continuum made sense. However, in reality, most recreational therapists were employed by health care organizations funded by third party payers who paid for treatment, not leisure education or recreation participation. While not negating the importance of this model, the environment in which therapists practiced limited them to the first level on the model, that of therapy. And herein lies the problem. Therapists working forty hours a week have only the "therapy" section of the model on which to base their whole practice. There is no standardized division or continuum on which to base delivery of services. This leads to a lack of unified direction and makes measurement of the benefits of treatment more difficult to obtain. Some attempt was made to provide reasonable divisions within the therapy level of the model. Three notable attempts divided therapy by domains, by purpose of service and by level of health.

During the 1980's and 1990's recreational therapy activities used for treatment interventions were frequently divided into *domains*, usually physical, cognitive, social, emotional and leisure (Austin, 1982; Coyle, Kinney, Riley & Shank, 1991; Grote, Hasl, Krider & Martin-Mortensen, 1995; Peterson & Gunn, 1984). These domains provided the therapist with functional divisions on which to base assessment and treatment. However, these divisions were just divisions and not a true model on which to base practice. An additional problem was the recreational therapist's inclusion of "leisure" or "leisure function" as a domain. This inclusion of a specialty area (e.g., "leisure") spoke more to the therapist's choice of modality of treatment than to a recognized domain.

The manner in which recreational therapists broke down each domain also lacked any national standardization. (An example of this lack of standardization can be found in Table 5.1.) This led to the development of testing tools and treatment protocols which lacked common categories, making the comparison of patient outcomes between facilities difficult. As health care credentialing agencies increased their emphasis on outcomes and efficacy research, the division of recreational therapy services by domains caused more problems for the therapist.

Another problem with dividing therapy into domains is that the other health care providers (e.g., physicians, nurses, occupational therapists) seldom use domains within their own research or literature. And at team meetings, the recreational therapist tends to be the only professional using domains.

Because they recognized problems with the Therapeutic Recreation Service Model, in 1987 the Board of Directors of the American Therapeutic Recreation Association (ATRA) divided recreational therapy into two levels (ATRA, 1993). Unlike the Therapeutic Recreation Service Model with its three levels, ATRA offered a definition (and implied a direction for a service model) by *purpose* of services: treatment services and recreation services. ATRA listed the purpose of treatment as encompassing three areas: "to restore, remediate or re-

Table 5.1: **Lack of Standardization in Domains**

Testing Tool	Category Divisions within the Domain of "Leisure"
Leisurescope Plus (Schenk, 1998)	Games, Sports, Nature, Collection, Crafts, Art & Music, Entertainment, Helping Others/Volunteering, Social Affiliation and Adventure
Leisure Diagnostic Battery (Witt & Ellis, 1989)	Outdoor/Nature, Music/Dance/Drama, Sports, Arts/Crafts/Hobbies and Mental Linguistic
Leisure Interest Measure (Ragheb & Beard, 1991)	Physical, Outdoor, Mechanical, Artistic, Service, Social, Cultural and Reading
Leisure Step Up (Dehn, 1995)	Community Spectator, Expressive Leisure, Physical Leisure and Cultural Leisure
STILAP (Navar, 1990)	Physical Skills/Solitary; Physical Skills/with Others, Regardless of Skill Level; Physical Skills/Requiring More than One Participant; Outdoor Environment; Physical Skills not considered to be Seasonal; Physical Skills with Carryover Opportunity for Later Years; Physical Skills with Carryover Opportunity and Vigorous Enough for Cardiovascular Fitness; Mental Skills/Solitary; Mental Skills/Two or More; Observation or Passive Response; Creative Construction or Self-expression through Manipulation, Sound or Visual Media; Enables Enjoyment/Improvement of Home Environment; Social Situations and Community Service

habilitate in order to improve functioning and independence as well as to reduce or eliminate the effects of illness or disability" (ATRA, 1993, p. 8). ATRA listed the purpose of recreation services as "to provide recreation resources and opportunities in order to improve health and well-being" (ATRA, 1993, p. 8). But ATRA's stated purpose of treatment and recreation services was not a true model. NTRS was still using the Therapeutic Recreation Service Model which it adopted in 1982, leaving the field with a lack of unified definition and service models. Even worse, none of these models matched the models being used by the other health care professionals.

Austin (1991) offered a model which he called the Health Protection/Health Promotion Model which is based on the patient's *level* of health. Like the Therapeutic Recreation Service Model, Austin's model contains three levels which represent a continuum of involvement by the therapist. The first level, "prescriptive activities," defines the therapist's role as activating the patient toward health (termed "stability tendency"). Treatment at this level is necessary to help the patient realize a more normal control over his/her health situation. Treatment, using activity, "becomes a necessary prerequisite to health restoration. In order to gain control over the situation and to overcome feelings of helplessness and depression, they [the patients] must begin to actively engage in life." (Austin, 1997, p. 146). The second level, "recreation," recognizes an increase in the patient's actualization and a decrease of the therapist's role allowing mutual participation in activities. The third level, "leisure," recognizes limited to no need for a recreational therapist's services as the patient engages in self-directed leisure activity.

Austin's model relies more heavily on psychological premises then the other two models, using terms such as "actualization, tendency, self-absorbed, feelings of helplessness, energize, passive victims of their circumstances, refresh the mind, body and spirit, control over their environment, feelings of self-efficacy and confront potentially threatening situation" (Austin, 1997, pp. 146-148). These terms are easily recognizable within the psychological treatment community but this model, as with the other two, does not match the continuum used by the health care community as a whole and the agencies which fund it.

World Health Organization's Model

Around the same time that the field of recreational therapy was searching for a model of service delivery, the rest of health care was also searching for a model. The World Health Organization (WHO) formed a committee in 1972 to develop a model which could be used by all health care providers, not just physicians. That committee recommended using a level model with a combination of body systems (e.g., circulatory) and scope of service (e.g., enhancing the body's own ability vs. augmenting with adaptive equipment). They recommended against using domains (e.g., cognitive, physical) or other categorization systems (e.g., prevention, intervention, restoration, rehabilitation). Once this model was accepted worldwide, coding systems for diagnosis, funding and research were developed using the WHO Model. The model became so ingrained in all levels of health care instruction, service delivery and fiscal management that many health care providers don't even give the model a second thought. Recreational therapy's use of service models which are different from the universally accepted model has proven problematic because our terminology, billing categories and basic conceptualization of delivery of services do not match the rest of the treatment team's.

The World Health Organization model of health care has four levels reflecting the consequences of disease and trauma. The model is published in a book called *The International Classification of Impairments, Disabilities and Handicaps* (ICIDH) (World Health Organization, 1980). This model goes beyond what is typically considered the "medical model" and recognizes causes for disease outside of the human organism itself, including conditions and barriers found in an individual's environment. In addition to offering practitioners a model for the continuum of care, this model has also established criteria for the types of reliability and validity needed for testing tools and treatment protocols for each of the four levels. Most importantly, this model establishes a common framework for the diagnosis, treatment, funding and outcome measurement of all health care services (including recreational therapy) worldwide.

WHO's four levels of care are (1) disease level, (2) impairment level, (3) disability level and (4) handicap level. Each level has its own definition of the scope of disease/trauma contained within that level, character of the types of treatment provided within that level, codes to use for billing and research, as well as descriptions of qualities required of the testing tools and treatment protocols used. Understanding this model is important because its levels are used for the first four levels of the Recreation Service Model.

Disease Level

Health concerns grouped within the *disease level* tend to be the roots of the disease process, having an etiology (e.g., from an infection), pathology (e.g., infection spreading through spinal fluid) and manifestation of disease and/or trauma which is found at the basic or cellular level (e.g., body temperature over 102° F). Health concerns at the disease level tend to be crisis situations and the recreational therapist's role is usually to help tide the patient over until the crisis has passed (e.g., providing bed play activities for a toddler in strict isolation). However, at the disease level the recreational therapist may also provide some preventative interventions to reduce the probability of another crisis (e.g., relaxation training to reduce blood pressure). See Table 5.2 for some interventions the recreational therapist may use for health concerns at the disease level.

Testing and treatment at the disease level require norm-referenced benchmarks to identify normal status versus pathological conditions. Desired scores

Table 5.2: **Recreational Therapist's Interventions at the Disease Level: Manage the Crisis**

Crisis	→	Intervention
high blood pressure	→	relaxation techniques
seizure activity	→	protect head & other body parts
autonomic dysreflexia	→	empty bladder
choking by patient with C3 quad	→	quad cough
severe, pulsating pain	→	pain management techniques
protective isolation	→	cleaning recreation supplies

and outcomes of treatment are based on normal function and are usually measured with interval scales. Both the testing tools used and the treatment protocols implemented should have internal consistency of the tools, inter-rater reliability with good content and construct validity.

Much of the testing and interventions that the recreational therapist implements at the disease level are interdisciplinary in nature. Recreational therapists working with patients who may not be medically stable should be trained to take someone's blood pressure, pulse and respiration rate (vital signs); know stages of skin breakdown to identify new damage due to activity (or lack of activity); be competent in CPR; and know which relaxation techniques work for different diagnoses (and as important, which techniques are contraindicated). In some settings the recreational therapist may also be trained in suction and bagging for patients on respirators, catheterization for patients at risk for autonomic dysreflexia and IV maintenance for patients involved in activities so that they don't need to leave the activity to have more IV fluid dropped.

Impairment Level

Health concerns at the impairment level address physiological, developmental, cognitive or emotional levels which are different from what would normally be expected. Patients at this level might have weaker muscles or even missing body parts, developmentally abnormal skills (e.g., autism), a low IQ or a loss of memory (e.g., dementia), hearing loss or impaired vision. Health concerns at this level tend to be "either/or" situations. Either the patient has an impairment in a specific area (e.g., executive function, muscle strength) or s/he does not. This doesn't mean that the measurement of impairment lacks any reference to degrees of impairment; it just means that thresholds have been established for determining if an impairment exists. Each threshold has previously been established through normative studies.

The criteria for testing tools and treatment interventions within the impairment level are the same as for the disease level. Recreational therapists seldom measure a patient's status at this level. Typically they rely on information obtained by other members of the treatment team. This information is then used to form clinical opinions about implied disability, opinions which are then tested and addressed during treatment. Because of the recreational therapist's need to use the impairment information obtained from the other team members, s/he must be familiar with the measurements (and scores) used. Recreational therapists should understand the ASIA levels of spinal cord injury (e.g., T2 Incomplete), muscle strength grades (e.g., +2), intelligence quotients (e.g., 65), grades of decubitus (e.g., stage 3), degrees of burns/percentage of body part burned (e.g., 3rd degree, 15%), staging in cancer (e.g., stage 2), degrees of range of motion (e.g., 65° elbow), Rancho Los Amigos Scale (e.g., Level 5) and visual acuity (e.g., 20/200 with correction).

While most of the measurement related to impairment tends to fall within the scope of practice of the other health care professionals, there are a few areas of impairment which recreational therapists measure and address. Reality orientation, basic social interaction and physical endurance are three areas related to impairment which fall into the scope of practice of the recreational therapist. The *Comprehensive Visual Neglect Assessment* (CVnA, Bond-Howard, 1998 — formally the Bond-Howard Assessment of Neglect in Recreational Therapy; BANRT), is a testing tool which measures the scope and density of visual neglect, and is a promising tool for recreational therapists to use to measure impairment.

Table 5.3 lists some of the areas for intervention listed by WHO for the impairment level. The column on the right side of the table suggests possible interventions to be implemented by the recreational therapist.

Interestingly, just because an individual has an impairment, does not imply that s/he also has a disability. An example would be a woman who had a hysterectomy. A lack of a uterus would be considered an impairment, but it is not necessarily a disability.

For billing and data gathering purposes, the disease level and the impairment level are placed together to ease coding in the *International Classification of Disease, Ninth Revision, Clinical Modification* (US Department of Health and Human Services, 1980). While they are placed together for coding purposes, they are still considered to be distinct levels (Anchor, 1996).

Table 5.3: **Recreational Therapist's Interventions at the Impairment Level: Maximize the Body's Ability**

Area of Function	→	Intervention
strength	→	exercise for strength
cognitive ability	→	exercise memory
range of motion (ROM)	→	ROM through activity
executive function	→	teaching for safety
edema	→	positioning for drainage
anhedonia	→	observe effects of medications; provide exercise and stimulation
attention seeking behaviors	→	teaching to wait
cardiovascular endurance	→	exercise to increase cardiovascular endurance

Disability Level

Health concerns at the disability level address any restriction or impairment-related lack of ability to perform an activity in the manner or within the range considered normal. The primary difference between the impairment level and the disability level is that impairment implies a loss of body function and disability implies a loss of performance function. Interventions at the disability level involve the development of skills and techniques or the use of adapted equipment to perform an activity. The majority of work that a recreational therapist does within a clinical setting falls into the disability level. The WHO (1980) lists pages of performance tasks which may be addressed through treatment to offset a disability. Many of the performance tasks listed by WHO fall within the scope of practice of the recreational therapist. Table 5.4 list just some of the performance tasks contained within the disability level.

Almost every aspect of function at the disability level is measured through some form of task analysis. Difficulty scales, most notably the FIM Scale (State University of New York Research Foundation, 1987), are used, along with other interval scales, to mark the patient's movement toward (or way from) being able to perform a task. The WHO has indicated that norm reference data is not required for assessment and treatment at this level. What is required is the ability to measure the degree to which a task can be performed. While norm reference is not critical for measuring disability, internal consistency, inter-rater reliability, construct and content validity are important.

The WHO (1980) stated clearly that clinical judgment is an important part of assessment and treatment at the disability level. Performance function has too much complexity (and cultural expectations blur expectations) for a single tool

Table 5.4: **Disability: Areas of Performance**

• punctuality	• transportation	• pro-social behavior
• comprehension	• work routine	• visual tasks
• performance rate	• personal safety	• social roles
• coping	• object identification	• walking/traversing
• locomotion	• listening	• cooking
• motivation	• problem solving	• cooperation
• noise tolerance	• eating skills	• self-awareness
• knowledge acquisition	• conduct appropriate for context	• appropriate crisis conduct
• transfers	• interpretation	• organizing routine
• time & space awareness	• temperature tolerance	• nonverbal expression
• ability to not wander purposelessly	• task fulfillment abilities	

to provide all the measurements required of the therapist for all of his/her patients. Testing tools which measure a patient's performance on specific tasks are widely available to the recreational therapist. Because interventions at this level relate directly to task performance, the recreational therapist has the option to also use standardized treatment protocols to measure performance. Some of the tools and protocols available to the recreational therapist include the *Community Integration Program, Second Edition* (Armstrong & Lauzen, 1994), the *CERT Psych/R* (Parker, 1997), *Protocols for Recreational Therapy Programs* (Kelland, 1995), *Therapeutic Recreation Activity Assessment* (Keogh-Hoss, 1993), the *Leisure Step Up* (with the *Global Assessment of Leisure Functioning*, Dehn, 1995) and the *Bus Utilization Screening Tool* (BUS, burlingame, 1989).

The Leisure Competence Measure (LCM) (Kloseck, Crilly, Ellis, Lammers, 1996) is one of the best testing tools developed in the field of recreational therapy and it uses the FIM scale as its scoring mechanism. However, the LCM should not be used as the sole testing tool to measure a patient's performance function. The therapist will need to first establish the patient's actual performance using assessments based on task analysis and then summarize the results on the LCM.

Many of the testing tools which measure leisure attributes do not comfortably belong in the disability level. Leisure interests are seldom pathological in nature, therefore falling more into the category of personal preference, just as a preference for Chinese food over Mexican food would. However, over consumption of food (of any ethnicity) would be considered pathological if it was the underlying cause of a disease, impairment or disability. One of the strengths of tools like the *Leisure Diagnostic Battery* (Witt & Ellis, 1989), the *Leisure Step Up* program (Dehn, 1995), the *Leisure Motivation Scale* (Ragheb & Beard, 1990a) or the *Free Time Boredom* (Ragheb & Merydith, 1995) is that they help identify extremes of leisure attributes which could cause pathology. The field's challenge over the next decade will be to identify which scores on these tools should be considered pathological (e.g., establishing a threshold for an impairment or a level of disability).

Handicap Level

Health concerns grouped within the handicap level relate to circumstances when the patient finds himself/herself with a barrier to full involvement in the community. Handicaps are circumstances where people who are disabled (disability level) are likely to find themselves at a disadvantage in relation to their peers when viewed from the norms of society. These circumstances, by definition, must lead to a restriction in a patient's social role due to a lack of: (1) orientation, (2) physical independence, (3) mobility, (4) occupation, (5) social integration, (6) economic self-sufficiency and/or (7) other handicaps.

By the WHO's definition, a handicap is a constraint or barrier caused either by the patient with a disability, by society or by both, which limits the patient's ability to fully engage in his/her community.

Using the term "handicap" is controversial with groups of individuals viewing that term as derogatory. The WHO (1980) and other authors (Badley, 1987; Badley; 1995; Schuntermann, 1996; Soder, 1987; Thorburn, Desai & Davidson, 1992) have discussed the use of this term. This literature says that much of the problem lies in the use of the term "handicap" in a pop psychology sense. The WHO has identified several terms which have been overused or mis-used, including the terms "depression," "addiction" and "handicap." "Because the term *addiction* has been so overused in pop psychology (e.g., addictive love, chocolate addiction) the World Health Organization has suggested that the term *dependence* be used in place of the term *addiction* when referring to dependence on drugs" (burlingame & Skalko, 1997, p. 8). However, after thoughtful review, the WHO decided to keep the term "handicap" and promote the correct use of the term. The WHO encourages professionals to make a determination of "handicap/non-handicap" in each of the seven areas instead of just listing the areas of handicap. This helps promote a whole person approach to health care and discourages the pop psychology use of the term handicap.

In acute care settings the recreational therapist finds that s/he may address a patient's needs on the disability level far more than barriers on the handicap level. However, full integration cannot be achieved if gross barriers to integration are not addressed. Failure to address significant handicaps (caused by pa-tient, society or both) leads to decreased health and well-being. Therapists working in long term care settings may find that as much of their practice in-volves issues at the handicap level as from all three other levels. The issues in-clude:

- modification of activities (instead of modifying the patient's performance);
- mixing and matching group participants (modifying the setting and situa-tion instead of modifying the patient's performance); and
- dealing with barriers to physical independence (e.g., not having enough nursing aides to transport residents to activities).

Dealing with these issues leads to a more normal "community" but it may take a considerable amount of time in some situations. Therapists working in community settings may find that the majority of their work falls into the handi-cap level.

Because the determination of handicap in each of the seven areas is such a complex task, the clinical judgment of the practitioner is used determine the degree of handicap in each area. This is done after the practitioner has com-pleted his/her assessment of the patient. The World Health Organization (1980)

Table 5.5: **Mobility Handicap Scale**

Scale Category	Description
0: Fully mobile	Not in categories 1-9.
1: Variable restriction of mobility	Restrictions are variable as with an individual with severe asthma with intermittent impairment of exercise tolerance.
2: Impaired mobility	Restrictions such that the ability to get around is not interfered with but getting around may take longer, e.g., a seeing disability makes the individual uncertain in getting around or the individual has difficulty, but can cope, with public transportation.
3: Reduced mobility	Reduction such that the ability to get around is curtailed, e.g., because seeing disability interferes with the ability to get around; due to cardiac or respiratory impairment, or inability to cope with public transportation.
4: Neighborhood restriction	Restriction to immediate neighborhood of dwelling, such as by disability on moderate exertion owning to cardiac or respiratory impairment.
5: Dwelling restriction	Confinement to dwelling such as by severe seeing disability or disability on mild exertion owning to cardiac or respiratory impairment.
6. Room restriction	Confinement to room, such as by disability at rest owning to cardiac or respiratory impairment.
7: Chair restriction	Confinement to chair, such as by disability when recumbent owning to cardiac or respiratory impairment, or by dependence on hoists or similar appliances for getting in and out of bed.
8: Total restriction of mobility	Includes bedfast or confined to bed.
9: Unspecified	

has developed a scale for each of the seven areas to be used when reporting the patient's degree of handicap. Table 5.5 provides a shortened version of the Mobility Handicap Scale (WHO, 1980).

Summary of WHO Levels

The World Health Organization's four level model provides a conceptual layout of patient needs and health care interventions. It was meant to provide all health care providers with a unified model. This, in turn, would help promote interdisciplinary teamwork; provide a structure for diagnosis, intervention and reimbursement; and allow better surveillance of trends, analysis of the utilization of services, service planning and performance measurement. A summary of all four levels can be found in Table 5.6.

Recreation Service Model

Developed by burlingame (burlingame & Skalko, 1997), the Recreation Service Model (RSM) is a conceptual scheme of clinical intervention and activity based on the World Health Organization's Model. burlingame was concerned that many of the models of service used in recreational therapy lumped all therapy into one category without providing a taxonomy for the provision of the different types of interventions. The premise of the RSM is that human beings experience varying degrees of health and well-being throughout their lifetime and that the use of activities can enhance individuals' health, well-being and quality of life. At times that enhancement will need to be prescriptive in nature, used to have an impact on a disease, impairment, disability or handicap. At other times little to no enhancement is needed. The goal of the RSM is to identity when enhancement is indicated and to provide the professional with guidelines as to the structure, scope and type of interventions called for. The Recreation Service Model divides clinical intervention (recreational therapy) into the

Table 5.6: **World Health Organization's Model**

	Disease Level	Impairment Level	Disability Level	Handicap Level
Scope	Interruption of, or abnormal presentation of normal body function on a basic or cellular level	Loss of normal function — maximizing the body's own ability	Development of skills, techniques or use of adaptive equipment	Application of skills, techniques and abilities within the community
Character	Attributes of normal biological function at the basic or cellular level	Attributes of normal physiological and developmental processes function based on threshold requirements	Attributes of normal skills (functional performance based on task analysis, adaptive skills and equipment)	Circumstances (which cause barriers or constraints)

WHO's four levels: disease level, impairment level, disability level and handicap level. Descriptions of these levels as they apply to recreational therapy have been provided in the previous section on the WHO Model. The Recreation Service Model also recognizes three additional levels of service: education, organized recreation programs and independent activities which are discussed in more detail below. The first two of the additional levels (leisure education and recreation participation) require that the professional providing the service be trained to provide the service but do not necessarily require a CTRS credential. The last level (independent activities) is not an actual service but a recognition that individuals can engage in a level of healthy involvement without the services of a professional. The Recreation Service Model provides the therapist with a taxonomy which organizes practice into a scientific model. The ICIDH has already established criteria for the characteristics of testing tools and interventions used on each level, as noted above. A diagram of burlingame's Recreation Service Model can be found in Table 5.7.

Education Level

The education level addresses a holistic approach to life and does not address a health concern. The Recreation Service Model recognizes the potential for the use of activity to promote a healthy, satisfying life without needing to address illness. At this level the purpose is to facilitate the acquisition of new skills, techniques and/or knowledge to engage in an activity of one's choice. Little to no additional modification is needed due to physiological or psychological impairment, disability or handicap. This does not imply that an individual engaged at this level is free of health concerns. It does imply that what is going on may be healthy, but is not related to treatment. (In fact, the individual engaging in a leisure education activity may be an individual with a C2 Complete Quadriplegia and require extensive assistance and technology to engage in the activity.) Leisure education is used to change behaviors so that they enhance positive capabilities which already exist, creating behaviors which cause health. The reader should note that "leisure" in this model is considered a state of mind as described by Neulinger (1990) and not an activity. Therefore, "leisure" can be experienced and enhanced through all seven levels of the Recreation Service Model, as can other aspects of life functioning. The services of the professional provide more than "leisure." Leisure education should not be confused with leisure counseling. Leisure counseling is used to eliminate (or reduce) a pathological pattern which is supporting a disease, impairment, disability or handicap (behaviors which cause harm) and is part of practice at the disease, impairment, disability or handicap levels.

Table 5.7: **Recreation Service Model**

Recreational   Therapy

Intervention and Treatment

Micro	Mezzo

Specific Levels of Intervention Provided by a Certified Therapeutic Recreation

Disease Level	Impairment Level	Disability Level
	Maximizing the Body's Own Ability	Development of Skills, Techniques or Use of Adapted Equipment
Scope of Service:	*Scope of Service:*	*Scope of Service:*
To reduce or prevent the interruption of (or interference with) normal physiological & developmental process. Most often associated with acute medical or psychiatric events. Therapists may also address issues of infection control and disease prevention.	To enhance cognitive, physiological or emotional function. Therapist addresses changes on a system level (cardiovascular, cognition, coordination, communication). Therapist may also observe for side effects of medication or address issues of edema and skin integrity through positioning.	To enhance performance of component (basic) skills required of an activity in a manner considered within the normal range. Therapist addresses the need to modify or enhance the individual's functional ability through adaptive techniques or equipment.
Examples:	*Examples:*	*Examples:*
• seizure • acute psych. crisis • catheter displacement • autonomic dysreflexia	• strength/endurance • cognitive retraining • coordination, ROM • executive function • anhedonia • tardive dyskinesia	• social skills • leisure counseling • anger management • relaxation training • advanced ADLs
Each level's goal is to promote competence, mastery, confidence and		

		Organized Recreation	Independent Recreation
	Promotion of Wellness		
Macro	**ADA Compliance Where Appropriate to Accommodate Individuals with Disabilities**		
Specialist (CTRS)	Assistance by Qualified Individuals		
Handicap Level Application of Skills, Techniques & Abilities in Community	**Education Level** Enhancing and Adding Skills	**Organized Recreation Programs** Facilitation	**Independent Activities** Autonomy
Scope of Service:	*Scope of Service:*	*Scope of Service:*	*Scope of Service:*
To facilitate the use of component (basic) skills within a community setting. To identify and help problem solve barriers. Therapist addresses the <u>application of component (basic) skills and techniques</u> along with the use of adaptive equipment to <u>integrate into the community.</u>	To <u>facilitate the acquisition of new skills, techniques and/or knowledge</u> to engage in activities of choice. Little to no additional modification is needed due to physiological or psychological impairment, disability or handicap.	Facilitating recreation through <u>the provision of facilities, staff and other resources.</u> Learning new skills is not the emphasis of the service, although the further development of skills may be.	<u>No direct service provided</u> by recreation professionals.
Examples:	*Examples:*	*Examples:*	*Examples:*
• identifying & using community resources • combining multiple tasks (plans/lists, transportation, shopping, cooking)	Instruction on: • Internet use • swimming • languages • skiing • painting • golf	• attend concert • golf course • baseball • hiking • summer camp	• writing poetry • walking along beach • talking with friends • painting

pleasure to encourage self-efficacy, empowerment, enjoyment & intrinsic motivation.

The field of recreational therapy has many testing tools to be used with the education level. They tend to fall into two categories: leisure attributes and skills/techniques.

Many of the tools used to measure leisure attributes at the education level are also used to measure leisure attributes at the disability level. The difference here is the same as the difference between leisure counseling (to eliminate or reduce a pathological pattern) and education (to promote behaviors which enhance health and well-being). Leisure attribute tools used for education increase the individual's awareness of himself/herself, knowledge of what helps make a more satisfying free time experience and how to make choices toward wholeness. Testing tools which measure leisure attributes include the *Leisure Diagnostic Battery* (Witt & Ellis, 1989), the *Leisure Step Up* (Dehn, 1995), the *Measurement of Social Empowerment and Trust (SET)* (Witman, 1991a), *Leisure Attitude Measurement (LAM)* (Ragheb & Beard, 1990b), *Cooperation and Trust Scale (CAT)* (Witman, 1991b), *Leisure Satisfaction Measure (LSM)* (Ragheb & Beard, 1991a), *Leisurescope Plus* (Schenk, 1998), *Leisure Interest Measure (LIM)* (Ragheb & Beard, 1991b), the *Leisure Motivation Scale* (Ragheb & Beard, 1990a) the *Free Time Boredom Measurement* (Ragheb & Merydith, 1995) or the other large selection of leisure interest measures.

The second category of testing tools at the education level includes tests which measure an individual's skill level or quality of technique for any given activity. A checklist which measures a swimmer's competency level to determine if s/he can swim in the deep end is an example of a skill testing tool. Measuring the strength of a skier's snowplow (wedge) to see if his/her technique is strong enough to allow the controlled decent with an injured skier in the toboggan is an example of a technique test.

Organized Recreation Programs

Organized recreation programs facilitate recreation through the provision of facilities, staff and other resources. Learning new skills is not the emphasis of the service, although the further development of skills may be. Organizations may provide the framework for individuals to participate, whether they have a disability or not, but the clear emphasis is on having fun and personal fulfillment and not new learning or treatment.

One would normally not find testing tools used at this level. Recreation staff are taking a more passive role, providing support services and facilities and not instruction. Peer feedback and self-evaluation are more likely to be the type of evaluation done.

Independent Activities

The vast majority of activities pursued by individuals are done without the support of recreation professionals. The ability to engage in such activity is one of the goals of almost any treatment intervention or education program. In this situation the recreation professional has let go of any control over the activity and the individual has the greatest degree of freedom for personal choice.

Why Use the RSM and WHO Models?

Recreational therapists would benefit by using the Recreation Service Model (RSM). It draws upon two models which are well known, have been tested over time and found to be generally workable. Using the RSM promotes better communication, enhances research and helps predict future trends.

Using the Recreation Service Model allows easier communication between professional groups and third party payers as it creates a unified taxonomy of practice. As recreational therapists adopt the world-wide use of the terms "impairment," "disability" and "handicap" they will be able to share a common understanding with health care providers around the world. Within these categories, the recreational therapist will find terms related to body function and performance function which the recreational therapist can use. Addressing standardized terms related to functional performance deficits that reduce a patient's ability to use his/her free time is far more palatable to third party payers than using terms such as:

- "leisure barriers" (relating to the handicap level which is generally not reimbursable)
- "leisure functioning" (the term *leisure* is not a recognized category under ICD-9-CM, it is recognized as a general modality domain of a health care group, just as speech, occupation and special education would be)
- "constraint" (a term generally associated with the handicap level, a level which is generally not reimbursable)
- "participation" (participation, in and of itself, does not relate to health care interventions or function)
- "leisure skills" (too general of a term; functional ability related to the ability to perform specific tasks, such as locomotion, object identification, problem solving are acceptable)
- "leisure education" (education is not generally considered to be part of the first three WHO levels; some insurance coverage which promotes wellness may allow education to be a billable service).

The RSM allows the recreational therapist to use nationally standardized categories to identify interrelationships between groups of patients. By being able to sort patient groups by impairment and disability, the therapist will be better able to compare the needs and impact of treatment provided. By understanding the interrelationships between groups, the recreational therapist will be better able to assign patients to groups, protocols and critical pathways.

As outcomes of treatment become more important, using the RSM simplifies research as this unified categorization allows prediction of pathology and prognosis based on the combined experiences of other patients previously in the same category. It also allows research and outcomes to cross occupational lines, allowing research done in one field to be applied to other fields.

A unified model simplifies surveillance of trends and analysis of the utilization of services, facilitates service planning and helps measure performance. This will help the facility's business managers anticipate staffing needs and physical plant space. It also allows management to compare one treatment group's cost-effectiveness to other groups serving similar patient groups and providing similar interventions.

Professionally it is beneficial to the recreational therapist to match the model and standards of the other health care professionals. As recreational therapists offset the limitations of the Therapeutic Recreation Service Model by inserting the WHO's model into the "therapy" category, the entire profession will come closer to truly being an integral part of the health care treatment team.

A Heuristic Analysis of the Recreation Service Model

Stevens (1979) proposed a procedure which helped define characteristics allowing for the testing, evaluation and refinement of models of practice. Gruver (1994) further defined Steven's procedures so that they could be specifically applied to models in the field of recreational therapy. Gruver suggests that two aspects be evaluated: whether the model is descriptive or explanatory in nature and whether the model contains both internal and external adequacy.

Descriptive versus Explanatory

A descriptive model describes a phenomenon where an explanatory model attempts to explain how and why the phenomenon happens. A descriptive model looks at the major components of the phenomenon it describes, in this case a classification system for information about the patients seen by recreational therapists and for the structure of and purpose of the treatment provided. The RSM does provide a description of each category and how each category fits in with the next. It also provides guidelines for determining what fits into each level. However, the RSM, drawing upon all of the research done on the WHO model, goes beyond descriptive terms and explains the relationship between impairments, disabilities and handicaps. Since the 1980 publication of *the International Classification of Impairments, Disabilities and Handicaps* (ICIDH) there have been extensive research efforts and other activities on an international basis resulting in more than a thousand publications (Schuntermann, 1996). This leaves the second half of the model open to discussion about being descriptive or explanatory. The second half of the model (education, organized recreation and independent activities) explains the relationship between the use of prescriptive activities, education and participation. It is descriptive in nature as it defines the scope of the service as well the purpose of each level. This portion of the RSM is not as strong as the first portion. The relationship between education (especially leisure education) and organized recreation (recreation participation) can be found in the literature but the depth and scope of this literature is not as extensive as that for the first four levels.

Table 5.8: **The RSM and Internal Adequacy**

Characteristic of Internal Adequacy	Characteristics of the RSM
Clarity: The model is easy to understand. The model may be complex in nature but well structured.	Model uses levels which are easily described by function (of patient) and action (of professional).
Consistency: The model consistently uses terms in the same way throughout, applies a similar pattern to interpret sections of the model, retains a uniformity in all value statements throughout and uses the same method of applying logic and support to justify the model throughout.	Model uses unified terminology based on function and action throughout, following a logical progression.
Logical Development: The model is based on reasoning which justifies and logically supports the development of and statements within the model itself.	The conceptualization underlying this model is grounded in both literature and health care practice from a variety of disciplines.
Level of Theory Development: The model is best if it exhibits a explanatory theory and not a descriptive theory.	The Model, especially the therapy aspect, goes beyond descriptive to explain the interrelationship between levels. Further work should be done on the activity aspects of the model to allow a greater level of explanatory theory.

Internal Adequacy

To determine how well a model is able to demonstrate internal adequacy one must examine the degree to which the model refrains from contradicting itself. Table 5.8 provides a summary of the internal adequacy of the RSM.

External Adequacy

To determine if a model has external adequacy an evaluation is needed of the degree to which the model allows and promotes the practice of recreational

Table 5.9: **The RSM and External Adequacy**

Characteristic of External Adequacy	Characteristics of the RSM
Theory Adequacy: Can the Model demonstrate enough strength to support research concerning the principles, interpretation and methods of the model?	Attributes of each level are distinctive enough to allow research. Therapy component has demonstrated ability to support principles, interpretation and methods.
Utility: Can the model be easily adopted by the profession to enhance the practice of the profession?	All components already implemented to some degree.
Significance: Are all important issues addressed by the model and can the model contribute to the development of practice knowledge?	Model addresses many issues including scope of practice; a pre-established set of criteria for research; integrates RT practice with other health care professionals.
Discrimination: Can the model help define professional boundaries? Does it help the profession define itself as a unique service?	Model, especially therapy section, clearly helps define professional boundaries. There is some necessary and expected overlap with occupational therapy and activity professionals but this model delineates the differences better than the other prevalent models.
Scope of Theory: Does the model help the profession construct a strong knowledge base on which to practice?	Model is applicable to populations within and outside of health care. Model uses well defined categories for further research.
Complexity: Does the model explain the interrelationship between the many elements of the theory?	Model is complex and, especially in the therapy section, has clear interrelationships explained.

therapy. Table 5.9 shows this evaluation.

In her discussion on models of practice Gruver (1994) states:

> Perhaps an issue that should be addressed as a profession is the goals of health care agencies, human services agencies, leisure services agencies and educational agencies in relation to therapeutic recreation practice, and appropriate practice models to be employed within difference agency structures in support of particular philosophies of treatment and sought outcomes. (Gruver, p. 9)

This seems to suggest that professionals who use activities and recreation to promote wellness may need to have more than one model of practice. The RSM provides these professionals with just one model which combines both a medical model and a wellness model with both descriptive and explanatory elements. While the promotion of wellness portions of the model would benefit from further research and refinement, the use of the RSM provides the field with a practical model on which to base practice.

Summary

The field of recreational therapy has had a variety of models related to the delivery of services. While many of them are closely aligned in their basic concepts and continuums, none of them provided enough structure to base the dynamic group of interventions which relate to the use of activity as a modality. The field of recreational therapy needed a taxonomy to base practice on which also allowed a structure common to all health care providers. The Recreation Service Model combines the taxonomy developed by the World Health Organization with Therapeutic Recreation Service Model. This model provides the field with a structure to base treatment, research and funding on, and recognizes the holistic nature of the use of leisure to bring about life satisfaction.

Learning Activities

1. Review different testing tools, treatment protocols and leisure education programs used within the field of recreational therapy. Creative a matrix similar to Table 5.1 in this chapter which lists the different divisions used by each. Compare and note any similarities and differences.

2. The *ICD-9-CM* provides professionals with categories and corresponding codes to help facilitate billing and research. Obtain a copy of the *ICD-9-CM* and review all three volumes. Select either a case study or an article about a treatment intervention from either the *Therapeutic Recreation Journal* or the *Annual in Therapeutic Recreation*. Using the *ICD-9-CM*, provide cod-

ing numbers for diagnoses and interventions discussed. (If your university does not have a copy of the *ICD-9-CM*, try your local medical center's medical library, your physician's office or a large public library.)

3.   Review a case study or article about a treatment intervention from either the *Therapeutic Recreation Journal* or the *Annual in Therapeutic Recreation*. Divide your paper into two columns. List all of the medical history, assessment results and interventions listed in the journal article down the left column. In the right column indicate in which of the four levels of the World Health Organization's Model the information in the left column belongs.

4.   Divide your paper into three columns. Take the disabilities listed in Table 5.4 and place them down the center column of your paper. Down the left of your paper list a possible impairment which may be the cause of the disability. In the last column list a handicap which may impact the individual as a result of the listed impairment and disability. Please list which one of the seven areas of handicap the barrier falls into, as well as the actual handicap.

Example:

Impairment	Disability	Handicap
visually impaired: total blindness	transportation	mobility: bus stop not adequately marked with Braille

Study Questions

1.   Explain why using domains (e.g., cognitive, social, leisure) proves to be problematic for the field of recreational therapy. What is one of the major impacts of the lack of standardized categories within each domain?

2.   List at least four of the strengths of the World Health Organization's Model of the health care continuum. Explain why each attribute you listed will also be a strength for the field of recreational therapy.

3.   What are the differences between leisure counseling and leisure education?

4.   What are some terms used by recreational therapists which are not part of the standardized terms related to functional performance deficits? How do these terms reduce a therapist's chance of receiving third party reimbursement. List at least six and state why these terms are not optimal to use in a treatment setting.

5.   What is the difference between a descriptive model and an explanatory model?

References

American Therapeutic Recreation Association. (1993). *Standards for the practice of therapeutic recreation & self assessment guide*. Hattiesburg, MS: American Therapeutic Recreation Association.

Anchor, K. (Ed.). (1996). *Disability analysis handbook: Tools for independent practice*. Dubuque, IA: Kendall/Hunt Publishing Company.

Armstrong, M. & Lauzen, S. (1994). *Community integration program* (2nd ed.). Ravensdale, WA: Idyll Arbor, Inc.

Austin, D. R. (1982). *Therapeutic recreation processes and techniques*. New York; John Wiley & Sons.

Austin, D. R. (1991). Introduction and overview. In D. R. Austin & M. E. Crawford (Eds.). *Therapeutic recreation: An introduction*. Englewood Cliffs, NJ: Prentice-Hall, Inc.

Austin, D. R. (1997). *Therapeutic recreation processes and techniques* (3rd ed.). Champaign, IL: Sagamore Publishing.

Badley, E. M. (1987). The ICIDH: format, application in different settings and distinction between disability and handicap. A critique of papers on the application of the ICIDH. *International Disabilities Studies, 9*(3), 122-125.

Badley, E. M. (1995, Feb-Mar). The genesis of handicap: Definition, models of disablement and role of external factors. *Disability and Rehabilitation, 17*(2), 53-62.

Bond-Howard, B. (1998). *Comprehensive visual neglect assessment* (CVnA). Mount Vernon, WA: Ptarmigan West.

Bullock, C. C. (1987). Recreation and special populations. In A. Graefe & S. Parker (Eds.). *Recreation: An introductory handbook*. State College, PA: Venture Publishing, Inc.

burlingame, j. (1989). *Bus utilization screening tool (BUS)*. Ravensdale, WA: Idyll Arbor, Inc.

burlingame, j & Skalko, T. (1997). *Idyll Arbor's glossary for therapists*. Ravensdale, WA: Idyll Arbor, Inc.

Coyle, C. P., Kinney, W. B., Riley, B. & Shank, J. W. (Eds.). (1991). *Benefits of therapeutic recreation: A consensus view*. Ravensdale, WA: Idyll Arbor, Inc.

Dehn, D. (1995). *Leisure step up*. Ravensdale, WA: Idyll Arbor, Inc.

Grote, K, Hasl, M, Krider, R. & Martin-Mortensen, D. (1995). *Behavioral health protocols for recreational therapy*. Ravensdale, WA: Idyll Arbor, Inc.

Gruver, B. M., (1994). Theories and models: An heuristic analysis of therapeutic recreation practice. *Annual in Therapeutic Recreation, 4*, 1-10.

Kelland, J. (1995). *Protocols for recreational therapy*. State College, PA: Venture.

Keogh-Hoss, M. (1993). *Therapeutic recreation activity assessment*. Ravensdale, WA: Idyll Arbor, Inc.

Kloseck, M., Crilly, R., Ellis, G. & Lammers, E. (1996). Leisure Competence Measure: Development and reliability testing of a scale to measure functional outcomes in therapeutic recreation. *Therapeutic Recreation Journal, 30*(1), 13-26.

Navar, N. (1990). *State Technical Institute leisure activities project (STILAP)*. Ravensdale, WA: Idyll Arbor, Inc.

Neulinger, J. (1990). *The road to Eden after all: A human metamorphosis.* Culemborg, The Netherlands: Giordano Bruno.

Parker, R. (1997). *Comprehensive evaluation in recreational therapy, Psych./Revised. (CERT Psych/R).* Ravensdale, WA: Idyll Arbor, Inc.

Peterson, C. A. & Gunn, S. L. (1984). *Therapeutic recreation program design; Principles and procedures.* Englewood Cliffs, NJ: Prentice-Hall, Inc.

Ragheb, M. G. & Beard, J. G. (1990a). *Leisure motivation scale.* Ravensdale, WA: Idyll Arbor, Inc.

Ragheb, M. G. & Beard, J. G. (1990b). *Leisure attitude measure (LAM).* Ravensdale, WA: Idyll Arbor, Inc.

Ragheb, M. G. & Beard, J. G. (1991a). *Leisure satisfaction scale.* Ravensdale, WA: Idyll Arbor, Inc.

Ragheb, M. G. & Beard, J. G. (1991b). *Leisure interest measure.* Ravensdale, WA: Idyll Arbor, Inc.

Ragheb, M. G. & Merydith, S. (1995). *Free time boredom measurement.* Ravensdale, WA: Idyll Arbor, Inc.

Schenk, C. (1998). *Leisurescope plus.* Ravensdale, WA: Idyll Arbor, Inc.

Schuntermann, M. F. (1996, March). The international classification of impairments, disabilities and handicaps: Results and problems. *International Journal of Rehabilitation Research, 19*(1), 1-11.

Smith, R. W., Austin, D. R. & Kennedy, D. W. (1996). *Inclusive and special recreation: Opportunities for persons with disabilities* (3rd ed.). Madison, WI: Brown & Benchmark Publishers.

Soder, M. (1987). Relative definition of handicap: Implications for research. *UPSALA Journal of Medical Sciences. Supplement, 44*, 24-29.

State University of New York Research Foundation (1987). *FIM Scale.* In j. burlingame and T. Skalko. (1997). *Idyll Arbor's glossary for therapists* (p. 116). Ravensdale, WA: Idyll Arbor, Inc.

Stevens, B. J. (1979). *Nursing theory: Analysis, application, evaluation.* Boston, MA: Little, Brown and Company.

Thorburn, M. J., Desai, P. & Davidson, L. L. (1992, Jul-Sept). Categories, classes and criteria in childhood disability — experience from a survey in Jamaica. *Disability and Rehabilitation, 14*(3), 122-132.

US Department of Health and Human Services. (1980). *The international classification of diseases, 9th revision, clinical modification, Vol. 1-3.* DHHS Publication No. (PHS 80-1260) Washington, DC: US Government Printing Office.

Witman, J. (1991a). *Measurement of social empowerment and trust (SET).* Ravensdale, WA: Idyll Arbor, Inc.

Witman, J. (1991b). *Cooperation and trust scale (CAT).* Ravensdale, WA: Idyll Arbor, Inc.

Witt, P. & Ellis, G. (1989). *The leisure diagnostic battery.* State College, PA: Venture Publishing.

World Health Organization. (1980). *International classification of impairments, disabilities and handicaps.* Geneva: World Health Organization.

Chapter 6

Recreational Therapy in Special Education

Charles C. Bullock
Danny E. Johnson

When we think of recreational therapy, we think of hospitals, institutions and increasingly, even outpatient clinics and community mental health centers. We think of myriad traditional treatment and rehabilitation settings, but seldom do we think of recreational therapy in the schools. The reason is that there are only a few recreational therapists who work in schools.

Since 1975 with the passage of Public Law 94-142, recreational therapy has been a legitimate function in schools when it enhances special education of students with disabilities. Yet until recently, neither the American Therapeutic Recreation Association nor the National Therapeutic Recreation Society even tracked recreational therapists in schools because there were so few working there.

In this chapter, first we will discuss the conceptual basis of recreational therapy as a part of special education. Following that, we will provide some background and legislative history about special education so that our explanation of the concept of "recreation as a related service" will be couched in the larger context of the statute and its rules and regulations as well as issues and trends in special education. Following a discussion of the roles of a recreational therapist in a school setting, we will then discuss important issues that must be faced if there is to be an increased presence of recreational therapy as part of special education in schools.

Leisure Needs and Education

The need for leisure has long been seen as a need of all people. Participation in leisure activities has a significant impact on the social and psychological adjustment of an individual. Leisure activity is instrumental in the individual's development of a sense of personal identity and self-worth and the ability of the individual to interact with others and his/her environment. Ford, Schnorr, Meyer, Davern, Black and Dempsey (1989) point out that a significant amount of time in a person's life requires participation using recreation skills which are constructive and personally satisfying in nature. They contend that using leisure time positively will affect where that person is able to live in the community, vocational success and the quality of relationships that they develop with others.

Through recreation, students with disabilities explore their own attitudes and values toward leisure and recreational involvement and plan ways to utilize recreation to assist them in their adjustment to school, community and, ultimately, independent living. Recreation activities and experiences are an important aspect of community adjustment and have an impact on total adjustment, especially in the transition from school to work and/or independent living.

Learning to Play

Children typically develop the skills and knowledge of leisure and leisure participation during the years in which they grow up. Most children are exposed to a variety of situations which provide opportunities to explore and to develop new recreation skills and awareness of a variety of recreation possibilities. For most children, recreation and the skills required for participation in recreation are taken for granted because they are a natural part of growing up. Unfortunately, children with disabilities often do not have the same opportunities to explore and learn about recreation and leisure as a direct result of their disabilities. They lack the knowledge and skills to participate in recreation activities of their choice. This means they are also denied the benefits derived from satisfying participation in recreation and leisure activities.

Education ostensibly teaches skills and provides experiences that will prepare a student for life. Recreation is an important component of every individual's life, yet preparation for recreation is not being adequately provided in schools. This is a source of concern for two reasons. First, a positive attitude towards leisure is correlated with increased life satisfaction (Iso-Ahola, 1980). Second, children with disabilities are usually subject to emotional, physical or cognitive impairments which affect their functioning in activities that are a part of daily life, such as education, self-care and recreation (Bender, Brannan & Verhoven, 1984). For the areas of traditional education and self-care, professional intervention is available to train children with disabilities in order to remediate their deficits and help them to function more successfully within contemporary society. Unfortunately, recreation has not been as strongly supported through our system of public education as an essential facet of an individual's life, development and contribution to society. Little academic or other formal training is provided for children with disabilities to develop their leisure awareness, clarify their leisure values, learn recreation skills, utilize leisure resources and participate in inclusive environments. This training is particularly important for children with disabilities, for whom recreation and leisure may be the primary context for social learning and integration.

Playing to Learn

Recreational therapy assists, augments and enhances the education and learning process. As an educational tool, recreational therapy can be used to achieve cognitive, social, emotional and physical objectives identified as learning needs. Recreational therapy, supplied as a related service, not only provides assistance, instruction and strategies to facilitate the short term objectives of special education, it is also crucial to the long-range life goals of students with disabilities. It facilitates social involvement and friendships and encourages and provides skills associated with opportunities for community integration. It is through leisure involvement that community connections can be established and re-established (Pelleiter, McWhorter & Kappel, 1985). Appropriate participation in leisure/recreation activities is associated with development of collateral skills, such as independent living and work skills. In fact, many of the first skills learned are learned during play. The possession of these advanced activity of daily living skills can play an important role in the successful community adjustment of individuals with disabilities (Schleien & Rynders, 1989). Therefore, it is an important part of a child's total education. Recreational therapy services for children with disabilities include assessment and the prescriptive use of activities to enhance function in school and community agencies.

One specific example of the connection of education and leisure is the area of self-determination and self-control strategies. Self-control strategies provide an important instructional link between self-determination and leisure education. Self-control strategy instruction has been proposed as a useful community-based process for facilitating educational outcomes for individuals with disabilities (Agran & Moore, 1987; Martin, Burger, Elias-Burger & Mithaug, 1988). The use of such strategies is supported by a plethora of scholars and practitioners who concur that a need exists for individuals who are disabled to learn to control their own behavior with as little external influence as possible (Agran & Moore, 1987; Martin, Burger, Elias-Burger & Mithaug, 1988). The process of self-control has been defined by Martin, Burger, Elias-Burger and Mithaug (1988, p. 157) as "the process of managing one's own behavior through self-regulation of antecedent or consequent stimuli." The intent of self-control training is to achieve internal control via external control procedures (Bandura, 1976). Self-control instruction has been used successfully in leisure education to facilitate both decision-making in leisure and independent leisure initiation (Mahon & Bullock, 1991). Keogh, Faw, Whitman and Reid (1984) and Matson and Andrasik (1982) also have utilized self-control techniques successfully in facilitating leisure behavior.

Work by Bullock, Mahon, Morris and Jones (1991); Mahon and Bullock (1991); and Mahon (1991) has begun to address self-determination by introducing a comprehensive leisure education program into classrooms for individuals with disabilities. Complimentary work in school-based leisure education curriculum development has been carried out by Voeltz, Wuerch and Wilcox (1982); Beck-Ford and Brown (1984); Wehman and Moon (1985); Putnam, Werder and Schleien (1985); Schleien, Olson, Rogers and McLafferty (1985); Schleien, Ray, Soderman-Olson and McMahon (1987); Fine, Welch-Burke and Fondario (1985); and Hambrecht, Forlifer, Peters and Wilson (1989).

Legislative History of Special Education

Before moving on to understanding the role of recreational therapy in schools, it is important to understand the historical progression of federal legislation pertaining to special education.

Public Law 94-142, the Education for All Handicapped Children Act (EHA) was passed in 1975 and went into effect in October of 1977 when the regulations were finalized. PL 94-142 grew out of and strengthened earlier acts of a similar name, including PL 91-230 and PL 93-380 (Ballard, Ramirez & Zantal-Weiner, 1987). The major purposes of PL 94-142 were to "assure that all children with disabilities have available to them, within specific time periods, a free and appropriate public education which emphasizes special education and related services designed to meet their unique needs, to assure that the rights of children with disabilities and their parents or guardians are protected, to assist States and localities to provide for the education of all children with disabilities, and to assess and assure the effectiveness of efforts to educate children with disabilities" (PL 94-142).

In 1983, through the Education of the Handicapped Act Amendments of 1983 (PL 98-199), Congress amended the law to expand incentives for preschool special education programs, early intervention and transition programs. All programs under EHA became the responsibility of the Office of Special Education Programs (OSEP), of the Office of Special Education and Rehabilitation Services, within the United States Department of Education.

In 1986, EHA was again amended through PL 99-457, the Education of the Handicapped Act Amendments of 1986. One of the important outcomes of these amendments was that the age of eligibility for special education and related services for all children with disabilities was lowered to age three. This amendment also established the Handicapped Infants and Toddlers Program (Part H of the Act) which provides early intervention services, as needed, for children from birth to their third birthday. In addition, under this program the infant or toddler's family may receive services that are needed to help them assist in the development of the child. State definitions of eligibility under this program vary. However, in order to continue to receive federal funds, each state must have a comprehensive, statewide, interagency service delivery system in place.

In October, 1990, Congress passed, and President Bush signed into law, the Education of the Handicapped Act Amendments of 1990 (PL 101-476). The new law has resulted in some significant changes. For example, the name of the law, the Education of the Handicapped Act (EHA), was changed to the Individuals with Disabilities Education Act (IDEA) to reflect, among other things, the emphasis on "people first" language. Many of the discretionary programs authorized under the law have been expanded. Some new discretionary programs, including special programs on transition, a new program to improve services for children and youth with serious emotional disturbance and a research and information dissemination program on attention deficit disorder, were created. Part B of IDEA mandates that beginning no later than age 16, each student now must also have included in their Individualized Education Program (IEP) a statement of the transition services which address employment, post secondary education, adult services, independent living and community participation. In addition, the law now includes transition services and assistive technology services as new definitions of special education services that must be included in a child's or youth's IEP. Also, rehabilitation counseling and social work services were added as related services under the law. Finally, the services and rights under this law were expanded to more fully include children with autism and traumatic brain injury.

The Individuals with Disabilities Education Act (IDEA) makes it possible for states and localities to receive federal funds to assist in the education of infants, toddlers, preschoolers, children and youth with disabilities. IDEA:

- calls for school systems to carry out a systematic search for every child with a disability in need of a public education.
- mandates a Free and Appropriate Public Education (FAPE) regardless of the nature and severity of an individual's disability.
- states that the education of children and youth with disabilities will be based on a complete and individual evaluation and assessment of the specific, unique needs of each child.
- makes it clear that education and related services must be provided at no cost to parents.

- requires an Individualized Education Program (IEP), or an Individualized Family Services Plan (IFSP) (in the case of infants and toddlers), be drawn up for every child or youth found eligible for special education or early intervention services, stating precisely what kinds of special education and related services, or the types of early intervention services each infant, toddler, preschooler, child or youth will receive.
- specifies that children and youth receiving special education have the right to receive the related services necessary to benefit from special instruction.
- has similar requirements to assure that testing and evaluation of a child's needs are not based on a single testing instrument.
- emphasizes the importance of educating children and youth with disabilities with their non-disabled peers to the maximum extent appropriate.
- regulates that parents have the right to participate in any decision related to the identification, evaluation and placement of their child or youth with a disability.
- specifies that parents must give consent for any initial evaluation, assessment or placement; be notified of any change in placement that may occur; be included, along with teachers, in conferences and meetings held to draw up individualized programs; and must approve these plans before they go into effect for the first time.
- gives parents the right to challenge and appeal any decision related to the identification, evaluation and placement of their child through due process procedures.
- grants parents the right to confidentiality of information. No one may see a child's records unless the parents give their written permission. (The exception to this is school personnel with legitimate educational interests.)

The Education of the Handicapped Act, PL 94-142 and its amendments, PL 98-199, PL 99-457 and now the Individuals with Disabilities Education Act, PL 101-476, represent the most important pieces of educational legislation in the history of educating children and youth with disabilities. Recreational therapy professionals should make every effort to familiarize themselves with these laws. The regulations, which further define these laws, can be found in the Code of Federal Regulations. They are called *CFR: Title 34, Education; Parts 300 to 399* and are available from the US Department of Education.

General Overview of Related Services

According to Public Law 101-476, The Individuals with Disabilities Education Act of 1990 (IDEA), formerly PL 94-142, all students are guaranteed a free and appropriate public education which emphasizes special education and related services. In the law, related services are described as "developmental, corrective and other supportive services as may be required to assist a child with a disability *to benefit from special education*, and includes the early identification and assessment of disabling conditions in children." Below is a list of related services specifically identified in PL 101-476.

1. Audiology
2. Counseling services
3. Early identification
4. Medical services for diagnostic or evaluation purposes
5. Occupational therapy
6. Parent counseling and training
7. Physical therapy
8. Psychological services
9. Recreation
10. Rehabilitation counseling
11. School health services
12. Social work services in schools
13. Speech pathology
14. Transportation

Recreation, as a related service for students with disabilities, must be administered in a manner consistent with other related educational services. Recreation, as defined in the regulations of the law, assists, augments and enhances the education and learning process. As with other related services, recreation can be used to achieve cognitive, social, emotional and physical objectives identified as learning needs for those children who need it to benefit from their special education. Recreational therapy personnel direct their energies toward analyzing and identifying students' strengths and weaknesses, and determining the appropriate programmatic response. Specific interventions and strategies are then developed to improve performance.

Components of Recreation as a Related Service

PL 101-476 clearly identifies recreation as a related service which enhances the educational goals of a child with a disability. If recreation is included in a child's IEP, it cannot be completed by a curricular service such as special education or physical education. Recreation and physical education are not the same from a statutory or a programmatic perspective. Unlike physical education, recreation, by definition, is *in addition to* regular special education and physical education. As a related service, recreation assists, augments and enhances the educational process. Recreation and leisure are essential parts of a total education. Recreational therapists must work with traditional service personnel such as special educators and physical educators to provide recreation services that assist and augment rather than duplicate. This is accomplished through cooperative working relationships that provide the highest quality and most comprehensive educational experience.

Recreation is further defined in the regulations as having four components. They are

- *Assessment of Recreation and Leisure Functioning*: Procedure to determine current functional strengths of students with disabilities in terms of skills, abilities and attitudes. This is the basis for IEP (Individualized Education Program) prescription and subsequent remediation.
- *Leisure Education*: Instruction to improve school and community involvement and social connectedness through the development of positive attitudes toward leisure, the development of skills necessary for recreation participation, knowledge of recreational resources and recognition of the benefits of recreation involvement.
- *Therapeutic Recreation*: The purposive use of recreation activities and experiences to ameliorate deficits in social, cognitive and physical functioning of students with disabilities.
- *Recreation in School and Community Agencies:* The provision of recreation services to students with disabilities in the most inclusive setting possible.

Any child with a disability is entitled to a free and appropriate public education which emphasizes special education. The child *may* receive any of the additional related services, but the services must assist a child with a disability to benefit from special education and must be specifically identified and written into the child's IEP. Although parents and teachers work together on writing the child's IEP, often recreation is not considered because it is not readily recognized as a related service. The precise role of the recreational therapist is dependent upon the size of the school system, the number and types of students with disabilities and the extent to which regular educators are available and prepared to provide programs for students with special needs.

Individualized Education Programs

An Individualized Education Program (IEP) is required by PL 101-476, the Individuals with Disabilities Education Act 1990, for any student in need of special education or related services. Prior to the development of an IEP, a school-based committee must review the records of the student in question and collect any additional evaluative information necessary to insure a comprehensive assessment of the student's present level of functioning. Once this committee has decided to initiate an Individualized Education Program, the IEP must include the following content:

- documentation of the student's current level of educational performance,
- annual goals or the attainments expected by the end of the school year,
- short term objectives, stated in instructional terms, which are the intermediate steps leading to the mastery of annual goals,
- documentation of the particular special education and related services that will be provided to the student,
- an indication of the extent of time a student will participate in the regular education program,
- projected dates for initiation and duration of services,
- appropriate objective criteria, evaluation procedures and schedules for determining mastery of short term objectives, at least on an annual basis.

Both the school and the child's parents or guardian must agree and sign the completed IEP before it is implemented. The IEP is a legal document, used by schools, which describes a child's unique needs for special education and coordinates a plan for the child's education. This plan can include recreation and leisure goals to enhance the child's overall education. The family can request that recreation and leisure goals be included if that area has been overlooked.

Yet, it is unusual to see "Recreation" written into an IEP. Few people would disagree that recreation is a vital part of everyone's life. Recreation is not excluded from IEPs because it is thought unnecessary. It is excluded because IEP teams are either unaware of "recreation as a related service" or are unaware of the expected benefits of this particular related service. Some public school personnel assume that if a child is receiving physical education that he does not need recreation as a related service. Whatever the reason, recreation as a related service is not being written into IEPs.

Which Students Could Benefit?

All children with disabilities as defined by federal mandate (PL 101-476) *may* receive recreation services. However, only students whose IEPs include recreation as a related service, receive assessment and subsequent remediation. Students can be referred for recreation services by regular or special education teachers, transition coordinators, counselors or other related service personnel. These are students who need a comprehensive recreation and leisure assessment or who have been identified by other assessment procedures as needing leisure education or remediation services. Some students may be referred to recreation services to assist in the completion of regular education goals or IEP objectives. Whatever the reason, any student with a disability who is referred for recreation services will receive recreation services as appropriate to extend and enhance the student's education in the most inclusive setting possible.

Depending on the services prescribed in the IEP, recreation services for students with disabilities are delivered in the most inclusive setting possible. These environments include self-contained developmental or remedial education classes, regular education classes, resource programs and other non-traditional school programs such as institutions and other treatment facilities. IEP prescribed services need not be restricted to school hours and could take place after school, in the home environment or in the community, as long as the intervention is connected to school-related needs.

The content of instruction will vary according to the ages, needs and abilities of students. At all levels, emphasis is on the assessment and subsequent remediation of recreation and play skills. Remediation, as defined by the regulations and discussed earlier, is accomplished through (1) recreational therapy, (2) leisure education and (3) recreation participation in the community. In early intervention and grade school settings, the student may receive recreational therapy primarily to ameliorate cognitive, social and physical deficits thereby assisting in the educational process. Later, special emphasis is placed on initial exploration of recreation and leisure skills, values and attitudes and on participation in activities consistent with their non-disabled peers. In middle schools and high schools, the emphasis may still be on assessment, remediation and participation, however, the greatest emphasis at this level tends to be leisure education. Leisure education is crucial to the pre-transitional and transitional phases as the students leaves school and transitions to adult life and community living. At the time the student is preparing for work, it is essential that s/he understand the importance of recreation and leisure to a well-balanced adult life.

Roles of Recreational Therapists in Schools

The role of a recreational therapist in a school system is dependent on a variety of circumstances including: the size of the school system, the staffing pattern of recreational therapists, the organization of special education services and the experience of the school system in utilizing recreational therapy services. The recreational therapist may provide any combination of services relating to assessment, direct service delivery, consultation and resource referral.

A recreational therapist may provide assessment services to a school system. This is often handled on a contractual basis for assessments as requested by teachers and/or parents. Often when an assessment is required for a child, it is because the parents have been assertive or insistent that an evaluation be completed. Contractual assessments are more likely to occur when a school system does not employ a recreational therapist. This role is critical to the expansion of recreational therapy services in schools because the assessment may lead to the recognition of the need for this related service which may not have been provided previously.

The recreational therapist can provide direct service to students as designated on their IEP. This may be on an individual or group basis providing therapeutic intervention, leisure education or facilitating inclusive recreation.

The recreational therapist may also serve as a consultant to teachers, parents, community and other agencies on strategies for providing appropriate recreation services and programs for persons with disabilities. This most often occurs in regular school environments, particularly in inclusive settings, but may occur in myriad settings.

Another area of consultation for the recreational therapist may be with classroom teachers on the inclusion of leisure in their curriculum. Specifically, this may mean working with teachers on how to conduct large group leisure education sessions for their class from standardized leisure education curricula. The recreational therapist may also consult with classroom teachers concerning the use of leisure activities as learning tools.

The recreational therapist in a school system may also provide referral services for the students and their families. Often students with disabilities have difficulty connecting to their community and finding accessible programs, both physically and socially. Recreational therapists can become experts on community recreation connections and provide a valuable referral and information service.

Responsibilities vary depending on the role or roles assumed. The duties of the recreational therapist are dependent on the referral and generally include:

- Assessing the recreation and leisure abilities, functional skills, impairments, knowledge and attitudes of students with disabilities,
- Planning an appropriate implementation/remediation strategy based on the assessment of the student with a disability,
- Implementing and conducting leisure education programs to assist the transition from school to work and adult life,
- Providing resource/consultative assistance to regular and special education teachers to infuse leisure education concepts into their ongoing curricula,
- Providing opportunities for recreation participation in the most inclusive environment in schools and community agencies,
- Providing supportive/resource services to special education classroom teachers and resource room teachers who incorporate recreation and play into the curriculum to enhance functional skills and
- Interacting and working with professionals and paraprofessionals from various disciplines, parents and community members who are concerned with students with disabilities.

The recreational therapist is not a teacher but rather is a supportive member of the educational team who works and consults with other education personnel. The recreational therapist works cooperatively with related service personnel, the adapted physical educator, the special educator and other educators to extend and enhance the students' total education.

Professional preparation is usually accomplished in an undergraduate or a master's degree program followed by certification through the National Council on Therapeutic Recreation Certification (NCTRC). Recreational therapists are not credentialed as teachers. Recreational therapists support teachers and educational goals by providing a related service. In order to function in school settings, professional recreational therapists must be recognized and certified as related service personnel by state education credentialing bodies.

Issues and Barriers

A variety of issues and barriers face the profession of recreational therapy in becoming an integral aspect of special education. A number of those issues are not unlike the pressing issues that are being dealt with by the entire profession such as assessment, efficacy research, funding and marketing.

In the area of assessment, there exists a need for the development and evaluation of a variety of age and disability appropriate assessment procedures which could be used throughout the country either in addition to or in conjunction with existing evaluations and assessments. This assessment procedure must be applicable and appropriate to the special education system and to the IEP process. Tools such as the General Recreation Screening Tool (GRST), the Recreation Early Development Screening Tool (REDS), the Fox and School/Social Behavior Scale are some testing tools which may be used by the recreational therapist working in school settings. However, even with some tools available, there is a need for other tools to be developed.

Efficacy research must look at the specific impacts of interventions on the student's education. Studies to identify the relationship between recreational therapy services and transition to employment and independent living are needed. Information relative to job satisfaction, adjustment to community life, friendship development and independent recreation participation could show the benefits of a comprehensive education which includes leisure education.

Funding of recreational therapy interventions and positions will become an increasingly important issue for school systems. As a profession, we need to expand our base of reimbursement and aggressively pursue funds from managed care systems, Medicaid, Medicaid waivers such as CAP-MR/DD (Community Alternatives Program for people who are severely mentally retarded/developmentally disabled) and other possible/creative sources.

Marketing is also important to the expansion of services in schools. Projects such as *Leisure Education in Teacher Preparation* from the Center for Recreation and Disability Studies (CRDS) at the University of North Carolina, Chapel Hill have been developed to increase administrators and teachers understanding of the meaning and importance of recreational therapy services in the schools. Additionally, it will become increasingly useful to help consumers and families connect the value of self-determination, free choice, friendship and community involvement in recreation to the child's education. Parents are potentially our strongest allies. Individual parents and family support groups often can articulate the importance of recreation, interaction and connectedness to school bureaucracies.

Other issues for recreational therapy that are more germane to school systems are Comprehensive Systems of Personnel Development, recreational therapist preparation and entry issues, expansion of the range of clientele and professional networking. There are a variety of issues and barriers which face a recreational therapy student or professional who wants to work as a recreational therapist in a school system.

University curricula, as well as individual therapists, are committed to developing new knowledge, methods, material and approaches which will facilitate the broader efforts of the nation's schools in fulfilling their commitment to a free and appropriate education for children and youth with disabilities. Yet, few state and local education agencies include recreation as a related service in their Comprehensive System of Personnel Development (CSPD), policies, administrative codes, training objectives or on a student's individualized education program form. Without addressing the need for recreation services through these processes, it is impossible for children with disabilities to receive appropriate and necessary recreation services as a part of their education.

From all of the available data, it is clear that there are not enough Certified Therapeutic Recreation Specialists to work as related service personnel in the nation's schools. Even though PL 101-476, the Individuals with Disabilities Education Act (formerly PL 94-142) allows this service, and has from its inception in 1975, it has been only within the past few years that school systems have begun to utilize this related service. To compound this situation, most recreational therapy curricula do not include sufficient content to prepare graduates to work specifically in schools. Curricula typically cover the applicable laws and the disabilities encountered by a recreational therapist in a school setting, yet do not comprehensively delineate the content and strategies necessary to be employed in a school setting. Consequently, very few universities provide this needed content as well as appropriate experiences during training. Training is needed to ensure that there are an adequate number of highly qualified recreational therapists to meet the identified needs in this specialty area.

It is very difficult for a recreational therapy student to use a school setting to meet the internship requirement or to gain specific experience with schools. This limited access also affects students in other ways. Many recreational therapy students develop their specific setting or disability interest while either volunteering or observing for a class assignment. Since a school setting is usually not a option, a student will choose a typical setting such as a hospital or nursing home for this experience. Again, the lack of school programs reinforces students not to consider this option.

Another barrier for recreational therapy students is certification by the National Council on Therapeutic Recreation Certification. Certification standards require that a student complete a 360 hour internship under the direct supervision of a full-time Certified Therapeutic Recreation Specialist. This problem is even more limiting when you take into account that many recreational therapists who work in schools are not employed full-time in recreational therapy because of limited contracts or part-time work and therefore cannot be an internship supervisor for certification purposes. A student will likely then intern in a traditional setting, not in a school setting. Once again a student is not prepared to enter the school system and the cycle continues.

The lack of written information for a recreational therapist who wants to work in a school system is another barrier. Because there is no "blue-print" to help a recreational therapist who wants to enter the school system, they are essentially on their own to figure out the exact services they can offer, who they should contact, the process they will go through and how they should present the potential benefits they can bring to students. The only exception to this lack of a "blueprint" is the *Model Program Guidelines for School-Community Leisure Link* from Center for Recreation and Disabilities at University of North Carolina — Chapel Hill and that is limited to starting a leisure education program.

Several universities in the last few years have been awarded personnel preparation grants by the Office of Special Education in the Department of Education to prepare recreational therapy students to work with children with disabilities in school settings. Both the University of New Hampshire and the University of North Carolina — Chapel Hill have developed specific courses on recreational therapy as a related service. Other personnel preparation grants to prepare recreational therapy students to work with children with disabilities in school settings have been awarded to Temple University, the University of Georgia, Indiana University, University of North Carolina — Greensboro, University of Minnesota, University of Tennessee, Pennsylvania State University, Florida International University and the University of Wisconsin — Milwaukee.

Traditionally, recreational therapy services have been delivered in schools to persons with mental retardation. Fewer programs have been developed for students with emotional and behavioral disorders, autism, severe and profound disabilities, students transitioning from clinical settings back into schools and students who are being included in regular classrooms. Additionally, the areas of recreational therapy involvement in early intervention and transition are sorely underdeveloped.

The universities mentioned above, along with practitioners employed by school systems, began networking nationally in 1993 through the *Therapeutic Recreation as a Related Service Newsletter* and through a special interest group of the American Therapeutic Recreation Association. These two steps have brought together hundreds of students and professionals interested in the provision of these important services. This networking has been important not only for sharing information but also in identifying recreational therapists working in schools. While only five Certified Therapeutic Recreation Specialists working in schools could be identified in 1992, by 1994 over thirty had been located.

Summary

For recreational therapy to become ingrained as a related service in school systems, it is important for new professionals become keenly aware of the legislation and regulations in education. A wide variety of special needs students can benefit greatly from recreational therapy services, yet most of them do not receive services. Just as recreational therapy has become commonplace in hospitals, rehabilitation centers and long term care facilities by finding its role in health care, recreational therapy must broaden its understanding of how it can help children in schools.

The National Organization on Disability/Harris Survey (Louis Harris and Associates, 1994) reported that people with disabilities socialize less, go out to shop, to worship or to attend sports or entertainment events less frequently, and are more likely to be unemployed than people without disabilities. The literature is replete with support that indicates that individuals with disabilities experience difficulties in the following areas upon leaving school: high levels of unemployment, economic instability and dependence, social isolation and limited opportunities for community integration. Young adults with disabilities experience little social interaction with other community members and little participation in community events (National Information Center on Handicapped Children and Youth, 1993). We must not forget that those whom we fail to help while they are in school are those we see later and more frequently in health and human services.

Learning Activities

1. Interview a public school teacher about the recreation and leisure needs of his/her students with disabilities. Find out the teacher's knowledge of recreation as a related service and his/her experience with recreational therapy.
2. Attend a meeting of a parent support group. Note the number of instances discussed that relate to potential recreational therapy interventions.
3. Obtain a copy of the regulations relating to IDEA and recreational therapy services. Prepare an overview to present to a recreational therapy or special education class.
4. Call your state department of education and obtain a copy of their CSPD. Discuss with one of these officials their procedure for gathering this data. Compare their figures with neighboring states.
5. Think back to the time when you were in high school. How did students with disabilities interact with students without disabilities?
6. Discuss potential marketing strategies for the expansion of recreational therapy services in schools. What strategies would you use for
    a. Parents?
    b. Teachers?
    c. Administrators?

Study Questions

1. Trace the federal legislative history of EHA, explaining the major provisions of the law.
2. Explain the distinction between "learning to play" and "playing to learn."
3. What should be included in an IEP?
4. If you were a parent of a child with a disability, how would you argue in an IEP meeting that your child needed a recreational therapy assessment?
5. Discuss the concept of related service and show how recreation is a legitimate "related service."
6. Describe at least two roles of a recreational therapist in a school setting.
7. Discuss the four components of recreation as a related service as defined in the regulations of the law.

References

Agran, M. & Moore, S. (1987). Transitional programming: Suggesting an adaptability model. *Advances in Mental Retardation and Developmental Disabilities, 3*, 179-208.

Ballard, R., Ramirez, S. & Zantal-Weiner, J. (1987). *Public Law 94-142, Section 504, and Public Law 99-457: Understanding what they are and are not.* Reston, VA: Council for Exceptional Children.

Bandura, A. (1976). Self-reinforcement: Theoretical and methodological considerations. *Behaviorism, 4*, 135-155.

Beck-Ford, V. & Brown, R. I. (1984). *Leisure training and rehabilitation: A program manual.* Springfield, IL: Charles C. Thomas.

Bender, M., Brannan, S. A. & Verhoven, P. J. (1984). *Leisure Education for the Handicapped.* San Diego: College Hill Press.

Bullock, C., Mahon, M. J., Morris, L., Jones, B. (1991). *The comprehensive leisure education program: A model for a school based leisure education program for children with disabilities.* Unpublished manuscript, University of North Carolina at Chapel Hill, Center for Recreation and Disability Studies in the Curriculum in Leisure Studies and Recreation Administration, Chapel Hill, North Carolina.

Center for Recreation and Disabilities Studies. (1992). *Model program guidelines for school-community leisure link.* Chapel Hill, NC: Center for Recreation and Disability Studies.

Fine, A., Welch-Burke, C. S. & Fondario, L. J. (1985). A developmental model for integration of leisure programming in the education of individuals with mental retardation. *Mental Retardation, 23,* 289-296.

Ford, A., Davern, L., Meyer, L., Schnorr, R., Black, J. & Dempsey, P. (1989). Recreation/Leisure. In A. Ford, L. Davern, L. Meyer, R. Schnorr, J. Black & P. Dempsey (Eds.). *The Syracuse community-referenced guide for students with moderate and severe disabilities* (pp. 63-75). Baltimore: Paul Brookes Publishing Co.

Hambrecht, G., Forlifer, N., Peters, J. & Wilson, B. (1989). *Leisure education curriculum for adolescents.* Silver Spring, MD: Montgomery County Government Recreation Department.

Iso-Ahola, S. (1980). *The social psychology of leisure.* Dubuque, IA: Wm. C. Brown.

Keogh, D. A., Faw, G. D., Whitman, T. L. & Reid, D. H. (1984). Enhancing leisure skills in severely retarded adolescents through a self-instructional treatment package. *Analysis and Intervention in Developmental Disabilities, 4,* 333-351.

Louis Harris and Associates, Inc. (1994). *National Organization on Disability/Harris Survey of Americans with disabilities.* New York: Author.

Mahon, M. J. (1990). *Facilitation of independent decision making in leisure with adolescents who are mentally retarded.* Unpublished manuscript, University of North Carolina at Chapel Hill, Division of Special Education, Chapel Hill, North Carolina.

Mahon, M. J. (1991). *The use of self-control techniques to facilitate self-determination skills during leisure in adolescents with mild and moderate mental retardation.* Unpublished manuscript, University of North Carolina at Chapel Hill, Center for Recreation and Disability Studies, Chapel Hill.

Mahon, M. J. & Bullock, C.C. (1991). Teaching adolescents with mild mental retardation to make decisions in leisure through the use of self-control techniques. *Therapeutic Recreation Journal, 26*(1), 9-26.

Martin, J. E., Burger, D. L., Elias-Burger, S. & Mithaug, T. (1988). Applications of self-control strategies to establish the independence of individuals who are mentally retarded. In N. Bray (Ed.). *International review of research in mental retardation.* New York: Academic Press.

Matson, J. L. & Andrasik, F. (1982). Training leisure time social interaction skills to mentally retarded adults. *American Journal of Mental Deficiency, 86,* 533-542.

National Information Center on Handicapped Children and Youth (NICHCY) (1993, March). Transition Services in the IEP. *Transition Summary, 3*(1).

Pelletier, J., McWhorter, A. & Kappel, B. (1985). Deinstitutionalization in Canada: Key issues and challenges. *Journal of Leisurability, 5*(3), 34-37.

Putman, J., Werder, J. & Schleien, S. (1985). Leisure and recreation services for handicapped persons. In K. C. Lakin & R. H. Bruininks (Eds.). *Strategies for achieving community integration of developmentally disabled citizens* (pp. 253-275). Baltimore: Paul Brookes Publishing Co.

Schleien, S. J., Olson. K. D., Rodgers, N. C. & McLafferty, M. E. (1985). Integrating children with severe handicaps into recreation and physical education programs. *Journal of Park and Recreation Administration, 2*(1), 50-66.

Schleien, S. J., Ray, M. T., Soderman-Olson, M. L. & McMahon, K. T. (1987). Integrating children with moderate to severe cognitive deficits into a community museum program. *Education and Training in Mental Retardation, 22*, 112-120.

Schleien, S. J. & Rynders, J. (1989). Integrated Community Recreation. *Impact, 2*(3), 1.

Voeltz, L. M., Wuerch, B. B. & Wilcox, B. (1982). Leisure and recreation: Preparation for independence, integration and self-fulfillment. In B. Wilcox and G. T. Bellamy (Eds.). *Design of high school programs for severely handicapped students* (pp. 175-209). Baltimore: Paul H. Brookes.

Wehman, P. & Moon, M. S. (1985). Designing and implementing leisure programs for individuals with severe handicaps. In M. P. Brady & P. L. Gunter (Eds.). *Integrating moderately and severely handicapped learners: Strategies that work* (pp. 214-237). Springfield, IL: Charles C. Thomas.

Chapter 7

Recreational Therapy in the Community

Betsy S. Kennedy
Nancy D. Montgomery

The provision of recreational therapy services in community settings has long been the subject of debate by professionals in the field. At the heart of ongoing discussions are questions such as:

- Can a Certified Therapeutic Recreation Specialist (CTRS) provide therapy/treatment in community settings?
- Are therapists currently providing therapy in community settings?
- Should therapists provide therapy in community settings?
- Is it the role of a recreational therapist to provide community recreation services for individuals with impairments and disabilities?
- Considering the status of health care and laws such as the Americans with Disabilities Act, what is the future of recreational therapy in the community?

Therapists in the community and the profession at large need to reconsider the role of the recreational therapist in community agencies. Therapists have been educated and trained to provide therapeutic interventions. Therapists also have the skills to train others to provide recreation for individuals with impairments and disabilities (special populations). The future of recreational therapy in the community is for therapists to provide comprehensive services with a focus on therapy while helping facilitate leisure education and the provision of organized recreation services as needed by the consumer.

Reinforcing this position is the health care reform initiative as well as decreases in patient lengths of stay due to the inception of Diagnostic Related Groups (DRG's), Prospective Payment Systems (PPS's) and managed health care. This has resulted in inpatients being placed in community settings earlier. Many patients are not ready to successfully transition to community-based recreation programs. These individuals would benefit from interventions which address functional disability or constraints due to handicaps even if they are no longer in traditional therapy settings.

Therapists in clinical settings find themselves with less and less time to achieve desired patient outcomes because of the shorter length of stay. Therefore recreational therapists in community settings are increasingly called upon to provide comprehensive services with an initial emphasis on treatment. This may be a new and different focus for some recreational therapists in community agencies. However, with time and education of community administrators, this focus of service will be a vital link to assuring appropriate, economical and effective service within the total continuum of care.

It is important for therapists to distinguish between therapeutic intervention (treatment based on disease, impairment, disability and handicap) and community recreation (leisure education and organized recreation programming) in order to meet the needs of clients, provide comprehensive services in all settings and promote consistency in our profession. The criteria in Table 7.1 are provided to assist with this effort.

For clarity, this chapter will use the definition of "recreational therapy" and of community "recreation services" provided by the American Therapeutic Recreation Association (ATRA):

> Treatment services, often referred to as recreation therapy, are to restore, remediate or rehabilitate in order to improve functioning and independence as well as reduce or eliminate the effects of illness or disability. The primary purposes of recreation services are to provide recreation resources and opportunities in order to improve health and well-being. (ATRA, 1993, p. 8)

The Recreation Service Model (burlingame & Skalko, 1997) further defines recreational therapy as having four levels of intervention provided by a Certified Therapeutic Recreation Specialist. The interventions used by the recreational therapist (CTRS) address illness at the disease level (to reduce or prevent the interruption of or interference with normal physiological and developmental processes), at the impairment level (to enhance cognitive, physiological or emotional function to maximize the body's own ability), at the disability level (to enhance performance of basic skills required by an activity in a manner considered within the normal range) and at the handicap level (to facilitate the use of

Table 7.1: Definitions

Clinical Orientation	Community Orientation
The primary purpose of the agency is the delivery of health care services and/or human services.	The primary mission of the agency is the provision of activities or services related to recreation, leisure and/or education.
The facility has the potential to be surveyed under HCFA, JCAHO, CARF and/or NCQA.	The facility does not hold any type of license or accreditation which would involve a survey by outside agencies related to health care.
The purpose of the services provided are to improve the client's functional skills as related to a *prescribed* course of intervention based on assessed health care needs.	The purpose of the services provided are to provide individuals and groups with the facilities and educational opportunities to improve their quality of life through recreation and leisure.
Client outcomes are geared toward improving functional ability to allow increased health and access to the community.	Client outcomes are geared toward the achievement of satisfying free-time experiences.
Services are based on an individualized assessment of the client's needs matched with available resources.	Services are based on consumer desires matched with available resources.

basic skills within a community setting) (burlingame & Skalko, 1997). The interventions at all four levels require an assessment of patient need, the use of clinical judgment and clearly stated treatment goals with an obvious starting point and obvious discharge point.

Community recreation is made up of services provided to the general public by either public, private, non-profit or volunteer entities for the purpose of enjoyment and constructive use of leisure time. Recreation services for individuals with disabilities may also be known as recreation for special populations (special recreation) in some areas of the country. These services may include leisure education (to facilitate the acquisition of new skills, techniques and/or knowledge to engage in leisure of choice with little or no modification required) and/or organized recreation programs (facilitating recreation through the provision of facilities, staff and other resources where learning new skills is not the emphasis of the service, although the further development of skills may be).

Background

Historically, the profession of recreational therapy has not been definitive concerning services for individuals with impairment or disabling conditions in community settings. This is evidenced in the broader scope of the profession as early as the 1950's with the Hospital Recreation Section of the American Recreation Society (ARS) and their philosophical position in relation to the National Association of Recreational Therapists (NART). The former organization basically supported the position that persons with illnesses or disabilities should receive the benefit of positive recreation experiences. The NART supported the position that recreation should be used with this segment of the general population as a means of treatment. Both organizations were concerned with defining the profession. The basis of discussions appears related to the orientation of the professionals by settings: clinical or community.

The same scenario seems to be repeating itself again in the 1990's as the result of changes in the health care system. The issue is much the same, only the two professional organizations have changed. The Board of Directors of the National Therapeutic Recreation Society (NTRS), a branch of the National Recreation and Park Association (NRPA) issued the following definition of recreational therapy in February of 1994:

> Practiced in clinical, residential, and community settings, the profession of recreational therapy uses treatment, education and recreation services to help people with illnesses, disabilities and other conditions to develop and use their leisure in ways that enhance their health, independence and well-being. (NTRS, 1995. p. 1)

The Board of Directors of the American Therapeutic Recreation Association (ATRA) published their definition of recreational therapy in 1993:

> Therapeutic recreation is the provision of treatment services and the provision of recreation services to persons with illnesses or disabling conditions. The primary purposes of treatment services, often referred to as recreation therapy, are to restore, remediate or rehabilitate in order to improve functioning and independence as well as reduce or eliminate the effects of illness or disability. The primary purposes of recreation services are to provide recreation resources and opportunities in order to improve health and well-being. Therapeutic recreation is provided by proccessionals who are trained and certified, registered and/or licensed to provide therapeutic recreation. (p. 8)

Comparison of these two definitions in relation to the practice of recreational therapy in community settings leaves some professionals with questions as to the uniformity of processes in the delivery of our services.

While the debate may be healthy, the need for professional uniformity and consistency as to what, where and how we do recreational therapy may impact considerably not only upon our profession, but on potentially large consumer markets in the future. Those markets include many clinical and long term care settings such as nursing homes, psychiatric hospitals, day treatment centers, physical rehabilitation hospitals and residential facilities. The larger market of the future, however, encompasses individuals who seek services in the community.

The Community

In order to formulate a position regarding the place of recreational therapy in the community one must first understand the agencies that are current and potential providers of services. While there are other populations that recreational therapists serve, looking at the population of people with disabilities provides an excellent view of the number of places that services can be provided. According to Kraus and Shank (1989), there are nine types of agencies that may provide recreation services to persons with disabilities in the community. These include:

1. *Public recreation and park departments* that are sponsored by government on federal, state and local levels, and that increasingly are initiating programs to serve individuals with impairments and disabilities.
2. *Voluntary, non-profit organizations*, such as YMCAs and YWCAs or Boy and Girl Scout groups, that serve the public at large, but may also provide services for individuals with impairments and disabilities.
3. *Specialized community organizations* that have been formed to provide education, counseling, vocational training and other services, including recreation, for a particular category of persons with a disability, such as individuals who are visually impaired or who are mentally retarded.
4. *Colleges and universities* that offer adapted physical education and other recreation opportunities to their students with impairments and disabilities, sometimes in connection with their professional curricula.
5. *Hospitals or rehabilitation centers* that frequently establish outpatient or satellite programs to serve their own patients/clients who have been discharged from the inpatient setting, or other individuals with impairments and disabilities who are living in the community.
6. *Group homes or other transitional living facilities* for individuals who are developmentally disabled or who have other impairments or disabilities,

and that provide a range of support services for them.

7. *Special recreation agencies* that have been established primarily to provide varied leisure services to a wide range of people with impairments or disabilities living in the community.

8. *Community councils or boards* that coordinate the efforts of various civic agencies and social groups, in meeting the human service needs of residents with impairments and disabilities.

9. *Consortiums of public agencies representing two or more communities* that provide special recreation through joint sponsoring arrangements (Kraus & Shank, 1989).

It is obvious that the term "community recreational therapy" goes well beyond municipal parks and recreation. Also included in this term are outpatient treatment services, partial hospitalization, day treatment centers, group homes and transitional living. All of these settings have the potential to provide recreational therapy with a treatment focus. Many related allied health professions such as speech language pathology, occupational therapy and physical therapy are currently providing treatment services in these settings. As our profession begins to accept this broader view of community-based recreational therapy services we are also seeing more and more treatment provided by recreational therapists within community settings.

Over the years, leaders in the field have attempted to define the role of recreational therapy in the community. At the heart of the discussion seems to be the fact that recreational therapy involves, as do other therapeutic interventions, a uniform treatment process. Peterson and Gunn (1984), describe this process to include:

> ...assessment of need, a statement of the problem, formulation of treatment goal(s), design of a treatment plan, implementation, monitoring and progress reporting, and designation of criteria for decision-making regarding termination, continuation, or change. (Peterson & Gunn, 1984, p. 15)

In some community agencies this process is not defined and/or specifically regulated like it is in clinically accredited agencies where operations are reviewed by external accrediting bodies such as CARF: The Rehabilitation Accreditation Commission and the Joint Commission on Accreditation of Healthcare Organizations (JCAHO). These external accrediting agencies provide numerous standards and guidelines for the agency's operation including services provided by recreational therapy. In the community, the development and operation of recreational therapy services have often been the result of the philosophy, training and experiences of the individual who directs the program in conjunction with the agency and its mission. Therapists in the community have, over the years, found themselves to be in a position where they determined how recreational therapy services would be delivered in community settings.

Treatment in the Community

Most of the professionals in our field acknowledge at least two levels of services that therapists provide: therapy and recreation. While both areas are accepted in professional practice, the issue is where and when each is appropriate. Clinicians feel that treatment encompasses the majority of their services with recreation serving as a diversion during non-treatment hours. (And, at times, diversional activities can be therapeutic in nature. The activity does not define the therapy; the intent and desired outcome define the therapy.) Recreation service providers usually say that they are providing recreation. Treatment is not within the scope of their practice. One of the distinguishing factors between the two is that treatment requires individual documentation and clinical judgment which make the therapist accountable in the therapeutic process, whereas recreation does not. Those in community agencies may not be required to "document" like their counterparts in clinical settings.

A primary goal of recreational therapy is to provide intervention to reduce the impact of a disease, impairment, disability or handicap of the clients served. To attain this goal recreational therapists must be acquainted with the physical, emotional and social needs of human beings (O'Morrow, 1980). Human behavior is the response to human needs (Gerow, 1992). Abraham Maslow proposed a hierarchy of needs which postulated that some needs are more basic than others. Needs at the lower level such as food, water and shelter must be met before higher level needs such as self-esteem can be attained (Carter, Van Andel & Robb, 1985). This is very pertinent to the recreational therapist who must know and address his/her client's current needs. Too often the therapist attempts to address needs that the client is not ready to attain.

The advent of PPSs and changes in the health insurance industry have decreased the client's length of stay. Recreational therapists working in traditional inpatient clinical settings usually cannot address important aspects of their client's needs. In the past, recreational therapists working in inpatient clinical settings were able to develop and implement treatment plans that addressed the client's needs up to the Ego/Esteem level of Maslow's Hierarchy of Needs. Today, recreational therapists in inpatient settings may only be able to address the client's needs up to the Safety/Security level prior to discharge. The resulting unmet needs can be addressed by community-based recreational therapists. Figure 7.1 shows this shift in treatment services. The initial focus of recreational therapy programs in community-based agencies will likely focus on a client's impairment and need to improve function, thus addressing the unmet basic needs of the client. Prior to integration into recreation programs and possible self-actualization, the client must have his/her lower level needs relatively well satisfied. Unmet needs related to impairment or disability or constraints to involvement in the community block the client's progression to meaningful quality of life and self-actualization. This requires therapeutic intervention.

Today, therapists working in community services are being provided guidance in many forms. For example, the Americans with Disabilities Act of 1990 has provided mandates to all levels of community services both public and private that require accommodation of individuals with disabling conditions into the mainstream of the community. Therapists in community agencies have responded by integrating programs and services wherever possible. This federal mandate to accommodate in community programs has resulted in an increased emphasis on equality and a de-emphasis of the need for special recreation programs at the community level. This increased emphasis in accommodation has been offset by the early discharge of many clients from inpatient settings. Many individuals with unmet needs related to an impairment or disability would greatly benefit from recreational therapy services provided in a community setting.

Adult day care and day care for children with impairments and/or disabilities are also being reviewed and regulated to insure that services are appropriate. Recreational therapy could play a much larger role in service delivery for these two segments of the population. Such services should include improved performance and appropriate adaptations to allow a greater involvement in free-time activities within the client's own community.

Standards of Practice

Standards of practice provide guidance and direction to a profession relative to professional practice. Both the American Therapeutic Recreation Association's and the National Therapeutic Recreation Society have developed separate yet similar, standards of practice. Both sets of standards may be applied to both clinical and community-based recreational therapy services. ATRA and NTRS do not have similar organizational structures for their professional standards of practice, so some compilation is necessary to compare what each states as a standard. The authors have examined both organization's standards of practice and have developed sample community practice applications and outcomes for each standard used below. It is clear that the standards can be applied to community-based recreational therapy programs with a treatment focus in addition to the special recreation and community recreation services that currently exist.

Figure 7.1: **Montgomery-Kennedy Model of Needs**

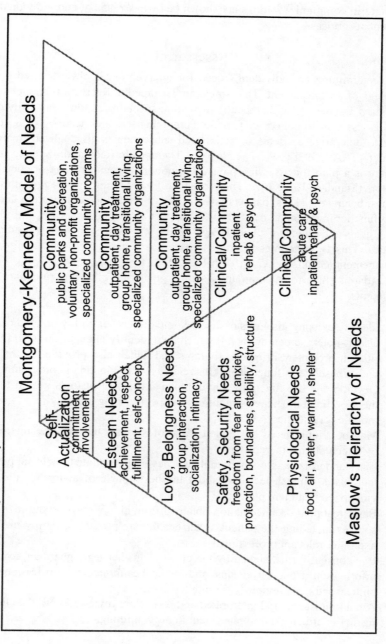

Montgomery-Kennedy Model of Needs

Community
public parks and recreation,
voluntary non-profit organizations,
specialized community programs

Community
outpatient, day treatment,
group home, transitional living,
specialized community organizations

Community
outpatient, day treatment,
group home, transitional living,
specialized community organizations

Clinical/Community
inpatient
rehab & psych

Clinical/Community
acute care
inpatient rehab & psych

Self-
Actualization
commitment
involvement

Esteem Needs
achievement, respect,
fulfillment, self-concept

Love, Belongness Needs
group interaction,
socialization, intimacy

Safety, Security Needs
freedom from fear and anxiety,
protection, boundaries, stability, structure

Physiological Needs
food, air, water, warmth, shelter

Maslow's Heirarchy of Needs

Two samples of applying standards of practice to recreational therapy services in community settings are shown below, assessment and individualized treatment services.

Assessment

Determining an individual's need for intervention is always based on the findings of an assessment. The American Therapeutic Recreation Association's Standard 1 states, "The therapeutic recreation specialist conducts an individualized assessment to collect systematic, comprehensive and accurate data necessary to determine a course of action and subsequent individualized treatment plan" (ATRA, 1993, p. 9). The National Therapeutic Recreation Society states, "There is a plan for assessing physical, emotional, cognitive and/or social behaviors (Standard 1.A.1.a.)... There is a plan for assessing knowledge, attitudes, values, behaviors, skills, barriers, and resources related to socialization and leisure functioning (Standard 1.B.1.a)... There is a plan for assessing and identifying goals and objective, client leisure needs, interests, competencies and capabilities. This is sometimes referred to as a needs assessment or benefit-based management (Standard 1.C.1.a.)" (NTRS, 1995, p. 2-4).

Adapting this for a community setting gives the following guidelines. Assessments:

- Identify existing instances of disease, impairment, disability or handicap.
- Use in-house screening tool(s) which help identify clients who would benefit from treatment-oriented programs and which also provide the therapist with a baseline of functional skills related to participating in programming.
- Develop and use functional-environmental assessment tools geared toward the specific competencies required for specific programming (e.g., the CIP module for aquatics).
- May be administered by trained paraprofessionals but must be interpreted by a recreational therapist.
- Use standardized assessment tools whenever appropriate to help support the therapist's clinical decisions about the best course of action for the individualized treatment plan.
- Base treatment on information obtained from all appropriate and legitimate sources including the patient, other health care providers, family members and other relevant professionals.
- Use consent forms, signed by the client or his/her legal guardian, to obtain information from physicians and other health/medical professionals in clinical settings previously serving the client.
- Are administered and interpreted and results are reviewed with the client or his/her guardian prior to placement in programming.

- Results of the assessment will be reported in an assessment report which identifies demographic information, the client's strengths and limitations, summary of client's functional status, goals, potential risks, recommendations for intervention and discharge criteria.
- Report assessment findings with appropriate individual involved in the client's care, such as family members, physicians, social workers, teachers as long as the client has granted consent for the information to be shared.

If these guidelines for assessment are followed, the following outcomes will be achieved:

- Determination of the client's needs including need for therapeutic intervention to address disease, impairment, disability or handicap and the client's needs and desires for involvement in leisure education and community activities.
- Determination of the role of the recreational therapist (therapist, educator, advocate, etc.).
- Appropriate placement into specific recreation programs to maximize client's enjoyment.
- Facilitated communication of client's needs to all individuals involved in the client's care.

Example

The recreational therapist in the Community Parks and Recreation Department requires an initial interview with new clients in order to obtain the history, determine interests and assure an appropriate initial placement. The recreational therapy staff conduct individual meetings within small groups in order to collect the information. The Leisurescope Plus is used, as this standardized test is structured to allow group administration and yet still retain its reliability. Portions of the Therapeutic Recreation Activity Assessment (TRAA) are also used to help obtain a baseline measurement for fine motor, gross motor, social skills and cognitive levels. The TRAA was also selected because it is another standardized testing tool which was developed to be administered to a group. The results of the tests help the therapists determine who is appropriate for which programs and what type of assistance and adaptive equipment will be required.

Individualized Treatment Services

The development and implementation of individualized treatment services should be based on assessed need, functional capabilities and patient interest. ATRA states that "The therapeutic recreation specialist implements the individualized treatment plan using appropriate intervention strategies to restore, remediate or rehabilitate in order to improve functioning and independence as well as reduce or eliminate the effects of illness or disability. Implementation of the treatment plan by the therapeutic recreation specialist is consistent with the overall patient/client treatment program" (ATRA, 1993, p. 12). NTRS states that "The therapeutic recreation specialist develops an individualized treatment/program plan for each client referred to the agency for therapeutic recreation services" (NTRS, 1995, p. 5). NTRS's standards also emphasize the need to have treatment based on assessment, with goals which are stated in measurable terms, periodically reviewed and modified as needed, documented as appropriate and reflect a cooperative team approach.

Treatment delivered in a community setting should:

- Determine appropriate staff to implement and/or oversee the recreational therapy programs.
- Determine procedures for monitoring each client's treatment plan.
- Determine appropriate client/staff ratios for specific treatment interventions.
- Determine appropriate treatment modalities, ensuring that each considers the client's age, developmental level, socioeconomic level and culture throughout the treatment process.
- Be based on client's needs and response to treatment interventions. Implementation may be modified or discontinued as appropriate.
- Include family/support system members in treatment interventions when appropriate.
- Consult with family and others involved in the client's care regarding procedures for intervention strategies such as behavior management.
- Have the treatment plan reviewed by a recreational therapist prior to program initiation in order to ensure consistency with overall client treatment/service plan.
- Document the client's progress and responses based on the department's plan of operations which address the types and frequency of documentation required.
- Provide the appropriate amount, content and frequency of communication with other individuals involved in the client's care.

The outcomes following these guidelines should include:

- measurable, desired client response/outcome achieved;
- discharge from recreational therapy programs, referral to integrated programming in the community and participation in leisure activities of his/her choice; and
- family/support system members actively participating with client in activities.

Example

The local Boys Club provides services to young boys with disabilities within their existing programs. This initiative is an effort to comply with the Americans with Disabilities Act. The Boys Club employs a recreational therapist who is responsible for all integration efforts. The recreational therapist assesses each individual who identifies himself/herself as requiring accommodation within the agency, develops a modified treatment plan (plan of action), identifies those that are involved in service delivery, provides all necessary training, assists with client orientation and identification of appropriate intervention strategies (behavior management, adaptive equipment, activity adaptations, etc.) and documents the course of action in the client's file. The recreational therapist follows up with the staff and client on the plan implementation and assures consistency with the community recreation programs. The recreational therapist confers with the client as to his/her comfort level and degree of independence and makes recommendations as necessary.

Summary

Recreational therapists are currently educated to provide services and interventions which are not necessarily location specific. As recreational therapists, we provide interventions to improve the client's functional ability to engage in meaningful activity in the variety of settings in which we are employed. Our skills are such that they are adaptable to the settings in which we work. We are trained in treatment processes in addition to the facilitation of accommodation into community recreation programs. We need to provide all of the dimensions of our services depending on the needs of our consumers. Certainly, the agency mission will dictate our service emphasis and intensity, but the need for and ability to provide recreational therapy and entry into community programs exists and needs to be carefully addressed in all agencies that purport to provide recreational therapy services.

The examples of community practice applications of the *Standards for the Practice of Therapeutic Recreation* found in this chapter are intended not only to illustrate their applicability, but to assist therapists in community settings with restructuring and or justifying various levels and intensities of service. It is foreseeable that the municipal parks and recreation department could provide recreational therapy to consumers as one portion of its overall service. It is possible that the psychiatric hospital might consider contracting with the community-based recreational therapists for the provision of intensive outpatient treatment programs; why not consider a recreational therapist employed by the Community Services Board to provide therapy groups for substance abusers and those in the community with chronic mental illnesses? A recreational therapist with training in child growth and development would be able to provide recreational therapy in infant stimulation programs or therapy groups for youth with behavior disorders in the community. The opportunities are there.

Answering the questions posed at the chapter's beginning is not a task that is so easy as to be done in one chapter of one textbook. Starting the dialogue that postulates a position such as the one stated in the chapter will encourage ideas and hopefully initiate programmatic changes by therapists that are at the heart of community practice as well as those in the leadership of the profession.

Learning Activities

1. Review the Standards of Practice from both ATRA and NTRS in Appendix B. What standards would apply to a recreational therapist working at a summer camp for youth with severe burns concerning the development of interventions related to self-image?

2. Using Maslow's Hierarchy of Needs in the Montgomery-Kennedy Model of Needs, list both impairments and disabilities which requires therapeutic intervention and examples of education or participation (non-therapy intervention) for each level.

Example:

Impairment/Disability	Physiological Needs	Education/Participation
• inability to feed oneself due to quadriplegia • inability to ask for a drink due to severe mental retardation • inability to stay warm due to homelessness as a result of psychiatric disorder	food, water, air & warmth	• class on the food pyramid • map and directions to all public drinking fountains downtown • class on how to improve air quality within your own home • cutting free wood from a clear cut for use in the wood stove

3. Write a paper discussing your view as to whether clinical services belong in a community park department. Discuss, among other issues, the differences you perceive related to clinical intervention versus accommodation for individuals with disabilities (ADA).

4. Review literature, interview current practitioners and access the Internet to determine what types of community-based *treatment* services are being offered. What types of patient populations are being served, what is the em-

phasis of the interventions being offered and where is the funding coming from?

5. The National Therapeutic Recreation Society endorses the philosophy that leisure education and advocacy are just as much a part of the recreational therapist's job as therapeutic intervention. Health care funding agencies tend to deny any payment for leisure education and advocacy services. Do clinical services belong only in health care settings and leisure education/advocacy belong only in community agency settings? To what degree should there be overlap? Support your positions on this topic.

Study Questions

1. What changes in the health care system are causing more individuals to be discharged into community settings prior to their treatment needs being addressed?
2. What are some of the differences between agencies with a clinical orientation and agencies with a community orientation?
3. List at least nine types of agencies which provide recreation services to individuals with disabilities in the community.
4. What types of locations/programs located within the community might be able to offer recreational therapy services as part of their treatment/intervention programs?
5. How has the ADA impacted all levels of community services, both public and private?

References

American Therapeutic Recreation Association. (1993). *Standards for the practice of therapeutic recreation & self assessment guide.* Hattiesburg, MS: ATRA.

Boskin, W., Graf, G. & Kreisworth, V. (1990). *Health dynamics attitudes and behaviors.* St. Paul, MN: West.

burlingame, j. & Skalko, T. (1997). *Idyll Arbor's glossary for therapists.* Ravensdale, WA: Idyll Arbor, Inc.

Carter, M. J., Van Andel, G. E. & Robb, G. M. (1985). *Therapeutic recreation: A practical approach.* Prospect Heights, IL: Waveland.

Gerow, J. (1992). *Psychology: An introduction* (3rd ed.). New York: Harper.

Kraus, R. & Shank, J. (1989). *Therapeutic recreation service* (4th ed.). Dubuque, IA: Wm. C. Brown.

National Council for Therapeutic Recreation Certification. (1994). *NCTRC candidate bulletin.* New York: NCTRC.

National Therapeutic Recreation Society. (1995). *Standards of practice for therapeutic recreation services and annotated bibliography.* Ashburn, VA: National Recreation and Parks Association.

O'Morrow, G. (1980). *Therapeutic recreation: A helping profession* (2nd ed.). Reston, VA: Reston Publishing Company.

Peterson, C.A. & Gunn, S. L. (1984). *Therapeutic recreation program design: Principles and procedures* (2nd ed.). Englewood Cliffs, NJ: Prentice-Hall.

Chapter 8

Efficacy Research in Recreational Therapy

Marjorie J. Malkin
Catherine P. Coyle
Cynthia Carruthers

A profession must have the ability to demonstrate that the work done is based on a specific body of knowledge. This implies that the professional group has a core that's founded in theory and research. While many who practice the profession may never formally conduct research, what they do relies heavily on the work of those who have done the research.

There are many areas that a profession must base on research. Areas the professional can work (scope of practice), skills needed to perform the work of the profession, benefits (outcomes) of the work and the best training methods are the major areas that need to be based on research.

The purpose of this chapter is to cover one aspect of research related to the profession of recreational therapy, namely, the benefits of the work that is done by the professional. This type of research is called efficacy research.

Efficacy research is used to determine which treatments provide the best "outcomes" (the results of the treatment). Research on outcomes is done when the professional places specific controls on both the environment and on the treatment that the patient receives. By controlling both aspects, the professional can measure what changes took place as well as what kinds of resources (e.g., staff time, equipment) were required to make those changes. Efficacy compares the success of the treatment with the cost of providing the treatment, usually for specific patient groups in specific treatment settings. The best results are usually defined as the treatments which produced an acceptable level of change in the patient while using the least amount of resources.

History

Efficacy research in recreational therapy has been influenced by many factors, including the various changes in the health care environment and the movement toward health care reform. For many years recreational therapy and other health fields have been expected to provide treatments which are both cost-effective and beneficial to recipients. This movement toward cost-effectiveness and "quality assurance" began in the early 1970's with the emergence of the Professional Standards Review Organization (PSRO) legislation. This federal law required hospitals to develop programs in quality assurance (measures to improve quality) and utilization review (measurement of the appropriateness of services delivered). To encourage cost containment and a standardization of treatment, this federal law also ordered the development of prospective payment systems (funding guidelines), such as diagnostic related groups (Ostrow & Kaplan, 1987).

Despite such measures, which impacted all health care professions, the "health care crisis" continued to develop. This crisis was described as the "high cost of health care and the lack of availability of medical insurance coverage to millions of Americans" (Malkin, 1993, p. 7). Costs kept on increasing. Part of the reason for this explosion in cost was because new treatment methods were continually being developed. Most of these tended to improve the quality of care for the patient and many increased the patient's chances of living. Health care providers were interested in providing the best care for their patients and many feared being taken to court if they didn't. As a result, the trend was to order any test or treatment that had a possibility of improving the patient's condition. Each patient tended to receive more services than were actually necessary. Those who had to pay the costs for these health care services started screaming for relief from the high cost of health care. The question for each patient was, which services were needed, which services were supplementary and which services were just a waste of time and money?

Efficacy or outcome research was started in all health fields to answer these questions. Because health care payers now tend to approve payment only for professional groups who can prove (through scientific study) that what they do both works and is an effective means of accomplishing the task, it is very important for each profession to demonstrate the efficacy of its treatment.

Purpose of Efficacy Research

The pressure and competition is intense for the limited health care dollar. To be competitive for funding, each field needs to base the treatment it provides on efficacy research and each professional in the field *needs to be able to articulate the results of that research.* The individual claims adjuster and utilization review staff have great power. If the staff on the floor providing the services cannot state the known benefits of the treatment, they give the impression that the entire field does not know the benefits. A poor showing at one facility may result in a denial of payment at another facility. Each professional must know about the efficacy studies related to his/her work and know how to measure outcomes.

"Outcome measurement is designed to manage health care costs and document treatment efficacy in order to determine which protocols and services are the most effective with respect to given illness, conditions and/or disabilities" (Seibert, 1991, cited in Coyle, Kinney & Shank, 1993, p. 228). Many therapists are finding that outcome measures are easier to obtain if they use clearly defined interventions called protocols. By using standardized treatment protocols like the *Community Integration Program, Second Edition* (Armstrong & Lauzen, 1994), the therapist can easily compare patient outcomes to the patient diagnoses and measure the expected result (outcome) against the average amount of time required to implement the protocol. Professions that can document effective and efficient outcomes will be those that survive the financial downsizing (Coyle, Kinney & Shank, 1993).

Health care outcomes or benefits are viewed from an economic perspective by the medical insurance industry (cost/benefit ratios) but may be viewed on a broader perspective as improvements, gains, a change that is advantageous to an individual, a group or society (Driver, Brown & Peterson, 1991, cited in Shank, Kinney & Coyle, 1993). Shank, Kinney and Coyle indicate two needs related to outcomes for the field of recreational therapy:

1. the need to provide definitive evidence of recreational therapy's value to outside groups and
2. the need to base professional practice upon a clearly established body of knowledge, based on empirical research.

Concerns about Research

As noted, demands to demonstrate efficacy and cost-effective beneficial outcomes to clients are common to all health fields. A review of the literature reveals articles and books on efficacy and outcome research in occupational, music, art and physical therapy, nursing, experiential education (outdoor adventure programs), psychiatry, psychology, health education, addiction treatment, as well as recreational therapy. Research texts in some of these fields have been published recently, indicating the increased emphasis on the research process. In terms of concepts and methods in recreational therapy, readers are referred to *Research in Therapeutic Recreation* (Malkin & Howe, 1993). Ostrow and Kaplan (1987) is also available. In both books the editors expressed concerns about efficacy research which were similar. The occupational therapy text defined efficacy as "what can be achieved through health care" (Ostrow & Kaplan, 1987, p. v) and effectiveness as "what is actually being achieved in each clinical setting" (p. v). While research develops theories and analyzes the treatment strategies of the profession, program evaluation and quality assurance demonstrate effectiveness and efficiency in applying treatment (Ostrow & Kaplan, 1987). Ostrow and Kaplan stated that both research and program evaluation are essential complementary aspects to demonstrate that a clinical service is valuable and cost-effective. Furthermore, they cited research which indicates the similarity and value of all activity therapies, including occupational therapy, recreational therapy and art therapy. These occupational therapy authors are echoed by Shank, Kinney and Coyle (1993) in recreational therapy, stating the necessity for theory-based practice. The lack of such a theoretical or conceptual framework in recreational therapy research has been noted previously (Malkin, 1993). A methodological review of research published in *Therapeutic Recreation Journal* from 1986-1990 concludes that such shortcomings remain to some extent (Bedini & Wu, 1994). These reviewers stated that only 26% of reviewed articles had a defined theoretical or conceptual basis.

Another criticism of research in recreational therapy has been the lack of sophisticated and valid research methods (Bedini & Wu, 1994; Malkin, 1993). There has been an increase in the number of experimental studies conducted in the profession but in articles reviewed by Bedini and Wu several problems surface. Research questions were often not stated, but implied. Quantitative (numerical) methodology was predominant. Design and statistical weaknesses were noted. Thirty percent of these articles were judged as poor in reporting implications for practitioners. Many studies lacked a control group, leaving many alternate explanations for the findings. Many researchers failed to report validity and reliability information to the readers. Bedini and Wu concluded by reminding professionals who undertake research "to be mindful of the ultimate purpose of research: testing and building theory to contribute to the body of knowledge" (Bedini & Wu, 1994, p. 96).

Despite continued demand for efficacy or outcome research in recreational therapy, problems remain. A think tank at the American Therapeutic Recreation Association Mid-Year Conference (Indianapolis, March, 1994), elicited constraints to conducting such research from both practitioners and researchers/educators (Malkin & Robbins-Sisco, 1994). The constraints reported by practitioners could be categorized into: (1) *support* (lack of time, money, agency support, networking, resources, mentors and grant/research writers); (2) *knowledge* (lack of knowledge, knowing where to begin, collection tools, understanding of the benefits of research, access to databases, national data, data analysis, training, exposure to allied health research and standardized assessments); and (3) *attitude* (feeling overwhelmed with responsibilities, lack of personal commitment, competency issues and fear based in ignorance).

Researchers/educators reported constraints in two categories: (1) *support* (lack of time, money, networking with practitioners/clients, collaboration with other universities, publication and grant/writing and administrative support; practitioner time constraints for collaboration; and an emphasis on teaching instead of research) and (2) *knowledge* (lack of clinical understanding, knowledge of research designs and measures and knowledge of topics that will benefit the practitioner). In order to address these concerns both the American Therapeutic Recreation Association (ATRA) and the National Therapeutic Recreation Society (NTRS) have conducted research methods workshops, networking projects, think tanks, etc. Most of these have emphasized collaboration among students, researchers, educators and practitioners.

Several Veterans Affairs Medical Centers (VAMC) have also been conducting efficacy research workshops. The efforts of these VAMCs and the professional organizations should begin to address the constraints above, by modifying attitudes toward research, increasing research knowledge and skills and providing ideas on securing support for these endeavors. Both the American Therapeutic Recreation Foundation (ATRF) and the National Therapeutic Recreation Society (NTRS) have established research funds or grants to promote efficacy research, although at present on a small scale.

Recreational Therapy Research

Despite the concerns expressed above, there are still many researchers who are doing useful efficacy research. It is instructive to evaluate the actual "state of the art" in recreational therapy research to see how research should be conducted. First reviewed is the grant received by Temple University to investigate the efficacy of recreational therapy in rehabilitation. Other individual studies are also shown.

National Institute on Disability and Rehabilitation Research Grant

One of the most comprehensive attempts to consolidate the research conducted in recreational therapy occurred in 1988 as part of a three year grant by the United States Department of Education's National Institute on Disability and Rehabilitation Research (NIDRR). This grant, received by Temple University's Therapeutic Recreation Curriculum, was designed to conduct research to determine the efficacy of recreational therapy in rehabilitation. The grant was funded by the Medical Sciences Division of NIDRR. The Medical Science Division of NIDRR primarily supports research associated with medical outcomes and the effect of specific interventions on medical outcomes. The grant was designed to address six competitive priorities established by NIDRR and published in the Federal Register (1987). The competitive priorities identified were

1. Determine the correlation between recreational therapy and successful re-habilitation outcomes in order to establish the effectiveness of this activity in rehabilitation;
2. Investigate the impact of various types of recreational therapy activities on the physiology of persons with disabilities and on psychological well-being;
3. Assess the effectiveness of recreational activity in reducing and preventing secondary disability and re-admittance to a rehabilitation hospital/facility;
4. Assess the effect of recreational therapy on the disabled individual's length of stay in a hospital or rehabilitation facility;
5. Investigate the comparative effects on the psychological well-being of par-ticipants in recreational programs that integrate disabled individuals with those who do not have a disability; and
6. Conduct a state-of-the-art meeting in the final year of the project to promote consensus on the benefits of recreational therapy in rehabilitation (Federal Register, 1987, p. 43302).

To address these priorities, the project staff from Temple University's Therapeutic Recreation Curriculum supervised a number of distinct research studies. Results from some of these studies have been published in rehabilitation and recreational therapy journals (cf., Coyle, Shank, Kinney & Hutchins, 1993; Santiago & Coyle (1995); Santiago, Coyle & Kinney, 1993; Shank, Coyle, Kin-ney & Lay, 1994). However, a significant part of the grant project addressed priority number six and has been an impetus for establishing consensus as to what was "state-of-the-art" in terms of research in recreational therapy. This occurred in 1991, at a National Consensus Conference on the Benefits of Thera-peutic Recreation in Rehabilitation.

This conference brought together experts (both practitioners and educators) in the field of recreational therapy and asked them to come to agreement re-garding uniform treatment outcomes associated with recreational therapy by reviewing existing research evidence. "A secondary goal of the conference was the development of research priorities and strategies which could serve as a guiding research agenda for the discipline during the coming decade" (Riley, 1991b, p. 1). The results of this consensus conference were extensively docu-mented in the text *Benefits of Therapeutic Recreation: A Consensus View* (Coyle, Kinney, Riley & Shank, 1991). This empirical review suggested that recreational therapy interventions did influence the attainment of health care outcomes. However, caution was urged in the text as to the rigor and gener-alizability of the research reviewed. In fact, much of the research reviewed had been conducted by other health care professionals, so recreational therapy researchers and practitioners were encouraged to work together to identify a systematic agenda for research in the profession of recreational therapy. This recommendation resulted in a national effort by the American Therapeutic Recreation Association's Research Committee to use the information derived from the consensus conference as a building block to the development of a national recreational therapy research agenda.

Current Research

The development of a systematic research agenda on the outcomes of recreational therapy interventions requires the conceptualization of a theoretical structure to group the results of research efforts. Shank and Kinney (1991) suggested that outcome research could be classified as being discipline specific (leisure functioning), client specific (concerned with the client's physical, social, emotional, cognitive functioning) or health care system specific. A summary of the research reviewed at the consensus conference has been reported in Malkin and Howe (1993, Chapter 15). This review, however, did not use the structure suggested above nor did it include research published later than 1991; therefore, the brief review of research studies presented below will give some of the summary information presented in Malkin and Howe using the structure suggested above. In addition, studies published since 1991 will also be included. This review will provide the reader with an overview of the status of research within the recreational therapy discipline and, in doing so, will give the reader:

- a reference point for identifying existing research associated with recreational therapy;
- direction for replication studies;
- an understanding of the different focuses for outcomes variables (discipline specific, client specific, health care system specific); and
- an overview of appropriate research methods for conducting studies that examine the clinical application of recreational therapy.

Discipline Specific Outcomes

Ellis, Maughan-Pritchett and Ruddell (1993) reported the results of a 3 X 3 research design that examined the effects of attribution based persuasion and guided mental imagery on self-efficacy judgments and video game playing scores of adolescents in a psychiatric institution. Results from their research suggested that the internal persuasion condition was most effective in improving performance on the outcome measures of persistence at task, game score, self-efficacy judgments, outcome judgments and generality of efficacy judgments.

Searle and Mahon (1993) used a randomized pretest-posttest control group design to examine the effects of leisure education programs on elderly individuals' well-being. They found that the treatment group (those receiving leisure education) had a significant higher mean score for leisure competence than did the control group immediately after the program and at three month follow-up.

Bedini, Bullock and Driscoll (1993), using a pretest-posttest control group research design, examined the effects of leisure education on factors that would enhance the successful transition of youth with mental retardation from school to adult life. They found that the leisure education program was successful in significantly increasing the students' leisure awareness, leisure appreciation, activity initiation and participation.

Using a multiple baseline design, Skalko's (1990) research with adults with chronic mental illness indicated that leisure education and recreational therapy programming increased the quality of discretionary time use. Earlier research conducted by Skalko (1982) compared experimental and control groups of psychiatrically impaired adults and demonstrated that those receiving leisure education interventions reported significantly greater degrees of perceived leisure well-being.

Schleien, Cameron, Rynders and Slick (1988) demonstrated that children with severe developmental disabilities could acquire and generalize recreation skills, social interactions and cooperative play behavior.

Client Specific Outcomes

Physical Functioning

Santiago, Coyle and Kinney (1993) used a pretest-posttest control group design to examine the effects of aerobic exercise on the physical functioning of adults with physical disabilities. Results indicated a statistically significant improvement in physical functioning (i.e., aerobic capacity) for the exercising control group.

A controlled study of exercise and asthma found that an exercise program involving physically active recreation (swimming and running) resulted in increased work tolerance and decreased heart rate for children with asthma (Rothe, Kohl & Mansfeld, 1990).

A water aerobics program held two times a week for 16 weeks significantly reduced diastolic blood pressure, body fat and body weight in 27 elderly community residents (Green, 1989).

Range of motion was improved in a quasi-experimental design using a structured cooking group as the intervention (Yoder, Nelson & Smith, 1989), while increased flexibility, hand strength and ambulation were demonstrated among older residents of a long term care facility through a development fitness program two times per week (Buettner, 1988).

Emotional Functioning

Mactavish and Searle (1992) used a matched-random assignment procedure to assign 26 older individuals with mental retardation to either a treatment or control group to examine the effects of a physical activity program. Results indicated that participation in physical activity may help increase self-control leading to enhanced perceptions of competence and self-esteem.

In a quasi-experimental study with adults with physical disabilities, Santiago, Coyle and Troupe (1991), using analysis of covariance (ANCOVA), found a lessening of depressive symptoms in the exercise group's adjusted post-test mean score on a depression scale of 59.3% in comparison to an increase of 2.0% in the control group.

Cognitive Functioning

Mahon and Bullock (1992) used a single subject alternating treatment design to examine the effects of a leisure education program using decision-making instruction for youth with developmental disabilities. Results suggested that the decision-making leisure education model is useful for promoting self-instruction and independent decision making in this population.

Peniston (1991), using an experimental pre-post test research design, reported that elderly individuals with mild and moderate memory loss who participated in a six-week computer games program demonstrated significant improvement in cognitive strategies, attention, memory and impulse control when compared to the control group who received no intervention.

Social Functioning

Dattilo and Light (1993) used a single subject design to examine whether communication patterns for adults using augmentative and alternative communication (AAC) systems could be enhanced so that these adults could initiate conversation. Results from the training program for facilitators demonstrated improvement in turn taking and initiation patterns of the adults using AAC systems.

Rancourt (1991a, 1991b) documented how individuals with substance abuse who were involved in a comprehensive leisure education program showed increased knowledge and skills in self-awareness, decision-making, social skills and social interactions.

Multiple Client Outcomes

Kunstler and Sokoloff (1993) reported the results from a multiple case study research effort that examined the effectiveness of intensive recreational therapy services provided by a private practitioner to clients with severe head injuries. Results indicated improvements for the five cases in the areas of physical condition, cognitive skills, leisure interests and mood.

System Specific Outcomes

Shank, Coyle, Kinney and Lay (1994/95) used ex-post facto research methods to examine variations in the amount of recreational therapy treatment time and their relationship to achieving improvements in community reintegration at discharge. Results indicated that clients receiving more than 30 minutes of treatment each day showed greater improvement in this outcome area.

Haight (1992) examined the long term effects of a structured life review process in a group of 51 homebound elderly clients. Using a longitudinal design with the treatment and control groups, Haight reported an upward trend in the experimental group on the outcome measure of life satisfaction and declines in all groups on measures of activities of daily living and depression.

Trader and Anson (1991) reported significant health differences between individuals with a spinal cord injury who had a commitment to leisure involvement and those who did not. Individuals with a leisure commitment reported a higher mean score for sitting tolerance, had spent fewer days in the hospital in the previous year and were two and one-half times less likely to have decubitus ulcers than individuals without a commitment to leisure involvement.

Creative dance and movement activities resulted in significantly improved life satisfaction scores for the elderly individuals in the experimental group compared with the matched controls, according to Osgood, Myers and Orchowsky (1990).

Szentagothai, Gyene, Szocska and Osvath (1987) reported that long term physical exercise programs (one to two years of regular swimming and gymnastic activities involving 121 youth between 5 and 14 years of age) were effective in reducing asthmatic symptoms, frequency of hospitalization and use of medication.

Using case study methodology, it was demonstrated that systematic recreational therapy intervention reduced hallucinatory speech (Wong, Terranova, Bowen, et al., 1987; Wong, Terranova, Marshall, Banzett & Liberman, 1983). Similarly, Liberman et al. (1986) determined that inappropriate laughter and bizarre behaviors were significantly reduced when psychiatric patients were engaged in structured recreational activities.

A sensitivity training program for personnel and non-disabled students in a community creative arts program resulted in improved community integration for the individuals with a developmental disability who participated (Schleien & Larson, 1986).

Reduced incidence of decubitus ulcers and urinary tract infections were found among wheelchair athletes compared to wheelchair non-athletes (Stotts, 1986).

Clients with dementia involved in recreational therapy programs showed reduction in need for medication (Schwab, Roder & Doan, 1985).

Recent Developments in Health Care

There are four recent developments within the health care environment which may affect future efficacy research in recreational therapy: (1) the trend toward organized governmental research agencies and programs; (2) the move towards outpatient treatment and health promotion; (3) trends toward interdisciplinary, multidisciplinary and transdisciplinary practice and research; and finally (4) the development of clinical pathways in health care settings.

In 1989, PL 101-239 established the US Agency for Health Care Policy and Research (AHCPR). This agency is responsible for establishing clinically relevant, voluntary guidelines for health care, including allied health fields. Practice guidelines, as well as effectiveness and outcome research, database development and dissemination of research findings are components of AHCPR's Medical Treatment Effectiveness Program (MEDTEP). MEDTEP activities are coordinated with the Health Care Financing Administration (HCFA), the Public Health Service and the National Institute of Health (NIH). These activities include large scale Patient Outcomes Research Team (PORT) projects. These are large scale group research efforts, featuring interdisciplinary collaboration and cooperation and Inter-PORT work groups. The primary goals are to coordinate research efforts in order to improve quality of care and to control health care costs (Raskin & Maklan, 1991). It is hoped that investigative recreational therapists will become involved in these research efforts to an increasing extent. Another organized research agenda is outlined in the Research Plan for the National Center for Medical Rehabilitation Research (NCMRR) (US Department of Health and Human Services, 1993). This publication details (among other topics) future directions for medical rehabilitation research, initiatives and opportunities for such research and support available. The usability of NCMRR's research classification scheme in recreational therapy research was recently reviewed by Shank, Coyle, Kinney and Boyd (1996). It would behoove recreational therapy professionals to become more informed about these national research programs and agendas.

Secondly, it is common knowledge that there is a trend away from inpatient treatment toward outpatient, day treatment and home health care approaches. Researchers need to be ready to evaluate treatment effectiveness in such alternate settings, including camps, schools and outdoor settings. Early childhood intervention is another developing treatment area. A related emphasis is on preventative measures, including the wellness and holistic health movements, as indicated by the popular text, *Healthy People 2000: Citizens Chart the Course* (Stoto, Behrens & Rosemont, 1990). It will be crucial to document the effectiveness of recreational therapy interventions in these new settings and in terms of health promotion.

A third trend to be aware of is the move from research limited to a single discipline, to inter-disciplinary (between disciplines), multi-disciplinary (many disciplines) and finally to transdisciplinary (across-disciplines) approaches. Sable, Powell and Aldrich (1993-94) introduced transdisciplinary concepts into the recreational therapy literature. Specifically they discussed transdisciplinary principles in the provision of recreational therapy services in inclusionary school settings. Readers are referred to Sable et al. for a more complete discussion of transdisciplinary principles and their implications for recreational therapy research. However, based on their work, the following model which applies transdisciplinary principles to the research process has been developed (see Table 8.1).

Disciplinary changes in practice should lead to changes in research methodology. The implications of the move toward a transdisciplinary approach to practice means, to many, a blurring of the distinctions between professions. Indeed, to some this trend may result in generic "rehabilitation counselors" rather than the specialties now employed. Others defend this transdisciplinary model, claiming that the role and value of each discipline will be enhanced when each works in such close collaboration and cooperative teams and "other team members tend to increase their knowledge, respect and value for therapists" (York, Rainforth & Giangreco, 1990). Within this model, some cross training of professionals is necessary.

A fourth trend with implications for recreational therapy research is the development of clinical pathways. Such an approach began as a means to coordinate complicated projects in industry, but has recently been applied to the health care setting (Hoffman, 1993). A critical path (clinical pathway) has been defined as "an optional sequencing and timing of interventions by physicians, nurses and other staff for a particular diagnosis or procedure, designed to minimize delays and resource utilization and to maximize the quality of care" (Coffey, Richards, Remmert, LeRoy, Schoville & Baldwin, 1992, p. 45). Such paths are often illustrated in tabular or graphic form, for example as flow charts, and efforts are underway to computerize these health care management tools. An interdisciplinary perspective is used to develop such clinical pathways and pilot data indicates such methods may reduce length of stay, reduce costs and improve communication (Coffey et al., 1992).

Table 8.1: **Multidisciplinary, Interdisciplinary and Transdisciplinary Research** (Sable, Powell & Aldrich, 1993-4)

I. Multidisciplinary Research (many disciplines)
   A. Separate activities and plans
   B. Informal lines of communication
   C. Function as individual team members
 	
II. Interdisciplinary Research (between disciplines)
   A. Some separate activities
   B. Share plans and information
   C. Responsible for own section of project
   D. Additive and collaborative
   E. Team effort
 	
III. Transdisciplinary Research (across disciplines)
   A. Team approach
   B. Work together across discipline boundaries to implement a unified plan
   C. Common set of goals
   D. Team members address same outcome
   E. Continuous meetings of team members to facilitate "transfer, of information, knowledge and skills across disciplinary boundaries" (p 73).
   F. Collaborative problem solving
   G. Coordinated planning
   H. Shared, discipline-free goals
   I. Professionals role release (role extension, role enrichment, role expansion, role exchange, role release and role support)

These paths may include staff actions and interventions, the expected problems, responses and outcomes and may be included as quality assurance materials "to document quality and variances" (Coffey et al., 1992, p. 50). Such an integrated overall plan can provide coordination of care and reduce variation on the processes and outcomes of care (Coffey et al., 1992). Recreational therapists have in fact participated in the development and implementation of such clinical pathways and such a procedure may help standardize practice interventions, document treatment variances and define expected outcomes in such a manner as to ultimately facilitate efficacy or outcome research. Outcome research could help justify the inclusion of recreational therapy professionals and interventions in the clinical pathways process.

Future of Efficacy Research in Recreational Therapy

The brief review of current research given above illustrates that recreational therapy can contribute to patient well-being. The recent trends in health care suggest that recreational therapy professionals must be aware of and support research efforts to prove the efficacy of their treatments if they want to insure the vibrancy of the profession.

It is with this purpose in mind that the recreational therapy profession has begun to create a national research agenda that will allow for more focused research in the discipline. This effort has been spearheaded by the American Therapeutic Recreation Association's (ATRA) Research Committee. The intent of the research agenda is addressed below.

Efficacy Research Agenda

One of the goals of the Benefits of Therapeutic Recreation in Rehabilitation Conference was the identification of research priorities that would guide the development of a national agenda for therapeutic recreation research (Riley, 1991b). Shortly after the conference, in the fall of 1992, the ATRA Research Committee established a formal goal of creating a national research agenda for recreational therapy.

The intent of the research agenda is to identify the gaps in therapeutic recreation knowledge and to encourage collaborative research in those areas (Russoniello, 1992). In addition, the research agenda will be used to guide the allocation of grant support for research projects. The involvement and input of professionals in the field was considered essential and fundamental to the formulation of the research agenda. Opportunities for professional input, from the generation of the items to the final prioritization of the items, were included in each stage of the agenda determination process. The remainder of this chapter describes the methods that were used in the development of the research agenda. The priorities of the national efficacy research agenda will also be presented.

The method used to identify the most important questions for recreational therapy efficacy research and the prioritization of the research questions was the Delphi technique. The Delphi technique is a method of eliciting expert opinion on an issue and through repeated polling, achieving some group consensus among those experts (Lindeman, 1981). The process consists of: (1) the development of the questionnaire, (2) distribution of the questionnaire to a group of experts, (3) tallying the returned questionnaires to determine areas of agreement and disagreement and (4) statistically summarizing the experts' opinions (as means for each item) and making them available (providing feedback) to the experts (Siegel, Attkisson & Carson, 1987). The experts are then asked to respond again to the same items. The statistical summary that accompanies each successive round of the questionnaire allows each of the experts to view the responses of the entire pool of experts. Each expert can then revise his or her responses on the basis of the feedback, if desired (A. Anderson & Co., 1987).

Because the Delphi technique is often used to make policy decisions based on informed opinion, it is very important that the "experts" are chosen in a way that does not allow a non-representative group with strong biases or personal agendas to unduly influence the results (Sackman, 1975). Therefore, the method of selection of the participating "experts" must assure a fair representation of varying opinions and perspectives. The Delphi technique has recently been used in recreational therapy to identify quality assurance monitors (Riley, 1991a) and to identify the expected outcomes of recreational therapy for people with chemical dependency (Rancourt & Howe, 1991). It has also been recommended as a suitable method for establishing research agendas in park and recreation systems (Ewert, 1990).

Sixty "experts" in recreational therapy were involved in this Delphi process. (See *Annual in Therapeutic Recreation*, Volume 7, for a complete description of this study.) These "experts" had either presented at national conferences, published in professional journals or been highly recommended by other "experts." The Delphi panel had expertise in a variety of areas, including developmental disabilities, aging, addictions, physical disabilities, psychiatric disorders and childhood disorders/illnesses. They were members of ATRA only, NTRS only or both professional organizations and represented a variety of geographic regions of the country. Most "experts" had over 11 years of experience in recreational therapy and a master's degree or higher.

The items for the instrument used in the Delphi process were generated from two primary sources. First, items were selected from the publication, *Benefits of Therapeutic Recreation*, which contained the efficacy research recommendations from the National Consensus Conference on the Benefits of Therapeutic Recreation in Rehabilitation. Second, additional items were generated by approximately 70 recreational therapy professionals at the ATRA midyear meeting in Spring 1993. This process resulted in the generation of 140 items that represented 11 areas for research. (See Table 8.2 for the 11 areas and sample items for each.) Twelve "experts" assisted in reviewing the 140 items generated through these processes. They edited for clarity and lack of redundancy and prioritized the research items in order of importance. On the basis of this review and prioritization, seventy-two items were retained for inclusion in the survey.

Each of the 60 recreational therapy "experts" was sent the 72-item survey. The subjects were asked to identify the degree to which they thought each item should be a research priority in recreational therapy. They responded on a scale from 1 to 5 (1 = very low priority, 3 = moderate priority, 5 = very high priority). The mean (average) score for each of the 72 items was then calculated.

Table 8.2: **Areas for Efficacy Research**

Leisure Functioning
Effect of leisure education on independent leisure functioning.
Effect of TR on perception of competence in leisure.
Effect of TR on participation in active leisure.

Cognitive
Effect of TR on decision making and planning ability.
Effect of TR on memory.
Effect of TR on ability to attend to tasks.

Emotional
Effect of TR on depression.
Effect of TR on ability to cope with stress.
Effect of TR on adjustment to disability.

Physical
Effect of TR on motor coordination skills.
Effect of TR on pain management.
Effect of TR on cardiovascular functioning.

Social
Effect of TR on community integration/reintegration.
Effect of TR on acquiring socially appropriate behaviors.
Effect of TR on ability to establish and maintain support networks.

Adjustment to Hospitalization
Effect of structured TR activity on elopement.
Effect of TR on alleviating pain associated with hospitalization.
Effect of TR on medication levels needed by clients.

Family Functioning
Effect of family leisure education on interaction between family members.
Effect of TR on the family caregiver role.
Effect of TR on anxiety of family members.

Prevention
Effect of TR as a preventative treatment of depression.
Effect of TR on substance abuse prevention.
Effect of TR on preventing deterioration associated with aging.

Table 8.2 (cont.)

Broad Health Care
Effect of TR on independent functioning.
Effect of perception of mastery and control on rehabilitation outcomes.
Effect of TR on recidivism/prevention of further illness.
Effect of leisure functioning on health.
Effect of TR on hospital costs/lengths of stay.
Effect of leisure education on quality of life.

Specific Types of Programs
Effect of adventure challenge experiences on positive behavioral change.
Effect of aquatic programs.
Effect of remotivation therapy.

Settings and Approaches
Effect of TR as a component of client follow-up support services.
Effect of service setting on TR outcome.
Effect of frequency and duration of contact with clients on TR outcomes.

Individual Differences
Effect of age, gender, socioeconomic status, level of disability and culture on treatment outcomes.
Effect of clients' level of motivation on response to treatment.

The sixty "experts" were then sent a second survey containing the 15 items with the highest mean scores from the first survey. Since the purpose of the Delphi process was to develop a prioritized research agenda, the systematic narrowing of the items was appropriate.

In addition to the 15 most prioritized research items, the "experts" received the mean scores for each of these items obtained through the previous survey. This allowed them to consider the priorities of the other experts when making their own ratings. The experts were again asked to identify the degree to which they thought each of the 15 remaining items should be a research priority in recreational therapy.

The mean scores were then calculated for each of the 15 items obtained from the second survey. A rank order list of these final findings appears in Table 8.3. The mean score of the top six items was above 4.0 which indicates that they were all considered a high research priority. The remaining nine items were above the mean of 3.0 which indicates that they were considered at least a moderate research priority by the experts.

Table 8.3: **Priority Ranking of the Efficacy Research Agenda Items**

TR on community integration/reintegration
TR on recidivism/prevention of further illness
TR on independent functioning
Leisure functioning on health
TR on hospital costs/lengths of stay
Increased efficacy and control through TR on rehabilitation outcomes
Leisure education on quality of life
TR on adjustment to disability
TR on depression
Leisure education on independent leisure functioning
TR on life satisfaction
TR on socially appropriate behavior
TR on decision making and planning ability
Leisure participation and addiction recovery
Leisure education and delinquency reduction

An analysis was also conducted to determine if there were significant differences between educators/researchers and practitioners. The only item on which the two groups differed was the importance of conducting research on the "Effect of therapeutic recreation on hospital costs/length of stay." Practitioners considered it a higher priority than did educators/researchers.

A final analysis was conducted to determine if there were significant differences between the research priorities of the members of ATRA only, NTRS only or both. The only item on which the three groups differed was again the importance of conducting research on the "Effect of therapeutic recreation on hospital costs/length of stay." Members of ATRA only considered that item their highest priority.

The results of this study indicated that there is fairly clear agreement on four of the top five efficacy research priorities for recreational therapy. Educators and practitioners, regardless of professional organization membership, placed a high priority on investigating the effects of recreational therapy on community integration, recidivism and independent functioning and the effects of leisure functioning on health. These areas represent strong areas for mutual collaboration.

Summary

The vibrancy of the recreational therapy profession within the health care system will depend on our ability to demonstrate the efficacy of our services (Shank & Kinney, 1991). The development of a focused research agenda will enhance these efficacy research efforts. The delineation of a research agenda has the potential to help recreational therapy focus its research studies, facilitate directed programs of research and foster collaboration both among researchers and between researchers and practitioners. The results of the Delphi study suggest that there are many potential areas of collaboration between practitioners and educators/researchers, and among members of NTRS and ATRA.

In 1997, the research committees of ATRA and NTRS began to investigate areas of possible research collaboration. In addition, mechanisms within both professional organizations are being established that will promote collaborative research between educators/researchers and practitioners. Collaborative initiatives such as these are essential to the advancement of the national efficacy research agenda.

The "survival of the profession" is often the reason cited for conducting efficacy research. Too often the profession's focus is on using research to justify itself or perpetuate current practices. It is important to remember that the ultimate aim of efficacy research is to assess the benefits of the work that recreational therapists do in order to better serve the consumers of our services. Through efficacy research, the profession can improve practice by identifying the services that most effectively and efficiently meet the needs of clients.

Learning Activities

1. Investigate and report on current issues and changes in the health care and social systems which might impact research in recreational therapy.
2. Review recent issues of *Therapeutic Recreation Journal* or the *Annual in Therapeutic Recreation* and evaluate the research studies in terms of where the results (outcomes) fit in the theoretical structure proposed: (1) Discipline specific outcomes; (2) Client-focused outcomes; or (3) Health care system outcomes.
3. As a class, divide into three teams and have each team develop a position statement that argues for the need for the recreational therapy profession to focus its research on discipline specific outcomes, client-focused outcomes or health care system outcomes. Each team should select one of the outcome categories and prepare their position. Have teams formally debate the priority of their position, as a class activity.
4. For each of the 11 areas for research from the Delphi project, generate three possible research topics.
5. The instructor should compile the list of topics. Have each student pick the five topics that they consider the most important priorities for recreational therapy research. Then have each student rank order the five items that s/he considers most important (5 =most important of five topics, 1 = least important of five topics). Have each student share his/her prioritized list and

provide a rationale. Determine if there is any consensus reached by students on the research topics considered most important. Compare the students' prioritized list with the "experts" prioritized list from the Delphi project.

Study Questions

1. How have changes in the health care environment affected recreational therapy practice and research?
2. What are some constraints to conducting research on the part of practitioners and educators?
3. What are the pros and cons of developing a national efficacy research agenda for recreational therapy?
4. What groups or individuals should be involved in the process of developing a national research agenda?
5. Identify the four items considered the highest research priorities regardless of the experts' organizational membership (in the National Research Agenda project).

References

Agency for Health Care Policy and Research. (1990, November). *Allied health perspectives on guideline development*. Rockville, MD: Department of Health and Human Services (Public Health Service).

Anderson, A. & Co. (1987). *Multi-hospital systems: Perspectives and trends*. Chicago, IL: American Hospital Association.

Armstrong, M. & Lauzen, S. (1994). *Community integration program* (2nd ed.). Ravensdale, WA: Idyll Arbor, Inc.

Bedini, L., Bullock, C. & Driscoll, L. (1993). The effects of leisure education on factors contributing to the successful transition of students with mental retardation from school to adult life. *Therapeutic Recreation Journal, 27*, 70-82.

Bedini, L. & Wu, Y. (1994). A methodological review of research in *Therapeutic Recreation Journal* from 1986 to 1990. *Therapeutic Recreation Journal, 28*, 87-98.

Brock, B. J. (1988). Effects of horseback riding on physically disabled adults. *Therapeutic Recreation Journal, 22*, 34-43.

Buettner, L. (1988). Utilizing development theory and adaptive equipment with regressed geriatric patients in therapeutic recreation. *Therapeutic Recreation Journal, 22*, 72-79.

Carruthers, C. (At press). Therapeutic recreation efficacy research agenda. *Annual in Therapeutic Recreation, 7.*

Coffey, R. J., Richards, J. S., Remmeil, C. S., LeRoy, S. S., Schoville, R. R. & Baldwin, P. J. (1992). An introduction to critical paths. *Quality Management in Health Care, 1*(1), 45-54.

Coyle, C., Kinney, W., Riley, B. & Shank, J. (Eds.). (1991). *Benefits of therapeutic recreation: A consensus view*. Ravensdale, WA: Idyll Arbor.

Coyle, C., Kinney, W. B. & Shank, J. W. (1993). Trials and tribulations in field-based research in therapeutic recreation. In M. J. Malkin & C. Z. Howe (Eds.). *Research in therapeutic recreation: Concepts and methods* (pp. 207-232). State College, PA: Venture.

Coyle, C., Shank, J., Kinney, W. & Hutchins, D. (1993). Psychosocial functioning and changes in leisure lifestyle among individuals with chronic secondary health problems related to spinal cord injury. *Therapeutic Recreation Journal, 27,* 239-252.

Dattilo, J. & Light, J. (1993). Setting the stage for leisure: Encouraging reciprocal communication for people using augmentative and alternative communication systems through facilitator instruction. *Therapeutic Recreation Journal, 27,* 156-171.

Driver, B., Brown, P. & Peterson, G. (1991). *Benefits of leisure.* State College, PA: Venture.

Ellis, G. D., Maughan-Pritchett, M. & Ruddell, E. (1993). Effects of attribution based verbal persuasion and imagery on self-efficacy of adolescents diagnosed with major depression. *Therapeutic Recreation Journal, 27,* 83-97.

Ewert, A. (1990). Decision-making techniques for establishing research agendas in park and recreation systems. *Journal of Park and Recreation Administration, 8*(2), 1-13.

Federal Register. (1987, November 10). *Federal Register, 52,* 217.

Green, J. (1989). Effects of a water aerobics program on the blood pressure, percentage of body fat, weight, and resting pulse rate of senior citizens. *Journal of Applied Gerontology, 8*(1), 132-138.

Haight, B. (1992). Long term effects of a structured life review process. *Journal of Gerontology, 47,* 312-315.

Hoffman, P. A. (1993). Critical path method: An important tool for coordinating clinical care. *Journal of Quality Improvement, 19*(7), 235-246.

Kunstler, R. & Sokoloff, S. (1993). Clinical effectiveness of intensive therapeutic recreation: A multiple case study of private practice intervention. *Loss, Grief and Care, 6*(4), 23-30.

Liberman, R. P., Mueser, K. T., Wallace, C. J., Jacobs, H. E., Eckman, T. & Massel, K. (1986). Training skills in the psychiatrically disabled: Learning coping and competence. *Schizophrenia Bulletin, 12*(4), 631-647.

Lindeman, C. A. (1981). *Priorities within the health care system: A Delphi survey.* Kansas City, MO: American Nurses' Association.

Mactavish, J. & Searle, M. (1992). Older individuals with mental retardation and the effect of a physical activity intervention on selected social psychological variables. *Therapeutic Recreation Journal, 26,* 38-47.

Mahon, M. & Bullock, C. (1992). Teaching adolescents with mild mental retardation to make decisions in leisure through the use of self-control techniques. *Therapeutic Recreation Journal, 26,* 9-26.

Malkin, M. J. (1993). Issues and needs in therapeutic recreation research. In M. J. Malkin & C. Z. Howe (Eds.). *Research in therapeutic recreation: Concepts and methods* (pp. 3-23). State College, PA: Venture.

Malkin, M. J. & Howe, C. (1993). *Research in therapeutic recreation. Concepts and methods.* State College, PA: Venture.

Malkin, M. J. & Robbins-Sisco, D. (1994, September/October). 2nd Annual ATRA research think tank. *ATRA Newsletter,* pp. 10-11.

Osgood, N., Meyers, B. & Orchowsky, S. (1990). The impact of creative dance and movement training on the life satisfaction of older adults. *Journal of Applied Gerontology, 9,* 255-265.

Ostrow, P. C. & Kaplan, K. L. (Eds.). (1987). *Occupational therapy in mental health: A guide to outcomes research*. Rockville, MD: The American Occupational Therapy Association.

Peniston, L. (1991, September). The effects of a microcomputer training program on short-term memory in elderly individuals. A paper presented at the Benefits of Therapeutic Recreation in Rehabilitation Conference, Lafayette Hill, PA.

Rancourt, A. M. (1991a). An exploration of the relationships among substance abuse, recreation, and leisure for women who abuse substances. *Therapeutic Recreation Journal, 25*(3), 9-18.

Rancourt, A. M. (1991b, April 7). Results of a past discharge survey of women who participated in a six month comprehensive leisure education program while in substance abuse treatment. Paper presented at the American Alliance of Health, Physical Education, Recreation, and Dance Symposium on Drugs and Drug Education, San Francisco, CA.

Rancourt, A. & Howe, C. (1991). A preliminary modified Delphi study of expected outcomes of TR services for persons with chemical dependency. *Abstracts from the 1991 Symposium on Leisure Research*, 27.

Raskin, J. E. & Maklan, C. W. (1991, June). *Medical treatment effectiveness research: A view from inside the Agency for Health Policy and Research*. Agency for Health Care Policy and Research (AHCPR Program Note). Rockville, MD: US Department of Health and Human Services: Public Health Service.

Riley, B. (Ed.). (1991a). *Quality management: Applications for therapeutic recreation*. State College, PA: Venture.

Riley, B. (1991b). Introduction. In C. Coyle, W. B. Kinney, B. Riley & J. Shank (Eds.). *Benefits of therapeutic recreation: A consensus view* (pp. 1-3). Ravensdale, WA: Idyll Arbor.

Riley, B. & Wright, S. (1990). Establishing quality assurance monitors for the evaluation of therapeutic recreation service. *Therapeutic Recreation Journal, 24*(2), 25-39.

Rothe, T., Kohl, C. & Mansfeld, H. J. (1990). Controlled study of the effect of sports training on cardiopulmonary functions in asthmatic children and adolescents. *Pneumologie, 44*, 1110-1114.

Russoniello, C. (1992). *ATRA Research Committee progress report and work plan*. Hattiesburg, MS: American Therapeutic Recreation Association.

Sable, J., Powell, L. & Adrich, L. (1993-94). Transdisciplinary principles in the provision of therapeutic recreation services in inclusionary school settings. *Annual in Therapeutic Recreation, 4*, 69-81.

Sackman, H. (1975). *Delphi critique*. Lexington, MA: Lexington Books.

Santiago, M. & Coyle, C. (1995). Aerobic exercise training and depressive symptomatology in adults with physical disabilities. *Archives of Physical Medicine and Rehabilitation, 76*, 647-651.

Santiago, M., Coyle, C. & Kinney, W. (1993). Aerobic exercise effect on individuals with physical disabilities. *Archives of Physical Medicine and Rehabilitation, 74*, 1192-1198.

Santiago, M., Coyle, C. & Troupe, T. (1991, November). Effects of twelve weeks of aerobic exercise in individuals with physical disabilities. Paper presented at 8th International Symposium on Adapted Physical Activities, Miami, FL.

Schleien, S., Cameron, J., Rynders, J. & Slick, C. (1988). Acquisition and generalization of leisure skills from school to the home and community by learners with severe multihandicaps. *Therapeutic Recreation Journal, 22*, 53-71.

Schleien, S. J. & Larson, A. (1986). Adult leisure education for the independent use of a community recreation center. *The Journal of the Association of Persons with Severe Handicaps, 11*(1), 39-44.

Schwab, M., Roder, J. & Doan, J. (1985). Relieving the anxiety and fear in dementia. *Journal of Gerontological Nursing, 11*(5), 8-15.

Searle, M. & Mahon, M. (1993). The effects of a leisure education program on selected social-psychological variables: A three-month follow-up investigation. *Therapeutic Recreation Journal, 27*, 9-21.

Shank, J., Coyle, C., Boyd, R. & Kinney, W. (1996). A classification scheme for therapeutic recreation research grounded in the rehabilitative sciences. *Therapeutic Recreation Journal, 30*(3), 179-196.

Shank, J., Coyle, C., Kinney, W. & Lay, C. (1994/95). Using existing data sources to examine therapeutic recreation outcomes. *Annual in Therapeutic Recreation, 5*, 5-12.

Shank, J. & Kinney, W. (1991). Monitoring and measuring outcomes in therapeutic recreation. In B. Riley (Ed.). *Quality management: Applications for therapeutic recreation.* State College, PA: Venture.

Shank, J., Kinney, W. & Coyle, C. (1993). Efficacy studies in therapeutic recreation research: The need, the state of the art, and future implications. In M. J. Malkin & C. Z. Howe (Eds.) *Therapeutic recreation: Concepts and methods* (pp. 301-335). State College, PA: Venture.

Siegel, L. M., Attkisson, C. C. & Carson, L. G. (1987). Need identification and program planning in the community context. In F. Cox, J. Erlich, J. Rothman & J. Tropman (Eds.). *Strategies of community organization* (pp. 71-97). Itasca, IL: F. E. Peacock.

Skalko, T. (1982). The effects of a leisure education program on the perceived leisure well-being of psychiatrically impaired active army personnel. Unpublished doctoral dissertation, University of Maryland, College Park.

Skalko, T. (1990). Discretionary time use and the chronically mentally ill. *Therapeutic Recreation Annual, 1*, 9-14.

Stoto, M. A., Behrens, R. & Rosemont, C. (1990). *Healthy People 2000: Citizens chart the course.* Washington, DC: National Academy Press.

Stotts, K. M. (1986). Health maintenance: Paraplegic athletes and non-athletes. *Archives of Physical Medicine and Rehabilitation, 67*(2), 109-114.

Szentagothai, K., Gyene, I., Szocska, M. & Osvath, P. (1987). Physical exercise program for children with bronchial asthma. *Pediatric Pulmonology, 3*, 166-172.

Trader, B. & Anson, C. (1991, September). The relationship of leisure commitment to health in individuals following spinal cord injury. Paper presented at the Benefits of Therapeutic Recreation in Rehabilitation Conference, Lafayette Hill, PA.

US Department of Health and Human Services. (1993, March). *Research plan for the National Center for Medical Rehabilitation Research* (NIH Publication #93-3509). Bethesda, MD: National Institute of Health.

Wong, S. E., Terranova, M. D., Bowen, L., Zarate, R., Massel, H. K. & Liberman, R. P. (1987). Providing independent recreational activities to reduce stereotypic vocalizations in chronic schizophrenics. *Journal of Applied Behavior Analysis, 20*, 77-81.

Wong, S. E., Terranova, M. D., Marshall, B. D., Banzett, L. K. & Liberman, R. P. (1983, May). Reducing bizarre stereotypic behavior in chronic psychiatric patients: Effects of supervised and independent recreational activities. Presented at the Ninth Annual Convention of the Association of Behavior Analysis, Milwaukee, WI.

Yoder, R., Nelson, D. & Smith, D. (1989). Added purpose versus rote exercise in female nursing home residents. *American Journal of Occupational Therapy, 43*(9), 581-586.

York, J., Rainforth, B. & Giangreco, M. F. (1990). Transdisciplinary teamwork and integrated therapy: Clarifying the misconceptions. *Pediatric Physical Therapy, 2*, 73-79.

Chapter 9

Healthy Caring

Melany Bailey Spielman
Thomas M. Blaschko

The health care industry is in the middle of a paradigm shift. Change is always anxiety producing but an even greater threat to our nation's health care system is looming. Arnwine (1990) reports that according to the United Nations Department of International and Social Affairs, consumers of health care will represent 14.2% of the population by the year 2020 compared to 6.7% for the *potential* caregivers. Compounding the problem of a smaller population base are the increasing career options for young people. Proportionately less people are choosing helping careers while the need for caregivers is increasing. Managers in health care need to create environments which attract qualified staff and promote well-being for helping professionals in their settings. Major barriers exist in many health care settings, including heavy patient loads, fear of downsizing, multiple reporting lines, volumes of paperwork and time demands for committee meeting to name only a fraction. The cost of retraining and the lack of potential new professionals makes it imperative that we create and help individuals create healthier work sites to prevent burnout and loss of present helping professionals.

Why did you choose to become a helping professional? Does it feel comfortable to you? Do you like being needed? There are great reasons to choose this very worthwhile profession. There also are serious reasons to become knowledgeable about the importance of healthy caring. The well-being of the professional has a profound effect on the dynamics of the helping relationship. The education process of becoming a professional is consumed with acquisition of knowledge and skills on how to care for others. Some of the student's attention must be focused on how to care for himself/herself as a professional to assure long term health and wellness, thus helping facilitate successful, continuous employment in the health care setting.

There are three major, intertwined issues which affect the ability of health care professionals to provide healthy caring: burnout and its causes, stress and codependency. This chapter will look at these issues and how they reinforce each other to make healthy caring more difficult. In addition, the chapter will talk about some ways to prepare yourself to provide healthy caring by guarding against stress, codependency and burnout.

Burnout

Burnout is a serious issue that affects the welfare of millions of helping professionals and tens of millions of their clients (Farber, 1991). Maslach and Jackson (1981) observed that burnout-prone workers exhibit three characteristics: (a) difficulty giving of themselves psychologically (emotional exhaustion), (b) negative feelings toward clients (depersonalization) and (c) a tendency to evaluate oneself and one's work negatively (lack of personal accomplishment).

Before looking at formal definitions of burnout, it is valuable to think about a real-world example. This short (and true) story is what burnout is all about:

Emily, a recreational therapist with 14 years of experience, had worked in a rehabilitation hospital for the past two and a half years. These two years included two high risk pregnancies, including one resulting in the birth of a premature baby who was in intensive care for a month. Emily returned to work a month after the baby came home from the hospital. She was in charge of the big event near Christmas and felt if she did not do it, it wouldn't get done. She worked full-time, stopping at lunch to run the carpool so her daughter could go to kindergarten. The baby was still nursing but right before the big event refused to nurse. The big event came and was a huge success. The next day Emily could not make herself walk into the hospital. She thought she was just tired and took a day off. An overwhelming feeling of dread became the overarching feeling any time she thought about going back into the hospital. She went to work anyway. Her first patient was a older woman with a right cerebrovascular accident. During a cognitive activity the patient was experiencing difficulty and was frustrated. Emily became very angry and yelled at the patient. Emily walked out of the room and got her supervisor who finished the treatment. Emily resigned that day and has never worked with clients on a daily basis since. It has been 12 years.

Work that was once exciting and fulfilling became a source of dread. The case is extreme but Emily is not unique.

One common theme in discussions of burnout is some sort of motivation erosion: dedication becomes apathy; altruism becomes contempt; insomnia replaces the impossible dream (Bersani, 1983). Burnout may not get all the way to an inability to walk back into a facility but it does reach the point where work is no longer enjoyable and the therapist is no longer as effective or committed as s/he once was. The implicit assumption in most work on burnout is that burnout must be preceded by commitment. For helping professionals, the focus of this commitment is fostering positive change — growth in their clients. Burnout may produce and perpetuate low levels of this motivation, but the process of burnout cannot begin unless the original level of motivation is high. Metaphorically, one must be "fired up before one can burn out" (p. 49). People who function minimally do not usually experience burnout.

There are two measures of burnout which seem especially appropriate for health care settings. The first is the Maslach Burnout Inventory (Maslach & Jackson, 1981). Golembiewski and Munzenrider (1987) developed a phase model of burnout to measure the incidence and virulence of burnout using this inventory. The phase model relies on 23 items from the Maslach Burnout Inventory and examines three sub-domains:

- ***Depersonalization***, on which high scores indicate the tendency to distance self from other, to think of others as things or objects (e.g., I have got to see the gallbladder in 302.)
- ***Personal Accomplishment*** (reversed), on which low scores indicate a decrease in feelings of competence and successful achievement.
- ***Emotional Exhaustion***, on which high scores indicate feeling emotionally overextended and exhausted by one's work. (Feeling "at the end of one's rope" emotionally.)

The phase model distinguishes individuals as High or Low on each of the three sub-domains, based on norms from a large population (Golembiewski & Munzenrider, 1984a), as shown in Table 9.1.

Using this model in a new study, Golembiewski, Boudreau, Goto and Mural (1993) found that in 7,500 health care workers a large proportion (47%) exhib-

Table 9.1: **Golembiewski and Munzenrider's phase model**

PHASE	I	II	III	IV	V	VI	VII	VIII
Depersonalization	Low	High	Low	High	Low	High	Low	High
Personal Accomplishments	Low	Low	High	High	Low	Low	High	High
Emotional Exhaustion	Low	Low	Low	Low	High	High	High	High

ited burnout in phases IV, VI, VII and VIII (high levels of burnout in two or more domains). This finding indicates that burnout is a serious issue for those concerned with the well-being of workers in health care settings. It may also have implications related to the quality of care which patients receive.

For the second measurement, George Everly (1981, 1985) stated that burnout was best conceived as a state of mental and/or physical exhaustion caused by excessive exposure to intense stress. He describes three stages of burnout shown in the Table 9.2. The stages progress sequentially from Stage 1 to Stage 3 as the degree of burnout increases. Of course, it is possible to change the situation (or the person) and stop the progression at any time as we will see later in the chapter.

Causes of Burnout

There are three major causes of burnout that must be studied: personal characteristics, dysfunctional workplaces and the level of stress inherent in even the best health care settings. As these are described, remember that it is often the interaction of personal characteristics and the workplace that lead to the worst situations.

Personal Characteristics

In some ways the personal characteristics associated with burnout are very simple. A person suffering from burnout is trying to do too much. Each of us has a limited amount of energy and when we try to do more than we have the energy to do, we burn out. The real question is, why is this a problem? Why don't people decide that they are doing too much and simply start doing less?

The answer is because people who get into health care are the type of people who want to take care of other people more than they want to take care of themselves. The term used to describe this process is "codependency." The authorities in the study of codependency have estimated that 80-90% of nurses and other helping professionals are codependent (Cermak, 1986; Kellogg & Harrison, 1991; Wegscheider-Cruse, 1982; Whitfield, 1990). However, all the reports were based on anecdotal data (Cermak, 1986). Bailey (1992) discovered that in a random sample of Certified Therapeutic Recreation Specialists (CTRS) from the states of California, Oregon and Washington, 42% have moderate to severe levels of codependency. These results indicate a significant number of recreational therapists are affected by codependency in varying degrees. While not as high as the results found by Kellogg and Harrison (1991), this total indicates that codependency is a serious problem.

Table 9.2: **Stages of Burnout (Everly, 1985)**

STAGE 1: The stress-arousal stage *(includes any two of the following)*
1. Persistent irritability
2. Persistent anxiety
3. Periods of high blood pressure
4. Bruxism (grinding your teeth at night)
5. Insomnia
6. Forgetfulness
7. Heart palpitations
8. Unusual heart rhythms (skipped beats)
9. Inability to concentrate
10. Headaches

STAGE 2: The energy conservation stage *(includes any two of the following)*
1. Lateness for work
2. Procrastination
3. Needed three-day weekends
4. Decreased sexual desire
5. Persistent tiredness in the mornings
6. Turning work in late
7. Social withdrawal (from friends and/or family)
8. Cynical attitudes
9. Resentfulness
10. Increased alcohol consumption
11. Increased coffee, tea or cola consumption
12. An "I don't care" attitude

STAGE 3: The exhaustion stage *(including any two of the following)*
1. Chronic sadness or depression
2. Chronic stomach or bowel problems
3. Chronic mental fatigue
4. Chronic physical fatigue
5. Chronic headaches
6. The desire to "drop out" of society
7. Desire to move away from friends, work and perhaps even family
8. Perhaps the desire to commit suicide

Let's look now at codependency as the major personal characteristic that leads to burnout. Kellogg (1990) defines codependency "as the process by which we learn to react to the needs, problems and dysfunction of those around us, rather than to our feelings, our reality, our needs and wants" (p. 37). Researchers started to look at people struggling with stressful situations and found they often exhibited problems with codependence. Weiss and Weiss (1989) further describe the phenomenon:

> Abuse, neglect and abandonment of the Inner Child are widespread in our culture; the result is codependence. We generally try to take care of ourselves and get our relational needs met in the same way we were parented, whether that parenting was functional or not. When it was dysfunctional, we tend to anesthetize and repress the pain of our unmet early needs through various addictions and compulsions and through codependent relationships. We search endlessly for love, for we have never learned to love ourselves. (p. xiii)

The first step in explaining the development of codependence requires the establishment of what is meant by functional and dysfunctional families. Black (1989) described characteristics that mark a nurturing or functional family as opposed to a dysfunctional family as shown in Table 9.3.

When a child is being a child (being vulnerable, imperfect, dependent and immature), the dysfunctional parent tells them that "There is something wrong with you. You are inadequate because you are not being perfect and acting like me. *You* are the problem." Greenleaf (1984) states, "Children are not born with standards for evaluating behavior, social skills or moral values. They learn what they see and they do not learn what they do not see" (p. 7). There is no way for the child to meet the expectation of this parent. No child and especially no infant is able to be perfect and act like an adult. The child develops survival skills because it is human nature to survive. *But the child learns his/her wants and needs are not important so s/he stops asking.* The natural characteristics go into hiding. S/he learns it is dangerous to be childlike. S/he learns that in order to not feel pain s/he can numb the pain. It is less painful not to feel. The child develops survival strategies (care taking, being adult-like, being over responsible) which are rewarded by authority figures in the environment.

People faced with their own recovery often ask, "How come I can do so well at work but feel so awful and empty inside?" The necessary development of responsible behavior created a pseudo-adult. This person learned what was necessary to insure his/her safety in a chaotic environment and taking care of everyone else's needs and wants was a key. When as a chronological adult it was necessary for the individual to choose a profession, s/he chose what s/he did well — care taking. And in the workplace s/he was rewarded for doing his/her

Table 9.3: **Functional and Dysfunctional Characteristics (Black, 1989)**

In a Nurturing Family...	In a Dysfunctional Family...
People feel free to talk about inner feelings.	People compulsively protect inner feelings.
All feelings are okay.	Only "certain" feelings are okay.
The person is more important than performance.	Performance is more important than the person.
All subjects are open to discussion.	There are many taboo subjects and lots of secrets.
Individual differences are accepted.	Everyone must conform to the strongest person's ideas and values.
Each person is responsible for his/her own actions.	There is a great deal of control and criticism.
Respectful criticism is offered along with appropriate consequences for actions.	There is punishment, shaming.
There are few "shoulds."	There are lots of "shoulds."
There are clear, flexible rules.	The rules are unclear, inconsistent and rigid.
The atmosphere is relaxed.	The atmosphere is tense.
There is joy.	There is much anger and fear.
Family members face up to and work through stress.	Stress is avoided and denied.
People have energy.	People feel tired, hurt and disappointed.
People feel loving.	Relationships lack love.
Growth is celebrated.	Growth is discouraged.
People have high self-worth.	People have low self-worth.
There is a strong parental coalition.	Coalitions form across generations.

job well. A problem may arise if the person stops and examines his/her life. A problem will certainly arise is there is a crisis which surpasses the person's underdeveloped coping abilities.

The coping strategies that were essential for the survival of the child in the dysfunctional family and assured the person's survival to adulthood are not necessarily robust enough to handle adult responsibilities. Lucas (1998) explains it this way. In childhood there was often one authority figure in the family. If the child did everything that the authority figure said, things usually were all right. As an adult, there are often many authority figures: the one from the childhood family, a spouse, the supervisor at work and, perhaps, the chairperson of a committee or two. As a child, there was often only one person to take care of, usually the same authority figure. As an adult, there are many more people to take care of including people at work, relationships and children. Meeting all of the conflicting needs of all of these people can become impossible.

Stress builds beyond the person's coping strategies. At some point coping mechanisms developed in childhood start failing. More complex problems and stress need more advanced (more adult) coping strategies. The major difficulty is unawareness, the person is not cognizant of the fact that his/her coping strategies are ineffective. If left untreated, more serious problems develop. The characteristics of codependency include denial, control, difficulty in trusting, low self-esteem, weak boundaries, over responsibility and difficulty in handling conflict and in giving and receiving love.

How does codependency lead to burnout? Codependency can be defined as the lack of sense of self. It is when a person "depends" on others to give feedback so s/he will know how s/he feels. (I am fine as long as someone gives me positive feedback.) We all know colleagues and maybe someone closer, who is always trying to please with no regard to his/her own needs. The problem is exacerbated because the need for approval is an addictive process. The person gets praise and then needs more praise to get the same sense of satisfaction. The problem also is compounded by the fact that the person is always looking for praise from others and doesn't have any intrinsic positive feedback strategies. S/he was taught not to trust him/herself. Everything must come from others. We all have a finite supply of energy. The analogy of an oil lamp is often used. Codependency is trying to keep dozens of wicks lit and burnout is the state when the oil is gone.

Codependence as it applies directly to recreational therapy was studied by Bailey (1992). She studied a random sample of Certified Therapeutic Recreation Specialists (CTRS) in Washington, Oregon and California, exploring the relationships among codependency, burnout and work motivation. In relationship to the normative data from Maslach, these recreational therapists exhibited lesser degrees of burnout in emotional exhaustion and depersonalization. The differences were not statistically significant. They were slightly more satisfied with their accomplishments than the norm group. However, when evaluating the relationship between burnout and levels of codependency a strong significant relationship was found. This study found a total of 42% of the recreational therapists were significantly affected by codependency and those therapists with high levels of codependency were more likely to experience high levels of emotional exhaustion. A multiple regression revealed that all three sub-scales of burnout were significantly related to codependency. If a group of people had high levels of codependency they would be more likely to experience burnout. The bar graph in Figure 9.1 clearly illustrates the effects of high levels of codependency on the three factors of burnout. A greater percentage of people with high levels of codependency experienced increased feelings of depersonalization and emotional exhaustion. And a greater number of people with high codependency felt a decrease in personal accomplishment.

When we experience burnout, one of the first things to do is to look at ourselves and try to understand why we are trying to do more than we are capable of doing. Codependence is one of the most likely answers.

Dysfunctional Workplace

Work sites can be dysfunctional (Jones, 1997; Wilson-Schaef & Fassel, 1989). Many times the way the facility is run feels irrational and illogical leading to stress for the workers. Other workplaces have managers who simply expect more than the workers can realistically be expected to do. Management gurus have been proposing solutions to workplace malaise for years with Blanchard and his *One Minute Manager* (1985), Peters and his *In Search of Excellence* (1985) and *Thriving on Chaos* (1987). These systems are effective in functional organizations but dysfunctional organizations are another matter.

Jones states that dysfunctional organizations have been around for a long time but they were called by different names. He believes that even though dys-

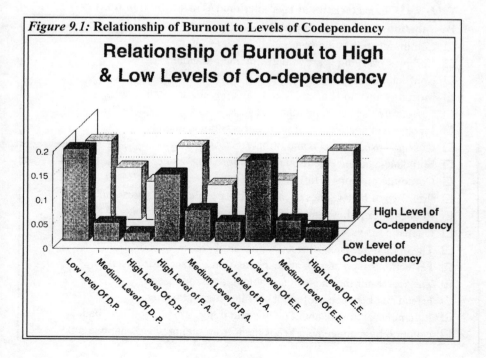

Figure 9.1: **Relationship of Burnout to Levels of Codependency**

functional is an uncomfortable term, it is the correct label. Table 9.4 has a list of dysfunctional work site characteristics.

Jones states in evaluating your work site, the more characteristics you iden-tify, the bigger problem you have. He also believes once you know where your organization is functioning it is possible to be healthier.

Other studies such as Golembiewski, Munzenrider and Stevenson (1986) put more emphasis on the workplace as the cause of burnout. They examined numerous variables in relation to burnout and indicate that, although there are probably several generic loci which contribute to the development of burnout, the most powerful one is the immediate work group practices. They state:

> Few work groups evidence mixed distribution of burnout phases. This suggests the significance of supervisory style and immediate work practices in inducing burnout and helps explain the apparently chronic character of most burnout. (p. 241)

In other words, if you are in a work group where one person is suffering from burnout, it is very likely that everyone in the group is at about the same

Table 9.4: **Characteristics of Dysfunctional Work Sites. (Jones, 1997)**

Dysfunctional Behaviors Checklist
☐ Communication is indirect.
☐ Complex procedures are initiated by memorandum.
☐ Conflict is not stated openly.
☐ Meetings have long agendas and end up going in circles.
☐ Secrets are used to build alliances.
☐ Inconsistent application of procedures is not challenged.
☐ Gossip is used to excite and titillate.
☐ Mundane announcements are given more time at meetings.
☐ Corporate memory is lost or forgotten.
☐ Promises of better times ahead seduces people into a status quo.
☐ Requests for policy clarification are ignored.
☐ Dualistic (us vs. them) thinking creates conflict and sets up sides.
☐ The open expression of true feelings is absent.
☐ Perfectionism creates an atmosphere of intolerance for mistakes.
☐ The search for the cause of a problem is personalized.
☐ Friendship between professional colleagues is lacking.
☐ Judgments are made about people and thing being "good" or "bad."
☐ Isolation by management keeps them from seeing what's happening.

burnout stage. Although they didn't study the question directly, it is certainly possible that particular supervisors select staff who have complementary characteristics. For instance, if a supervisor is very controlling, hypersensitive and constantly seeking approval, it is likely that s/he would choose people with high levels of codependency who would not question the unreasonableness of demanding behavior.

Health care settings may be especially prone to being dysfunctional. The medical culture is such that long hours of work are the norm and demands put on support staff are high. Add to that the fact that a large percentage of the other workers are contending with issues of codependency and it seems likely that dysfunctional situations would be common.

More research needs to be done to understand all of the interpersonal variables in the workplace but it is clear that the workplace is a strong component of the causes of burnout in health care settings.

Job-Related Stress

Even if a workplace is functional, it may still be a highly stressful place simply because of what goes on in it. Health care settings are one of the most stressful places to work for several reasons. The first is that the work that is being done can literally be a matter of life and death. If person is not paying attention at a McDonalds and puts a quarter-pounder burger into a regular cheeseburger bun, it's no big deal. If a nurse puts Mr. Smith's medicine into Mrs. Jones IV, it matters. In a health care setting, the hundreds of actions taken in a day each need to be done exactly right or there may be serious problems. That level of accuracy and attention to detail requires a great deal of energy and attention.

Another reason that health care settings are stressful is that people die. People who work in hospitals are there because they care about other people. With or without codependence, they want to help other people get better. Sometimes even with the best possible care, the patient dies. It is extremely hard to go on caring for each patient, one after the other, when any one of them may die.

A third reason that health care settings are stressful is that the people who are being served by them need to be, in one way or another, taken care of. People at a McDonalds may be rushed but people in a hospital may be terminally ill, criminally insane or watching their children die. Some places where you can work, the people smile and thank you for helping them. In a health care setting, it happens less. In some health care settings, it may not happen at all.

The fourth major reason that health care settings are stressful is that they are dangerous. The danger comes in two varieties. The first is the inherent and obvious danger of being around people who have a disease. Needle stick injuries can easily transmit HIV or Hepatitis B. You will probably meet more people with life-threatening, communicable diseases in a day in a hospital than in a month outside of one. The second danger is less apparent. A recent study (reported in Beason, 1998) looked at workplace assaults in the state of Washington. "One of the panel's most striking findings was that more than half of the nonfatal workplace violence reported statewide occurs in health-care-related fields" (p. E2). Beason went on to note that "the top five most violence prone industries in Washington involve psychiatric care, nursing care and job training" (p. E2). What the study also found was that most of the violent acts were not committed by colleagues or supervisors. Most were violence by customers and clients.

Dealing with stress requires energy, the same energy that goes into doing work or taking care of a family. If too much of the energy is used up and too little is put back in, stress by itself can lead to burnout. In combination with the other issues described, it can be even more serious.

Studies with Recreational Therapy

Several studies over the past two decades have looked at burnout among recreational therapists. In addition to Bailey (1992), discussed earlier, Robertson (1980) found burnout and suggested it was the result of trying to do too much. Chamberlain (1982) found a significant relationship existed between emotional exhaustion and managerial practices in recreational therapists in Oregon. Wade-Campbell and Anderson (1987) revealed recreational therapy personnel experienced low levels of emotional exhaustion, moderate levels of depersonalization and somewhat lower levels of personal accomplishment. Wade-Campbell and Anderson (1987) looked at work environment variables and found that they played a crucial role in the perceived levels of burnout in recreational therapists.

Interventions

There are things that we can do to prevent burnout. Most people don't do them. More realistically, what we do is recognize burnout when it happens to us and try to recover from it. The actions we take start with ourselves and then expand into the workplace as we get a better understanding of the situations that are causing us to burn out.

Intervention can begin whenever realization of the burnout process occurs. Usually people experience some form of unpleasantness which moves them to action. There is a danger of trivializing the symptoms. Often people change jobs and sometimes they change professions. Everly (1981) stated that burnout was caused by excessively prolonged or excessively intense stress arousal. Using the metaphor of the lamp, it would be as if the lamp were burning and no one was putting any fuel back in. End stage burnout would occur when the fuel was gone.

In the scenario at the beginning of this chapter, Emily experienced all the symptoms listed in Everly's model but was unable to intervene in a positive way. Part of the reason was constant, unmitigating pressures and, probably more important, was her dysfunctional coping strategy. She believed she had to keep going despite compelling reasons to cut back. She had a baby who was born prematurely and weighed three pounds at birth, a two year old and a five year old. She had a husband in his medical residency who had to go to another city for the month between Thanksgiving and Christmas (her pressure time). She received no support from her spouse and had the children in two different child care arrangements. This all was on top of the big event she was in charge of at the hospital, in addition to a full load of patients on the rehabilitation unit. Her belief was that she *had* to do it all. She had to take care of everyone. The end result was tragic. Twelve years later it is still anxiety producing to enter a hospital and she has never worked in a setting with clients again. What would have been the healthier path?

The first step is knowing what is healthy behavior. How do you balance the needs of your clients with your psychological needs? First, realize that you need to be as healthy as possible. You need to examine your reasons for helping. What is your motivation for helping? Wanting to be needed is not bad. Needing to be constantly reinforced that you are needed is unhealthy.

Our bodies react to stress. Our first line of defense is to be highly skilled in stress management. We often cannot control the stress we face, but we can learn to manage it. The other first order task is to evaluate coping strategies. Take the Friel Adult Codependency Assessment Inventory (Friel & Friel, 1989) shown at the end of the chapter or some other hardiness scale. If there is an indication of codependency, work on your issues either in a group, with a counselor and/or by yourself by reading self-help books.

If you identify yourself in the Exhaustion Stage or Stage 3 of Everly's Stages of Burnout (Table 9.2), you need to get help immediately. A student in a recreational therapy programming class repeatedly broke down crying. She removed herself from patients and busied herself sorting beads for a craft project. She was very ashamed at crying and felt everyone thought poorly of her. When she explained what had been going on in her life, it was clear that this was a reaction to an extended period of extreme stress. She was carrying 37 units, had three children, was having to be away from her family, was recovering from pneumonia, found out her husband was being transferred to the mid-west so she'd have to move after 20 years of living in the same town and her oldest son was going away to college. She believed that she had no choice. She had to successfully deal with this all. She believed that she was a failure if she asked for help. She needed help and she needed help immediately. After an extensive discussion of options, it was pointed out to her that any one of these events was stressful in and of itself. Why did she think she had to deal with all of them simultaneously? She sought assistance from her husband, children and professors and came up with a more reasonable plan of action. One very simple suggestion was made to her that she had never entertained before — stop striving for straight "A's." She was taking several classes pass/no pass and it never occurred to her to do only what was necessary. This prevented further progression towards meltdown (end stage burnout).

Personal Issues

There are things each person can do to relieve burnout. The place to start is to look at your motivation for your work to see if codependency is an issue. Check your personal motives to see what you are motivated by. Examine if what you are doing is driven by your need to help or the patient's actual need for help. Over helping is harmful for our clients and ourselves. Wegscheider-Cruse (1989) used the term "Professional Enabler" and she believes that most untrained and all untreated helping professionals fall into this category. She further describes the professional enablers as:

> Any helping professional who engages in the same kinds of dysfunctional behavior as the family Enabler — denial, avoidance, covering up, protecting, taking responsibility for someone else ... may not realize that helping in the normal sense of the word — that is trying to fix things — is not helpful in this situation. (p. 53)

Our task is to maximize the client's ability to function in leisure and empower the client's goal to be as independent as possible. Each helping professional must look at his/her motivation for helping. The help given needs to be dictated by the amount of help needed. Help beyond the appropriate level is codependency, trying to take on responsibilities that are not possible to take on. To avoid burnout, you must deal with issues of codependency first.

Identifying the symptoms and changing behavior is the key to ameliorating burnout. It is hard to identify people hurting from codependency. Often they are the highest achievers and appear very successful. Their codependency has served them well. However, professionals must learn to care for themselves with as much love and caring as they give their patients. We often erroneously think someone will take care of us. But the truth is that you need to care for yourself and you are not being selfish, you are being smart. Codependency is a coping mechanism. It was learned and it can be unlearned. The first step is awareness. You need to realize what you are doing and then work to do things differently. You need to take care of yourself. Rest when you are tired. Eat when you are hungry. And probably the most difficult, feel what you are feeling instead of stuffing it. Cry when you are sad and express anger to someone who is being unkind to you. It requires hard work but it is possible to learn new coping strategies designed to empower and validate who you are. Insanity is defined as doing the same thing over and over and expecting different results. You need to do things differently. Consider what you need to be healthy and do it. What does a functional person look like?

Functional People...
- Feel free to talk about inner feelings.
- Know all feelings are okay.
- Know the person is more important than performance.
- Know all subjects are open to discussion.
- Accept individual differences and expect to be accepted unconditionally.
- Know each person is responsible for his/her own actions.
- Offer respectful criticism along with appropriate consequences for actions.
- Believe there are few "shoulds."
- Hold to clear, flexible rules.
- Live in a relaxed atmosphere.
- Experience joy.
- Face up to and work through stress.
- Have energy.
- Feel loving.
- Celebrate growth and change.
- Have high self-worth.

The second step is to deal with the other stresses in your life. Table 9.5 contains suggestions for dealing with different kinds of stress.

Workplace

Golembiewski, Boudreau, Goto and Mural (1993) identified that burnout occurs in similar distributions in work groups. This could be a factor of the leadership style of the supervisor. Be certain you are managing using healthy rules. Look over the chart in Table 9.4 again and ask which list most accurately reflects the "rules" governing your workers. Ask your staff which list reflects their understanding. Discuss in a non-threatening manner what is and how everyone would like it to be. As a group develop norms of acceptable behavior. Ask the whole group if they have concerns or are uncomfortable about anything.

Table 9.5: **Techniques For Controlling Stress**

Category	Techniques for Controlling Stress
Adaptive Stress	Establish routines Sleep well Eat regularly and healthfully Plan for change — adopt belief that change is consistent and to be expected Write plan for specific changes
Frustration	Express feelings Deal with what is, rather than what you think it should be (fairness) Examine personal beliefs that produce frustration Learn personal and interpersonal behavior skills
Overload	Ask for support Learn to delegate Express your feelings Negotiate Use time management Reduce the number of tasks you do Be more realistic in expectations of self
Deprivation	Ask for what you are feeling deprived of Engage in physical activities Join a social group Learn to ask for human contact Examine beliefs that keep you deprived
Bio-ecological	Noise reduction or modification Light manipulation (full spectrum lights) Visual calming (mess reduction) Work during peak effectiveness times
Self-Concept	Accurate assessment of assets List personal resources Accept compliments Assertiveness Interpersonal effectiveness Positive self-talk Examine beliefs blocking positive self-image
Anxious Reactivity	Thought stopping (very useful technique) Write fear journal Take action Give away fear Examine beliefs about fear

Each person can contribute to the discussion. For instance, one person might feel non-valued by both the supervisor and others in the group. Ask what would it look like for this person to feel valued. S/he might answer that when s/he shares an experience with a patient, the rest of the staff will give feedback in a non-critical manner. S/he may want the supervisor to give frequent positive comments. Or if there are frequent critical statements made by staff members, the group can decide that critical comments can only be made to the person they concern and they need to be as helpful as possible. Setting groups norms helps clarify rules and makes sure everyone is aware of the rules.

Burnout needs to be addressed by everyone in a work group. Golembiewski, Munzenrider and Stevenson (1986) suggested that sending one person to an isolated workshop would have little effect on either the person attending or the group as a whole. Burnout can be stopped. Cooley and Yovanoff (1996) evaluated the combined and differential effects of two interventions designed to support special education personnel. They found that improvements in burnout, job satisfaction and organization commitment were a function of the interventions. The members in the treatment group tended to improve on all measures while the control group members tended to get worse. The treatment group members also perceived the skills and strategies to be valuable in preventing or alleviating burnout. So if burnout is identified as a problem, interventions need to occur for all members of the work group.

Excessive stress is the main contributing factor in burnout. Lee and Ashforth (1996) reported that in a meta-analysis of three dimensions of burnout, demand and resource correlations were more strongly related to emotional exhaustion than to either depersonalization or personal accomplishment. All three dimensions of burnout were related to intentions of leaving the position, organizational commitment and control coping (possibly codependency). This study confirmed that burnout can be caused by dysfunctional coping strategies and/or from overwhelming work demands. Another recent study by Flett, Biggs and Alpass (1995) further confirmed that professionals can help themselves by learning healthy coping strategies during their professional education process. They suggested that clarification of roles, responsibilities and policies and the development of effective communication can reduce stress. They also found that social support, good communication skills and interpersonal skills were essential topics in the education of rehabilitation professionals.

What can supervisors do to help staff therapists become healthy helping professionals? A fundamental structure which has nothing to do with union rules but is essential for mental health is working a normal shift and going home at quitting time. There will always be times when special circumstances occur making it necessary to work overtime. The supervisor should be sure to communicate his/her concern for the employees' health. Most supervisors are under pressure from upper administration to get the most production out the front line therapists. It is important to have a big picture perspective when managing people. If you teach and *model* healthy work habits the long term results will be less sick leave, less turn over and a happier work group. Ask your staff how they think they could accomplish needed tasks in the most efficient manner. All people need basically two things. First, they need to know you see them. You recognize them as people with strengths and needs. Secondly, they need to know you hear them. Listen, ask for their input and, most importantly, empower them to work effectively and efficiently.

When you *model* healthy behavior you are sending a very powerful message to your staff. You need to work reasonable hours, communicate your wants and needs clearly, have and enforce healthy rules and not a laundry list of "shoulds." When you are feeling sick let your people know and ask for support. When they ask for support, model giving it appropriately. Talk about balance and how that contributes to wellness. Work out schedules to the best of your ability to maximize peoples' time off. Communicate that you want them to be healthy caregivers.

If you notice the characteristics of your work place as being dysfunctional, what are your options? First complete the characteristics evaluations in both Tables 9.3 and 9.4. Find out what is going on. In your own work group, agree on strategies to address the most disturbing symptoms. You can choose to always tell the truth and refuse to keep secrets. The first step is to name the problem. Keep asking others in the environment what are their perceptions. If you can form a critical mass of people who identify a problem, it is possible to work on a solution. People need to see what is happening and agree to choose healthier ways of interacting. Often communication is non-direct. Say your work group has a project with another department and you are experiencing difficulty. Call a meeting and name the problem as you see it and ask for solutions. Listen to the impressions of the other group and come to consensus. It is possible to create a better working environment with less stress and less chance of burnout.

School

Prevention of burnout should be a concern for organizations, supervisors and therapists but especially for professors in recreational therapy. All helping professions will be faced with a shortage of manpower in the next 20-30 years. Attention needs to be addressed to the emerging therapist today who will be the supervisor or administrator of the future. Vessel (1980) and Bailey (1992) illuminated the need to educate to the risks and appropriate coping strategies as students are developing.

Wade-Campbell and Anderson's (1987) first suggestion for preventing burnout is education. They believed that new therapists need to know the signs of developing burnout. Awareness of the dangers and awareness of the developing symptoms can increase an individual's ability to cope and function.

Behavior in school is practice for life. If individuals overcommit and overwork themselves in school, it is likely they will function the same way after graduation. Going through the education process is an orientation to the work world. Behavior demonstrated in school is a good indication of work behavior later.

The education of recreational therapists is a stress-filled time with multiple demands for acquiring new knowledge, meeting graduation requirements (major, option, general education and maybe a second major), meeting certification requirements, work demands and maybe a personal life. Many of today's students are also parents with jobs, a house and children. There is pressure to finish as soon as possible. Where in this quest do you pay attention to the most important person, *you*?

There is a premise that says you can't love another until you love yourself. This is often quoted but seldom held to by the general public. In the case of helping professionals, it is often a difficult lesson to learn. Professionals see such suffering and need which makes them feel that their own needs are less important. That is not true. Professionals need to learn to balance the patient's needs and their own needs to stay healthy. Professionals must learn to trust their own voice and judgment. If they learned from their family of origin that their needs are not real, overstated or selfish, they need to work on changing that perception to understand that their own needs are important.

What can be done with the student who feels s/he has no choices? What about the student in the recreational therapy programming class in the example cited earlier in this chapter? What can the school do to help? What lessons must the student learn? The most important and first task is for the person to break through his/her dysfunctional thinking. You always have choices even when those choices are difficult. Dysfunctional thinking must be identified. Often this is a case of unawareness. One task the school can help with is facilitating a discussion of the danger signs and characteristics of codependency. Another way could be to institute self-paced lessons so students could accomplish their learning at their own pace and create asynchronous learning environments which are supportive to working adults. Sessions on healthy helping and its characteristic should be mandatory.

Summary

In recreational therapy, many practitioners come into the field "fired up." It may be that many who choose recreational therapy are enthusiastic, idealistic and positive. What happens to professionals over the next 3-10 years impacts on if or when burnout occurs. This chapter explained some of the issues surrounding burnout and offered the following ideas to help make sure that your career will be an effective one. Enjoy your quest for wellness and a long productive career. Model healthy caring to those around you as you take care of yourself. This is a radical concept for some people. Realize that being a caretaker for others does not mean that if you take care of yourself you are selfish. Keep yourself healthy and educate those around you and you will see systems getting healthier. Do not accept unacceptable behavior from those around you.

Many times no one calls people on their bad behavior. One day at the nurses' station on rehab, a nurse was on the phone to a patient's family. The doctor asked her to hand him a chart (which he was closer to). When she did not respond, he started yelling and throwing a temper tantrum. The recreational therapist, who had entered the nursing station to pick up a chart, said to the doctor, "Oh Mario, be quiet, stop throwing a temper tantrum and get the chart yourself." He replied, "Okay." The nurses were in shock. But no one has the right to be rude and unreasonable. You may not always work in a healthy environment so, if you don't, work to make it healthier.

Learning Activities

1. Sarah is the Chief of Rehabilitation in a large hospital. She is very stressed and runs her life by a set of strict rules. Upon becoming Chief she instituted many rules for her supervisors and expected them to apply them to front line therapists. One of her rules increased the therapists load to 20 patients and required no one to go home until they had completed their entire quota for the day. All documentation and multiple team meetings were also required. What is an explanation of Sarah's behavior and how might the supervisors approach this problem?

2. Amy is working with juveniles in a drug rehabilitation program. There are 30 clients and only one recreational therapist. Recreation is part of the treatment protocol so Amy gets referrals for all 30 clients. She is expected to assess each client within 24 hours and design treatment plans, run groups, run an evening recreation program for the clients and their families and she has just been given the approval to create a community integration program. What should she do when she talks with the facility administrator? How would you determine a reasonable work load?

3. George is a student at mid-western university studying recreational therapy. He has finished all his classes and is doing his internship at a state facility for the developmentally disabled. His assigned unit has clients with serious behavioral problems. He has an excellent site supervisor and is anxious to do a good job. His family, however is experiencing a significant crisis. His mother has had a stroke and George has always been the caretaker in his family. His family expects him to fulfill this role during this crisis. He at-

tempts to complete his internship and take care of his mother. Within three weeks his university supervisor is called by the site supervisor with a warning. George is not functioning adequately, he is missing too many days and the days he comes in he is late and forgetful. You are the university supervisor. How would you handle this situation?

4. Go back to the scenario at the beginning of this chapter. Emily was in serious trouble. In your small groups decide if you were her supervisor: What could have helped prevent the final outcome? Can you think of a way to help Emily now? What could you have said to Emily to help her see that there was more than one way of accomplishing things?

5. Where are you in your quest to be a healthy helper? After reading this chapter what are the areas of concern for you? Make a plan of wellness and look at it often. How can you achieve a healthy balance?

6. Take the Friel and Friel Codependency Test at the end of the chapter.

Study Questions

1. What is burnout? Maslach's Burnout Inventory lists three sub-domains of attributes which help measure burnout. What are these three sub-domains? Over the last three months have you experienced any of the attributes listed in the sub-domains? If so, describe them.

2. Compare the Black's characteristics of functional and dysfunctional families to Jones' characteristics of dysfunctional work sites. What similarities and differences do you find?

3. What are Everly's three stages of burnout? List the characteristics in each level. What are some potential interventions for people who are demonstrating at least two of the signs of Stage 2?

4. What are some of the characteristics of functional people (i.e., people who are coping well and not demonstrating signs of burnout)? Select one of the characteristics and develop a treatment intervention/patient education program to help a patient develop the skills to demonstrate the characteristic.

References

Arnwine, D. (1990). Human resources managers should prepare for the "big one." *Modern Health-care, 20*(34), 38.

Bailey, M. (1992). *The relationships among codependency, burnout and work motivation in thera-peutic recreation specialists.* (Doctoral dissertation, University of Oregon) Dissertation Abstracts International.

Bailey, M. (1993). Codependency's impact on helping professionals. *AAL Reporter, 18*, 4, 5-6.

Beason, T. (1998, June 22). Watch you back: Your job description probably doesn't include looking out for assault. Perhaps it should. *The Seattle Times.* pp. E1-E2.

Bersani, H. (1983). Perceived stresses and satisfactions of direct care staff in community residences for mentally retarded adults. *Dissertation Abstracts, 43*(12-A), 3869.

Black, C. (1989). *Double duty.* New York: Ballantine Books.

Blanchard, K., (1985). *The one minute manager.* New York: William Morrow and Company.

Cermak, T. (1986). *Diagnosing and treating codependence: A guide for professionals who work with chemical dependents, their spouses and children.* Minneapolis, MN: Johnson Institute Books.

Chamberlin, T. (1982). *Burnout and managerial practices among therapeutic recreation professionals in the state of Oregon.* Unpublished Master's thesis, University of Oregon.

Cooley, E. & Yovanoff, P. (1996). Supporting professionals-at-risk: Evaluating interventions to reduce burnout and improve retention of special educators. *Exceptional Children, 62*(4) 336-355.

Eriksson, E. H. (1963). *Childhood and society.* New York: Norton.

Eriksson, E. H. (1986). *Identity youth and crisis.* New York: Norton.

Everly, G. (1985). *A clinical guide to the treatment of the human stress response.* New York: Plenum Press.

Everly, G. & Girdano, D. A. (1981). *The stress mess solution: The causes and cures of occupational health promotion on the health behavior in the workplace.* New York: Prentice Hall.

Farber, B. A. (1983). *Crisis in education: Stress and burnout in the American teacher.* San Francisco: Jossey-Bass.

Flett, R., Biggs, H. & Alpass, F. (1995). Job stress and professional practice: Implications for rehabilitation educators. *Rehabilitation Education, 9*(4) 275-291.

Friel, J. & Friel, L. (1988a). *Adult children: The secrets of dysfunctional families.* Deerfield Beach, FL: Health Communications.

Friel, J. & Friel, L. (1988b). Excellent word, lousy diagnosis? Clarifying the concept of codependency. *Focus on Chemically Dependent Families, 11*(6), 30-31.

Friel, J. & Friel, L. (1989). *Friel adult codependency assessment inventory.* Arden Hills: Friel & Associates Lifeworks.

Golembiewski, R. (1987). Diagnosing health-care providers and their systems: An entry design and its supporting theory, *Consultation, 6*(4) 265-280.

Golembiewski, R., Boudreau, R., Goto, K. & Mural, R. (1993). Transitional perspectives on job burnout: Replication of the phase model among Japanese respondents. *International Journal of Organizational Analysis, 1*(1) 7-27.

Golembiewski, R. & Munzenrider, R. (1984a). Phases of psychological burnout and organization covariants: A replication using norms from a large population. *Journal of Health and Human Resources Administration, 6*, 290-323.

Golembiewski, R. & Munzenrider, R. (1984b). Active and passive reaction to psychological burnout. *Journal of Health and Human Resources Administration, 7*, 264-289.

Golembiewski, R. & Munzenrider, R. (1987). Social support and burnout as covariants of physical symptoms: Where to put marginal dollars? *Organizational Development Journal, 5*(4), 92-96.

Golembiewski, R., Munzenrider, R. & Stevenson, J. G. (1986). *Stress in organizations.* New York: Praeger.

Greenleaf, J. (1984). *Co-alcoholic/para-alcoholic: Who's who? in codependency.* Deerfield Beach, FL: Health Communications.

Jones, T. (1997, October). *Dysfunctional worksites.* San Francisco Chronicle.

Kellogg, T. (1990). *Broken toys, broken dreams.* Amherst, MA: Brat.

Kellogg, T. & Harrison, M. (1991). *Finding balance: 12 priorities for interdependence and joyful living.* Deerfield Beach, FL: Health Communications.

Lee, R. & Ashforth, B. (1996). A meta-analytic examination of the correlates of the three dimensions of job burnout. *Journal of Applied Psychology, 81*(2), 123-133.

Lucas, K. (1998). *Outwitting your alcoholic: Exploring and escaping from the strange world of alcoholism.* Ravensdale, WA: Idyll Arbor, Inc.

Maslach, C. (1986). *Burnout — the cost of caring.* New York: Prentice Hall.

Maslach, C. & Jackson, S. (1981). The measurement of experienced burnout. *Journal of Occupational Behavior, 2*, 99-113.

O'Gorman, P. (1993). Codependency explored: A social movement in search of definition and treatment. Special Issue: *Contemporary Topics in Drug Dependence and Alcoholism.*

Peters, T. J. (1987). *Thriving on chaos: Handbook for a management revolution.* New York: A. A. Knopf.

Peters, T. J. & Waterman, R. H. (1985). *In search of excellence: Lessons from America's best-run companies.* New York: Warner Books.

Robertson. (1980). *Burnout and motivation in therapeutic recreation specialists.* Unpublished Master's theses, University of Oregon.

Uhle, S. (1994). Codependency: Contextual variables in language and speech pathology. *Issues in Mental Health Nursing, 15*(3), 307-317.

Vessel, K. (1980). *Managerial perceptions of motivation using Herzberg's model.* Unpublished Master's thesis. University of Oregon.

Wade-Campbell, M & Anderson, S. (1987). Perceived levels of burnout of Veteran's Administration therapeutic recreation personnel. *Therapeutic Recreation Journal, 3*(3) 52-63.

Wegscheider-Cruse, S. (1982). *Choice making for codependents, adult children and spirituality seekers.* Deerfield Beach, FL: Health Communications.

Wegscheider-Cruse, S. (1990). Co-dependency and dysfunctional family systems. In R. C. Engs (Ed.). *Women: Alcohol and other drugs.* Dubuque, IA: Kendal Hall.

Weiss, L. & Weiss, J. (1989). *Recovery from codependency: It is never too late to claim your childhood.* Deerfield Beach, FL: Health Communications.

Whitfield, C. (1990). Codependence: Our most common addiction. *Alcoholism Treatment Quarterly, 6*(1), 19-36.

Wilson-Schaef, A. W. & Fassel, D. (1989). *The addictive organization.* San Francisco: Harper and Row.

Friel Adult Codependency Assessment Inventory[1]

Below are a number of questions dealing with how you feel about yourself, your life and those around you. As you answer each question, be sure to answer honestly, but do not spend too much time dwelling on any one question. There are no right or wrong answers. Take each question as it comes and answer as you usually feel. Check true for those items that are true about you most of the time and check false on those items that are not reflecting you.

T	F	Statement	T	F	Statement
		1. I make enough time to do things just for myself each week.			9. I am very satisfied with my intimate love life.
		2. I spend lots of time criticizing myself after an interaction with someone.			10. I've been feeling tired lately.
		3. I would not be embarrassed if people knew certain things about me.			11. When I was growing up, my family talked openly about problems.
		4. Sometimes I feel like I just waste a lot of time and don't get anywhere.			12. I often look happy when I am sad and angry.
		5. I take good enough care of myself.			13. I am satisfied with the number and kind of relationships I have in my life.
		6. It is usually best not to tell someone they bother you; it only causes fights and gets everyone upset.			14. Even if I had the time and money to do it, I would feel uncomfortable taking a vacation myself.
		7. I am happy about the way my family communicated when I was growing up.			15. I have enough help with everything that I must do each day.
		8. Sometimes I don't know how I really feel.			16. I wish I could accomplish a lot more than I do now.

---

[1] Friel, J. C. and Friel, L. D. (1989). *Friel Adult Codependency Assessment Inventory*. Used with the permission of Friel & Associates Lifeworks, Suite 328, Arden Plaza Office Building, 3585 N. Lexington Ave., Arden Hills, MN 55126.

T	F	Statement	T	F	Statement
		17. My family taught me to express feelings and affection openly when I was growing up.			28. When a close friend or relative asks for my help more then I'd like, I usually say "yes" anyway.
		18. It is hard for me to talk to someone in authority (boss, teachers, etc.).			29. I love to face new problems and am good at finding solutions to them.
		19. When I am in a relationship that becomes too confusing and complicated, I have no trouble getting out of it.			30. I do not feel good about my childhood.
		20. I sometimes feel pretty confused about who I am and where I want to go with my life.			31. I am not concerned about my health a lot.
		21. I am satisfied with the way that I take care of my own needs.			32. I often feel like no one really knows me.
		22. I am not satisfied with my career.			33. I feel calm and peaceful most of the time.
		23. I usually handle my problems calmly and directly.			34. I find it difficult to ask for what I want.
		24. I hold back my feelings much of the time because I don't want to hurt other people or have them think less of me.			35. I don't let people take advantage of me more than I'd like.
		25. I don't feel like I'm "in a rut" very often.			36. I am satisfied with at least one of my close relationships.
		26. I am not satisfied with my friendships.			37. I make major decisions quite easily.
		27. When someone hurts my feelings or does something that I don't like, I have little difficulty telling them about it.			38. I don't trust myself in new situations as much as I'd like.

T	F	Statement	T	F	Statement
		39. I am very good at knowing when to speak up and when to go along with others' wishes.			50. I tend to think of others more than I do of myself.
		40. I wish I had more time away from work.			51. More often than not, my life has gone the way that I wanted it to go.
		41. I am as spontaneous as I'd like to be.			52. People admire me because I'm so understanding of others, even when they do something that annoys me.
		42. Being alone is a problem for me.			53. I am comfortable with my own sexuality.
		43. When someone I love is bothering me, I have no problem telling them so.			54. I sometimes feel embarrassed by behaviors of those close to me.
		44. I often have so many things going on at once that I'm really not doing justice to any one of them.			55. The important people in my life know "the real me," and I am okay with them knowing.
		45. I am comfortable letting others into my life and revealing "the real me" to them.			56. I do my share of work, and often do quite a bit more.
		46. I apologize to others too much for what I do or say.			57. I do not feel that everything would fall apart without my efforts and attention.
		47. I have no problem telling people when I am angry with them.			58. I do too much for other people and then later wonder why I did so.
		48. There's so much to do and not enough time. Sometimes I'd like to leave it all behind me.			59. I am happy about the way my family coped with problems when I was growing up.
		49. I have few regrets about what I have done with my life.			60. I wish that I had more people to do things with.

Score Sheet

1. Add 1 point for every "True" marked in the even numbered items.
2. Add 1 point for all the "False" responses marked on the odd numbered items.
3. Add the two sums together for your level.

Friel and Friel report:

        10-20 mild codependency/adult child concerns

        21-30 mild-moderate range

        31-45 moderate-severe

        over 45 severe codependency/adult child concerns

Rather than keeping score, though, we suggest that you use this inventory as a means for self-exploration. We invite you to arrange for a one-session evaluation with a professional if you feel that you have some of these issues interfering with your happiness and sense of well-being.

Chapter 10

The Right Stuff

Carmen V. Russoniello

The purpose of this chapter is to suggest a "character" to serve as a guide for the delivery of recreational therapy services. This information is intended for both the clinician who can rely on the framework as a touchstone for clinical decisions and the student who wants to understand the implications of their chosen profession. Overall, this information will help individuals decide if they have the "right stuff" to be a good recreational therapist. The six questions are, quite simply, what, where, when, who, why and how.

Standards, be they ethical or practice oriented, provide the *what*, *where*, *when* and *who* of services rendered. A therapist is always searching for the answers to these questions, admitting when s/he does not have the answers and continuing to search for better understanding of the problems and better solutions. The "character" applied to the actions addresses the *how*. The character of a recreational therapist's action is how the recreational therapist conducts himself/herself while delivering services. Since success with therapy is contingent upon the character by which services are delivered, a willingness to study the requirements for this character becomes imperative. *Why* is implicit in the question — we provide health care services to improve health. If we don't truly care about the health of our patients, we are in the wrong field, as caring is an important part of the healing process.

Why

A requirement for establishing a character of action for any profession is the understanding and acceptance of the profession's purpose. According to Newman and Sime (1991), a health care profession is differentiated by its "domain of inquiry that represents a shared belief among its members regarding its reason for being" (p. 1). Newman and Sime continue by noting that a profession is distinguishable by its focus statement and cite several examples such as physiology, the study of the function of living systems, and medicine, the study of the diagnosis and treatment of human disease. As such, the term recreational therapy implies the prescriptive use of techniques of, or related to, recreation that produce positive health outcomes. Among other things, the recreational therapy process seeks to assist individuals to obtain and maintain health through the use of recreation much the same as a physician uses medicine, surgery or other devices or a psychologist works with thought processes. The difference between the professions is the method, modality and technique that is chosen to derive the end result.

Agreement with this principle presupposes the acceptance of the underlying definitions of the words *health* and *care*. Whereas "health" is the end to which therapy is directed, treating with "care" or in a "caring manner" is the expected character of action when operating within the health service paradigm. Health is the physical, mental and social well-being of an individual with an absence of illness, disability or other abnormal condition (Anderson, Anderson & Glanze, 1994). This perspective does not exclude preventive care, management and/or prediction of disease, impairment or disability as these processes are strategies to link and maintain the whole (health). The definition of health presented here includes services for individuals with disabilities because these individuals have, to some degree, lost their wholeness or health. The recreational therapist, therefore, uses adaptive equipment, counseling and rehabilitation skills to assist the individual in regaining and maintaining health.

What, Where, When and Who

If the overall directive of the recreational therapy profession is to develop and implement techniques and processes that promote health, then it does not matter whether the technique is an exercise-oriented treatment to decrease depression or leisure education used as a behavioral medicine intervention to counteract the negative effects of stress. In other words, the choice of intervention should be contingent upon its potential for treatment success. The physical setting where practitioners deliver their services becomes important only as it relates to maximizing the processes which facilitate health. The important issue is that the recreational therapist must study and improve the delivery throughout his/her career regardless of the setting.

Sir William Osler (1981) in his classic work entitled "A Way of Life" addresses the importance of establishing standards for successions of actions (habits) that become more or less automatic (standards of practice). Moreover, he implores the professional to develop a character for these actions. Of course, habits are not enough. The effective recreational therapist will not keep to old roads, but will study the new ones to find better ways to treat patients.

Perhaps the foremost contemporary thinker on health care ethics is Edmund Pellegrino, renowned Georgetown University professor and medical philosophy scholar for the Kennedy Institute on Ethics. Dr. Pellegrino (1981) offers a theoretical foundation for health care professions based on the caring concept, and challenges professionals and their associations to abide by the fundamental principles which underlie the concept of "health care professional." He specifically states the need to have education, standards of practice and ethical foundations to be a professional. Clearly he states that the professional has an obligation to be able to honestly say, "I can help. I have the tools and skills and if I do not have I will get them before I will make such a claim."

Dr. Pellegrino asserts that health care is founded on three phenomena specific to health care: the fact of illness, the act of profession and the act of medicine (treatment).[2] The interrelationship between these three phenomena have the potential to impact an individual and his/her significant others so completely that it calls for a special kind of human relationship. This relationship must be grounded in honesty and competency. According to Dr. Pellegrino, the same moral and ethical imperatives apply to all health care professions and have evolved for over twenty-five hundred years. These principles are readily applicable to the literal interpretation of health expounded upon earlier.

The Fact of Illness

Health care exists because people become ill. When ill, individuals experience a loss; a change from being "whole." Often the individual is very aware of the new limitations to his/her customary routine, functional ability and, potentially, his/her dreams. This situation leaves the individual vulnerable and needing to rely on others. A loss of autonomy is realized; decisions may be left to others, freedom of movement may be lost, cherished relationships may be negatively impacted. "The state of being ill is therefore one of wounded humanity, of a person compromised in his fundamental capacity to deal with this vulnerability" (Pellegrino, 1981, pp. 207-208).

The Act of Profession

Being a professional is more than sharing a common educational background with others, adhering to the same standards associated with practice and following common ethics. Being a professional means that you are willing, and able, to say that you have the knowledge, skills and desire to help heal; and all

---

[2] Albert Johnson (1988), another preeminent thinker in medical ethics agrees and offers a "test" to decide whether the principles are being followed. All recreational therapists and students are encouraged to review Dr. Johnson's work on this subject.

the actions taken to help will be based on the patient's interests and not your own needs.

The Act of Treatment

The act of treatment has one end goal — all helping and healing actions are to be taken in the interest of the patient. Treatment is based upon three questions: (1) What is wrong? (2) What can be done? and (3) What should be done? The clinical judgment used by the therapist is based on the learned answers, as well as the art of helping. The knowledge learned and the art practiced help achieve "a right and good healing action taken in the interest of a particular patient" (Pellegrino, 1981, p. 211).

Pellegrino emphasizes that the relationship between the health care provider and the patient must be one based on truthfulness. The fundamental center of this truthfulness lies in the expectation that the therapist has a technical competence to practice and heal. If the therapist does not have the specialized knowledge of his/her profession (holding a basic competency), then, no matter what the outcome of the treatment is, the entire therapist/patient relationship is based on a lie. Without basic competency, the therapist lacks the character required to be a professional.

Moreover, the professional's obligation to be competent is never static. Once s/he passes his/her schooling, internship and national exam, the therapist has the moral obligation to continue increasing his/her knowledge and competencies. The characteristics which go along with this moral obligation are the willingness to submit his/her work to peer review; the willingness and ability to confess ignorance or error to a patient or peer; and a "concentrated and sustained effort to deepen his clinical craftsmanship." (Pellegrino, 1981, p. 213). Competence is an essential element of professionalism, one that is defined as morally imperative to the professional's code of standards.

Dr. Pellegrino's pithy discussion about competency accurately describes the modern health care professional and his/her related obligations. He differentiates between purposeful intervention and happenstance. He acknowledges the struggle to become and remain competent. In other words, if purposeful intervention (therapy) is expected by consumers, then therapists need to learn certain techniques and processes before they can be considered as competent. These processes require standardization and so does the way they are implemented. Dr. Pellegrino (1981, pp. 209-210) calls this commitment the Act of Profession saying it "is an active, conscious declaration, voluntarily entered into and signifying willingness to assume the obligations necessary to make the declaration authentic." Thus, the recreational therapist, like the physician and other health care professionals, makes an Act of Profession each time a patient is approached for treatment.

Furthermore, the integrity of a recreational therapist's act of profession can be measured by his/her ability to confidently assert that s/he is competent to carry out the standard for action in a caring manner. Hence, caring for the patient requires the therapist to constantly seek to improve his/her clinical skill. Moreover, the recreational therapist must develop a "character" for the application of these clinical skills. This character of action can best be articulated through the concept of caring which has, as its cornerstone, the empathic bond.

How

Agreement that the overall purpose of recreational therapy is to provide effective health-related services begets other inherent responsibilities such as the manner in which these health-related services are provided. How recreational therapists deliver health-related services may be just as important as the intervention delivered and therefore must also be targets for continued improvement. Caring is the implied manner in which actions are to be measured when delivering health-related services. This is evident in the term "health care" which describes both the services to be delivered (health) and the character of delivery of these services (care). What is caring? How is it used when providing recreational therapy services?

Caring implies that an empathic relationship or bond between the server and the served exists. Caring is tantamount to ensuring success. Yet, the contributions of caring in the healing process are just beginning to be explored and, to date, no single definition has emerged. (Morse, Solberg, Neander, Bottorff & Johnson, 1990). The number and diversity of factors that affect the concept of care suggest that it will continue to change. (An additional contribution to the discussion is found in Chapter 9, *Healthy Caring*.)

While it has been difficult to objectively define caring, its emotional components of compassion and empathy have been felt and reported. Here are the often cited concluding remarks from the classic 1927 essay by Francis Peabody entitled "The Care of the Patient" in which he poignantly addresses this emotional bond. Brackets were added for emphasis.

The good physician [recreational therapist] knows his patients through and through, and his knowledge is bought dearly. Time, sympathy and understanding must be lavishly dispensed, but the reward is to be found in that personal bond which forms the greatest satisfaction of the practice of medicine. One of the essential qualities of the clinician is interest in humanity, for the secret of the care of the patient is in caring for the patient. (p. 877)

The desire and ability to "care" is, therefore, not only important when deciding whether to join a profession but also provides a "litmus test" for clinicians deciding whether to remain in the profession. Most importantly, as Dr. Peabody pointed out, caring is essential to successfully treat a patient.

The acceptance of caring, especially "always taking care of others," as a way of life is not required for one to be a competent professional. In fact, the idea that there is a responsibility to live "a therapists' life" is often obscure or vague and consequently causes personal and professional conflict as well as treatment ineffectiveness and even patient harm. Caring is not done to meet your need to take care of someone else. Effective caring is done to meet the needs of your patients. If you don't understand how to separate (and set aside) your needs when you are working with patients, this may not be the right profession for you. What you do need is a desire to learn the ability of seeing each patient as an individual and finding a way to put him/her on the road to better health.

The following is a testimonial for Sir William Osler that appeared in a 1920 *Life* magazine obituary entitled "The Best Doctor of All" (Wheeler, 1990). It not only speaks to the quality of the man but also about the principles that guided his medical practice. Students seeking to join the recreational therapy profession and those already practicing should be willing to live according to:

> His errand in life … not only concerned the bodies of men and women, but their spirits. He lived in constant contact with all manner of people, giving out incessantly the kindness and wisdom that were in him… He was always directing human life, and wherever he touched it, it seemed to go lighter and more blithely. (p. 1544)

Another eloquent affirmation of this character is evident in Dr. Phillip Lee's (1992) Commencement Address at the Mayo Clinic. Here, using Professor Alvin Tarlov's (1980) words he poignantly depicts the character to which Sir William Osler alluded. These words are applicable to the recreational therapist.

> Beyond the intellectual competence required for making correct diagnoses, there are qualities of the spirit upon which effectiveness as a physician depends. I speak of honesty, integrity, dependability and the courage to stand tall with personal accountability. These qualities form the substance of the doctor/patient relationship, the most powerful of all tools for healing… Honesty, integrity, dependability and accountability are your treasure. Attend to them; do not suspend them for an instant; use them in every aspect of your personal and professional lives.

Finally, Francis Peabody's 1927 article in the *Journal of the American Medical Association* specifically addressed this character and the importance of the caring aspect of health care. While Peabody was discussing the practice of medicine, his points clearly apply to the practice of recreational therapy.

Practice, in its largest sense, encompasses the relationship between the therapist and his/her patient. This relationship is made up of more than learned technique and knowledge; the relationship is lacking without also applying the art of therapy. The therapist will find that the science of recreational therapy practice complements the art of practice. The good therapist will feel with his/her "gut" the right action to take, the right word to say, even when the science falls short.

While the treatment of disease, impairment and disability may be entirely impersonal, "the care applied to the patient must be completely personal" (Peabody, 1927, p. 877). The ability to initiate a personal relationship with the patient, and nurture that relationship while maintaining professional boundaries, is vital. For without this level of personal bonding and established trust, too much about the patient and his/her needs/desires will be missed. Too often newer therapists fail in being able to treat patients because they are not able to establish this relationship, a relationship which must be built on professional competency and putting the patient's needs first.

The therapist is called upon to develop a true "clinical picture" of the client during the initial assessment process and to continue defining this picture as time goes by. A clinical picture includes much more than the patient's disease, impairment or disability; it also includes "an impressionistic painting of the patient surrounded by his home, his work, his reactions, his friends, his joys, sorrows, hopes and fears" (Peabody, 1927, p. 877). For the therapist to try to treat a patient without taking into consideration the patient's emotional life is to be unscientific in the application of the science of recreational therapy, and clearly falling short in the art of recreational therapy.

While the techniques and modalities used to obtain and maintain health are very different from what they were in 1927, the basic requirement for caring remain the same. Caring is the universally accepted standard for the delivery of health-related services and therefore transcends the population or setting in which the services are provided.

Summary

Pursuing recreational therapy as a health care profession requires commitment to excellence in both service techniques and personal character. The purpose of health care is to deliver services which assist patients in obtaining and maintaining health or wholeness. This charge assumes the practitioner is competent to provide these services and is continually seeking to improve. Caring is the operative standard of how services are to be applied. Caring becomes the character of action by which recreational therapists not only conduct their business but also their lives with competency and honesty. An act of profession occurs every time a therapist delivers services to a patient. The act of profession, therefore, begins for recreational therapists when they accept the responsibilities of their professional actions throughout their lives.

Learning Activities

1. Review the paragraph under "The Fact of Illness." How can the therapist use both the science and the art of recreational therapy to address illness?
2. Imagine yourself as a new therapist working in a large nursing home. The facility has just admitted a 70 year old male patient in the middle stages of Alzheimer's. This patient is also a convicted, untreated sex offender; a diagnostic group you have not worked with before. What would you need to do to be able to have "the right stuff?"

Study Questions

1. What defines the difference between professions as they work toward an end result?
2. Discuss the three phenomena specific to health care as defined by Dr. Pellegrino. How do these apply to recreational therapy?
3. What is meant by "The Act of Treatment?" What is the therapists obligation in this case?
4. What is meant by the "character" of practice?
5. What is meant by a "true clinical picture?" How does it apply to the assessment process?

References

Anderson, K., Anderson, L. & Glanze, W. (Eds.). (1994). *Mosby's medical, nursing & allied health dictionary* (4th ed.). St. Louis, MO: Mosby — Year Book, Inc.

Johnson, A. R. (1988). Ethics in the practice of medicine. In J. B. Wyngaarden & L. H. Smith (Eds.). *Cecil textbook of medicine*. Philadelphia: W. B. Saunders.

Lee, P. R. (1992). Changes in the scope and responsibility of medicine. *Mayo Clinic Proceedings, 67*, 876-878.

Morse, J. M., Solberg, S. M., Neander, W. L., Bottorff, J. L. & Johnson, J. L. (1990). Concepts of caring and caring as a concept. *Advances in Nursing Science, 13*(1), 1-14.

Newman, M. A. & Sime A. M. (1991). The focus of the discipline of nursing. *Advances in Nursing Science, 14*(1), 1-6.

Osler, W. (1951). *A way of life and other selected writing of Sir William Osler*. New York: Dover

Peabody, F. W. (1927). The care of the patient. *Journal of the American Medical Association, 88,* 877-882.

Pellegrino, E. D. & Thomasma, D. C. (1981). *A philosophical basis of medical practice.* New York: Oxford.

Wheeler, H. B. (1990). Shattuck Lecture — healing and heroism. *New England Journal of Medicine, 332*(21), 1540-1548.

Tarlov, A. R. (1980). The responsibilities of the medical class of 1980. Commencement address presented at West Virginia, May 17, 1980.

Issues of Facilities

Chapter 11

Health Care Delivery Systems

Nancy Rickerson
joan burlingame

There are a variety of systems used to deliver health care services which strive to manage the balancing of the three major concerns of health care: the fiduciary relationship between the caregiver and the patient, cost and availability of health care and quality of health care. The three major health care delivery systems for the last fifty years are fee-for-service, managed care and critical pathways. These systems of delivering health care services all try to address the fiduciary relationship, cost and availability and quality of care to some degree. This chapter will present the reader with a historical perspective to explain why health care has changed so much in the last fifty years and an overview of each system along with strengths and weaknesses.

Delivery System History

A delivery system is an organizational approach to providing services and products. The actions, processes and resources of the entire organization are structured in such a manner as to deliver an end product. In this case, the end product is health care which, hopefully, provides a balance between the relationship of the provider and patient, the cost and availability of the product and the quality of the product. Delivery systems are not location specific; that is, the actions, processes and resources may be delivered in many settings including inpatient, outpatient, home health care, day treatment and/or residential facilities.

The work a recreational therapist does, whether it is a treatment intervention or a service provided to a patient, can generally be defined as a distinct action or process. Teaching a patient how to use the city bus or teaching activities which do not encourage the use of alcohol are pretty basic. The techniques, knowledge and clinical skills would be similar whether the patient is an inpatient at a large teaching hospital, attending a day treatment program or a home health care client. However, the teamwork involved, the scope and depth of service provided and the type of documentation vary, depending on the health care delivery system used. In the last twenty years there have been three major health care delivery systems used in the United States. These three systems are physician led, fee-for-service systems, managed care systems and critical pathway systems. Each system is not necessarily exclusive of the others, with hybridization being common.

The physician led fee-for-service system is a system directed by the patient's physician who orders services which s/he feels appropriate for the patient. This system led to a steep inflation in the cost of health care, as the provider was paid for the services which s/he ordered (National Center for Health Statistics, 1995). To help curb the inflationary impact of the physician led fee-for-service system of health care delivery, managed care was developed (American Therapeutic Recreation Association, 1996; Blegen et al., 1995). Managed care is a system directed by a managed care organization which is functioning as both the insurance company and the health care provider. This system helped slow the increase in health care costs but often led to necessary services being omitted. To help overcome this problem, critical pathways (also known as clinical pathways) were developed to make sure necessary services were not omitted (Pearson, Goulart-Fisher & Lee, 1995). Critical pathways is a system of health care delivery which is directed by the treatment team that has determined the critical health care treatments and services required of a patient with a specific diagnosis. The treatment team outlines which assessments, treatments and services are required for each day of the patient's admission. This information is placed in a calendar format and called a critical pathway. Critical pathways are used in both fee-for-service and managed care systems and try to address the quality of care provided within a cost containment environment.

A fourth delivery system which includes health care along with a wide variety of other services is used in the United States. This system is typified by the federal legislation for Intermediate Care Facilities for the Mentally Retarded (ICF-MR). Individuals who qualify for this government program are provided with room, board and vocational training as well as health care. This is a capitated system. In this system the provider of the service has a maximum amount of funds to spend and cannot usually exceed that amount except for certain health care services. Within the ICF-MR system, health care services are generally provided using managed care and care similar to critical pathways.

Fee-for-Service

For hundreds of years the physician was considered to be the one to make decisions about the treatment a patient received. Because of this, it is hard to separate the concept of the physician as the head of the treatment team and health care costs. Many of the regulations and standards of health care today address the conflict between what the physician would order for a patient's care and the cost of the care. Originally individuals would pay for their health care themselves. As the cost of health care grew and the idea that individuals had the right to receive care developed, private health insurance became more readily available.

Typically, health care delivery systems which are physician led, fee-for-service provide treatment based on the patient's assessed need and ability to pay. Many facilities are mandated by their mission to treat patients regardless of their ability to pay. In these cases, treatment is based upon the patient's assessed need tempered by what the facility can afford to provide. The physician is almost always the head of this treatment team. The entire team works from a care plan which is usually interdisciplinary in nature. The patient's care plan lists the goals and objectives of treatment. The goals within the care plan tend to be interdisciplinary (e.g., patient will be able to return home) with the objectives within each goal tending to be service specific (e.g., contact will be made with visiting nurse services by 7/12/99 — social work; will be able to use public bus to attend outpatient clinic by 7/14/99 — recreational therapy). The medical chart is the repository for all assessments, test results and documentation related to the patient's response to treatment. Services and interventions contained within the care plan and not funded through the room rate typically require a physician's prescription.

Generally, what the physician orders, the patient receives. The services ordered by the physician are paid for using a fee-for-service billing system. While fields such as occupational therapy established systems during the 1970's and 1980's to unify the types of services which could be billed, recreational therapy was not a major player of that development (American Therapeutic Recreation Association, 1996). Even so, a study done by Hutchinson-Troyer (1987) found that 41% of the facilities responding to her survey billed for some of the services they provided. (This may or may not have been the primary source of the income for the department.) In a survey conducted by the American Therapeutic Recreation Association in 1989 only 16% of the departments responding listed direct charges (fee-for-service) as their *primary* source of funding for therapeutic recreation services (Skalko & Malkin, 1992). In that survey it was reported that 60% of therapists who charged directly for services required a physician's order prior to providing treatment.

A fee-for-service system of reimbursement is a system in which each service above and beyond the basic room rate is billed separately (burlingame & Skalko, 1997). UCR (Usual, Customary and Reasonable), CPR (Customary, Prevailing and Reasonable) and Fee Schedules are examples of fee-for-service systems (Knaus & Davis, 1993). Using fee schedules (the amount typically reimbursed for any given service), the dollar amount reimbursed is based on three elements:

> ...computation of the total work, practice cost, and malpractice cost involved in performing a procedure. Each of the three elements of the value is modified by a geographic index. After the geographic modification, the three values are summed to reach a single value. (Knaus & Davis, 1993, p. 53)

Inherent in this system is the physician as the head of the treatment team. The physician orders (prescribes) services and treatments which s/he feels in the best interest of the patient and his/her health. But, as noted by Knaus and Davis above, the cost of malpractice is also included in the equation to determine the cost of care.

The increasing burden of health care costs driven by new technology, physician ordered services and the cost of malpractice began to force a change. During the 1980's the percentage of the gross domestic product spent on health care increased an average of 3.2 percent a year in the US, while the average for the other developed countries was 1.2 percent (National Center for Health Statistics, 1995). Despite the amount spent by the US on health care services, its health care outcomes lagged behind those in many other developed countries. Pressure was placed on the health care industry to begin to rein in the spiraling cost of health care. In 1991 Senator Jay Rockefeller told the staff at the American Hospital Association

> unless the private insurance industry can demonstrate that they are about the business of managing and controlling costs in health care and not just avoiding them, which is what they do now, I predict that they will not survive this decade. (Pozgar, 1996, p. 541)

The US Congress followed up Rockefeller's warning with its health care agenda to both manage the cost of health care and to help offer health insurance to individuals who currently were priced out of the market. The Health Security Act of the 103rd Congress started out with stating its purpose as

> To ensure individual and family security through health care coverage for all Americans in a manner that contains the rate of growth in health

care costs and promotes responsible health insurance practices, to promote choice in health care, and to ensure and protect the health care of all Americans. (United States Congress, 1993, p. 1)

The changes being implemented in how health care was managed (i.e., physician as the primary decision maker) was not because of physicians making decisions unhealthy for the patient. The changes were being driven by the expenses incurred as a result of the increased cost of the care prescribed by physicians. Cries to manage costs grew in the 1970's and 1980's (American Therapeutic Recreation Association, 1996) to the point that alternative systems were developed. The most broadly adopted system was managed care.

Managed Care

Managed care is a system of delivering medical services to an identified and prepaid population of patients for a fixed premium. It is essentially an agreement or contract between a health care facility or provider and an individual (patient or receiver of health care), which is managed or controlled by a managed care organization. This system is significantly different than the physician led health care system. Note that while the physician is usually still the head of the treatment team, decisions about care are frequently pre-determined by the agreement or contract. The physician (and the rest of the treatment team) are expected to work within the contractual agreement which outlines what may be provided, not just what is best for the patient.

One of the main goals of managed care is to increase health care efficiencies and thus decrease excess services and costs. The ultimate goal is to reduce the need for health care and, to this end, includes illness prevention, health promotion activities and increased community-based care. Realistic outcomes are required and must be outlined in measurable terms (Olsen, 1994). "Managed care models have been used to decrease costs while maintaining health care quality for large groups of consumers" (Blegen, Reiter, Goode & Murphy, 1995, p. 809). Specific questions managed care organizations ask of providers include:

- Is the care/treatment effective?
- Is the hospitalization/treatment medically necessary?
- Is the care cost efficient (with a low cost/high benefit ratio)?
- Can the care be provided in a more cost-effective way by a different provider (e.g., outpatient rather than inpatient, or non-surgical intervention)?
- Can the care be provided in a shorter period of time? (Lewing & Sharfstein, 1990)

The need for managed care developed after the period of health care expansion (1950-1970) when there were numerous developments in medical science and technology, rapid growth in the number of hospitals and physicians and health care insurance was extended through Medicare and Medicaid. Over time, the problem seemed to be "too much of a good thing" with resultant abuses of the medical system. (See Table 11.1 for some examples.) Health care costs were rising over the years, abuses including provision of unnecessary treatment procedures, duplicate provision and billing of service, inflation of charges, provision of unnecessary specialty services and continuing treatment when it was no longer medically necessary. In addition, serious mal-distribution of health care services resulted in very little for poor elderly, children and minorities, and excess services to privileged groups. This, together with a drastic reduction in the amount of federal funds to support medical allied health, resulted in a health care crisis. The public began questioning ethical and financial motivations for professions and service provision. People became more aware of economic efficiencies. Managed care became a legislatively mandated solution and an era of cost containment began (Sederer & Mirin, 1994).

The mechanisms of managed care shift the responsibility of patient care management from the physician and professional groups to third party players: insurance companies and managed care organizations contracted with treatment facilities. Thus care is more centralized, focused and organized in design. Primary care physicians, nurses and case managers oversee coordination of patient

Table 11.1: **HCFA's Believe It or Not**

While some charges of fraud may seem as mere hair-splitting, others are downright hair-raising. Here are a few examples, culled from a long list:

- A nursing home billed for the equivalent of 240 yards of gauze bandages per resident per day.
- A doctor billed for $350,000 in fees over two years without every seeing a single patient.
- An equipment supplier routinely charged $5,000 for the most basic $200 wheelchairs.
- A psychotherapist submitted fees for sessions with a 106 year old comatose woman and a resident who spoke not a word of English (the doctor's only language).
- A psychiatrist submitted hundreds of thousands of dollar's worth of false claims — and then pleaded that a mental disturbance provoking "fits of grandiosity" had forced him to do it. (He's now in prison.)
- A hospital coded card games and spelling bees as psychotherapy.
- A podiatrist racked up $100,000 in one year for the "minor surgery" of toenail removals — including 11 from one person. (Sullivan, 1998, p. 54)

care. Prior to hospitalization, prospective payment is established (a predetermined and fixed payment for a patient requiring hospital level of care). Services and payments are capitated; specifically, a maximum amount, or cap, is placed on the amount of services provided in days, number of treatments or dollar amounts. While patients are in the hospital, concurrent utilization reviews occur where care is reviewed during provision to determined the continued necessity for hospitalization.

In managed care the physician is no longer fully in control of the patient's care. The individual determining the type, frequency and duration of treatment services is frequently the case manager. While there is a national certification program for case managers, there is no one occupational group which fills this position and it is not mandated that the case manager be certified. The physician is typically still the head of the treatment team but his/her decisions (as well as the decisions of the rest of the treatment team) can be overridden by the case manager. The patient's written care plan is based upon assessed need, fulfilled by services approved by the managed care organization. As with the fee-for-service delivery system, the care plan's goals are interdisciplinary in nature. The medical chart is used to document all of the patient's responses to treatment as well as the results of all tests and assessment. Services rendered by non-physicians do not always require a physician's prescription. Frequently the case manager can make the decision that a service is required, separate from a physician's orders.

Health care experienced some positive outcomes as a result of managed care. Decreased medical costs to facilities and patients, elimination of duplicate services, shorter hospital stays and more efficient service provision are some of the positive results of managed care. However, some undesirable results have also developed. In theory, managed care to increase benefits while holding down costs makes sense. Translating that theory into practice has not always been smooth. For example, a shorter length of hospital stay may only be effective if adequate outpatient, community and home care services are available for follow up. Otherwise, the patient quickly returns to the hospital for additional inpatient days and costs. In addition, lower cost care does not necessarily mean quality care, consistent with the old adage, "You get what you pay for." Furthermore, what the managed care or insurance company considers "medically necessary" may be far less than what the physician and treatment team consider medically necessary. A patient may leave the hospital before s/he feels ready and blame the physician and hospital staff for caring only about money and not about the patient.

In order to ensure quality in the managed care environment (and it can be done), certain efficiencies must be utilized. For instance, a case manager or primary nurse coordinates care under the direction of a primary physician and frequent health care team meetings are held to plan and efficiently coordinate patient care. Quality treatments are administered in a timely, efficient manner. One of the more formalized methods of achieving this goal is the critical pathway.

Critical Pathways

The critical pathway is a tool used to plan and document patient care within a case management system for high volume and high cost diagnoses and procedures for which inefficient variations in care extend or decrease quality of patient care. The purpose and goals of critical pathways are to increase the efficiency of service provision, specifically to lower costs of health care by better coordinating systems, improving patient outcomes, providing good patient satisfaction and decreasing hospital lengths of stay. In short, the critical pathway is a tool to articulate and implement the highest standard for provision of patient care. Critical pathways are also known as optimal care paths, care maps and clinical pathways. Whatever term is used, (and for the purposes of this chapter, the term critical pathway will be used) the goals and functions remain the same.

Critical pathways are based on best practices. A critical pathway is the product of the therapist's and treatment team's understanding of what is the best set of interventions and services for patients with a specific diagnosis. "Best" includes the use of clinical experience, research on outcomes of interventions and clinical judgment on the appropriate timing for the delivery of each service or treatment.

A recreational therapist working on a rehabilitation unit knows that an intake assessment which obtains information about the patient's current medical status, expected medical status, levels of impairment and disability, personal interests and desires, and family and/or disposition situation is important. This information must be obtained prior to treatment (from a practical standpoint as well as a standards of practice and regulatory standpoint). Since some of the information required for the recreational therapist's intake assessment will come from the physician's report, the recreational therapist's assessment takes place after the physician's. Given this clinical experience, the physician's (and usually nursing's) intake assessment is scheduled on a critical pathway prior to recreational therapy's intake assessment.

When implementing treatment protocols such as the *Community Integration Program, Second Edition* (Armstrong & Lauzen, 1994), it is generally expected that every patient will be assessed for his/her ability to be safe in the community (Module 1A: Environmental Safety) prior to taking on more specific community integration training such as eating out (Module 2B: Restaurant), using public transportation (e.g., Module 4A: Taxi/Taxi Vans, Module 4E: City Bus) or engaging in community-based recreation programs (e.g., Module 2D: Sporting Event, Module 3A: Shopping Mall, Module 5A: Aquatics, Module 5C: Leisure Activities). Many facilities require that a patient be evaluated using Module 1A:

Environmental Safety prior to being able to go on a pass out of the hospital with family or friends. These policies, based on the past clinical experience of the practitioners and research, are built into a critical pathway.

Additional experiences of recreational therapists get built into the critical pathway. Not every treatment session offered by recreational therapy leads to improved care for patients within a specific diagnostic group. Experience may show that the provision of specific services do not positively impact a patient's outcomes enough to justify *requiring* them as part of the critical pathway. Medical play to help a young child cope with a rehabilitation procedure may not benefit an adult who developmentally can grasp the purpose of a procedure. In such a case, medical play may be a key component of a critical pathway when working with young children with a C-4 Complete spinal cord injury but not a key component of a critical pathway when working with adults with a C-4 Complete spinal cord injury.

Experience also points out what types of service are best implemented before others. Take an example of an individual with a head injury who will be communicating using sign language. An interdisciplinary assessment should be completed to determine what types of words should be taught to the individual, including words related to activities and recreational pursuits. The individual should be taught such signs first, and then have the use of the sign language supported throughout the remainder of the course of treatment. The management of this interdisciplinary schedule would be laid out on the critical pathway.

Goals of Critical Pathways

Critical pathways clearly display and thus alert staff to common diagnostic symptoms, corresponding tests, treatments and goals for patients. They help by outlining the ideal sequence and timing of staff actions for achieving those goals with optimum efficiency. Multidisciplinary communication is therefore necessary and often improved through use of the tool. Patient and family education and satisfaction may be improved as well when the patient and multidisciplinary team involve the patient in treatment decisions and progress through the use of critical pathways. Specific goals include:

- Identification of optimum patient care practice (best practice)
- Improved efficiency and continuity of care
- Provision of a documentation framework that shows frequency and reasons for patients failing to follow an expected course during hospitalization
- Clearly defined outcomes
- Decreased amount and redundancy of documentation
- Patient centered design
- Improved patient satisfaction

- Decreased length of stay
- Reduced use of resources and required documentation
- Decreased cost of care without decreased quality.

Means to the above ends generally include:

- Defining needed tests and treatments
- Defining achievable daily objectives
- Comparative benchmarking
- Analyzing relationship of treatments, staff actions, patient responses and length of stays
- Creating a common game plan for multidisciplinary staff and defining roles in the process
- Using the critical pathway as a central multidisciplinary communication tool
- Educating patients and families about care and involving them throughout the process.

Development of Pathways

A critical pathway is much like a calendar which lists not only when something is going to happen, but also the content and quality of the event. A useful pathway addresses the issues involved with patient care: treatments, observations that need to be made, expected patient outcomes, evaluation of patient progress, length of stay and documentation. In choosing which patient populations are appropriate for the use of critical pathways, high volume, high cost and high risk populations are considered. Many larger hospitals find their cardiovascular services fit into all three of these categories. Coronary artery bypass graft, uncomplicated myocardial infarction and congestive heart failure are common diagnoses for which critical pathways are developed. Other pathways developed include total hip or knee replacements, medical management of acute renal failure, total abdominal or vaginal hysterectomy and schizophrenia. Critical pathways are utilized throughout all services in large hospitals now, including medicine, surgery, orthopedics, physical medicine and rehabilitation and psychiatry. Successful pathways are developed by multidisciplinary teams, including a member from each discipline and a medical staff or director. This is important, not only for inclusion of all critical and appropriate treatment factors, but to ensure document credibility and "buy-in" from all members of the treatment team. Common failures of pathways emerge from a lack of physician involvement and support in the process and from lack of staff education regarding the purpose, goals, roles and methodology and lack of balance between standardization and individuation of patient care documentation. Steps in developing pathways vary, yet must include:

- Selection of patient diagnoses or groupings
- Identification of the current process in care
- Identification of specific outcome criteria for treatment milestones and timely discharge
- Determination of specific test and treatment appropriateness per diagnosis, according to medical requirements
- Formatting tools and forms
- Extensive staff education and training in critical pathway purpose, goals and method of use
- Data analysis and project evaluation.

Structure of the Pathway

There is no "right way" to design and use pathways. They should reflect the unique clinical and organizational characteristics of each facility. Nevertheless there are some standard components of successful critical pathways. They are generally set up in a table format with a time-task matrix that maps out an expected course of care, thus the name "care map." Components of care are listed on one axis of the matrix and days on the other with specific staff tasks identified per care component on each day of hospitalization. Key components of the critical pathways are multidisciplinary in scope and thus coordinated. They specify goals and timelines for each outcome. Key indicators, issues which must be addressed specifically to attain an outcome, are noted and tracked. Overall documentation is decreased since all expected interventions and outcomes are predetermined and charting therefore involves simply initialing each item. Every member of the multidisciplinary care team can scan the pathway and know at a glance exactly where the patient is in terms of progress toward goals. They can also easily see where the last caregiver has left off without reading a long narrative note.

Detailed charting is written for "variances" to outcomes or practice only. Variances are staff actions or patient outcomes that do not match expected patterns. These may be omissions or additional occurrences. The most common of these are outcomes which are not accomplished "on time." For any variance, an explanation of cause is provided along with a plan for returning to the expected course. Evaluating variances provides the framework for continuous quality improvement. Treatment techniques and staff action can be easily monitored and adapted to improve outcomes.

Multidisciplinary Function and Recreational Therapy's Role

Collaborative practice is an important part of case management and critical pathways can greatly facilitate this collaboration. The recreational therapist must be involved in development of the critical pathway in collaborative way with all other disciplines. All disciplines involved in patient care work together to assist the patient attain goals. This requires mutual respect, keen awareness of each professional's role and trust that all are doing their job. Open communication is essential for management of progress and efficient provision of care. This eliminates the potential problem of recreational therapy being misunderstood or an adjunct rather than integral part of patient care. Particular skills assessed include community safety and integration, leisure knowledge and skills and awareness of community resources for independent and healthy functioning. Clear behavioral goals are listed with reasonable timelines for accomplishment. The expected and defined day of community involvement for each patient population, with clear behavioral milestones and discharge goals greatly assists the treatment team in planning and implementing a timely and well facilitated hospital discharge. Clear, measurable outcomes are key and already established in critical pathways. Because the treatment and service outcomes are predetermined within the critical pathway, care plans are not used. Generally, physicians serve as the head of the treatment team when a critical pathway is used. Recreational therapists, occupational therapists and physical therapists, because of their expertise in evaluating and treating functional outcomes, are vital members in critical pathway development, documentation and implementation.

Drawbacks of Critical Pathways

Despite positive clinical anecdotes, pathways are controversial. Many case studies have reported reductions in hospital stays from 4-40% and cost reductions of up to 33% with significant improvements in readmission rates, wound infections and other clinical outcomes (Pearson et al., 1995). However, other reports have been less favorable. A well-controlled study of a critical pathway for patients with strokes showed no significant effect on costs or clinical outcomes. For treating strokes "no controlled study has shown a critical pathway to reduce the duration of hospital stay or to decrease resource use, nor has any study shown critical pathways to improve patient satisfaction outcomes" (Pearson et al., 1995, p. 945).

Critical pathways work best for surgical or medical procedures with little variation in the care process from patient to patient. For medical diagnoses in which symptomatology and thus treatment response is very individualistic, critical pathways become cumbersome documents due to the amount of variance which must be documented. For example, a critical pathway for schizophrenia requires frequent variance recording due to wide range of patient response and symptomatology. Psychiatry is one medical practice area in which multiple variables in patient diagnoses, presentation and care make critical pathways controversial.

Summary

A delivery system is an organizational approach to delivering a service or product. In health care settings three types of delivery systems are the fee-for-service, managed care and critical pathways. The underlying premise of all three is that they try to address the balance between the fiduciary relationship between the caregiver and the patient, the cost and availability of health care and the quality of care provided. The organizational approach to a delivery system describes how the product is to be deliver and by whom; it does not imply a location (e.g., inpatient versus outpatient). A summary of the three types of delivery systems discussed in this chapter is shown in Table 11.2.

A fee-for-service system usually is a physician led team which develops an individualized care plan for the patient based on assessed need (and usually

Table 11.2: **Summary of Delivery Systems**

Type	Fee-For-Service	Managed Care	Critical Pathways
Service Based On	assessed need and ability to pay	assessed need tempered by contracted services	defined needs of specific diagnostic group
Head of Treatment Team	usually physician	physician and/or case manager	usually physician
Type of Treatment Document	care plan with treatment goals and objectives and medical chart to note patient response	care plan with treatment goals and objectives on allowed services; medical chart to note patient responses	critical pathways flow sheet; usually no care plan document separate from flow sheet; medical chart used only to document deviations from clinical pathway
Physician Prescription for Recreational Therapy	desired, generally considered required	varies	assumed if included in critical pathway

ability to pay). This type of system has led to significant increases in the cost of health care over the last thirty years.

A managed care system provides services which are based on assessed need tempered by a contractual agreement which specifies the type, duration and frequency of services that will be available. The case manager leads the team as much or more than the physician does.

Critical pathways, otherwise known as care maps or clinical pathways, are frequently used tools to organize and ensure completion of necessary and efficient patient care. Service delivery structures are clearly defined and the expected medical outcomes identified. Finally, patient/customer satisfaction is enhanced through collaborative goal setting and treatment planning. Research performed by Colleen Goode (1995) in the University of Iowa Hospitals showed

> patients who were cared for under the care map [critical pathway] delivery system had greater satisfaction with their care and greater satisfaction with their participation in decision making [than patients in the control group who were not part of a critical pathway approach]. There was greater job satisfaction for the multidisciplinary hospital staff on the unit. These findings are consistent with those reported by Cohen and Cesta (1993) regarding job satisfaction with Case Management and with those reported by Abbott, Young, Haxton and Van Dyke (1994) regarding job satisfaction with a practice model using clinical pathways. (Goode, 1995, p. 347)

Using critical pathways increases the likelihood of quality patient care and managed care success.

Learning Activities

1. Develop a schedule for recreational therapy interventions for a critical pathway for patients with depression who average seven days of inpatient stay. Support your proposed scope of treatment and schedule based on literature and interviews with professionals.
2. Search the web for web sites on critical pathways. Summarize the type of information you find. How much of it is educational and how much of it is commercial? What type of information can you find which can be applied to the practice of recreational therapy? How do you see yourself being able to use that information?
3. Search the web for information on managed care. What are the issues being discussed at the various web sites? How would some of the issues impact how recreational therapy delivers services?

4. Using the Internet go to a site which allows you free access to Medline. Search for articles which discuss fee-for-service which have been published over the last two years. Read the abstracts of the articles. What issues are being brought up by the authors of the various articles? How could these issues apply to or impact recreational therapy?

Study Questions

1. What are the three major concerns of health care which a variety of delivery systems try to address? What are the primary delivery systems in the US to address the major concerns of health care?
2. Compare and contrast a fee-for-service and a managed care delivery system.
3. What are considered the strengths and the drawbacks of managed care systems?
4. What is a critical pathway and what are the goals of this delivery system?
5. Discuss the differences in team leadership and documentation requirements between the three main types of delivery systems.

References

American Therapeutic Recreation Association. (1993). *Standards for the practice of therapeutic recreation & self assessment guide*. Hattiesburg, MS: American Therapeutic Recreation Association.

American Therapeutic Recreation Association. (1996). *The next generation of reimbursement*. Hattiesburg, MS: American Therapeutic Recreation Association.

Armstrong, M. & Lauzen, S. (1994). *Community integration program* (2nd ed.). Ravensdale, WA: Idyll Arbor, Inc.

Blegen, M., Reiter, R. C., Goode, C. J. & Murphy, R. R. (1995). Outcomes of hospital based managed care: A multivariate analysis of cost and quality. *Managed Care, 86*(5), 809-814.

Bruner, R. F., Eaker, M. R., Spekman, R. E. & Olmsted Teisberg, E. (1998). *The portable MBA* (3rd ed.). New York; John Wiley & Sons, Inc.

Bryant, M. R. (1995). Critical pathways: what they are and what they are not. *Tar Heel Nurse, 57*(5), 18-19.

burlingame, j. & Skalko, T. (1997). *Idyll Arbor's glossary for therapists*. Ravensdale, WA: Idyll Arbor, Inc.

Capuano, T. A. (1995). Clinical pathways practical approaches, positive outcomes. *Nurse Manager, 26*(1), 34-37.

Danish, A. (1995). Critical care pathways: The basics of development and implementation. *Continuum, 15*(2), 3-8.

Ebener, M. K. (1996). Proving that less is more: Linking resources to outcomes. *Journal Nursing Care Quality, 10*(2), 1-9.

Edwards, W. H. (1996). Resource utilization and pathways: Meeting the challenge of cost containment. *American Surgeon, 62*(10), 830-834.

Forkner, J. (1996). Clinical pathways benefits and liabilities. *Nurse Manager, 27*(11), 35-38.

Goode, C. J. (1995). Impact of a care map and case management on patient satisfaction and staff satisfaction, collaboration, and autonomy. *Nursing Economics, 13*(6), 337-348.

Hague, D. A. (1996). Clinical pathways: The careplans of the 90's, an independent study. *Ohio Nurses Review, 71*(5), 15-18.

HealthSTAR (1996). The prognosis for pathways: A study of clinical path trends in health care. *Health Systems Review, 29*(1), 48-54.

Hutchinson-Troyer, L. (1987). Third-party reimbursement update. *ATRA Newsletter, 3*(6), 4.

Ibarra, V., Titler, M. G. & Reiter, R. C. (1996). Issues in the development and implementation of clinical pathways. *AACN Clinical Issues, 7*(3), 436-447.

Knaus, D. & Davis, J. (1993). *Medicare rules and regulations: A survival guide to policies, procedures and payment reform*. Los Angeles: PMIC.

Lewing, R. & Sharfstein S. (1990). Managed care and the discharge dilemma. *Psychiatry, 53*, 116-121.

Lumsdon, K. (1994). Clinical paths: A good defense in malpractice litigation? *Hospitals and Health Networks, 68*(13), 58.

National Center for Health Statistics. (1995). *Health United States 1994*. Hyattsville, MD: Public Health Service.

Olsen, D. P. (1994). The ethical considerations of managed care in mental health treatment. *Journal of Psychosocial Nursing, 32*(3), 25-28.

Pearson, S. D., Goulart-Fisher, D. & Lee, T. H. (1995). Critical pathways as a strategy for improving care: Problems and potential. *Annals of Internal Medicine, 123*(12), 941-948.

Pozgar, G. D. (1996). *Legal aspects of health care administration*. Gaithersburg, MD: Aspen Publishers, Inc.

Rasmussen, N. (1994). The route to better communication. *Nursing, 24*(2), 47-49.

Sederer, L. I. & Mirin, S. M. (1994). The impact of managed care on clinical practice. *Psychiatric Quarterly, 65*(3), 177-187.

Skalko, T. & Malkin, M. J. (1992). Current status of third party reimbursement for therapeutic recreation services: Where do we go from here? *Annual in Therapeutic Recreation, 3*, 80-89.

Sullivan, J. G. (1998). Unusual suspects. *Contemporary Long Term Care, 20*(8), 52-57.

United States Congress. (1993). *Health security act*. Publication #151-183 O-93-4. Washington, DC: 103rd United States Congress.

Windle, P. (1994). Critical pathways: An integrated documentation tool. *Nursing Management, 25*(9), 80F-80L.

Chapter 12

Outcomes

Linda O. Niemeyer
joan burlingame

Outcomes are the results of actions you have taken. If you provide treatment to a patient, measuring the outcome tells you how effective the treatment was in causing the desired result. Often therapists will declare (with tongue-in-cheek) that treating patients gets in the way of all of the "required" work: patient assessment, documentation in the medical chart, running quality assurance programs and, lately, the process of determining *outcomes*. At issue here is whether gathering information about the cause and effect of your actions (treatment) produces a greater benefit than the loss of direct patient contact caused by gathering the data. To be truly able to answer this question, each therapist must be able to measure the actual benefit of his/her services. Can the therapist improve delivery of services and reduce treatment which does not cause significant benefit? Do specific recreational therapy interventions have a reasonable cost/benefit ratio? Are patients really getting the quality of services which they (or others) are paying for? This chapter will discuss how outcomes fit into the facility's strategic planning, how to establish databases from which you can analyze your services and how to analyze and display the results.

Why Do Outcome Research?

Why is it important for the therapist to spend time and resources doing outcome research when we already have a difficult time meeting the requirements for patient care and documentation? In reality, we have no choice but to start doing outcome research. Payers are in the driver's seat. We do not have the luxury of waiting to develop research programs when we reach a management position. The future of any program depends not only on how well our patients do, but also on whether we are able to document this success. Payers, health policy makers and investors are all looking for objective evidence of efficacy and cost-effectiveness. Tom Chapman (in Framrose, 1995) outlines four reasons why we must integrate the process of outcome research into our practice on a daily basis:

- There is a tremendous oversupply in the marketplace of health care services, so payers are asking for competitive pricing and quality.
- Providers are continuing to come under the microscope. Insurers are doing provider profiling which entails keeping records of provider track records, captured from billing information.
- It's about computers. Computers are capturing the data in great detail and, for those who have the talent to put the data into meaningful formats, that data is going to be their competitive advantage.
- It's going to be harder to get away with abuse of the system. Providers should get their house in order.

Outcome research answers the big "so what" in therapy. In other words, how do we know the value of the therapy we provide if we don't know the final result (outcome)? How does the payer know the value of one provider over another? They look at final outcomes. Providers are being held accountable for knowing their outcomes. Measurement of outcomes is tied in with the issue of accountability. Accountability implies that the facility and its staff know how to correctly identify patient needs and then use interventions which cause the desired change. Accountability means that the staff do more than guess how to bring about the changes for which they are receiving reimbursement. Moving beyond guessing to purposeful manipulation is possible when they analyze the cause and effect of services provided. A facility which provides good care (is accountable) does so because all of its staff coordinate efforts in purposeful manipulations to achieve good outcomes.

Outcome-Oriented Collaborative Care

In health care, looking at the "bigger picture" is important, especially in managed health care systems. In the larger scheme of things, what is the application for the data you obtain through outcome research? The data contribute to several aspects of a facility's ongoing strategic planning framework.

Figure 12.1 presents a model of a strategic planning framework that is supported by outcomes research. In the outer circle are seven areas of focus in strategic planning that are vitally important to the continued success of any health care provider in the current managed care marketplace. These are (1) predicting care needs, final outcomes and costs; (2) development and use of outcome measures and indicators; (3) total quality management (TQM) and continuous

Figure 12.1: Outcome Research Part of a Strategic Planning Framework

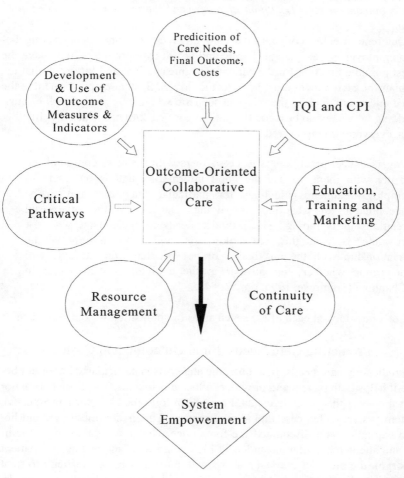

© 1995 Linda O. Niemeyer

performance improvement (CPI); (4) education, training and marketing; (5) continuity of care; (6) resource management and (7) critical pathways.

Each of these seven areas of focus benefits from the application of outcome data, and they are all interrelated. In other words, as one is developed, it will support the development of all the others. In fact, one large, well-designed research project would support the development of all seven simultaneously. This model might be visualized as an umbrella, with each spoke essential to maintaining the integrity of the fabric of the system as a whole. The hub or dynamic focus is *outcome-oriented collaborative care* and the mission is *system empowerment*.

Outcome-oriented collaborative care involves coordinated partnering between employer, payer, patient, family and health care providers to achieve the highest possible function for the patient. This means, first and foremost, that the care plan for each patient must be outcome-driven. System empowerment is the desired end result. This is the win-win scenario where everybody stays in business doing what they do best and the patient goes back to his or her life. In other words, everyone is empowered.

> Payers expect practitioners to be partners with them, to communicate better with them, to use the good information that is out there to employ treatment guidelines for particular diagnoses and to be accountable for what they are doing. The day of the adversarial relationship is fading. The provider needs to understand who the customer is, what they are looking for, and strive to improve the relationship with them. Whether or not you have this attitude will determine whether you prosper in the evolving system. — Tom Chapman (Framrose, 1995, pp. 52, 54)

Let's now look at each of the seven areas of application for outcome data.

Predicting Care Needs, Final Outcome and Costs

Predicating care needs, final outcome and costs is particularly important because it helps both payers and providers allocate resources. There are two major applications for this predictive data. First, it can form the basis for a prospective payment system called case rate reimbursement. This is the middle ground between capitation and discounted fee-for-service. Under capitation (e.g., Medicare outpatient rehabilitation under TEFRA, paid as a single rate per patient discharge), the provider may take a loss with patients who are difficult to treat so there is a disincentive to take on patients with high-cost health care needs. With case rates, each patient is assigned on admission, following an initial assessment, to a classification based on projected length of stay and complexity of care needs. Then the provider can negotiate with the payer to receive a lump sum for that case that is keyed into the patient's classification. Of course, this payment system only works if the method of classification is a valid predictor, and that requires outcome research. For example, two studies (Harada, Kominski & Sofaer, 1993; Stineman, Escarce, Goin, Hamilton, Granger & Williams,

1994) used a classification system called Functional Related Groups (FRG's), based in part on a standardized measure of function at time of admission, to predict care needs more accurately than by diagnosis alone. This same type of research can also be used by payers to adjust capitation rates so that facilities seeing a greater proportion of complex cases can be reimbursed accordingly (Manton, Newcomer, Vertrees, Lowrimore & Harrington, 1994).

Second, predictive data are used by facilities and insurance companies for long-range planning and major research on the outcomes and cost of care. The goal is to have a database that matches certain case characteristics with expected cost and length of treatment for medical care and/or rehabilitation. Then, for designated groupings of patients in particular facilities, it can be determined whether costs and clinical outcomes are within predicted ranges. Insurance companies may use this information as a kind of "report card" to look at a facility's cost-effectiveness. To keep up with the kinds of analyses that insurance companies are doing, more and more providers are using software packages designed to compare cost to outcomes.

Development and Use of Outcome Measures and Indicators

Each discipline has the responsibility of developing and testing appropriate outcome measures. Historically, rehabilitation medicine, psychiatry and, as a discipline, recreational therapy have been slow in quantifying what they do. Occupational and physical therapists have been accustomed to quantifying changes in edema, range of motion, strength and sensation, but recently the importance of developing standardized measures of function has come to the forefront. While recreational therapists have tools to measure leisure attributes and leisure barriers, they have yet to incorporate the results of these tests into studies of outcome. Recreational therapists can make intelligent guesses as to anticipated meanings of test results and how they might affect outcomes, but cannot support these judgments with outcome research. Why? Because recreational therapists who see patients don't realize that data collection is an integral part of everyday treatment — just like patient care and documentation.

Outcome research is the means to develop and test ways to quantify function in real-life by analyzing community integration, patient satisfaction with outcome and functional change. These are difficult things to measure and it takes time to come up with suitable tools. Indicators must include "red flags," which might be psychosocial factors indicating that this patient will be more difficult to treat than medical severity alone might indicate. The CERT Psych/Revised (Parker, 1997) could prove beneficial in identifying behavioral patterns which have correlated with longer stays. Treatment programs such as the *Community Integration Program, Second Edition* by Armstrong and Lauzen (1994) can provide us with measurement tools to use to identify indicators. After the measurement tools are in place, we need to collect the outcome data and correlate the outcomes with the indicators. At that point the indicators can be used to improve outcome-oriented collaborative care.

TQM and CPI

Total quality management (TQM) and continuous performance improvement (CPI) are buzzwords describing a process that has been used successfully in industry and is now being applied to health care service providers. These are other terms for quality assurance. The ideal in TQM is to ask openly and honestly:

- Are we doing the right things?
- Are we doing things right?
- Is it done right the first time, every time?

Outcome research provides the feedback information needed to monitor and implement change.

Education, Training and Marketing

Education, training and marketing are ongoing processes involving both internal and external partners of the treatment team. Staff get feedback regarding their treatment philosophies, goals and methods. Education of employers, physicians and insurance companies is a means of marketing, of selling potential referrers and consumers on the efficacy of your services and also of getting cooperation. The most convincing way to share the vision of a unified effort is to give the results of outcome research. Since each player speaks a different language, has a different focus and area of interest, outcome data has to be formulated differently for each audience.

Continuity of Care

Managed care systems are holding providers more accountable for final functional outcome, meaning function in the community. Outcome research can help to justify the cost of special programs that go beyond the walls of the facility. You have to sell employers and insurance carriers on these services. What combination of return-to-community services is most effective, and with what types of patients? And the bottom line is how many dollars in health care expenditures are saved in the long run by improving continuity of care? Research that answers these questions can be a powerful, persuasive tool.

Resource Management

Resource management refers to management of all cost factors. Resources are both human and fiscal. The payers must determine the dollars they are willing to spend for each patient's case. You, as the provider, have to manage dollars that are paid on each patient's case to keep costs down while at the same time achieving the desired or highest outcome. This requires making hard decisions regarding allocation of resources, such as, who is going to deliver the care and how it is going to be delivered. Only routine outcome research can tell us the best way.

Critical Pathways

A critical pathway is another concept that has been borrowed from industry and applied to the health care arena. A treatment protocol represents a type of critical pathway. Right now, most critical pathways are general descriptions of a preferred route to get from point A to point B, from where you start to the desired outcome or goal. They have an educational value in promoting the concept of the total care plan. Physicians, employers and insurers who review a critical pathway for a patient gain a sense of what is going to be done during the total course of care and the amount of time and effort that will be going into the program. Insurance companies are already beginning to establish what they see as "care paths" or critical pathways. Outcome research can be used to define critical pathways and then look at whether treatment followed a critical pathway or deviated, and whether deviations affected the outcome.

Designing an Outcome Study

Determining End Use of the Data

The end use of the data should be considered when determining all aspects of the study design. Those who will be using or reviewing or benefiting from the data can include individual patients and families, therapists, physicians, case managers, hospital administrators, payers and health policy makers. The data will likely be used for educational or marketing purposes, to promote the program or to change the program.

Each audience has different concerns and will view the data in different ways. We will come back to this point periodically. In general, doctors are interested in clinical measurements, but insurers and case managers are not. They are interested in cost, length of stay, number of treatments and whether you were able to do what you said you could do. Insurers want to set rates. They want data showing a program's effectiveness in treating a particular impairment. Insurers have software packages that can project outcome ranges based on assessment data from an individual patient. They want to see if you are within or exceed predicted ranges.

Determining Levels of Data Aggregation

You must be able to determine how broad your scope of study will be and how you bring all of the data together to make an understandable picture (or *data aggregation*). Data aggregation is the process of collecting information and bringing it all together to form an honest, complete picture of what is going on. (See Figure 12.2.)

At the center is the patient, the person served. This is the most fundamental and this is how we have been accustomed to looking at outcomes. This is essentially at the level of a case study. Therapists, physicians and case managers find this information particularly useful. You are comparing, in an individual person, initial versus discharge function.

The next level is to aggregate across groups of patients to programs or diagnostic groupings. For example, what are the outcomes for the stroke program, the head trauma program? You can compare outcomes of initial versus discharge function for the entire group. Or you can subdivide the group further and compare the outcomes for subgroups. For occupational therapists, the question might be what are the outcomes for patients admitted for upper extremity treatment versus back strengthening; or patients with post surgical versus conservative care carpal tunnel treatment; or patients with a right hemi versus left hemi.

Figure 12.2: **Levels of Data Aggregation**

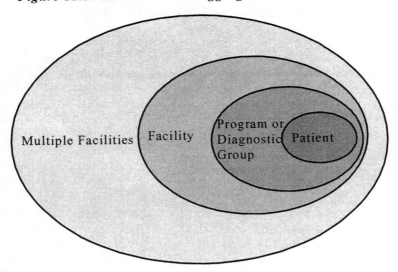

Recreational therapy might ask what is the impact of cognitive training on patients with Alzheimer's versus head injury; what is the frequency of readmission rates due to drug abuse for patients with depression versus schizophrenia who have completed the *Leisure Step Up* (Dehn, 1995); what is the degree of independence in using the city bus for youth with ADHD versus moderate mental retardation? Who is interested in this data? Case managers, school districts and insurance companies who might be deciding whether to choose your program over another. Your facility administrator might need documentation on program effectiveness to justify funding.

Next is the facility level with regard to costs, outcomes and documentation. Again, insurance companies are interested in comparing your results with the results from other facilities.

The last level aggregates information for multiple facilities, with a regional or nationally complied database. This, of course, requires a common language of outcomes. An example of a multi-facility project that strives to work within a common language to measure occupational and physical therapy outcomes for upper extremity injuries is UE NET (upper extremity network) sponsored by the American Society of Hand Therapists. Another multi-facility project called Focus on Therapeutic Outcomes (FOTO) looks at physical therapy outcomes for cervical, knee and lower back injuries.

Choosing Which Outcomes to Measure

What outcomes should you measure? The first step in addressing this aspect of the design of an outcome study is to answer the question, "So what?" with regard to the therapy you are providing. In other words, were you instrumental in bringing about positive change in a patient? What makes your therapy valuable to the patient? to the doctor? to the payer? For example, recreational therapy can positively influence functional ability, quality of life and life satisfaction.

The next step is to consider where the disease or condition is impacting the life of the patient and subsequently where intervention is being targeted. This requires a conceptual scheme or taxonomy, which is a scientific model that serves as a basis for a uniform language underlying evaluation, goal-setting, intervention and measurement of outcomes. There are two major conceptual schemes in use today. One was developed by the World Health Organization (WHO) in 1980 and called the International Classification of Impairments, Disabilities and Handicaps (ICIDH). The other came out of the work of the sociologist Saad Nagi and was adopted by the National Center for Medical Rehabilitation Research (NCMRR) (Verbrugge & Jette, 1994). They are both presented in Table 12.1. Both taxonomies are in wide use, but note that the two systems use slightly different terms to refer to similar concepts. For your outcome study, choose the system most in keeping with the language used at your facility. In this discussion, we will use the WHO terminology.

Look at Table 12.1. Note that a disease or condition can impact the individual from the "micro" level (*disease*), where it interferes with tissue physiology,

Table 12.1: **Functional Outcome Targets**

	Micro	Mezzo	**Macro**

Level:	Underlying Cause	Anatomical Part	Person	Environment
World Health Organization	Disease	Impairment	Disability	Handicap
NCMRR	Pathophysiology	Impairment	Functional Limitation	Disability
Definition:	Interruption of or interference with normal physiological and developmental process or structures.	Loss or abnormality of cognitive, emotional, physiological or anatomical structure or function.	Restriction or lack of ability to perform an activity in the manner considered within the normal range for a human being.	Inability or limitation in performing tasks, activities and roles to levels expected within physical and social contexts.
Problem Areas	Edema Wound, lesion Infection Skeletal compromise Cardiovascular Metabolic	Strength, endurance Range of motion Sensibility Loss of body part Executive function Pain Depression Cognition, memory Coordination Spasticity Speech	Activity Deficit ADL Mobility Communication Work demands (handling, fingering, bending, stooping, lifting, carrying, reaching)	Independent living Recreation Working Parenting Social Activities Transportation

all the way to the "macro" level (*handicap*), where it affects the individual's ability to participate in his or her customary social roles in the community. In between at the "mezzo" level are *impairment*, which is loss of structure or function of an anatomical part, and *disability*, or restriction in ability to perform normal activities of daily living. In each of these four domains — disease, impairment, disability and handicap — there are specific kinds of problems, as well as evaluations, goals, treatments and outcome measurements available to health care professionals. If a condition impacts the patient in all four domains, it is often necessary to deal with problems at the more micro level before moving on to those at the macro level.

Let's use the example of an individual with a closed head injury. A physician first determines the negative impact of the condition on the physiology of the brain and prescribes treatment to minimize or reverse that impact. The desirable outcome is prevention of as much permanent tissue damage as possible. The next step is to address problems of impairment, which for this individual might include deficits in cognition, memory, speech and coordination. For each of these deficits there are specific measures designed to ascertain the severity of the problem. It may take the combined efforts of a team of various rehabilitation professionals to evaluate and treat all areas of impairment. Outcome is determined as the change in each impairment measure from beginning to end of therapy, hopefully from more severe to less severe or normal. As problems in the impairment domain resolve, problems related to disability and handicap come to the forefront. For example, the individual may be unable to purchase groceries. During evaluation, the rehabilitation professional looks at component functional skills for grocery shopping such as making a grocery list, counting money and selecting items in keeping with a budget. The desired outcome at the disability level is mastery of the component skills, usually measured by therapist observation and rating of performance. The desired outcome at the handicap level is successful completion of a shopping trip in the community. Though the patient might have the functional skills for shopping, s/he may need access to community services (e.g., public transportation) to minimize any handicap.

Note that, when moving from micro to macro domains, the kinds of measures available to determine outcomes become less "objective" (i.e., clinical tests) and more "subjective" (i.e., rating of performance by a skilled observer). Subjective ratings tend to have more variability due to natural differences between observers. When used in an outcome study, the method of conducting subjective ratings must be structured and standardized as much as possible to reduce this variability. This in itself may require a major research effort, so whenever possible, search the literature for measures that have already been developed and tested by reputable research groups. Other factors to consider when choosing outcome measures to use include:

- *The type of program and patient population.* In a facility handling an acute or subacute population you will be dealing with problems in the more "micro" domains and using more clinical testing procedures to determine outcomes. If the facility is handling patients much farther along in the recovery process, your outcomes will be focused on problems in the more "macro" domains and you will be measuring component skills for performance of activities of daily living as well as function in the community.
- *Who is reviewing the results.* Physicians tend to be more interested in changes in strength, sensibility, range of motion, reality orientation, decision making/judgment, degree of independent initiation of activity and coping skills. The case manager and insurer tend to be more interested in the final functional outcome (minimizing or eliminating disability and handicap), for example return to work, self-maintenance to avoid skin breakdown, abstention from drug abuse.

A final word: The medical and rehabilitation community until fairly recently has been focused to a greater extent on reducing impairment and disability and to a lesser extent on reducing handicap. That focus is now shifting. It is time to stretch our view of therapy outcomes beyond the doors of the inpatient or outpatient center into the community. Increasingly, providers will be held accountable by those paying the bill for final functional outcome in the community.

Measuring Outcomes

There are many outcome measures that are established, reliable and well-validated. Use them if they fit into the diagnostic group you are working with, provide a measure appropriate to the target domain where intervention takes place and if they are available for you to use (measures that are licensed and/or copyrighted can require written permission for use or purchase from a designated supplier). As you move from micro to macro levels of outcome, good measurement tools may be more difficult to locate. Here are some examples of outcome measures for each domain used by therapists:

- *Measures for the disease domain:* There are no measures specifically for recreational therapy. An example is measurement of change in edema in a limb using a tape measure or volume of water displaced.
- *Measures for impairment:* Includes test of muscle strength, joint range of motion, sensibility, coordination/dexterity, memory, cognition, attention span.
- *Disability/functional limitation:* The field of recreational therapy has a variety of tools which can measure functional ability pre- and post-treatment.

Some of the tools include the twenty-two pre- and post-test functional measures found in the *Community Integration Program, Second Edition (CIP)* by Armstrong and Lauzen (1994), the *Bus Utilization Scale* (BUS) by burlingame (1989) and the *CERT-Psych./Revised* by Parker (1997). All three are testing tools used to measure the patient's functional status. There are also some interdisciplinary tools which are available as software packages. These include the Functional Independence Measure (FIM) (State University of New York Research Foundation, 1987), Minimum Data Set (MDS), Functional Assessment Scale from the Rehabilitation Institute of Chicago (RIC-FAS) (1992), and the SF-36 from Medical Outcomes Trust (1990) which is a measurement of quality of life. The *Leisure Competency Measure* (Kloseck, Crilly, Ellis, Lammers, 1996) is specifically developed as an outcomes measure. This testing tool is not intended to be an assessment used face-to-face with the patient, but a tool which summarizes the data obtained from the patient's assessment, allowing comparisons from pre- and post-treatment, from patient to patient, unit to unit and facility to facility.

- *Measures for handicap:* Determination about the presence of a handicap in all of the seven areas of handicap requires the therapist to evaluate all the information s/he has on the patient. The World Health Organization recommends that practitioners use the scales contained in *The International Classification of Impairments, Disabilities and Handicaps* (1980) to make a determination of handicap. (See Chapter 6, *Clinical Practice Models.*)

Forming Research Questions

An important aspect of measuring outcomes is to select the right research questions. Most outcome research studies are designed to help guide improvements in an existing program. The majority of questions you will ask will fall into one of three standard questions:

1. *Are we achieving our goals?* (Is this patient or group of patients achieving his/her or their therapy goals? Is this program or facility achieving its goals?)
2. *Are we worth it?* (Was the therapy effort worth it for this patient? Did s/he get the right level of care? Was the care cost-effective?)
3. *Are we better than the alternative?* (Was the program better than no program or better than somebody else's program? Is our facility doing better than the facility across town?)

Notice that these three questions can be used in a variety of ways: to compare patient to patient outcomes, diagnostic group to diagnostic group or facility to facility.

Once you have decided on the question(s) you want to ask, the next step is to decide what independent variables you should measure. Independent variables are also known as "input data elements." Since you want something that will help explain the pattern of outcomes, you will want to look for variables that are related to, or might contribute to, the outcomes. You are looking for factors whose presence or absence will influence outcome and red flags that might present barriers to rehabilitation. This knowledge will allow you to establish divisions of your population requiring distinct levels or intensities of care, with different outcome expectations.

Look in the literature for your diagnostic groups to pick out things that might influence outcomes for this population. Don't forget the insurance literature. This information may come through partnerships with insurance companies. Research can provide severity indicators.

An example of a severity indicator is to examine what factors impact the patient's recovery from injuries received at work. Severity indicators may include stress on the job or pre-existing depression or somatization disorder, and history of prior claims. You can also select elements from the patient's initial assessment to divide a population. Harada et al. (1993) and Stineman et al. (1994) showed that using the FIM (Functional Independence Measure) helped distinguish patient populations requiring different levels of care.

Organizing an Outcome Database

An outcome database (as shown in Figure 12.3) is the combination of information on many patients put together to analyze the information more easily. The outcome database will have three parts: (1) input data, (2) process data and (3) outcome data.

Basically, you collect data by diagnostic or impairment categories based on patient characteristics and then measure functional status at admission, discharge and post discharge. You can then statistically look at outcome ranges for patients with similar characteristics, and possibly generate a model to predict expected outcome for future patients who are similar to the study population.

Input Data

Your input data elements are independent variables. These data elements are crucial to explain the pattern of outcomes so that you know what to do with the outcome information in your program.

Figure 12.3: **Anatomy of a Database**

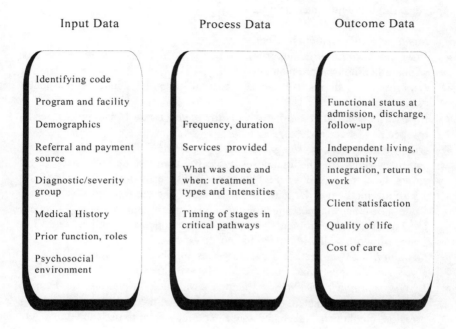

Input Data   Process Data   Outcome Data

Identifying code

Program and facility

Demographics   Frequency, duration

Referral and payment   Services provided
source
                        What was done and
Diagnostic/severity   when: treatment
group   types and intensities

Medical History   Timing of stages in
                         critical pathways
Prior function, roles

Psychosocial
environment

Functional status at
admission, discharge,
follow-up

Independent living,
community
integration, return to
work

Client satisfaction

Quality of life

Cost of care

© 1995 Linda O. Niemeyer

Why do you need to have patient characteristics in a database? You need to put enough patient information in so you can retrieve important information. The information you might want includes:

- Which patient groups do best with specific treatment protocols?
- Which patient groups should not take part in certain programs?
- Are the scores on the CERT Psych/R good indicators for success in certain programs?
- What is the readmission rate of patients who have completed the different treatment protocols?
- What is the back-to-work rate for patients who complete certain protocols?
- Which patients report better short term and long term satisfaction with their treatment?

To obtain this information your database has to be flexible enough for you to divide the data by patient diagnosis, by treatment received, by assessment results, by length of stay, etc. When you sort the data in these various ways, patterns of results may turn up which you did not expect. The following types of input data might go into the database.

- *Identifying code*: patient number
- *Program and facility*: important if research includes several programs within a facility or more than one facility
- *Demographics:* things like age, sex, marital status, ethnicity, religion, education
- *Referral and payment source*: who is the payer, type of insurance, referral by specialty, specific doctor
- *Diagnostic and/or severity group.* You can use the DRG or ICD-9 classification systems for the diagnoses typically seen. Some diagnoses (e.g., stroke, head injury, MI, COPD) have medical severity codes like grade I, II, III; small, medium or large (infarct); or scales like the Rancho Los Amigos Scale. For other diagnoses a skilled clinician might assign a level of severity. For orthopedic problems you may use an impairment rating. The FIM scale will work well with many diagnostic groups.
- *Medical history*: time since onset, surgeries, number of admissions
- *Prior function*: customary roles, residential status
- *Psychosocial/environment*: social support systems (you can use the Family APGAR scale, Smilkstein, 1978), functionality of the family, history of depression, alcoholism, substance abuse. You may want to use the Global Assessment of Functioning (*DSM-IV*, American Psychiatric Association, 1994) or the Global Assessment of Leisure Functioning (Dehn, 1995).

Process Data

Your process data elements are the change factors of treatment. Relating interventions to outcome is the missing piece in most systems. This is the next big frontier in outcome measurement systems. Process data elements include four primary areas: (1) frequency/duration, (2) services provided, (3) treatment types and intensities and (4) critical pathways.

- *Frequency, duration*: The most basic measurement of process. Frequency describes how many visits, over how many weeks. Duration describes the length of time for the visits.
- *Services provided:* Who saw the patient (e.g., OT, PT, RT, SLP)? Did the patient participate in any special services like return-to-work or location-specific community integration training?
- *Treatment types and intensities*: This is where data collection begins to be a challenge. The National Center for Medical Rehabilitation Research

(NCMRR), a new grant agency within the National Institute of Health (NIH), supports this measurement as an overriding need in all of rehabilitation. Here is an opportunity to look at billing and treatment coding systems to see if there is a way to refine or add onto the codes to better describe the definition of the treatment provided. An example would be dividing your exercise program into steps, stages or types and then adding a dot or dash and a number or letter to the end of the code used for exercise group.

- *Critical pathways*: There are many critical pathway methodologies. This work is just starting to take off. In the simplest sense, a critical pathway defines steps in a process of rehabilitation and outlines the timing of the steps for a patient going through the process. The simplest documentation is to look at whether certain critical processes or steps happen for a given patient and when, and to what extent there is variation from the expected path. A research question might be, *do people with more steps or who are given different interventions have better or worse outcomes*? An example might be the use of the *Community Integration Program, Second Edition* by Armstrong and Lauzen (1994) with adults with head injuries. Let's say that your critical pathway called for patients to go through Modules 1A (Environmental Safety), 1B (Emergency Preparedness), Module 4E (City Bus) and Module 6A (Independent Plan). Would your patients who are homeless do better or worse if Module 1C (Basic Survival Skills) was substituted for Module 4E? When there is a mismatch, do we alter the pathway? The best way to answer these questions is to use your process data along with your outcome data.

Outcome Data

The traditional dependent variable is the change in functional status at admission, discharge and follow-up. We might also compare functional status outcomes between populations with different characteristics or between facilities.

There are newer outcome measures we need to add to this list. It is becoming more important to document what happened to the patient in the community beyond the doors of the program. (We will come back to this.) Outcome data should include something about independent living, community integration and living arrangements. Your measurements should include the degree to which the patient was able to get out in the community after receiving your services.

Consumer satisfaction is an outcome just as much as functional status or return home because health care is becoming increasingly consumer-driven. There are two parts to measure concerning consumer satisfaction. The first is whether s/he was satisfied with "customer service" while in the program: were people competent, polite and did they listen? The second is whether s/he is satisfied with the degree to which his/her own outcome goals were achieved.

Relating outcomes to cost may be more crucial for the provider than for the purchasers. The provider needs to know how much it is costing to provide services for particular types of individuals compared to what is charged and/or paid for the service. This relates directly to resource management and to economic survival.

Collecting and Analyzing Data

Data Coding

The ability to examine the data requires that it be in a form that can analyzed. All the data will need to be reduced to some type of numerical coding system. The system you use will be determined by the type of data you are collecting. Some coding will be dictated by the scoring system of particular measures that you are using (e.g., the Likert scale used on the Idyll Arbor Leisure Battery, Ragheb & Beard, 1991). Also be cognizant of the type of statistical analysis you plan to do. Make sure that the data form chosen will work well with the statistical model you will be using.

You will have three basic "types" of coding styles to choose from: (1) nominal or naming, (2) ordinal or rank order or (3) interval and ratio scales as shown in Table 12.2.

Nominal or naming codes include classification or categorization coding such as "yes/no" questions and "male/female" data. You may also be gathering data which include names, such as the names of insurance companies or facility names or types (e.g., nursing homes, general medical hospitals, schools or day treatment centers). A number can be assigned to each category to facilitate analysis. Some data, such as diagnostic groupings already have a numbering system in the ICD-9-CM diagnostic codes. Nominal or naming coding lends itself to both descriptive statistics (mode or median as central tendency, frequency distribution, percent distribution) and comparative statistics (contingency table, generating a Chi-square value, contingency coefficient).

Ordinal or rank order codes are a series of classifications indicating an increasing or decreasing magnitude. Examples would be the 1-5 muscle test categories used by physical and occupational therapy, 1-7 FIM rating scales and various severity categories such as the Rancho Los Amigos scale for recovery after a head injury. Ordinal or rank order codes lend themselves to both descriptive statistics (mode or median, frequency distribution, percent distribution) and comparative statistics (Mann-Whitney U test, Kolmogorov-Smirnov two-sample test, Kruskal-Wallis one-way analysis of variance, Spearman rank correlation coefficient and Kendall rank correlation coefficient).

Interval and ratio scales are a series of classifications where there is an equal interval between each group. A ratio scale is an interval scale which has a zero point. Interval scales include the number of admissions, number of patients taken out on community integration trips per month, time from onset to admission, age of patients, number of questions answered correctly in a *CIP* pre-test. Interval scales lend themselves to both descriptive statistics (mean, standard deviation, variance) and comparative statistics (T-test, ANOVA, correlation coefficient, multiple regression, higher-order statistical analyses). You can also translate raw scores from different measures into scale scores based on deviations from the mean and then compare different measures.

Table 12.2: **Ways of Coding Data and Statistical Options**

Type of Coding	Nominal, Categorical	Ordinal Rank Order	Interval or Ratio
Examples	yes/no, ICD-9 diagnostic codes, type of insurance, male/female	1-5 muscle test categories, 1-7 FIM rating scale, level of severity categories, Rancho Los Amigos Scale	number of admissions, number of outings, age, time from onset to admission, answers correct on CIP pre-test, SF-36 1-100 scale
Definition	Numbers are used to designate classification of an object, person or characteristic.	A series of classifications indicating an increasing or decreasing magnitude. Numbers indicate a rank order classification, but not an amount.	The distances between any two numbers on a scale are equal. The numbers actually indicate a value. Ratio scale starts with zero.
Statistical Options	**Descriptive:** mode, median, frequency distribution, percent distribution. **Comparative:** contingency table, Chi Square, contingency coefficient.	**Descriptive:** mode, median, frequency distribution, percent distribution. **Comparative:** Mann-Whitney U test, Kolmogorov-Smirnov two-sample test, Kruskal-Wallis one-way analysis of variance, Spearman rank correlation coefficient, Kendall rank correlation coefficient.	**Descriptive:** mean, standard deviation, variance. **Comparative:** T-test analysis, correlation coefficient, multiple regression, higher-order statistics.

When you develop your coding system, think practically. Use a category grouping system which will be the most useful to you. In other words, develop coding categories which can be used in a variety of situations and which staff can easily understand.

Many therapists use the Module 1A: Environmental Safety protocol from the *Community Integration Program, Second Edition (CIP)*. Part of the protocol requires the patient to read a set of pathfinding instructions like the sample below.

1. From the Emergency entrance of the hospital, go North on 9th, crossing Jefferson and James. Then stop.
2. On the corner of James and 9th, facing East (toward the corner store), cross the street and turn left. Stop.
3. Proceed three blocks, turn right, and walk two blocks. Stop.
4. Cross Boren, turn right, and proceed to James. Stop.
5. Give the card back to the therapist.

Once the therapist and the patient have followed all of the steps on the card, and the therapist has the card back, s/he instructs the patient to retrace his/her steps back to the emergency room entrance. Encoding the data from a group of patients to compare scores could help the therapist anticipate which diagnostic groups are more likely to fail this pathfinding test and which ones will need more therapy time (or memory books). Encoding the data using a system of pass/fail on specific functions versus pass/fail on counting the blocks from "James" or reading the name "Jefferson" may make the data more useful. Some of the data to be collected could include the ability to ambulate, the ability to distinguish left and right, the ability to read the steps in sequence, the ability to count blocks, the number of errors and staff cues required to return to the hospital, etc. The *CIP* itself has 20 specific skills already outlined on the behavioral checklist. The instructions give the therapist the option of using a +/- coding system or FIM scale. The +/- system gives a nominal score for each skill. A FIM scale is ordinal data, more detailed than the simple +/-. You could also record the total number of skills demonstrated which is an example of ratio data. What you choose to record depends on how you want to analyze the information.

Data Collection and Inputting

The next step is to decide how you will collect and input the data. You have four questions to answer before you can resolve the collection and input problem.

- *Will you use a prospective or a retrospective method of data collection?* Prospective data collection is the collection of data as the event happens. Retrospective data collection is the collection of data after the patient has been discharged.
- *What type of form or chart will you use to record the data?* Most therapists use a data input form. Make sure that your data input form matches your medical chart forms as much as possible for ease of extracting the data without leafing through the chart. You can also design chart forms that double as data input forms. The fewer times the data is copied, the more efficient and less open to errors your data collection is.
- *Who will input the data into the computer?* Your typical choices are clerical or therapy staff. Clerical staff will usually be faster and make fewer errors. Therapists may not have time for data input, but will be better at coding or rating medical information. You could split the task between the two different types of staff.
- *Can you use a system which allows the direct transfer of data?* The automatic transfer of information from charting done on the computer to a database is probably the most efficient means of data collection and causes the fewest amount of errors. (That is, as long as the database system itself is well-written and error free.) This kind of system also allows your patients to answer questionnaires directly on a computer.

Having the data on the computer helps expedite your analysis. But how are you going to analyze the data? You may use existing software packages like SPSS, Statview or SIS Plus. Or you may input your data into a spreadsheet like Excel or a database like Access (Microsoft) or Paradox (Borland). Data contained in databases can be sorted and rearranged. Portions can be selected and saved as text and then imported into a statistical program. You can always start this way and upgrade your software later. Some spreadsheets have statistical analysis functions and charting functions built in. Another choice is to employ an analysis service to "crunch" your data for you.

Displaying Data

Once you have analyzed your data, you will want to display it in a manner that can be easily understood. Consider who will be reviewing the data. Some people relate to tables better than to graphic presentations. Many of the computer programs generate the charts and graphs you need without having to re-enter the data. Below are some examples of charts and graphs which help present outcome data.

Figure 12.4 shows two tables which illustrate one technique of displaying your data using tables. Figure 12.5 shows an example of a Spider-Web Profile using the FIM scale (1-7 scale) to compare the patient's functional ability at admission and discharge.

Figure 12.4: **Displaying data using tables**

Contingency Table

X (Columns): Cumulative Trauma? 1 = yes, 2 = no
Y (Rows): 1 = male, 2 = female   Total Chi Square = 23.151
Degree of Freedom = 1   p = 1.000E -4
Contingency Coefficient = .374

	1	2		
1	33.18	42.82	76	**Expected**
2	28.82	37.18	66	**Frequencies**
	62	80		

		1	2	
Observed	1	19	57	76
Frequencies	2	43	23	66
		62	80	

Figure 12.5: **Spider-Web Profile**

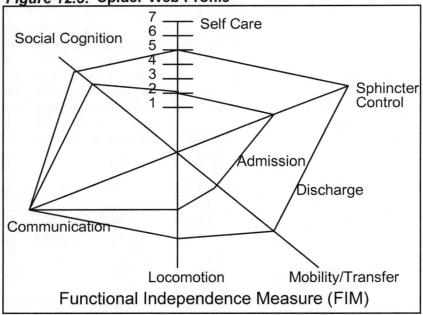

Functional Independence Measure (FIM)

Trouble-Shooting

What do you do if the results don't look right, are not what you wanted or what you expected? First, look for an error in your data. Sort columns and look for numbers that don't seem to fit. If the problem does not seem to be in the translation of the data into the database, look for problems related to staff training, the measurement tool selected or the design study. Were the therapists and data entry people adequately trained in how to rate or code data? Is their reliability good? Were errors made in the data entry itself? Was there a problem with the measurement? Was it not sensitive to the changes that needed to be detected? Look at the case mix. Was the population too heterogeneous so that meaningful differences were buried or exaggerated? For example, maybe one program had a greater number of difficult or severe cases than another, so their outcomes appeared poorer. Or maybe there was a difference in acute versus cumulative trauma between the groups. Maybe scores were aggregated that should have been separated. For example, a composite score for function which combines mobility, Activities of Daily Living (ADL) and cognition cannot be meaningfully averaged. Also, while some therapists use the total score on the Free Time Boredom Scale, the use of the subscores tends to be much more useful in pinpointing problematic areas.

Summary

The ongoing measurement of outcomes is as much a part of the therapist's job as patient assessment, patient treatment and documentation. Using established measurement tools (and the development of other tools as needed), the therapist measures outcomes in an ongoing process of inputting data, processing data and then analyzing data. This process allows the therapist to use this information as part of the facility's strategic planning framework. The purpose of this strategic planning is to encourage outcome-oriented collaborative care which, in turn, produces the win-win situation of system empowerment. System empowerment allows the provision of quality services and promotes the ongoing fiscal health of the facility.

Learning Activities

1. Develop a mock-up of a patient data base for just one patient which reflects all three levels of data. Use resources such as the DSM IV (*Diagnostic and Statistical Manual of Mental Disorders, Fourth Edition*), a CPT (Current Procedural Terminology) Code Book and journal articles in your chosen specific diagnostic group, etc. to develop as realistic a data base as possible. Write it up as a case study.

2.   Divide the class into two groups. Each groups is to develop a "treatment plan" to teach the members of the other group a new skill (e.g., dance, card game). Prior to implementing the "treatment plan" have a form to document data from all three levels (input, process and outcome). Determine what type of data coding you will use. Run the "treatment plan" and then analyze your data. Show at least two different ways to display your data.

Study Questions

1.   Explain the different ways outcome data is used in health care.
2.   What is the process for designing an outcome study?
3.   At what level(s) of the WHO's ICIDH Model would the therapist be most likely to use a clinical test? A skilled observer test? Why?
4.   What are the different types of coding styles you can choose for your outcome data? Give five examples of data (e.g., frequency of re-admission due to skin breakdown) for each of the three coding styles.
5.   What do you do if the results from your collected data don't look right?

References

American Psychiatric Association. (1994). *Diagnostic and statistical manual of mental disorders* (4th ed.). Washington, DC: Author.

Armstrong, M. & Lauzen, S. (1994). *Community integration program* (2nd ed.). Ravensdale, WA: Idyll Arbor, Inc.

burlingame, j. (1989). *Bus utilization screening tool (BUS)*. Ravensdale, WA: Idyll Arbor, Inc.

Dehn, D. (1995). *Leisure step up*. Ravensdale, WA: Idyll Arbor, Inc.

Framrose, A. (1995). 24-hour managed care: A conversation with Tom Chapman. *Rehab Management, 8*(2), 51-52, 54, 56-57, 131.

Harada, N. D., Kominski, G. & Sofaer, S. (1993). Development of a resource-based patient classification scheme for rehabilitation. *Inquiry, 30*, 54-63.

Kloseck, M., Crilly, R., Ellis, G. & Lammers, E. (1996). Leisure Competence Measure: Development and reliability testing of a scale to measure functional outcomes in therapeutic recreation. *Therapeutic Recreation Journal, 30*(1), 13-26.

Manton, K. G., Newcomer, R., Vertrees, J. C., Lowrimore, G. R. & Harrington, C. (1994). A method for adjusting capitation payments to managed care plans using multivariate patterns of health and functioning: The experience of social/health maintenance organizations. *Medical Care, 32*(3), 277-297.

Medical Outcomes Trust. (1990). *SF (MOS 36 item short form)*. Boston, MA: Medical Outcomes Trust.

Parker, R. (1997). *Comprehensive evaluation in recreational therapy, Psych./Revised. (CERT Psych/R)*. Ravensdale, WA: Idyll Arbor, Inc.

Ragheb, M. G. & Beard, J. G. (1991). *Idyll Arbor leisure battery*. Ravensdale, WA: Idyll Arbor, Inc.

Rehabilitation Institute of Chicago. (1992, September). *Rehabilitation Institute of Chicago functional assessment scale*. Chicago: Rehabilitation Institute of Chicago.

Smilkstein, G. (1978). The family APGAR: A proposal for a family function test and its use by physicians. *Journal of Family Practice, 6*, 1231-1239.

State University of New York Research Foundation. (1987). *FIM Scale*. In j. burlingame & T. Skalko. (1997). *Idyll Arbor's glossary for therapists* (p. 116). Ravensdale, WA: Idyll Arbor, Inc.

Stineman, M. G., Escarce, J. J., Goin, J. E., Hamilton, B. B., Granger, C. V. & Williams, S. V. (1994). A case-mix classification system for medical rehabilitation. *Medical Care, 32*(4), 366-379.

Verbrugge, L. M. & Jette, A. M. (1994). The disablement process. *Social Science and Medicine, 38*(1), 1-14.

World Health Organization. (1980). *International classification of impairments, disabilities and handicaps*. Geneva: World Health Organization.

Section IV

Issues of Consumers

Chapter 13

Customer Service

joan burlingame

Customer service is a relatively new management concept for health care. During the past few decades health care has been concerned with improving the quality of services provided to the consumer but customer service, while related, is not the same thing. Work on improving quality of service has led to new theories, standards and, most importantly, ways to measure the quality of services provided. Now the health care industry, driven by increasing competition for limited health care dollars, is looking at the concepts of customer service and customer satisfaction to increase its ability to attract and keep health care customers. Today the health care industry is in the early developmental stages of understanding customer service from a management standpoint.

The business world has long worked on the concept of customer service and is far ahead of the health care industry concerning theories, models and measurement. Health care is a service industry and, as such, must be careful to adapt the correct models from business in its quest for improved customer service. Industry and manufacturing are not good models, but retail sales seems like it can provide some valuable ideas. There are differences, of course, so modifications to standard models and measurements of customer service will need to be developed specifically for health care. Some of what health care has learned about quality assurance can also help with the development of models of customer service, but it is important to understand that quality assurance is not the same thing as customer service. burlingame and Skalko (1997) define quality assurance as

The way in which a facility (1) identifies (potential) problems, (2) determines a systematic way to decrease the problems and (3) monitors the success of the facility in decreasing the problems. The purpose of a quality assurance program is to safeguard and improve the quality of care each patient receives. (burlingame & Skalko, 1997, p. 213)

Customer service, on the other hand, is broadly defined as whatever it takes to make a customer satisfied. Davidow and Uttal state that "satisfaction, or lack of it, is the difference between how a customer *expects* to be treated and how he or she *perceives* being treated" (Davidow & Uttal, 1989, p. 19). That leads to three questions which this chapter will address: How are health care professionals going to measure the differences between expectations and perceptions, allowing changes in the way services are provided? What components make a good customer service program? How do health care services work as a business and provide good customer service with all of the regulations and standards imposed upon them?

Health Care as a Business

When people mention the need to treat health care as a business, a distaste is often felt. It seems almost sacrilegious to treat an area which deals with life and death as a seemingly cold, indifferent monster concerned only with the "bottom line." But, in reality, there are some reasons for doing just that. Not only are we dealing with people's well-being and lives, but also with the need to perpetuate a system which can bring healing. Our health care system in the United States seems to be like a family who is always in dire need of consumer debt counseling and, because of that, putting health care on a business footing may not be a bad idea. Still we have the concern that business is cold and unfeeling. Perhaps this perception of business is the problem. Health care as a business does not need to be unfeeling. In fact, many very successful businesses prosper because they are able to provide services in a customer-friendly manner. What could be the problem is the manner in which those who work in health care provide the "business" of health care. While watching the bottom line and use of resources is important, equally important is the treatment of the consumer himself/herself. Does providing good customer service require over-extending health care resources? Does customer satisfaction increase in proportion to the amount of services provided? Or would better tailoring of services both save money and increase satisfaction?

Health care is clearly an industry. Health care expenditures in the United States tops $666 billion dollars a year (1990). Compare that expenditure with the amount we spend on automobiles ($132 billion a year, 1990) and clothing ($94 billion a year, 1990) and it is easy to see that health care is a huge industry (Kurian, 1994). While health care is in the business of providing services to modify the health status of its customers, compared to other industries it only gives "lip service" to customer service. Part of the reason for this "lip service" is because the concept of customer service has been, up to now, left relatively undefined in modern health care.

Surprisingly little has been published concerning customer satisfaction with recreational therapy services in the last decade. The most notable piece of literature on customer satisfaction was by Rhodes (1991). In his chapter he discussed the use of patient satisfaction data as part of a quality assurance program which was measuring treatment outcomes. Since 1991 the two primary journals in recreational therapy (the *Therapeutic Recreation Journal* and the *Annual in Therapeutic Recreation*) had only one article which focused on patient satisfaction (Leonard & Schwind, 1996).

Another reason for lip service is because of the overwhelming amount of regulatory and voluntary oversight into how health care is delivered. Health care is a highly regulated field, allowing only limited flexibility to staff. While the trend in the last five years has been to move away from prescriptive standards (standards which stated how health care was to function), the newer, outcome-oriented approaches still contain a large amount of prescriptive rules. It is hard to be flexible to meet the needs of a divergent patient population while following prescriptive rules.

An example of this limitation due to regulations occurred when the author was working as a surveyor for the state of Washington. The state of Washington is in Region Ten of the Health Care Financing Administration. Also in Region Ten is the state of Alaska. An immediate jeopardy citation was leveled against a nursing home in Alaska because of some dead, unskinned, ungutted animals being stored in the walk-in refrigerator. The residents in the nursing home were primarily from the local Inuit tribe. The activity professional had scheduled an animal skinning and gutting contest the next day at the request of the residents. A local hunter had trapped and killed the animals needed for the next day's contest and the animals were being stored in the walk-in refrigerator. As luck would have it, the state survey team walked in the morning of the skinning contest to find the dead animals oozing some body fluids onto the floor of the walk-in refrigerator. Citing a grave threat to resident safety due to the contamination in the walk-in, the clock started ticking for a threatened shut-down of the facility. By offering the requested activity, the activity professional was treating the residents in the culturally sensitive manner in which they expected to be treated. The residents' perceptions were that such activities as the skinning and gutting contests provided them with a portion of what it took to make them (the customers) satisfied. However, the desired activity was carried out in such a manner as to violate one of the many regulations which dictate what goes on (and what doesn't go on) in health care.

Components of Customer Service

One of the current mantras of health care is "customer service." But what is customer service? Is it as simple as polling patients about what they liked, didn't like or wanted to be different about their experience? Or is it so complex that good customer service may be beyond the reach of many facilities?

Many health care facilities have been able to provide good customer service in the past, but little formal structure has been offered to provide a systematic approach to providing good customer service. With cost containment pressures being felt throughout health care, concerns have developed that important aspects of customer service are being lost to cost cutting. Health care, becoming increasingly a business versus a fiduciary relationship between provider and patient, is looking toward management techniques to provide structure. Just as the development of formalized quality control systems received definition from leaders such as Deming, Juran and Crosby, formalized systems of customer service are being developed today. Davidow and Uttal (1989) divided customer service into six components. By using these six components, health care providers will able to develop statistical and organizational methods to quantify customer service. The six components of customer service are strategy, design, infrastructure, leadership, personnel and measurement.

Strategy

The first step toward organizing a facility's customer service program is to develop a strategy. No health care system can be everything for everybody. By focusing resources into packaged services, the facility tends to produce better customer satisfaction (Davidow & Uttal, 1989). Taking a "shotgun approach" and trying to cover all services desired by patients will stretch the facility's budget and other resources so thinly that it cannot provide a good product. Many people in health care are aware of this and are grouping similar services together into a package now. "Re-engineering" departments such as the recreational therapy department into service units such as rehab services is based on the strategy of product packaging. Grouping rehabilitation services in one place and general medicine services in another tends to lead to better customer satisfaction than mixing differing needs together. However, for the professionals within each treatment team, this re-engineering can produce significant stress, as it isolates the professional groups in different services from their peers at the facility. Some facilities are attempting to deal with this by having peer group meetings (e.g., all the recreational therapists within the facility) in addition to service unit meetings (all the treatment professionals working on the unit).

Matching the facility's service abilities to the expectations of the patients it decides to target may be a good strategy (at least from a business standpoint, not always from a humanitarian viewpoint). An example of business not planning for customer satisfaction is when the facility plans a strategy to draw patients who have good health insurance policies over those who do not. That facility is matching an expectation of the business owners (bottom line economics) instead of the expectations of the customer.

Recreational therapists who function within a facility may need to evaluate the services that they can provide and, instead of taking a shotgun approach, develop a strategy to target the patient groups which they can serve the best. Yes, a recreational therapist can offer treatment beneficial to a woman on prolonged bedrest due to complications of pregnancy. But a broader range of services can usually be offered to patients on the rehabilitation unit. Developing a strategic plan for the delivery of recreational therapy services is not only a good business decision but a good customer service decision. Developing the department's strategic plan requires a knowledgeable, flexible staff, an awareness of customer expectation, strong leadership and coordination with other team members.

Leadership

The best customer service tends to be possible when the staff having face-to-face contact with the customer have the greatest discretion to modify the service or product to meet that specific customer's needs. The type of leadership which promotes this must be willing to let go of a top-down management style and trust each staff person's judgment.

When trying to define what types of services and attitudes lead to outstanding customer service, it is best to examine a company which is world renowned for its customer service. A handful of companies are well known for their customer service including Westinghouse, Motorola and Federal Express, but almost without question, Nordstrom is identified as the world leader in providing good customer service.

Nordstrom is a department store which originated in Seattle, Washington. Providing customer service is not a new idea, but Nordstrom has clearly defined today's standard. Today, Nordstrom is the measure of customer service to which all other companies are compared and few, if any, come close. Why is that? How has the Nordstrom family defined and implemented customer service to become the world's benchmark?

The Nordstrom family, now with its third generation of family running the business, has always been strong on customer service. One of the Nordstromisms for which they are so famous is "We out service, not out smart." The two elements which Nordstrom feels are key to providing good service are, first and foremost, a workforce which is motivated to walk the extra mile to satisfy a customer (the personnel component) and, second, the materials the workforce needs to provide that service (a broad range of items and a culture which encourages the entrepreneurial spirit of the motivated staff).

Nordstrom feels that providing good customer service can only be achieved if every employee, from the top down, supports that goal. It is not enough to have the staff smile and treat the customers with courtesy. Employees must be empowered by their supervisors to provide the depth of service required to satisfy the customer. This type of company philosophy requires an attitude that the short term cost may be greater than desired, but the long term outcome will be financial security for the company. Some may argue that such an attitude would never work in health care because of the competitive nature of today's health care environment. But isn't the retail industry just as competitive? When employees take the personal responsibility to satisfy the customer's needs within the customer's budget, with the courtesy that goes along with good customer service, the customer tends to feel that s/he is dealing with an owner of the business. And the employee, feeling ownership in the company, has a vested interest in taking actions which help guarantee the long term health of the company.

The "Nordstrom Way" is to empower all their employees with the right, and the responsibility, to make decisions. This action requires that management is willing to live with those decisions. Jamie Baugh, an executive vice-president with Nordstrom, states, "Giving away responsibility and authority is the ultimate expression of leadership. At Nordstrom, we create an environment for empowerment. We assemble a team and allow them to fail, but obviously, we're there for them when they need us" (Spector & McCarthy, 1995, p. 25). This type of leadership also requires employees who are willing to set high goals for themselves and the company. New employees at Nordstrom all receive the following greeting from Nordstrom management:

> We're glad to have you with our Company. Our number one goal is to provide outstanding customer service. Set both your personal and professional goals high. We have great confidence in your ability to achieve them. Nordstrom Rules: *Rule #1: Use your good judgment in all situations. There will be no additional rules.* Please feel free to ask your department manager, store manager or division general manager any questions at any time. (Spector & McCarthy, 1995, pp. 15-16)

The first Nordstrom store was opened in 1910 and the company has continued to grow since that time, despite the volatile ups and downs of the retail industry. Its strength is a result of the care it takes in hiring its employees and its realization that the future of the company lies in the hands of the employees who have direct face-to-face contact with their customers. While many managers would feel uncomfortable having only one rule (as Nordstrom does), this rule has worked well for Nordstrom. Nordstrom has many keys to success, all of which support their rule. Some of their keys to success are listed in Table 13.1

Design

Products and services should be designed from the beginning to make access to and use of the services and products easy, with little "down time" due to being out of service or otherwise not functioning. In health care, the products the therapist provides are primarily services. The environment to offer a quality product (therapy services) is created by the facility for which the therapist works through the facility's commitment to standards developed by the Joint Commission on Accreditation of Healthcare Organizations (JCAHO) and CARF: The Rehabilitation Accreditation Commission. The therapist also has his/her professional standards of practice to draw from. All of these standards, along with the company's actions in hiring qualified staff, create the environment for the therapist to "out serve, not out smart" the competition.

Designing access to quality recreational therapy services must be a critical and ongoing process. Recreational therapy services should be based on the pa-

Table 13.1: **Keys to Success** (Spector & McCarthy, 1995)

- Nordstrom empowers its employees with the freedom to make decisions, and is willing to live with those decisions. Delegating authority and accountability is the ultimate expression of leadership. (p. 35)
- Because Nordstrom pushes decision-making responsibilities down to the sales floor, shopping with a Nordstrom salesperson is like working with the owner of a small business. (p. 35)
- Nordstrom is informally organized as an "inverted pyramid," with the top positions occupied by the customers and the salespeople, and the bottom position filled by the co-chairmen. Every tier of the pyramid supports the sales staff. (p. 129)
- All managers are hired from the sales floor. Nordstrom has created, through expansion, fast career tracks for energetic, entrepreneurial people, who are rewarded for their performance with advancement and increased responsibility. Promoting from within is an essential ingredient in Nordstrom's success.
- Nordstrom doesn't acquire other chains (or parts of chains) and convert them to Nordstrom stores because it is too difficult for those employees to break old habits. A distinctive culture separates Nordstrom from the competition. When the company expands to other regions, it dispatches an advanced force of veteran "Nordies" who carry the culture with them and impart it to new employees. (p. 95)

tient's assessed needs with all treatment being geared to address at least one of the assessed needs. While many activities may be fun, the therapist must strive to make the activity "count" by using activities which are very likely to achieve the desired effect within a reasonable amount of time. All treatment should be clearly addressing and solving problems which the patient (and/or his/her significant others) have. As treatment progresses, it should follow a logical flow with each session building upon the last. Each session should be planned to allow the patient to assume the greatest degree of control possible within his/her own comfort level. And, as much as possible, treatment should be available to the patient on a schedule which is convenient for him/her.

Fitting the intervention to the customer's expectations means that standardized approaches will need to be modified to meet the patient's unique situation while still maintaining the integrity and quality of the intervention. Salcido (1997) addresses this when he writes:

> Function and usability are important to a consumer. To a small child, it means the ability to play, crawl and investigate his or her world (habitation). To a teenager, it may mean the ability to blend in. To an adult, it might mean returning to work, the ability to care for oneself, or becoming independent. Cultural issue and norms should be considered as well. In many Native American cultures, for example, independence is not valued as highly as interdependence. Therefore, outcomes should be viewed as age-, gender- and culture-specific. (Salcido, 1997, p. 50)

Designing a quality product requires that the therapist and the entire treatment team keep their focus on the patient and his/her perceived needs, not just on what research and practice have previously dictated. Recently the National Rehabilitation Hospital in Washington, DC reported an embarrassing example of health care providers not paying attention to their customer's individual desires and needs. They found that a large majority of equipment issued to patients was abandoned within one month (Salcido, 1997). This leads to the question of whether the equipment (and the therapy sessions which supported the issuance of the equipment) were meeting the therapist's or the patient's ideas of what was needed and practical.

To maximize the patient's experience and to achieve the patient's desires, coordination with other team members will be critical. This may mean that the physical therapist works in coordination with the recreational therapist to ensure that a wheelchair selected for the patient's use also allows the patient to engage in his/her normal leisure activities. Or that the recreational therapist supports the patient and nursing to modify a treatment schedule to allow dressing changes. Nordstrom staff are well aware of the need to work with staff from different departments and instead of begrudging the need to pass the customer on to another department, they do so with a positive attitude. That is what good customer service is about — meeting the customer's needs.

The sales staff at Nordstrom are provided with quality products by their management. Each sales person not only knows the products within his/her own department but also has a working knowledge of the products offered by other departments. After the salesperson determines what the customer perceives s/he needs (and what s/he does not want), the sales person can begin to provide the customer with what s/he wants. This may include combining items from the sales person's own department with items from other departments. The sales person does not resist asking another sales person to help out. Since Nordstrom staff work on commission, in the short run the sales person would receive a reduced commission. But if s/he makes the customer happy, the customer will come as regular customer, increasing the sale person's long term income. To be able to provide this cross department, or "seamless" customer service, the facility must have an infrastructure which allows this coordination between disciplines.

Infrastructures

Support, both in human resources and physical structures, should be well thought out to provide efficient and timely support for the services and products. Infrastructure includes staff education, building space, support staff and adequate supplies. Motorola, a company long recognized as a leader in customer service, has the philosophy that "there are two kinds of people who work at Motorola — people who serve customers and people who serve people who serve customers" (Bruner, Eaker, Freeman, Spekman & Olmsted-Teisberg, 1998, p. 105). In business, the process of overseeing the transformation of all of the products (services) into the final product (health care) is called operations management. The emphasis of the operations manager impacts all areas of service, including customer service. If the operations manager's emphasis is to obtain the best "bottom line" (profit), all support services, room allocations and priority will be given to saving and making money. The customer will find longer waits for service, limited service and limited access to service. If, on the other hand, the operations manager's emphasis is on providing good customer service, all support services, room allocations and priority will be given to matching the patient's treatment with his/her expectations.

Personnel

The staff who meet with the customer face-to-face are a critical component of good customer service. All other components of customer service must be geared toward supporting front-line personnel in their quest to provide quality customer service. A motivated, well-trained, respectful and respected staff provide management with satisfied customers, low staff turnover and good outcomes.

Because the field of recreational therapy has a nationally recognized credentialing program, all staff should be able to demonstrate a basic level of competency. However, well-trained staff become that way because they are life-long learners who are supported by their employer with many opportunities for learning. This does not mean that every employer must send their staff to regional or national conferences. Learning can take many avenues. Learning along the lines of professional competencies can be achieved through reading, attending rounds, local inservices and through mentoring. Training in conflict resolution, stress management and methods to interact with people are also important.

Eric Berne, in his 1964 book *Games People Play*, proposed an approach to defining the roles people "play" as they interact with each other. In his book on transactional analysis he proposed that people tend to fit into one of three roles during any interaction with others: the role of a parent, the role of an adult or the role of a child. Providing good customer service requires the therapist to assume the role of an adult, not that of a parent or child.

Berne defines the role of a parent as having two main functions. The first function is to act as an authoritarian figure over an actual child, guiding the child through childhood so that s/he may be learn his/her roles and to be safe, thus promoting the survival of the human race. This role tends to take on the pattern of using automatic responses, as if to say "That's the way it's done" (p. 27) and expect that attitude to be enough to motivate the recipient/child to follow through on what was said. This second function (that of automatic responses) saves the adult from having to spend time on trivial matters to, hopefully, provide time for hashing out the important matters.

The role of the child is twofold, just as the adult's. Berne refers to these two roles as the natural child and the adapted child. The natural child exhibits the traits of being creative, charming, somewhat rebellious and taking pleasure in life. The adaptive child exhibits the trait of being able to modify his/her behavior in response to the parent's authoritarian role; exhibiting some rebellion but complying to the other's wishes.

The last role, the role of an adult, is considered by Berne to be the desired role to be assumed by adults when interacting with other adults. The adult role is one which "processes data and computes the probabilities which are essential for dealing effectively with the outside world" (p. 27). Berne felt that many of our failures in getting along with others are because we have tried to interact with another adult using either the role of a parent (thus treating them as a child) or using the role of a child (thus influencing them to take on the role of a parent). One of the biggest "faults" made by health care workers is to take on the role of the parent while treating the patient as a child. It is hard to provide quality customer service without allowing the patient to take the role of an adult, the same role the health care worker should be using.

Management can also have a big impact on how their personnel interact with the patient/customer. One of the major reasons that service people give disrespectful service is because they mirror the way they are treated by their supervisors, passing that treatment on to their customers (Glen, 1992). One of management's best roles is to support and motivate their staff. Nordstrom uses a variety of methods to motivate their staff including the use of honest compliments, role plays and rewards.

Honest compliments go a long way toward motivating staff. Being recognized for good performance by a supervisor not only motivates the staff person to repeat the performance but also increases the staff's self-esteem. Self-esteem is a strong motivator when matched with self-confidence.

Nordstrom builds the self-confidence of its staff by using role plays of difficult situations on a regular basis during their staff meeting time. Nordstrom feels that staff meetings are not only for the purpose of dispensing and discussing information about the business of the department, but also an important continuing education time. Management and staff select examples of difficult situations recently encountered. Staff then assume the roles of the people involved and role play through various scenarios so that the whole department can problem solve to improve the situation. This problem solving role play not only helps staff learn from each other but builds camaraderie.

Rewards, especially money rewards, do motivate staff. Financial rewards alone seldom provide enough incentive to produce an outstanding customer service environment but, used with honest compliments and role playing, they can significantly increase performance. Nordstrom feels that when the staff provide great customer service a direct result will be an increase in sales. To promote this, Nordstrom runs contests to see who can achieve a perfect "customer service score." Evaluators who are not known by sales staff pretend to be customers. Sales staff with top scores for customer service have received up to $2,500 in cash bonuses. While health care managers would love to experience the performance increase experienced by Nordstrom during its cash reward incentive drives (up to 22% increase), the health care environment does not generally allow cash bonuses. However, donated gifts such as dinner tickets for two, a weekend at a ski resort or a gift certificate to a local store may be possible.

Measurement

The measurement of how well a facility is providing customer service is important. Three types of measurements are used to quantify customer service: (1) *process measures* (comparing staff performance to standards of quality and quantity), (2) *product measures* (also known as outcomes of treatment) and

(3) *satisfaction measures* (customer perceptions compared to customer expectations) (Davidow & Uttal, 1989).

Process measures help determine how well a group delivers a product, in this case the product is "recreational therapy." Professional groups, accreditation agencies and governments have all developed standards which measure how well and how frequently therapists are able to meet what is considered to be good practice. Different terms are used for measuring processes including standards of practice, competency measures, compliance with regulations (surveys) and patient contact quotas (percentage of staff time spent in direct patient care). This type of measurement compares what industry has set as benchmarks for good practice to what is actually provided. Of the three types of measures used for customer satisfaction, process measures come closest to quality assurance measures. The assumption is that individuals within the professions have a high degree of knowledge related to what is considered to be best practices within their field and in health care in general. So, just as a crash engineer would know best what types of cars survive car crashes, so would health care providers know, through research, what makes good care.

The field of recreational therapy has a variety of tools to measure the process of how the product of recreational therapy is delivered. However, the most important one developed so far is the *Standards for the Practice of Therapeutic Recreation and Self-Assessment Guide* (American Therapeutic Recreation Association, 1993). This document goes beyond listing standards of practice by providing the therapist with an actual testing tool measure the process of delivering recreational therapy services.

Product measures help determine the inherent value of the product. In health care, product measures are more frequently called treatment outcomes. Product measures help document what change, if any, was derived as a direct result of the service provided. Just as health care has previously encouraged the development of quality assurance systems, it is currently stressing the need to measure the actual quality of the product delivered. This topic is covered in great detail in Chapter 12, *Outcomes*. Providing a good product is an important element of providing good customer service.

Satisfaction measures are the most common type of measurement thought of when customer service is mentioned. As a result, the measurement of this element of customer service has been fairly well defined and measured in health care. What have the consumers of health care indicated as top components of good customer service? Press, Ganey Associates, Inc. in a study of 139,830 former patients at 225 hospitals, identified and ranked the factors that correlated most closely with patient satisfaction. They identified the following 14 factors, listing in the order of importance to patients:

(1) staff's concern for patient privacy, (2) staff's sensitivity to the inconvenience of sickness and hospitalization, (3) adequacy of information given to family members concerning the patient's condition and treatment, (4) overall cheerfulness of the hospital's environment, (5) promptness and attitude of the nursing staff when called by patient, (6) extent that nurses took patient problems seriously, (7) nurses' attention to the personal and special needs of the patient, (8) courtesy of the technician who took blood, (9) technicians' explanation of tests and treatments, (10) likelihood that the patient will recommend the hospital to others, (11) friendliness of the nursing staff, (12) information available from the nursing staff about tests and treatments, (13) technical skills of the nurses and (14) skill level of the technician who took the patient's blood. (Kreitner, Hartz & Pflum, 1994, p. 25)

Kreitner, Hartz and Pflum (1994) divide patient satisfaction measures into three elements: satisfaction with service received, satisfaction with information received and satisfaction with the overall experience. Table 13.2 lists sample questions for each of the three elements of patient satisfaction.

Summary

Customer service as a separate entity from quality assurance is a fairly new management concept in health care. Good customer service is the patient's per-

Table 13.2: **Patient Satisfaction Questions** (Kreitner et al., 1994, p. 26)

Element	Sample Questions
Service Received	What do you think about the service you received? Was it effective? Did it solve your problem? Did the people serving you seem competent? Was the service efficient and well coordinated? Was it timely? Was the cost reasonable?
Information Received	What do you think about the information you received? Was it relevant and complete? Was it provided on a timely basis? Was it clear and understandable? Was is useful?
Experience	What do you think about the experience you had? Were you treated with dignity and respect? Did those who served you seem to be genuinely interested in you? Would you recommend this service to a friend or relative?

ception that his/her care matched his/her positive expectations. Good quality assurance is the process of identifying problems, identifying ways to decrease those problems and then monitoring to ensure that the problems were addressed. The management of health care with customer service in mind has six components: strategy, leadership, design, infrastructure, personnel and measurement. Measurement of customer service tends to fall into one of three types of measurement; process measures, product measures and satisfaction measures.

Learning Activities

1. Develop a process measure questionnaire which covers two standards using the internship standards from either NTRS, ATRA or your own university.

2. Select a treatment protocol, leisure education course or treatment intervention. Develop a product measure questionnaire to be used to measure any performance and/or attitudinal change which is a direct result of the protocol/course/intervention.

3. Ask five non-health care professionals/non-health care students and also five health care professionals/health care students the following question: "What can your doctor's office do to provide you with good service?" Using a table like Table 13.3 divide up the answers. Summarize the information which you received and note if there was any difference between individuals in health care versus not in health care.

4. Develop a satisfaction measure using the question in Table 13.2 as your guide. Attend a class, training course or other similar activity. Arrange with the person in charge of the class/course/activity to give the questionnaire to the participants at the end. Summarize your results.

5. Divide a piece of paper into three columns. In the first column list ten different decisions which an operational manager may need to make (e.g., square footage of the patient waiting room versus staff office space). In the second column list the decision likely to be made by an operational manager who is primarily concerned with "the bottom line." In the third column

Table 13.3: **Table to Analyze Good Service**

Type of Service for Measurement	Health Care Workers	Non Health Care Workers
Process (staff performance)	(write in responses from individuals interviewed)	(write in responses from individuals interviewed)
Product (outcomes)	(write in responses from individuals interviewed)	(write in responses from individuals interviewed)
Satisfaction (perceptions)	(write in responses from individuals interviewed)	(write in responses from individuals interviewed)

list the decision likely to be made by an operational manager who is principally concerned with customer service.

Study Questions

1. What is the difference between customer service and quality assurance? Why might they not be the same thing? In what ways might they be the same thing?
2. What are the six components of customer service?
3. What are the two primary elements identified by Nordstrom as key to providing good service?
4. Explain the differences between the three roles people play as described by Berne.
5. What are the three types of measurements used to quantify customer service?

References

American Therapeutic Recreation Association. (1993). *Standards for the practice of therapeutic recreation and self-assessment guide*. Hattiesburg, MS: American Therapeutic Recreation Association.

Berne, E. (1964). *Games people play: The basic handbook of transactional analysis*. New York: Ballantine Books.

Bruner, R. F., Eaker, M. R., Freeman, R. E., Spekman, R. E and Olmsted-Teisberg, E. (1998). *The portable MBA* (3rd ed.). New York: John Wiley & Sons, Inc.

burlingame, j & Skalko, T. (1997). *Idyll Arbor's glossary for therapists*. Ravensdale, WA: Idyll Arbor, Inc.

Clifton, D. (1995, April/May). Diversifying for success in the '90s. *Rehab Management, 8*(3), 52-60.

Davidow, W. & Uttal, B. (1989). *Total customer service: The ultimate weapon*. New York: HarperPerennial.

Glen, P. (1992). *It's not my department: How America can return to excellence giving and receiving quality service*. New York: Berkley Publishing Group.

Kreitner, C., Hartz, A. & Pflum, R. (1994, April/May). Patient-centered care. *Rehab Management, 7*(3), 25-30.

Kurian, G. T. (1994). *Datapedia of the United States 1790-2000*. Kanhan, MD: Bernan Press.

Leonard, D. & Schwind, B. (1996). Through the patient's eyes: Understanding and promoting patient-centered care. Book review in *Therapeutic Recreation Journal, 30*(3), 233-235.

Rhodes, M. (1991). The use of patient satisfaction data as an outcome monitor in therapeutic recreation quality assurance. In B. Riley (Ed.). *Quality management: Applications for therapeutic recreation*. State College, PA: Venture Publishing.

Salcido, R. (1997, Dec/Jan). Consumer participation and outcome research. *Rehab Management, 10*(1), 48-51.

Spector, R. & McCarthy, P. (1995). *The Nordstrom way: The inside story of America's #1 customer service company*. New York: John Wiley & Sons, Inc.

Chapter 14

Confidentiality

joan burlingame

To keep something confidential is to keep information secret from individuals who do not have the right to know the information. While this seems like a relatively simple concept, its application on a day-to-day basis requires the therapist to understand the laws, standards, court cases and ethics of guarding confidential information in different situations. The therapist also needs to know what constitutes informed consent related to the patient releasing his/her right to privacy. This chapter will help the therapist understand the important aspects of confidentiality as it applies to practice.

What is Confidentiality?

Privacy is the right to share information as well as the right to exclude information. Confidentiality is the professional's responsibility in response to the patient's right to privacy. The Supreme Court of the United States has upheld that the right to privacy is implied in the Constitution. This right to privacy includes the right to be free from unwarranted or unwanted publicity and the right to be left alone without undo exposure to public view. Pozgar defines the right to be without undo public view as "the right to live one's life without having one's name, picture or private affairs made public against one's will" (Pozgar & Pozgar, 1996, p. 72). In health care, this right to privacy includes two elements: the right to share *privileged* information with health care workers and the right to be free from *unnecessary probes* into personal affairs.

Privileged information implies that the patient is able to share private information with his/her health care provider and that the provider has the obligation to maintain the confidentiality of that information. The scope of this privileged information has four primary elements: the patient's identity, the patient's physical or psychological condition, the patient's emotional state and the patient's financial situation (Coastal HealthTrain, 1996). Except in very limited situations, the health care provider is not allowed to share information from any of these four elements without the patient's prior, written permission.

The right to be free from unnecessary probes into personal affairs implies that health care workers must have a reason for each question asked, each test given and each procedure undertaken and that the reason directly relates to the patient's condition. Probes into the patient's condition, lifestyle or work which do not have a measurable impact on why the patient is receiving treatment should be left unexplored and unexposed.

Circles of Privilege in Confidentiality

How can the therapist know who may obtain confidential information? Envision two circles, one inside the other. Individuals inside the center circle are not required to obtain specific permission from the patient before releasing information to other people in the inner circle. This group includes the staff members who are on the patient's treatment team, clinical supervisors (and the student interns they supervise who are on the treatment team) and consultants. Individuals in the outer circle may not receive information about the patient without prior, written consent. This larger circle includes the patient's family and friends, the patient's insurance company, law enforcement agencies, employers, attorneys and other health care providers (including recreational therapists or specialized recreation professionals) who have seen the patient in the past, or will see the patient in the future.

The Inner Circle of Confidentiality

Health care standards and federal, state and local laws require that the health care team provide reasonable care for each and every patient. Experience has shown that the quality and continuity of care relies heavily on communication between members of the treatment team. It is for this reason that anyone who cares for and consults with patients at or for your organization who has legitimate reasons to have access to private information about the patient, is included in the inner circle of confidentiality. However, within this inner circle there is also a rule called the "need to know" rule. While it is logical that the medical and therapy staff associated with a patient's care have full access to information which impacts the patient's overall care, volunteers, dietary aides, housecleaning staff and others have a more limited scope of information that they "need to know" to carry out their jobs. (For example, the housecleaning staff may need to know that a patient is in drainage/secretion precautions isolation but not that the infection is due to being homeless and sharing needles with others.)

Recreational therapists usually use some type of notebook or Kardex to communicate patient needs to volunteers. Since volunteers are limited to confidential information on a "need to know" basis, the therapist must be both careful in selecting the information shared and skillful in writing the information down. The general guidelines for placing information in Kardexes (shown below) provides the therapist with some basic rules to follow when communicating information to volunteers.

1. The therapist needs to balance the volunteers' need to know how the patient's situation is impacting his/her life with the patient's need for privacy. Patient confidentiality comes first while keeping overall safety in mind.
2. When the patient's injuries are due to abuse, write down the actual injuries and not the kind of abuse.
3. If the patient is experiencing family crises like a pending divorce, a lost child or other stressful events, ask yourself if the volunteer really needs to know about the stressful events. It is usually best just to write that the patient is under a lot of stress in addition to the injury/disease and suggest that the volunteers be extra sensitive to the patient's need for support and privacy.
4. In the case of child abuse or failure to thrive of unknown origin, it is best to write "please observe parent-child interaction." This helps take the implied blame off of the parents. (It might not be the parents who are causing the problem.)
5. One of the best rules for determining what to write in the Kardex is to ask yourself if you would feel uncomfortable telling the patient that you are sharing the information with volunteers. (burlingame & Skalko, 1997, p. 157)

The Larger Circle of Confidentiality

Explicit consent must be given by the patient before any confidential information is shared with individuals (or agencies) who are in the larger circle. Many of the individuals who are contained within this larger circle will have an appropriate, logical and vested interest in learning more about the patient and his/her condition. Their knowing may actually benefit the patient, especially when this knowledge relates to insurance coverage or allows improved care. Nonetheless, the therapist must obtain permission directly from the patient for the release of any information concerning his/her identity, physical or psychological condition, emotional status or financial situation.

The patient's insurance company does not have a legal right to obtain information about the patient's condition or care without prior, written permission from the patient. In most cases, the patient will sign a release for the insurance company to have access to the records because, without the release, it is unlikely that the insurance company will pay for the care. Recreational therapists, especially therapists in private practice, may not submit any bills for treatment to the patient's insurance company without first obtaining written permission from the patient to share the information. Just because the patient provides the therapist with his/her health insurance company's name, address and phone number, along with his/her policy number does not mean that the therapist has obtained permission to share information with the insurance company.

Another situation where it seems "logical" for the therapist to discuss the patient's situation is with family members, especially during the intake assessment or discharge planning. In some situations the therapist will be able to get a more accurate patient history or other information if s/he interviews the patient's family and friends. This can be a difficult task, however, because the therapist must be able to elicit the needed information without divulging the patient's condition or other information which is considered confidential. In most cases, the admitting staff obtain a blanket consent upon admission to services. It is the therapist's responsibility to be sure that this consent exists prior to talking with the family. If the consent form obtained does not explicitly include family members or friends within this larger circle, the therapist's job becomes harder. The therapist will need to become a master at gathering information, offering hope or caution without revealing information which the patient does not want released.

At times the therapist will be approached by police officers or lawyers (even the patient's own lawyer) for information about the patient and his/her situation. The therapist is not allowed to even acknowledge that s/he is seeing the patient without prior, written approval from the patient. The only exceptions to this rule are covered in the next section.

A situation which seems logical for the therapist *not* to share information with the larger circle, but seems the hardest to implement, is to not talk about the patient in a public area or around others who are not contained within the inner circle. Staff will frequently discuss a patient's care while riding the elevator, while having a "lunch" meeting in the cafeteria or while participating in a walk-through "rounds." Do not discuss patients while in the hallway, open charting area, dining room or any other location where individuals outside the circle of confidentiality might be present. Make sure all charts and patient notes are covered when people come into your office to use the phone or to talk to you. When families are taking pictures of their family member, make sure that other patients who might be in the picture are consenting to having their picture taken. Care must be taken in all situations so that the patient's privacy (and the therapist's responsibility) are not violated. This need to protect the patient's privacy also extends to after work hours. Many staff become very sloppy in this aspect of practice. Professional ethics and standards of practice require the therapist to maintain a high "moral" ground on this issue: legally and ethically the therapist is obligated to protect the privacy of a patient.

Exceptions to the Confidentiality Rule

There are seven situations which allow health care providers to disclose confidential information without prior written consent from the patient. The seven situations are

1. reporting suspected abuse of minors, the elderly or domestic violence;
2. providing information in a medical emergency (e.g., your patient develops autonomic dysreflexia while on an outing and "911" is called);
3. reporting to police (or the appropriate authorities) a situation where there is a high likelihood that the patient will violently harm himself/herself or another person (*disclosure to safeguard*) following the guidelines in Tarasoff I and Tarasoff II as discussed below;
4. responding to litigation (subpoenas);
5. providing information related to administrative activities (e.g., peer review, risk management, utilization review, quality assurance activities);
6. notification of the appropriate authorities in the case of a gunshot wound (not within the scope of practice for recreational therapists — usually reported by the emergency room staff);
7. reporting communicable diseases to the Health Department (not within the scope of practice for recreational therapists) (Coastal HealthTrain, 1996; Pozgar & Pozgar, 1996).

Reporting Suspected Abuse

While the laws vary from state to state, the bottom line is that any *suspected* abuse must be reported to the appropriate government agency. This is especially true when the potential victim is a minor or is unable to take responsibility for himself/herself.

The important word here is *suspected*, not *proven*. Confidentiality may be broken if the therapist or treatment team has a reasonable suspicion that an individual has been, or is being, abused. And yet this breach of confidentiality is very limited, because the report is made to a governmental agency and not shared with anyone outside of the inner circle of confidentiality. (This excludes any staff person or volunteer who is on a "need to know" basis.)

When the recreational therapist is working as a member of a treatment team, it is seldom the recreational therapist's responsibility to make the phone call himself/herself to report the suspected abuse. It *is* his/her responsibility to have knowledge that the report has been made to the appropriate governmental agency. Some situations which place the recreational therapist in the position to make the phone call are when s/he is the treatment team leader, the Qualified Mental Retardation Professional in a ICF-MR (training team leader), in private practice and working outside of a treatment team or in the rare situation where s/he has reported the suspected abuse to the team leader and the team leader has not reported the suspected abuse to the appropriate agency.

Medical Emergencies

When a patient who is with a recreational therapist has a medical emergency outside of a medical center, the therapist becomes a vital link with the emergency medical team. In the case of an extreme medical emergency, the patient may not be able to provide important consent which may impact emergency medical care related to his/her physical or psychological condition. If the patient is unable to provide the necessary information to the medical team in an emergency, the therapist is allowed to breach confidentiality. However, if the patient is at all able to give (or decline) consent for the release of information, the therapist has the obligation to hold the information. The same guidelines hold true if the patient is legally not able to give his/her own consent (in the case of a minor or an individual who has been determined by the courts as unable). The therapist should attempt to reach the legal guardian (or have his/her agency provide the notification) as soon as possible.

Disclosure to Safeguard

A situation which may warrant breaking confidentiality of the patient's physical or psychological condition is when the patient makes a clear statement that s/he intends to harm herself/himself or to violently assault another person. While the therapist's relationship to the patient does imply an obligation to maintain confidentiality, the courts have ruled that, at times, the therapist has a greater obligation to the community.

In *Tarasoff v. Regents of University of California* (1976), the California Supreme Court ruled that physicians and psychotherapists must warn a potential victim, the potential victim's family or authorities if a patient has threatened violent harm. This ruling came after a student at the University of California indicated that he was going to kill a fellow student. The therapist (employed by the University of California), after consulting with a colleague, documented the threat and called campus police. The police found the student who made the threat and detained him. During that time, the two therapists' supervisor learned about the "breach of confidentiality" and ordered all of the patient's records destroyed. The supervisor also ruled out the use of the state's 72-hour emergency psychiatric detention provision of the commitment law. The campus police no longer having legal grounds to hold the student, released him on his promise to not harm his intended victim. Two months later the student did kill the intended victim and the dead victim's parents subsequently sued the University of California. The court's findings, referred to as the Tarasoff I ruling, stated that a therapist has the legal obligation to *warn*. In 1982 the California Supreme Court issued a second ruling on Tarasoff (referred to as Tarasoff II) which stated that therapists have the obligation to *protect* in addition to warn. Tarasoff rulings have been upheld to mean acts of violence only. Numerous court cases have tried unsuccessfully to include the threat of spreading the HIV virus to others.

The American Psychiatric Association has developed three guidelines for the therapist to follow in determining if the Tarasoff rulings apply. After careful review and prudent judgment the therapist may break confidentiality if:

1. A patient will probably commit murder, and the act can be stopped only by the psychiatrist's notification of the police,
2. A patient will probably commit suicide, and the act can be stopped only by the psychiatrist's notification of the police, or
3. A patient, such as a bus driver or an airline pilot who has potentially life-threatening responsibilities, shows marked impairment of judgment.

The Supreme Court rulings do not provide grounds for a recreational therapist to breach confidentiality in the case of a threat. As a member of the team, the recreational therapist is obligated to work with his/her medical supervisor, providing objective, clinical data to support a decision to apply (or not to apply) Tarasoff. As changes in health care progress, more and more teams are led by non-physicians. This makes it harder for the team to determine when the Tarasoff rulings apply, or how to apply them. Figure 14.1 shows the flow chart to use when trying to decide if the Tarasoff ruling applies.

Responding to Subpoenas

In the United States, information about a patient's identity, physical or psychological condition, emotional status or financial situation is considered available to the government without the patient's prior approval if it is for use by "governmental investigative agencies, licensing and accrediting bodies and peer review or quality assurance committees" (Scott, 1990, p. 91). This definition does not include most courts of law which are required to issue subpoenas for the confidential information desired by the court. Subpoenas are court orders which compel the therapist to appear before the court at a specific time and place. There are two different types of subpoenas. The first, *subpoena ad testificandum*, is a court order for the therapist to come to the court and testify about a

Figure 14.1: **Flow chart for applying the Tarasoff ruling.**

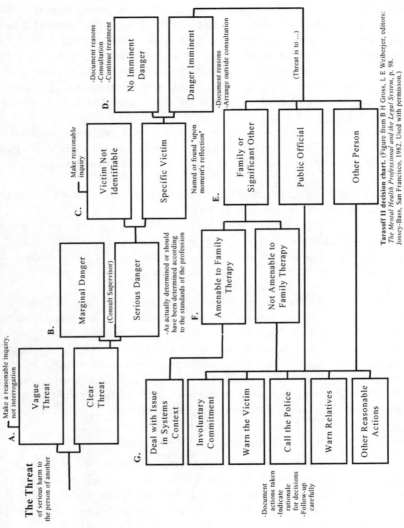

The Threat
of serious harm to
the person of another

A. ⌐ Make a reasonable inquiry,
    not interrogation.

Vague
Threat

Clear
Threat

B.

Marginal Danger

(Consult Supervisor)

Serious Danger

-As actually determined or should
have been determined according
to the standards of the profession

C. ⌐ Make reasonable
    inquiry

Victim Not
Identifiable

Specific Victim

Named or found "upon
moment's reflection"

D.

No Imminent
Danger

-Document reasons
-Consultation
-Continue treatment

Danger Imminent

-Document reasons
-Arrange outside consultation

(Threat is to ...)

E.

Family or
Significant Other

Public Official

Other Person

F.

Amenable to Family
Therapy

Not Amenable to
Family Therapy

G.

Deal with Issue
in Systems
Context

Involuntary
Commitment

Warn the Victim

Call the Police

Warn Relatives

Other Reasonable
Actions

-Document
 actions taken
-Indicate
 rationale
 for decisions
-Follow-up
 carefully

Tarasoff II decision chart. (Figure from B H Gross, L E Weibejer, editors:
The Mental Health Professional and the Legal System, p. 98.
Jossey-Bass, San Francisco, 1982. Used with permisson.)

specific patient or situation. The second, *subpoena duces tecum*, is a court order for the therapist to provide the court with specific notes, charts, assessments or other confidential patient information. Because the existence of a subpoena does not give the court a right to all of the confidential information, the therapist will benefit from the advice and presence of an attorney before and during the hearing. The amount of confidentiality required to be breached by the therapist may vary from court to court (e.g., county court versus federal court) or from state to state (e.g., depending on state law, previous court findings on patient confidentiality).

Confidential Information Related to Administrative Activities

The information the recreational therapist wrote concerning a patient's condition, status or situation is available for review by individuals outside of the inner circle of confidentiality without written permission from the patient. In this situation, the breach of confidentiality must be related to improving or maintaining overall quality of care and be carried out by individuals who are functioning as members of a recognized peer review, quality assurance or survey team. A recreational therapist is most likely to be involved in administrative activities related to conducting quality of care reviews and outcome measurement for his/her department or facility. A fine line is drawn between outcome measurements and research. If the recreational therapist is conducting experimental research related to treatment interventions and not just measuring the outcomes of standard treatment, a specific consent is required (for both the experimental treatment and for use of the confidential information generated).

Release of Confidential Information Outside Scope of Practice

There are a few areas where a medical professional (physician or nurse) is allowed to release confidential information without the patient's consent which is considered outside the scope of practice of recreational therapists. These areas include the reporting of infectious diseases to the Health Department and the reporting of gunshot wounds to the police.

Managing Confidentiality

Confidentiality is a key aspect of treatment and a facility's policy and procedure manual should outline the administration's stance on the subject. While each staff person is expected to know to keep the patient's identity, physical or psychological condition, emotional status and financial situation concealed, the "hows" (and possibly, the "whys") should be clearly stated so that all staff can follow them.

The administration's policies (what should be done) relating to patient confidentiality should outline the areas that impact the recreational therapist as s/he provides care and services. Each procedure associated with a policy should state who does what and when the action(s) should be taken. The specifics of how to carry out tasks, (e.g., which form to have the patient sign to allow his/her photograph to be taken) are a necessary part of policies and procedures which address confidentiality.

What are some of the specific issues relating to confidentiality which are addressed by the recreational therapist? The recreational therapist assists the patient with many aspects of functional ability and one of the key areas of functional ability is integration into the community. In this area, recreational therapy needs to address confidentiality on almost a day-to-day basis. If the therapist helps the patient fill out an application for a discounted gym or pool pass from the local YMCA, the therapist will have the patient sign the application. However, the therapist must also have the patient sign a release which states that the therapist is allowed to provide information relating to the fact that the patient was a patient (identity) and to release the information as to why the patient qualifies for the discounted pass (condition, emotional status or financial situation). Photographs are frequently taken during activities (by families, participants and observers). Proper releases are required before a patient's picture may be taken during an activity to guard his/her confidentiality rights. Table 14.1 shows some of the four areas of confidentiality and their related issues.

Confidentiality as a Standard of Care

Because confidentiality is a concern in health care, all major regulating and accrediting agencies provide professional standards associated with the maintenance of patient confidentiality. Most federal health care laws address patient confidentiality. An example can be found in 42 CFR §483.10 (e) (OBRA — Nursing Home Regulations), "The resident has the right to personal privacy and confidentiality of his or her personal and clinical records. Personal and clinical records include all types of records the facility might keep on a resident, whether they are medical, social, fund accounts, automated or other" (Department of Health and Human Services, 1995, pp. 23-24). Voluntary accreditation organizations also have strict standards for confidentiality of patient information. The Members' Rights and Responsibilities Standard in Table 14.2 is from the National Committee for Quality Assurance (1996), the national organization which sets standards for accreditation of managed care systems. The Joint Commission on Accreditation of Healthcare Organizations and CARF: The Rehabilitation Accreditation Commission also have similar standards relating to confidentiality.

Table 14.1: **Areas of Confidentiality**

Area	Examples of Confidentiality Issues Requiring Releases
Identity	• Photographs. • Newspaper releases, press releases, professional presentations. • Involvement with community integration programs while out with a treatment group (e.g., is the hospital's name on the side of the van really treating the patient's identity and the fact that s/he is receiving treatment confidentially?). • Applications for discounted participation fees.
Physical or psychological condition	• Disclosing, even in general terms, the patient's physical or psychological condition, even when helping the patient search for appropriate resources in the community if enough information is given for someone to make an intelligent guess as to the identity of the patient. • Releasing information to other professionals during the referral process. • Releasing information in the process of obtaining adapted equipment.
Emotional Condition	• Disclosing clinical opinion about a patient's emotional ability to handle community programs. • Sharing information about a patient's coping skills, anger management or parenting skills.
Financial Status	• Releasing information on a patient's ability to afford community recreation programs.

Professional Ethics

The field of recreational therapy has two professional organizations which represent practitioners. Both have statements about the ethical need to maintain confidentiality. The ethical statements from each are shown below.

Therapeutic recreation personnel are responsible for safe-guarding information about individuals served. Individuals served have the right to control information about themselves. When a situations arises that requires disclosure of confidential information about an individual to protect the individual's welfare or the interest of others, the therapeutic recreation professional has the responsibility/obligation to inform the individual served of the circumstances in which confidentiality was broken. — American Therapeutic Recreation Association (1993, p. 30)

Table 14.2: **Sample of Confidentiality as a Standard of Care**

Standard RR 7: The managed care organization protects the confidentiality of member information and records.	
Number	**Standard**
RR 7.1	The managed care organization adopts and implements written confidentiality policies and procedures to ensure the confidently of member information used for any purpose.
RR 7.2	The managed care organization's contracts with practitioners and providers explicitly state expectations about the confidentiality of member information and records.
RR 7.3	The managed care organization affords patients with the opportunity to approve or deny the release of identifiable personal information by the managed care organization, except when such release is required by law.

Rationale: As a part of business operations, employees of the MCO [managed care organization] have access to individuals' records that contain private and privileged information. It is vital that this information not be divulged to any person or agency that does not need to use it or that might use it to the detriment of the member.

To ensure that everyone who handles patient information keeps it confidential, the MCO sets standards for its own employees and for all the sites of care that participate with the organization. The MCO incorporates those policies into its contracts with participating practitioners. Furthermore, the MCO has policies to obtain the member's permission before releasing confidential information outside the organization.

Documents to Be Reviewed: (1) Confidentiality policies and procedures, (2) Practitioner contracts and (3) Employee confidentiality agreements, if any.

Persons to Interview: Members of member services staff, if documents are problematic.

Scoring Interpretation: MCOs should have policies and procedures about confidentiality that apply to practitioners and practitioner offices, members of claims processing staffs, members of UM [utilization management] and case management staffs, members of QI [quality improvement] staffs, and members of all other staffs who have access to any patient information. *(Note: "Staff" includes participating practitioners who serve on committees.)* Policies should address all of the following:

* Maintenance of confidentiality of information within the organization.
* Protection of medical record information (both original information and documentation used for UM, QI activities, and case management).
* Protection of claim information.
* The right of the member to approve the release of information beyond the MCO.
* Orientation of employees regarding the MCO's confidentiality policies and procedures.

The MCO's contracts should also require that all contracted practices, including the offices of PCPs, have appropriate policies and procedures to preserve patient confidentiality. There should be a process to assess the adequacy of the PCP offices' polices and procedures during site visits.

Delegation Policy: An MCO *may not* delegate authority for performing this function to another entity.

Professionals respect the privacy of individuals. Communications are kept confidential except with the explicit consent of the individual or where the welfare of the individual or others is clearly imperiled. Individuals are informed of the nature and the scope of confidentiality.
— National Therapeutic Recreation Society (1990, p. 2)

Keeping Records Confidential

Keeping patient information and records confidential is a legal requirement, a standards of practice expectation and an ethical obligation. Records should be maintained so that access by individuals outside the inner circle is controlled. While it obviously points to the need to obtain prior authorization to share information, the application of this concept on the hospital unit can be much simpler. If a therapist finds a medical chart left in a public area of the hospital, s/he should return it to the appropriate location. If the therapist notices a patient leaning over the nursing counter, reading another patient's medical chart, the therapist should politely say "excuse me" and close the chart. More than once the author has been asked for a chart by a professionally dressed individual unknown to her who did not have a hospital name tag. In each case, she asked for some kind of identification and for the reason the person felt authorized to review the patient's confidential information. Not everyone who asked actually had the authority to look at the chart. One of the individuals asking had been the patient's pastor, who did not have permission from the patient to review his information.

Information (including medical charts) should not be shared in any manner which allows unauthorized individuals to obtain confidential information. While this seems obvious, the application of the concept off the hospital unit becomes more complex. Guidelines have been developed for notifying potential readers of the material about the nature of its confidentiality, for use of online medical charts, for using faxes and e-mail and for standardized ways to obtain consent.

Notices Relating to Confidentiality

Generally, any time confidential material leaves the therapist's office, the patient's medical chart or travels outside the inner circle of confidentiality, a notice of confidentiality should be attached to the information. It is never adequate to just stamp the word "confidential" or "for professional use only" on material relating to the patient's private information. Zuckerman (1995) lists four directions for providing a notice of confidentiality which should be attached (at minimum) to the front of the confidential material, or (preferably) to each page of the confidential material. He suggests indicating:

1. the information in this report is to be used for a stated/specific purpose
2. the report is to be used only by the authorized recipient
3. the report is not to be disclosed to any other party, including the patient/client (any exceptions to this must be clearly and specifically stated)
4. the report is to be destroyed after the specified use has been made/stated need has been met. (Zuckerman, 1995, p. 289)

Computerized Records and Confidentiality

Restricting the flow of confidential information to "secondary users" (generally insurance companies, researchers and other groups in the larger circle of confidentiality) is becoming more and more difficult as more records go online. In the past, staff in the inner circle of confidentiality had a physical hold on the material contained within the patient's medical chart. As records go online, it is harder to restrict access on a "need to know" basis or to limit the scope of access as outlined by the patient's written release. Increasingly the therapist will hear the word "security" in association with "privacy" and "confidentiality." "*Security* refers to technical and organizational procedures that protect electronic information and data-processing systems from unauthorized access, modification, destruction or misuse" (Gostin et al., 1993). This security is achieved through four main avenues:

- encryption of information (scrambling the material so it can only be read by computers with specialized devices to decode the material),
- authentication techniques (use of passwords, specialized keys and other automated identification systems to verify the identity of individuals seeking access to the record),
- ethical conduct by all health care providers (self-policing themselves and others in their field to set and maintain a high standard of conduct in relation to confidentiality and security of records) and
- standardization of confidentiality laws.

As computers became more commonplace in health care, some individuals felt that "reasonable" give and take related to a person's constitutionally guaranteed right to privacy was needed because of the complexity of providing security online. Partly in response (or reaction to) this expressed need, the United States Government passed a law called the Federal Privacy Act of 1974 (codified as 5 USC Section 552a). The law was meant to address many of the concerns related to the government's (and computer technology's) invasion of the individual's privacy. While inadequate to address the complex challenges of online medical charts, the *fair information practices* contained in this law were a beginning. These protections are

1. The law covers records which pertain to medical information on individuals (medical records, not all medical information);
2. Individuals are given the right to access much of the personal information kept on them;
3. Limits are placed on the disclosure of certain personal information to third parties;
4. Health care personnel are required to request information directly from the individual to whom it pertains, whenever possible;
5. When a government entity requests personal information from an individual, laws require the individual to be notified of the authority for the collection of data, whether the disclosure is mandatory or voluntary;
6. The individual may contest the accuracy, completeness and timeliness of his or her personal information and request an amendment;
7. Health care personnel must decide whether to amend the information within a fixed time, usually 30 days after receiving a request;
8. The individual whose request for change is denied may file a statement of disagreement, which must be included in the record and disclosed along with it thereafter;
9. The individual can seek review of a denied request. (Office of Technology, 1995, p. 118)

Even though most federal health care laws and the Federal Privacy Act of 1974 include regulations concerning the patient's right to privacy, the laws do not cover many aspects of care with specific, enforceable interpretations. The Office of Technology Assessment of the Congress of the United States (1995) noted that:

The present system of protection for health care information offers a patchwork of codes; State laws of varying scope; and Federal laws applicable to only limited kinds of information, or information maintained specifically by the Federal Government. The present legal scheme does not provide consistent, comprehensive protection for privacy in health care information, whether it exists in a paper or computerized environment. (p. 116-117)

To address this concern, the Office of Technology Assessment has recommended that the Congress of the United States take the following actions concerning an individual's right to privacy and the provider's obligation to confidentiality:

1. Define the subject matter of the legislation, health care information, to encompass the full range of medical information collected, stored and transmitted about individuals, not simply the patient record.
2. Define the elements comprising invasion of privacy of health care information and provide criminal and civil sanctions for improper possession, brokering, disclosure or sale of health care information, with penalties sufficient to deter perpetrators.
3. Establish requirements for informed consent.
4. Establish rules for educating patients about information practices; access to information; amendment, correction and deletion of information; and creation of databases.
5. Establish protocols for access to information by secondary users, and determine their rights and responsibilities in the information they access.
6. Structure the law to track the information flow, incorporating the ability of computer security systems to monitor and warn of leaks and improper access to information so the law can be applied to the information at the point of abuse, not to one "home" institution.
7. Establish a committee, commission or panel to oversee privacy in health care information. (Office of Technology Assessment, 1995, p. 122)

Fax and Electronic Transmissions of Confidential Material

Information on patients is frequently transmitted over facsimile ("fax") lines or via e-mail. Confidential information transmitted in this manner has a higher risk of arriving in unintended hands than does material which is hand carried or mailed. Because of the risk associated with both fax and e-mail, the therapist should:

1. Always include a cover letter which provides the sender's name, phone number and address; the receiver's name, phone number and address; and, in prominent lettering, a notice relating to the confidential manner of the transmission.

2. Confirm that the fax number or e-mail address is correct prior to any transmission being sent.
3. Once the fax number or e-mail address has been punched/typed in, again, double check the entry to make sure that no sending errors will occur.
4. Keep a log of what records were transmitted and to whom (including fax number/e-mail address used).

When receiving confidential information on patients from others, the therapist should keep in mind that thermal fax paper fades over time. While fax copies meet the standards of practice for inclusion in medical charts, it is a good idea to make a photocopy of the faxed material. In either case, it is not required that an original, signed copy be in the medical chart.

Patient Consent Guidelines

Generally, when a patient is admitted to any health care service, s/he is asked to sign multiple consent forms, including consent related to care and treatment, consent for the treatment team to confer with specialists related to the patient's care, for the use of local anesthetics or other routine anesthetics in the course of treatment, for the right to use discarded specimens for research purposes, for the right to use information within the medical record for research purposes, for the use of still or motion pictures for educational purpose or hospital publicity and for permission to release medical information to other physicians, health care providers or other facilities/health care professionals who may provide (or who have provided in the past) health care services for the patient.

When a patient is asked to sign a consent to release information form, the professional should provide the patient with all of the information that is needed for them to make an informed decision. This would include *who* will be told *what*, and in what *manner*. An example would be when the recreational therapist asks a patient to sign a photo release form. This form should let the patient know what types of photographs will be taken (e.g., during community outings or inpatient activities), what format they will be in (e.g., snap shots, video tape) and how the photographs will be used (e.g., promoting the recreational therapy service and/or educational purposes). The patient should also be told that they have the right to decide not to release the information. All consent forms used by the recreational therapist should be reviewed by the appropriate professionals within the facility prior to being used. If the therapist finds that the majority of patients require a specific consent form to be signed, s/he may be able to have that specific consent added to the consent forms signed upon admission.

Not all patients have the right to sign legal papers on their behalf. When the recreational therapist is seeking to determine who can sign consent papers for specific activities or consent to release information, s/he should check the patient's chart to see who signed the original consent papers. Individuals who may not have the right to sign their own legal papers include minors or individuals who have been determined to be mentally incompetent by a court of law.

Patient Consent Guidelines
when the Patient is a Minor

The degree of confidentiality the therapist retains between a minor patient and his/her parents related to testing and treatment results will be directly inverse to the child's age. The younger the child, the more appropriate it is for the therapist to share testing and treatment results directly and fully with the parents. As the minor patient reaches adolescence, the therapist will find that a lesser degree of disclosure may be appropriate.

The treatment team should have established criteria for the amount of privacy allotted adolescents. However, the legal ability to share (or not share) information must be based on who has the legal right to make decisions for the minor. It is not always the child's parents who have the right to make decisions about sharing confidential information. In most states, a *minor* is an individual who is under eighteen years of age and has not been declared an emancipated minor by the courts. An *emancipated minor* is an individual who is under eighteen years of age and married or who has obtained a court order declaring the child emancipated from his/her parents or legal guardian. A child who is a w*ard of the court* usually will need the signature of his/her caseworker or legally designated guardian to authorize consent. Foster parents are rarely designated as legal guardians. Step parents frequently also lack the legal ability to sign consent papers.

In general, the therapist/minor patient relationship is better off if the therapist lets the child know that s/he is there to work *with* the patient. This may involve letting the patient know that what goes on during treatment will generally remain "just between us" but some of the information will be shared. A developmentally appropriate, open conversation about the parent's need to know versus the child's concerns for privacy will help both the therapist and minor patient understand each other's needs better. Especially with children who are latency age or older, asking the patient to give the therapist the most important piece of information that the child wants shared with the parent helps. This process, when used each time, helps the child recognize that information will be shared, but that s/he has some control over one aspect of that sharing.

What is Trust?

What happens when health care workers break trust and breach confidentiality? Trust is a learned belief system held by individuals which has three parts:

"(1) the belief in the validity of one's own perceptions, (2) the belief in the potential of another person to respond in mutually respectful ways and (3) the belief in one's own capability to assess the trustworthiness of another person accurately" (burlingame & Skalko, 1997, p. 252). When health care workers breach confidentiality, they are negatively impacting the patient's ability to believe that health care workers will respond in mutually respectful ways and cause the patient to call into question his/her own ability to know who to trust.

When trust is broken, a patient is more likely to be hesitant to seek further care and to not share vital information with providers in the future (Coastal HealthTrain, 1996). The long term effects of the professional's unethical breaching of confidential information could be a decrease in the patient's health.

Professionals who unethically breach confidentiality are also subject to reprimand, possible lawsuits, loss of credential and/or criminal prosecution.

Summary

Patients have a right to privacy as guaranteed by the Constitution of the United States. It is the recreational therapist's obligation (legally, ethically and professionally) to honor that right. However, confidentiality is not always a simple concept to apply in everyday practice. The standards for the professional's responsibility toward patient confidentiality is defined through laws, standards of practice, standards of ethics and court rulings. The therapist must be aware of who has the legitimate right to privileged information, the appropriate manner to obtain the patient's permission to allow others this right and when it is legally and morally ethical to breach confidentiality. The maintenance of confidentiality may become more difficult as computers are used more frequently. It is the therapist's responsibility to understand security in relationship to privacy and confidentiality.

Learning Activities

1. Review the confidentiality policies and procedures for a selected health care facility to see if they meet the requirements outlined in this chapter.
2. Practice writing up imaginary patient information to be shared with volunteers. Pass the entries to other students in your class to evaluate whether the correct balance of information sharing versus privacy was achieved.
3. Sit in a hospital cafeteria for an hour during mealtime and count how many times you hear potentially confidential information being discussed inappropriately.
4. Review patient confidentiality release forms from different facilities. Compare the scope of the forms.

5. Compare the confidentiality training material for volunteers in hospitals versus volunteers in a community treatment setting. See which one provides the volunteers with the information they need to protect client confidentiality appropriately.

Study Questions

1. What is confidentiality? What are the four elements of confidential information? How does the concept of privilege and unnecessary probes affect the therapist's assessment of a patient?
2. Explain the inner circle and larger circle concept of confidentiality. Why are individuals within the inner circle allowed to share information freely with each other? How does "need to know" apply to the inner circle?
3. What are the exceptions to confidentiality which allow the therapist to breach the patient's privacy? How do Tarasoff I and Tarasoff II impact the therapist?
4. What types of activities are considered "administrative activities?" Why is it important to allow this type of review of confidential material?
5. How was the Federal Privacy Act of 1974 a reaction to both this type of review and the increased use of computers? What avenues are being taken to increase the security of electronically stored medical information?

References

American Therapeutic Recreation Association. (1993). *Standards for the practice of therapeutic recreation & self assessment guide*. Hattiesburg, MS: American Therapeutic Recreation Association.

burlingame, j. & Skalko, T. (1997). *Idyll Arbor's glossary for therapists*. Ravensdale, WA: Idyll Arbor, Inc.

Coastal HealthTrain. (1996). *Patient confidentiality: It's everybody's job, not everybody's business*. Virginia Beach, VA: Coastal HealthTrain.

Department of Health and Human Services. (1995). *State operations manual*. Washington, DC: Author.

Gostin, L., Turek-Brezina, J., Powers, M., Kozloff, R., Faden, R. & Steinauer, D. D. (1993). Privacy and security of personal information in a new health care system. *The Journal of the American Medical Association, 270*(20), 2487-2493.

Kaplan, H., Sadock, B. & Grebb, J. (1994). *Kaplan and Sadock's synopsis of psychiatry* (Seventh Edition). Baltimore, MD: Williams & Wilkins.

National Committee for Quality Assurance. (1998). *1998 Standards for accreditation of managed care organizations*. Washington, DC: National Committee for Quality Assurance.

National Therapeutic Recreation Society. (1990). *National Therapeutic Recreation Society code of ethics*. Ashburn, VA: National Recreation and Parks Association.

Office of Technology Assessment. (1995). *Bringing health care online: The role of information technologies*. Washington, DC: Congress of the United States.

Pozgar, G. & Pozgar, N. (1996). *Legal aspects of health care administration* (6th ed.). Gaithersburg, MD: Aspen Publishers, Inc.

Scott, R. (1990). *Health care malpractice: A primer on legal issues for professionals*. Thorofare, NJ: SLACK, Inc.

Uniack, A. (1996). *Documentation in a SNAP*. San Anselmo, CA: Skilled Nursing Assessment Programs.

Zuckerman, E. (1995). *Clinician's thesaurus: The guidebook for writing psychological reports* (4th ed.). New York: Guilford Press.

Chapter 15

Attitudes Toward Disability

Leandra A. Bedini

Attitudes toward people with disabilities are an important area for professionals working in health care to explore. Appropriate attitudes of health care providers can contribute significantly to the successful rehabilitation of people with disabling conditions. Further, when patients are discharged from medical treatment facilities, the attitudes of health care professionals dealing with the transition process are important for the empowerment and successful integration of people with disabilities into their respective communities.

There are several reasons why recreational therapists, in particular, should understand the types and effects of attitudes toward people with disabilities. First, people who become disabled do not instantly become enlightened about what it is like to have a disability. As a result, some people with disabilities will have the same range of attitudes (both positive and negative) as people without disabilities. Once an individual finds himself/herself in that group (having an disability), s/he may have a difficult time understanding his/her rights, choices and opportunities. Recreational therapists have the opportunity to foster positive attitudes through their choice of recreational therapy treatment techniques. Also, since recreational therapists interact not only with patients, but also with their families, the therapists will have the opportunity to help the patients and families learn more about the implications of having a disability.

Another reason recreational therapists should understand the dynamics of attitudes relates to their goal of empowering people with disabilities to meet the challenges of living and participating in the community. The more people with disabilities are able to participate in public leisure and recreation programs, the more opportunities people in the community will have to interact with and accept these individuals.

A final reason for understanding attitudes deals with the recreational therapist's own beliefs. Recreational therapists themselves may need to evaluate their own attitudes and subsequent behaviors to make sure that their services are free from bias and, indeed, empowering to the patients.

The purpose of this chapter is to examine how attitudes are defined, how attitudes are formed and how negative attitudes toward people with disabilities can be changed within and through the delivery of recreational therapy services. Attitudes towards disability have a long history. This chapter will also address significant events that have influenced attitudes toward people with disabilities in society.

What Are Attitudes?

There are many definitions of attitude, most of which associate attitude with potential behavior. For example, Allport (1935) defined attitude as a precondition to behavior. Triandis (1971) defined an attitude as an individual's tendency to respond to a given situation in a given manner. Perhaps the most common definition of attitude is Ajzen's (1988) which proposed that "an attitude is a disposition to respond favorably or unfavorably to an object, person, institution or event" (p. 4). Thus, the core characteristics of attitudes are that they contain an element of evaluation toward or against something and have an impact on how people behave. If a person's life experiences contribute to the development of negative attitudes toward someone or something, then s/he might develop negative behaviors as well.

Meanings of Being Different: A Historical Perspective

Throughout history, people with disabilities have experienced a variety of reactions from society. In some cultures, physical anomalies were perceived to be a good omen. For example, in Dahomeans's culture of Western Africa, children born with abnormal physical characteristics were believed to be protected by supernatural beings. Similarly, for the Palaung people, extra fingers or toes were considered to be good luck (Wright, 1983). In some ancient Roman cultures, people with psychological conditions that would cause hallucinations or seizures were thought of as charmed and chosen by the gods.

In other times in history and in other cultures, however, people with disabilities have been labeled and treated as monsters, animals and creatures. For example, the Roman wealthy class kept "deformed slaves" for amusement (Welsford, 1935). People with physical and mental disabilities ("morios") were bought and sold at the "Forum Morionium" (marketplace of the disabled). Parents actually stunted the growth of their own children so they could later sell them for a profit (Duran, 1969). Sometimes people who were short-statured or mentally retarded were kept as household pets (Duran, 1969; Welsford, 1935). Likewise, in the middle ages, royalty in Europe exchanged people of short stature as gifts (Clair, 1968; Duran 1969).

Despite the oppression of the middle ages, many social changes over the past few centuries have contributed to more humane treatment and greater understanding of people with disabilities. The 1800's witnessed changes in philosophies of the medical world toward viewing people with disabilities as humans rather than as animals. The use of recreation in institutions for people with mental illness made its debut during this period (Zwelling, 1985). By the turn of the 20th century, the beginning of organized recreation programs for people with disabilities was clearly evident.

The deinstitutionalization movement in the middle of the 20th century had a significant impact on society's attitudes toward people with disabilities. This movement began during the early 1960's when President John Kennedy called for a plan that would address the community needs of people with mental retardation. A decade later, in the early 1970's, President Nixon continued this sentiment calling for one-third of the individuals in public institutions for the mentally retarded to re-enter their community.

This deinstitutionalization movement sought to take people with disabilities out of the institutions and place them back into their communities. Meyer (1973) identified the shift in the 1960's from total institutionalization to community-centered mental health programs as instrumental to the developing attitude of acceptance of people with disabilities. In addition to a growing political push from families, much of this activity and growth was based on the concept of normalization proposed by Nirje (1969) and Wolfensberger (1972) which identified the rights of all individuals to experience "culturally valued lives." Wolfensberger proposed that people with disabilities should be allowed opportunities and treatment equal to people without disabilities. His principle of normalization included elements of physical and social integration, dignity of risk (being allowed to try) and the right to self-determination.

Several other events of the last few decades also affected attitudes toward people with disabilities. Legislation in the last 30 years has had a big impact on the rights of people with disabilities. Through passage of various acts, people with disabilities are now able to access and participate in educational, work and recreational environments that previously were denied to them. For example, the Architectural Barriers Act of 1968 was strong legislation that addressed the issue of physical accessibility. Although change was not quick, modifications warranted by this act afforded opportunities not available before. Requirements of ramps and curb cuts, for example, opened up numerous physical environments for individuals with physical limitations.

Additionally, it is hard to imagine that just over 25 years ago in the United States, children who had disabilities were not entitled to free public education.

The Individuals with Disabilities Education Act (originally called the Education for All Handicapped Children Act of 1975), provided a legal support system for children to receive a public education. This eventually led not only to mainstreaming and inclusion of children with disabilities in the classroom, but also assured their legal rights to assessment, leisure education, recreational therapy and recreation services in the public schools.

Employment, as well as support for recreation research and demonstration projects addressing the needs of people with disabilities, was made possible through legislation called the Rehabilitation Act of 1973 and its Amendments in 1974 and 1978. These pieces of legislation authorized funding for specific training of recreation personnel as well as research about recreation and people with disabilities. Additionally, they endorsed the idea that recreation services be consistently provided in rehabilitation and community settings.

Finally, the most significant legislation of this period was the Americans with Disabilities Act (ADA) of 1990. Specifically, the ADA addresses access and opportunity in areas of employment, accommodations (which include recreation facilities and services), transportation and communication for individuals with disabilities. This legislation is similar to the Civil Rights Act of 1964 in that it focuses on issues dealing with rights for people with disabilities specifically. For example, the Americans with Disabilities Act identifies separating programs or services for people with disabilities from those without (separate but equal) without also providing the choice of integrated opportunities as a form of discrimination.

In addition to the effects of legislation, technology is another force in society that is having a great impact on the opportunities of people with disabilities. Improved medicines are providing people with severely limiting conditions, such as cancer or epilepsy, the opportunity to function successfully with non-disabled peers in work, school and community environments.

Improved appliances and assistive devices such as prosthetics and communication equipment are also allowing people with disabilities to participate in more mainstream activities in their communities. For example, voice activated computers that print in Braille allow people with visual impairments to work in many more jobs than were possible in the past. Similarly, for recreation, equipment like the Monoski (a single railed seated ski) allows individuals without the use of their legs to downhill ski.

The combination of advances in technology and increased legislation provides the foundation for helping society become more receptive to people with disabilities as equals in the work, school and community environments. Through increased accessibility (physical and conceptual), people with disabilities are more able to "be present" in society. As a result, people without disabilities have the chance to see, interact with and learn about people with disabilities and thus are more able to understand and accept any differences.

In summary, modern American society can claim great strides in acknowledging the rights of people with disabilities. From the time of deinstitutionalization to the 1990's, social, legislative and technological advances have accelerated the rights and opportunities of all individuals with disabilities, providing opportunities for work and play not available before.

What is a Negative Attitude?

Negative attitudes can be just as restrictive as an architectural barrier to a person with a disability (Bedini, 1991). A negative attitude can take many forms. Initially, the reaction of feeling avoidant or resistant comes to mind when considering negative attitudes. In these situations, people with negative attitudes see little good or value in the object of their attention. Negative attitudes with regard to perception of people with disabilities, however, can also include inappropriate attitudes. For example, being overly protective and treating an adult with a disability like a child are ways of demonstrating poor or negative attitudes. Makas (1988) did a study which compared the responses of people with and without disabilities about what they considered positive attitudes toward people with disabilities. She found that there were major discrepancies between the two groups' perceptions. People with disabilities identified behaviors such as dropping the specific category of "disability" as well as promoting attitudes that defended civil and social rights of people with disabilities as examples of positive attitudes. Meanwhile, the people without disabilities suggested that a desire to be nice and helpful was a reflection of a positive attitude toward people with disabilities. People without disabilities tended to consider people with disabilities as needy or "special." Thus, being overprotective, although well intended, becomes an inappropriate and sometimes detrimental perception.

Ways Society Treats People with Disabilities

Wolfensberger (1972) listed several ways that society treats people with disabilities based on attitudes that were formed without education or interaction. Several of them include the following:

Subhuman. Wolfensberger suggested that people who devalue others as subhuman rarely admit it since this perception clashes so greatly with the average values held by society. In other words, we think we are more accepting and tolerant than we actually are. As a result, in function, people with disabilities are often relegated to a second class or subordinate status in society. Linveh (1980) suggested that society's tendency toward avoidance of people with disabilities could be based not only in fear but also in the challenge of the subhumanness of people with disabilities. While subhumanness suggests classlessness of people with disabilities, at the same time it poses a threat to non-disabled individuals' feelings of security and superiority. Drimmer (1991) proposed that society has a morbid fascination with humans who are different and uses it to reinforce its perception that the non-disabled are better, more beautiful or more competent than others. Goffman (1963) stated that society, based on the assumption that a person with a disability is not quite human, creates its own theories to explain feelings of superiority and animosity toward those that are different.

Menace. People in society view disability as a stigma that marks people who are different as objects to be feared. Fiedler (1978) suggested that people who are different or "freaks" elicit both curiosity and fear from the average person and pose a threat that is disruptive to the observer. This is evident from most horror movies where the "bad guy" or evil creature usually has some striking physical or mental "difference" or anomaly to identify him or her as the "monster."

Object of Pity. When people with disabilities are perceived and treated as individuals always in need, as not deserving to have this (disease or disability) happen to them, as needing help and care at all times, then they are objects of pity in society's eyes. Perhaps the best illustration of how people with disabilities are perceived by society as objects of pity are some of the telethons that are conducted to raise money for selected charities. Poster children (always cute, smiling and under 12 years of age) are used to represent the horrible "toll" the illness in question is taking on our youth and society. This exploitation manifests in that diseases such as muscular dystrophy strike many types of people, adults as well as children, and plain looking children as well as cute. These types of telethons use pity to solicit funds based on the assumption that if we see a cute child who is disabled, we will say, "Isn't that a shame. I will donate money." Unfortunately, and probably correctly, they believe that if people in society were presented with just the facts about the disease, they might not be inclined to donate.

Holy Innocent. The assumption that people with disabilities are "special" casts them into the role of "holy innocents" or "children of God." This connotation brings with it the assumptions that these individuals have been sent by God for a special purpose (perhaps as a reminder of our own mortality) and, therefore, are incapable of sin.

Eternal Child. Somewhat similar to the perception of holy innocent is the perception that people with disabilities are and always will be developmentally equal to a child. This assumption prohibits any potential regarding growth or adaptation. The individual with the disability is presumed to be limited in intellectual abilities, sense of responsibility, competence and related factors that signify adulthood.

The above examples are by no means all of the negative attitudes which society holds about people with disabilities. At the same time, it is unfair to assume that no one in society has fair and appropriate attitudes toward individuals who are different. Although as a society, we are learning and interacting more often with people with different abilities, negative attitudes are still pervasive, contributing to much discrimination in our world.

Causes of Negative Attitudes

Linveh (1991) identified two major sources of negative attitudes for society: psychodynamic (process or from within) and sociocultural (content or from outside). Selected elements are described below.

Psychodynamic Influences on Attitudes

According to Linveh (1991), unconscious psychological processes can be responsible for how one perceives and reacts to another. There are many ways that individuals in society respond to people with disabilities based on their personal experiences and on what is going on in their own lives.

Spread. Wright (1983) described the concept of "spread" as bringing together different characteristics. For example, a person who cannot speak because of a muscular disorder may be perceived as mentally retarded as well. Another example is the assumption that one must speak louder to a person who cannot see, spreading the blindness to deafness as well. This "spread" of assumptions of traits and abilities poses additional barriers to people with disabilities in their activities of daily living and also denies them opportunities to be "normal."

Fear of Association. Often people who are able-bodied are afraid that "society" will ignore and discriminate against them as well if they are "connected" to those with disabilities. Unfortunately, this fear of "guilt by association" (Siller, Chipman, Furguson & Vann, 1967) directs how people interact with others. Some people will avoid being seen in public with someone who has a disability because they do not want to be treated poorly as if they, too, were disabled.

Associating Responsibility with Etiology. This source of negative attitudes is based on the belief that individuals with a disability could somehow have avoided acquiring the disability or that they caused it to happen. In other words, the individual with the disability is blamed by society for having this "problem." Bordieri and Drehmer (1987) studied attitudes of college students majoring in business toward people with disabilities. They found that social acceptance of people with disabilities was correlated with how much responsibility the students placed on the individual with the disability. Therefore, when a person is perceived by others to have control over a certain situation, s/he is often held responsible for its consequences.

Guilt for Being Able-bodied. People without disabilities often avoid or withdraw from people with disabilities because they feel guilty that they can walk or see and those with whom they are interacting cannot. Many situation comedies have used the theme of guilt in this context. For example, in an episode of Golden Girls that featured a man with short stature, another character offered him appetizers, saying "Shrimp?" and then spent several minutes apologizing to redeem herself. Similarly, a common comic "bit" is trying to talk to someone who is blind without saying, "Do you *see* what I mean?" The discomfort that is experienced in these circumstances is based on the fact that the person who is able-bodied feels guilty for having abilities and would rather not recognize or acknowledge the other's "losses" so avoids situations and language that would bring attention to the disability.

Minority Status. Linveh (1991) also discussed how people with disabilities are viewed as a minority, thus marginalized by people in society. Perceiving people with disabilities as a minority has been credited to Roger Barker in 1948. This way of thinking supports the premise that problems experienced as a result of having a disability are bred by society and not the disability. Minorities are often perceived as "fringe" populations. These marginalized groups are not completely accepted by society but at the same time are not completely ostracized. Being a minority makes a group a "second" or inferior class.

Sociocultural Influences on Attitudes

Society, as well as individual cultures within our society, has a major impact on what and how we think. Expectations and assumptions about how we should act, what we should wear and what we should do with our lives often determine our attitudes and behaviors. Similarly, these expectations and assumptions encourage us to judge others who are atypical or "different" from the norm. The following are some of the ways society influences our attitudes about people with disabilities.

Physical Image. American society has always put a lot of emphasis on how we look. Attractiveness is a valued commodity and is used daily to sell everything from make-up to lawnmowers. This "body beautiful" craze encourages the everyday media consumer to lose weight, have pearly white teeth, long flowing hair, beautiful expensive clothes and physical competence. Although not many people in the real world have the attributes of these models and actors, we, as a society, subscribe to the message that is being sent, "If you don't look like this, you are not acceptable." For people who might be atypical in terms of missing limbs, using adaptive devices, or being shorter, taller, wider or smaller than the "average," expectations of the perfect physical image can be detrimental.

Media. Media consist, among others, of film, newspapers, magazines and television. Many studies have analyzed how the media often exploit people with disabilities (e.g., Bedini, 1991; Byrd & Elliott, 1988; Thurer, 1980). Additionally, literature and art can have an impact on how people with disabilities are perceived. For centuries, media and literature used characteristics of disability to convey evil, inferiority or comedy. Zola (1992) suggested that societal and political influences have a much greater impact on disability than the actual disability itself. Therefore, depiction of disability as "inappropriate" can reinforce society's perception of people with disabilities as second class or fringe citizens.

In some cases, these depictions even encourage fear and animosity toward people with disabilities. Thurer (1980) stated that metaphors in art and literature have been used as symbols of evil or inferiority. For example, scars or hunchbacks symbolize evilness of one's character. Zola (1992) did an analysis of crime fiction finding that villains are often identified by their features (i.e., scars, clubfoot, disfigurement). Similarly, classic and popular literature are full of these metaphors in characters such as Long John Silver, Captain Ahab, Cain, Richard III and villains in stories like Dick Tracy and James Bond (Bedini, 1991). Perhaps one of the most intense areas of subtle exploitation comes from horror movies. These movies often (and unfairly) portray an individual with a history of severe and persistent mental illness as the maniacal murderer who is evil and exhibits unpredictable and dangerous behaviors.

Byrd and Elliott (1985) studied 1051 feature films finding that 11% of the characters had a disability. From that group, 44% had a severe and persistent mental illness, 80% of which were portrayed in a negative manner (dangerous or "psychotic killer" type). Weinberg and Santana (1978) studied comic books and found "deformed" characters were usually evil. Conversely, the media often presents the opposite end of the spectrum. Longmore (1987) noted that the film and television industries create a specialness or super-humanness for people with disabilities. Many of the studies about how people with disabilities are portrayed in literature and media conclude that they are more often represented as very bad or very good but seldom "average."

Work Ethic. The goal instilled in children in the United States is to be productive and successful. As we become adults, falling short of this goal is often perceived as failure and worthlessness. Some people with disabilities are not able to be productive in the same way as people without disabilities. As a result, Western society sees them negatively as non-contributing members of society.

Stigma. In the early 1960's Irving Goffman presented the concept of stigma. Stigma is a form of labeling which originated centuries ago when criminals or slaves were branded to mark them as inferior citizens. This mark or brand was a symbol of disgrace. Today, we stigmatize people through words rather than marks that label them as less important. Disparaging nicknames such as "cripple" or "psycho" deny the subject their identity as a person. Stigma also perpetuates negative images of these individuals which are not only untrue but also unfair.

Results of labeling include the assumptions that are generated from the images created. Fine and Asch (1988) presented several assumptions about what disability means. First, it is assumed by society that disability is all biological and is synonymous with the person. Second, society also assumes that when a person with a disability faces problems, it is because of the impairment. The third assumption states that the person with a disability is a "victim." Fourth, society assumes that the disability is central to the person's life (self-concept, self-determination, social comparisons and reference groups). The final assumption is that having a disability is the same as needing help and social support.

While these assumptions are clearly untrue, people in society perpetuate them because they lack education about or opportunities to interact with people who have disabilities. If people in society know more about each other, they would be less likely to make and reinforce these assumptions.

Factors Affecting Attitudes

Linveh (1991) presented various factors that affected the attitudes one develops toward people with disabilities.

Functionality. Disabilities which appear to be most functional are usually perceived with the most positive attitudes. For example, people usually are more receptive of someone on crutches than someone in a wheelchair because the are more "normal." Similarly, we are more likely to feel comfortable around someone with partial sight or hearing than with someone who is completely blind or deaf.

Visibility. The more visible a disability is, the more negative the attitude becomes. For example, people's attitudes toward someone with epilepsy or heart trouble usually are more positive than toward someone who has cerebral palsy because the hidden disabilities are easier to avoid acknowledging.

Contagiousness. The more contagious a condition is perceived to be, the worse the attitudes are. People fear "catching" disease and disabilities. If a disability is even just perceived to be contagious, the attitude toward that group of people is clearly negative. The best example today involves people who are HIV positive or who have AIDS. Although medical professionals clearly state that this disease is not transferable through average daily contact, people who are HIV positive or who have AIDS have been denied access to every public opportunity ranging from recreation programs to education services. People in society ostracize anyone whom they perceive threatens their well-being. Unfortunately, once again, it is the lack of education about this disease that is reinforcing these negative attitudes and behaviors.

Body Part Affected. If one were to experience severe burns on his/her hands or feet, attitudes would be more positive than if these burns were on the face. Certain parts of the body are essential for our communication and self-image. If these parts are threatened or disfigured, society is more likely to consider us in a negative manner than if other, "less important" features are affected.

Predictability. In Goffman's (1963) analysis of stigma, he stated that "blemishes of character" were one of the three dimensions of stigma. Today, blemishes of character refer to people with psychiatric or social disabilities such as homelessness. Perhaps the reason why people with psychiatric disabilities are feared more than most physical disabilities is a combination of their supposed unpredictability and the fact that society tends to blame the people with the disability for their condition as if they could control it. Predictability also refers to the potential for a cure. Notably curable diseases such as tuberculosis are more likely to be perceived positively by society than those like schizophrenia whose prognosis is unknown.

A study by Safilios-Rothschild (1982) summarized the factors that affect attitudes toward people with disabilities. The results of her study suggested a hierarchical structure for negative stigma ranging from least threatening to most threatening. People with sensory disabilities are less threatening to society than people with mobility limitations such as paraplegia or cerebral palsy. People with physical deformities (misshapen body parts) are more discriminated against than both of the former disabilities. People manifesting perceived rationality or morality disabilities such as alcoholism, mental retardation or severe and persistent mental illness are discriminated against the most.

Effects on Leisure from Negative Attitudes about People with Disabilities

It is important to look not only at the causes of negative attitudes but also at the effects or impact that negative attitudes can have on people with disabilities. Much has been written about the psychosocial impact of having a disability. Within these discussions, research notes how different people with disabilities react to being teased, excluded or pitied. For example, West (1984) studied the barriers to recreation participation presented by "social stigma" or the labels that society places on an individual or group. He found that individuals with disabilities experienced negative reactions from the community because of their disability. As a result of these bad experiences, many of the people interviewed stated that they chose to avoid future community recreation programs and opportunities.

Additionally, Bedini and Henderson (1994) studied women with physical disabilities who lived independently in the community and found that the women felt limited in their opportunities for leisure because of society's expectations. These women also described the "emotional toll" of being pitied and stared at which often forced them to curtail their public and leisure activities. Several of these women also described how the attitudes of medical personnel with whom they dealt made them feel unimportant and ashamed to have a disability. They expressed how these bad experiences manifested in feelings of low self-esteem, insecurity in social situations and poor body image.

Finally, research about the attitudes of health care personnel toward people with disabilities suggests that despite the image of "empathetic helper," negative attitudes toward clients with disabling conditions can exist among health care professionals. Geskie and Salasek (1988) summarized studies about the attitudes of health care personnel toward people with disabilities done in the last three decades. They found that patterns existed based on occupational group, age, sex, education, job function and socioeconomic status. They also noted that the philosophical model (medical versus psychosocial) under which one works might have an impact on the level of attitudes expressed by different health care personnel. They concluded, however, that few consistencies existed because of the many diverse factors that come into play. In addition to the demography and personal characteristics of the staff, client diagnosis, setting and administrative philosophies might contribute to the development of both positive and negative attitudes toward people with disabilities. More comparative research is warranted.

The above research suggests that the attitudes of not only people in the community but also medical personnel can affect the recreation choices and pursuits of people with disabilities. Recreational therapists as well as community recreation professionals need to be aware of this potential for negative experiences in recreation environments. With this insight, they can work to prepare clients before discharge, both through leisure education and by "walking" the client through their first ventures into a new leisure activity in the community. Clients tend to be less reticent to participate in a leisure activity if they are supported through their first experience with activity. Professionals can also strive to make the community environment more accepting. McClain and Todd (1990) showed that with appropriately presented information about accessibility, therapists can have a positive impact on the community's accommodation.

Encouraging Positive Attitudes

Every recreational therapist has an obligation not only to be sensitive to how s/he is treating people with disabilities, but also how s/he can help others develop appropriate attitudes. Gartner and Joe (1987) suggested that we note that individuals possess both strengths and limitations and that we use those to build our programs. They also stated that limitations should be viewed as something to be overcome, not as defining characteristics.

According to Donaldson (1980), attitude modification requires unbalancing and unfreezing current attitudes by reducing restraining factors or increasing driving forces. Applying Fishbein's (1963) attitude theory to facilitating change of attitudes of individuals without disabilities, the key element of attitude change is the conditioning process so that old responses become unbalanced and new appropriate evaluation responses can be generated. With proper evaluation responses, new attitudes can be developed and retained.

Several techniques for changing negative attitudes toward people with disabilities exist including: (a) direct contact with or exposure to a person with a disability, (b) education (factually accurate information about disability), (c) persuasive messages, (d) disability simulation and (e) group discussion (Donaldson, 1980).

Exposure and Direct Contact. Often unfamiliar situations breed anxiety. We are never really given any rules or techniques for dealing with someone who is different than we are. When people are anxious they tend to deal with their fears by either under of over reacting. For example, some people will make a particular effort to avoid contact with people with disabilities. Others will try to compensate for their fears by being overly protective or helpful to people with disabilities.

Direct contact is perhaps one of the most successful techniques in changing attitudes. Yuker (1988) studied the effect of contact with people with disabilities and positive attitudes and found that 51% of the studies identified positive differences in attitude while only 10% showed negative changes. Hamilton and Anderson (1983) studied undergraduate students in a leisure studies curriculum specifically examining both education and experiential interactions. The experiential group (contact with people with disabilities) showed significant improvements over the group that did not interact with people with disabilities.

Donaldson (1980) suggested, however, that direct contact be engaged in under certain conditions only. Direct contact must take place within a structured context to make the difference. Incidental interaction with a person with a disability will not assure positive impact. Studies reporting the use of direct contact alone as a technique were not significant in positive changes. Similarly, it is important that using direct contact as a technique must assure that the person with a disability and the target audience represent equal roles, rather than a helper/helpee relationship between individuals. Differentials of power and control actually can create negative effects on the attitudes of the non-disabled toward people with disabilities (Donaldson, 1980; Makas, 1988). Although the resultant attitudes of the individuals who were not disabled can be considered "positive," they are often sympathetic and demeaning rather than identifying the person with a disability as a social equal.

Education. Factual information about disability is another technique for decreasing negative attitudes. According to Ibrahim and Herr (1982) increased information leads to decreased negative attitudes. Monson and Shurtleff (1979) studied the effects of informational filmstrips on attitudes of non-disabled children toward people with disabilities. Results showed that these films produced positive changes. Other studies with college students demonstrated that through education techniques the attitudes of the subjects not only improved in post-test scores but also showed positive results six weeks later (Bedini, 1992; Ibrahim & Herr, 1982).

Education could include different forms of media including props and speakers themselves. An example of this are the puppets, "Kids on the Block." These are large puppets of children with different types of disabilities who talk in the first person about what it is like to be disabled (Aiello, 1988). It is important to note, however, that frequency was an important factor in changing attitudes with exposure and meaning. Therefore, an incidental film or particular information regarding people with disabilities might have no impact at all unless presented often.

Linveh (1980) noted that language can contribute to the perceptions of people with disabilities. For example, terms like "blind as a bat" and "sick as a dog" use comparisons to animals to create an inferior image. The careful use of terminology and language is also a form of indirect education. Dattilo and Smith (1990) emphasized how the use of terminology can affect the quality of life for a person with a disability. How we depict people with disabilities in word or in writing is important. The words we choose to describe a person with a disability can be very powerful. How one characterizes a person with a disability affects reactions to that person (Hannah & Midlarsky, 1987).

Persuasive Communication and Sensitivity Training. A technique where the message is communicated with the intent of convincing the audience of its suggestions is called persuasive communication (Kennedy, Smith & Austin, 1991). When effective, the message is sent by someone who is trusted or liked enough to change the beliefs and attitudes of those to whom it is sent. Additionally, the strength and content of the message are important.

Several studies have been done using training for camp counselors or non-disabled peers of children with disabilities in schools (Sasso & Rude, 1988; Rynders, Schleien & Mustonen, 1990). In most cases, the training alleviated many of the typical unfamiliar and uncomfortable situations that previously turned into problems.

Simulations and Role Play. Using the opportunity to simulate what it is like to have a disability may help people get a sense or "feel" of having a disability. Commonly used as a classroom experience, "becoming disabled for a day" can encourage students to try to understand disability from the inside. Ibrahim and Herr (1982) used role play simulations of speech and audiology disabilities with college students to elicit attitude change. They found that positive changes not only resulted but also remained at six weeks.

McGill (1984) stressed that these simulations must be guided experiences if they are to work. It is important that the instructor make sure that students not only understand the purpose and procedure of the exercise, but also that they truly complete the entire task as designed. Additionally, it is important that the experience is processed with professional guidance and put into context appropriately for it to have potential in attitude change.

Combination of Techniques. Although all of the aforementioned techniques individually have generated some success in changing attitudes toward people with disabilities, it seems from the literature that combinations of the methods have more potential for attitude change than applying them independently. For example, Dewar (1982) used simulations, direct contact and group discussion in combination and generated positive results. Similarly, a combination of research information, role play and direct contact with people with disabilities increased positive attitudes of community recreators (Stone, 1987). More specific to recreational therapy, Bedini (1992) used a combination of direct contact, discussion, role play and education to successfully improve attitudes of students in leisure studies classes.

Other Considerations for Changing Attitudes

Mindfulness versus mindlessness. Langer and Chanowitz (1988) developed the concept of "mindfulness versus mindlessness" which suggests that when society perceives someone as being disabled, the people perceived as disabled have been *categorized* by society. Traditional approaches to changing this tendency to label try to eliminate categories and to view all people as "human beings." Unfortunately, this perspective is not realistic as it is natural for people in society to use labels and categories. Langer and Chanowitz (1988) proposed, therefore, that being mindful or consciously creating categories, is potentially positive as opposed to being mindless and relying on already constructed categories. Being mindless is to assume certain similarities among a particular group beyond those that actually exist. In other words, it is better to be cognitively active or to discriminate differences and construct our own categories based on what we see at the time, rather than just going along with what has already been constructed and assume it is applicable to all people in all situations. The authors suggested that programs that encourage mindlessness in an attempt to change attitudes toward people with disabilities will probably not succeed. Mindfulness will teach us that we are all deviant (Langer & Chanowitz, 1988) in reference to some attributes. Therefore, to be disabled is not merely belonging to a particular groups. In a study by Langer, Bashner and Chanowitz (1985), any attempt to change attitudes of children toward people with disabilities through encouraging mindfulness was successful. According to Langer and Chanowitz, "...we decreased prejudice by increasing discrimination" (p. 81).

Encouraging Self-Advocacy. Helping individuals with disabilities become empowered can contribute to changing society's negative attitudes toward disabilities. Empowerment involves not only being acknowledged but also gaining control over one's life. According to Chesler and Chesney (1988), the attitudes of significant others can be "dis-empowering." These significant others can include family, friends, medical personnel and community agencies. Chesler and Chesney (1988) suggested that self-help groups or self-advocacy groups can enhance and encourage empowerment. They identified six benefits of self-help groups: (a) promoting disclosure and networking or "going public," (b) sharing emotional experiences, (c) gaining access to information, (d) gaining new coping skills and practical resources, (e) contributing to welfare of others and (f) mobilizing and acting for change. The benefits from these groups can increase one's sense of control and, in turn, have an impact on the negative attitudes of society.

Implications for Recreational Therapy

Recreational therapists are in a prime position to facilitate positive attitudes of individuals who are not disabled and also of individuals who are newly disabled and their families toward people with disabilities. Several implications are important for recreational therapists to consider.

First, keep in mind that we are all just temporarily able-bodied. The "minority" group of disability is the only group that is completely non-discriminating. Anyone can join regardless of age, race, sex, culture or competence (Stanat & Gray, 1995). Maintaining this thought will allow the recreational therapist to do an occasional "humility check" whereby we realize we are all eligible candidates for this experience.

Second, remember that our attitudes can direct our behavior. It is important for each recreational therapist to do a "self-evaluation" regarding his/her own attitudes toward different groups of disabilities. As Geskie and Salasek (1988) found, different types of health care professionals demonstrated a full range of attitudes toward different disability groups. Just because we are working in health care fields does not mean that we are exempt from or inappropriate in having a negative attitude. The important thing is that we do the work necessary to mindfully get in touch with those feelings and deal with them. As therapists, we are in a position of power. It is possible that we might slip into addressing our own needs by nurturing rather than the needs of empowering our clients. We must be careful to avoid creating dependence in our clients by overemphasizing the helper/helpee relationship. It is also important, however, that we do not alienate our clients by being too demanding. As Donaldson (1980) and Makas (1988) noted, the difference in power (between therapist and client) can encourage negative attitudes toward dis-empowered individuals. Thus, a recreational therapist's attitude in combination with his or her position of power can have a major effect on the treatment outcomes for the clients.

Third, the kind of language we use when describing our clients is a reflection of our attitudes. Dattilo and Smith (1990) suggested that even in health care professionals, the use of insensitive language may occur due to lack of knowledge of appropriate words or phrases to use. They presented several considerations for helping professionals to be sensitive in their language. The first consideration was the concept of "people first" language. Rather than referring to someone as the "epileptic" or the "retarded man," people first language encourages using "a person with epilepsy" or "a man with mental retardation." This type of phrasing places emphasis on the person and puts the disability in the place of a modifier, thus taking the focus off the disability. A second consideration regarding language was communicating dignity and respect for individuals. This means that terms such as "moron" or "idiot" are demeaning and should be excluded. Third, Dattilo and Smith recommended using consistent terms to enhance understanding. They stated that the terms impairment, handicap and disability are distinct terms with separate meanings. (See Chapter 5, *Clinical Practice Models*, for definitions of these terms.) We should be careful not to use them interchangeably. Finally, they suggested that we should avoid the use of the term "normal" when referring to people without disabilities. Use of this word suggests that those with disabilities are outside the norm and "deviant." "Non-disabled" can be used instead. It is the therapist's responsibility to keep up with the most recent information about language and perceptions of people with disabilities.

Additionally, it is important to encourage the use of proper terms from other clients and families. Our environmental input can have just as much impact as direct interaction. Hershenson (1992) noted that different concepts of a disability by therapists, clients and significant others can impede the rehabilitation process.

A fourth implication for recreational therapists regarding attitudes toward people with disabilities is related to proactive propaganda. Often recreational therapists have the opportunity to publicize their programs in the media ranging from public service announcements to sponsored community events. Thoughtful consideration needs to go into every news release, banner and presentation to assure that your clients are being presented as people first. Matthews, White and Mrdjenovich-Hank (1990) studied the effects of a slide presentation by an independent living center and found that the presentation had an impact on not only the attitudes of the community toward people with disabilities but also toward the center. How we prepare and present ourselves and our clients to the community can be very powerful.

Related to how recreational therapists present themselves is the importance of normalizing community outings as much as possible. Often field trips are taken on large buses with the facility's name on the side. To truly create a normalized environment, recreational therapists should consider ways to eliminate labels for the clients. Smaller vans that are more "normal" in appearance can facilitate the integration of groups and individuals into community events and settings.

Last, recreational therapy programs should attempt to incorporate assertiveness training methods of empowerment into all treatment plans. Empowering individuals within the medical setting can prepare and facilitate their integration into the community upon discharge. West (1984) studied social stigma as a barrier to accessing community recreation opportunities for people with disabilities. In his study, people with disabilities experienced negative attitudes from people without disabilities in their community settings. Because of this, many individuals with disabilities chose to terminate their activities in these settings. Helping clients become more assertive can not only empower them to face these challenges, but also help them present themselves in a way that is less threatening for individuals who are not disabled.

Summary

Attitudes are very powerful elements in our society. An attitude can be the greatest barrier to a person with a disability, greater than any other architectural, communication or environmental obstacle. As recreational therapists, we have the ability and the responsibility to explore ourselves, our colleagues, our clients and their significant others to determine how attitudes affect the rehabilitative process and the ultimate success in leisure independence. To achieve complete normalization, people with disabilities should be allowed access, choice and opportunities afforded to anyone else in society (Leisure is for Everyone, 1988). Understanding how attitudes work and how to change them can contribute greatly to the ultimate goals of recreation and leisure independence and integration for our clients.

Learning Activities

1. *Insider/Outsider Activity.* On a piece of paper, have each person in class write down their worst handicap or disability. Ask them each to write the same handicap/disability on a second piece of paper. When everyone is finished, collect one set of papers from the class and ask them to keep the second piece and not let anyone see it. Mix up the pieces from the first set and redistribute them so that no one gets his/her own. When everyone has a new disability/handicap, ask them to compare the two (their own and the newly acquired one). How many would trade their own handicap/disability for the one they just received? Take a count and figure what percent of the

class would not trade. Wright (1983) conducted this experiment in several forms and found that 62 to 95 percent of the subjects reclaimed their own disability/handicap. Encourage discussion as to why they decided what they did. This result is due to the familiarity of their own disability and how they have learned to cope.

2. *Interview a Person with a Disability.* Interview a person with a disability asking questions about his/her history, his/her perceptions of having a disability, what attitudes s/he has about himself/herself, what attitudes s/he has experienced from others, how attitudes of others has helped or hindered his/her life and leisure pursuits and so forth. Video presentations such as Stanat and Gray's (1995) taped interviews of nine people with different disabilities provide similar experiences.

3. *Media Analysis.* Gather at least 60 articles about disabilities from newspapers and magazines. Then organize them as to topics. You might find they fall into categories based on disability types, political versus educational, categories such as technology, human interests and so forth. Next, using the materials about attitudes from this chapter, analyze what the purposes of the article are, to inform, raise consciousness, elicit pity or others. Finally, examine the presentation of the article. Look for where it was within the page; how big it was; how long it was; whether there was a picture; whether it was in color or black and white; if there were people in the picture, what the people were doing; whether the article portrayed them in a negative or positive light. Feel free to add your own analysis, then summarize this group or subgroup of articles.

4. *Accessibility Survey.* Get the standards for accessibility and conduct a survey on a recreation/leisure facility in your community. Write a report about what met and what failed to meet standards. Share the information with the proprietor of that facility. Explore facilities such as museums, libraries, restaurants, bowling alleys, moving theaters. (Standards for accessibility may be found in material from the Architectural Barriers Compliance Board, Washington D. C., the *Community Integration Program, Second Edition* by Armstrong and Lauzen (1994) from Idyll Arbor, Inc. or the Americans with Disabilities self-evaluation materials from the National Recreation and Parks Association, Ashburn, VA).

5. *Sponsor a Disability Awareness Day.* Students and faculty alike can learn a great deal from having the opportunity to become informed about and interact with people with disabilities. Recreational therapy students can take the lead by sponsoring a disability awareness day (or week). Events and activities could include: (a) demonstration wheelchair basketball or beep ball where students and faculty have the opportunity to participate, (b) popular films about disabilities such as *Mask, Waterdance, Elephant Man,* (c) architectural barriers scavenger hunt, (d) lectures about disabilities by

professionals, students or faculty with disabilities and (e) information tables with written literature about disabilities and recreational therapy. Add your own ideas. If your college or university has an Office of Disabled Students Services, involve them as much as possible.

Study Questions

1. What is "attitude?" How do attitudes affect behavior? What are some key actions which help change attitudes? Would the actions which change attitude work the same way on someone with a disability versus someone without a disability?

2. How have people historically viewed people with disabilities? How have these views changed over the last twenty years? How do these changes impact your patient's ability to function within his/her community?

3. What were some of the initial laws enacted which regulated access for individuals with disabilities? What types of barriers were removed first? What barriers seem to remain? Give several specific examples of the remaining barriers which you have found within your own community.

4. What are some negative attitudes toward disability? How can negative attitudes become barriers? Explain how the term (or concept) of "special" (as in "special recreation programming") actually may promote inappropriate attitudes and barriers?

5. What are the five attitudes toward individuals with disabilities described by Wolfensberger? Give at least two examples of how each attitude could negatively impact treatment or integration into the community. How would you address the negative impact?

References

Aiello, B. (1988). The Kids on the Block and attitude change: A 10 year perspective. In H. E. Yuker (Ed.) *Attitudes toward people with disabilities* (pp. 223-229). New York: Springer Publishing Company.

Ajzen, I. (1988). *Attitudes, personality and behavior*. Chicago, IL: The Doresey Press.

Allport, G. W. (1935). Attitudes. In C. Murchinson (Ed.). *A handbook of social psychology* (pp. 798-844). Worcester, MA: Clark University Press.

Armstrong, M. & Lauzen, S. (1994). *Community integration program* (2nd ed.). Ravensdale, WA: Idyll Arbor, Inc.

Bedini, L. A. (1991). Modern day freaks?: The exploitation of people with disabilities. *Therapeutic Recreation Journal, 25*(1), 60-69.

Bedini, L. A. (1992). Encouraging change in attitudes toward people with disabilities through undergraduate leisure studies and recreation curricula. *Schole: A Journal of Leisure Studies and Recreation Education, 7*, 44-54.

Bedini, L. A. & Henderson, K. A. (1994). Women with disabilities and the challenges to leisure service providers. *Journal of Park and Recreation Administration, 12*(1), 17-34.

Bordieri, J. E. & Drehmer, D. E. (1987). Attribution of responsibility and predicating social accountability of disabled workers. *Rehabilitation Counseling Bulletin, 30*, 218-226.

Byrd, E. K. & Elliott, T. R. (1985). Feature film and disability: A descriptive study. *Rehabilitation Psychology, 30*(1), 47-51.

Byrd, E. K. & Elliott, T. R. (1988). Media and disability: A discussion of research. In H. E. Yuker (Ed.). *Attitudes toward people with disabilities* (pp. 82-95). New York: Springer Publishing Company.

Chesler, M. A. & Chesney, B. K. (1988). Self-help groups: Empowering attitude and behavior of disabled and chronically ill persons. In H. H. Yuker (Ed.). *Attitudes toward people with disabilities* (pp. 230-245). New York: Springer Publishing Company.

Clair, C. (1968). *Human curiosities*. London: Abelard Schuman.

Dattilo, J. & Smith, R. W. (1990). Communicating positive attitudes toward people with disabilities through sensitive terminology. *Therapeutic Recreation Journal, 24*(1), 8-17.

Dewar, R. L. (1982). Peer acceptance of handicapped students. *Teaching Exceptional Children, 14*(5), 188-193.

Donaldson, J. (1980). Changing attitudes toward handicapped persons: A review and analysis of research. *Exceptional Children, 46*(7), 504-514.

Drimmer, F. (1991). *Very special people: The struggles, loves and triumphs of human oddities*. New York: Citadel Press Books.

Duran, J. (1969). *The history of court fools*. London: Richard Bentley.

Fielder, L. (1978). *Freaks: Myths and images of the secret self*. New York: Simon and Schuster.

Fine, M. & Asch, A. (1988). Disability beyond stigma: Social interaction, discrimination and activism. *Journal of Social Issues, 44*(1), 3-21.

Fishbein, M. (1963). An investigation of the relationships between beliefs about an object and the attitude toward the object. *Human Relations, 16*, 233-240.

Gartner, A. & Joe, T. (Eds.). (1987). *Images of the disabled, disabling images*. New York: Praeger.

Geskie, M. A. & Salasek, J. L. (1988). Attitudes of health care personnel toward people with disabilities. In H. H. Yuker (Ed.). *Attitudes toward people with disabilities* (pp. 230-245). New York: Springer Publishing Company.

Goffman, I. (1963). *Stigma: Notes of the management of spoiled identity*. Englewood Cliffs, NJ: Prentice Hall.

Hamilton, E. J. & Anderson, S. C. (1983). Effects of leisure activities on attitudes toward people with disabilities. *Therapeutic Recreation Journal, 17*(3), 50-57.

Hannah, M. E. & Midlarsky, E. (1987). Differential impact of labels and behavior descriptions on attitudes towards persons with disabilities. *Rehabilitation Psychology, 32*(4), 227-238.

Hershenson, D. B. (1992). Concepts of disability: Implications for rehabilitation. *Rehabilitation Counseling Bulletin, 35*(3), 154-160.

Ibrahim, F. A. & Herr, E. L. (1982). Modification of attitudes toward disability: Differential effect of two education modes. *Journal of American Rehabilitation Counseling Association, 26*(1), 29-36.

Kennedy, D., Smith, R. W. & Austin, D. (1991). *Special recreation: Opportunities for persons with disabilities* (2nd ed.). Dubuque, IA: Wm. C. Brown.

Langer, E. J., Bashner, R. S. & Chanowitz, B. (1985). Decreasing prejudice by increasing discrimination. *Journal of Personality and Social Psychology, 49,* 112-120.

Langer, E. J. & Chanowitz, B. (1988). Mindfulness/mindlessness: A new perspective for the study of disability. In H. H. Yuker (Ed.). *Attitudes toward people with disabilities* (pp. 230-245). New York: Springer Publishing Company.

LIFE Center for Recreation and Disability Studies. (1988). *Leisure is for everyone.* Chapel Hill, NC: Author.

Linveh, H. (1980). Disability and monstrosity: Further comments. *Rehabilitation Literature, 41*(11-12), 280-283.

Linveh, H. (1991). On the origins of negative attitudes toward people with disabilities. In R. P. Marinelli & A. E. Dell Orto (Eds.). *The psychological and social impact of disability* (3rd ed.). (pp. 181-197). New York: Springer Publishing Company.

Longmore, P. K. (1987). Screening stereotypes: Images of disabled people in television and motion pictures. In A. Gartner & T. Joe (Eds.). *Images of the disabled, disabling images.* New York: Praeger.

Makas, E. (1988). Positive attitudes toward disabled people: Disabled and non-disabled persons' perspective. *Journal of Social Issues, 44*(1), 49-61.

Matthews, R. M., White, G. W. & Mrdjenovich-Hanks, P. (1990). Using a slide presentation to change attitudes toward people with disabilities and knowledge of independent living services. *Rehabilitation Counseling Bulletin, 33*(4), 301-306.

McClain, L. & Todd, C. (1990). Food store accessibility. *American Journal of Occupational Therapy, 44,* 487-491.

McGill, J. (1984). Training for integration: Are blindfolds really enough? *Leisureability, 11*(2), 12-15.

Meyer, L. (1973). Recreation and the mentally ill. In T. Stein & H. D. Sessoms (Eds.). *Recreation and special populations* (pp. 137-170). Boston: Holbrook Press.

Monson, D. & Shurtleff, C. (1979). Altering attitudes toward the physically handicapped through print and non-print media. *Language Arts, 56*(2), 163-170.

Nirje, B. (1969). The normalization principle and its human management implications. In R. Krugal & W. Wolfensberger (Eds.). *Changing patterns in residential services for mental retardation* (pp. 179-195). Washington, DC: President's Committee on Mental Retardation.

Rynders, J. E., Schleien, S. J. & Mustonen, T. (1990). Integrating children with severe disabilities for intensified outdoor education: Focus on feasibility. *Mental Retardation, 28*(1), 7-14.

Safilios-Rothschild, C. (1982). Social and psychological parameters of friendship and intimacy for disabled people. In M. G. Eisenberg, C. Griggins & R. J. Duval. *Disabled people as second class citizens* (pp. 40-51). New York: Springer Publishing Company.

Sasso, G. M. & Rude, H. A. (1988). The social effects of integration on non-handicapped children. *Education and Training in Mental Retardation, 3,* 18-23.

Siller, J., Chipman, A., Furguson, L. T. & Vann, D. H. (1967). *Studies in reaction to disability: XI. Attitudes of the non-disabled toward the physically disabled.* New York: New York University School of Education.

Stanat, F. C. & Gray, J. *Like You and Me: Different But Not Disabled: Eliminating Handicappism* [Video]. Ravensdale, WA: Idyll Arbor, Inc.

Stone, C. F. (1987). Examining attitudes of non-disabled individuals toward disabled individual through use of L.I.F.E. inservice training. Unpublished manuscript, University of North Carolina at Chapel Hill.

Thurer, S. (1980). Disability and monstrosity: A look at literary distortions of handicapping conditions. *Rehabilitation Literature, 41*(1-2), 12-15.

Triandis, H. (1971). *Attitude and attitude change.* New York: Wiley and Sons.

Weinberg, N. & Santana, R. (1978). Comic books: Champions of the disabled stereotype. *Rehabilitation Literature, 39*(11-12), 327-331.

Welsford, E. (1935). *The fool: His social and literary history.* London: Faber.

West, P. C. (1984). Social stigma and community recreation participation by the mentally and physically handicapped. *Therapeutic Recreation Journal, 18*(1), 40-49.

Wolfensberger, W. (1972). *The principle of normalization in human services.* Toronto: National Institute on Mental Retardation.

Wright. B. A. (1983). *Physically disabled — A psychosocial approach* (2nd ed.). New York: Harper and Row.

Yuker, H. E. (1988). *Attitudes toward people with disabilities.* New York: Springer Publishing.

Zola, I. K. (1992). "Any distinguishing features?" The portrayal of disability in the crime-mystery genre. In P. M. Ferguson, D. L. Ferguson & S. J. Taylor (Eds.) *Interpreting disability* (pp. 233-250). New York: Teachers College Press.

Zwelling, S. S. (1985). *Quest for a cure.* Williamsburg: VA: The Colonial Williamsburg Foundation.

Chapter 16

Excess Disability

René P. Katsinas

A significant issue in the general field of health care and the specific field of recreational therapy is excess disability. Excess disability is used to describe the condition of a patient whose impairment is greater than expected for a specific disease process. Katsinas and Gugel (1992, p. 1) defined excess disability as:

> encompassing a decline of functional abilities, alertness, cognitive status, orientation, communication, physical status and socialization attributed to the environment and not specifically to a disease process.

In other words, excess disability is functional limitations induced by factors other than the disease or impairment.

This condition affects the economics of health care, the practice of the therapists, the need for intervention services and potential success of services. It has a profound impact on quality of life issues for the individuals in question. Problems resulting from excess disability show up in patient dysfunction, poor rehabilitation progress, increased need for intervention services and even early or unnecessary institutionalization. The decline in the quality of life, increased costs of care and added intervention requirements have a significant impact on our health care system in terms of economics, labor demands and potential abuse issues.

Symptoms

Symptoms of excess disability vary from individual to individual. Assessment of the condition requires examination of an individual's functional limitations. General symptoms can be divided into three domains related to function: physical, cognitive and psychosocial.

A classic presentation of excess disability involves extreme physical deconditioning. Symptoms of deconditioning include: problems with general endurance, fatigue and endurance for sustained activity such as walking, stair climbing and activities of daily living (ADLs) (Seines, 1990). The presence of deconditioning is also seen in reduced respiratory volume, increased breathlessness and changes in cardiovascular function (Seines, 1990). Individuals suffering from deconditioning frequently have elevated resting heart rates and post-exertion heart rates which remain high for extended periods following mild activity. Other physical symptoms include dysfunctions in connective tissue and joint movement. Reduced flexibility and strength are common examples. Further investigation may also reveal deficits related to neurologic function and metabolic function, as well as bowel and bladder functional ability.

Cognitive impairments may include reduction in reasoning speed and increased response time to stimuli, as well as inability to remain engaged for sustained periods in appropriate activities or conversations. Other impairments include confusion and pseudodementia, which may present slow response time to questions and word finding problems. Disorientation to place, time and even to person may also be seen. Other cognitive deficits may exist in problem solving, abstraction and retrieval and storage of information.

Psychosocial impairment of function from excess disability is difficult to quantify. Observations of social functioning may reveal increasing dependence on others. In addition, lack of confidence in one's own actions, low self-esteem and poor perceptions of self-competence should be assessed as possible deficits. Individuals suffering from excess disability may perceive themselves as impaired and may act accordingly even when no concrete deficits are observed during situational assessments. Motivational problems indicated by lack of willingness to initiate or carry out activity without frequent prompting and/or lack of engagement within the environment are symptoms of the condition.

Depression, regressive social behavior and low and foundering levels of engagement within social and home environments may also be indicators of profound excess disability. It is difficult, however, to sort out the factors of depressed affect from the other indicators of the condition of excess disability. A significant portion of individuals exhibiting symptoms of this condition suffer from depression either as a result of their functional impairment or as a precursor to the condition itself.

Etiology

The increased loss of functional ability attributed to excess disability may be traced to several factors found singularly or in combination. These factors may be located within the physical and social environments, influenced by the patient's capacity to perform and may also result, in part, from the effects of medications (Katsinas, 1996, Osterweil, 1990).

Physical environments include the nature of the lighting, signage and furniture, as well as overall physical accessibility. The physical environment must also include the degree to which the individual is homebound.

Assessment of the social environment includes examination of the attitudes expressed verbally and nonverbally by family and peers. It also includes the interaction of the individual with helping professionals. The individual's perception of what s/he is capable of accomplishing is colored by the perception of those groups. If the perception, intentionally or unintentionally, expressed by family, professional or para-professional caregivers or peers is that the person is dysfunctional or incapable of performance and/or choice, then the individual may assume these characteristics. Learned helplessness and external locus of control are frequently seen in individuals who are not performing up to their capacity (Baltes & Skinner, 1983). When individuals do not perform up to potential in functional living skills, they are exhibiting excess disability.

Model For Understanding Excess Disability

Excess disability can be conceptualized through the model presented in Figure 16.1. This figure has three overlapping circles. One represents the disease process, the second the environment and the third represents the patient's capacity to perform or function. In an ideal situation, with the best care and the best environment, the three circles overlap minimally. The area in which all three overlap depicts true disability. The worst case scenario involves circles overlapping to a great degree. Whenever two or more circles overlap, such as with environment and patient's capacity to perform, the area shared by both circles represents excess disability (Katsinas, 1996).

As the shared or overlapping areas increase, the amount of excess disability increases. Depictions of extreme excess disability are represented by the greatest degree of overlap.

Situations in which the individual experiences low motivation, lack of opportunity or poor environment, may hamper or reduce the individual's ability to interact with the environment in a meaningful way and thus reduce functional ability (Katsinas, 1996).

Problems arising from the use of prescription and over-the-counter drugs frequently contribute to excess disability. Medications that are over-used, or inadequately monitored and/or adjusted, may result in difficulty in concentration, reduced reasoning abilities, confusion and general lethargy. In the elderly and severely mentally ill populations, the problems of inadequate supervision,

Figure 16.1: A model for understanding excess disability.

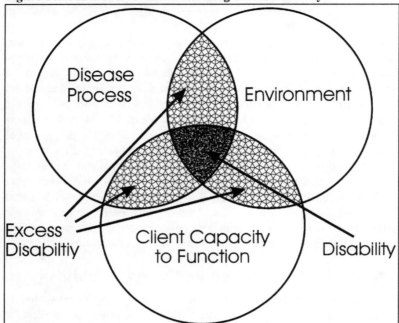

self-prescription and a lack of monitoring of medications are an ongoing dilemma for individuals who are either community-based or institutionalized.

Excess Disability and Health Care

Excess disability is an issue within the general field of health care because of its economic impact and also because of the perception by some that it can be classified as a form of abuse (Katsinas & Gugel, 1992). Economics are a concern because of three factors: (1) labor intensive rehabilitation and custodial care associated with the condition, (2) the unconfirmed theory that individuals with excess disability may be receivers of "repeat" treatment in home-based, inpatient and residential care service delivery systems and (3) the speculation that excess disability is a significant factor leading to institutionalization and consequently increased cost of care compared with home or outpatient based services.

Persons with excess disability require labor intensive rehabilitation on the front and on the back end of the treatment process. An individual entering the acute rehabilitation phase of treatment post injury/illness may appear severely debilitated and disabled. In many situations a significant portion of the presenting dysfunction may be traced to pre-incident functional limitations, excess disability induced by the physical and social environments, medications and/or the individual's capacity and desire to perform. In this type of situation, the intervention team must overcome the disability not attributable to the current medical incident or pre-existing disease process as well as dealing with the losses accrued from the recent medical incident. These expenditures of professional time and labor, medical intervention services, hospital or rehabilitation stays, in addition to the effort of the afflicted individual, are not cost-effective health care. Such a situation could be considered similar to the scenario of attempting to bail the water out of a rowboat, loaded with rocks and having several holes in the bottom, prior to trying to plug the holes.

On the back-end of the treatment process, preventing excess disability in someone who has already been a victim of this condition requires intensive education of the individual, the family, peers and professional caregivers, both within the rehabilitation setting and in the "home" environment. It may involve reconfiguration of the physical environment as well as intensive re-education of others within the social environment. The same is true for preventing excess disability among individuals who have suffered a severe medical incident, leaving them with functional limitations. They, too, have the potential to accumulate excess disability in addition to the functional limitations attributable to the medical incident. Ongoing monitoring of patient functional ability is recommended for both situations. Some circumstances even require "refresher" sessions to preserve and promote independent functioning. Hence, the amount of intervention necessary to remediate the excess disability is in addition to the services needed to rehabilitate the medical incident. The presence of excess disability may also signify the need for ongoing services of a periodic nature in order to prevent regression.

The existence of excess disability may lead to an increased need for community-based health care services to maintain the person in the community in two very different ways. The first involves preventing a person who has recovered from excess disability from relapsing. Factors related to patient functional ability, such as motivation and the impact of conditions within the physical and social environments, must be monitored in order to prevent a recurrence. For example, when an individual returns home from an inpatient stay, it is very easy for him/her to fall into a motivational trap of letting others do too much. It is also understandable when family members and professional caregivers find it easier to do for a individual. In some situations, the patient also refuses to do for himself/herself. In these circumstances an individual may lose skills from being "helped" too much (Avorn, 1982) and the cycle of excess disability is triggered.

Individuals whose motivation to remain independent and functional is extrinsically motivated by others and/or by their various physical and social environments may develop into repeat users of inpatient, outpatient and home-based services. These individuals may have great rehabilitation potential during active treatment, but post discharge they lose skills and become increasingly dysfunctional. The intermittent or periodic need for rehabilitation or "refresher" services is an evident and real need for a significant number of these persons. Active case management and early intervention may prevent inpatient stays, inappropriate hospitalization or institutionalization. Without active case management, these individuals may overuse the health care system through repeat needs for inpatient or crisis hospitalization. A more practical and economic approach involves ongoing preventive maintenance services and ongoing facilitation of functional ability through home and community-based case management services.

The inability to meet one's own needs, the functional disability and the motivational/behavioral aspects of this condition sometimes lead to early or inappropriate institutionalization. On admission into health care facilities from homes with poor social and physical environments, numerous individuals may exhibit symptoms of severe disabilities. After placement within an enriched environment, many symptoms and functional losses disappear as the individuals spontaneously regain functional skills and ability. In some cases the recovery is sufficient for the individual to return home or at least go to a less restrictive environment such as independent or assisted living.

Early institutionalization due to excess disability is common in our society. Frequently, instead of treating the excess disability, depression or re-configuring the home environment, the individual is "rushed" into institutional care. It doesn't matter whether this institution is a nursing home or a group home for individuals who are severely and persistently mentally ill. By and large, an institutional environment promotes and encourages further excess disability by discouraging and limiting choice, standardizing care and doing for, rather than encouraging the individual to do for himself/herself. That is to say, the cycle of excess disability is nurtured as the level of environmental challenge and stimulation is reduced. Accordingly, the lower levels of patient function and increased levels of dependence and dysfunction raise the cost of institutional care.

As an abuse issue, excess disability is a factor in functional limitation not attributable directly to the disease process (Roberts, 1986). The individual has become more disabled as a result of factors in the physical and social environments (Rogers, 1990). The social environment is frequently viewed as a major contributing factor. Low levels of stimulation, as well as low expectations expressed by peers, caregivers, family members and the individual, are usually reflected in decreasing levels of functional ability. By allowing conditions which encourage an individual to lose skills, become more impaired or regress behaviorally, excess disability may be considered a form of abuse.

Quality of life is an issue of great concern. As functional ability is reduced, the control the individual possesses over life choices and self diminishes. Due to the subjective viewpoints of the individual and his/her responsible family members, quality of life is extremely hard to quantitatively assess.

Elements of Excess Disability Relevant to Recreational Therapy

Three elements which are important in the practice of recreational therapy include: decline of functional ability, poor follow-through in therapy and high recidivism rates.

The decline of functional ability is an important factor to the recreational therapist on two fronts. The therapist is at the front line both to prevent and to ameliorate the condition described as excess disability. To ameliorate the condition, the therapist can increase the level of environmental stimulation and target specific skills and experiences in each of the major domains of function through activities and skillful leadership. Such purposeful activity intervention allows the individual to practice "old" skills and to gradually and, sometimes dramatically, regain function. The secondary goal of this treatment is to maintain the "re-gained" skills and facilitate further skill re-acquisition over time.

Prevention of excess disability includes the purposeful use of activities to stimulate and challenge the individual to use functional skills. Facilitation of functional skills and decision-making within enriched environments (physical and social) to achieve and maintain functional skill gains are a prime directive for activity intervention services.

In order to prevent and/or ameliorate excess disability, the therapist must examine the preskills, skills, habits and perceived self-competence of the individual with regard to leisure/recreational experiences and activities (Roberts, 1990). Preskills are factors generic to many tasks such as manipulative ability, hand-eye coordination, attention, memory, problem-solving and communication (Roberts, 1990). Preskills can be evaluated formally through standardized assessment, skill/task challenge activities and general observation.

The next area focuses on the assessment of specific skills connected to particular activity requirements. The therapist must examine skill deficit areas related to leisure experience and activities. It is necessary to determine whether the deficit occurs during the initiation of tasks, sequencing of tasks or performance of tasks. Once the assessment is completed, the therapist can devise intervention strategies using re-training, alternate skill acquisition or facilitation of appropriate tasks, skills and behaviors.

Habit observation is another important factor in the assessment process. Observation within the "home" environment allows the therapist to investigate whether the deficits of performance and initiation are situational or skill-related (Roberts, 1990). Roberts indicated that observational assessment within the "home" environment may allow the therapist to determine whether deficits occur because of skill dysfunction due to disuse, failure to learn a skill, skill breakdown or inflexibility with regard to activity pattern. An additional area of assessment includes an evaluation for a disorganized and ineffective lifestyle (Roberts, 1990).

Perceived competence is influenced by the individual's perceptions of what s/he is capable of doing, direct observation of functional capability and the influence of others' perceptions of the individual's competence. If a family member, a caregiver or a peer perceives that the individual is incapable of performance or choice, then the individual's own perceptions of function will usually reflect this perception. Thus, low perception of competence becomes a self-fulfilling prophecy. Frequently when direct observation and task challenges are presented to the individual, discrepancies between self-assessment and situational assessment are discovered. Self-competence affects the day-to-day functional ability of the individual, as well as the ability to follow through on tasks both during the active treatment phase and post discharge. It is critical that the therapist document the discrepancies and work with individuals to build up their perception of competence as a distinct part of the intervention process. Frequently the most difficult part of this process involves the re-education of other professional caregivers and family members as to the potential of the individual to take part in activities and make choices for him/herself. Post discharge care is critical in maintaining the skills and perceptions of self-confidence/competence gained during the active treatment phase in order to prevent deterioration and return to active treatment.

An Example in Rehabilitation

A common rehabilitation problem among patients with traumatic brain injuries, post-initial-injury and post-discharge from short term rehabilitation, is excess disability. Some individuals within this population are particularly prone to this condition as their motivation and ability to structure their lives have been damaged by their injury. Sometimes the physical and social environments in which they reside also contribute to their loss of functional skills. These individuals frequently make progress in short term rehabilitation centers after their accident. They are frequently discharged into the community or to long term rehabilitation training programs with significant improvements in skills and independent functioning. In some situations, individuals discharged to the community experience a significant decline in functional ability over time. Without the day-to-day structure of the rehabilitation unit and staff and their support and motivation, these individuals may actually experience a decline in functional skills resulting in either transfer to a group home setting or re-entry into a short term rehabilitation center, a long term rehabilitation program or custodial care.

The reasons for excess disability in this population are complex, including but not limited to: limited accessibility within the community, isolation, depression, loss of status, loss of family and/or loss of work skills. Another significant factor is the lack of intrinsic motivation. Frequently, motivation for daily care skills, socialization and independent living appear to be extrinsically motivated where there is functional impairment. With the absence of consistent and systematic extrinsic motivation, the patient declines over time, exhibiting severe loss of functional skills.

On the opposite end of the spectrum is the patient who is placed within a social or physical environment where too much is done to and for him/her. This type of situation can also result in loss of functional ability in some individuals with head injuries because the patients lose function due to impairment, lack of skill practice and motivational problems.

An Example in Psychiatry

Long term problems with over-medication, environmental and social deficiencies may severely impair the function of individuals with psychiatric disabilities. Individuals with dual diagnoses of either developmental impairment and mental illness or mental illness and substance abuse are particularly susceptible. Additionally, individuals who are severely and profoundly mentally ill may also show excess disability due to common problems associated with medication, socialization, access to activities and services in general. An individual who is severely mentally ill and resides in a community-based independent residence, group home or state facility is at extreme danger of acquiring excess disability traits due to the nature of his/her physical and social environment. The causes include a number of factors: over-medication, medication side effects, social isolation, low levels of stimulation, lack of access to appropriates services on a daily basis, transportation issues and financial stress. Many communities within our country are unable to provide active treatment or adequate maintenance activities for persons with severe mental and/or developmental disabilities. These individuals may be isolated due to a combination of one or more of the factors listed above. In addition they frequently experience multiple deficits in functional ability attributable to medication side effects; inappropriate behaviors; lack of appropriate social skills, leisure skills, resource knowledge; and simple lack of experience. The lack of acceptance by society is another element that negatively affects their ability and perception of self-competence. Over time, many of these individuals actually lose skills and become more functionally disabled than expected from their mental/developmental condition. In many situations low expectations and low levels of stimulation actually make these individuals appear much more dysfunctional than their disease process or their medications suggest. In some cases, the individuals have not acquired or have lost basic survival skills related to self-maintenance, nutrition, finance, socialization, leisure and basic wellness.

An Example in Long Term Care

Examples of excess disability abound in long term care settings including problems induced in residents with dementia as well as individuals of supposedly "sound faculties." For example, one long term care facility in Florida stored wheelchairs in the rooms of residents capable of ambulation with or without assistive devices. After approximately one year, a significant majority of the residents had become dependent on the wheelchairs for their mobility needs. It took a major rehabilitation plan and effort by all facility staff to assist and encourage a very small number of residents to attempt to walk one way to one meal, one time a day. The inability of these particular residents to ambulate short distances under their own power was not attributable to a disease process but to disuse resulting in excess disability as illustrated by deconditioning, low perception of self-competence and problems with gait and sway.

Implications for the Future

Due to the nature of disability and the current economic crunch, health care programs are under financial attack. These economic and restricted service conditions may result in an increase in the frequency of excess disability diagnoses in the future due to the following: further reductions in the length of treatment stays; decreasing availability of partial and full day treatment programs within rehabilitation, psychiatric and geriatric settings; lack of reimbursement at the state level (Medicaid) for activity services in long term, psychiatric and home-based care; and the inability for many patients to meet the expectations of Medicare Part B with regard to progress and minimum hours of treatment per day. Other issues facing recreational therapists are the proposed changes in social security disability compensation for individuals who are severely mentally ill or developmentally disabled which may result in a loss of funds and services. All of these potential scenarios could lead to increased incidence of excess disability in a wide variety of populations with vastly different needs for intervention and amelioration. Further education of the public, other professional caregivers, families and regulatory bodies is necessary to prevent the widespread, accidental encouragement of excess disability and the label of enforced disability/abuse by benign neglect.

Summary

Excess disability is an artificial condition of functional inability caused by factors other than disease or impairment. In many cases, this condition can be prevented and/or ameliorated to a great degree. Understanding the essence of this condition rests on the realizing that "if you don't use it, you'll lose it." It is a complex condition affected by self-perception of competence and the perception by others of an individual's competence and capacity for performance and choice. At its worst, it affects physical, cognitive and psychosocial domains of function. The losses, when present, are very real and require the concerted effort of recreational therapists, members of health care intervention teams, the families and the individuals themselves to overcome.

Learning Activities

1. Discuss the difference between true disability and excess disability. List circumstances besides the ones in the text which can cause excess disability.
2. Describe the excess disability caused by family members. What reasons would the family have for treating the patient in a way that causes excess disability? How can a therapist change their perception to increase the effectiveness of treatment?
3. Discuss, as a class, whether you feel that excess disability should be considered a form of abuse.
4. Discuss why task assessment is a vital part of treatment for excess disability. Take a task such as preparing a meal (from getting food to serving it) and find the ways excess disability may prevent a person from successfully completing the task. Consider alternatives that would make the task easier.
5. Compare and contrast the causes and indicated treatment for the three examples of excess disability discussed in the chapter: traumatic brain injury, psychiatric disorder and long term care.

Study Questions

1. What are the three types of changes seen as a result of excess disability? What are some of the symptoms?
2. What are the causes of excess disability?
3. Why is excess disability an issue in health care?
4. How can active case management lower the risk of excess disability occurring?
5. What interventions by a recreational therapist will help prevent and/or reduce excess disability?

References

Avorn, J. (1982). Induced disability in nursing home patients. *Journal of American Geriatric Society, 30,* 397.

Baltes, M. M. & Skinner, E. A. (1983). Cognitive performance deficits and hospitalization: Learned helplessness, instrumental passivity or what? Comment on Raps, Peterson, Jonas and Seligman. *Journal of Personality and Social Psychology, 45*(5), 1013-1016.

Katsinas, R. (1996). Therapeutic programming to alleviate and prevent excess disability. In G. Hitzhusen, L. Jackson & M. Birdsong (Eds.). *Global Therapeutic Recreation IV. Selected papers from the 4ᵗʰ International Symposium on Therapeutic Recreation.* Columbia, MO: Curators of University of Missouri.

Katsinas, R. (1997). Leadership techniques as methods of intervention for adults with dementia. *Expanding Horizons XXV, 25ᵗʰ anniversary edition: Selected papers from the 1995-1996 Midwest Symposium on Therapeutic Recreation.* Columbia, MO: Curators of University of Missouri.

Katsinas, R. & Gugel, R. N. (1992, March). Excess disability as elder abuse. Paper presented at the meeting of the Southern Gerontological Society. Memphis, TN.

Osterweil, D. (1990). Geriatric rehabilitation in the long term care institutional setting. In B. Kemp, K. Brummel-Smith & J. W. Ramsdell (Eds.). *Geriatric rehabilitation* (pp. 347-356). Boston, MA: College-Hill of Little, Brown and Company.

Roberts, A. (1986). Excess disability in the elderly: Exercise management. In L. Teri & P. M. Lewinsohn (Eds.). *Geropsychological assessment and treatment: Selected topics* (pp. 87-120). New York: Springer Publishing Company.

Rogers, J. C. (1990). Improving the ability to perform tasks. In B. Kemp, K. Brummel-Smith & J. W. Ramsdell (Eds.). *Geriatric rehabilitation* (pp. 137-155). Boston, MA: College-Hill of Little, Brown and Company.

Seines, H. (1990). Deconditioning. In B. Kemp, K. Brummel-Smith & J. W. Ramsdell (Eds.). *Geriatric rehabilitation* (pp. 177-191). Boston, MA: College-Hill of Little, Brown and Company.

Chapter 17

Accessibility: A Bridge to a More Inclusive Community

Patti Gorham
Frank Brasile

One of the more important, yet often overlooked, roles of the allied health professional is to function as an advocate for the profession and for the individuals whom they serve. This chapter will focus on one particular means of serving as an advocate for persons with disabilities, accessibility. More specifically, the focus will be on the role of the recreational therapist in relationship to accessibility issues.

Background

The road to equal access for individuals with disabilities in the United States has been a long one — one which is far from being finished. The modern movement toward equal rights concerning accessibility gained momentum during the 1960's and the Vietnam War. During the 1960's, Martin Luther King helped bring equal rights and accessibility for people of color to the forefront of the news. As this movement gained momentum, the concept that accessibility for all: individuals of color, women, adults with physical disabilities and children with disabilities (who had, up to that point, been denied an education), joined the equal rights movement. The young adults who were the Vietnam Veterans or the parents of children with disabilities (the "Baby Boomers") had gone through their adolescent years witnessing the profound changes they could make in their world through political activism. They believed that they could make a difference and acted on that belief. Just as the struggle for racial equality was not based on one speech or one march, the road to today's level of accessibility has involved many laws and court cases. The activism that was prevalent in the 1960's and 1970's is still needed today to help achieve true accessibility. We are not there yet.

Accessibility is an often misunderstood term. Most people focus on structural accessibility related to wheelchair use when discussing accessibility. However, accessibility is a more complex topic. When considering accessibility, the recreational therapist must be aware of issues related to architectural accessibility, program accessibility and the skills required to access the resources now available to people with disabilities. The recreational therapists' interventions related to accessibility make it easier for participants with disabilities to pursue recreation and leisure activities in an inclusive atmosphere. This atmosphere should take into account the physical, cognitive and emotional needs of every person in the program as well as the physical structure of the environment.

Architectural Accessibility

Architectural accessibility focuses on the physical environment related to buildings, transportation and recreation areas (parks, lakes, stadiums, etc.). In their first report to Congress, the Architectural and Transportation Barriers Compliance Team (ATBCT) (1974) described the accessibility issues this country and the world face as follows:

For the most part they [persons with physical disabilities] are a hidden population, isolated in a household environment and restricted from contributing their talents as active members of the community. One of the major obstacles to their participation in societal endeavors is the physical design of our man-made environment. The transportation systems, buildings and facilities that are an integral part of our urban environments are designed and built to accommodate only a portion of its residents, the physically unimpaired.

Over the past thirty years legislation and court rulings have served to make our environment more accessible to person with disabilities. See Table 17.1 for a summary of the major milestones to accessibility.

The first major legislative act was the formation of the National Commission on Architectural Barriers authorized in 1965 by the amended Vocational Rehabilitation Act. This Commission recognized the guidelines for architectural accessibility developed by the American National Standards Institute (ANSI) as being appropriate for evaluating architectural accessibility. In 1967 the Commission recommended to Congress that these ANSI standards be used for legislation requiring accessibility in all buildings leased or owned by the government or constructed with federal funds.

Table 17.1: **Milestones on the Way to Accessibility[3]**

Event	Description
Brown v. Board of Education (347 US 483) (1954)	This court case dealt only with racially segregated schools but lawyers applied it to youth of color who were disabled. Even as late as 1971, only sixteen states had requirements which outlined the public education rights of children who were disabled. Within five years another thirty-two states enacted legislation ensuring access to education for children with disabilities.
National Commission on Architectural Barriers (1965)	An amendment to the Vocational Rehabilitation Act (1920, with major revisions in 1943, 1954 and 1965) recognized architectural accessibility standards developed by the American National Standards Institute.
Federal Architectural Barriers Act of 1968	Required that architectural barriers be eliminated in all new buildings, but lacked enforcement, so therefore was not very effective.
Federal Urban Mass Transportation Act of 1972	Specified that only metropolitan transportation systems which provided accommodations for individuals with disabilities would qualify for an 80% federal match on funding for the project. This law had little "bite" and did not require architectural accessibility for individuals who used walkers or wheelchairs.
Urban League v. WMATA, Civil No. 776-72 (1973)	This was a lawsuit which sought to establish the requirement that the stations and trains for Washington, DC's new subway must be accessible. This case was a precursor to the Americans with Disabilities Act.
Rehabilitation Act of 1973 (Section 503 and Section 504) (1973)	Made it illegal to discriminate against individuals due to a disability. This law called for affirmative action programs for the hiring of individuals with disabilities and for the prohibition of discrimination against individuals with disabilities (the penalty being the loss of federal funds). This bill was vetoed twice by President Nixon before there was enough political pressure from individuals and groups (both disabled and non-disabled) to force passage and signing of this bill.

---

[3] Modified with permission from burlingame and Skalko, 1997. *Idyll Arbor's Glossary for Therapists*. Ravensdale, WA: Idyll Arbor, Inc.

Table 17.1: **Milestones on the Way to Accessibility (cont.)**

Event	Description
Education for All Handicapped Children Act (1975)	President Ford signed a bill in 1975 which mandated each state to provide an education for all children, regardless of disability. This was called the *Education for All Handicapped Children Act* (Public Law 94-142). Public Law 94-142 provided a formula for federal and state governments to share in the cost of educating children who were disabled. The Individuals with Disabilities Education Act (IDEA) re-authorized and amended the Education for All Handicapped Children Act in 1991.
Civil Rights Attorney Fees Act (Public Law 94-559) (1976)	Many lawyers were hesitant to take on litigation concerning the violation of the civil rights of an individual with a disability because they seldom got paid for their services. The Civil Rights Attorney Fees Act (Public Law 94-559) (1976) authorized federal courts to order the payment of attorney fees if it is found that the claimant had, indeed, been discriminated against due to his/her disability.
Coordinated sit-in affecting eleven offices of the Department of Heath, Education and Welfare (April 28, 1977)	The American Coalition of Citizens with Disabilities held sit-in protests in the ten regional offices as well as the Washington, DC office of the Department of Health, Education and Welfare (HEW), forcing HEW Secretary Califano to sign regulations which ordered accessibility for individuals with disabilities which the administration had delayed for three and a half years. These regulations were designed to carry out Section 504 of the Rehabilitation Act of 1973.
Americans with Disabilities Act of 1990 (ADA)	Prior to the *Americans with Disabilities Act of 1990* (ADA), individuals with a disability had little legal recourse to end discrimination based on their disability. The ADA provided a clear and comprehensive mandate to eliminate accessibility barriers and set up enforceable standards which were lacking in earlier efforts.
Americans with Disabilities Act of 1990 (ADA)	The ADA was modified to reflect problems with the original standards and to provide standards for buildings designed for use by children.

The following year Congress passed the Architectural Barriers Act of 1968. This legislation helped but it was not until 1990 with the passage of the Americans with Disabilities Act (ADA), that these standards became mandatory for most publicly accessed structures and transportation systems.

The Americans with Disabilities Act, signed into law by President George Bush on July 26, 1990, is the most significant piece of civil rights legislation passed since the early 1960's. The act extended civil rights protection to an estimated 49 million Americans with disabilities, making it illegal to discriminate on the basis of disability in the areas of employment, public services, public accommodations, transportation and telecommunication. The ADA has a three-fold purpose (McGovern, 1992):

> First, to eliminate discrimination against people with disabilities; second, to state a proper national goal towards people with disabilities; and third, to enable the further independent growth of such individuals by the guarantee of access to every area of American life. (p. 7)

The ADA did not magically ensure a society free of discrimination or access to "every" area. It did, however, provide the basis for building a partnership between the able-bodied community and people with disabilities that will result in tearing down many barriers that restrict access to the community.

There have been some problems and misunderstandings in implementation which have delayed full compliance. One of the responsibilities of professionals, such as recreational therapists, who work with people with disabilities is to help make full compliance a reality. The ADA presents an opportunity for people with disabilities to work cooperatively with business owners, government officials, transportation authorities and other entities to ensure a community's voluntary compliance with the law. Through positive, thought-provoking discussions, a community can chart its course for compliance in a spirit of cooperation.

One of the best ways to ensure compliance is through Community Partnerships. Successful implementation of the ADA requires far more than providing instruction in its regulations. Education and training based on the facts about and implications of the ADA provide a basis for understanding how the law can have a positive impact on the community. However, more importantly, a community needs to understand the advantages of full inclusion of people with disabilities. Once this is understood, interest in the goal can spawn the development of community partnership projects which involve the entire community.

In order for a community partnership initiative to be successful, it must involve and engage representatives from the private and public sectors including government officials, business people, representatives from educational institutions, medical and rehabilitative professionals, people with disabilities and their families and friends, organizations serving people with disabilities, transportation authorities and media representatives. Many perspectives need to be available for a successful effort.

Ideally, one person or organization will emerge to steer the community partnership effort. The knowledge and experience base of the community leader will vary greatly from one community to another. One may have an extensive background in providing ADA implementation support while another may have had no formal ADA training at all. The real requirement is an innate interest in ensuring full community integration of individuals with disabilities.

Once the group is formed, it needs to follow a workable process to achieve its goals. The goals, once defined, can be broken down into workable tasks. These required tasks include collecting data, developing a plan, putting the plan into action, marketing and project promotion, and monitoring and revising the plan.

Data Collection

The first task is to survey the community to ascertain its level of compliance with accessibility requirements. Effective surveying may be accomplished in many different ways including the use of key informants, community forums, case studies, statistical analysis, official surveys and formal studies. Any or all of the methods can be employed to collect data for the development of a comprehensive community plan.

The use of *key informants* consists of soliciting information from individuals whose testimony or description of what exists for the targeted population is credible because of the informant's level of expertise. Such key informants may include service providing organizations; representatives from business, industry and Chambers of Commerce; teachers and other school officials; people with disabilities or their representative organizations; and other individuals or organizations.

A *community forum* is a hosted or sponsored public meeting. A great deal of information can be obtained by providing an opportunity for individuals to express opinions or present verifiable information about the issue of accessibility and accommodation.

Case studies consist of selecting individuals to describe their experiences related to disability issues. The individual case studies provide a realistic description of the current community climate relative to ADA compliance and other disability concerns.

Statistical analysis is the use of existing data to develop a picture of the community: census records, government reports, etc. This information is helpful in validating the demographics of the community.

Official surveys involve the use of questionnaires, interviews or observations to gather information. This method is very effective in gathering information in a non-invasive, anonymous manner if respondent confidentiality is ensured.

Formal studies cite relevant research in the field of community needs assessment and response. This method allows valid information to be gathered from other communities which have undertaken projects similar to those envisioned.

Developing the Plan

Whatever methods of data collection are employed, the results are used by the community committee to develop a comprehensive plan which effectively addresses the community's needs regarding accessibility, accommodation and other ADA issues. To simplify the process, the community committee can use the data to respond to the issues of "what, where, when, who and how." Answers to these five basic questions will serve as the basis for the development of the plan.

The plan can address both tangible and intangible ideas. For example, installing a ramp outside city hall or a stair lift in the public library may be the number one priority, or ongoing ADA education and training and/or disability awareness and sensitivity programming for the community may emerge as the number one goal. Whatever the priority is, it must be presented in such a manner as to thoroughly define the issue and determine the course of action to be taken. Inherent in that determination will be the identification of who will be involved in the process and when and how it will be accomplished.

The community plan should be thorough, comprehensive and, most importantly, contain goals and objectives which are measurable and attainable. The community as a whole should be involved in its design, development and implementation.

Putting the Plan into Action

Communities are often criticized for developing plans that are never put into effect. In order to ensure that this is not the case with the community's ADA plan, assign individual team members to be responsible for overseeing the successful implementation of certain sections of the plan or divide the team into subcommittees responsible for addressing various portions of the plan. Whatever approach is adopted, make certain that the plan is enacted in a timely and effective manner.

Communities are fluid and priorities change over the course of time. It is important to keep the plan current and responsive to the needs of the community. For this reason, the plan should be reviewed and updated on an annual basis. By doing so, the compliance team ensures that the plan they are implementing represents both the current and future needs of the community.

Marketing and Project Promotion

Throughout the course of the project, the work of the committee and the resultant plan must be promoted and marketed in the community. For the project to be successful, it is imperative that the general public be kept informed of the committee's work. Their support is mandatory for success and you may find new committee members who are interested in the overall work of the committee or in specific components of the plan's development and implementation.

A well-organized marketing/promotion effort has several components. A project brochure explaining the purpose of the project and outlining the tasks is vital to the project's success. Press releases for mass media assist in creating awareness of and interest in the project. Articles describing the project written for newsletters of organizations who are part of the project keep their members informed of the progress that is being made because of their efforts.

A speaker's bureau should be available to talk about the project with local professional, civic and social organizations. Formal presentations to city councils, county boards and school boards should be arranged on a regular basis to keep the local officials informed of the project's progress. Obviously, many opportunities for marketing and promotion exist. Use the ones that will advance your goals.

Monitoring and Revising

As with any plan, ways to evaluate progress should be developed as part of the overall plan. Monitoring and evaluation helps the team decide which strategies are working and which are not. This information is required for revising the plan to meet the changing needs of the community.

Well-designed community partnership projects take on many different looks. No two communities are alike; therefore no two projects will be alike. They key to a successful project is to enlist and maintain broad-based community support for the team's work. The community, as a whole, must be adequately assessed to ensure that the plan reflects current and future needs. It is also important that the project is proactive so it can respond to the changing needs of the community. Finally, the project must be implemented in a way that actually works. The Americans with Disabilities Act has often been described as a "common sense" law. The development of community partnership projects is a common sense approach. The role of the recreational therapist in the development or implementation of these partnerships should not be overlooked. Recreational therapists emphasize functional ability — the actual experience of doing something. Hopefully the recreational therapist can bring his/her down-to-earth, practical experiences in implementing a program that works into the process and end-product of the community partnership.

Making a Difference

Students can make a difference within the community even prior to joining a community partnership. Examples of the positive impact that students can have on a community's accessibility can be found throughout the literature. As an example, one set of students conducted a survey to measure the wheelchair accessibility of twenty stores. They then shared this information with the manager of each store. When students re-surveyed the same stores six months later, they found that five out of the twenty stores had made corrections (McClain & Todd, 1990).

If done with diplomacy, students can have a positive impact on the accessibility of the community. This usually involves using the forms found in the ADA Accessibility Guidelines (Architectural and Transportation Barriers Compliance Board, 1991). The ADAAG is a manual which contains checklists for all of the ADA architectural and transportation requirements, including all the necessary measurements. Your university library or instructor should have a copy of the ADAAG 1991. The next version of the guidelines are expected out in late 1998.

Program Accessibility

While architectural accessibility is of major importance to the person with a physical limitation, there is also another type of accessibility that the recreational therapist must be aware of, program accessibility. Architectural accessibility relates to buildings and transportation. Program accessibility focuses on the design and implementation of specific activities and other events. Program accessibility issues are related to administrative policies, transportation, equipment and attitudes. It is the responsibility of the recreational therapist to provide clients with an inclusive and equal atmosphere and the modifications related to his/her functional limitations. (For example, an individual who has a hearing impairment may require an interpreter in order to attend and enjoy a lecture at the art museum.) The recreational therapist, in designing programs, plans for minimum modifications which allow inclusive participation in recreation and leisure pursuits for all individuals. The ADA implies that the individual must be able to enjoy as full and appropriate a recreation experience as possible in the least restrictive environment.

Administrative Policies

Administrative policies can have a significant impact on the participant's ability to access the recreational activities and programs. If the facility does not have a TTY hook-up to accept registrations by phone for individuals with hearing or speech impairments, programs are not equally accessible to all potential participants. If the facility's policies do not allow animals into the weight room due to perceived sanitation concerns, an individual with a guide dog may experience a barrier caused by an administrative policy. If the Wildlife and Game Department does not allow hunting from within a vehicle for individuals with mobility impairments, then individuals who have a paresis may not be able to hunt.

In most of these instances the administration may believe that they are adhering to the mandates of equal treatment for all individuals. However, the ADA makes it clear that equal treatment may in some instances be considered to be discriminatory. In many instances an adaptation or modification of rules and procedures may be all that is necessary to provide equal access to persons with disabilities.

Transportation

Transportation is a problem for all participants. In fact, a study by Hauber, et al. (1984) found that the inability to use public transportation was one of the most common reasons for (re)admission to an institution instead of being able to stay in the community. Ability to get to and from programs is a necessity for participation. If a community does not have a system available for a person with disabilities, then participation in employment and recreation programs by a person with disabilities will suffer. The ADA specifies that public transportation must be available and useable by all persons with disabilities. When planning programs that require transportation, such as field trips, the recreation programmer should take into consideration the needs of persons with disabilities. Today there are many modes of transportation that make travel accessible to persons with disabilities.

Equipment

One of the most important and easiest ways of making programs accessible is to purchase and use adapted equipment or auxiliary aids. Over the past ten years equipment to make programs more inclusive for persons with disabilities has become a major focus of many equipment manufacturers. Items such as hydraulic lifts for pools, basketball hoops that can be lowered or raised, exercise equipment that is easily accessible to persons who use wheelchairs and other game equipment have made it easier for persons with physical limitations to participate in recreation programs with their peers. In many instances this equipment is essential for participation. In other instances this equipment is used as the first step toward the end goal of participating without any adapted equipment.

For example, recreational therapists may use adapted equipment to teach bowling to a person who has recently become impaired as a result of a stroke. The recreational therapist may use a bowling ramp at first to assist in developing the initial physical, psychosocial and cognitive skills for participation in the activity. As the individual progresses through the rehabilitation process, s/he may use a bowling ball push stick and eventually become strong enough to use a bowling ball that has a retractable handle. The same sequence of equipment choices are available for many other sports including swimming, bike riding, skiing and hiking.

It is important that adaptive equipment be used to make the program accessible to the individual only when it is necessary. The responsibility of the recreational therapist is to take into consideration the unique needs of the individual and consider the path that rehabilitation and integration should take. Knowledge of the equipment available to allow participation by his/her clients is a basic tool for the recreational therapist to posses.

Attitudes

Physical barriers are only one of the types of barriers individuals with disabilities encounter. Individuals with disabilities also experience barriers due to the attitudes which others hold. There are three primary attitudes which place barriers to accessibility:

- attitudes which artificially limit someone's opportunities to participate in or benefit from programming and services,
- attitudes which cause individuals with disabilities to have unequal benefits compared to able-bodied individuals,
- attitudes which insist that individual with disabilities use separate or special services.

Artificial Limitations

One type of barrier which people with disabilities encounter is a restriction to activity which is not based on similar restrictions placed on individuals without disabilities. Often these restrictions are due to false beliefs about the capabilities of individuals with any type of disability. An example would be restricting individuals who use wheelchairs from dockside activities with the fear that their chair may somehow slip off the dock and plunge into the water. The false belief is that individuals in wheelchairs cannot control their mobility were someone who is ambulatory would, "of course," never walk backwards off the edge of the dock. Another restriction often cited is that an individual with a disability cannot participate in a program because the organization running the activity is afraid that their insurance won't cover someone with a disability. Johnson (1992) states

> "Our insurance won't cover you!" is a frequent excuse many of us have heard when told we can't participate in a program. The Department of Justice says, "a public accommodation cannot refuse to serve a person with a disability because its insurance company conditions coverage or rates on the absence of persons with disabilities."
> "This is a frequent basis for exclusion [of disabled people] from a variety of community activities," says the Department, "and is prohibited by the law." (p. 39)

Individuals with disabilities are too frequently required to take ground-floor accommodations at resorts instead of the rooms with better views for fear that they will not be able to escape in case of a fire. Once at the resort, the same individual may be denied the right to use golf carts or boats, even if they normally use this equipment and have good safety records. And, of course, if the individual who uses a wheelchair wants to attend a concert that evening, they will be required to sit in the back of the viewing area. (The thought here is that the individual would get out right away being by the door, therefore not blocking an aisleway in the case of a fire.) The Department of Justice's rules state that any restrictions imposed must be on actual, documented risks and not just mere speculation.

Unequal Benefits

It is imperative that the individual with a disability who is participating in a recreation program feel that s/he is being treated no differently than others who are participating in the same program. The key term when discussing this area of program accessibility is *desirability*. The participant with a disability may be able to get to and into the building, as well as use the equipment necessary for successful participation in an activity. However, if they feel they are not welcome or not treated as an equal, then this program is not a fully accessible program.

Issues in desirability can take two twists. First, the person with the disability may be given special (unequal) treatment or unwarranted (unequal) attention because of his/her disability. For example, a special rule might be made for the individual with an impairment, e.g., "We'll give your team two points for every score by the individual with the disability instead one point." This points the finger at the individual with the disability, giving the impression that s/he needs to be treated as if s/he were a small child. Modifications to the activity or equipment should attempt to "equal the playing field" thereby allowing the individual with a disability to compete on a more even level.

Secondly, the individual with the disability may be "tolerated" by staff or other participants during his/her involvement in programs at the facility. Frequent irritation from the leader/staff or comments made about the individual with a disability, related to the disability, are attitudinal barriers. This kind of attitudinal barrier can lead to another type of barrier — imposed specialized programming.

Specialized Programming

It is a common practice for parks departments, schools and other groups which offer recreational programs to also offer "special" programs. While the concept of special programs makes sense on one level (offering activities geared toward an individual's specific skills and needs) on a whole other level special programs are nothing but segregated programs. The Americans with Disabilities Acts allows the provision of special programs but prohibits the insistence that people with disabilities use the special programs. A resort may not require an individual who uses a wheelchair to use the accessible room on the ground floor when s/he would rather have a room on the top floor. If an individual who qualifies to use handicap parking decides not to use that parking space, the owner of the parking lot cannot force the individual to use it. A parks department which offers a special swim time for individuals with disabilities cannot prohibit an individual with a disability from using the free swim time open to the general public. One of the fundamental tenets of the Americans with Disabilities Act is the right to participate in activities in an integrated manner. Johnson (1992) states

"The provisions of Title III," says the Department of Justice, "are intended to prohibit exclusion and segregation ... and denial of equal opportunities enjoyed by others, based on, among other things, presumptions, patronizing attitudes, fears and stereotypes ... Modified participation for persons with disabilities must be a choice, not a requirement." (p. 38)

Facilities should be able to reduce the barriers caused by attitudes through using some common sense and providing employees with some basic training. Entities which offer recreational programming should follow the general premise that "the customer knows best," whether the customer is disabled or not.

Asking the individual with a disability is a good place to start to ensure that unintended discrimination does not happen.

Assisting Accessibility

If an individual is not taught the advanced activities of daily living skills required to use accessible facilities and programming, has the individual's world actually been made accessible? While facilitating architectural and programmatic accessibility is a major concern for the recreational therapist, teaching individuals how to use what is accessible, or how to problem solve around that which is not, tends to be the therapist's primary job responsibility. Armstrong (personal communication, March 11, 1998) states:

> We are never going to make the world fully accessible. The law says equal access. We can't make Mount Rainier accessible, so we need to analyze the needs of the clients and teach them the potential mechanisms for problem solving.

All too frequently there are patients who are able to pass all of their physical and occupational therapy goals who still cannot access resources in the community. These patients are able to walk fast enough and far enough to meet community standards, but they still cannot integrate back into the community. Why? Because mobility, and the ability to access community resources, also requires the ability to tolerate stimulation and to have adequate social support.

Individuals may also be limited by other barriers to accessibility. One of the largest barriers is the patient's own internal feelings (e.g., a lack of motivation, low self-esteem, fear of failure). Humans are social creatures and, as such, the recreational therapist should help provide each one with the skills to access social experiences. Patients who do not have these skills become more isolative and develop the health problems associated with isolation. Practice in the clinic alone does not work. We need to teach patients the skills required for true access by helping them practice in the community.

This section covers advanced activities of daily living skills, also known as life management skills; reviews studies which point to the importance of mobility training to facilitate the use of accessible systems; and provides the reader with some specific examples of one department's community integration program.

Advanced Activities of Daily Living

While occupational therapists tend to dominate treatment related to the basic activities of daily living (ADLs), the recreational therapist dominates the treatment modalities related to the advanced activities of daily living (AADLs). burlingame and Skalko (1997) list the advanced activities of daily living as

(1) basic environmental community safety skills, (2) community mobility skills, (3) consumer skills, (4) community resource identification, (5) advanced dressing skills, (6) time management skills and (7) social interaction skills. (p. 9)

These life management skills are important precursors to being able to avail oneself of opportunities in the community. The World Health Organization (1980) lists specific skills related to AADLs which are considered to be key "survival roles" (p. 184). The six survival roles are orientation, physical independence, mobility, occupation, social integration, economic self-sufficiency. Any limitations in these survival roles (or any other disadvantages) are considered to be "handicaps." The World Health Organization uses the term "handicap" to refer to barriers which are a combination of personal disability and constraints which originate with the community. Table 17.2 lists burlingame and Skalko's (1997) list of AADLs on the left side with the World Health Organization's (1980) disability classification on the right side. Handicaps arise when the individual is not able to access community resources as a result of limitations due to a disability, a restraint due to architectural or attitudinal barriers or both. The recreational therapist is trained to identify these limitations and barriers and then to implement a treatment intervention to reduce their impact.

Importance of Teaching AADLs

There can be no substitute for trying out newly learned advanced activities of daily living in the community itself. Especially with individuals who are newly disabled, the need to try out skills learned in a clinic (inpatient, outpatient or day treatment setting) is vital to achieving carryover of skills. Bandura's (1977) self-efficacy theory emphasizes the importance of providing the patient with many opportunities, each progressively more challenging, to develop a mastery. Based on this theory, individuals with disabilities will benefit from multiple chances to practice skills in a community setting under the support and guidance of the recreational therapist. Armstrong and Lauzen (1994) also point out that performance in a clinic setting does not directly correspond to performance in the community. As a general rule, individuals with traumatic head injury did more poorly on the pre-trial/cognitive section of the *Community Integration Program, Second Edition* (Armstrong & Lauzen, 1994). Their score in the community, when they were actually able to demonstrate skills, tended to be better than their pre-trial score. On the other hand, individuals with newly ac-

Table 17.2: Skills Necessary to Utilize Accessible Programs

AADLs	World Health Organization
basic environmental community safety skills	{13.1}* Personal safety disability in special situations. This includes being in hazard in special situations, such as those related to travel and transport, occupation and recreation, including sport.
community mobility skills	Includes three areas: {40-45} ambulation disabilities including being able to negotiate, {41 & 43} discontinuities in terrain; confining disabilities including transfers, {46.0, 46.1 and 46.2} and transport disability including {47.0} personal transport, {47.1} other vehicles and {47.2} other difficulty with remote shopping, i.e., parking spaces too far from store.
consumer skills	{17.0} Disability in participation in household activities.
community resource identification	{15} Knowledge acquisition disability; {18.5} recreation disability ... including efforts to obtain information.
advanced dressing skills	{10.2} Personal uncleanness, {10.3} Other disturbance of appearance, {10.4} Other disturbance of self-presentation.
time management skills	{11} Disability relating to location in time and space, {18.3} disability in organizing daily routine.
social interaction skills	Disability relating to situational behavior including {14.0} comprehension disability, {14.1} interpretation disability and {14.2} coping disability. Other behavioral disabilities including {19.0} antisocial behavior, {19.1} indifference to accepted social standards and {19.4} other severe behavior disorders such as aggressiveness, destructiveness, extreme over activity and attention seeking.

*The numbers in braces {} refer to WHO's diagnostic category numbering system. This system allows comparisons of outcomes across facilities and countries.

quired spinal cord injuries showed poorer performance in the community than they did on their pre-trial test.

    Community mobility skills training is vital for individuals who lack independent skills. McInerney & McInerney (1992) found that teaching adults with developmental disabilities how to ride the bus using an individualized sequential skills training program allowed these individuals to maintain their use of the public transportation system a full year after they left the program. Wehman and Schleien (1981) found that the ability to use public transportation was an important prerequisite skill for adolescents and adults who are mentally retarded to being able to plan recreational outings alone or with others. Other researchers found the same results with different population groups (Gaule, Nietupski & Certo, 1985; Hauber, et al. 1984; Welch, Nietupski & Hare-Nietupski, 1985).

Armstrong and Lauzen (1994) found that patients who used wheelchairs for mobility and who completed at least five of the *Community Integration Program, Second Edition* modules reduced readmissions due to skin breakdowns over the next 12 months by 50%.

Assisting patients to feel comfortable in the community is important for the patient's general health and for their ability to use accessible facilities. Patients feel comfortable because the therapist has helped "run interference" and this helps the patient problem solve other barriers to accessibility. The final result is greater use of the community by the patient and reduced secondary disability due to isolation.

Harborview Medical Center

Many facilities across the country have recreational therapists as part of their treatment teams. One specific hospital, Harborview Medical Center, is internationally known for the services provided by its recreational therapists, especially related to community integration training. Harborview Medical Center is a 411 bed community hospital affiliated with the University of Washington. It is located in the heart of downtown Seattle and right on the edge of Puget Sound.

The recreational therapists who work at Harborview, whether it be in psychiatry, rehabilitation, burn/plastics, pediatrics or partial hospitalization, provide three primary functions: functional leisure skills, leisure education and community integration training. The recreational therapists are viewed as a vital part of the treatment team and are reinforced by the other disciplines. They provide opportunities for the patients to take the skills learned in clinical settings and use them in the community. Accessibility is not guaranteed if the patient cannot use adaptive techniques or equipment, so using the skills in a real life setting under the supervision of a therapist is an important step which should not be omitted.

What the Harborview staff have found is that simulated experiences do not exactly match reactions to the outside environment. Following the World Health Organization's model/continuum of impairment/disability/handicap, the acquisition of adapted techniques and equipment is only one step toward function. The next step which must follow is the actual experience of applying the adaptations in the community setting. Usually this step should be supervised by a health care professional trained in integrating adaptive techniques and equipment. The recreational therapists at Harborview have found this second step an important one to promote accessibility for their patients. Barriers to accessibility are identified during the assessment phase of patient care. Throughout the treatment phase these barriers are taken from discussion to experience. The treatment teams at Harborview understand the importance of ensuring that the skills taught "in house" are also competencies the patient can demonstrate in the community. For this reason it is a hospital policy that the patient must demonstrate these core skills to the recreational therapist while in the community prior to their first pass with family or friends.

For example, a patient with a spinal cord injury must demonstrate pressure release techniques in a public setting without cues prior to being granted a weekend pass. A patient with a traumatic brain injury must demonstrate the ability to access a community-based leisure site through an assessment of safe street behaviors, the ability to problem solve emergency situations, pathfinding and other core skills prior to being cleared for unsupervised community activity (you can't go to play if you can't cross the street safely).

Patients with behavior and cognitive issues, who have problems with lack of exercise and inability to initiate activity may be directed to demonstrate core competencies. The recreational therapists use aquatic therapy (safe transfer in and out of the pool, safe swimming techniques), behavioral control during leisure skills (an in-house activity), ability to develop community resources near their discharge area, identify costs, transportation, time management, management of ADLs and the ability to maintain aerobic activity for a fixed period of time before being cleared for unsupervised community activity or supported through a scholarship program. It is not unusual for any one recreational therapist to take one to three outings into the community with patients each day.

Summary

Accessibility is an important area for recreational therapists to become involved in as part of their professional responsibility. The ADA spells out the rights of persons with disabilities as well as the responsibilities of the community to make sure that equal access to all public programs and services is available for these individuals. It is the responsibility of each recreational therapist to understand the legislation as it relates to programs and the client.

It is the job of the recreational therapist to ensure that his/her patients are able to access the programs and facilities in the community. This is accomplished by having the patient actually practice the necessary skills, first learned in the clinic, within the community setting.

Learning Activities

1. Familiarize yourself with community-based organizations providing services to people with disabilities. Organizations such as centers for independent living, local Easter Seal or March of Dimes chapters and other agencies should be contacted to develop a comprehensive listing of services provided in the community.
2. Meet with members of an ADA accessibility or compliance team. Describe the members of the team and summarize the goals and objectives of their plan.
3. Access current documents and publications relative to accessible recreation facilities, programs and services. Review information and keep updated on new requirements and the latest trends in the provision of services to the targeted population.
4. Develop and conduct a survey to indicate the attitudes of both persons with disabilities and persons without disabilities regarding recreation program accessibility in your community.
5. Develop a list of incentives for community businesses to make their programs and faculties more accessible to persons with disabilities.
6. Obtain four or more of the checklist forms from the latest version of the ADA Accessibility Guidelines and evaluate at least two different sites in the community using the forms.

Study Questions

1. List the steps that have been taken in the last 50 years to assure accessibility to all people.
2. What are the different types of accessibility that a recreational therapist must consider when providing equal access?
3. Who must be involved to make a community partnership successful?
4. List the steps required to implement a community partnership.
5. List the types of barriers that may affect program accessibility.
6. List the types of barriers which a recreational therapy intervention can help a person overcome through therapeutic interventions.
7. List the six survival roles that are part of life management skills.

References

Architectural and Transportation Barriers Compliance Board. (1974). *First report of the architectural and transportation barriers compliance board to the Congress of the United States.* Washington, DC: United States Department of Health, Education and Welfare.

Architectural and Transportation Barriers Compliance Board. (1991). *Americans with disabilities act accessibility guidelines checklist for buildings and facilities.* Washington, DC: US Government Printing Office.

Armstrong, M. & Lauzen, S. (1994). *Community integration program* (2nd ed.). Ravensdale, WA: Idyll Arbor, Inc.

Bandura, A. (1977). *Social learning theory.* Englewood Cliffs, NJ: Prentice-Hall.

burlingame, j. & Skalko, T. (1997). *Idyll Arbor's glossary for therapists.* Ravensdale, WA: Idyll Arbor, Inc.

Gaule, K., Nietupski, J. & Certo, N. (1985). Teaching supermarket shopping skills using an adaptive shopping list. *Education and Training of the Mentally Retarded, 20,* 53-59.

Johnson, M. (Ed.). (1992). *People with disabilities explain it all for you.* Louisville, KY: Advocado Press.

Hauber, F. E., Bruininks, R. H., Hill, B. K., Lakin, K. C., Scheerenberger, R. C. & White, C. C. (1984). National census of residential facilities: A 1982 profile of facilities and residents. *American Journal of Mental Deficiency, 89*(3), 236-245.

McClain, L. & Todd, C. (1990). Food store accessibility. *American Journal of Occupational Therapy, 44,* 487-491.

McGovern, J. (1992). *The ADA self-evaluation: A handbook for compliance with the Americans with Disabilities Act by parks and recreation agencies.* Ashburn, VA: National Parks and Recreation Association.

McInerney, C. A. & McInerney, M. (1992). A mobility skills training program for adults with developmental disabilities. *American Journal of Occupational Therapy, 46*(3), 233-239.

Recreation Access Advisory Committee, US Architectural and Transportation Barriers Compliance Board. (1994). *Recommendations for accessibility guidelines: Recreation facilities and outdoor developed areas.* Washington, DC: US Government Printing Office.

Salzberg, C. L. & Langford, C. A. (1981). Community integration of mentally retarded adults through leisure activity. *Mental Retardation, 19,* 127-131.

Wehman, P. & Schleien, S. (1981). *Leisure programs for handicapped persons: Adaptations, techniques & curriculum.* Baltimore: University Press.

Welch, J., Nietupski, J. & Hare-Nietupski, S. (1985). Teaching public transportation problem solving skills to young adults with moderate handicaps. *Education and Training of the Mentally Retarded, 20,* 287-295.

World Health Organization. (1980). *International classification of impairments, disabilities and handicaps: A manual of classification relating to the consequences of disease.* Geneva, Switzerland: World Health Organization.

Issues of Education, Training and Credentialing

Chapter 18

Adult Learning: Andragogy and Adults with Learning Disabilities

joan burlingame
Judi Singley

    Recreational therapists may assume different roles in the process of their work. They may be direct service providers, supervisors and/or consultants, but within all of these duties there is another role — the role of educator.

    Regardless of the setting (facility inservice, formal classroom or clinical work), recreational therapists are charged with the task of developing human resources and potential. As therapists, they educate patients about choices, techniques and resources. As supervisors, they are responsible for training their own staff as well as staff from other disciplines. As consultants, they help others learn how to build upon their own experiences within the workplace. And, the recreational therapist, as a life-long-learner, continues to expand his/her own knowledge because "Who dares to teach must never cease to learn" (Dana, 1912, p. 55). As the therapist takes on all the various aspects of the role of educator, it is important that s/he do so in a knowledgeable, effective and efficient manner, always making sure that s/he is getting the information across.

    To successfully fulfill the educator's role, a foundation must be laid. This chapter looks at some elements of the role of the recreational therapist as an educator. It provides the philosophical underpinnings for understanding the learning process of adults and the principles for facilitating adult learning based upon educational philosophy. Learning styles and the implications of an interactive learning environment are also discussed. Instructing adults with learning disabilities is also covered, as a significant number of adults bring special needs to the learning process. This information provides understanding and tools for facilitating learning that the therapist can use in multiple settings.

Learning

Learning is generally defined as behavioral changes resulting from experience. While there are many theories about the *process* of learning (including Brookfield, 1986; Knowles, 1978; Knox, 1977; Maslow, 1972; Rogers, 1951; and Skinner, 1968). Hilgard and Bower (1966) point out that there is little disagreement about *what* education is between all of the theories. Crow and Crow (1963) summarize:

> Learning involves change. It is concerned with the acquisition of habits, knowledge and attitude. It enables the individual to make both personal and social adjustments. Since the concept of change is inherent in the concept of learning, any change in behavior implies that learning is taking place or has taken place. (Crow & Crow, 1963, p. 1)

Learning can be divided into three components: learning as a function, learning as a process and the learning as a product (Harris & Schwahn, 1961). *Learning as a function* refers to the internal physiological and psychological processes which must take place for learning to happen. *Learning as a process* refers to what happens in the environment during the process of learning. *Learning as a product* emphasizes the end result of learning. Table 18.1 depicts the learning equation which outlines the relationship of the components of learning.

Learning as a Function

Learning as a function is a key knowledge and skill area required of the recreational therapist, as many of the individuals the therapist will be expected to work with will have impairments, disabilities or handicaps which impact their ability to learn. Knowing what may limit learning on a physiological level helps the therapist approach learning in the manner most appropriate for the learner's

Table 18.1: **The Learning Equation**

Learning as a Function +	Learning as a Process =	Learning as a Product
physiological & psychological process of learning + (internal changes)	impact of the environment on learning (external events impacting change)	• change in habits = • change in knowledge • change in attitude

abilities and situation.

In the past, although there were many theories about the physiological process required for learning, there were very few tools which could measure the physiological function of learning. The typical way of measuring learning was to measure some aspect of performance. However, measuring performance is measuring the product of the learning and not the functionality required to learn. In addition to not measuring physiological functions, performance has another significant drawback. It requires motivation, opportunity and reciprocal interactions between the learner and teacher to demonstrate learning. It was difficult to tell how learning was actually taking place with all of the indirect measurements. As Grandjean points out

> Neurophysiology, psychology and other branches of science try very hard to get some degree of insight into the basic processes of mental effort. The well-known neurophysiologist Penfield makes the following comparison: "Anyone who studies mental processes is like a person who stands at the foot of a mountain range. He has cut himself a clearing on the lowest foothill, and from there he looks toward the mountain top, since that is his objective, but the summit is obscured in dense cloud." (Grandjean, 1988, p. 144)

On the physiological side, researchers were looking at the physical structure of the brain. One of the first researchers to document the neurophysiological aspects of learning was Clark L. Hull (1884-1952). Hull described learning as an interaction between a stimulus in the environment and the body's reaction to that stimulus by its transmitting nerve impulses to and from the sensory neurons and to the central nervous system.

Recent research with more sophisticated tools has suggested that all learning can be explained by changes in neurological synapses as a result of external and internal stimuli. The primary neurobiological structures of the brain involved in the formation and retention of information are the hippocampus, the cortex and the cerebellum. "One hundred billion neurons in the brain are involved in forming memories, including a layer of 4.6 million cells in the hippocampus" (Kaplan, Sadock & Grebb, 1994, p. 170). Information is taken in as the neurons react to environmental stimuli. This information is processed along what is called a memory link. A memory link is not a true anatomical structure but a description of the process. The synapsing of the neurons as they pass on the stimuli through an electrical/chemical process triggers the formation of connections (synapses) between brain cells. Generally, the more the environmental stimulation is processed, and the greater the variety of sensory neurons stimulated in the process, the more likely the information will be stored in the brain.

Three events help embed information into long term memory: the use of multiple sensory inputs, the repetition of the sensory inputs and the ability to associate new information with previously learned concepts. These events allow increased connections (pathways) between neurons. The more the information is accessed, the greater the chance for long term storage of the information.

The function of learning is affected not only by the stimuli coming in but also by how well the person limits the stimuli. Reduction of the sensory input into the brain is normal, and actually desirable. If the human body did not have a process to limit the amount of information processed, the brain would be overwhelmed. There are more than one billion receptors in the body for stimulation, which could be processed at over three million nerve junctions. However, humans are only able to have a conscious awareness of around sixteen bits of information with a capacity to remember between zero and seven bits (Grandjean, 1988). Therapists frequently see patients who are unable to filter (inhibit) and process the incoming information. Their learning is significantly slowed because they are not able to attend to a task.

Adrenaline, when experienced in moderate amounts, can increase the body's ability to retain information learned through stimulation. However, too much adrenaline (as with significant stress) inhibits learning. Lesions in the brain also negatively impact learning.

Learning as a Process

Learning as a process refers to not only the specific events which led to the change but also to what happened in the rest of the environment during the process to facilitate (or block) learning from happening. The experience that most people had in elementary through high school was a teacher who stood in front of the classroom lecturing to students who sat, row after row, hopefully taking in what the teacher was presenting. Much of the time spent in school was dedicated to the passive activity of listening to the teacher presenting information and providing an interpretation. This type of education is considered to be a classic example of pedagogy — or the art and science of teaching youth.

> The term comes from the Greek derivatives "ped" (meaning child) and "agogos" (meaning leading). Somewhere along the line, though, the focus on "children" was dropped and pedagogy became accepted as the process for teaching everyone, regardless of the setting — school workplace or community. (D'Antonio-Nocera, DeBolt & Touhey, 1996, p. 188)

Pedagogy is a classic example of teacher-centered learning. The model describes the student/learner as an empty vessel which must be filled by the teacher who is directing both the content and the interpretation of the content which fills the vessel. The teacher assumes an active role while the student assumes a passive role. With such roles, the teacher is clearly the player with the authority and final judgment, while the student lacks authority and is evaluated by what the teacher perceives as being correct. The student is only right when s/he agrees with the teacher.

Knowles (1984) presented other assumptions about learners within the pedagogy model. They are

- The learner is not voluntarily motivated to participate but rather is there because of an external requirement.
- The content of the course is previously determined and learning objectives reflect the content, not necessarily the students' needs.
- Education (in this model) is a "process of the accumulation of a reservoir of subject matter, knowledge and skills to be used later in life" (Knowles, 1984, p 48).

The pedagogical model has been the primary experience of children in schools. While increased emphasis has been on using such methods as "whole language" and other ways of integrating curriculum, much of a child's time in school is still spent with a teacher in the front of the classroom lecturing. This style of teaching/learning is well ingrained in the memories of most adults who teach, whether they teach children or adults. However, adults and children are at different stages of development. The pedagogical model may not be the most appropriate way to facilitate change in adults.

The pedagogical model should not be thrown out completely. There still is a place for a lecture format with the teacher being the center of the process delivering specific information. This is especially true when the content is material that must be memorized, such as standards of practice or federal regulations. However, without the person who is instructing also allowing reasonable interaction from the students to help them grasp the material, and without the information being presented using multiple sensory inputs, the "change" due to learning will be lessened.

The field of education has understood the drawbacks to using the pedagogical model with children for quite a while and has worked to develop models which have greater impact (D'Antonio-Nocera, DeBolt & Touhey, 1996). This change has greatly increased the use of interactive processes between the teacher and the student in pedagogical situations.

A somewhat slower evolution has occurred in the field of andragogy. burlingame and Skalko (1997) state that andragogy is the study of how adults learn. Malcolm Knowles (1978, 1984) theorized that since adults don't learn the same way as children, the educational techniques used with adults should be different from what is typically seen in schools. Adults learn differently for four primary reasons: (1) They are more self-directed than children, (2) They come to the learning environment with significantly more real-world experience, (3) They identify learning closely with their social and occupational role(s) in life, so learning has an important place in their lives and (4) They usually have an immediate application for the learning which is taking place, unlike children who are not sure where they will use the information. (burlingame & Skalko, 1997, p. 20)

The research done in andragogy has demonstrated how vital it is to approach adult learners in a manner which recognizes the very nature of the adult learner (Godbey, 1978) whether they be patients, peers or college students. The orientation with which adults approach learning is different than that of children, so using a classic pedagogical approach falls short of maximizing the adult's learning. This need to approach teaching from an andragogical model requires that the teacher take a learner-centered/patient-centered approach. The unique experiences, orientation to learning and motivation of each learner provides him/her with reasons to actively engage in the learning process, making the teacher's role that of a facilitator, not lecturer. See Table 18.2 for a summary of pedagogy and andragogy.

The concept of andragogy impacts almost every element of treatment provided to adults by the recreational therapist. The assessment process both identifies the patient's strengths and needs and also his/her *need to know* how the impairment/disability and treatment will impact day-to-day life. The treatment program is developed mutually between the patient and the therapist because of the patient's (healthy) need to be responsible for himself/herself (*learner's self-concept*). The assessment evaluates the patient's experience and draws upon the experience as the foundation for all treatment (*role of experience*). *Readiness to learn* new techniques, skills and life patterns is enhanced when the content being taught is based on the patient's need to cope successfully with his/her roles, *orienting learning* to the patient's specific situation. Working to recover (or to even maintain one's current level of health) can be extremely taxing. An internal *motivation* is needed to learn and change. The therapist's role is that of a facilitator of learning.

The therapist's role of facilitator is different only by degrees when instructing non-patients. An understanding of the learner's need to know, experience and roles in life are key to allowing learning to come alive.

Table 18.2: **Contrasting Pedagogy and Andragogy**

Assumptions About Learner	Pedagogy	Andragogy
The Need to Know	The goal of learning is to pass coursework. Application to day-to-day experience is not perceived as necessary.	The need to know how content will impact learner's day-to-day experience is perceived as a critical element of learning.
The Learner's Self-Concept	Teacher's perception of learner is that of a dependent needing to rely on teacher. Learner frequently accepts this role.	Adults generally perceive themselves as being responsible for their own well-being. They expect others to share this perception.
The Role of Experience	Learner has little experience in the new information or in related subjects. The techniques for learning (e.g., lecture, assigned readings, videos) are generally one-way transmissions of information — from teacher to student.	Learner has acquired considerable experience and knowledge. Learning can be much more dynamic with two-way transmission being a larger part of learning.
Readiness of Learner	Learners are mentally prepared to learn what the teacher decides to present.	Learners are mentally ready to learn content which helps them cope with their current life situations. They have greater demands on their time (family, job, health) and may be less able to focus on learning.
Orientation to Learning	Learning is perceived as revolving around subjects (e.g., algebra, US History) which are frequently isolated from each other and from the learner's day-to-day experiences.	Learning is perceived as revolving around roles taken on by learner (e.g., parent, supervisor, therapist, family member).
Motivation	Motivation is primarily external (teachers, grades, parents).	Motivation is primarily internal (desire to perform better, increased life satisfaction, self-esteem).

The existence of multiple roles may have a significant impact on the learner's ability and willingness to participate in new learning. While a facility inservice may be scheduled during the normal workday, attending a professional conference or seminar or enrolling in a college course will involve a commitment of time, energy and often financial resources beyond minimum expectations. As educators we hope that participating in a course or seminar is a top priority, but we must recognize that this may not be the case. The existence of these multiple roles impacts greatly the learner's priorities and the overall process of learning.

Patients come to the therapist with pre-existing conditions, attitudes and prejudices. Some patients may not realize that most of the "skills" necessary to function at work (or as a parent) were first learned through leisure (play) activities. Until the patient is able to understand the direct connection between learning through leisure and critical life functions, the patient may not be motivated to participate in recreational therapy. The therapist should also realize that the patient's priorities may logically lie outside of skills and function learned through activity or leisure.

Similar concerns may be seen outside the "treatment" realm. Responsibilities students face outside of the "classroom" must always be recognized and at times given priority. Educators must acknowledge that their teaching and students' learning does not occur in a vacuum.

Learning as a Product

The last element of the learning equation is the actual product of learning. This product can be seen by changes in habits, changes in knowledge and changes in attitude. The change sought as a product of learning is identified by many terms including "outcomes," "goals," "performance" and "education." Education is a major outcome of health care. Patients are able to modify behaviors which negatively impact health because they have learned how to do so through information provided by the heath care community. They also learn new skills to help overcome impairments, disabilities and handicaps to allow a greater integration back into their community and to improve their quality of life.

Education is one of the two primary outcomes or products of health care; the other being service. Education is a change that comes about through learning. It is measured by the products of learning where internal changes + external events impacting change = change in habits, knowledge and/or attitude. Some examples include learning how to use the bus system, how to move around in a wheelchair or understanding reasons to eat a balanced diet. Service, on the other hand, is the result of actions taken by staff or equipment which bring about change (external events caused by staff action = change in health, independent of patient learning). Examples of service include providing medication, providing passive range of motion, changing dressings, casting and ordering health care equipment.

Different health care professions have different ratios of education and service. Recreational therapy usually provides a higher ratio of education to service than most other health care disciplines. Professionals in nursing, physical therapy and medicine, for example, usually spend more of their time providing service. Most of the treatment objectives written by recreational therapists are educational where the success of the intervention is measured by the product of the learning.

In addition to the patient learning, there is also the issue of staff learning. The types of products of learning we expect to see in staff include improved staff performance, increased customer satisfaction and increased cost/benefit ratio. Supervisors in health care settings expect their staff to engage in continuing education opportunities that create change: the development of a skill (learning how to run a specific treatment protocol) or the acquisition of knowledge about a concept or topic previously unknown (new state regulations for documentation or service provision). Supervisors need to make sure that they put the proper emphasis on the education of staff, including appropriate amounts of time and money. They will find that the change resulting from education has a domino effect. A change in the individual enhances the professional standing of the staff, which prompts a positive change in the field of recreational therapy, thus promoting greater integrity for allied health.

In the learning done by patients and the learning done by therapists, it is important to understand that there is more to providing education than making the material available. To satisfy the needs of health care, the person providing the education needs to take into account the function of learning and the process of learning. Then the educator needs to accurately measure the product of learning to make sure that his/her goals have been met.

Effective Teaching

The application of the principles of andragogy will increase the learners' ability to learn and change. Brookfield (1986) has identified six principles of andragogy as shown in Table 18.3.

Anytime one or more of these elements are missing from the therapy or learning session, the therapist will have a suboptimal learning climate. In reality, especially in a treatment setting, there are many elements which make learning difficult. The patient may have disabilities or impairments which negatively impact the ability to learn. The treatment facility may have treatment schedules, policies or facilities which also detract from optimal learning. The skilled thera-

Table 18.3: **Brookfield's Six Principles of Effective Teaching**

1. Participation is voluntary.
2. Participants demonstrate a mutual respect for each other's self-worth.
3. The learner takes an active role in the facilitation of learning (collaborative facilitation).
4. Praxis is at the heart of effective adult learning.
5. The learning strategies applied aim at fostering a spirit of critical reflection.
6. The overall goal of adult learning is to nurture so the learners become empowered to be self-directed. (Brookfield, 1986)

pist will be able to take all of these elements into consideration as s/he modifies the material to be learned to the characteristics of the learner.

It is important to utilize andragogical theory by implementing Brookfield's principles. If educators only recognize how adults approach learning differently than children but do not adjust their teaching strategies, they will fall short of their potential. A discussion follows on each of the six principles and examples of their application.

Participation is Voluntary

burlingame and Skalko (1997) point out that "participation is not the same as attendance" (p. 195). Participation includes the performance of patient (or learner) controlled behaviors which are appropriate for the situation. Individuals who are happy in their work or therapy are generally motivated to learn. They will be more eager to learn if they feel it will directly benefit their work or treatment efforts (D'Antonio-Nocera, DeBolt & Touhey, 1996). Therefore it is critical for the therapist to present the need for learning in such a way that encourages individuals to participate. Once the individual holds this perception of the value of the material, his/her participation will be voluntary. Motivated individuals are more willing to participate in active learning experiences such as group discussions, small group tasks and role-playing. Interactive learning methods allow the use of multisensory input of the material being taught. This, in turn, helps facilitate the function of learning, the storage of information into short term and long term memory.

- In almost every health care setting the patient has a personal choice to engage in treatment. It is to the therapist's benefit to have the patient voluntarily participate in treatment and the therapist's responsibility to ensure that the patient knows his/her right to refuse treatment.
- By providing information about the learning session or treatment session prior to the session, the individual has a chance to make a choice about whether to participate. If there is material to be read, consider allowing the

learners the opportunity to read the material prior to discussing it. This allows small groups the opportunity to discuss their own interpretations of the material based on their own past experiences.

Mutual Respect

Mutual respect is an important aspect of any learning situation. Respect should flow between the learner(s) and the therapist(s) who take part in the learning activity. Each member of the group should feel that s/he is a valued, unique individual within the learning situation. Mutual respect helps acknowledge the role of experience within each member's contribution to the group. Nathan and Mirviss (1998) talk about the elements of mutual respect:

- Support. Group members should be encouraged to be supportive, not negative. Negative feelings damage group cohesiveness.
- Acceptance. All members, including the therapist, need to feel accepted into the group in order for the group to function effectively.
- Willingness to share ideas/feedback. Members need to be active participants (most of the time) in order for the group to progress and be fruitful. There may be times when this is not psychologically possible, in which case a person's mental state should be respected.
- Commitment to being there. This should be established in the early stages of the group. When members do not show up, their absence affects the rest of the group.
- Ability to work with the therapist and each other. A member cannot function if there isn't the ability/desire to work within the established structure.
- Willingness to engage in the creative process. If a member doesn't really want to be in the group and/or isn't interested in the activities, it wastes everyone's time and energy. (Nathan & Mirviss, 1998, p. 22-23)

Facilitation is Collaborative

A collaborative environment is one where all members work together, supporting each other's efforts to reach a common goal. Whether the learning situation is a classroom, a work setting or a treatment session, promoting and maintaining the spirit of collaboration helps promote a positive self-concept and supports the learner's role (orientation to learning) within the group.

- Whenever the therapist works with a patient to create a contract to work together to decide what the patient's treatment plan, schedule and desired outcomes will be, they are working in a collaborative manner.
- When employees develop a work plan with their supervisor for improvements they anticipate developing over the next year, and then both work toward that agreement, they are working in a collaborative manner.

Praxis is Placed at the Heart of Facilitation

Praxis is the Greek word meaning "to practice," and is the opposite of theory. Key to learning, praxis involves alternating the acquisition of knowledge with the application of the knowledge. Brookfield (1986) describes the process as "...[centering] on the need for educational activity to engage the learner in a continuous and alternating process of investigation and exploration, followed by action grounded in this exploration, followed by reflection on this action, followed by further investigation and exploration, followed by further action and so on" (p 15).

- Alternating back and forth from teaching new skills or providing new knowledge to using newly learned material within a community setting greatly enhances a patient's ability to integrate into the community. An example would be a therapist covering the content of the questions in Module 4E (City Bus) of the *Community Integration Program, Second Edition* (Armstrong & Lauzen, 1994). After reviewing the material verbally with the patient, the therapist would then join the patient on a trial run using the city bus. Upon returning, the patient and the therapist would review both the knowledge and skill required for the activity and then go on to learn more about the skills required, take another trial run and so on.
- Recreational therapy students are required to complete at least one practicum under the supervision of a Certified Therapeutic Recreation Specialist prior to obtaining their college degrees and sitting for the National Council for Therapeutic Recreation Certification exam. This process support the cycle of learning and practice which is the basis of praxis.

Fostering Critical Reflection

As adults learn and experience more, they begin to realize that many of the beliefs, ideas and theories they have held may not hold up in newly presented contexts. What is true in one case may not be true in all situations. This ability to realize that not all "truths" hold up to scrutiny is part of the maturation process. As children, we are taught to accept the "truth" handed down from authority and are not encouraged to question the validity of that truth. Brookfield says, "an awareness that the supposed givens of work conduct, relationships and political allegiances are, in fact, culturally constructed, means that adults will come to question many aspects of their professional, personal and political lives" (Brookfield, 1986, p. 10). It is normal to learn to challenge "facts," as long as a healthy skepticism is appropriately demonstrated. Encouraging professionals to think critically about information that is presented and compare it to what they know to be true from their experiences will help establish a climate where the learners are ready for change. Self-reflection is an essential criteria for personal and professional development.

To encourage learners to engage in critical reflection, the environment must be set for them to do so relatively safely. This involves not only having peer and supervisor support to question long standing beliefs but also, and just as importantly, providing the resource material and experiences from which to draw new knowledge.

- When a patient feels that there is no way for him/her to engage in community recreation programs because s/he is in a wheelchair for the first time, the therapist can help by providing both knowledge and experience to help the patient challenge that belief.
- When presenting a new methodology for facilitating activities, it is necessary to give the people learning it for the first time the freedom to work through their objections and compare what they previously thought with new information in an interactive way.

Nurturing of Self-Directed, Empowered Adults

Individuals who perceive themselves as being empowered tend to be more effective, goal directed and productive (D'Antonio-Nocera, DeBolt & Touhey, 1996). Supporting staff or patients goes beyond just providing them with information, by providing them with input on their own performance goals, the process to achieve them and the manner in which they are to be evaluated. burlingame and Skalko (1997) also point out that empowerment goes beyond supporting individuals with words. They state that empowerment is

the feeling that one can influence one's own life and the events surrounding it. Many therapists are assigned the job of helping the patient to feel empowered. By the nature of empowerment, this cannot be done through talking or self-help programs. Empowerment only comes from the actual experience of being able to control a significant aspect of one's environment. (burlingame & Skalko, 1997, p. 104)

- The therapist's role again is that of a facilitator, working with the learner to set out benchmarks for change.

- The goals should be difficult, but attainable. This helps the learners to feel empowered by taking control and succeeding. To structure success, the therapist must have skill and solid clinical judgment.

Adults with Learning Disabilities

While the term *learning disabilities* has been used for at least one hundred years (with one of the first reports in scientific literature dating back to P. Broca, a French physician, in 1861), the community as a whole has not agreed on a unified definition for learning disability (Goldenson, Dunham & Dunham, 1978). In fact, learning disability is not a recognized medical diagnosis although mental retardation, attention deficit hyperactivity disorder and autism are. The American Psychiatric Association (APA) recognizes only four categories of learning *disorders* (reading disorder, mathematics disorder, disorder of written expression and learning disorder not otherwise specified). (American Psychiatric Association, 1994). A lack of a unified definition has led to many "statistical" reports as to the prevalence of learning disabilities. Reports on incidence of learning disabilities range from

- 50-80% of all students in literacy and basic education courses
- 15-30% of all participants in job training programs
- 25-40% of all adults on welfare (National Institute for Literacy, 1998)

However, without being able to clearly determine who falls into the general category of having a learning disability, it is hard to obtain scientifically solid numbers. The National Institute for Literacy defines learning disability as

> an umbrella term that encompasses a wide variety of disorders, including basic psychological processes involved in understanding or using spoken or written languages. Learning disabilities may manifest themselves as significant difficulty in listening comprehension, speaking, reading, writing, spelling, computational and problem solving skills needed by adults to function effectively as parents, employees and citizens. People with learning disabilities are recognized as having a disability under federal law. This means that they are entitled to "reasonable accommodations" and certain other federally-supported services. (National Institute for Literacy, 1998)

Knowing what a learning disability is requires the therapist to know about the "normal" performance abilities of adults. The State of Oregon has established benchmarks of normal adult learning performance. The purpose of establishing these benchmarks is to have indicators of functional literacy skills in adult Oregonians who share English as a primary language. They looked at the ability of adults to answer questions of various degrees of difficulty from information in newspaper articles, warranties and other documents (advertisements, graphs, pay slips, bus schedules, menus, unit pricing information, etc.). It was felt that workers needed a broad range of learning performance to be successful at work. Table 18.4 depicts the results of the study done using a testing tool developed by the Educational Testing Service and the US Department of Labor (Oregon Progress Board, 1992).

Whether the adult who needs to learn falls into a formal category of learning disabilities or just has difficulty learning, there are techniques for the therapist to use (Adult Learning and Literacy Clearing House, 1990). The key to working with adults with learning disabilities is to apply the concept of praxis — alternating information with actual experience using the new information. The instructor will be learning along with the learner, with the learner taking an active role in the facilitation of learning. Learning how the learner was successful in acquiring knowledge previously allows using the same techniques with new learning. This requires a period of trial-and-error using clinical judgment, ongoing evaluation and an interactive process between the instructor and the learner. In the process of finding out who the learner is (discovering his/her strengths and areas of weakness) also concentrate on what truly interests the learner. Establish the learner's baseline of skills which can be built upon. Since many learning disabilities impact an individual's ability to read, limit the number of written or read testing tools. If written testing material is used, be sure that the reading material is at the right reading level for the learner.

Teaching Methods

The process of acquiring new knowledge and practicing new skills requires the instructor to apply four principals in instructing individuals with learning disabilities (D'Antonio-Nocera, DeBolt & Touhey, 1996).

1. Knowing the learner's *needs, abilities and strengths.*
2. Reaching *mutually agreed upon goals and priorities*, as well as her/his preferences for the type of learning experiences.
3. Using *multi-sensory teaching techniques* — always approaching the delivery of information from at least two different sensory directions.
4. Using *adaptive tools and techniques* — double checking that each will have carry-over and will work in the learner's every day life.

Needs, Abilities and Strengths. To draw upon the learner's abilities and strengths to address his/her needs, the therapist must start from a basic understanding of the learner's capabilities. This information may come from assess-

Table 18.4: **Adult Skill Proficiency**

	Prose Literacy (understands text information)	Document Literacy (can understand and use graphs, text, maps, etc.)	Quantitative Literacy (can understand math and apply it)
Basic Proficiency 21-25 Year Olds	77.7%	78.2%	76.9%
Basic Proficiency All Adults	78.0%	76.1%	80.0%
Intermediate Proficiency 21-25 Year Olds	38.0%	37.1%	27.4%
Intermediate Proficiency All Adults	41.1%	35.5%	39.0%
Advanced Proficiency 21-25 Year Olds	5.5%	6.2%	3.6%
Advanced Proficiency All Adults	8.7%	6.3%	7.6%

ment results (both recreational therapy and from other professionals) as well as the learner himself/herself. When the learner is a volunteer or another staff person, a formal assessment may not be practical or appropriate. Rely on the learner for guidance. Obtaining initial information may include feedback from the learner as to ways which s/he felt s/he learned well previously. If possible, have the learner get tested for hearing and vision problems. Be sure that any reading material that is used is at the correct reading level and font (letter) size. By listening to the learner, through discussion and observation, discover what truly interests the learner.

Teach new concepts by relating them to practical applications, especially ones which the learner is familiar with, to build upon past learning. Build upon the student's own strengths and modify how the information is presented to work around the student's weaknesses. Spend time teaching the learner how to correct his/her own mistakes — it is a skill which will improve the learner's ability far more than any other single skill you can teach. Whenever possible, be flexible concerning time schedules for getting work done. If learning the content of the lesson is the outcome desired (learning as a process), then it may be more appropriate to push out the date that the end product (learning as a product) is due.

Mutually Agreed Upon Goals and Priorities. The learner should be involved throughout the goal setting and priority setting process. Together, the teacher and the learner develop a written work plan which is fully understood and agreed upon as reasonable by both parties. The goals set should be realistic, with short term goals which allow incremental success. Be creative and flexible in determining how the goals will be met. All along the way involve the learner in deciding how his/her work will be evaluated and also in the actual evaluation process. Learning how to manage a learning disability, and how to work around it, is an important skill for adults with a learning disability to learn.

Multi-Sensory Teaching Techniques. It is easier for the therapist to adjust his/her teaching approach than it is for the individual with a learning disability to change the way s/he learns. Using multisensory strategies helps many learners develop full mental images of what is being presented. Being able to see, say, hear and touch increases the learner's ability to make sense of the material. When presenting any information, whether it is instructions concerning class expectations or the actual content to be learned, both oral and written forms of the material should be presented. Be creative and vary your teaching style. Add color, drama and objects which support what you are teaching. Whenever possible, have an example or model of what you are presenting or what you want turned in for the learner to examine. Prior to covering new content, review major points of previous sessions. Provide the learner with a preview of the main points to be covered during the current session. Outline both in several ways: written on the white board, presented orally and outlined in a handout. Some learners may benefit from tape recording or videotaping instructions or the complete session so that they can review it at a later date.

Movement and eye contact are important multisensory approaches the instructor can use to help enhance the student's learning. Make eye contact frequently; this helps in maintaining attention and encouraging participation. Be demonstrative while presenting to allow your body language to punctuate the content.

Adaptive Tools and Techniques. Using adaptive tools and techniques to help the learner overcome an impairment or disability is an important aspect of the therapist's work. Talk with the learner about what techniques worked well for him/her in the past. Help him/her identify techniques which may enhance learning further. Simple modifications include using larger type, incorporating keyboards or having the learners sit in front of the group where they can hear well and have a clear view of the white board. Incorporating keyboards (word processing) can be especially important. Studies show that some learners produce 15 times more writing with a word processor than they can with a pencil or pen. Encourage the use of other learning aids and tools besides the keyboard (e.g., calculators, highlighter pens, extra worksheets, computerized learning programs, records, tape recorders, films, demonstrations, maps, charts, figures, rulers).

Ensure that the learning environment is also conducive to learning. Many individuals with learning disabilities do better if the learning environment is free of visual and auditory distractions. Also, create a positive environment which supports the learner's feeling of self-worth and perceived competencies separate from learning. Praise the learner's accomplishments often during the learning session. The better a learner feels about the learning experience, the harder s/he is likely to work at learning. Allow the climate for learning to emphasize cooperative work, not competition. Humor is an excellent component of each lesson, but how humor is used can make a tremendous difference in the learning climate.

> Laughing *with* someone tends to be based on mutual respect and caring for the other. The laughter develops empathy between groups, giving each a greater confidence. This brings individuals closer together, providing support and emotional nourishment through amusement. Healthy laughter breaks down emotional barriers instead of creating or reinforcing them.

> Laughing *at* others tends to be based on contempt and insensitivity toward others. This type of laughter divides people and destroys confidence. This division excludes some people, offends others and tends to reinforce negative stereotypes by singling out individuals or groups. When a person doesn't have a choice about being the butt of a joke, hurt feelings develop and grow, even if the teller of the sarcastic joke is the butt of the joke. This type of laughter is often abusive in nature and chills any hope of developing a closer, open group. (Nathan & Mirviss, 1998, p. 194)

In addition to nurturing the learner/teacher relationship, encourage the learner to find a mentor to help the learner review information and apply classroom skills to practical situations.

As noted in the discussion of Brookfield's second principle for facilitating adult learning, mutual respect, it is important to further highlight the concept that adults will bring varying levels of educational and field experience to the training environment. It is conceivable that many learning styles or learning preferences will be found in any group of learners. Some staff will be more motivated to read and debate concepts, while other staff will appear to be "engaged" only when practical applications are made. Still others may prefer to listen to presentations and then take some "time out" to reflect upon what has been presented. It is important for the teacher to understand that all learning preferences are valid and that trainees should be encouraged to participate in a variety of learning activities, with the intent that, with such variety, something will help reinforce the learning for each participant.

It is also quite possible that the therapist will face the challenge of working with a staff member with a learning disability. While it is not expected that a therapist will have extensive knowledge and training in working with adults with learning disabilities, it is essential that the therapist be prepared to present content and engage staff with content in ways that they will allow them to learn successfully. This may include utilizing approaches that have been found to be effective with adults with learning disabilities. This information will also serve as an effective tool when working with adult patients engaged in leisure education.

The Future

Because of recent cutbacks in allied health care due to rising costs of service provision, increased demands and shifting political agendas, allied heath care workers find themselves doing work that might have traditionally been done by other disciplines. Where a facility may have contracted out for professional development services in the past, they now look to in-house staff to provide training. The professional development needs of staff are changing, too. As a means to hold human resource budgets in check, facilities may hire more part-time, para-professionals to fill positions previously held by full-time professionals. These para-professionals work under the direct supervision of trained professional staff, but will require more on-the-job training and support in order to be effective in meeting patient needs.

While a recreational therapist may not initially think of himself/herself as an educator, given the rapidly changing demands of professionals in the allied health care field, it is possible that the responsibility for training staff will be a challenge commonly faced. In order to meet this task effectively, recreational therapists need to have an understanding of adult learning and be able to access tools to promote learning effectively in many different settings.

Summary

The assumptions and characteristics of adult learning provide a foundation on which to develop principles for effective facilitation. Adult learners are different from children as learners in respect to the following: a change in self-concept, orientation to learning, the role of life experience and readiness to learn. These differences must be closely considered when designing education and training sessions for adults.

Just as students seek out opportunities for practical applications that support and reinforce what they know to be true, the way in which the learning environment is created and established must also be a practical application of the theories regarding adult learners. Teaching strategies must be supported by theory. Six principles for the effective facilitation of adult learning include: participation is voluntary, mutual respect should be fostered, facilitation is collaborative, praxis is placed at the heart of facilitation, critical reflection should be fostered and the overall goal is to nurture self-directed, empowered adults. When these six principles are used to develop strategies for teaching, then effective learning will occur. The principles are easily applied to adult learning in a variety of settings: inservice training, professional development workshops and seminars, college courses and in working with patients for whom therapy goals have been identified.

Attention must also be paid to the variety of learning styles/preferences and needs of adult learners. Therapists should strive to include different learning activities in training sessions in an effort to effectively "reach" all learners. A working knowledge of guidelines for working with adults with learning disabilities will enhance the therapist's ability to promote learning for learners with different needs and abilities.

Changing demands in allied health care will result in continually changing responsibilities for recreational therapists. As the demand for inservice and staff training increases, it will be critical for recreational therapists to be able to effectively perform this function. Recreational therapists, who are also effective adult educators, will have the opportunity to contribute to the further growth and development of the field by playing an active role in both providing and improving continuing education offerings for themselves and their peers.

Learning Activities

1. Compare Knowles' four assumptions about the adult learner (andragogy) with the three assumptions of the classical pedagogical model. How would these differences impact a leisure education program for youth between the ages of 12 and 15 years and for adults over the age of forty?
2. Look up the definition of learning disability in a variety of federal laws, journals and books. How are the definitions similar? How are they different?
3. Develop a leisure education session for adults with learning disabilities applying both Knowles' andragogy and Brookfield's principles.
4. Obtain a copy of a published leisure education program. Critique it using Knowles' and Brookfield's principles.

5. Read material on the physiological function of learning as it applies to either long or short term memory. What are the basic anatomical structures involved in the memory process and what enhances the process?

Study Questions

1. What is "learning?" What are the three components of learning as discussed by Harris and Schwahn?
2. What are the differences between the andragogical and pedagogical approaches to teaching?
3. What three events help embed information into long term memory?
4. What are four principles for teaching adults with learning disabilities?
5. What is "praxis" and how does it apply to learning the requirements for a student in recreational therapy?

References

Adult Learning and Literacy Clearinghouse. (1990). *Instructional strategies for adults with learning disabilities*. Washington, DC: US Department of Education.

American Psychiatric Association. (1994). *Diagnostic and statistical manual of mental disorders* (4th ed.). Washington, DC: American Psychiatric Association.

Armstrong, M. & Lauzen, S. (1994). *Community integration program* (2nd ed.). Ravensdale, WA: Idyll Arbor, Inc.

Brookfield, S. (1986). *Understanding and facilitating adult learning*. San Francisco: Jossey-Bass.

Brookfield, S. (1990). *The skillful teacher*. San Francisco: Jossey-Bass.

burlingame, j. & Skalko, T. (1997). *Idyll Arbor's glossary for therapists*. Ravensdale, WA: Idyll Arbor, Inc.

Cross, P. (1983). *Adults as learners*. San Francisco: Jossey-Bass.

Crow, L. D. & Crow, A. (Eds.). (1963). *Readings in human learning*. New York: McKay.

Dana, J. C. (1912). In a report to Newark State College as reported in The New York Times Book Review, March 5, 1967.

D'Antonio-Nocera, A., DeBolt, N. & Touhey, N. (Eds.). (1996). *The professional activity manager and consultant*. Ravensdale, WA: Idyll Arbor, Inc.

Godbey, G. C. (1978). *Applied andragogy: A practical manual for the continuing education of adults*. College Station, PA: Continuing Education Division, Pennsylvania State University.

Goldenson, R. M., Dunham, J. R. & Dunham, C. S. (Eds.). (1978). *Disability and rehabilitation handbook*. New York: McGraw-Hill Book Company.

Grandjean, E. (1988). *Fitting the task to the man* (4th ed.). Bristol, PA: Taylor & Francis, Inc.

Harris, T. L. & Schwahn, W. E. (1961). *Selected readings on the learning process*. New York: Oxford University Press.

Hilgard, E. R. & Bower, G. H. (1966). *Theories of learning*. New York: Appleton-Century-Crofts.

Kaplan, H. I., Sadock, B. J. & Grebb, J. A. (1994). *Kaplan and Sadock's synopsis of psychiatry* (7th ed.). Baltimore: Williams & Wilkins.

Knowles, M. (1978). *The adult learner: A neglected species.* Houston, TX: Gulf Publishing Company.

Knowles, M. (1984). *Andragogy in action: Applying modern principles of adult learning.* San Francisco: Jossey-Bass.

Knox, A. B. (1977). *Adult development and learning.* San Francisco: Jossey-Bass.

Kolb, D. (1984). *Experiential learning: Experience as the source of learning and development.* New York: Prentice Hall.

Library for the Blind and Physically Handicapped. (1987). *American basic education and general educational development programs for disabled adults.* Philadelphia, PA: Free Library of Philadelphia.

Maslow, A. H. (1972). *Motivation and personality.* New York: Perseus.

Nathan, A. A. & Mirviss, S. (1998). *Therapy techniques using the creative arts.* Ravensdale, WA: Idyll Arbor, Inc.

National Institute for Literacy. (1998). National resources for adults with learning disabilities. http://novel.nifl.gov/nalld/resource.hmt#checklist. 6/29/98 11:44 a.m.

Oregon Progress Board. (1992). *Oregon benchmarks: Standards for measuring statewide progress and government performance.* Salem, OR: State of Oregon Progress Board.

Polson, C. (1993). *Teaching adult students.* Idea Paper No. 29. Kansas State University: Center for Faculty Evaluation and Development.

Rogers, C. R. (1951). *Client-centered therapy.* Boston: Houghton-Mifflin.

Ross-Gordon, J. M. (1989). *Adults with learning disabilities: An overview for the adult educator.* Columbus, OH: ERIC Clearinghouse.

Skinner, B. F. (1968). *The technology of teaching.* New York: Appleton-Century-Crofts.

Chapter 19

The Recreational Therapy Degree Program: Trends in Education

Frank Brasile

According to the Occupational Outlook Handbook (Department of Labor, 1991), recreational therapy is a relatively new field whose employment is expected to grow much faster than the average for all occupations through the year 2005. As recently as the 1980's many individuals who were recognized as being qualified for positions as recreational therapists were individuals with degrees in physical education, psychology, sociology, social work and other human service areas. However, this no longer is the case because, increasingly, formal preparation in recreational therapy is expected. The acceptance of the national credential for employment is one of the biggest factors in this change and has led toward the professionalization of the field. Nowakowski, Nowakowski and Lane (1983) refer to five specific categorical means of measurement which are used in evaluating professional competence: professional standard setting, evidence of entry and educational process, certification and licensure, specialization and continuing education.

With the development of professional standards of practice (See ATRA and NTRS Standards of Practice in Appendix B), a national certification examination coupled with the continuing education requirements for recertification and an optional curriculum accreditation path, it would appear that the field of recreational therapy is well on its way to reaching an acceptable level of professionalization. Yet, the issues of evidence of entry and educational process and specialization need to be addressed in more depth, especially taking into consideration the rapid growth in the knowledge base of the profession and the current demands in the provision of health care services.

The Impact of Credentialing

The establishment of the National Council for Therapeutic Recreation Certification (NCTRC) and its credentialing process has had an instantaneous impact on the educational process of the professional. In effect, the NCTRC standards for sitting for the national certification examination has set minimum requirements for the education of those interested in entering the field. To become a Certified Therapeutic Recreation Specialist (CTRS) an individual must first meet these sitting requirements and then pass a national certification examination which is administered through the Educational Testing Service (ETS). This certification exam for recreational therapy personnel was implemented on November 10, 1990.

When considering that the NCTRC minimum requirements to sit for the certification examination are three courses in recreational therapy (one of which can be a swing course), three courses in general recreation, a 360 hour practicum combined with additional requirements of content courses in human growth and development, abnormal psychology and anatomy and physiology along with other "specialization courses," the question arises: is this really a thorough educational and experiential background to prepare a student for current professional practice?

Even before this examination was established, there were concerns that the profession was putting the cart before the horse in the quest of establishing a strong educational foundation for the profession. In fact, Brasile (1984) stated: "It is hoped that prior to the development and use of this competency test, more of an emphasis will be placed on the development of consistent and standardized curriculum in therapeutic recreation throughout our colleges and universities as well as on the development of more stringent standards to be used in the hiring of Therapeutic Recreation Specialists" (p. 28). In agreement with this concern Casteen (1984) wrote: "Proper tests, properly used, sustain learning and document compliance. They do not replace or compete with education and training" (p. 11).

Even though the intent of the certification standards developed by NCTRC has been to assure better accountability of practicing professionals, it does not specifically address the issue of extreme diversity among college and university programs that offer degree options or specializations in recreational therapy.

The Impact of Curriculum Accreditation

In the late 1970's The National Recreation and Park Association and the American Association for Leisure and Recreation (NRPA/AALR Joint Council on Accreditation) implemented a curriculum accreditation program as a means of assuring that minimal competencies were being met within Recreation and Leisure Studies curricula. In addition to a general accreditation of a degree program, a college or university could consider having an option (i.e. recreational therapy, outdoor recreation, programming, etc.) accredited through this process. As such, basic option competency areas were established and all colleges and universities who pursued and were granted accreditation in an option were required to address these minimal areas of competency for their professional preparation programs. However, it must be noted that this is a voluntary accreditation and the majority of institutions of higher education that offer a recreation and leisure studies degree have chosen not to participate in this program for one reason or another.

With these efforts toward professionalization through certification and accreditation, educators and the profession in general have become better aware of the pre-professional educational components deemed necessary for entry level competence in recreational therapy. The task of defining appropriate curriculum is not completed yet because professionals have begun to realize that curriculum needs to be a better match to the demands of the profession as it enters the 21st century. Taking into consideration the information acquired by NCTRC related to the scope of practice in recreational therapy and used to assist in the development and updating of the national certification examination, it appears that there is a reference point for the educational foundation of the profession. It would also seem that this information, combined with the information included in the recently published *Self-Assessment Guide on the Competencies for Practice as a Therapeutic Recreation Specialist* (ATRA, 1996), could serve as a point of departure to develop a road map for the standardization of curriculum at our colleges and universities. However, before discussing the issue of the standardization of the degree components for the profession it would first be appropriate to review a brief history of professional preparation in recreational therapy.

Historical Information

Recreational therapy is a growing allied health profession. Even though there were individuals employed in positions related to hospital recreation prior to the 1940's, the first attempt to professionalize the occupation and its educational process did not occur until the late 1940's. An acceleration to the hospital recreation movement occurred as a result of World War II. This was a period when the American National Red Cross recruited large numbers of individuals from allied health fields to participate in preparation programs to train them to work as hospital recreators. A training program at the American University was established for newly employed staff (O'Morrow, 1980). This training program was an intensive four week course in basic recreation. This represented one of the earliest attempts to educate individuals to be competent recreation specialists in hospital settings. One of the first committees of the Hospital Recreation Section of ARS was the Standards and Training Committee which, as early as 1953, made recommendations for the educational preparation of future personnel.

The majority of professional education programs for hospital recreation workers evolved around institutes and workshops. During the 1950's, biennial institutes in hospital recreation or recreation for the ill and disabled were held on the campuses of the Universities of Minnesota and North Carolina (Frye & Peters, 1972).

Prior to the mid 1960's most of the formal educational preparation for professionals entering the field was found at the graduate level (Frye & Peters, 1972). The majority of these curricula led to degrees in Parks and Recreation or Health, Physical Education and Recreation. Many of these programs required one course related to Special Recreation or Recreation for Special Populations and a fieldwork experience or thesis in their area of specialization.

In the 1960's the term therapeutic recreation was selected over the term recreational therapy as described in Chapter 2, *The Conceptual Development of Recreational Therapy*. The first study related to status of therapeutic recreation education was published by Stein (1970). In this study Stein identified 35 institutions that indicated they had an option in therapeutic recreation. From this study it was reported that there were 37 full time faculty positions in therapeutic recreation and that there were 531 individuals who were students in this specialization. These numbers indicate that there were on average 14 students per faculty member and 15 students per option.

The 1970's represented a decade where the growth of professional preparation programs at colleges and universities was phenomenal and more and more of these universities were beginning to hire at least one qualified therapeutic recreation educator to serve as the primary faculty member for the majors in this area.

Many institutions were also developing specific options which required students to take more than one course in the specialty area. The body of knowledge was growing rapidly; however, it was also evident that there were not enough qualified educators to meet the demands. Anderson and Stewart (1980) reported that the total number of students enrolled in therapeutic recreation options witnessed an increase that could not have been predicted by anyone. The results of this survey also indicated that there were 137 programs offering concentrations in therapeutic recreation with 7,992 students enrolled in these programs. Additionally, it was reported that there were 253 faculty directly involved in therapeutic recreation education. These numbers indicate that their were on average 32 students per faculty member and 58 students per option.

As a complement to this growth in curricula, educational opportunities during this decade were manifested by a proliferation in therapeutic recreation related workshops and symposia throughout the country. Pioneering most of these efforts was the first Midwest Symposium on Therapeutic Recreation in 1969. The impact of this symposium led to the development of many similar local, regional and international symposia.

During the 1980's, as a result of this rapid growth in professional preparation programs and a reciprocal growth in the numbers of qualified professionals in the field, a critical focus was placed upon professionalization issues. Professional preparation programs at colleges and universities experienced a peak in the late 1970's and during the past decade the number of institutions offering programs in therapeutic recreation has declined. In their most recent study, Stewart and Anderson (1990) reported a decrease in concentrations in therapeutic recreation with a similar decrease in faculty positions and student enrollment. In this study it was reported that there were 105 programs offering concentrations in therapeutic recreation with 4,267 students enrolled. Also it was reported that their were 173 faculty members directly involved in therapeutic recreation education. These numbers indicate that their were on average 25 students per faculty member and 41 students per option. Much of this decline is directly related to the loss of financial support for higher education programs that prepare individuals to work with special populations.

As such, what may be an even more important issue here is, if this knowledge base is an indication of current professional practice needs, is there a consistency in our pre-professional preparation programs and curricula across the nation? If we feel that certain competencies are necessary and we have taken the time and effort to document an entry level knowledge base, is it also not important to develop some kind of standardized curriculum for the profession?

In addition to showing a decline in the number of programs and majors in therapeutic recreation, the 1980's were also a decade in which more stringent regulations for allied health professions were implemented. Funding for most services in clinical facilities dropped to a low level and many programs suffered as a result. This has carried over into the 1990's and all indications are that it will continue in the next century. A new paradigm for allied health services has emerged; accountability and reimburseability are of utmost importance.

Recreational therapy must not stagnate or it may become extinct. It must endeavor to evolve like any other profession and it is now time to seriously consider developing a specific degree programs for the professional area of recreational therapy.

The education of clinically oriented health care professionals can no longer exist as a specialization or emphasis. There is an ever-growing body of knowledge in the professional area and future professionals need to keep abreast of this body of knowledge to meet the ever-growing demands of the consumer and provider in the new era of health care in our country. Prior to discussing this new educational design it is necessary to review some of the more recent studies related to curriculum and competencies of practice in the profession.

Current Educational Research

Stumbo (1986) set out to define the knowledge base of the profession by identifying, refining and validating entry level knowledge needed for professional practice. As a result of this investigation, it was suggested that these results be examined by recreational therapy professional organizations and also be used as the basis for and provide direction to a variety of professional activities.

McGhee (1987) surveyed recreational therapy professionals to determine which educational experiences were most appropriate for acquiring specific therapeutic recreation competencies. This investigation reveled significant differences in the perceptions of appropriateness among educator/researchers, administrator/directors and practitioner/leaders. Most interesting were results which indicated that educators tend to place a higher emphasis on the bachelor's degree experience than do the other groups. There was also an indication that the bachelor's level program may not be the appropriate place in which to garner the management cluster competencies needed for professional practice.

Oltman, Norback and Rosenfield (1989) heeded Stumbo's suggestion and set the stage for the development of an examination to be part of the certification process for entry-level therapeutic recreation practitioners. Their job analysis provided the profession with a core body of knowledge that had substantial professional agreement and eventually served as the basis for the National Certification Examination.

Skalko and Smith (1989) examined the status of recreational therapy within state personnel systems. Results indicated a lack of standardized national criteria related to titles, credentials and employment criteria. It was suggested that a standardization of recreational therapy curricula may assist in the quest to further advance the field.

Brasile (1992) surveyed the membership of the American Therapeutic Recreation Association in relation to their perceived needs related to professional preparation. As a result of this survey it was recommended that the ATRA Board of Directors create a task force to develop guidelines for the standardization of therapeutic recreation curricula, that this task force also examine its potential to initiate a dialog with the American Medical Association Curriculum Accreditation Council in developing new curriculum accreditation options and suggested further research to define the divergence in undergraduate and graduate curricula in therapeutic recreation. Results also indicated that the membership of ATRA believed it was now time to become more aligned with other allied health curricula and develop a professional specialization that was more clinical oriented.

Addressing the suggestions from Brasile (1992), the ATRA Board of Directors established a Task Force on Higher Education. This task force, which was co-chaired by Dr. Terry Kinney and Dr. Jeff Witman, published a self-assessment guide on the competencies for practice as a therapeutic recreation specialist (American Therapeutic Recreation Association, 1993). When reviewing these competencies and those that have been approved by NCTRC and mixing in the recreational therapy domains described by JCAHO, it is hard to imagine that they all can be addressed in just three specific recreational therapy classes and a 360 hour practicum. Thus, it certainly is evident that it is now time to develop a professional standardized curriculum for training recreational therapists of the next millennium. As such, the best place to start is at the undergraduate level. The graduate level can then be used for the specialization component of the profession as described in Nowakowski et al. (1983).

Recreational Therapy Degree

Recreational therapy has been described as one of the oldest yet one of the youngest human service professions (Carter, Robb & VanAndel, 1988), and as a field of specialization within a broad profession of recreation and leisure services (Austin, 1997). Over the past forty years recreational therapy has also been described as a process which utilizes recreation services for purposive intervention in physical, emotional, cognitive and social behavior to bring about desired change in behavior and to promote the growth and development of the individual (Frye & Peters, 1972), and as a helping profession (Kraus, 1983). More recently both the American Therapeutic Recreation Association (ATRA) and the National Therapeutic Recreation Society (NTRS) have identified the use of recreation as a modality to address health needs [italics added]:

> …as the provision of treatment services and the provision of recreation services to persons will illness or disabling conditions. The primary purposes of Treatment Services which are often referred to as *Recreational Therapy*, are to restore, remediate or rehabilitate in order to improve functioning and independence as well as reduce or eliminate effects of illness or disability. The primary purposes of *recreation services* are to provide recreation resources and opportunities in order to improve health and well-being. (American Therapeutic Recreation Association, 1993, p. 8)

Practiced in clinical, residential and community settings, the profession of *therapeutic recreation* uses treatment, education and recreation services to help people with illness, disabilities and other conditions to develop and use their leisure in ways that enhance their health, independence and well-being. (National Therapeutic Recreation Society, 1995, p1)

These definitions makes it obvious that the purpose of recreational therapy is different than the purpose of recreation. The services are provided differently and may require different resources. It is time to advance our profession as a health care profession, not just a recreation profession. Health care has its own continuum: disease, impairment, disability and handicap and its own set of services: ambulatory services, inpatient services, outpatient/day treatment services, long term care services, home health services and human services. These services are not just unique to the clinical or hospital setting and thus must be combined with community services. As such, we must train and educate our future professionals as allied health professionals who have a basic understanding of the foundation of the profession which is the use of recreation and other activities to promote health and well-being in a wide variety of settings.

A major step in the development of the prototype recreational therapy degree program began in October, 1982, when the Therapeutic Recreation Degree Program at Longwood College in Farmville, Virginia, became the first specific degree program in recreational therapy to be accredited by the NRPA/AALR Joint Council on Accreditation. This program had already been in existence since the late 1970's when the State Council on Higher Education awarded this institution the right to award a specific baccalaureate degree in recreational therapy. This curriculum required students to take a minimum of six recreational therapy specific courses along with a minimum of four general recreation courses and also participate in three practicums during the four year degree process. One of these practicums was to be performed in a general recreation setting and the other two were to be performed in treatment settings. In addition, students were required to take introductory biology, anatomy and physiology, basic psychology, abnormal psychology, physiology of exercise, human growth and development, motor learning and adapted physical education. Other specialized courses that were required were Music for Special Populations and Arts and Crafts for Special Populations. In a sense it was an intense specialization.

It is evident, upon reviewing this degree program, that this was the most clinically-oriented, treatment-intervention-focused curriculum in existence in the country at that time. In fact, the degree program was almost turned down for accrediting because the NRPA/AALR Joint Council on Accreditation stated that they did not accredit specific degree programs in recreational therapy. However, because the degree title and content was a mandate of the Commonwealth of Virginia and also because it adhered to all of the competency areas addressed in the accreditation standards, there was no sound reason not to accredit the program.

If a program like this could exist and produce quality students from the late 1970's through today, why can't the profession venture forward and develop a unique degree for the future that will address a treatment orientation? It is time to take the Longwood approach to its next level, a specific degree as an allied health profession, and it is the responsibility of the entire profession to bring this issue into the forefront.

Recreational Therapy Degree Components

As mentioned earlier, the entry degree for the profession should be the undergraduate degree and the graduate degree should be a degree of specialization (e.g., related service, gerontology, mental health, physical medicine). The undergraduate degree should have six primary components; liberal arts, science, allied health, recreation and leisure, recreational therapy and practicum.

Liberal Arts, Humanities and Behavioral Sciences. Studies in this particular component of the degree program should dominate the first two years of a student's educational process. Courses may include: English Composition, Literature, Anthropology, Psychology, Sociology, Mathematics, Philosophy, Biology, Speech, Introduction to Computers and Cultural Diversity.

Biological Behavioral and Health Sciences. During this phase of the undergraduate curriculum, the student should focus on courses that deal with the structure and function of the human body and on recognition of normal and abnormal conditions. Also, a focus on human behavior as it relates to the life cycle (including sensorimotor, cognitive and psychosocial components), as well as in the context of socio-cultural systems and beliefs need to be considered. Courses related to these areas include: Anatomy, Physiology, Kinesiology, Human Growth and Development, Ethics, Cultural and Gender Diversity, Developmental and Abnormal Psychology, Health and Wellness, Stress Management and Drug Awareness to mention a few.

Recreation and Leisure (Theory and Practice). The vast majority of professionals employed in the delivery of recreational therapy services would agree that the one component of our profession that sets us apart from all other allied health professions is a strong background in recreation and leisure. Courses related to this aspect of the profession should include: Introduction to Recreation, Recreation Leadership Techniques, Recreation Administration, Outdoor Recreation and/or Camp Counseling and Leisure Philosophy. Also, each student should be required to participate in a practicum or minimum number of hours in the delivery of general recreation services prior to the recreational therapy practicum phase.

Allied Health. It is important for the recreational therapy major to establish a relationship with other allied health professionals as early in her/his career as possible. One of the ways this can be accomplished is by taking certain introductory courses with these allied health peers.

Most colleges or universities have pre-professional training for allied health careers as options for students who are attending the school (examples of such programs are those in Pre-OT, Pre-PT and Pre-Nursing). In fact, many colleges that offer the recreational therapy option are on the same campus or close to a campus that offers professional training for these other allied health fields. There is no reason that a relationship cannot and should not be established between these allied health professional options and the recreational therapy degree program. Many of these pre-professional training programs have specific requirements such as: Introduction to Allied Health Professions, Medical Terminology, Anatomy and Physiology and Introduction to Pharmacology.

Recreational Therapy (Theory and Practice). It is currently required that all individuals who wish to be considered for certification by NCTRC have successfully completed a minimum of three courses specifically related to recreational therapy. However, because the focus of this specific degree program is on recreational therapy and should no longer be considered an emphasis, it becomes more important to make sure that all of the documented competency areas are covered with the depth that is necessary for today's entry level professional.

Areas such as theoretical approaches, human performance, activity adaptation and modification, diversional and purposeful activity, education, assessment, evaluation, intervention techniques, writing skills, group intervention, management, values and attitudes and research need to be considered. Courses which may be related to these components include: Introduction to Recreational Therapy, Recreational Therapy Intervention and Facilitation Techniques, Clinical Aspects of Recreational Therapy, Recreational Therapy Programming, Issues and Trends in Recreational Therapy, Assessment and Evaluation in Recreational Therapy, Leisure Education, Research in Recreational Therapy and Administration of Recreational Therapy Services. Along with these courses, additional course work with specific diagnostic groups as a more in depth focus should be considered. The vast majority of employment opportunities for the profession today are found in community mental health, physical medicine and gerontology; therefore courses such as: Recreational Therapy Intervention for the Aging, Recreation and Sport for the Physically Disabled and Recreational Therapy Intervention in Mental Illness need to be considered.

Additional Supportive Coursework. NCTRC standards spell out specific supportive courses such as anatomy and physiology, abnormal psychology and human growth and development. Each of these competencies can be acquired in meeting the demands of the Biological and Health Sciences requirements or in the General Education — Liberal Arts portion of the degree program. Some of the other, more important considerations for the supportive area might be Sign Language, Introduction to Special Education, The Hospitalized Child, Stress Management, Physiology of Exercise, Adapted Physical Education, Psychodrama, Psychology of Disability and Health Aspects of Aging. This part of the student's curriculum should be selected to fit her/his unique area of interest for employment.

Fieldwork or Practicum Experiences. Probably the most important component in any professional preparation degree program is the practical experience component. Currently, the National Council on Therapeutic Recreation Certification (NCTRC) requires that each student who wishes to become certified under their plan have a minimum of 360 hours of practicum under the supervision of a CTRS. Most practitioners believe this is not enough time for them to do the student any justice in this most important learning experience. Thus, it is suggested that the fieldwork or practicum experience be a major component of this degree program. Fieldwork experiences should be clearly described in written documents that are available to the student, the practitioner and the administration.

Each student should be required to have three separate practicum experiences. Each experience should relate to a certain phase in their educational development. The first experience should take place during the sophomore or early junior semesters and should be a general recreation leadership experience of a minimum of 120 contact hours. This particular practicum could be integrated into specific requirements in the general recreation component of the educational process.

The next two experiences should be accomplished in recreational therapy settings under a CTRS. The first of these could be a single experience or a group of varied experiences designed as an integral part of the didactic courses for the purpose of directed observation and participation in recreational therapy. Prior to beginning their senior or final year in the major, each recreational therapy major should have accumulated a minimum of 200 contact hours in these types of experiences. Lastly, and most importantly, the third experience should serve as the bridge to becoming a professional and, as such, this pre-professional practicum experience should be a semester long (minimum of 15 weeks at 40 hours a week) experience in a treatment-oriented recreational therapy setting. The student should be involved in hands on recreational therapy practice under the supervision of a CTRS. This practicum should be the last requirement in the student's educational program. As such, all course work must be completed prior to beginning this experience.

Now that an overview of content is in place there are other questions which need to be addressed such as where is this specific degree program housed, who should serve as faculty members, how can these programs be reviewed for quality assurance purposes and what about the graduate degree component.

Administrative Concerns: Sponsorship and Resources

As one reviews the curriculum content listed above, it appears to be consistent with the demands of the profession. Such a degree specialization can be implemented in various academic settings. The sponsorship of such a program, at minimum, should be located in a college or university authorized to grant a baccalaureate degree. This college or university should be recognized by appropriate regional accrediting bodies. While the major concern should be consistency in recreational therapy education throughout the country, it is clear that the specific department or academic discipline area in which this degree curriculum is located does make a difference. With the emphasis moving toward an associations with other allied health professionals and a desire to have course work in the allied health professions as part of the recreational therapy curriculum, it seems desirable to be in a college or university which has allied health programs. We may, in fact, be seeing the beginning of a trend for the recreational therapy program to move away from sponsorship in health, recreation and physical education to sponsorship in schools of allied health.

The recreational therapy degree program should have at the minimum one faculty member who is a CTRS and access to competent part-time adjunct faculty who are also NCTRC certified. Because health care is changing so quickly, previous *and* current experience in the profession as an administrator or therapist is imperative. If the degree program has a graduate degree component, the faculty member should eventually be encouraged to obtain a terminal degree, however, the profession should stress to higher education administrators that it is acceptable to hire competent practitioners as educators for these faculties. In effect, a terminal degree is not necessary to be a competent recreational therapy educator at the undergraduate level. Each particular program should take into consideration the existing market and the demands of the profession. What is of greatest importance during this developmental phase is that the faculty member be a Certified Therapeutic Recreation Specialist (CTRS), have an advanced degree, be knowledgeable, be a competent clinician, be effective in teaching the content assigned and be effective in the supervision of practicum students.

NCTRC could play a major role in the educational process if it would establish a new requirement for the acceptance of the recreational therapy specific courses: that the courses must be taught by a CTRS. It would appear to be easy to ask that the educator's name and certification number be listed next to the course title on the student's application. This would be similar to the method that is presently used in assuring that the clinical field work supervisor is a CTRS. If the educator is not a CTRS, then the course should not be accepted. The same holds true for the college/university recreational therapy fieldwork supervisor. The majority of professionals who responded to the survey by Brasile (1992) strongly believed that the college or university field work supervisor should be a CTRS. These requirements would add more credibility in the professionalization process.

Accreditation Issues

A standardized degree program in recreational therapy must be subject to some outside peer review. The most obvious would be through the already existing NRPA/AALR accreditation process. What would be needed, as was not available in the Longwood situation, is the addition of guidelines for a specific degree program in recreational therapy. This could be accomplished through working with the existing professional organizations to establish the specific recreational therapy standards.

Other possibilities worthy of consideration include developing an accreditation program in connection with an already existing allied health curriculum accreditation body, or developing a specific recreational therapy curriculum accreditation body for the profession. Another consideration may be to develop a peer review process that a local advisory committee of certified practicing professionals could implement.

Graduate Degree Specialization

Graduate study should deal with more complex ideas and demands, sophisticated techniques, research and analysis, creative thinking and time than undergraduate study. The research should be extensive in both primary and secondary sources and a high quality of writing should be expected. Graduate students should be expected to do work of high caliber and, if not, it should result in at least temporary dismissal from the degree program or from graduate standing.

It is now time for the professional education process of the recreational therapist to meet these demands; therefore, no student should be admitted into a graduate degree program that specializes in recreational therapy unless s/he is already a CTRS. The competencies that are needed to practice in the field should be met prior to reaching the next level of the educational hierarchy. The graduate level should serve as an intense specialization area, as discussed earlier by Nowakowski et al. (1983) and also have a strong focus on efficacy research for the profession.

For too long now, graduate and undergraduate students have been attending the same classes and have been educated at the same level for entry into the field. This does not lead to professional development and in a sense devalues the

graduate degree and potential of the graduate student in the profession. It would
be in the best interests of the profession to establish the graduate degree as a
specialization degree area. In many cases this can be accomplished in a transdisciplinary manner. Some examples of this are a management specialization that is
completed in cooperation with a public health graduate program, a gerontology
specialization that is completed in cooperation with a gerontology graduate program, a related services specialization that is completed in cooperation with a
special education graduate program or a rehabilitation medicine specialization
that is completed in cooperation with either a rehabilitation counseling or exercise science graduate program. Graduate specializations are not a new concept;
in fact, in the past many students chose to attend certain colleges or universities
based upon the specialized background of the educator/mentor from whom they
wanted to learn.

Summary

This chapter represents an appeal for sophistication in the process of educating recreational therapy personnel. It should not in any way be construed as
belittling the importance or impact of the current educational programs. However, it is time to plan for the future and build upon the past. The recreational
therapy profession must enter the new millennium with an open mind regarding
its continuing development and acceptance as a caring and accountable profession. One of the most important issues facing this profession is the standardization of the training of its professionals based upon the mandates of current practice. How this issue is addressed could very well be the key to acceptance as a
viable allied health profession in the twenty-first century.

Learning Activities

1. Obtain the curriculum requirements for another allied health field at your
    university (or at a university in your state). These may include nursing, oc-
    cupational therapy, physical therapy, speech and language pathology, social
    work. Divide that curriculum into the classifications found in this chapter.
    What similarities and differences do you find?
2. Take the 87 professional job responsibilities listed in the NCTRC National
    Job Analysis (available from NCTRC, 7 Elmwood Dr., New York, NY
    10956, 914-639-1439) and a list of the recreational therapy/recreation
    classes required by your university. For each job responsibility, list the class
    which covers that responsibility. Are there any job responsibilities which
    are not currently covered by your curriculum?
3. Take the recreational therapy treatment competencies from JCAHO as
    listed in this chapter. Match each competency with the classes that teach

you the skills required. What skills are not being taught in available classes? Where will you learn the skills required?

Study Questions

1. What are the five specific categories used as a means to measure professional competence (Nowakowski, Nowakowski and Lane)?
2. Discuss the major trends in the historical development of professional preparation programs from 1940 to present.
3. What are the types of courses and course content which a student in recreational therapy should take in order to have a strong knowledge base?
4. What types of practicum experiences are appropriate for a recreational therapy student at the undergraduate level?
5. What should be the emphasis of a graduate degree and what are the concerns discussed about the way that many graduate programs are run today?

References

American Therapeutic Recreation Association. (1993). *Standards for the practice of therapeutic recreation & self-assessment guide*. Hattiesburg, MS: Author.

American Therapeutic Recreation Association. (1996). *Self-assessment guide on the competencies for practice as a therapeutic recreation specialist*. Hattiesburg, MS: American Therapeutic Recreation Association.

Anderson, S. & Stewart, M. (1980). Therapeutic recreation education: 1979 survey. *Therapeutic Recreation Journal, 3*(4), 4-10.

Austin, D. (1991). *Therapeutic recreation process and techniques* (3rd ed.). Champaign, IL: Sagamore Publishing, Inc.

Brasile, F. (1984). Measuring professional status through self-regulatory standards and competency testing, does therapeutic recreation measure up? *TRENDS*. Richmond, VA: Virginia Parks and Recreation Society.

Brasile, F. (1992). Professional preparation; Reported needs for a profession in transition. *Annual in Therapeutic Recreation, 3*, 58-71.

Carter, M., Robb, G. & VanAndel, G. (1988). *Therapeutic recreation: A practical approach*. St. Louis: Times Mirror/Mosby.

Casteen, J. (1984). The public stake in proper test use. In C. D. Davis (Ed.). *The uses and misuses of tests*. San Francisco: Jossey-Bass.

Department of Labor. (1991). Recreational Therapists. *Occupational Outlook Handbook*.

Frye, V. & Peters, M. (1972). *Therapeutic recreation: Its theory philosophy and practice*. Harrisburg, PA: Stackpole Books.

Kraus, R. (1983). *Therapeutic recreation service: Principles and practices* (3rd ed.). Philadelphia: Saunders.

McGhee, S. (1987). Professional preparation: Matching competency acquisition with appropriate educational experiences. *Therapeutic Recreation Journal, 21*(4), 63-73.

National Therapeutic Recreation Society. (1995). *Standards of practice for therapeutic recreation services and annotated bibliography.* Ashburn, VA: National Recreation and Parks Association.

Nowakowski, J., Nowakowski, A. & Lane, K. (1983). Measurement and the professions: Lessons for accounting, law, and medicine. *New Directions for Testing and Measurement, 20,* 77-93.

O'Morrow, G. (1980). *Therapeutic recreation: A helping profession* (2nd ed.). Reston, VA: Prentice Hall.

Oltman, P., Norback, J. & Rosenfeld, M. (1989). A national study of the profession of therapeutic recreation specialist. *Therapeutic Recreation Journal, 23*(2), 48-58.

Reynolds, R. & O'Morrow, G. (1985). *Problems, issues and concepts in therapeutic recreation.* Englewood Cliffs, NJ: Prentice Hall, Inc.

Skalko, T. & Smith, M. (1989). Status of therapeutic recreation in state personnel systems: A national survey. *Therapeutic Recreation Journal, 23*(2), 41-47.

Stein, T. (1970). Therapeutic recreation education: 1969 survey. *Therapeutic Recreation Journal, 4*(2), 4-7.

Stewart, M. & Anderson, S. (1990). Therapeutic recreation education: 1989 survey. Paper presented at the American Therapeutic Recreation Association Conference, Kansas City, MO.

Strenio, A. J. (1981). *The testing trap.* New York: Rawson, Wade.

Stumbo, N. (1986). A definition of entry level knowledge for therapeutic recreation practice. *Therapeutic Recreation Journal, 20*(4), 15-30.

Chapter 20

Health Care Credentialing

Peg Connolly

Certification, licensure and registration, referred to as credentialing, are critical attributes of a defined and established profession. Credentialing efforts originate with the profession's definition of quality practice and provide a schemata for examining who is and who is not qualified to practice a professional service. The origins of the credentialing of professionals began in medieval times when the public sought to protect itself from unqualified professional practitioners, particularly in the area of medicine (Young, 1987). Today, certification, licensure and registration are benchmarks used to define minimum competence to practice. As Young (1987) states:

> Professionalism in the United States generally refers to the provision of expert, high-quality service to consumers. Underlying this definition of professionalism is the assumption that professionals are granted the privilege of self-regulation in exchange for providing services at a fair price... In other words, professionals are charged with serving the public interest. (p. 2)

Definitions of Certification, Registration and Licensure

Traditional definitions of certification, registration and licensure have long existed in the professions. "Licensure and certification were viewed as appropriate mechanisms to ensure the minimum competency of health professionals and the adequacy of health care services. While there is complementary association between certification and licensure, each can exist in the absence of the other" (National Commission for Health Certifying Agencies, 1986, p. *v*). Licensure traditionally occurs at the state level. Registration and certification have more often been enacted at the national level by non-governmental agencies. In current practice, one will often see licensure, registration and certification enacted by state legislation. To date, there has been no licensure program instituted for health care professions by a national governmental authority.

The American Hospital Association publishes a directory of national health care certification programs (1993). This publication examines 53 certification programs and includes information on the National Council for Therapeutic Recreation Certification (NCTRC). The American Hospital Association Publication offers definitions of registration, certification and licensure. According to the American Hospital Association (1993)

> *Registration* requires an individual to file his or her name and address with a designated agency. In some instances the agency also may establish minimum practice standards. For example, under the Omnibus Budget Reconciliation Act of 1987 (OBRA), to be registered by the state, nurse aides in long term care settings must have completed a training and competency evaluation program. (p. 1)

Young (1987) indicates that registration is the simplest form of credentialing "which usually requires little more of individuals than listing their names on official rosters" (p. 5). According to Young 643 occupations require registration in the US.

The American Hospital Association (1993) states that "*certification* can be statutory — provided by a state agency — or voluntary — awarded by a private agency" (p. 1). Certification requirements may include "education, experience and examination or a combination thereof" (American Hospital Association, 1993, p. 1). Certification restricts the use of a professional title but does not restrict an individual from practicing the regulated profession. Certification "may include graduation from an approved training program, a certain amount of work experience, passage of qualifying examinations and such personal characteristics as age, residence, citizenship and moral character" (Young, 1987, p. 5).

Licensure is considered the strictest form of regulation for a profession. "*Licensure* is the process by which an agency of government grants permission to an individual to engage in a given occupation upon finding that the applicant has attained the minimum degree of competence necessary to ensure that the public health, safety and welfare will be reasonably well protected" (American Hospital Association, 1993, p. 1). In a state where a profession has licensure, an individual cannot practice the profession without being licensed in the state. Licensure requirements are similar to certification requirements. "The key difference, of course, is that lack of certification does not bar someone from practicing the certified trade; it only prohibits him from presenting himself to the public as a 'certified' practitioner. Licensure, on the other hand, prohibits practice without the license" (Young, 1987, p. 5). Young (1987) identified 490 occupations that were licensed to practice in the United States.

Considering these definitions, there is little regulation or control of qualifications in registration and a greater control of qualifications in certification and licensure. When both certification and licensure are used in state legislation, the processes of both will be very similar but the enforcement effect differs significantly. In other words, both certification and licensure may involve criteria of scope of practice, education and experience requirements, examination and related criteria such as mental and physical fitness for practice, age, citizenship, etc. The major difference between the two in state law is that certification is often referred to as "title protection" while licensure is often termed as "practice protection." Title protection would assure that only individuals who have been certified to practice may use the restricted title. It does not, however, restrict non-certified individuals from practicing the occupation; they simply cannot use the certification title to identify themselves. Licensure, on the other hand, restricts both title and the ability to legally practice the occupation in a state with such laws, thus protecting not only title but also practice. A profession may be licensed in some states while being registered or certified in other states (Young, 1987).

Registration is rarely used in recreational therapy today. Most efforts have focused on certification and licensure over the past 15 years. Therefore, the remainder of this chapter will deal primarily with certification and licensure.

According to the American Hospital Association: "Licensure is a more encompassing regulation of a profession than certification because it establishes scope of practice and prohibits unlicensed persons from performing specific functions cited in the statute" (1993, p. 1). Professionals appear to believe that the strongest form of public protection is to regulate who can practice a profession. It is also more difficult for a profession to gain licensure today than it was in the past. The cost and political process that control state laws and authority to regulate a profession have been tempered over the past twenty years and there have been efforts in many states to reduce the number of licensed professions.

Advances in establishing national standards for certifying agencies (Davis, 1990) have led to the development of higher quality professional certification programs. Young (1987) states that "certification and other non-intrusive schemes have been shown to afford substantially the same protection to consumers as licensure, but without the cost or violation of basic freedoms" (p. 94). New efforts also point to a greater emphasis on national certification standards as the US Congress in 1994 enacted legislation to develop a program of national skill standards for occupations (Geber, 1995). The field of recreational therapy has been successful in developing a nationally recognized certification program but has been less successful at creating licensing programs in the states. Still, there has been renewed interest in obtaining licensure for recreational therapists in the past few years. Is this the best approach for our profession? Is the motivation a demand from consumers for better quality services or our own search for more recognition, reimbursement and improved income for practitioners? These questions must be addressed before the field embarks on a program of seeking licensure at the state level.

In 1977, the National Therapeutic Recreation Society (NTRS) Board of Directors under the leadership of President Gary Robb initiated the study of several critical issues facing the field. Robb established several committees to conduct national investigation of six critical issues: (a) the philosophy of the profession, (b) legislation, (c) standards of practice, (d) accreditation of academic programs, (e) branch governance or how the professional society should be organized and governed and (f) credentialing. This effort would bring the field together to forge its future and the effects on the professionalization of the field were dramatic. Many of our accomplishments today can be traced to this initiative by Robb. The initiative and study of critical issues affecting credentialing had a dramatic effect on the directions our profession would take and led, ultimately, to the establishment of the NCTRC certification program.

While the committee report on credentialing in 1978 did not provide exact answers on a course of action, it did conclude that professionals desired a stronger credentialing program for the field and that such a program should be more in line with comparable health care professions such as occupational and physical therapies. This led to further committee work to examine trends and options that would help the profession institute a stronger credentialing program. The field of allied health was studied and the National Commission for Health Certifying Agencies (NCHCA) was identified as the source of national standards for voluntary certification programs:

> In the early 1970's, the initiative of the United States Department of Health, Education and Welfare (now Health and Human Services) and the extensive participation and commitment of private-sector health certifying agencies and professional associations provided the format and arena for the creation of the National Commission for Health Certifying Agencies (now the National Organization for Competency Assurance)... The Commission's mission and primary purpose is to develop and promulgate national certification standards which are universally applicable across agencies and occupations and to continually review and refine such standards in applying its objective membership criteria to test and determine the sufficiency and appropriateness of applicant organizations' certification programs. (NCHCA, 1986, p. v-vi)

The leadership of NTRS studied these national standards, surveyed the professionals of therapeutic recreation on potential revisions of existing registration standards and, by 1981 recommended the formation of a new credentialing authority and the use of a two-level (i.e., professional and paraprofessional) certification program.

The name of the National Commission for Health Certifying Agencies was changed to the National Organization for Competency Assurance (NOCA) in the late 1980's. Agencies involved with certification may be in NOCA on two levels: (a) as a member of NOCA or (b) as an accredited certifying agency based on evaluation by NOCA's review body, the National Commission for Certifying Agencies (NCCA). NCTRC has been a charter member of NOCA since 1987.

From its founding, the leadership of NCTRC steadily moved forward on creating the therapeutic recreation certification program to meet national certification standards. NOCA's standards (Davis, 1990) include the following concepts which must be demonstrated by any national certification program desiring accreditation:

- a certifying agency has the purpose of evaluating individuals and issuing credentials to those who meet the required level of competence
- the certifying agency must be non-governmental and be administered independently in matters pertaining to certification
- all policy decisions relating to certification are the sole decision of the certifying body and not subject to approval by any other body
- the governing body of the certifying agency shall include individuals from the profession, public or consumers and employers
- the certifying agency must have the resources and staff to properly conduct certification activities
- the mechanism used to evaluate individual competence must be objective, fair, reliable, valid and based on knowledge and skills needed in the profession
- the certifying agency must publish public information about the agency, test construction, validation, administration and a summary of certification activities
- the agency shall not discriminate among applicants as to age, sex, race, religion, national origin, handicap or marital status
- there must be periodic review of the application and testing procedures
- proctored testing sites must be accessible to all areas of the nation at least once annually
- there must be a means for individuals who have obtained skill or knowledge outside the formal education setting to be evaluated and obtain certification
- there must be an appeals process

- the certifying agency must have a formal policy for discipline, including revocation for conduct which may cause harm to the public health and safety and this program must incorporate due process
- there must be a plan for recertification

In May 1985, NCTRC met the standard of administrative independence from the parent professional group (i.e., NTRS) by becoming incorporated as a separate organization. In 1988, NCTRC completed the first National Job Analysis Study of the Profession of Therapeutic Recreation (Oltman, Norback & Rosenfeld, 1988) and, thus, defined the minimum knowledge and skills necessary for competent practice in the field. In 1990, NCTRC engaged the nationally recognized expertise of the largest and most well-established testing company in the United States, Educational Testing Service, to institute the first national certification exam for the profession. Instituting this exam allowed NCTRC to meet the standard of having a valid and reliable mechanism for determining competence. At the time of implementation of the national exam, a recertification requirement for Certified Therapeutic Recreation Specialists (CTRSs) was also put in place. In 1991, NCTRC restructured its certification standards and instituted a disciplinary action policy with appropriate due process procedures, thus meeting the standard of having a policy on discipline and the ability to revoke or deny certification for conduct that is considered a threat to the public health and safety.

The culmination of meeting these standards and refining the NCTRC certification program was the award of national accreditation by the National Commission for Certifying Agencies. On March 18, 1993, NCTRC was awarded accreditation for the Therapeutic Recreation Specialist credential by NCCA. While the CTRS credential was accredited in this review, the Certified Therapeutic Recreation Assistant (CTRA) paraprofessional credential was not considered acceptable by national certifying standards. This was one of contributing factors in the decision to phase out the CTRA credential and focus on the continued development and strengthening of the CTRS credential. Accreditation by NCCA is for a five year period. This is truly a significant achievement. NOCA's NCCA is the only recognized organization which offers national voluntary standards for certifying agencies.

How does NCTRC benefit from NCCA accreditation of the CTRS credentialing program? There are several benefits, including: recognition that NCTRC's CTRS program has met the highest national standards for private certification; demonstration of the quality of the NCTRC CTRS program to employers, peer organizations, governmental agencies and regulatory groups; increased ability to defend the integrity of the CTRS credential in legal challenges and competitive situations; and enhanced overall reputation of the CTRS credential. It had taken the profession 12 years to structure the NCTRC certification program with operational proof of meeting all national standards to accomplish this recognition. NCTRC became the 27th national certification program to gain accreditation from NCCA, including the following professions: orthotics and prosthetics, opticianry, medical technologists, nurse anesthetists, clinical radiography technologists, music therapists, dietary managers, rehabilitation counselors, dental assistants, ophthalmologists, surgical technicians, counselors, respiratory therapists, podiatrists and others.

Another milestone was accomplished in 1993 by the Council. After several years of legal research, NCTRC was awarded federal trademark of the title "Certified Therapeutic Recreation Specialist" and its mark "CTRS" by the United States Patent and Trademark Office (USPTO). This was another important step in recognition and credibility for the profession. The "CTRS" designation is intended to protect the consumer. It lets consumers know that professionals have demonstrated the minimum skills necessary to provide services as Therapeutic Recreation Specialists. Consumers can be harmed by individuals who represent that they are "CTRS" certified by NCTRC when they have not met the standards for certification. With USPTO trademark registration, the ability to protect the consumer by enforcing NCTRC's trademark rights is strengthened. The trademark registration provides significant legal protection against unauthorized users of NCTRC's marks. Any reports of unauthorized use of the "CTRS" and "Certified Therapeutic Recreation Specialist" credentials to NCTRC are fully investigated.

Health Care Reform and Its Impact on Credentialing

Health care reform is not a new movement in our country. There has been increasing momentum in the health care reform initiative since the 1970's. In 1993 President Clinton placed priority emphasis on the demand for health care reform and began a national effort to address a serious problem that had been festering for many years. For many reasons, the crisis in health care has escalated. The main symptoms of the problems have been rapidly growing costs, increasing demands for services and lack of perceived access to care for some sectors of our society who do not possess the financial or insurance resources to purchase services. Thirty years ago, the overall population assumed basic, quality health care as a birthright of citizenship. Today, a third of our society is not covered by basic health care insurance and many consider quality health care a benefit not available to all Americans.

How does the health care reform initiative relate to NCTRC and its CTRS credential? The certification movement in the United States was impacted by the early stages of the health care movement in the late 1970's. In fact, NCTRC's basic structure and focus on consumer protection arose from following guidelines developed in the early days of health care reform. The field of recreational therapy experienced its greatest period of growth and development during the period of the most competitive health care environment ever experienced in our society. New professional health care specialties were growing rapidly during the 1960's and 1970's, and the majority of these new occupations sought reimbursement for their services.

The federal government underwrote a feasibility study during the early 1970's to attempt to clarify the validity of credentialing of the diverse health care occupations competing for reimbursement of services. It was decided that the program to regulate health care credentialing should be handled in the private sector on a voluntary basis with involvement of not only the professions but also of consumers and employers. The tide was to turn the professions from self-serving interests into more public protection interests, legitimizing those credentialed occupations devoted to valid criteria for determining the requisite knowledge, skills and abilities for competent practice. The criteria established through this governmental health care reform effort became the basis of establishing the National Organization for Competency Assurance (originally NCHCA). NCTRC represents professional responsibility in health care reform and has passed the test of national independent review to be recognized as a valid and credible certifying agency.

During a very active stage of health care reform in 1993-94, several pieces of legislation were proposed in the US Congress. Within these proposed bills was a definition of health professionals eligible to receive reimbursement for services. Health professions were defined as those individuals legally authorized to provide health services in a state. This concept of legally authorized health professions was interpreted by some individuals to mean that only licensed health professions would be authorized to receive reimbursement for services. Not all legitimate health professionals are licensed in every state. NCTRC legal counsel indicated that it was plausible that rigorous national certification could be defensible to fit the definition of legally authorized. It is the author's opinion that those who interpreted legally authorized to mean only licensed professions have promoted the increased emphasis on recreational therapists seeking licensure as a means of gaining greater recognition and the opportunity for reimbursement authority at the state level.

By 1995, these national legal efforts toward health care reform had come to a halt due to other societal priorities. Still, the profession of recreational therapy continued its public policy effort to define itself as a viable health care profession. As the profession of recreational therapy continues its involvement in health care reform, the value of our national credentialing program and its recognized strength as compared to other health professions will continue to be examined. Thus far, the strength of certification and number of certificants has been a point of demonstrating the quality of the profession. While health care reform has been reduced in emphasis at the national level as of 1995, the problem is not solved. More will be done in the coming years as we continue as a society to define the price we are willing to pay for the quality of health care we expect. The field of recreational therapy has made great strides in this dialogue, but has yet to fully prove itself as a reliable and accepted health care service. Much of the ability to define the quality of this profession lies in our definitions of a qualified practitioner and the services society can expect to consistently receive from recreational therapists. Continued development of our national certification standards helps clarify, define and defend the qualifications of recreational therapists.

Licensure in Recreational Therapy

The original purpose of providing for regulation of professions was to protect the public from fraudulent or unqualified practitioners. "Regardless of the profession or trade, practitioners seeking new licensing laws or toughening of existing ones always invoke the public interest: protection of public health, morals or safety ... licensing is believed to protect consumers from incompetents, charlatans and quacks" (Young, 1987). However, those protected under these laws often have certain privileges that benefit the professional. By the 1960's, many professions were licensed and it was costly to the states who governed these professions. Licensing costs include the review of credentials, administration of examination and review boards and enforcement of licensing laws through disciplinary and legal proceedings that monitor professionals' adherence to the laws. Additionally, new information began to amass supporting the notions that licensing raised costs to the consumer, raised the income of the licensed professional and restricted entry to licensed professions, thus damaging the free trade concept (Young, 1987). Young documents the problems with licensure in the US and cites the Stigler Theory of Economic Regulation. According to Young, this theory refuted the "public interest" rationale for creating licensing of the professions and suggested instead that the "capture model" was being used by professionals to obtain licensure:

> ...professional groups used the coercive power of government for their own economic advantage. In effect they capture the regulatory apparatus and use it to restrain competition and raise income. (p. 6-7)

Thus, while most had stated that licensure was created to protect the public interest, common practices of licensed professions showed that more often the licensing act was sought by the profession. Further, professions used their political power to "capture" and restrict an area of service or practice which enhanced their own income, often restricted trade and, in some cases, actually limited access to services for the public (Young, 1987).

Many things came together in the 1970's to affect the licensing movement in the US. The consumer movement increased and some consumers objected to the restrictions of services caused by licensing. Also, the first evidence of the health care crisis and need for reducing health care costs began to surface. In an effort to reduce state tax payers' fiscal responsibilities for maintaining these professional licensing programs, the sunrise and sunset laws were enacted as a means of regulatory reform. The first sunset law was passed in Colorado in 1976 and the first sunrise law was passed in Minnesota in the 1980's (Young, 1987). The intent of these laws was to assure that any licensed profession could prove that there was a need to protect the public by licensing a profession, rather than the licensing law protecting the professionals involved by limiting other individuals from practicing the profession. In other words, the purpose of the licensing law had to be proven to protect the public and not to protect the profession from others practicing their trade or to provide the profession greater opportunity for reimbursement of its services.

The sunrise laws were placed in effect to have any new profession seeking licensure justify how such a law was needed to protect the public from the potential harm of nonlicensed individuals providing the same services. The sunset laws placed a limit on the licensing of all professions in a state and called for periodic review of the continued need for licensing to protect the public. In other words, the "sun would rise" on licensing a profession if sufficient evidence existed that without the licensing law, consumers of the professional practice would somehow be harmed. In like manner, all licensed professions would be reviewed and the "sun would set" on those professions where evidence showed little or no threat to the public by not licensing the professional practice. If public harm could not be proven, a profession would not be licensed under a sunrise law in a state. And licensing acts would be eliminated for professions where public protection was no longer proven to be necessary.

An example of the effect of the sunset law on licensing in recreational therapy is evident in the state of Georgia. In 1975, the Georgia licensing act for "Activity Therapy" was signed into law. Because the state of Georgia had instituted sunset laws, the licensing act for "Activity Therapy" was reviewed for the need to continue the law. In an audit of the licensing act, the law was not renewed fully, but was extended for a brief period of time. In the early 1990's, the law was not renewed and licensing ceased in the state since the state authorities determined that the regulation of "activity therapy" was not necessary to protect the public from harm in the state. How could the state at one point regulate a professional practice and later repeal such a protection of the public?

To initiate licensing at the state level the profession has to compile not only evidence of potential harm to the public should the profession go unlicensed, but also clearly define a scope of practice and defensible qualifications for practitioners of the profession to deliver the practice. The profession's practice has to be different enough from other, already licensed professions to demonstrate that the service is not already being provided by another profession and there have to be sufficient numbers of qualified professionals practicing in the state to warrant the regulation. This has often been difficult for the profession of recreational therapy as, until recently, there were not large numbers of professionals consistently trained and qualified to deliver professional services.

After initiation of the licensing law, the profession must continue to regulate both those practicing under the law and those found to practice without being licensed. This is how the public is protected, by continuous monitoring of the scope and nature of practice and the resultant effect of the practice on the public who receives the profession's services. This continuous monitoring was probably one of the reasons the Georgia law was ultimately repealed. When a licensing law is in effect in a state, it is against the law to practice the profession regulated by the law unless the practitioner has been licensed to do so by the state. When sufficient efforts are not instituted soon enough to regulate or enforce a licensing law on those practicing without a license, questions begin to arise as to the need for the law.

Because of concerns regarding the cost and feasibility of adequately regulating professions via the state legal system of licensing, a voluntary, non-governmental effort to improve the certification programs of professions at the national level was instituted in the late 1970's. This national effort sought to create standards for certification programs that would assure protection of the public. "The effective management of health care in the United States became increasingly complex during the late 1960's and early 1970's. Governmental efforts to provide consumers greater protection from incompetent providers was prompted by the need to examine and explore alternative mechanisms for credentialing health professionals" (National Commission for Certifying Agencies, 1986, p. *v*).

There was another purpose in the government's efforts to develop national certification criteria and health care reform in the 1970's. State licensure was going through a period of reform as well. It was assumed that the establishment of national certifying standards might be as strong, if not stronger, than state licensure programs. Licensure is also intended to protect the public. However, one would be hard pressed to find a handful of state licensing programs in any discipline that were initiated by the public. Most professional licensing laws, including those in recreational therapy, have been initiated by professionals rather than by the public.

Licensing acts are usually initiated by the profession and its interpretation of what the public needs. Licensing acts have become a means of restricting the practice of a profession to those indicated as qualified by its own professional standards for a given state. And to the licensed profession often goes the right to health care reimbursement, not necessarily because of the quality standards the credential has been determined to meet, but more likely because of the ability to monitor the practice. NOCA criteria for certifying agencies appear to be much stronger than the diverse criteria of public protection instituted by the fifty independent states.

The use of state regulation in the field of recreational therapy has been less consistent over the years. Licensure in the field has been less often sought on the state level until recently. In 1974, a licensure bill for recreational therapy was passed in the state of Utah. In 1975, the state of Georgia passed a licensing bill for the regulation of activity therapy. The next successful passage of a title protection act was accomplished in the state of North Carolina in 1985. Here, the title of "Therapeutic Recreation" was protected for use by individuals who were evaluated as meeting minimum standards in the state. In 1985, a licensing act was passed in the District of Columbia for "Therapeutic Recreation Specialists."

More recently, there has been an increase in activity to gain licensing or title protection at the state level. Indication that professionals are beginning to organize to seek licensure acts has been received from various states at the time of this writing. The heightened interest in state regulation of the profession parallels national efforts in health care reform and comes from those who believe that only licensed professions will be eligible for health care reimbursement in the future.

Title Protection Through State Law

Licensure restricts the practice of a profession; certification restricts the use of certain titles but not the practice of a profession. When it became more difficult for professions to obtain licensure because of its powerful restrictions, some states moved to create a form of professional regulation between licensure and certification. This became known as title protection. During the 1980's, title protection was used by professions who were able to justify protecting professional titles but not able to justify restriction of a professional area of practice. North Carolina has a title protection act for therapeutic recreation. In the state of North Carolina, an individual may not use the title "Therapeutic Recreation Specialist" without application to and approval from the North Carolina Therapeutic Recreation Certification Board because of the regulatory law protecting that title in the state. However, the North Carolina law does not restrict the practice of recreational therapy.

In the 1990's, title protection was challenged in the Supreme Court. A ruling by the Supreme Court in 1992 (Abrahamson v. Gonzalez, No. 90-4099, 11th Cir. 1992) found a "title protection" law in the state of Florida to be unconstitutional (Zeitlin & Dorn, 1992). The professional title protection law was found to violate first amendment rights. The Court ruled that while this law prohibited the use of a protected title, it did not restrict an individual's right to practice the occupation the title reflected. Thus, the law did not protect consumers from the practice. Further, those allowed to practice had their First Amendment rights violated by not being able to use the title of the occupation they were legally allowed to practice. In this landmark decision, title protection was found to be unconstitutional and an argument was made that such laws did not protect the consumer of services. While many states still use "title protection" or certification laws, it will be interesting to watch the effects of this Supreme Court ruling on further activity to restrict professional titles without restricting practice. One must question if title protection laws at the state level protect the public interest or the interests of professions.

National Certification and State Licensure:
A Comparative Developmental Perspective

For most professions, there is a close relationship between national and state regulation of the profession. Oftentimes, the profession has significant control of its national plan for credentialing. Usually operated via a voluntary, non-governmental structure, the profession establishes an organization to develop, implement and monitor adherence to minimum standards of competence for recognition as qualified practitioners in a specific arena of professional practice.

Again, this practice of professional development and monitoring of personnel standards has been closely overseen by the federal government. When the US Government assisted in establishing a national organization to set credentialing standards for the professional certifying agencies, it wanted to assure that credentialing was being pursued to assist the public and not for the personal gains of professionals. In this way, the government was addressing two concerns at the time: (a) a means of adding consistency to the concept of a "credentialed profession" and (b) a means of providing for rigorous standards for credentialing in view of the desire to reduce regulation at the state level and reduce reimbursement to non-recognized occupations.

NCTRC is the recognized personnel credentialing authority in the field of therapeutic recreation. NCTRC has followed national standards for certifying agencies in its own development and received accreditation from the NCCA of NOCA. The NCTRC certification program parallels the standards followed in medicine by the American Board of Medical Specialties and by other related professions such as the American Occupational Therapy Certification Board and the Certification Board for Music Therapists. Currently, several states seeking licensure or title protection in recreational therapy are attempting to use the NCTRC Standards and exam within their proposed state laws. In essence, this is the same model that has been used in Occupational Therapy and other professions. One set of standards is used at the national and state level. The national level standards are voluntarily sought, while state law may require the qualified professional to register and pay fees again to use the same national credential on the state level.

Protecting the Public:
NCTRC's Public Education Effort

While the first twelve years of NCTRC's development focused on refinement of the certification standards and the credentialing program, NCTRC's recent emphasis on public relations represents the overall mission of the Council to protect the consumer by promoting quality therapeutic recreation services. The consumer is not protected if it is unaware of NCTRC and how to access qualified therapeutic recreation personnel.

NCTRC currently employs two major approaches to educate the public on the value of the CTRS credential. First, NCTRC has initiated a national marketing campaign to educate employers and the public on the value of the CTRS credential. Secondly, NCTRC has developed an ongoing educational campaign with governmental and non-governmental regulatory groups such as the Health Care Financing Administration (HCFA), the Joint Commission for the Accreditation of Healthcare Organizations (JCAHO) and CARF: The Rehabilitation Accreditation Commission.

CARF (1994) defines Therapeutic Recreation Specialist in its Glossary of Terms as: "An individual who is a graduate of a therapeutic recreation program in an accredited university, who currently meets applicable legal requirements, and/or who is certified or eligible for certification by the National Council for Therapeutic Recreation Certification as a therapeutic recreation specialist." JCAHO included NCTRC's CTRS certification in the 1995 definitions of qualified professionals. JCAHO (1995), in the Interpretation of Terms section of the *Comprehensive Accreditation Manual for Hospitals,* currently defines a qualified recreational therapist as: "An individual who, at a minimum, is a graduate of a baccalaureate degree program in recreational therapy accredited by a nationally recognized accreditation body; is currently a Certified Therapeutic Recreation Specialist (CTRS) by the National Council for Therapeutic Recreation Certification (NCTRC); meets any current legal requirements of licensure, registration or certification; or has the documented equivalence in education, training and experience; and is currently competent in the field."

These national organizations exert considerable influence on health care service delivery systems. By educating these regulatory and policy setting agencies, the public interest is better protected by more widespread awareness and recognition of the CTRS credential as a sign of quality. Until consumers and employers understand how to identify and access a qualified therapeutic recreation practitioner, they may accept services with questionable value to an individual's health care needs. This scenario exists in the health care market today because one non-certified individual is employed in the labor market for each qualified CTRS practicing. Individuals practicing in therapeutic recreation who have not demonstrated *minimum* qualifications for competent practice cause potential confusion to the consumer and cloud the value and worth of therapeutic recreation in health care. Consumers and employers may not know what to look for in terms of quality practices in therapeutic recreation. The struggle for identity and the recognition of the worth of a profession will continue as long as individuals other than qualified recreational therapists are allowed to dominate the practice arena. NCTRC's focus on consumer education and protection seeks to offer information that allows employers and consumers to make informed choices about the quality of therapeutic recreation practitioners and services presented to them.

Current Issues and Implications for the Future

Currently, the national certification program provided by NCTRC continues to be the strongest means of regulating the profession of recreational therapy. As of January 1, 1995, 13,600 individuals hold certification by NCTRC. This is a growth of 450% since the Council was founded in 1981. The effect of the accreditation of the NCTRC certification program by the National Commission for Certifying Agencies is directly related to the Council's continued growth and the recognition by others of the quality and respectability of the Council's certification. Following these national certification program standards has aided the Council in establishing a reliable and valid national certification exam, instituting and monitoring adherence to disciplinary standards and refining the professional certification standards for recreational therapists.

At the same time that the NCTRC program continues to become refined and to gain greater acceptance in the health care arena, many professionals desire the type of protection provided through licensing laws. Several groups are exploring the possibility of state licensing for recreational therapy. Questions of whether state licensure efforts will become an organized professional movement across the United States are still unanswered. During the 1980's, very little emphasis was placed on pursuing licensure. The advent of the health care reform initiative of the 1990's has led to an increased interest in licensure. What remains to be seen is whether the profession can organize itself to mount the political effort that will be needed to institute more licensing laws in more states. A few states have begun to seek title protection at the state level. However, this form of regulation has been found to be unconstitutional (Zeitlin & Dorn, 1992) and may be further contested in other states in the future. Another critical issue related to the licensure of recreational therapists still remains to be resolved. This issue is to clarify our intent in seeking licensure. Is the effort to truly protect the consumer from unqualified practitioners or is it to foster better opportunities for recreational therapists? We could argue that both sides of this issue are possible. However, as a profession, we must honestly examine our motives for licensure as well as the gains we may receive.

Another issue that faces recreational therapy is a movement to define core or general health care skills at the national level. Health care continues to undergo dramatic changes. More emphasis recently is being placed on examination of generic skills that all health care workers need to possess to create a more effective and efficient service delivery system. A recent study by the National Health Care Skill Standards Project of the US Department of Labor and Education (Far West Laboratory, 1995) is studying national skill standards for health care workers. Preliminary reports indicate this study has defined core health care skills that will also be useful for training and certification in specific occupations. This project has defined both an industry core and a therapeutic/diagnostic core for health care workers.

The industry core would take into consideration such competencies as academic background, legal responsibilities, ethics, communication and safety. The therapeutic core includes skills in client interaction, client status evaluation and intra-team communication. The skills of therapeutic recreation fit within the "therapeutic cluster" of occupations where the function of the professional is to change the health status of the client over time. Skills needed would include: data collection, treatment planning, ability to implement procedures and client evaluation. Many of the skills defined in the Job Analysis for Therapeutic Recreation relate to these proposed standards and skills and further exemplify the benefit of including therapeutic recreation professionals as team members in health care.

In 1980, Alvin Toffler presented his views on what he termed the "third wave." In his book, Toffler spoke of three waves in society: the first was the agricultural civilization, the second was the industrial revolution and the third was the future world of high technology and integrated information. In the second wave, there was a need to specialize and standardize. Recreational therapy has been involved in this specialization and standardization with other health care professions for the past thirty years. Scope of professional practice defines specialization and boundaries of a profession to deliver health services. However, a new wave of civilization is upon us. It is the age of information and integration of services, the age of high technology. While we have become specialized in our professional practice, we are now being called on to also be flexible and to possess generalized "core skills" for health care. In this "wave," the blending and sharing of certain skill areas by health professions will be implemented to accomplish more effective and efficient client care. The extent to which we are able to maintain developmental efforts in specialized skills which are unique to the profession of recreational therapy and to also be a functioning, flexible, integrated member of the health care team may well be our greatest challenge for the future.

Summary

This chapter has defined the terms certification, registration and licensure. Information has been provided on the state of certification in the field of recreational therapy, analysis of the relationship of certification and licensure in recreational therapy, comparison of developments in the certification and licensing of recreational therapists to efforts in other health care professions and possible future directions for the field of recreational therapy with regard to certification and licensure. In the field of recreational therapy, the term registration is rarely used. Certification has been the dominant means of recognizing qualified recreational therapists. Until the past few years, there has been little activity to obtain state licensure. However, there appears to be an increased interest in obtaining licensure at this time. Whether licensure will be obtained or useful to the field remains to be answered.

Licensure has not been as well developed in the profession of recreational therapy. Only two states had obtained licensure by 1980. It was not until the health care reform initiative of the 1990's that a renewed interest in licensure arose in the field. It is questionable whether the current emphasis on licensure is really in the interest of public protection or the interest of professionals seeking greater recognition and reimbursement for services. Additionally, it is uncertain whether state licensure will be as necessary as we move toward a core definition of health care skills for the United States.

Learning Activities

1. *Interview a professional.* Interview a recreational therapist in your state in regard to opinions of what recreational therapists need to do to advance national certification and whether or not licensing of recreational therapy in your state will be helpful to the clients. Ask this CTRS to explain why they hold the beliefs they do.

2. *Hold a debate on the pros and cons of licensing.* Divide into two groups in class and have one group study and present the issues in favor of seeking licensure and the other group study and present issues against seeking licensure. For each group, consider such issues as: How will the public be protected from harm by licensing? What evidence of public harm from recreational therapy practice is known? How many professionals in your state will be affected by licensing? How will they feel about the additional cost they

will have to pay to be licensed? What additional health care costs are associated with licensure? How will the practice of licensed and nonlicensed professionals be monitored?

3. *Learn about licensure in your state.* Contact your local legislator to learn about how a profession is licensed in your state. Ask your legislative representative for information on the state's administrative law to license professions, find out the department or state office that monitors these laws and ask what the opinion of your legislative representative is toward the licensing of health care professions. Also contact the department or state office that regulates the health professions in your state. Ask for resources on how it works and what a profession would have to do to become licensed. Then, develop a mock plan to gain licensure for recreational therapy in your state. What would you do first? What resources would you need? What national professional organizations would you contact for information and support? How would you gain the support of other recreational therapy practitioners to make this effort successful? What evidence would you collect to insure that this licensing is necessary to protect the consumer?

4. *Find an article on licensing or certification from another profession.* Go to the periodical section of your library and find a current article on licensing or certification. Current issues that you may find include the value of continuing education to the protection of the public, the types of disciplinary cases being examined, the constitutionality of some laws, etc. Read the article and consider what the implications to recreational therapy might be. Share your article and your opinion of the implications with your professor and your fellow students.

5. *Obtain the copy of a licensing or title protection law in recreational therapy.* Write to one of the states that currently has licensure or title protection in recreational therapy (Utah, North Carolina) and ask for a copy of the law or go to the legal research section of your library on campus and obtain a copy of the statute (ask the librarian for assistance with your search). Review the law and discuss the following issues: How is the scope of recreational therapy practice defined? What qualifications are delineated for professionals? How is the law administered? Is it a title protection law or a licensing law? What is the difference and what are the pros and cons of each?

Study Questions

1. What is the difference between certification and licensure? Many state-owned facilities do not require formal training as a therapist for individuals hired as "therapists." How would state certification impact this practice? How would state licensure impact this practice?

2. What were the steps that NCTRC took to be able to meet the standards set by the National Organization for Competency Assurance? Why is it important that NCTRC took these steps?
3. One of the standards set by the National Organization for Competency Assurance states that the credentialing body must be politically and organizationally separate from governmental and professional membership organizations. In what ways does this standard safeguard the integrity of the credentialing process?
4. How have health care reforms impacted the credentialing process? How have these reforms impacted state licensure of professionals? In what ways have these reforms benefited the consumer?
5. Almost half of the individuals working in the capacity of a recreational therapist are not certified. How does this impact the delivery of recreational therapy services, the development of treatment standards and the demand for credentialed therapists (Certified Therapeutic Recreation Specialists)?

References

American Hospital Association. (1993). *Report on voluntary certification of health care personnel.* Chicago, IL: Author.

CARF: The Rehabilitation Accreditation Commission. (1994). *Standards manual, interpretive guidelines, and self-study questionnaire.* Tucson, AZ: CARF: The Rehabilitation Accreditation Commission.

Davis, N. M. (1990, February). Who certifies the certifiers? *Association Management*, 38-43.

Far West Laboratory for Educational Research and Development. (1995). *National health care skill standards.* San Francisco: Author.

Geber, B. (1995, February). The plan to certify America. *Training*, 39-44.

Joint Commission for the Accreditation of Healthcare Organizations. (1995). *Comprehensive accreditation manual for hospitals.* Chicago: Joint Commission for the Accreditation of Healthcare Organizations.

National Commission for Health Certifying Agencies. (1986). *Sourcebook on health occupations.* Washington, DC: Author.

Oltman, P. K., Norback, J. & Rosenfeld, M. (1988). *A national study of the profession of therapeutic recreation specialist.* New York: National Council for Therapeutic Recreation Certification.

Oltman, P. K., Norback, J. & Rosenfeld, M. (1989). A national study of the profession of therapeutic recreation specialist. *Therapeutic Recreation Journal, 23*(2), 48-58.

Toffler, A. (1980). *The third wave.* New York: Bantam Books.

US Department of Labor, Bureau of Labor Statistics. (1984, April). *Occupational Outlook Handbook* (Bulletin 2205). Washington DC: Author.

US Department of Labor, Bureau of Labor Statistics (1991, Fall). *Occupational Outlook Quarterly.*

US Department of Labor, Bureau of Labor Statistics. (1992, May). *Occupational Outlook Handbook* (Bulletin 2400). Washington DC: Author.

US Department of Labor, Bureau of Labor Statistics. (1992, Spring). *Occupational Outlook Quarterly.*

Young, S. D. (1987). *The rule of experts: Occupational licensing in America.* Washington, DC: CATO Institute.

Zeitlin, K. A. & Dorn, S. E. (1992, January). Professional credentialing: Title law declared unconstitutional. *Association Management*, 5-7.

Chapter 21

NCTRC Certification

Peg Connolly

The field of recreational therapy has had a national credentialing plan for 40 years. The National Council for Therapeutic Recreation Certification, Inc. (NCTRC) is currently recognized as the national credentialing body for recreational therapists. NCTRC provides a quality program for therapeutic recreation professionals and has gained national recognition by attaining accreditation from the National Commission of Certifying Agencies (NCCA) of the National Organization for Competency Assurance (NOCA). NCTRC's certification program has national recognition as providing a valid and reliable method for identifying recreational therapists with minimum competence to practice. This chapter will review basic information for recreational therapists related to the development of a credentialing program, the current program of certification, expected standards of conduct and the process for insuring the continuance of professional competence.

For the past eighteen years, NCTRC has been the main focal point for addressing the certification needs of the profession. Significant strides have been made in refining the Certified Therapeutic Recreation Specialist® (CTRS®) credential by adding standardized testing, as well as standards for both professional conduct and continued professional competence. There has also been an increased emphasis on education of the public regarding the meaning and value of the credential for assuring minimum competence and quality in the delivery of therapeutic recreation services. Overall, the value of the CTRS credential has increased. These advances in the credentialing of therapeutic recreation personnel parallel the efforts in other professions and the national movement to establish core skill standards (Geber, 1995) for US occupations in health and other industries.

NCTRC was founded as a non-profit organization in 1981. NCTRC's mission is to protect the consumer of therapeutic recreation services by promoting the provision of quality services offered by the NCTRC certificants. When NCTRC was founded, it took in approximately 3,000 individuals who had been registered by other professional membership organization programs between 1958 and 1981. By 1995, it had credentialed over 13,600 active therapeutic recreation professionals which is 45% of the estimated United States practitioner population.

There has been a national registration or certification plan for recreational therapists since the early 1950's. In 1953, three professional groups joined efforts to create a national registration program for the field which, at the time, was referred to as Hospital Recreation. The Hospital Section of the American Recreation Society, the Recreation Therapy Section of the American Association for Health, Physical Education and Recreation and the National Association of Recreational Therapists joined together in the Council for the Advancement of Hospital Recreation (CAHR) (Folkerth, 1986; Grubb, 1958). They created the first set of credentialing standards for recreational therapy and preceded the development of similar standards for personnel in the field of recreation and leisure (Carter & Folkerth, 1989; Folkerth, 1986). The first meeting of the Board of Registration of CAHR was held in March 1957 and there were three levels of certification standards: (a) Hospital Recreation Director, (b) Hospital Recreation Leader and (c) Hospital Recreation Aide (Grubb, 1958).

This pioneer effort in the profession set the stage for future development and refinement of a credentialing program. The Hospital Recreation Director and Hospital Recreation Leader levels of certification relate to professional level skills while the Hospital Recreation Aide level can be defined as paraprofessional skills. The first organized study to investigate personnel and qualifications in hospital recreation was conducted by the National Recreation Association in the late 1950's (Stilson, Cohen & Hill, 1959):

> The study's overall purpose was to determine the number of hospitals in the country with organized recreation programs and the program content. In addition, data was sought regarding the number of personnel engaged in this work, their qualifications and training, and the resources available for their education in the field. (p. 2)

Surveys were sent to 6,776 US hospitals and responses were received from 3,500. From these responses, Stilson, Cohen and Hill (1959) drew the following conclusions about hospital recreation personnel at the time:

- Less than half of the respondents had been employed in recreation for as long as five years, even though the mean age was over 37,

indicating that a high proportion had come into the field from other disciplines.
- Over half were males and a great majority were married.
- Less than half had any professional license or registration.
- Only two-fifths were members of any professional organization in the field.
- Their educational qualifications ranged from grade school level to master's degrees, with about one third who had not gone beyond high school. Salaries varied from under $2400 to over $8400, with a mean of about $4300. The over all picture of even this self-selected group is therefore not one of very high professional status. Both qualifications and functions appear to vary widely. (p. 65)

This early research provides perspective on how the profession of recreational therapy has advanced in the minimum standards for personnel, salary levels, nature of services provided and educational opportunities for professional preparation.

The CAHR Registration Program continued until the National Therapeutic Recreation Society (NTRS) was formed and established the National Therapeutic Recreation Society Voluntary Registration Plan in 1968 (Folkerth, 1986). The profession had changed significantly by this time and revised personnel registration standards were placed in effect.

The NTRS Voluntary Registration Program grandparented all registered Hospital Recreation personnel from the CAHR Registry into the new program. Standards were revised to reflect the changing nature of therapeutic recreation practice which had begun its expansion beyond the confines of hospital-based services (Folkerth, 1986). The numbers of registered professionals with the NTRS program began a slow but steady increase over the years.

Personnel registration standards were revised to include six levels. The first three were professional levels of registration requiring a minimum baccalaureate degree, and the next three were paraprofessional levels with requirements ranging from on-the-job experience to an associate's degree in therapeutic recreation (Carter, 1981; Folkerth, 1986). By 1977, there were six levels of registration which included 18 categories or configurations of qualifying standards (Carter, 1981).

By 1977, a movement of increased professionalization in the field of therapeutic recreation was undertaken by NTRS. The credentialing program for the field was examined and extensive research was undertaken through 1980 to improve the profession's credentialing program (Carter, 1981; Carter & Folkerth, 1989). In 1980, the NTRS Board of Directors "accepted a proposal from the NTRS Registration Board to approve, in principle, a plan having two levels, a professional and a paraprofessional level" (Carter, 1981, p. 21). This new plan for credentialing, which created NCTRC, closely paralleled programs from other *health care* professions and it became the basis for the standards used today. On October 19, 1981, the National Council for Therapeutic Recreation Certification held its first meeting in Minneapolis, Minnesota, and a new era of credentialing for the field began. At the time, approximately 3,000 individuals were grandparented into the new NCTRC certification program.

The most significant change in the credentialing program since that time was the elimination of the paraprofessional credential. On November 7, 1992, NCTRC's Board of Directors voted to discontinue the CTRA credentialing program. The NCTRC Board reached this difficult decision after considerable discussion of how the conclusion of the program would affect current CTRA certificants, as well as employers and the public. The last date to submit applications for CTRA certification was November 15, 1997. The last date for renewal of CTRA certification was December 31, 1997. After December 31, 1999, NCTRC will no longer grant or otherwise recognize the CTRA credential.

Professional Certification

While the NCTRC certification program has changed in many ways since it began, its basic structure of professional certification standards has remained intact. There are two paths of certification. The paths are *academic*, i.e., obtaining the qualifications for certification via a college degree with a major in the profession and the *equivalency* path where equivalent college education and/or course content and experience are delineated by standards. The professional path to certification requires a baccalaureate degree or higher, passing a national standardized certification exam and leads to the award of the Certified Therapeutic Recreation Specialist (CTRS) certificate.

There are three sets of standards that govern certification as a professional with NCTRC: (a) entry-level or initial certification standards, (b) conduct standards and (c) recertification standards. Together these three sets of standards govern the expectation of professional knowledge, skills and conduct that are expected as minimum competence for as long as the individual holds the CTRS credential. Entry-level or initial certification standards include education and experience requirements and the passing of a national certification exam. Conduct standards govern and monitor certain professional behaviors to assure the public health and safety of the consumer as a recipient of therapeutic recreation services. Recertification standards must be met every five years by the CTRS to show continued professional competence.

All NCTRC standards are defined based on the analysis of the role and function of the CTRS on the job or in practice. The first comprehensive Job Analysis Study was conducted by NCTRC and the Educational Testing Service (ETS) in 1988 (Oltman, Norback & Rosenfeld, 1989). The purpose of this national study was to define entry-level, competent practice of professional therapeutic recreation personnel. The results of this study provided detailed information about what professional therapeutic recreation personnel do on the job and about the knowledge and skills necessary for competent performance. These job skills and knowledge areas are considered to be the minimum and important criteria that CTRSs must possess and use in their practice. More importantly, the skills and knowledge are used by NCTRC to define the therapeutic recreation process. From this inventory of the therapeutic recreation process, certification standards are developed and implemented. Applicant experience or education is compared to this definition of the therapeutic recreation process in making judgments of those qualified to receive certification. Additionally, the knowledge areas are the basis for the content of the national certification examination. Thus, the NCTRC certification program is tied directly to research from the field that describes the knowledge and skills necessary for competent practice in recreational therapy.

Initial Certification Standards

There are two paths to professional certification as a CTRS. The academic path is for individuals who have completed a baccalaureate degree or higher with a major in therapeutic recreation. The equivalency path is for individuals with a related baccalaureate degree. Both certification paths have requirements related to: (a) the academic degree, (b) content course work in therapeutic recreation and general recreation, (c) supportive course work and (d) experience in therapeutic recreation practice. The structure of these professional standards has not changed significantly since the Council was founded in 1981, however, interpretive guidelines within each path have at times been changed to reflect changes in the profession. For complete information on the certification standards currently in effect, please contact NCTRC.

For the professional level *academic path* to CTRS certification, the exam eligibility requirements are a baccalaureate degree or higher from an accredited college or university with a major in therapeutic recreation or a major in recreation with an option in therapeutic recreation. For current academic path requirements please contact the NCTRC office.

The professional *equivalency path* refers to an alternate route to certification based upon specific academic preparation and full-time, paid work experience. This path was developed for individuals who have taken an "equivalent path" to developing their knowledge and skills for competent practice in the field in a way other than an academic degree in therapeutic recreation. The requirements are equivalent to those of the academic path. For current equivalency path requirements please contact the NCTRC office.

Individuals demonstrate that they have met the standards for either the academic or the equivalency path by applying for "professional eligibility" for certification with NCTRC. In this application process, the transcripts and documentation of applicants' skills are reviewed against the current standards. All work and field placement experiences are verified directly by NCTRC. The results of these comprehensive reviews are to award or deny professional eligibility. Once individuals receive professional eligibility from NCTRC, they may apply to sit for the national certification exam. The CTRS credential is not awarded until an individual passes both the review for professional eligibility and the national exam.

The National Certification Exam

In 1987, NCTRC contracted with the Educational Testing Service (ETS) to develop a national exam for the Certified Therapeutic Recreation Specialist. The NCTRC Exam is based on the National Job Analysis Study of the Therapeutic Recreation Specialist, which assures that the test specifications and the exam are related to the practice of therapeutic recreation.

The NCTRC National Certification Exam is administered twice a year in November and May. Only individuals who have been awarded professional eligibility or are actively certified as a CTRS are eligible to sit for the national exam. The exam is required for initial or entry level certification as a CTRS and may also be used as one of the options for recertification for those renewing their CTRS credential. Complete information on registration, scoring, reliability and testing accommodations for individuals with special needs is available in the *Candidate Bulletin* of NCTRC. The content of the exam is based on the knowledge areas defined in the NCTRC Job Analysis. As new information is defined in revisions of the Job Analysis, the exam is revised to match new knowledge requirements for competent practice in therapeutic recreation.

Initial professional eligibility is awarded for a period of five years to allow new applicants sufficient and fair opportunity to sit for and pass the national certification exam. For individuals who do not pass the examination, a score report is provided which indicates that they were unsuccessful in achieving the required passing scaled score along with diagnostic indicators for the content areas included in the exam. The diagnostic indicators are intended to help identify areas of strength and weakness. The indictors say whether the exam score is at or above the minimum acceptable competency level, somewhat below the minimum competency level or considerably below the level of minimum competency. Matching these scales of indicators to the content areas of the exam aids candidates in preparation for a future exam.

Conduct Standards

There has been a heightened awareness of the importance of ethics, professional conduct and the very worthiness of professional acts in our society over the past few decades. As technology has risen and the crises of human events in health care have become more complicated, educated consumers have begun to question professional motives and conduct more often. While professional societies and organizations develop and promote Codes of Ethics, a credentialing program cannot monitor professional competence by ethical values. Ethics deal with moral issues and values — they are beliefs and underlying principles. Certification deals with concrete, observable measures of competence for practice. The National Job Analysis lists knowledge and skills for competent practice in recreational therapy. The professional skills can be observed in practice and the knowledge areas can be tested in a national standardized exam. So, how does a credentialing program address the concern for protecting the public from harm in regard to incompetent or negligent practice? The answer is through the development, monitoring and evaluation of professional conduct.

Certain types of conduct from health and human service providers are unacceptable to consumers. It is expected that professionals operate at the highest level of honesty and integrity and that they are concerned about protecting the lives and rights of the people they serve. The public expects no less than professional competence in education, experience and continuing professional education, as well as truthfulness, integrity and professional appropriateness. NCTRC has established 14 statements regarding professional conduct. All NCTRC certificants must agree to abide by these conduct rules and to report truthfully information regarding any violation of a conduct matter. NCTRC may deny professional eligibility, revoke eligibility or certification or take other appropriate action if a candidate for certification or a CTRS violates any of the 14 conduct statements. In this way, NCTRC monitors adherence to standards to assure that cases involving potential harm to public health and safety are investigated fully and that appropriate sanctions of reprimand, suspension and/or denial are instituted as needed. Through this effort, NCTRC encourages public recognition of the CTRS credential as an indicator of professional competence and appropriate conduct. NCTRC is the organization in the field of therapeutic recreation which acts as an overseer in the interest of the public.

As a condition of professional eligibility for certification and to retain NCTRC certification, all certificants agree in writing to follow conduct standards. The current 14 statements of conduct for which NCTRC may revoke, deny or otherwise take appropriate action appear in Table 21.1.

Table 21.1: **NCTRC Conduct Statements**

NCTRC may take action with regard to certification should any one of the following events occur:

1. Ineligibility for NCTRC certification as a CTRS. Ineligibility includes, but is not limited to, a failure to meet any educational or experiential standard set by NCTRC;
2. Irregularity in connection with any NCTRC exam. This includes, but is not limited to, copying answers, permitting another to copy answers, falsifying information required for admission to exam, impersonating another examinee, falsifying education or credentials, or providing and/or receiving unauthorized advice about exam content during the exam;
3. Failure to pay fees required by NCTRC;
4. Unauthorized possession of, use of, distribution of, or access to (i) NCTRC exams, (ii) certificates, (iii) logo of NCTRC, (iv) abbreviations relating thereto, and (v) any other NCTRC documents and materials;
5. Obtaining or attempting to obtain certification or recertification for oneself or another by a false or misleading statement or failure to make a required statement, fraud or deceit in an application, reapplication or any other communication to NCTRC;
6. Misrepresentation of NCTRC certification;
7. Failure to provide any written information required by NCTRC;
8. Failure to provide timely update of information required by NCTRC;
9. Habitual use of alcohol or any drug or any substance, or any physical or mental condition, which impairs competent and objective professional performance;
10. Gross or repeated negligence or malpractice in professional work;
11. Limitation or sanction, including but not limited to revocation or suspension by a health care organization, professional organization, or other private or governmental body, relating to therapeutic recreation practice, public health or safety or therapeutic recreation certification;
12. Conviction of, plea of guilty to, or plea of nolo contendere to a felony or misdemeanor directly relating to therapeutic recreation practice and/or public health and safety. An individual convicted of a felony directly related to therapeutic recreation practice and/or public health and safety shall be ineligible to apply for certification or recertification for a period of three (3) years from the exhaustion of appeals or final release from confinement (if any), whichever is later. Convictions of this nature include, but are not limited to, felonies involving rape, sexual abuse of a patient or child, actual or threatened use of a weapon, violence, and prohibited sale, distribution or possession of a controlled substance.
13. Knowingly assisting another to obtain or attempt to obtain credentialing by fraud or deception.
14. Any other violation of an NCTRC bylaw, standard, policy or procedure, or any other rule, standard, or procedure as may be adopted by NCTRC.

In addition to these 14 specific statements, candidates for certification and CTRSs must also comply with the following:

1. To Comply with NCTRC Standards, Policies and Procedures. No individuals are eligible to apply for or maintain certification unless they are in compliance with all NCTRC rules and standards, policies and procedures. Each individual bears the burden of showing and maintaining compliance at all times.
2. To Adhere to NCTRC Application and Notification Requirements. Each candidate for CTRS certification must truthfully complete and sign the appropriate application provided by NCTRC. Candidates and certificants must notify NCTRC within sixty (60) days of any change in name, address, telephone number and any other facts bearing on eligibility or certification.
3. To Respect the Property of NCTRC. The examination, certificates, logo, emblem and the name "NCTRC," the designation "Certified Therapeutic Recreation Specialist" and abbreviations relating thereto are all the exclusive property of NCTRC and may not be used in any way without the express prior written consent of NCTRC. In the event of suspension, limitation, revocation or resignation from NCTRC, or as otherwise requested by NCTRC, each individual shall immediately relinquish, refrain from using and correct at his or her expense any outdated or other inaccurate use of NCTRC's certificate, logo, emblem, the name "NCTRC," the designation "CTRS" and related abbreviations.
4. To Report Pending Litigation, Sanctions and/or Criminal Convictions. Candidates must notify NCTRC within sixty days of any indictment or charge directly relating to the field of therapeutic recreation pending before a state or federal regulatory agency or judicial body, including but not limited to the following actions to the extent such actions relate to therapeutic recreation or public health and safety: filing of any civil or criminal charge; indictment or litigation; conviction; plea of guilty; plea of nolo contendere; or disciplinary action by a health care organization, professional organization or other private or governmental body.

NCTRC requires that all applicants adhere to professional standards and report only truthful information in regard to their education, experience and professional conduct. All applicants who truthfully disclose information relating to the 14 statements have the opportunity to present all relevant circumstances and to explain why they should be eligible for certification. These issues governing the CTRS's behavior are not unique to the field of recreational therapy but are in fact representative of conduct standards held by most legitimate health care professions. The critical importance that ethics and conduct matters play in the delivery of competent, effective and credible health care services to clients has become more and more evident over the past twenty years of technological advancement in the health care industry. These conduct standards, coupled with procedures for implementation and the development of national peer review committees for enforcement (i.e., Standards Review and Standards Hearing Committees), keep NCTRC focused on its mission of consumer protection and quality therapeutic recreation services.

Continuing Professional Competence

Everything changes over time. The profession of recreational therapy is constantly developing new techniques and new knowledge for better services for clients and consumers. What practitioners learned in their educational programs in 1980 is different from what they learned in 1990. And what we will learn in 2010 should represent further advances in knowledge and skill. Recognized certification programs, therefore, have a responsibility not only to set minimum standards for entry level certification, but also to establish a system to periodically reassess a practitioner's competence. This system of reassessing practitioner competence for professional practice is referred to as "recertification."

When NCTRC first established a national standardized exam in 1990, it required over 9,000 individuals who already held the CTRS credential at the time to take and pass the exam just as a new applicant for certification would be required to do. This was the first attempt of the Council to reassess the CTRS's competence for practice based on individual possession of knowledge areas as defined in the Job Analysis and verified by passing the national exam. Once individuals are certified by passing the national exam, they are then subject to periodic reassessment of their competence by the NCTRC Recertification Program. The period of reassessment is every five years and the evidence of competence must relate to the knowledge and skills delineated in the National Job Analysis.

The NCTRC Recertification Program is designed to allow certificants to maintain continuing professional development and high professional standards. Recognizing the fact that professional careers take a variety of different paths, the program is flexible to allow individual professionals choices on how they demonstrate maintenance of competence to practice recreational therapy. There are many ways to continue competence for practice. We can complete more education on innovative skills and the requisite knowledge for practice, we learn by practicing the profession and some learn by reading and studying new techniques and knowledge. As with other educational and experiential requirements, NCTRC developed a means of evaluating evidence that CTRSs were maintaining competency.

During the five year certification period, the CTRS must choose two of three potential Recertification Components. Each CTRS must earn a total of 100 points to renew certification at the end of the five year cycle. The three components by which a CTRS can demonstrate continued professional competence are professional practice or experience in therapeutic recreation, continuing education in therapeutic recreation or passing the national exam at the end of the five year period. The CTRS must complete at least two of the three components in order to recertify and retain the CTRS credential.

The *professional experience* component must include a minimum of 360 hours of therapeutic recreation professional experience and must be earned within the five (5) year recertification cycle. These hours can be earned through the performance of one or several of the following professional roles: Direct Service Deliverer, Supervisor, Administrator, Educator, Consultant, Volunteer or Professional Service on a recreational therapy professional board or council, or by doing legislative work, standards development, curriculum development, etc. Both paid and non-paid experience, and full-time as well as part-time experience are accepted.

The *continuing education* component for recertification includes a wide range of activities that are typically available to the CTRS. A certificant can accumulate recertification points in one or several of three categories: continuing education courses and experiences, academic courses or professional publications and presentations. The continuing education must be in therapeutic recreation as defined by the knowledge areas of the National Job Analysis and must receive Continuing Education Credits as defined by the International Association for Continuing Education and Training (IACET). Academic Courses in recreational therapy may be completed for recertification credit and must also meet the knowledge areas of the National Job Analysis. A CTRS may also earn recertification credit for professional publications and presentations as this is another measurable way to show continued professional learning.

The third and final recertification component is *reexamination*. This component requires the CTRS to take and pass the current examination used for professional level certification. Certificants who choose the reexamination component must take and pass the exam within the last 18 months of their five year active certification cycle.

Each year of the five year active certification period, the CTRS must submit an annual maintenance application and fee to retain certification. At the end of the five year cycle, certificants must submit a recertification application documenting the completed continuing professional competence requirements. In order to complete the recertification process, all maintenance fees must be paid and current. During any period of time that an individual's certification is inactive, that individual is prohibited from (i) representing that he or she is a "Certified Therapeutic Recreation Specialist" or "CTRS" and (ii) accepting the role of supervisor for a proposed internship requiring a supervisor that is certified by NCTRC as a CTRS. If an individual is not recertified for failure to meet the recertification requirements, that individual must return the NCTRC CTRS certificate and refrain from using the title "Certified Therapeutic Recreation Specialist" or "CTRS." Any individual who uses CTRS, or represents himself or herself as being NCTRC certified without having fulfilled the requirements of the NCTRC certification process is deemed in violation of the credentialing procedure and may be denied the right to future certification or may be subject to legal action.

Growth of the Council

As of 1995, NCTRC had over 13,600 certificants and continues to experience steady growth as it refines its certification standards and promotes the credibility of its certification marks. The growth in numbers of certified individuals has been most dramatic during the decade of 1985 to 1995. In 1985-86, certificant numbers grew from just over 3,000 to over 6,000 when the Council initiated a standard requiring field internships to be supervised by certified CTRSs in order for the field internship to be acceptable toward certification standards. This action was a vote of confidence by the Council in the competence of its own certificants to be the best means for supervising new entrants to the field. Between 1986 and 1990, the number of certificants grew to 11,000.

When the exam was instituted in 1990, NCTRC required all incumbent certificants to sit for and pass the exam as well as using the exam as an entry requirement for new applicants. This action was essential to assure that all NCTRC certificants had demonstrated possession of minimum knowledge for practice in the field. It was a bold step and a difficult time for the profession. Some who were certified at the time objected to taking the exam as veteran certificants with experience in practice, even though they did not object to the exam requirement for new certificants. This was the only period of NCTRC's history where there was a decrease in the numbers of certified individuals. At the close of 1992, NCTRC had lost over 1,000 certificants who did not take the national exam and therefore forfeited their certification. There are many reasons why these individuals did not step forward. Some were no longer working in the field and saw no reason to continue their certification, some were close to retirement, some did not consider certification necessary to their employment and some simply followed through on their objections to the national exam. By 1993, the numbers again began to rise and at the beginning of 1995, NCTRC held a registry of its highest number of certificants — well over 13,000. Growth in the number of certificants is expected to continue and it is a goal of the Council to have over 20,000 certified by twentieth anniversary of NCTRC in 2001.

Summary

According to the United States Department of Labor (Spring, 1992), "Recreational Therapy" is listed as number 12 of the 20 fastest growing occupations requiring a bachelor's degree or more education. Recreational therapy is a unique, alternative helping profession with a focus on recreation and activities as a means to psychological and physical recovery, health and well-being. While the number of certificants and jobs in recreational therapy continue to grow, the Council's mission will not be fully realized until the majority of the labor pool in therapeutic recreation has demonstrated competence through attaining certification. Only then will the public recognition of and protection by qualified therapeutic recreation services be accomplished.

The strongest and most reliable means of recognizing qualified recreational therapist practitioners is the NCTRC certification program. The NCTRC program has been developed following national standards for certifying agencies. The NCTRC's CTRS credential is recognized in the arena of health care services. NCTRC's history of development coincides with ongoing efforts toward greater fiscal responsibility in health care delivery and continues today as the health care reform discussion heightens. The credential is directed toward the protection of the consumer and delivery of quality health care services.

NCTRC fulfills its mission of protecting the consumer through three important functions. First, NCTRC standards are based on current knowledge and skills necessary for competent practice in therapeutic recreation. Second, NCTRC evaluates individual qualifications for certification and recertification through a comprehensive system of review, verification and standardized national testing to assure that each individual awarded the CTRS has met the qualifications to hold this credential. Third, employers who hire NCTRC certificants can rely on the CTRS credential as evidence that the employee has demonstrated competence for practice in recreational therapy. This employer will also be assured that the CTRS must adhere to standards of conduct and will continue professional development by meeting recertification requirements.

Learning Activities

1. *Required Coursework.* Obtain a current copy of the course content requirements. Compare the requirements to the courses you have already taken and the courses which you plan to take prior to graduation.

2. *NCTRC Conduct Statement.* Compare the NCTRC Conduct Statement with the ethics statements from both the American Therapeutic Recreation Association and the National Therapeutic Recreation Society found in the back of the book. What do the three documents have in common? What unique elements may be found in the NCTRC Conduct Statement?

Study Questions

1. What is the mission of the National Council for Therapeutic Recreation Certification (NCTRC)? How is this mission carried out in the work that it does? In what way does NCTRC's mission impact the work that you will be doing as a therapist?
2. How did credentialing for recreational therapists evolve? How has the number of credentialing levels an individual may apply for changed over the years? How have the changes in health care and professional credentialing, in general, influenced these changes?
3. What are the three standards that govern professional certification as a Certified Therapeutic Recreation Specialist? What are the components which make up each standard? How is your university coursework preparing you to meet these standards?
4. What are the three components of recertification for the Certified Therapeutic Recreation Specialist (CTRS)? How often is the CTRS expected to go through the recertification process? What must the CTRS do on a yearly basis to ensure that his/her status as a CTRS is maintained?

References

Carter, M. J. (1981). Registration of therapeutic recreators: Standards from 1956 to present. *Therapeutic Recreation Journal, 15*(2), 17-22.

Carter, M. J. & Folkerth, J. E. (1989). The evolution of the National Council for Therapeutic Recreation Certification, Inc. In D. M. Compton (Ed.). *Issues in therapeutic recreation: A profession in transition* (pp. 505-510). Champaign, IL: Sagamore Publishing.

Folkerth, J. E. (1986). Certification historical perspectives: The first thirty years, 1956-1986 [Monograph]. *Twentieth Anniversary National Therapeutic Recreation Society*, 51-59.

Geber, B. (1995, February). The plan to certify America. *Training*, 39-44.

Grubb, A. (1958, October). Are you registered? *Recreation for the Ill and Handicapped*, 8-9.

Oltman, P. K., Norback, J. & Rosenfeld, M. (1989). A national study of the profession of therapeutic recreation specialist. *Therapeutic Recreation Journal, 23*(2), 48-58.

Stilson, J. E., Cohen, E. M. & Hill, B. (1959). *Recreation in hospitals: Report of a study on organized recreation programs in hospitals and of the personnel conducting them*. New York: National Recreation Association.

US Department of Labor, Bureau of Labor Statistics. (1991, Fall). *Occupational Outlook Quarterly*.

US Department of Labor, Bureau of Labor Statistics. (1992, Spring). *Occupational Outlook Quarterly*.

Young, S. D. (1987). *The rule of experts: Occupational licensing in America*. Washington, DC: CATO Institute.

Zeitlin, K. A. & Dorn, S. E. (1992, January). Professional credentialing: Title law declared unconstitutional. *Association Management*, 5-7.

Chapter 22

Mentorship: Transitioning from Student to Practitioner

Michael Rhodes

We are all apprentices in a craft where no one ever becomes a master.
— Ernest Hemingway

Obviously, Hemingway was not referring to the profession of recreational therapy, but life itself, when he made this famous statement. However, in looking at the profession we call recreational therapy, if learning stopped after the academic and internship experience, then we would all be cursed to be apprentices in a craft where no one ever becomes a master. Hopefully, we all continue to seek and gain knowledge in an effort to "master" our craft.

There are many ways in which we polish the skills of our profession. We read our professional journals, we attend and participate in continuing education experiences, we network with our colleagues, we actively participate in professional associations, we take classes and so forth. This chapter will explore the concept of mentorship and its role in assisting us in our quest to master our profession.

Roles in Mentorship

The word mentor has its roots in Greek mythology. Bezuidenhout (1993), Grossman (1993) and DeMarco (1993) all note that in Homer's *The Odyssey*, Odysseus, (Latin: Ulysses), King of Ithaca, left home to wage the battles of the Trojan War. He asked his good friend, Mentor, to be the guardian of his household and tutor his son, Telemachus. Mentor's role as a tutor included serving as a guardian, teacher and friend to Telemachus. Thus, such duties as serving as a guardian, teacher and friend have evolved into essential roles that a mentor performs.

Webster (1989) defines a mentor as a wise advisor or a teacher or coach. Bohannon (1985), a physical therapist, offers a more complex definition of mentorship as "a process by which a senior interacts one-to-one in a personal relationship with a less powerful and less experienced subordinate to develop the subordinate. The more senior participant in the relationship, the mentor, must be a model with skills and qualities assumed by the subordinate to be lacking in himself." Bohannon (1985) also cites Levinson's biographic research that indicates most mentors are 8-15 years older than the mentees and the relationship lasts two to three years, although it could last much longer. Sarah C. Slater (1993, p. 55), the Director of the American Speech and Hearing Association's Research Information and Analysis Branch, states that mentoring "is the process by which one person learns from the knowledge and experience of another." Rogers (1986, p. 79), an occupational therapist, states that "mentors teach what textbooks cannot." Rogers (1986, p. 79) goes on to list five major functions of the mentor:

Teacher — develops the mentee's textbook and clinical skills;
Sponsor — eases the mentee's entry into and advancement in the work environment;
Host and Guide — welcomes the mentee into the professional world;
Exemplar — serves as a role model for the mentee; and
Counselor — provides support, reassurance and appropriate alternatives.

There were numerous other definitions in the literature, but for the purpose of this chapter, we will assume that the process of mentorship in recreational therapy combines many of the features previously noted, including a relationship where a less experienced individual learns from a more knowledgeable and experienced individual, who is usually older, in a relationship that lasts at least two to three years. The mentor roles include that of teacher, sponsor, host/guide, exemplar and counselor.

Webster (1989) defines a protégé as a person guided and helped in his career by another person. We will utilize the terms protégé and mentee interchangeably throughout the chapter to mean the individual, male or female, in the mentorship relationship other than the mentor. Webster (1989) defines the word preceptor as a teacher. Ellis (1993, p. 154), a teacher of nursing in the United Kingdom, states that in the United States, the "term 'nurse-preceptor' is used to describe a unit-based nurse who carries out one-to-one teaching of new employees or nursing students in addition to her regular unit duties." If we utilize Webster's (1989) definition of a preceptor, then recreational therapy college professors are our preceptors in the classroom. Likewise, the recreational therapy clinical internship supervisor is likely to play the role of preceptor to students during their clinical affiliation. Although the preceptor relationship that most students, professors and clinical internship supervisors experience could evolve into a mentoring relationship, most remain at the preceptorship level.

Webster (1989) defines an apprentice as a person being taught a craft or a trade, now usually as a member of a union. For the purpose of this chapter, we will define the word "apprentice" in a traditional manner, as in teaching a specific trade through a union. The closest we come to an apprenticeship in recreational therapy is the internship experience, the main difference being that recreational therapy is not considered a unionized trade.

Mentorship

Mentorship seems to have its roots in the business world. DeMarco (1993) notes that affirmative action lawsuits in the 1970's prompted large corporations, such as AT&T, to utilize mentors in an attempt to improve the employment of women and other minorities in management positions. Bohannon (1985, p. 921) notes that "testimonies by successful individuals, such as Andrew Carnegie and Dwight D. Eisenhower, bear witness to the role mentors played in their professional development." Bohannon (1985) goes on to note that Peters and Waterman, in their classic work *In Search of Excellence*, identified important role progressions among employees of successful organizations known as "product champions" and "executive champions" that have roles that correspond well to those of protégé and mentor. He further identifies the natural evolution of product champion (protégé) into executive champion (mentor).

With mentoring having its roots in the business world, it was not surprising that some individuals compared the similarities between characteristics of leaders and mentors. Chandler (1993, p. 343), a nurse, notes the similarities in the Table 22.1.

Table 22.1: **Comparison of Leader and Mentor Characteristics**

Leader (Kouzes & Posner, 1989)	**Mentor** (Vance, 1982)
Enabler	Teacher/Guide
Encourager	Sponsor
Model	Exemplar
Coach	Counselor
Visionary	Visionary

If we are looking for whom our mentors are in recreational therapy, we need only to look at our leaders. This is not to suggest that all leaders are willing mentors, but clearly the leaders have the characteristics that parallel those of mentors.

This brings us to the question of why someone would want to play the role of mentor. If the literature is correct, then today's protégés are tomorrow's mentors. If we assume that our mentors are our leaders, then it is clear that rather than re-inventing the wheel, it is to our advantage as professionals to assist the future leaders in order to continue to improve. Valadez and Lund (1993, p. 260), two nurses in the Veterans Affairs System, note that mentoring "promotes job satisfaction, self-discipline, honesty and persistence and more mentors." They go on to say that mentoring is reciprocal. They note that the mentor's rewards include the ability to teach, lead and develop new practitioners while the protégé's rewards center on application of their textbook knowledge under the guidance of an experienced professional. They note in a case study that the mentor is expected to be the teacher, but the successful mentor also learns from the experience, using the example of a mentee teaching a mentor about computers. Slater (1993, p. 55), notes that a speech and language pathology survey that identified the benefits gained by the mentee through mentoring. Table 22.2 summarizes this survey:

Table 22.2: Benefits Gained Through Mentoring by the Mentee

Benefits	Respondents Noting This Benefit
Advice	85.3%
Confidence	80.1%
New Skills	76.6%
Opportunities	54.2%
New Contacts	44.7%
Less Stress	34.5%
No Benefits	1.7%

Career Transitions

As we grow from student to practitioner, we evolve from mentee to mentor. Rogers (1986), an occupational therapist, describes three career transitions: non-professional (student) to professional (clinician), generalist (clinician) to specialist (senior clinician) and specialist (senior clinician) to academician (professor). I would add a fourth career transition and that is specialist (senior clinician) to leader (program manager). It is important to review these critical career transition stages if we hope to understand the role of mentorship. We will start with the evolution of the non-professional (student) and continue through the development of the professional (clinician).

Student to Clinician

Many who have successfully made the transition from student to clinician have fond memories of key individuals that assisted in this important stage of professional development. Certainly all of us have had someone that played a key role in our lives. Most have had preceptors that have taught us the skills needed to do our jobs. But a select few have had the true opportunity of a mentoring experience to assist us as we blossomed into recreational therapists.

In recreational therapy, much has been written about the gap between academic preparation and entry into the workforce. In looking at practitioners' evaluations of college preparation, Smith (1976, p. 156) concluded that "overall, the findings tended to support the premise that the undergraduate training experience had not, in many cases, properly trained the bachelor level practitioner to meet the job situation or given him/her a strong philosophical base from which to work." Austin (1974), in writing about the limits of academia to meet the needs of the student, came to similar conclusions. Littlefield (1975, p. 107) wrote that, "I would rather suspect the common phrase 'when I graduated, I put my books on the shelf and learned my job from scratch,' is more truth than fiction." Fortunately, we have come a long way since the 1970's in our academic preparation. The National Council for Therapeutic Recreation Certification, with its work on the job analysis and the examination, has taken major strides in narrowing the gap between student and clinician by identifying key job responsibilities and testing to assure knowledge to perform these duties.

We must realize that the gap from academic preparation to clinician is not unique to recreational therapy. In physical therapy, Bohannon (1985, p. 922) notes that "those who teach physical therapists are by and large philosophically and practically isolated from the very practice that they are attempting to pass on to the future generations." He further notes another study which indicates that physical therapy students identify more strongly with their clinical supervisors than with their professors. In occupational therapy, Rogers (1986, p. 80) notes that "occupational therapy students frequently complain that they have difficulty identifying with their classroom instructors because they rarely observe their instructors applying theory and techniques that they teach as the solution to real patient problems." She goes on to say that it is no wonder that students select clinicians over instructors as their role models since the clinicians apply the theory into actual concrete practice. In nursing, Ellis (1993, p. 154), a nurse in the United Kingdom, notes "In the United States, the term mentor was seized upon as a means of reducing 'reality shock' (Kramer 1978) which occurs when the values instilled in newly registered nurses by the school come into conflict with the bureaucratic values of their workplace." Cullen, Rodak, Fitzgerald and Baker (1993, p. 227), noted that "one profession, nursing, has realized that the new professional commonly needs a transition period to acclimate into the clinical setting." It appears clear that many nursing and allied health professions struggle with the same gap between the classroom and the clinic.

Clearly outlining expected competencies and then requiring the student to demonstrate these competencies is one way to bridge this gap from the classroom to the clinic. The American Occupational Therapy Association (1987) has done an outstanding job of standardizing clinical competencies and holding all interns responsible for demonstrating these competencies on their clinician affiliations. This standardization of internship clinical competencies should be carefully looked at by the American Therapeutic Recreation Association and the National Therapeutic Recreation Society. The National Council on Therapeutic Recreation Certification requires us to articulate our knowledge of recreational therapy practice through the national examination process to become a Certified Therapeutic Recreation Specialist, or CTRS. We need to take the next step and demonstrate knowledge of basic clinical competencies during our internships for the jobs we seek.

Peer program review is the last method of note that should not be overlooked when discussing ways to assist the young professional in closing the gap between the knowledge of the new graduate and the demands of the workplace. Coyne and Turpel (1984) discussed this in their article on peer review. They note that peer review by professional associations that utilize set standards can be an effective approach to teaching new skills to the new graduate. They go on to discuss how both speech and language pathologists, through the American Speech and Hearing Association and physical therapists, through the American Physical Therapy Association Quality Assurance Board, have demonstrated the ability to ease the transition from student to clinician through peer program review. The National Therapeutic Recreation Society first published *Standards of Practice for Therapeutic Recreation Services* in 1980 and revised the *Standards* in 1994. The American Therapeutic Recreation Association published their set of *Standards for the Practice of Therapeutic Recreation* in 1991 and has field tested these *Standards* (1993) for compliance. It appears we have the opportunity of utilizing peer review as another means to assist in the development of the entry-level professional. The challenge is seeking all means necessary to improve service delivery by the new clinician. These are the tools by which the profession is measured.

Mentoring could also play an important role in assisting the individual in transition by preparing him/her for the profession though observation of competent intervention and knowledge sharing with someone that already possesses the skills needed to be successful. Clinicians that step forward and accept this challenge will greatly assist the new graduates in successfully making the transition from the classroom to the clinic and from student to recreational therapist.

Clinician to Specialist or Senior Clinician

The second career stage transition is that of clinician to specialist or senior clinician. Universities cannot be expected to teach specialized skills to all students and therefore the transition from clinician to specialist is best done through the mentoring process. Clinicians who wish to develop an expertise beyond entry level knowledge should seek out a willing mentor. The potential mentor should have demonstrated competence and expertise in the areas in which the mentee wishes to acquire skills or knowledge. For example, the individual wishing to learn more about the use of behavioral medicine interventions, such as relaxation and stress management techniques, should seek out an individual who has specialized training and the appropriate credentials, such as a CTRS with experience and certification in the use of biofeedback. The need for mentoring opportunities is clear. However, the ability to meet this need is questionable. With the 1990's being the decade of health care reform and "doing more with less," the opportunity for mentoring is often limited by the reality of the workplace.

Many of us have worked in facilities that have entry level recreational therapy positions that can be filled with the skills of the new graduate. There may also be senior or specialist positions that require a more experienced individual with additional skills. At the facility where this writer works, the recreational therapist position on the inpatient rehabilitation unit is an example of a position that lends itself well to the new graduate. It is a traditional recreational therapy position, located in a hospital, where other recreational therapists practice. This type of position provides the new graduate with the assistance needed to successfully do his/her job. This is not to suggest that all individuals working on inpatient units are entry level practitioners. Some of these individuals evolve into senior or specialized areas of responsibility, such as assuming supervisory or management duties or becoming specialists themselves in working with individuals with unique needs, such as individuals with traumatic brain injuries. In most cases, the young professional looks to other recreational therapists who have the skills they seek, as their preceptors or mentors, to gain the knowledge they lack.

By contrast, the recreational therapy position in the outpatient comprehensive chronic pain management program is a more non-traditional position that requires a clinical specialty in the cognitive-behavioral approach to treatment. This is a good example of specialized training beyond the foundation of knowledge one would expect to acquire at the university level. This clinical program is located in a community recreation center and the recreational therapist is isolated from the support offered at the main hospital. Again, if we assume the mentor or preceptor is going to teach us the skills our textbooks cannot teach, then who might a recreational therapist seek out to gain knowledge in this type of situation? Often, it is not a recreational therapist, but another member of the clinical treatment team. In this example, it is the program psychologist. Why psychologists, one might ask. Simply because they have the knowledge and skill needed to successfully initiate this type of treatment. They understand the cognitive-behavioral approach and the difficulties associated with implementation. They often serve as preceptors or mentors not only to the recreational therapists, but also to the physical and occupational therapists and other team members that seek this knowledge and understanding. In most cases, this type of specialized knowledge is not available through the more traditional means of classroom learning and shows how mentoring aids in the transition from clinician to specialist.

Senior Clinician to Academician

The third career transition stage is that of senior clinician to academician. If mentors are needed to teach us about the politics of the workplace, then there seems to be no area with a greater need for mentoring than that of senior clinician to academician. The logical cycle would seem to be student to clinician, clinician to specialist and specialist to academician. The academician would then start the cycle again by training students. However, in looking at academicians in recreational therapy, this cycle appears broken. Many recreational therapy professors have never practiced as clinicians. Some that have practiced have been out of the field for many years. This writer is one of the few who have had the opportunity to make the transition from student to clinician, clinician to specialist and specialist to academician. In making the transition from the clinic back to the classroom, this writer was fortunate enough to have met a terrific individual that served as his mentor when he taught for three years at Wayne State University. This individual was a leader in the park and recreation movement and assisted this writer greatly in understanding the politics of the park and recreation movement and of education. However, like most curricula, the recreational therapy program was housed in the Department of Health, Physical Education, Recreation and Dance in the College of Education and there was little opportunity to network and learn from professors in other allied health professions taught at the University, such as the departments of physical or occupational therapy. If we accept recreational therapy as an allied health profession and we agree that allied health includes all health care professions except physicians and nurses, then we must improve our opportunities for mentoring at the academician level by housing our curriculum and our professors in the appropriate location. It is this author's opinion that without an immediate movement toward this change, we will widen the gap between the needs of the health care providers and the abilities of the recreational therapist to meet those needs.

Rogers (1986, p. 81) notes that academia is very different from the health care environment. "Work standards are largely determined by unwritten rules handed down informally rather than by detailed policies and procedures." For the clinician making the transition to the classroom, the assistance of a mentor is almost always required to understand the politics of academia.

Mentoring takes place at the university level. The question this writer raises is who is doing the mentoring. The knowledge needed to survive in the increasingly competitive world of health care is simply not available to the average recreational therapy professor, working in the department of park and recreation resources, in the college of education.

Senior Clinician to Manager

The final stage of career transition is that of senior clinician to manager. Everyone knows that the world of health care delivery is rapidly changing. In the last ten years, health care has gone from a retrospective payment or straight fee for service system where the more services a facility provides, the more money it makes, to a prospective payment or capitated system where the less services a facility provides, the more money it makes. This obviously presents the challenge of obtaining quality outcomes with less time and energy. We have seen the evolution from diagnostic related groupings to managed care and capitated costs in the last few years. The future promises even more change if we finally become the last industrialized nation, besides South Africa, to offer our citizens national health care.

Twenty years ago, the recreational therapist most likely reported to the director of the activity therapy department. That individual frequently happened to be an occupational therapist. Slowly the trend developed for free-standing departments. This provided an introduction to the world of supervision and management. Since that time, many recreational therapy roles have evolved into those of administrative directors of programs, with duties such as the executive director of Comprehensive Outpatient Rehabilitation Facility (CORF), Qualified Mental Retardation Professional (treatment team leader) and Industrial Rehabilitation Program Manager. The management matrix has shifted from clinical department director, such as director of recreational therapy, to service line delivery manager, such as manager of traumatic brain injury services. This shift in health care delivery has eliminated many recreational therapy and activity therapy director positions but has offered the opportunity for new challenges in program management.

There are many theories as to why so many recreational therapy directors have evolved into health care program managers and administrators. One theory is that since, in most instances, recreational therapy is not a "billable service," making the recreational therapy supervisor a manager does not reduce the ability of the institution to generate revenue. Another theory is that recreational therapy has treated the individual as a whole, unlike physical therapy which works on the lower extremities, occupational therapy which works on the upper extremities or speech and language pathology which works on speech and cognition. It is because of this holistic approach that recreational therapists may have better insight into the needs of the individual. However, more than one hospital administrator has noted that recreational therapists make good managers because they are good leaders. Before we revise our educational programs, we must be sure that we do not "throw the baby out with the bath water."

Health care delivery is changing dramatically. Our leadership skills will offer many opportunities for us to meet the changing needs in health care. However, with the changes in health care delivery, opportunities for mentoring to polish these skills have also dramatically changed. Those who seek knowledge are faced with the challenge of finding the individuals who can provide them with the knowledge they seek. These individuals are not as obvious as they once were when the leaders in recreational therapy naturally evolved into recreational therapy/activity therapy department directors. It has been said that the only people who like change are babies with wet diapers. We do not have to like change. We do, however, have to accept change and be prepared to be proactive rather than reactive if we are to be successful.

Outcomes of Mentoring

This chapter has been reviewing the role of mentoring in various career stages. However, we must ask ourselves, does mentoring produce outcomes? Cullen, Rodak, Fitzgerald and Baker (1993) note that a study of psychology graduate students showed that the students with sponsorship by mentors produced more publications and conference presentations and generally had greater research productivity than students without mentors. Bohannon (1985) notes two relevant sociological studies. Vaillant (1977) studied 268 men who graduated from 1939 to 1944 from a prestigious Eastern university. The study, using interviews and questionnaires, examined the men's adaptation to life. The findings showed that those who were highly successful at 47 years of age no longer recalled the role models of their university years. The early role model had been replaced by a "mentor acquired in young adulthood, the master craftsman as it were, to whom they had apprenticed themselves" (Bohannon, 1985, p. 921). The second sociological study Bohannon (1985) cites is by Dalton, Thompson and Price (1977). It involved interviews with accountants, engineers, university professors and scientists. The study showed that the 550 people interviewed included both high and low rated performers. High rated performers differed from low rated performers in that they had progressed through four stages in their professional careers. The first and third of these stages corresponded to those of mentee and mentor.

There are numerous other examples of studies that have demonstrated positive outcomes from mentoring in such areas as physician supervision of emergency medical personnel (Pepe, Mattox, Duke, Fisher & Prentice, 1993), mentoring nursing students to write (Davidhizar, 1993), mentoring minority college nursing students to improve retention (Alvarez & Abriam-Yago, 1993), mentoring students from disadvantaged backgrounds (Baldwin & Wold, 1993), mentoring dental students (Romberg, 1993) and so on. Mentoring produces results.

However, is recreational therapy meeting the challenge of providing mentoring opportunities? If we are a health care profession and we are not physicians or nurses, then we are part of the family called allied health professions. In allied health, much has been written about the state of mentoring. Powers and Wheeler (1993), two dietitians, noted that in a survey by the American Dietetic Association of its members, only 28% reported that they had a mentor. Slater (1993) from the American Speech and Hearing Association, conducted a similar study and found that 36% of members surveyed have or have had mentors. Although mentoring opportunities have not been surveyed in recreational therapy, it may be safe to assume that as an allied health profession, we probably fall somewhere between the 28% having or had a mentoring experience reported by the dietitians' association survey and the 36% as reported by the speech and language association survey. Maggs (1994) notes that additional research is needed regarding the effect of mentorship on health care professions. Recreational therapy could contribute to this body of knowledge by researching our practice of mentoring.

Finally, what unique challenges does mentoring face in recreational therapy? One appears to be that most mentors are of the same sex as their mentees. Slater (1993) again cites the American Speech and Hearing Association report that 71% of male audiologists have had male mentors and over 75% of the female speech and language pathologists have had female mentors. Over 93% of speech and language pathologists are female. Various recreational therapy professional association membership studies have demonstrated that over 85% of recreational therapists are female. If we tend to migrate to our comfort zone in mentoring relationships, do we foster the production of mentees that are similar to us? Does this produce obstacles for those who may be different in race, religion or other characteristics? De Marco (1993, p. 1243) notes that "mentoring aligns itself with long established male apprenticeship professions such as philosophy, arts, letters, military, medicine, law and sports." We hear accusations in the media about the lack of minority representation in areas such as professional sports management. Through 1994 in the National Football League, 65% of the players were African American, yet there have only been two African American head coaches in the history of the league (Art Shell and Dennis Green). This is not because African Americans are not capable of managing professional sport teams. The explanation is in the reality of the workplace that thrives on mentoring for success. Current head coaches select mentees as their assistants and these mentees are the individuals that then evolve into future head coaches and who, in turn, select mentees to become their assistants. This selection of mentees is discriminatory in nature since individuals tend to select mentees that remind them of themselves. Mentoring by old white male head coaches has produced mentees that are white males, not because of some conspiracy to not allow African Americans to coach, but because, as mentors, they selected mentees that reminded them of themselves. We migrate to our comfort zones.

We must move cautiously or we will make the same mistakes so clearly demonstrated in professional sports management. The stereotype of the park and recreation department director as one of the "good old boys" could be interpreted as a sexist statement. However, working in city government requires the understanding of the complexity of politics and city politics is not taught in the classroom. City politics is a great example of what is taught during a mentoring experience. All professions tend to breed clones of themselves through the mentoring process. As a new profession, we have the opportunity to understand this process and do things to improve the mentoring opportunities for minorities. There are politics in health care as well as in city government. The new professionals will need assistance in learning the unwritten rules of practice. A question we must continue to ask ourselves is are we becoming the "good old boys or girls?"

There are numerous examples of health care professions that have recognized the discriminatory nature of mentorship and have been proactive in responding. The nursing profession has published several studies on the topic including mentoring ethnic-minority students as a strategy for retention (Alvarez & Abriam-Yago, 1993) and mentoring nursing students from disadvantaged backgrounds (Baldwin & Wold, 1993). A radiology study (Cullen, Rodak, Fitzgerald & Baker, 1993) also indicates that minority students benefit from mentoring programs. Asking if recreational therapy should become proactive and establish a mentoring process for minority students and professionals is like asking if the Pope is a Catholic. The need exists. Can recreational therapy meet this challenge?

Ernie Harwell, the Hall of Fame Detroit Tiger baseball announcer, likes to use a familiar phrase when describing a batter that takes a called third strike. He says, "He stood there like the house by the side of the road and watched that one go by." The challenge to our profession is to not stand there like the house by the side of the road while health care changes and watch our profession go by. We have a great opportunity to demonstrate our ability to meet the future needs of health care. Alternative medicine, behavioral medicine and preventative medicine all utilize interventions that we have used daily in our service delivery.

Summary

Progressing through our career transitions and understanding the role mentoring can play in the evolution of our profession can be complex. It seems clear that mentoring is an important component in the development of the recreational therapy profession. This text contains the names of the contributors to this textbook. Many of these individuals are leaders in the profession of recreational therapy. Some have been fortunate enough to not only have had opportunities to learn as mentees, but to have also served as mentors. Review the chapters. Ask yourself if the authors have the knowledge you seek. Remember, the more knowledge you seek, the more knowledge your mentor must possess. This process of mentorship is the essence of the mastering of the craft we call recreational therapy.

Learning Activities

1. Meet with a health care manager who was a recreational therapist earlier in his/her career and discuss his/her transition from clinician to manager. What obstacles did s/he overcome? What classes or continuing education has s/he pursued? Did s/he have a mentor and has s/he served as a mentor?
2. Meet with a university professor and explore his/her development as a professional. What career stages did s/he evolve through? Did s/he have a mentor in academia?
3. Meet with a recreational therapist who is currently in the clinician stage of development. Ask about his/her transition from the classroom to the clinic. Did s/he have a mentor? From whom does s/he seek knowledge at this point in his/her career?
4. Write down the knowledge you seek from a mentor. Try to identify at least three individuals who have the knowledge you seek. Is the development of a mentoring relationship possible with any of these individuals?
5. Discuss how recreational therapy can avoid the pitfalls that professional football has so clearly outlined in the discriminatory nature of the mentoring experience. What can be done to assist in limiting the unconscious discrimination inherent to mentoring?

Study Questions

1. Discuss the discriminatory nature of mentorship. Why is it unconsciously discriminatory? What can be done to change this?

2. Discuss the four career transitions noted in the chapter and the role of mentoring with each. Where do you think the greatest need for mentoring exists? At what stage?
3. Define mentorship and preceptorship. Have you had a mentor or preceptor in your life? If yes, describe the relationship.

References

Alvarez, A. & Abriam-Yago, K. (1993). Mentoring undergraduate ethnic-minority students: A strategy for retention. *Journal of Nursing Education, 32*(5), 230-232.

American Occupational Therapy Association. (1987). *Field work evaluation for the occupational therapist.* Bethesda, MD: Author.

American Therapeutic Recreation Association. (1991). *Standards for the practice of therapeutic recreation.* Hattiesburg, MS: Author.

American Therapeutic Recreation Association. (1993). *Standards for the practice of therapeutic recreation & self-assessment guide.* Hattiesburg, MS: Author.

Austin, D. R. (1974). The university can't train therapeutic recreators. *Therapeutic Recreation Journal, 8*(1), 24.

Baldwin, D. & Wold, J. (1993). Students from disadvantaged backgrounds: Satisfaction with a mentor-protégé relationship. *Journal of Nursing Education, 32*(5), 225-226.

Bezuidenhout, M. (1993). Mentoring. *Nursing RSA, 8*(7), 24-26.

Bohannon, R. W. (1985). Mentorship: A relationship important to professional development. *Physical Therapy, 65*, 920-923.

Chandler, G. E. (1993). The RN mentor program: An exercise in leadership. *Nln Publications*, (14-2511), 339-354.

Coyne, P. A. & Turpel, L. T. (1984). Peer program review: A model for implementation of standards. *Therapeutic Recreation Journal, 18*(2), 7-13.

Cullen, D. L., Rodak, B., Fitzgerald, N. & Baker, S. (1993). Minority students benefit from mentoring programs. *Radiologic Technology, 64*(4), 226-231.

Dalton, G. W., Thompson, P. H. & Price, R. L. (1977). The four stages of professional careers: A look at performance by professionals. *Organizational Dynamics, 6*, 19-42.

Davidhizar, R. (1993). Mentoring nursing students to write. *Journal of Nursing Education, 32*(6), 280-282.

DeMarco, R. (1993). Mentorship: A feminist critique of current research. *Journal of Advanced Nursing, 18*(8), 1242-1250.

Ellis, H. (1993). Teaching roles in critical care — the mentor and preceptor. *Intensive and Critical Care Nursing, 9*(3), 152-156.

Grossman, M. (1993). Mentorship: Bonds that strengthen professions [editorial]. *Canadian Journal of Nursing Research, 25*(3), 7-13.

Kouzes, J. & Posner, B. (1989). *The leadership challenge.* San Francisco: Jossey-Bass.

Kramer, M. (1978). *Reality shock: Why nurses leave nursing.* London: Mosby.

Littlefield, S. R. (1975). So, you're a recreation therapist. *Therapeutic Recreation Journal, 9*(3), 106-108.

Maggs, C. (1994). Mentorship in nursing and midwifery education: Issues for research. *Nurse Education Today, 14*(1), 22-29.

National Therapeutic Recreation Society. (1980). *Standards of practice for therapeutic recreation services.* Ashburn, VA: National Recreation and Park Association.

National Therapeutic Recreation Society. (1994). *Standards of practice for therapeutic recreation services — revised.* Ashburn, VA: National Recreation and Park Association.

Pepe, P. E., Mattox, K. L., Duke, J. H., Fisher, P. B. & Prentice, F. D. (1993). Effect of full-time, specialized physician supervision on the success of a large, urban emergency medical services system. *Critical Care Medicine, 21*(9), 1279-1286.

Powers, M. A. & Wheeler, M. L. (1993). Model for dietetics practice and research: The challenge is here, but the journey was not easy. *Journal of the American Dietetic Association, 93*(7), 755-757.

Rogers, J. C. (1986). Mentoring for career achievement and advancement. *American Journal of Occupational Therapy, 40*(2), 79-82.

Romberg, E. (1993). Mentoring the individual student: Qualities that distinguish between effective and ineffective advisors. *Journal of Dental Education, 57*(4), 287-290.

Slater, S. C. (1993). Mentoring — an enriching experience. *ASHA, 35*(5), 55.

Smith, S. H. (1976). Practitioners' evaluation of college courses, competencies and functions in therapeutic recreation. *Therapeutic Recreation Journal, 10*(4), 152-156.

Vaillant, G. E. (1977). *Adaptation to life.* Boston, MA: Little Brown and Company.

Valadez, A. M. & Lund, C. A. (1993). Mentorship: Maslow and me. *Journal of Continuing Education in Nursing, 24*(6), 259-263.

Vance, C. (1982). The mentor connection. *Journal of Nursing Administration, 4*, 7-13.

Webster's New World Compact School and Office Dictionary. (1989). New York. Simon & Schuster, Inc.

Chapter 23

Copyrights and Practice

Alice Gustafson
joan burlingame

Health care professionals need to know more about their jobs than just how to care for residents or patients. There are many laws which regulate what they do, how they do it and when they do it. One such area of law is copyright law. In the United States, federal laws provide rules related to the ownership of word combinations. This ownership is protected just as is the ownership of your car or house. Other countries, including Canada, also have laws on copyrights. The laws relating to copyright are, for the most part, straightforward. This chapter will help you understand your responsibilities (and your rights) when you want to use something written by someone else or when you want to protect something that you wrote.

What is a Copyright?

A copyright is a legally protected right that an author has which allows him/her to control who makes copies of his/her written, spoken or video taped statements. The person who wants to exercise this right must meet two primary requirements with his/her work:

1. The statements must be original to the author. While ideas cannot be copyrighted, the combination of words used to describe the ideas or statements must be expressed in the author's own words and should be noticeably different from the ones someone else used.
2. The statements must be contained in a "tangible medium." A tangible medium is any way of saving word combinations like writing, typing, word processing, audio taping, video taping or other means of sharing statements with multiple people.

It is recommended *but not required* that an author place a copyright notice on his/her work. If the author's statements meet the two criteria listed above, then the material is copyrighted whether or not the work contains a copyright notice.

People who create original works are entitled to certain rights of ownership. Generally referred to as copyrights, these rights are controlled by the creator(s) and include the following:

1. the right to copy the work;
2. the right to distribute copies of the work to others;
3. the right to prepare "derivative works" based on the original work; and
4. the right to perform and display the work in public.

Except in a few, very limited situations, no one may take someone else's copyrighted work and copy it, give it to anyone else, combine it with other material to create a new work or use the material in public (e.g., to give a speech) without prior approval of the individual who owns the copyright. (In the same sense, someone is not allowed to come and use your house to eat, shower and sleep without your permission. Without permission, the law is clearly broken and the house owner has the right to stop the person violating his/her right to determine the use of his/her house.)

Copyright laws do not differ from state to state; they are a federal law and apply equally anywhere within the United States and its protectorates. The copyright laws which are currently applied in the United States underwent significant changes in the late 1970's.

What Can Be Copyrighted?

While this chapter addresses the laws concerning an author's right to protect his/her written work, copyright law actually applies to a much broader group of original works. Categories of protected works include literary, musical, dramatic and a number of others. Literary works are those expressed in words, numbers or other verbal or numerical symbols. It doesn't matter how the literary work is presented. Common forms of literary works include books, manuscripts, periodicals, disks, tapes, films and material found on the Internet. Literary works may also include assessment and other types of medical forms and testing tools.

The copyrighted work does not have to be of any great length to be able to be protected. Material of almost any length can be subject to copyright protection. Thus, excerpts from copyrighted material, such as quotes, appendices and chapter summaries, are also protected.

Copyright law applies to materials on the Internet. Think of the Internet as just another form of publication. If it would be a copyright violation to copy and distribute an article if you found it in a magazine, it would also be a copyright violation to copy and distribute the same article if you found it on the Internet. As with other types of publications, copyright notice is not required on the Internet to maintain copyright protection.

This means that purchasing information on the Internet or downloading information or images from a web site does not give any automatic right to use that material for your own purposes. If your use would be a "fair use," there is no copyright infringement. If your use would not be "fair use" (as described later in the chapter), however, you may need permission to incorporate the material into your work. Since failure to find out if permission is needed is not a defense to a claim for copyright infringement, check with the source of the material first to determine if you need further permission to use it.

Testing tools, assessment tools and forms that the therapist uses may be copyrighted. In most cases the therapist must buy a copy of the form for each assessment that s/he gives. S/he may not make additional copies of blank forms. Most owners of copyrights realize that, by law, patients are allowed to have copies made of the material in their charts to share with their other health care providers. Most owners of the copyrights in those forms will allow the therapist to make copies of only those tools or forms which are already filled out for use in additional charts. If you are unsure whether you can make a copy, call the owner of the copyright.

What is Not Copyrightable?

Copyright protection is not available for any idea, procedure, concept, system, process, method of operation, principle or discovery. Rather, it is the expression of the underlying idea, procedure, concept, etc. that is protected. See Table 23.1 for a summary of what is and what is not copyrightable.

Table 23.1: **What is Copyrightable?**

Not Copyrightable	Copyrightable
• an idea	• literary works
• a procedure	• musical works
• a concept	• dramatic works
• a system	• charts
• a process	• drawings
• a method of operation	• photographs
• a principle	• diagrams
• a discovery	• models

You may develop a new treatment program which increases your patient's response to the environment. The program that you develop would not be protected under copyright law, but the way that you wrote up the program, including the specific combinations of words in your policy and procedure would be protected.

Copyrights of Material
Which Uses Other People's Work

In some cases an author may legally claim copyright in something which contains pieces of material found in another person's work. There are two categories of this type of copyright: *derivative works* and *compilation works*.

A derivative work is based on one or more preexisting works, but the preexisting material is edited, recast, condensed or similarly transformed to such an extent that it becomes a new work. If the preexisting work is copyrighted, the owner must first give permission for creation of a derivative work.

At times an author may want to use the "raw" data, or the basic information that another person used to write about a given topic. An example might be the use of information from the OBRA regulations to develop an intake assessment for patients. The intake assessments developed by therapists in two different facilities may be remarkably similar. The information to develop the assessments was taken from the same underlying material (OBRA Regulations). The therapists in each case used basic information on categories from the same source to develop their activity assessments and created nearly identical intake assessments. As long as the similarity in the two forms came because they used the same underlying material and not because one copied the other's work, they would not be violating each other's copyright.

A compilation is a work formed by the collection and assembly of preexisting materials or data that were selected, arranged or coordinated in such a way that the result amounts to an original work. A state professional organization may want to publish a book on treatment ideas as a fund raiser. By obtaining permission from each therapist submitting treatment ideas and then editing and formatting the activities so that they can be made into one publication, the state organization may claim a copyright in the new work (book). The original author of each written treatment idea is able to retain his/her copyright ownership in his/her original work. Such a book would be an example of a compilation work.

Copyright protection is available for compilations and derivative works which contain preexisting copyrighted material, but only if the preexisting material is being used lawfully (with permission or under one of the exemptions discussed below). The creator of the compilation or derivative work is also only entitled to copyright protection for his/her own contributions to the new work.

The owner of the copyright in the preexisting material may still retain his/her copyright.

Limitations on Copyrights

While the creator of a copyrighted work does have extensive rights, guaranteed by federal law, to protect his/her work, there are some limitations to the owner's exclusive rights.

A copyright owner is not entitled to stop all use of his/her work. For example, a library or archive open to the general public may reproduce and distribute one copy of a copyrighted book without permission, so long as it is done for a noncommercial purpose and the copyright notice is included in the reproduction. This limitation to the owner's exclusive right is very specific and seldom applies to health care settings. (Most medical and departmental libraries are open only to staff, not to the general public.)

In very limited cases, a "fair use" exclusion may apply. A fair use is recognized by copyright law as any use that is "insignificant" enough that the copyright owner should not be able to stop the use (and is insignificant enough that the copyright owner would probably not be upset by the limited use of his/her work). Unlike the fairly clear ability of a public library or archive being able to make one copy without permission, the fair use laws are quite complicated, almost never giving a straightforward answer.

The federal law gives examples of some of the possible cases where a fair use of copyrighted material may be used without the owner's prior permission. These include the use of someone else's material when you are quoting a piece of the work for a critical review; when you are quoting a piece of the work to then comment on that material; when you are using the material as part of a news report; and when you are including limited parts of the work for scholarship and research.

Copying Material for Teaching Purposes

In unique situations copyrighted material may be copied for teaching purposes. Very specific guidelines have been developed concerning making multiple copies of copyrighted material without permission for classroom use. Whether a specific instance of copying is lawful may depend upon the amount copied from a particular work, the time pressures involved (whether there was time to seek permission in advance — there usually is for college classes) and how many other instances of multiple copying have occurred during the same class. In any event, only one copy may be made per student and each copy must include a notice of copyright.

Considerations for Fair Use of Someone Else's Work

The federal laws give us some guidelines to follow when trying to decide if a use could be considered a fair use. The statute says that the following factors should be considered when deciding if something is a fair use:

1. the purpose and character of the use, including whether it is of a commercial nature or for nonprofit educational purposes;
2. the nature of the copyrighted work;
3. the amount and importance of the portion used in relationship to the copyrighted work as a whole; and
4. the effect of the use upon the potential market for or value of the copyrighted work.

Determining whether there is a fair use in a particular situation can be difficult, since the rules are not straightforward and their application to specific facts not usually obvious. The following two common sense considerations might help focus the decision of whether you need to contact the copyright holder for permission prior to using the material:

1. If you would object if another person did the same thing to you, there may be a copyright infringement problem.
2. If a copyrighted work is being used without permission in order to save money or time (too expensive to pay a license fee or "buy" the product, too time-consuming to track down the author, etc.), it is likely to be a copyright infringement to use the work.

Because these exceptions to the copyright laws are so complex, and because the fines are so significant, you should consult with your lawyer before making any copies under the "fair use" provisions.

Liability for Copyright Infringement

Civil liability for copyright infringement can include the actual damages caused to the copyright owner (e.g., you made 30 copies of a chapter from a book, the book cost $40, the potential loss of sales would be $1,200), plus any profits that you might have gotten from making the copies (e.g., selling the copies for $5.00 each — the amount it cost you to make the copies and the amount you collected which would be $150). If the copyrighted material had been formally registered with the government before you made the copies, an additional payment of up to $100,000 may be ordered by the court. The lawyer's fees that the copyright owner incurred fighting for his/her ownership right may also be passed on to you. It is potentially very expensive to violate some-one's copyright!

Who is the Owner of a Copyright?

Generally, the creator of the work owns the copyright in that work and is the person (or entity, e.g., a company) from whom permission must be obtained before any of the copyrighted material may be used.

When a work is prepared by an employee as part of his or her employment, the legal author of the work is considered to be the company or group that the employee is working for. This is called a *work for hire*. Unless agreed otherwise in writing, the employer in that situation owns the copyright in the work created by the employee. If you write a manual for the orientation and supervision of therapy assistants at work, your facility is the owner of the copyright.

Frequently therapists assume that it is an acceptable practice to share mate-rial which they have developed at work (works for hire) with individuals outside of the facility. Unless the therapist has an agreement in writing that s/he will own the copyright to his/her work, s/he does not have the legal authority to share the material (release the copyright) to assessments, protocols, policies and procedures or other material developed by him/her while at work.

Works made by special order or commission may be owned by the party giving the order or commission or by the creator, depending on the type of work involved and the written agreements between the parties. Consultants may be wise to stipulate in their contract with facilities that the copyright in any work that they write to be used by the facility remains with the consultant. Failure to address copyright ownership in advance in writing in the case of a special order or commission can have unintended (and unhappy) results for the therapist.

Joint Ownership of Copyrights

More than one person or company may jointly own a copyright in a work. This usually happens when the authors intended that their contributions to a particular work be merged into interdependent or inseparable parts of a whole.

A collective work is a work containing a number of contributions, each of which constitutes a separate and independent original work in itself. Each con-tributor retains the copyright in his or her individual contribution, separately from the copyright in the whole. The assembler of the individual contributions is the owner of the copyright in the whole, but as such is essentially only entitled to reproduce, distribute and revise the collective work.

Claiming Copyright

There are two ways to claim a copyright on an original work. One is to identify on the work that you are claiming your rights to restrict the copying of the material by others. You may also formally register the copyright with the federal government.

Although no longer required in all instances, a copyright notice should be placed on all works in which copyright is claimed. The purpose of such a notice is to advise others that the material is considered to be subject to copyright and that the copyright owner intends to enforce his/her exclusive rights. This notice also helps facilitate contact by others seeking permission to use all or part of the copyrighted material.

The notice should include the name of the owner, the year of the first publication of the work and the word "copyright" or the symbol "©". The notice should be displayed in a place where it will be easily seen.

Under the federal law that went into effect in 1978, a copyright exists from the moment an original work is created. It is therefore not necessary to register a copyright in order to have the exclusive rights of a copyright owner.

To formally register a copyright in a literary work you must obtain FORM TX from the United States Copyright Office. After completing the form, the owner of the copyright sends it back to the Copyright Office with a check for the appropriate amount and a copy of the work to be copyrighted. The address for the United States Copyright Office is Register of Copyrights, Library of Congress, Washington, DC 20559-6000. You can obtain more information on copyright registration and applications by calling the Copyright Office at (202) 707-3000.

The owner of a copyright, whether it is formally registered or not, still has legal rights to the copyrighted work. In the event of copyright litigation, however, there are certain advantages to the copyright owner if the copyright was registered before the infringement occurred. In most situations, registration is required before the litigation can actually be started. Since copyright registration is a relatively simple and inexpensive process, it should be considered even if the possibility of infringement seems remote.

Litigation, or going to court, over violating someone's copyright can be expensive. Civil liability for copyright infringement can include actual damages caused to the copyright owner plus any profits from the infringement. If the copyright is registered before the infringement, damages of up to $100,000 and the lawyer's fees of the copyright owner may be what you are required to pay the owner of the copyright. In addition, a court can order the allegedly infringing items to be impounded at any time while the lawsuit is pending, and after the lawsuit is concluded, may order any infringing items to be destroyed. Copyright infringement is also a criminal offense, punishable by fines and incarceration.

Duration of a Copyright

The copyright in a work created on or after January 1, 1978 (the effective date of the last major revision of the federal copyright law) begins when the work is created and continues for the life of the author (or the surviving author in the case of a joint work) plus fifty years. The copyrights in works made for hire and in pseudonymous and anonymous works endure for the shorter of two periods, 100 years after the work is created or 75 years after the work is first published.

Copyrights in works created before January 1, 1978 are governed by a number of different aspects of copyright law. If you want to use material from before this time period you may want to contact a lawyer who specializes in copyright law, or a copyright search firm to determine the status of the material. Direct contact with the author may also be an option.

Temporary or Permanent Transfer of a Copyright

The owner of a copyright has many options of temporarily or permanently, partially or fully giving another person the right to make copies. The three most common types of transfer that the therapist may experience are (1) a one time use permission, (2) a restricted "license" and (3) outright transfer.

"One time use permission" is frequently given when someone wants to include already copyrighted material into another, larger publication. The professional may submit an article to a newsletter but want to retain his/her copyright ownership in what was written. In this case the author would grant the newsletter a one time permission to make many copies of the work, but each copy must be contained within that issue of the newsletter (e.g., if the newsletter goes out to 2,000 people, the newsletter is given a one time use permission to make 2,000 copies of the copyrighted material). This chapter was published with a one time use permission.

It is becoming more and more common to see "licenses" assigned to individuals. This license may permit the purchaser of the product to use the copyrighted material for a predetermined number of times or may allow that purchaser unlimited usage. One example of this is the software that you bought for your computer. Generally you are "licensed" to load the software onto only one machine. Allowing others to make copies of your purchased software is a violation of your license and a violation of the copyright law.

In health care you will also find that some books allow the purchaser of the copyrighted material to make unlimited copies of the forms in the book. This type of license does not allow you to share those forms with another facility or another therapist who works outside of your facility. That would, again, be a violation of copyright. If you are wondering if the book you bought allows you to make copies, you can usually find the answer on one of the first pages inside the cover of the book. There you will find a copyright notice and a paragraph which explains any rights to copy that the purchaser may have.

At times the owner of a copyright may do an "outright transfer" and give all rights to another person or company. In this case the owner of the copyright gives up his/her rights to control the use of the material unless some exceptions are noted in writing.

The fees, if any, to be paid for a copyright assignment or license must be negotiated between the copyright owner and the person who wants to temporarily or permanently obtain the right to use and copy the material. Any assignment of copyright should be in writing; should indicate what, if any, payments will be made and should be signed by everyone involved.

Copyright law helps protect the ownership rights of authors. Respecting the rights of authors and making sure that they receive fair payment for the works they produce will encourage the development of quality written material. Quality written materials are one of the factors which will increase the credibility of recreational therapists among other health care professions and ensure continued advances in the field.

Patents Are Different than Copyrights

A patent is a government grant to an inventor of a device that embodies a newly discovered idea or principle. The inventor applies for a patent and if it is granted, the inventor is entitled to exclusive rights to use, make and sell the invention for 17 years. The right of exclusive use is not generally available to copyright owners, who instead control access to their work through control of copying and distribution. Nor is copyright protection preserved for works based only on newly discovered ideas.

A "design patent" can be obtained to protect the appearance of a manufactured object if its design is unique, original and ornamental. Design patents offer protection against duplication and last for 14 years. Some designs (such as a game board) may be both copyrightable and eligible for a design patent.

Learning Activities

1. Compare the copyright statements of textbooks with protocol or treatment books to see which ones allow copying of material in the book and what limits are put on copying.

2. Imagine that you are a director of a new recreational therapy department. Write policies and procedures regarding the issues of what may be copied and who owns the copyright of material produced by facility employees.
3. The proper way to make a copy of an article for a university resource file is to include a copy of the page with the copyright notice with the copy of the article. Go through your resource file and find an article which is missing this information. Locate a copy of the copyright page and attach it to the article.

Study Questions

1. What is a copyright? What are the legally protected rights that an author has? What are the criteria to determine if someone can claim a copyright?
2. Not everything is copyrightable. What is not copyrightable?
3. When is making a copy of copyrighted material (without prior consent) permitted? Would fair use allow making and handing out multiple copies of a chapter for a university course or multiple copies of material for patient education?
4. What are the differences between derivative, compilation and collective works? If you want to use a diagram found in a compilation work, do you contact the copyright owner of the compilation work or the copyright owner of the specific section which contained the diagram?
5. In what situations may you not claim copyright in an original document you created? In what situation does your employer not own the copyright in anything you write?
6. What are the ways to transfer copyright ownership? If you get permission (or a license) to make copies of a treatment protocol for use within your facility, is it legal and ethical for you to give a visiting therapist a copy for use in his/her facility? As an employee of the recreational therapy department, do you have the legal right to give that visiting therapist permission to use an intake assessment you developed at work?

Issues of Outside Agencies

Chapter 24

Reimbursement

Thomas K. Skalko

We must convince by reason, not prescribe by tradition.
— Cyprian

Over the past several years, a number of subjects have repeatedly emerged as critical issues in the field. Among those items considered to be acute is the issue of reimbursement for the delivery of recreational therapy services. Surveys of professionals indicate that third-party reimbursement repeatedly ranks in the top ten concerns facing our profession (Grote, 1990; Skalko, 1992). The issue of reimbursement for the delivery of recreational therapy as an active treatment service has been pervasive within the literature and may continue to be among the profession's salient challenges for years to come (Esneault, Malkin & Sellers, 1992; Malkin & Skalko, 1992; Reitter, 1984, 1989; Russoniello, 1992; Skalko & Malkin, 1992; Teaff & Van Hyning, 1988a, 1988b; West, 1984). It is critical, therefore, that the emerging entry level professional have an understanding of health care financing and the role of third-party reimbursement in the fiscal management of recreational therapy services (Skalko & Malkin, 1992). Although health care reform will alter existing reimbursement practices, knowledge of reimbursement practices will continue to be essential.

In order to establish a foundation from which to understand the role of third-party reimbursement to the profession, a basic understanding of health care financing and reimbursement for services is needed. This chapter will provide an overview of reimbursement and the role of reimbursement in health care financing. In addition, this chapter will include a brief overview of the status of third-party reimbursement for the provision of recreational therapy services as an active treatment and basic guidelines on reimbursement for future consideration.

The mid 1990's included a major initiative in health care reform by President William J. Clinton. President Clinton introduced a plan that would have made profound changes in the way health care is provided and financed in the future. This plan was revised by several committees of the United States' 103rd Congress and legislative acts were forwarded for consideration. Although defeated by the 103rd Congress, the subsequent compromise legislation that has since been passed by the United States Congress has increased the application of managed care and has significantly impacted health care with regard to the financing of health care services including recreational therapy services. Health care reform, however, will continue for years to come and recreational therapy professionals will need to continue to be active in the legislative process.

Basics of Health Care Financing

Before the emerging professional can comprehend third-party reimbursement, a basic knowledge of health care financing is useful. It is through an understanding of financing that the implications of third-party reimbursement become evident.

To make the concept of health care financing less elusive and complicated, it may be useful to examine the evolution of health care financing. Initially, costs of health care were the responsibility of the individual. Each person or family was responsible for medical costs incurred and made arrangements with the family physician for payment either through currency or barter. This system was replaced by the emergence of health care financing from both private sector (insurance companies) and government supported sources. The passage of the Social Security Act of 1935, the subsequent amendments, and the expansion of private insurance carriers each played a role in evolution of today's system.

The Social Security Act Amendments of 1965 (PL 89-97) established a structure for health care financing where hospitals were reimbursed for "reasonable costs" incurred in the treatment of the patient. This system is referred to as "retrospective cost-based reimbursement." Per diem reimbursement was provided for "routine services" such as meals, nursing and housekeeping and additional reimbursements were made for "ancillary services" such as diagnostic services and medically necessary treatment ordered by a physician. Since hospitals were reimbursed at a reasonable rate for services provided, hospitals were reinforced financially for delivering more services (Reitter, 1989). As a result, health care costs increased dramatically in the decades of the 1960's and the 1970's.

In 1983, the Social Security Act Amendments (PL 98-21) changed Medicare reimbursement from a retrospective to a prospective payment system (PPS). The prospective payment system reimbursed health care costs based on diagnostic related groups (DRGs). Thus payment for medical costs were reimbursed based upon the individual's primary diagnosis. The incentive became one of treating the patient for less than the designated DRG payment. Hospital administrators began focusing on reduced costs, reduced length of stay, cost-containment, cost-effective services and efficiency (Reitter, 1984). A criticism of this system was the perception that quality patient care became less of a priority.

The prospective payment system gave incentive to third-party carriers to contract with health care systems to receive discounted medical services. The use of preferred provider organizations (PPO) and health maintenance organizations (HMO) further defined what services were reimbursable. Ultimately, hospitals and other health care professionals have again been required to demonstrate efficient, effective, outcome-oriented services in order to receive reimbursement for services rendered.

The managed care explosion currently sweeping the system will further promote the provision of the most economical yet effective set of services for the treatment of specific diagnostic categories. Such an approach allows agencies to determine the most appropriate and cost-effective approaches to meet the needs of the individual client. Recreational therapy services have a role in such a system.

Speculation on the future predicts a capitated system for financing. Hospitals and health care provider networks will receive pre-payment for services by purchasing groups (employers or groups of employers) to enroll their employees for health care services. The health care provider will then be responsible for ensuring that the enrollee receives a guaranteed range of benefits or services. In such a system, many of the services currently covered as a reimbursable service will be a standard benefit and not reimbursed as a separate treatment service and only the most cost-efficient providers will survive (Zimmerman & Skalko, 1994). See Table 24.1 for a timeline of health care financing.

Health Care in the 1990's and the Future

The 1990's have witnessed an increase in the implementation of managed care practices in health care and the initiation of a capitated system for health care financing. In this system of health care, the consumers incurs up-front premium costs and the provider assumes the risk of being in a position to supply the needed health care services. The system offers basic health care options but the full-service menus are more limited. In addition, basic health care services are delivered by a more restrictive listing of pre-designated, preferred providers. Insurance carriers identify health care "gate keepers" to the system for access to more costly specialized services and the consumer is required to see the designated provider for that particular need. The managed care organization determines what services persons are entitled to access and restricts experimental

Table 24.1: **History of Health Care Financing**

Early 1900's
- Out-of-pocket expense.

Social Security Act of 1935
- Offered federal support for medical costs.

Late 1930's and early 1940's
- Blue Cross emerged as a private sector carrier.

Social Security Amendments of 1965 (PL 89-97)
- Enacted the Medicare program providing coverage for reasonable medical costs: per diem rates including routine charges, rates for room, board, housekeeping, etc. and ancillary service charges.

Social Security Amendments of 1972 (PL 92-603)
- Established Professional Standards Review Organizations (PSRO) to promote effective, efficient and economical use of medical services of proper quality.

Tax Equity and Fiscal Responsibility Act of 1982 (TEFRA) (PL 97-248)
- Changed health care reimbursement for services. A per case system replaced the per diem system. Case-mix was incorporated into the payment system. Rate of increase in reimbursable Medicare costs per case was limited. Peer Review Organizations (PROs) replaced PSROs and changed the focus from provider services to cost containment.

Social Security Amendments of 1983 (PL 98-21)
- Retrospective system was replaced by the prospective payment system. Pre-fixed rates were paid based on diagnostic related groups (DRGs). The incentives for hospitals changed from services provided to cost containment and efficient operations. If costs were less than the DRG allotment, the hospital made money. If costs ran over, the hospital lost revenue or had to secure the over-run from the consumer. Focus was on reduced length of stay and cost containment. Private insurance carriers adopted PPS.

Health Care in the Future
- Implementation of managed care practices.
- Initiation of a capitated system for health care financing.

approaches. For persons with chronic disabilities, this managed health care approach has resulted in greater hardship since access to specialists is restricted.

Regardless of the system implemented, hospitals must compete for the health care dollar and must strive to provide the highest quality of care to the consumer at the most reasonable cost. Consumer satisfaction, in turn, is paramount and drives health care business practices. Hospitals have adopted corporate business procedures, realized the impact of competitors and have concentrated on quality product line services.

Simply put, hospitals are businesses. Each receives a budget from a combination of sources. Governmentally sponsored hospitals such as state hospitals, Veteran's Administration Medical Centers, university hospitals and county hospitals each receive a significant percentage of funding from governmental budget allocations. In addition, governmentally sponsored hospitals must generate additional revenue from various sources. Each system will have different rules and regulations governing sources of revenues. Non-governmental agencies support operations in a similar manner but must rely much more heavily on their ability to compete for a limited number of clientele while generating revenue for services rendered. Regardless of the type of hospital, services delivered must be cost-effective and revenue producing from a designated source whether that be the individual consumer or a third-party source (insurance company, Medicare/Medicaid, etc.). Sources of revenue for most health care agencies are presented in Figure 24.1.

Reimbursement from Public and Private Insurance Companies

Fund Raising and Foundation Support

Direct Payment for Services

Government Budget Allocation

Other (special projects, donations, research, etc.)

Grants (governmental and private sector)

Reimbursement for Medicare and Medicaid

Figure 24.1: **Sources of Revenue for Most Health Care Agencies**

Financing in Recreational Therapy

Financing for recreational therapy departments will also come from different sources. Typically, the recreational therapy department will receive operational support as either a "routine service" (as part of the per diem charges) or as an "ancillary service" (reimbursed as a diagnostic or treatment service). As a routine service, recreational therapy services are considered a customary service similar to nursing. The department is supported as a cost center and justified based upon the benefits derived by the provision of services to the patient. In some systems, such as state hospitals, recreational therapy services are generally considered customary services for all clients of the hospital and include treatment as well as patient recreation services.

With the expanded pressure to contribute to the revenue base of the hospital, recreational therapy departments are increasingly expected to pursue reimbursement as an ancillary service. This push demands that practitioners provide quality treatment services, demonstrate the efficacy of services offered through patient progress and outcomes and receive reimbursement for services rendered. By pursuing reimbursement as an ancillary service, recreational therapy departments can contribute to the financial stability of the hospital by operating as a revenue center rather than a cost center. As a revenue center, the recreational therapy department is in a better position to enhance or compete for the allocation of resources. Note that although the trend today is to move to capitated practices, the current system continues to emphasize reimbursement for ancillary services.

Reimbursement in Recreational Therapy

Third-party reimbursement will continue to be among the issues that command the attention of the profession. Third-party reimbursement (or simply reimbursement) within the health care arena can be viewed as *payment by another agency for the delivery of active treatment services*. To be considered as active treatment, the service must be

1. furnished under an individualized plan of treatment or diagnosis;
2. considered a reasonable and necessary service expected to improve the patient's condition or required for diagnostic purposes; and
3. supervised and monitored by a physician (Reitter, 1984).

Therefore, the recreational therapy department must provide an array of services that constitute active treatment for the individual health care consumer. Typically such services as individual or group treatment programs for cognitive or affective stimulation, gross and fine motor development or social skills development, among others, may constitute active treatment. These services must be indicated in the individual's treatment plan, be expected to improve the patient's condition and be supervised and monitored by a physician. Recreational therapy departments must evaluate programs and services to ensure that a sensible balance of services delivered meet the criteria for active treatment.

It is important to note that the delivery of diversional recreation services or leisure outings do not constitute active treatment. Although they may be healthy activities for the consumer, activities that are strictly of a recreational or leisure nature are an end in themselves and are not considered necessary, active treatment services. Leisure activities may produce positive outcomes but do not withstand the test to demonstrate that the activity is medically necessary for the consumer. In addition, it is difficult to illustrate resource and outcome accountability through diversional recreation and leisure activities. Table 24.2 lists the major reimbursement issues for recreational therapy.

The Reimbursement Process in Recreational Therapy

When active treatment services are provided to meet the needs of the health care consumer, the agency may forward a claim (or bill) to a third-party carrier (e.g., commercial insurance company, Medicare or Medicaid, health maintenance organization) for the reimbursement of the costs of providing the service. This claim is reviewed and processed by an insurance adjuster and a determination is made as to whether the services are covered under the particular policy or plan. The adjuster may approve all or part of the charges as active treatment, or may deny the claim as being unnecessary or not covered under the particular plan or benefits package.

The provision of functional social skills training provided by a qualified recreational therapist (i.e., Certified Therapeutic Recreation Specialist), for instance, may be submitted to a carrier for reimbursement as a component of active treatment for the patient. The service is provided based upon an order from the physician, an assessment of the health care consumer's needs and the development of an individualized treatment plan. The service must meet the criteria for active treatment services. If the service delivered does not meet the criteria, it may be denied for reimbursement. For instance, some agencies may submit community outings as an aspect of treatment. If the outings cannot be justified as necessary and reasonable for the treatment of the patient's condition and designed to produce active treatment outcomes, the adjustor may deny the request

Table 24.2: **Third Party Reimbursement Issues in Recreational Therapy**

- Too often recreational therapy is seen as diversionary activity.
- Recreational therapy must begin to justify services and expenditures and demonstrate efficacy.
- Recreational therapy must move from "routine service" classifications to an ancillary service cost code.
- The field must establish a consistent definition for recreational therapy services.
- A standardized curricula responsive to health care competencies must be established.
- The field must increase interactions with third-party carriers.
- Coding for services must follow the established categories for impairment or disability; new codes should be developed along these lines.

for reimbursement. Therefore, involvement in a community bowling outing for the patient may very well be viewed as an unnecessary service claim.

With the changing health care market, the profession is left with the responsibility to demonstrate its worth. For recreational therapy to demonstrate its value at least the following must be accomplished:

- Secure administrative support for third party reimbursement for recreational therapy services.
- Determine cost of department per case, DRG or critical pathway.
- Train recreational therapy staff in techniques to reduce length of stay (inpatient, outpatient or day treatment).
- Gear patient evaluations to length of stay problem areas.
- Be involved in effective treatment and discharge planning for inpatient stays, outpatient and day treatment.
- Concentrate on DRGs or critical pathways where recreational therapy is successful.
- Work with physicians to demonstrate the efficacy of recreational therapy services.
- Improve management skills of recreational therapy directors.
- Ensure that accurate documentation standards are in place and are followed by all recreational therapy staff.
- Establish fee schedules and standardized codes for itemized billing of services.
- Streamline paperwork (or computer input) to increase patient contact hours.
- Communicate departmental successes with administration.
- Engage in research to demonstrate the efficacy of recreational therapy services at your agency.

The issue of reimbursement for services is central to the fiscal stability of the allied health treatment modalities. The leadership of a progressive recreational therapy department must continuously evaluate the appropriateness of pursuing separate reimbursement as an ancillary service or ensuring their status as a routine and customary service covered under daily room rates or per diem charges. See Table 24.3 for a comparison of the two methods of paying for recreational therapy services. Each method has both advantages and disadvantages. The current debate regarding health care financing and reform, however, will set the ground-rules for future health care reimbursement practices. In the existing system and in the foreseeable future, the need will continue to exist for recreational therapy services to address the issue of third-party reimbursement.

Table 24.3: **Room and Board Charges vs. Ancillary Service**

Recreational Therapy Under Room and Board	Recreational Therapy as an Ancillary Service
Recreational therapy is provided as a customary service such as room, board, nursing, etc.	Recreational therapy is promoted as necessary treatment service to address impairment and disability.
Recreational therapy may not need to be involved in as rigorous a level of documentation, billing and accounting. In turn, administrative costs are reduced for billing. At the same time, the recreational therapy department is a cost center not a revenue center for the agency.	Recreational therapy must conform to the rigors of all treatment modalities.
Recreational therapy services can combine treatment and recreational services. The danger exists, however, of being relegated to a diversional role.	Recreational therapy can determine the level of fiscal contribution to the agency. The recreational therapy service can demonstrate its role as a revenue vs. cost center.
Recreational therapy services are more readily available to all patients.	Recreational therapy services will focus on the treatment aspect of service delivery. Services must, however, be accountable for producing patient treatment outcomes.

Current Status and Future Directions

The field has embarked on a series of efforts to secure third-party reimbursement since the late 1970's. These efforts have resulted in mixed successes and shortfalls. The early efforts were led by members of the National Therapeutic Recreation Society (NTRS) and have been continued by the leadership of the American Therapeutic Recreation Association (ATRA) into the 1990's. Most of the efforts have revolved around survey formats to identify the status of securing reimbursement in the field. In 1982, NTRS, in conjunction with North Carolina Memorial Hospital, implemented a survey to determine the state of third-party reimbursement in therapeutic recreation. Of the respondents, 21% indicated that they received third-party reimbursement for therapeutic recreation services. This initial effort was followed by efforts by ATRA (Hutchinson-Troyer, 1987; Malkin & Skalko, 1992) and by an effort by Teaff and Van Hyning (1988b). Reimbursement for services were reported for recreational therapy or therapeutic recreation as an ancillary service and on a per diem basis. The surveys, however, also identified questions to be addressed.

Areas for consideration with regard to third-party reimbursement for recreational therapy services include:

1. The need to evaluate the inclusion of recreational therapy as an ancillary service versus inclusion in overhead, room and board or daily charges;
2. The practice of billing for recreational therapy services under the codes of other allied health disciplines such as occupational therapy or physical therapy should not be continued;
3. Recreational therapy practitioners and administrators should become more knowledgeable of third-party reimbursement and health care financing;
4. Recreational therapy services must establish well-founded rates for services based upon documented costs, regional differences, diagnostic categories and specific procedure;
5. The need exists to begin to establish of a set of standardized services as active treatment protocols for reimbursement (Skalko & Malkin, 1992); and
6. Recreational therapy administrators and practitioners need to understand the coding and billing process for treatment services in order to better address the reimbursement issue.

Although progress has been made, continued research and concerted efforts are needed. Both the American Therapeutic Recreation Association and the National Therapeutic Recreation Society continue to generate a database to update knowledge regarding the status of reimbursement practices in recreational therapy. Historically, however, the field has faced a number of barriers that have thwarted progress in securing third-party reimbursement. It is noteworthy that these obstacles are consistent with those of all evolving professions. Overcoming these barriers will have a profound impact on our ability to secure reimbursement as an active treatment service.

Hutchinson-Troyer and Gillespie (1991) listed ten steps for securing third-party reimbursement in recreational therapy:

1. Secure administrative support.
2. Open discussions with primary third-party carriers.
3. Develop fee structure/charge slips.
4. Establish program treatment protocols.
5. Incorporate physician's orders into system.
6. Establish evaluation process and documentation.
7. Formalize treatment planning and goal setting.
8. Discharge summary.
9. Answer denials.

10. Periodic review of reimbursement or fiscal responsibility of department manager.

Reimbursement Related Barriers

Recreational therapy as a profession has come a long ways in the last decade toward eliminating barriers to reimbursement. Nonetheless, five barriers remain which we will need to address in the coming decade. These five barriers are (1) lack of a unified philosophy, (2) lack of the application of our standards into everyday practice, (3) inconsistency in college curriculum, (4) lack of public awareness of recreational therapy and (5) fast-paced change within health care itself.

Unified Philosophy

The field has continuously debated the issue of whether we are a treatment modality (recreational therapy) or a recreation service (recreation for all). Efforts to adopt philosophies and definitions that attempt to embrace the diversity of the field of therapeutic recreation to include treatment (recreational therapy), leisure education and recreation services for persons with disabilities confuse outside parties. The adoption of the philosophical position by the National Therapeutic Recreation Society in 1982 struck a compromise in philosophies for the field while at the same time obscuring the primary mission of therapeutic recreation (recreational therapy) as an allied health care discipline. (The newly adopted definition continues to embrace a similar concept focusing on independent leisure functioning).

The Recreation Service Model (RSM) presented in this book (burlingame, 1998) provides an answer to these concerns. There are, indeed, different levels and types of service provided by people in the field. Services provided in the first four levels of the RSM (disease, impairment, disability and handicap levels) are the true clinical services and may be reimbursable. Services in levels five through seven (leisure education, organized recreation and leisure activities) are generally not considered reimbursable. Residential facilities such as nursing homes, intermediate care facilities for the mentally retarded and long term psychiatric facilities tend to consider all seven levels as part of a per diem (roomrate) charge, recognizing that the clients need both the therapeutic intervention required to maintain or improve health and the normalization of recreation and leisure activities.

The need exists to delineate the primary mission for recreational therapy to that of treatment and to embrace terminology, professional preparation and practices consistent with that mission. When the terminology and practices are compatible with the health care environment, the field will resolve the issues of reimbursement as a necessary treatment service.

Unified Standards of Practice

In 1980, the National Therapeutic Recreation Society published *Standards of Practice for Therapeutic Recreation Service*. These standards of practice were marginally integrated into practice over the decade of the 1980's. NTRS's document was revised in 1995 as *Standards of Practice for Therapeutic Recreation Services and Annotated Bibliography*. In 1991, the American Therapeutic Recreation Association published a similar document entitled *Standards for the Practice of Therapeutic Recreation* (reissued in 1993 as *Standards for the Practice of Therapeutic Recreation & Self Assessment Guide*). As with NTRS's documents, its widespread implementation has not occurred. To date, the field has not fully implemented a document on standards of practice. Such inaction impairs our ability to pursue third-party reimbursement based upon the delivery of consistent, quality services and standards of care.

Practices in Professional Preparation

Despite the existence of an educational accreditation program, appropriate accreditation standards for recreational therapy professional preparation continue to be elusive. The National Recreation and Park Association (NRPA) in conjunction with the American Association for Leisure and Recreation (AALR) implemented an accreditation program for recreation and park curricula with standards to address therapeutic recreation. The accreditation program, although perhaps a first step, has been questioned by practitioner surveys (American Therapeutic Recreation Association, 1992; Skalko, 1992; Skalko & Goldenberg, 1994). In addition, as presented by the Philosophical Statement Committee (1981) of the National Therapeutic Recreation Society and Skalko and Goldenberg (1994), the acceptance of a philosophical position that therapeutic recreation, as a treatment modality (i.e., recreational therapy), requires the development of a separate and distinct curriculum and accreditation process.

Today, the pursuit of third-party reimbursement will continue to be hindered without professional preparation standards consistent with practice. Entry level practitioners and administrative personnel will continue to lack the skills necessary for formulating active treatment programs and the documentation needed to justify reimbursement practices.

Public Policy, Public Relations and Educational Services

Despite the progress made, the field must continue with efforts to influence public policy as it relates to the identification of recreational therapy services as an aspect of the basic benefits package for federally supported health care programs. These efforts include consistent public relations activities with private carriers and health care accrediting bodies.

In recent years, efforts by the consumers of our services, in concert with efforts by the American Therapeutic Recreation Association (ATRA) and the National Therapeutic Recreation Society (NTRS), have been instrumental in identifying recreational therapists as members of the core treatment teams for acute traumatic head injury, inpatient rehabilitation and outpatient services under the standards established by CARF: The Rehabilitation Accreditation Commission. Such activities are necessary if recreational therapy services are to be recognized as standard benefits and potentially reimbursable as an ancillary service.

Educational and public relations efforts must continue to be extended to private third-party carriers, public officials, accrediting agencies and related allied health disciplines. In addition, the message must depict a unified mission and entail consistent terminology for the discipline. If we continue to confuse our audiences, efforts to secure third-party reimbursement will be hampered.

Position in the Health Care Reform Initiative

Recreational therapy, as a discipline, has not yet developed a cohesive, politically active lobby. Legislative initiatives have continually listed traditional services such as occupational therapy, physical therapy and speech-language-pathology but do not list recreational therapy within the standard benefits package, despite an organized effort by ATRA's and NTRS's Committees on Public Policy. We must educate public policy makers, third-party intermediaries and health care providers of the role of recreational therapy services in active treatment. These messages must be consistent and continue to deal with health care and treatment issues.

A consistent message will be easier to deliver if our field focuses more on the levels of service as provided in the Recreation Service Model (burlingame, 1998) which parallels the terminology and treatment structures of the other health professions. If the field continues to give mixed messages by confusing philosophy with commonly held diagnostic and treatment structures it will be hard for others to take us seriously. By confusing missions of recreation and therapy and continuing to use the same terminology (i.e., therapeutic recreation) to describe both recreation services and recreational therapy, public policy makers will continue to disregard the recreational therapy discipline as a unified active treatment discipline. Furthermore, recreational therapy will not be included in future health care reform and will not be listed as a standard benefit either as a routine service or as an ancillary service.

Summary

Throughout the remainder of the 1990's and into the 21st century, health care reform and financing will be one of the top items on the nation's agenda and, in turn, the agenda of the recreational therapy discipline. Current and future decisions may employ new paradigms for funding and the issue of third-party reimbursement may take on new meaning. Diagnostic related groups may receive and be reimbursed for a designated bundle of services as part of the standard benefits package. Reimbursement policy will set new limits for services rendered. Increasingly, consumer satisfaction, quality of life and functional independence (or perhaps interdependence) will become hallmarks. The emerging recreational therapy professional of the 21st century must lead the effort to: validate the efficacy of our services; ensure the inclusion of recreational therapy as a standard health care benefit; secure, when appropriate, the reimbursement for recreational therapy as an ancillary service; and demonstrate competence as a qualified, multi-skilled professional. Ultimately, recreational therapists must demonstrate the value of their services as an active treatment and as an essential component in the recovery of the individual and subsequent quality of life. This can only occur through well-qualified, well-trained professionals committed to the excellence of quality services provided to the health care consumer.

Learning Activities

1. Have groups assume separate sides of the issue of having the recreational therapy department pursue reimbursement as an ancillary service and to maintain coverage under a "per diem or room and board" format.
2. Identify the benefits of recreational therapy services and justify their reimbursement to an administrator.
3. Establish a team to operate as a Department of Recreational Therapy. Assign members different task for securing third-party reimbursement and developing a specific plan of action for each task group.
4. Establish a rationale for the inclusion or exclusion of recreational therapy as a reimbursable service.

Study Questions

1. Identify and discuss the five barriers to securing third-party reimbursement as identified in the chapter.
2. Identify and discuss sources of financing for hospitals.
3. Address the impacts of Prospective Payment Systems and Capitated Systems on recreational therapy services?

4. Describe how the recreational therapy department receives funding under the following systems: retrospective reimbursement, prospective payment and managed care.

References

American Therapeutic Recreation Association. (1992). Status of therapeutic recreation in higher education. Study conducted by D. Compton. Unpublished report.

American Therapeutic Recreation Association. (1993). *Standards for the practice of therapeutic recreation & self assessment guide*. Hattiesburg, MS: American Therapeutic Recreation Association.

burlingame, j. (1987). CPT's impact on therapeutic recreation. *ATRA Newsletter, 3*(2), 5-6.

burlingame, j. (1998). Clinical practice models. In F. Brasile, T. Skalko & j. burlingame (Eds.). *Perspectives in recreational therapy: Issues of a dynamic profession*. Ravensdale, WA: Idyll Arbor, Inc.

Esneault, C., Malkin, M. J. & Sellers, L. (1992). Third-party reimbursement for outpatient therapeutic recreation services. *Annual in Therapeutic Recreation, 3*, 90-95.

Grote, K. (1990, May/June). Strategic planing. *American Therapeutic Recreation Association Newsletter, 6*(3), 8-9.

Hutchinson-Troyer, L. (1987). Third-party reimbursement update. *American Therapeutic Recreation Association Newsletter, 3*(6), 4.

Hutchinson-Troyer, L. & Gillespie, A. (1991). *First steps to reimbursement: An overview*. Hattiesburg, MS: American Therapeutic Recreation Association.

Malkin, M. J. & Skalko, T. K. (1992). ATRA's third-party reimbursement survey. In G. Hitzhusen & L. T. Jackson (Eds.). *Expanding horizons in therapeutic recreation XIV* (pp. 23-51). Columbia: University of Missouri.

National Therapeutic Recreation Society. (1980). *Standards of practice for therapeutic recreation service*. Ashburn, VA: National Recreation and Park Association.

National Therapeutic Recreation Society. (1995). *Standards of practice for therapeutic recreation services and annotated bibliography*. Ashburn, VA: National Recreation and Park Association.

Olsson, R. (1986). The prospective payment system: Implications for therapeutic recreation. *Therapeutic Recreation Journal, 20*(1), 7-17.

Philosophical Statement Committee (1981, February 1). *Report from the Philosophical Statement Committee*. Ashburn, VA: National Therapeutic Recreation Society.

Powell, L. G. (1984). Fiscal management in therapeutic recreation: A perspective on educational preparation. *Therapeutic Recreation Journal, 18*(4), 37-41.

Reitter, M. S. (1984). Third-party reimbursement: Is therapeutic recreation too late? *Therapeutic Recreation Journal, 18*(4), 13-19.

Reitter, M. S. (1989). Third-party payers: Are we getting our share? In D. M. Compton (Ed.). *Issues in therapeutic recreation: A profession in transition* (pp. 239-256). Champaign, IL: Sagamore Publishing.

Russoniello, C. (1992, January/February). President's message. *American Therapeutic Recreation Association Newsletter, 8*(1), 3.

Skalko, T. K. (1992, May/June). Clearing the confusion: Therapeutic recreation as a treatment modality. *American Therapeutic Recreation Association Newsletter*, *8*(3), 3-4.

Skalko, T. K. & Goldenberg, R. (1994, September). Practitioners' perspective on educational preparation: A national survey. Poster Session conducted at the American Therapeutic Recreation Association Annual Conference, Orlando, FL.

Skalko, T. K. & Malkin, M. J. (1992). Current status of third-party reimbursement for therapeutic recreation services: Where do we go from here? *Annual in Therapeutic Recreation, 3*, 80-89.

Smith, L. (1986, October). Speaking the language of reimbursement. Paper presented at the National Recreation and Park Association Congress, Anaheim, CA.

Teaff, J. D. & Van Hyning, T. E. (1988a, April). Leisure service financing in US health-care settings. *Journal of Physical Education, Recreation, and Dance, 58*(3), 25-26.

Teaff, J. D. & Van Hyning, T. E. (1988b). Third-party reimbursement of therapeutic recreation services within a national sample of United States hospitals. *Therapeutic Recreation Journal, 22*(2), 31-37.

West, R. E. (1984). Productivity analysis as a method of fiscal accountability for therapeutic recreation. *Therapeutic Recreation Journal, 18*(4), 27-36.

Wilson, J. L. (1989). Alternate sources of funding: Potentials and pitfalls. In D. M. Compton (Ed.). *Issues in therapeutic recreation: A profession in transition* (pp. 257-269). Champaign, IL: Sagamore Publishing.

Zimmerman, D. & Skalko, J. J. (1994). *Reengineering health care: A vision for the future*. Franklin, WI: Eagle Press.

Chapter 25

The Role of
Information Technologies

joan burlingame

We are at the beginning of an age where three concurrent changes in information technology are occurring simultaneously. First, technology is changing the way practitioners work including: new processes for documentation, new standards for benchmarking quality indicators and new methods for billing right from the medical record. Second, computer technology is changing what is done for patients: incredible advances in medicine have been made because of hundreds of improved diagnostic and treatment options which practitioners have been forced to learn about and use. Finally, computer systems, especially databases, are allowing health care payers and providers to analyze treatment at a depth and comprehensiveness that was never possible before. Practitioners have to understand and record new and more detailed sets of data about new types of treatment on machines they are just beginning to understand. Any one of these changes would have been difficult to cope with. All three at once can be overwhelming. In the past the "old hand" had the advantage. There are many aspects of practice where this is true but, in this era, it is possible that the new graduate will be better versed in computer basics than his/her supervisor.

The changes in technology are fast paced and the applications are expanding exponentially. To help bring some order to this phenomena, the Congress of the United States established a Technology Assessment Board (TAB). The TAB, along with industry (both software and health care), is setting new standards concerning information technologies which will impact the recreational therapist in almost every area of practice.

After discussing the trends in information technology, information on databases and standards related to software will be presented. Lastly, this chapter will provide the reader with a scenario depicting how the changes will impact the recreational therapist's work. For the reader who is not familiar with some of the terms related to information technology, databases in particular, the end of the chapter contains a glossary of terms.

Overview

Not too long ago therapists hand wrote their notes in the patients' medical charts, being careful to use black ink pens. (The black ink made photo copying patient notes easier.) Problems arose when the therapist wanted to maintain a copy of the notes, or of an assessment, for records kept within the department, separate from the medical chart. Access to a copying machine, and the time it took to reach the machine, wait in line and copy the material made for an awkward and time consuming task. Some departments used NCR paper or carbons trying to address these problems. Gathering information for quality assurance reviews or for outcomes research required labor intensive work. This pen to paper process may have once been the method for communication and history of patient care but the expectations associated with all aspects of patient care have changed. The new expectations are that all professionals will become familiar with and use the new, rapidly developing standards associated with communication, documentation and reporting. Roger Herdman, Director of the Office of Technology Assessment states:

> Information technologies are transforming the way health care is delivered. Innovations such as computer-based patient records, hospital information systems, computer-based decision support tools, community health information networks, telemedicine and new ways of distributing health information to consumers are beginning to affect the cost, quality and accessibility of health care. Changes in the health care delivery system including the emergence of managed health care and integrated delivery systems, are breaking down the organizational barriers that have stood between care providers, insurers, medical researchers and public health professionals. Old distinctions between clinical health information and administrative health information are gradually eroding as new health care delivery patterns emerge that are supported by, and in some cases reliant on, the widespread use of networked computers and telecommunications. (Congress of the United States, 1995, p. iii)

As health care moves increasingly toward managed care systems and practitioner's sophistication using computers develops, we will see an increased reliance on information technologies. Providers and insurers are placing increased value on digital information. Using computers makes it easier to answer the question, "Is the patient receiving the right treatment in the right frequencies to experience maximum benefit without over-utilizing resources?" "What we'll be most interested in as an accreditor is how organizations are using data," says JCAHO vice president for performance measurement Deborah Nadzam. "Are they digging deeper to understand why their rates are what they are? Do they follow up and accomplish that improvement?" (Brooks, 1998, p. 41). More than any other time in the past, health care is mixing the clinical use of data (assessment results, treatment interventions, treatment outcomes) with the administrative use of data (utilization review, billing, gate-keeping activity).

There are three trends which are impacting both the provider of health care and the information technologies. The first trend is the aggressive management of costs in health care, the second is the continued integration of health care services and the third is the explosive change in the technologies themselves.

There have been increasingly aggressive moves to manage the cost of health care. This includes controlling the access to services (gate keeping), containing costs of the services received, managing utilization of resources (making sure that the services provided are known to provide desired outcomes), conducting concurrent review (double checking that progress is being made as the services are being provided) and providing financial incentives or penalties to modify practitioner and user actions. These moves have been taken because of the staggering increase in the cost of health care combined with the aging of the baby boomers. "Health care expenditures increased from 5.9 percent of gross domestic product in 1965 to 13.9 percent in 1993. Total expenditures for health care in 1993 were $884.2 billion. Government sources pay for about 43 percent of this total; the federal government alone pays nearly 32 percent" (Congress of the United States, 1994, pp. 5-6).

Part of this movement to control the cost of health care using information technologies is the development of managed care systems. The Office of Technology Assessment (OTA) defines managed care as "a vaguely defined term referring to various systems of health care delivery that attempt to manage the cost, quality and accessibility of health care" (Congress of the United States, 1995, p. 220). By 1992 managed care systems had 50% of all people covered by employer provided health insurance (Congress of the United States, 1993). Even fee-for-service systems are implementing aspects of managed care to stay competitive. Only the use of computers has made the administration of managed care systems possible.

The process of requiring all treatment and billing to be reported via computer has already started with all nursing homes who receive Medicare and Medicaid reimbursement. As of June 1998 all of these facilities were required to submit data on patient status and billing to the Health Care Financing Administration (HCFA) using electronic transfer of information. If the staff do not document in a timely manner, the services received by the patient and any change in patient status, the facility stands to lose thousands of dollars. A facility is most likely to achieve cost savings only if they are almost totally online. Harpool and Yancy state, "The mix of manual and automated systems in most long term care organizations leads to excess paperwork, duplicated efforts, a lack of timeliness, increased costs and operational complexity" (Harpool & Yancy, 1997, p. 73). This change to an online system to manage information is forcing many changes in how long term care is delivered.

> "Operationally there will be some changes to make," says John P. Barber, executive vice president and CFO of White Oak Manor, based in Spartanburg, South Carolina. "You'll need a computer tracking system that can maintain appropriate logs. You will have to make sure your rehab department is efficient, your nurses are able to recognize changes in patient status on a timely basis, and that information gets to the proper people in order to be documented in the MDS [Minimum Data Set]." (NovaCare, 1998, p. 4)

Another trend in health care has been the integration of health care services. Health care has historically been run by many different "players" with little continuity between the primary physicians office, the hospital, the nursing home or public health services. In the past, the amount of money an insurance company would pay for a service depended a lot on *where* the service was provided. Outpatient services were frequently denied coverage in the 1980's, while now insurance companies give incentives to provide services on an outpatient basis. Increasingly, insurance companies and accrediting agencies are emphasizing the use of continuum of care where one entity follows the patient from acute care to rehabilitation to home care and even preventative care. But developing a system to deliver this continuum of care has proven a challenge, if for no other reason than for the sheer numbers of people and providers involved. In 1995 there were over 1.2 million providers and 3,000 private insurance companies in the United States. The ideal would be to have a continuum of care concept with contracts uniting the various players. To help provide cost containment information, ideally all of the insurance companies and health care providers would also be linked by computers to analyze utilization and outcome data. However, currently, many are competitors for each other's business.

Any linking of data may help one's competitors. It has been a difficult task to encourage professionals to change how they did things in the past and work together, not necessarily for just their own good and professional identity, but for the preservation of services to consumers. Four major systems are already in place which are helping "break the ice" and lead others to integrate their data systems. They are the Uniform Data System for Medical Rehabilitation, the

MDS for long term care facilities (HCFA), the Health Plan Employer Data and Information Set (HEDIS) developed by the National Committee for Quality Assurance (NCQA) and the ORYX System (JCAHO). While all four data-driven systems allow the comparison of outcomes across facilities, none are fully integrated with the patient's medical chart.

The first, and oldest, is the Buffalo-based Uniform Data System for Medical Rehabilitation which collects data throughout the entire physical medicine and rehabilitation service industry using the functional independence measure (FIM) as its basis for measurement. This is a voluntary system separate from any government reporting requirements.

The MDS reporting system mentioned above obtains information on each patient admitted to a nursing home in the United States. The MDS is the standardized assessment tool which contains a summary of all of the assessments done by professionals working in a nursing home with that specific patient. The MDS started out as a "paper/pencil" assessment tool in the early 1990's and has developed into a nationally integrated database. This integrated database is required by HCFA. All reimbursement to the nursing home (and therapists billing fee-for-service) comes directly off this electronically submitted data.

The HEDIS system collects data on 56 measures in its standard set and 30 measures in its testing set related to the performance of managed care systems. In 1997 98% of the HMOs with Medicare contracts who were required to report performance data to HCFA did so using the HEDIS system.

The newest system is the ORYX program of statistical process control (SPC) through the Joint Commission on Accreditation of Healthcare Organizations (JCAHO). JCAHO plans to use the data collected by a facility to help analyze comparative data and turn it into valuable information to be used in improving the quality of services a facility provides. The ORYX system will be used in both hospital and long term care settings.

The third change is the explosive growth in hardware and software development, and the change is already here! The use of phone systems and paging, the capacity of hardware, industry-wide standards for integrated and interactive software, the Internet and personal aids such as personal digital assistants (PDAs) have already greatly changed the options available to health care. Gone are the days when most hospitals paged staff using an overhead public address system. Pagers today not only allow the wearer know that s/he has a phone call, they can also display messages on their small screens. It is not uncommon for unit assistants to have a keyboard which allows messages to be sent to the therapist without the therapist ever having to answer the page. Phone messaging systems allow many options using menus, mailboxes, voice messaging and priority notification systems (which allow you to have the staff's pager notify him/her that an important message is waiting).

Computers tend to be doubling their speed and capacity every two years. The computer's increased ability to handle word processing, data collection and analysis and desktop publishing have allowed more realistic options for the professional. Match that with the computer industry's drive for standardization of architecture and the options begin to multiply. Integrated and interactive software allow increased options for building a computer system to meet the facility's specific need, including the use of user defined formats to integrate with grouper software and databases. Add to this desktop publishing and the facility can create its own promotional material using information gleaned from its database to create specific reports which will look appealing to potential customers.

One of the most promising of the personal aids is the PDA (personal digital assistant). The PDA is a type of computer which uses radio transmission technology to download information from the hospital's computer network. It can also upload information from the therapist such as chart notes, assessment reports, time cards, etc. Radio receiving wires are strung along the ceiling right on top of the ceiling tiles. These wires connect to the hospital's networked computer system. PDAs are portable and fit easily into one's hand. The display screen is not very large and the user has choices of keypad types, including menu driven keypads and keyboards. PDAs lack a hard drive but employ a high-performance computer processor and wireless communications.

The advancement of the Internet has had phenomenal effects on health care. The Internet has not only offered the professional access to thousands of sites for research, but has also created easier communication between professionals and between agencies. The impact of increased contact between agencies is already having significant impact, as the Health Care Financing Administration (HCFA), the Joint Commission on Accreditation of Healthcare Organizations and other entities are now requiring that data be transmitted electronically through the Internet. In the case of HCFA, the reimbursement rate for nursing home patients will be determined by the information transmitted to HCFA from the facility over the Internet. No other avenue for billing is available.

Changes Which Need to Take Place

To allow both the aggressive management of costs in health care and the continued integration of health care services, some major changes will need to take place. The introduction of information technology into health care has not been a smooth one. Such changes have been impeded by issues which need to be resolved concerning the use of information technologies. These issues can be grouped into three general problem areas: conceptual barriers, organizational barriers and technical barriers.

Conceptual Barriers

Conceptual barriers can be defined as problems associated with how people think. The delivery of health care services creates a lot of data, everything from information associated with the patient's care, to billing systems, to management needs (e.g., quality assurance, utilization review, outcomes management). This vast amount of data can only be understood if it is organized into concepts, or logical ways of thinking. This requires a unified approach to thinking within each professional group as well as between professional groups.

One conceptual barrier is the reluctance of professionals to follow the treatment protocols developed by national "experts" instead of developing their own in house treatment program. Each professional group will need to have clearly defined treatment protocols. Using standardized protocols will allow the integrated database to better recognize and analyze the information. The treatment protocols used will come from national organizations, health care corporations and private companies. While some protocols will retain a "local flavor," the integration of data from the protocols, including the assessments and documentation in the medical chart, will need to fit into the data collection system used across the country.

To be part of the national databases used by regulators and third party payers, the recreational therapist will need to produce data that will fit into the frameworks currently being developed. These frameworks include standardized service models (e.g., the World Health Organization's ICIDH Model), methods of electronic documentation and the development of decision making tools. Therapists need to think globally when they decide which protocols and coding systems to use. Unified definitions of such terms as advanced activities of daily living/life management skills, community integration skills/community re-integration skills and constraints/barriers associated with activity will need to used nationally within the appropriate field on the screen. Coding systems such as the FIM scale will increasingly be used as the primary method of denoting functional ability.

The field of recreational therapy will need to be able to reach compromises which provide quality service using unified language and approaches.

Organizational Barriers

Organizational barriers are problems inherent with different groups with different or competing goals needing to work together. This goes beyond the need for departments within a single facility to work together and professionals to agree on specific terminology. The greatest challenges may prove to be felt by governmental entities, human resources and fiscal resources.

As health care documentation and reimbursement systems go fully online, the team working with the patient (and the patient's third party payer) may be working outside the geographic area normally covered by licensure and other regulatory boundaries. An example would be a CTRS who practices in Twin Falls, Idaho and works for a corporation which owns multiple subacute care units (nursing homes) in many states, including Utah. Utah requires recreational therapists practicing in Utah to be licensed by the state while Idaho does not. As more of our nation's treatment goes online, practitioners will be providing consultation and even treatment (via satellite links) to areas governed by other states.

> Thus, they may challenge the existing structure of state medical licensing and malpractice laws, as well as "pen and quill" laws that require paper-based medical record keeping. Consolidations and mergers among the many companies offering managed health care reflect the ability of computer networks and digital telecommunications to act as a nervous system that can connect previously independent parts of the health care delivery and administrative systems, forming new bodies known as integrated delivery systems. (Congress of the United States, 1995, p. 4)

Another organizational barrier (as well as a conceptual barrier) is the use of paraprofessionals in some tasks historically done only by certified or licensed professionals. The use of information technologies tends to reduce the need for multiple layers of personnel, flattening organizational structures and creating a crisis among those who find comfort in rigidly defined job roles. As the field of recreational therapy gains more experience with online documentation and the use of standardized protocols, it will be more able to know when to use a specific protocol. The formally defined rules for determining which protocols to use with specific diagnoses and specific situations are referred to as "clinical decision systems." As more and more clinical decision making applications develop, increased responsibility will be given to the entry level professional and the paraprofessional. This causes both an organizational barrier and a conceptual barrier — therapists are uncomfortable with letting paraprofessionals provide some of the services restricted to certified therapists in the past. The Office of Technology Assessment reports:

> In some cases, role changes are induced by other organizational changes in which information technology is a facilitator. For example, one way that health care organizations are reducing costs is by redesigning work so that tasks once done by high-cost personnel are now done by lower cost personnel. For example, much primary health care previously done by physicians is now being done by physician extenders like physician assistants and nurse practitioners. In some

hospitals, work previously done by licensed and registered nurses is now done by nursing aides — sometimes labeled patient care technicians, while nursing takes on the role of managing a team of caregivers. This trend is typical of a "reengineering" movement in hospital management known as patient-centered care or patient-focused care as opposed to department-focused care. Computer technologies including computer-based decision support tools and treatment protocols, online patient information systems, patient monitoring devices and teleconferencing systems — can support and assist people giving care in these new ways. (Congress of the United States, 1995, p. 5)

Technical Barriers

Technical barriers are problems related to the inability of the current software and hardware to handle the immense amount of data required for even one patient, let alone for every patient within a specific geographic area. Health care is an extremely complex system offering many reasonable options and courses of treatment based on current knowledge and the patient's own unique needs. "Despite the ongoing efforts of standards-setting bodies, no unified conceptual model exists that is powerful enough to construct the mapping between the information that must be stored in computer databases and medicine as it is practiced" (Congress of the United States, 1995, pp. 2-3). While standards have been proposed for software "engines" (the programs which run the application software), the workflow software interoperatives and common request broker architecture (COBRA), none of the standard-setting bodies have achieved full integration of all these basic systems to be able to actually run online medical records as they need to be run. The hardware needed to contain such a large database is also proving difficult to create. As of yet, the technology is still lacking.

One element of health care has set hardware standards for its national database. The Health Care Financing Administration (HCFA) has set minimum specifications for hardware and software specifications for MDS computerization. HCFA's minimum standards are matched with what has been recommended as specifications for best performance in Table 25.1.

The Joint Commission on Accreditation of Health Care Organizations (JCAHO) has also set minimum standards for software used for reporting outcomes. As of the beginning of 1998, JCAHO had already approved 67 measurement systems for use in long term care facilities (Brooks, 1998). By the end of March, 1999, all long term care facilities wanting to be accredited by JCAHO will be required to submit data collected from electronic databases.

Table 25.1: Specifications for MDS Computerization

Minimum Specifications (HCFA)	Recommend Specifications
486 Personal Computer, connected to a network or standalone. • 8 megabytes of RAM • 100 or more megabytes of hard disk space • Windows 3.1 or higher • 14 inch color monitor • 28.8 Kbps modem for telecommunication • Data communications software, such as Netscape or Internet Explorer	Pentium 166 Personal Computer, connected to a network or standalone. • 32 megabytes of RAM • 4 gigabyte or larger hard disk • Windows 3.1 or higher • 15 inch color monitor with a 600 x 800 or higher resolution • 56 Kbps modem for telecommunication • Data communications software, such as Netscape or Internet Explorer
Source: HCFA Final Rule: Resident Assessment Instrument for Long Term Care Facilities.	Source: Accu-Med Services, Inc. (1998). *Contemporary Long Term Care 21*(6), p. 7.

Databases

Working with databases will be part of a recreational therapist's day-to-day job, just as using a pen with black ink was previously. Until the issues discussed above become resolved, the therapist is likely to use a computer database for some of the medical chart and a narrative file for other portions. At some point, the entire chart should be integrated into some type of database.

A database is the collection of information which is organized in such a manner that data can be retrieved quickly. It allows the creation of different configurations of data to allow analysis by staff and others. For the information to be readily available from the database, the entry of the data should be done in a systematic, organized manner. Professionals will need to define terms (e.g., what is *depression*? what constitutes a *barrier*? what constitutes a *name*?) and use these terms consistently throughout the region and the country. The use of standardized testing tools and forms, like the MDS (nursing homes), the Leisure Competency Measure (LCM) and the CERT-Psych/R will all help unify the nation's databases, thus allowing better patient care by helping identify outcomes and quality measures. While this system of using standardized terminology and tools is initially easy to conceptualize, the implementation is difficult.

Trying to set up an information system to track quality measures is like becoming a student of philosophy. It requires a new way of thinking, a way of seeing data collection as more than just a bureaucratic chore.

Internally, data can help you determine your real costs and identify and improve areas in which your facility's performance is weak. Externally, the right data can convey a positive story about your organization to prospective payers and clients. (Hawver, 1997, p. 100)

Integrated databases using data from many facilities has proven difficult to achieve. "There's no agreement yet in the hospital arena as to which measures to use and which data should be collected. Most measurement systems in the long term care setting base their measures off MDS" (Brooks, 1998, p. 43). One of the first steps to having integrated databases is for each facility to work to bring the entire facility online. This section on databases will provide information about making decisions toward acquiring and integrating a database.

Databases in Health Care

The database which is purchased by the facility will likely be a standardized database developed to address many needs. The primary need will be for the facility to comply with health care regulations, standards and reporting (billing and outcomes) requirements. "... the Joint Commission on Accreditation of Healthcare Organizations (JCAHO) will soon require all accredited long term care facilities to report outcomes. A JCAHO survey shows that 33 percent already are. The rest must choose a measurement system by March 2 of this year and start reporting by March 31, 1999" (Brooks, 1998, p. 39). If the recreational therapist is to be able to have input in the database or other applications used in the facility, s/he needs to know more than just how the database runs (Brooks, 1998). To improve the efficiency with which the facility collects data, the facility should start by understanding what is currently being done (with or without computers), identifying areas where the facility can improve performance and understanding how improved performance can be brought about. Once this information has been collected and some basic plans for improvement have been designed, the facility should take the following steps to allow technology to simplify the process (Harpool & Yancy, 1997):

- Organize a steering committee of decision makers and an advisory committee of department managers. The steering committee guides the process while the advisory committee helps clarify scope and boundaries of service and identifies realistic changes for each department.
- Review current systems to identify the relationship between technology, processes and people. Important systems and relationships of the current system and desired system should include information on "critical clinical, operational and financial activities and how the information systems support them" (Harpool & Yancy, 1997, p. 73).

- Bring together representatives from different departments to analyze the flow of core business and treatment processes and identify major bottle-necks. Make sure that the team identifies all the core requirements neces-sary (including documentation, assessment, risk indicators, etc.).
- Identify vendors who seem to have software that fits the facility's needs. Use the information the steering committee and advisory committee have developed concerning critical activities as a checklist of requirements for the vendor's database.
- Re-evaluate what's currently being done in the facility and whether each step is still necessary. The vendor should be able to compare your current systems of operation to what the database can do to identify ways in which your facility can cut duplication for staff.
- Monitor and evaluate quality outcomes. Once the database is online and all the staff have been trained to use it, develop an ongoing program to monitor and evaluate your system.

When selecting a database for the facility, there are a set of questions to be answered (Brooks, 1998; Accu-Med Services, Inc., 1998):

- How easy is the database to use? Does the database follow logical se-quences similar to what the staff currently use? Does it reduce the amount of typing required?
- How is information entered into the system? Is it clear, logical and easy, allowing for decreased errors due to data entry failures? Is the data entered then shared with other parts of the system? For example, do the staff have to continually re-enter the patient's entire personal data including name, age and diagnosis, or does the system automatically carry that information over to the other applications?
- What else is in it? What kind of data can it collect in addition to its primary function? How flexible is it in generating outcomes data? Can it collect pa-tient satisfaction information? Does it use any standardized questionnaires or testing tools so that data can be compared to other facilities, regions and nationally? Can it compare cost information to services and clinical inter-ventions provided?
- Does it have a care plan system integrated into the database, so that an ini-tial care plan will be generated for staff review after the assessment infor-mation is entered?
- How long has it operated? Has it had time to have bugs worked out? How experienced in health care is the firm that developed the database?
- Does it audit data? "To protect the integrity of its data, Care Computer runs MDS reports through a probability analysis. For example, an MDS that re-

ports cognitive difficulties in one section might be suspect if another section reports few problems with activities of daily living" (Brooks, 1998, p. 43).

- How may facilities are linked? Benchmarking is more effective if your data can be compared to the data generated by other facilities. A benchmark repository requires that hundreds of facilities be interconnected to be able to compare against industry averages (Brooks, 1998).

The reader may also want to include questions from Table 25.2 to make sure the program is user friendly.

How to Collect the Data

Once the facility has database software, it will need to decide what types of data it wants to collect. In some cases, as with the MDS, some types of data collection are required. In others, especially for data related directly to the delivery of recreational therapy services, some decisions will need to be made. Hawver (1997) suggests:

- Categorize your data and establish key indicators.
- Start with what you know.
- Identify information you haven't collected but should.
- Require staff involvement.
- Standardize on an information system to house and analyze the data.

Even with the establishment of your key indicators and identifying what else could be done concerning information gathering and staff involvement, your system requires more (Oatway, 1997). The facility's work concerning the selection and use of a database is never really over. Systems work best when they have dedicated staff who run the information system (they don't run themselves). To help coordinate the use of the system by all staff, policies and procedures should be set up and reviewed as requirements change, upgrades are installed or staff changes. The facility will need to conduct regular audits of the system, examining patterns of use (and misuse). Reviewing and updating the policies and procedures should follow each audit cycle.

Benchmarking Indicators

Moore (1997) describes benchmarking as "a comparative analysis of industry factors, ratios and practices and answers the question, 'How does my community stack up in comparison to my immediate competition and similar operations on a regional and national basis?' " (Moore, 1997, p. 33). Benchmarking is the second step to establishing a database. By analyzing the information (data) collected on patients, the facility can determine what works, what doesn't and what is close. Because very soon databases will be connected be-tween facilities, each service unit will be able to compare its performance against other, similar service units. This interconnectedness will allow competi-tors and non-competitors alike to learn from each other's successes and failures. "Successful benchmarking efforts usually involve extracting relevant informa-tion based on 'best practices' vignettes rather than copying another organiza-tion's complete strategy" (Moore, 1997, p. 34). Moore lists some of the im-provements which may be realized through benchmarking:

- improve treatment outcomes
- improve the use of resources allocated to your department and justify an increase of resources allocated
- improve your department's ability to operate efficiently
- develop an understanding of what your services *really* are, and adjust both the amount charged and/or delivery system to match costs with resources
- increase patient satisfaction
- support (to administration) quality of life initiatives
- enhance the patient's and administration's perception of the value of your services
- clarify misconceptions about what your department does

Issues of Standards

The acceptance of standardization as a key element in all aspects of practice (terminology, assessment, protocols, etc.) is a necessary component of practic-ing in today's (and tomorrow's) health care system. Critical linking between providers and payers will be necessary to make sure that the most important element — the patient — does not lose out. This section will make a plea for standardization for integrated and interactive software. It will also review the type of attributes which make software more "user-friendly."

A profession sets standards for the minimum performance acceptable for work done within its own scope of practice. An individual who has gone through the formal educational process and who has taken the NCTRC national exam understands that certain competencies are required to practice the art and science of recreational therapy. There are many techniques, theories and core knowledge areas to learn before one can practice. So why is it that recreational therapists feel that they can also develop and sell software without paying atten-tion to the published international standards for minimum components and per-formance for software? Coding skills alone are not enough. Strict adherence to the standards for published software should be the minimum expectation for software developed by anyone.

Because so many computers are networked today, standards are being set so that information on networked computers can operate together.

An example would be the new standards being developed for workflow interoperative software. "Workflow management is a growing need as information about a project must be exchanged between more and more different users and departments" (Mohan, 1996, p. 16). Because of this multiple user reality, especially in health care when all the medical charts go online, every aspect of the software written for the recreational therapy program must interface smoothly with software from other vendors. It is no longer adequate to write a program which meets the departments needs and which does not crash easily. Nor do programs which run testing tools or leisure education programs meet standards if those programs cannot interface with the other systems, especially databases, on the network. As we are entering a time when our patient's medical records and the billing for our services will be taken directly off of our software programs, it is expedient for us to have them interface with the other programs. There are many places to begin searching for standards related to software. Two good places to begin are the Web site for the IEEE Engineering Standards Committee (http://www.computer.org/standard/sesc/overview.htm#standards) and the *Encyclopedia of Computer Science* edited by Ralston, Reilly and Dahlin (1993).

User Friendly Software

Whether the recreational therapist is writing his/her own code or purchasing a software package, there are certain features which make the software more "user friendly" for both the therapist and the patient. Table 25.2 is a summary of the information found in the Alliance for Technology Access (1994) publication. It may be used as a checklist against future software purchases.

A Scenario

But what will this look like? How will all the changes in information technologies change the recreational therapist's job? The following scenario will help show what it may be like.

Sally is an on-call (per diem) recreational therapist at a large county hospital. Working per diem and covering six different units (rehab medicine, pediatrics, burn-plastics, chemical dependency/dual diagnosis, general psychiatric and a locked psychiatric unit) is a challenge, especially since she spends an average of fifteen days on any one unit per year. She has just been called to work on the locked psychiatric unit — a unit she has not been on for eight months.

Table 25.2: **Checklist for User Friendly Software**

Feature	Description	• Issues of Accessibility
Easy-to-Read Screens	Key components of easy-to-read screens are uncluttered screens, simple text, menu items in both graphics and text.	• Option to make text larger on screen for individuals with visual impairments. • Text in single columns with no asterisks, dashes or other non-alphabetical characters used (not readable by voice-synthesis software).
Consistency	Predictable placement of menus and objects within the window. Predictable response of objects and menus throughout the program.	• Consistently placed menu items are especially important for individuals who use programs which enlarge the screens, as the menu item may not always be on the screen in such situations. • Consistency in the use of key commands helps adapt shortcuts.
Intuitive Characteristics	Clear and logical options for using the program increase the user's comfort level.	• Some intuitive programs adjust their speed and other characteristics by learning the user's interactive patterns. This makes the program easier to use.
Logical Labels	The use of graphics and terms which are self-explanatory.	• Logical labels are especially important for individuals using a screen reading program.
Instructional Choices	For educational software, a program which allows a variety of levels of difficulty and personalization.	• Allows adjustment of the program to the client's functional level. • Many allow adjustment to reaction time needed.
Graphics	If well presented and used logically, graphics expand the usability and understandability of the program.	• Graphics support reading skills, especially for individuals with graphic input disorders. • With scanning ability, can help personalize memory book.
Friendly Documentation	The documentation written to support the program should be clear and easy to read.	• The written document should help the user understand how to modify the usage/speed/control of the functions of the program to allow for greater adaptation.

Table 25.2: **Checklist for User-Friendly Software, continued**

Feature	Description	Issues of Accessibility
On-Screen Instructions	Steve Job of Apple Computers once said there are only two rules which apply to on-screen instructions: (1) assume that the user lost the written manual and (2) assume that s/he lost the manual before s/he read it.	• Following logical sequencing and allowing the reader to advance the screens at his/her own pace is important. • On-screen instructions should follow the guidelines under "easy-to-read screens" for use with screen readers.
Auditory Cues	Using either a voice synthesizer and/or a sound card, many programs can make sounds to alert the user to problems or as part of the entertainment.	• Best when the auditory cues can be modified to meet the individual's specific needs. • Tends to increase attention span of those using the program.
Visual Cues	Program which uses graphics and hidden text to cue the user for everything from spell check to prompts to help use the program.	• Visual cue programs may not function as well with screen-enlargement programs, as the visual cue may be in another location on the screen.
Built-In Access Methods	The ability to use devices other than the keyboard or mouse to run program.	• Allows the client to use the adaptive device with which s/he is familiar.
Built-In Utilities	Multiple programs packaged into one unit.	• Reduces amount of system conflict and increases ease of navigation between features.
Alternatives to a Mouse	Allows more than one way to make menu choices.	• Increases options for individuals with disabilities who have trouble using a mouse.
Optional Cursors	A program which allows changes to the shape and size of the cursor.	• Allows option of a cursor which is easier to see with a visual impairment.
Creation of Custom Programs	A program which helps you use its elements to create your own customized software program.	• Opens up many options for the therapist to customize programs to help the client improve function at his/her own pace.

This is a ten hour shift on a unit with thirty beds which seldom has an empty bed for more than a few hours. The majority of patients are court ordered onto the unit because they have been determined to be dangerous either to themselves or to others. Usually a third of the patients have committed a violent assault just prior to being admitted. Sally knows that the primary job of the recreational therapist on this unit is threefold: (1) To complete an assessment on each patient within 72 hours of admission, (2) To observe the patient for possible side effects of medications and (3) To determine the basic knowledge, functional ability or resources needed by the patient prior to discharge.

Sally uses the computerized key pad to gain access to the unit and picks up her personal digital assistant (PDA). She calls up all of the policy and procedure changes on the locked unit since last time she worked on it. She scans the changes, noting the items that are relevant for her work. Next she asks for her schedule for the day including a list of the groups she is to run together with the names of the patients assigned to each group. There are two groups so she calls up the protocols for each group. Each protocol lets her know the functional level of patients assigned to that protocol, how to run the protocol/activity and risk management guidelines.

Her computer generated schedule also provides her with a list of the six patients who need an initial assessment and the date and hour which they need to be completed and into the chart. Usually the therapists talk face to face to divide up the assessments. Sally was glad that the face to face communication between staff could never be fully done away with. Contact with co-workers was so critical! Since recreational therapy and occupational therapy share an intake assessment, Sally sends a voice mail to the occupational therapist to see if she has a preference of the two patients who must be assessed before 5:00 that evening. Sally then calls up a list of patients referred to recreational therapy for specific services and a list of cautions concerning patients. She notices that four patients are on close observation for suicide watch, one patient had a positive (for cocaine) urine screen after being on the unit for seven days (a visitor must have brought some in), five patients were considered to be assaultive, three were known to be HIV positive and two patients were from rival gangs and could not be in groups together. In addition, one patient was medically unstable coming off a drinking binge (detox), one patient spoke only Hmung and another was deaf and communicated in sign language. Her screen noted that both patients who needed interpreters were in her evening activity. The computer verified that two interpreters were scheduled for her evening activity. The patient who spoke Hmung was one of the two patients who required an intake assessment and had a recreational therapy/occupational therapy assessment scheduled for 2:00 p.m. An interpreter was already scheduled. She then voice mailed the OT again to say that she could do the 200 p.m. assessment if the OT could not.

Sally realized that 30 minutes had gone by and she hadn't even been on the unit yet. It usually took on-call staff at the hospital a full half hour to become oriented to the changes on the unit, the daily schedule and memorizing important information about the patients she would be seeing. Sally left her office and entered the unit. She said "hi" to staff she remembered, introduced herself to the rest and introduced herself to the various patients she saw. When she met a patient with whom she was to have formal interactions, she talked to the patient about that interaction. Three patients had referrals for a county bus pass. While most people in the community who were disabled needed to pay for the passes, the recreational therapist had the authority to waive the required fee and issue the bus pass. Sally had read that the policy concerning this had been modified slightly since the last time she had worked on the locked unit. The previous criterion was that any patient who lacked transportation and was planning to attend an outpatient counseling program qualified for a free pass. Now, if the patient needed transportation but was going to attend only a substance abuse program, s/he no longer qualified for a free county bus pass. (The Americans with Disabilities Act does not recognize substance addiction as a disability. This lack of recognition caused the policy to change.) She had actually received four referrals for bus passes but the computer had also indicated that one, the patient medically unstable because of detox, did not qualify. She arranged for the three patients who qualified to meet her by her office door in ten minutes so she could take their pictures for the pass. As she walked by the nursing station she logged on that computer and entered into each patient's computerized medical chart that the bus referral was received and was being processed. On the fourth, she recorded that the patient did not currently meet the criteria for a free bus pass. Sally signed all four charts with her electronic signature then went to meet the three patients.

After using a digital camera to take the patient's pictures she asked the computer to print out the passes, pictures and all, on the bus pass printer three floors down. She would stop by on her way back from dinner tonight and pick them up. Sally's PDA was indicating that she had voice mail. The OT said that she couldn't do either of the intakes before 5:00 p.m. but could pick up two of tomorrow's before she went home at 9:00 p.m. Sally quickly checked her schedule, the two patients' schedules and then decided that she had time for one (hopefully quick) assessment before her one o'clock group. The patient was available, so she entered the intake assessment onto his schedule and went to find the patient. On the way she called up the patient's history and key information on her PDA and read it. Sally remembered having to use pen and paper to enter the patient's assessment results in the past. All Sally had to do now was to press "send" and her finished assessment would be wirelessly transferred into the patient's medical chart. Once in front of the patient, the display scrolled through the questions and Sally selected answers from a set of pre-approved selections. Because information on each patient had to be compiled into a regional database, Sally had to use words with regionally accepted definitions. She remembered back to the discussion, at times heated, when the recreational therapists across the country had to agree on the exact meanings of specific words. They had to agree on what constituted barriers (constraints) to involvement and finally agreed to the categories suggested by Jackson (1993). They then worked through what constituted a mild, moderate or severe barrier. But is had paid off. Because of the computerization of medical charts and other patient database systems, recreational therapist now knew that a patient with bipolar disorder and a moderate barrier to leisure took five more hours of intervention if the patient also had problems with substance abuse. For patients on the voluntary unit, this actually resulted in patients with bipolar disorder and substance abuse being authorized for two more days of inpatient stay.

Within five minutes of Sally sending the patient's assessment to his medical chart, the patient's computerized schedule had the activities (protocols) the patient would (statistically) benefit from the most. Sally reviewed these with the patient and together they decided that one additional activity should be added because of the patient's interest in learning about the food pyramid (a group the OT ran). The patient had indicated a desire to know about scholarships for swimming pool passes and parks programs. This request had also been keyed in, along with the assessment and the results. Once everything was agreed upon, she cued the computer to integrate all of the activities and information throughout the system. The computer system was very good at ensuring that staff and patients were not double scheduled. The list had been developed after the database had compared the patient's residential, leisure interests and financial information to available parks programs on the appropriate bus routes and available scholarship programs. Sally reviewed this information with the patient.

Sally now had thirty minutes before her group activity. The activity dealt with basic survival skills in the community. She longingly remembered when the outdoor survival skills she learned in college were used in Outward Bound summer programs. Now she used the same skills — how to keep warm and dry, what kind of vegetation was okay to eat and what to do with free time between basic survival activities — with patients who were homeless in an urban environment. The statistics from the last year indicated that 23% of the patients on this unit were homeless. She had the computer print off the locations of all the public drinking fountains, soup kitchens, free recreation centers and free public showers for each patient coming to the group based on the city they were going to be discharged to. After the activity Sally keyed in each patient's response to the group including some specific functional measurements and sent these along to each patient's medical chart.

Sally had just two things to do before dinner. One of the referrals was a request from a community mental health specialist for the inpatient recreational therapist to determine if a specific patient was ready to go on to step six of the *Leisure Step Up* program. Many of the patients had multiple admissions, so much so that they were referred to as "frequent fliers." This allowed both the inpatient and outpatient therapist a chance for continuity — since they both used the *Leisure Step Up* as the leisure education program. She also asked her PDA to tabulate her patient stats — what percentage of time she had spent on "patient care." She was running at 83%, just 3% above what was expected of a per diem staff. She definitely did not have much room for slack after dinner!

Summary

Just as the rest of the business world has had to think fast and work smart to keep up with changes in technology, so will the recreational therapist. Not only will each recreational therapist need to understand the basics such as word processing, databases and adaptive technologies, but s/he will also need to put aside many strong feelings s/he feels toward specific philosophies and terminology to coordinate documentation, allowing it to fit into today's (and tomorrow's) databases. Two trends in health care which have helped drive this change are the aggressive management of costs in health care and the continued integration of health care services. Three issues which need to be resolved as information technology is embraced more are conceptual issues, organizational issues and technological issues. While the basic service recreational therapists provide will not change, the manner in which that service is provided and how it is documented, will change dramatically.

Glossary of Computerese[4]

Architecture: A model or blueprint used to develop how a computer handles the information that is entered into it. It includes hardware, software and components.

Computerized Reports: Computers can generate a report, or summary of information, by extracting certain elements from a variety of documents and combining them in meaningful ways for the user. For example, from the MDS, the user can create a list, or report, of patients with diabetes or a list of referral sources. Depending upon the software, these reports come in three formats: (1) standardized, pre-formatted reports, in which the user can make no changes, (2) templates, in which the report

---

[4] Reprinted with permission from Accu-Med Services, Inc. © 1998 Accu-Med Services, Inc.

is pre-defined but can be tweaked by the user to add or change certain elements or (3) totally designed by the user, in which format and all elements are chosen.

Database: A collection of information or data, organized for rapid search and retrieval by the computer. Various elements of the database can be called up and sorted to create specific reports. For example, all the MDS forms completed by a facility are stored in a database in the computer. Any one element, such as patient diagnosis, can then be extracted to create a separate list.

Field: A particular area, or line, in a form on the computer screen in which the same type of information is regularly recorded. For example, name, address and telephone number are three fields in which specific information is entered.

Grouper Software: Special software designed to translate MDS data on clinical complexity of a patient into a case mix analysis. It automatically assigns patients to predetermined groups — classifications used by the Resource Utilization Group System (RUGS) for the purpose of reimbursement. Grouper software works behind the scenes in your computer, so that after completing the MDS, you push a key and the RUGS category is automatically assigned for that patient.

Integrated Software: Computer programs that make it possible for two different systems or programs to share data. Applications from one or more vendors can thus communicate with each other, although each maintains its own database.

Interactive Software: A step above integrated software in which computer programs not only share information, but draw from the same database, making retrieval faster. Also, any information entered into one program automatically transfers to the other modules.

Menu: Just as with a restaurant menu, this is a list of choices available at any point in the computing process that allows the user to select which task or option the computer should perform next.

Prompt: The computer wait-state that indicates it is the user's turn to take an action. A prompt can be a blinking cursor at the point in the document where data can be entered, or a box appearing on screen with a question to be answered.

User Defined: Software that supports the user's ability to alter or redefine formats set up by the manufacturer in order to create a more personalized document or report. For example, if your admissions form on the computer lists patient name first, and you would prefer the patient's social security number first, software with a user-defined format will allow you to change the order of the information on the screen.

Learning Activities

1. Go to a store which sells database software or to a review in a magazine and compare the features available on four different databases, the machine requirements (e.g., memory, disk space) and the price.
2. Using the criteria for selecting a database for a facility from Brooks (1998) and Accu-Med Services, Inc. (1998), analyze a database which you have available to review.
3. Review the conceptual barriers listed in the chapter including the suggestions about the use of "canned" protocols and standardized nomenclature. What problems do you see associated with implementing these two suggestions? What steps could be taken to move the field in this direction (or, do you feel that it should go in this direction)?
4. The use of paraprofessionals in recreational therapy services is likely to increase over the next ten years. Develop a scenario which includes one treatment protocol (if possible, use a standardized protocol such as one from the *Community Integration Program, Second Edition* by Armstrong & Lauzen, 1994) and list what types of responsibilities would fall to the recreational therapist and what to the paraprofessional in the execution of the protocol? Include areas such as responsibility for teaching, observing, modifying approaches, documenting, interpreting actions, etc.
5. Using Table 25.2: Checklist for User Friendly Software, evaluate a software program available to you. How does the program rate for issues of accessibility?

Study Questions

1. What are the three concurrent changes in information technology which are impacting the practice of recreational therapy?
2. What are four national systems which currently use data submitted electronically?
3. What is the relationship between a database, integrated software and interactive software?
4. How has the Internet affected health care?
5. List at least seven barriers to the use of information technology.

References

Accu-Med Services, Inc. (1998). What and why of three-tier architecture. *Software solutions: Special advertising section of Contemporary Long Term Care, 21*(6), 2-3.

Alliance for Technology Access. (1994). *Computer resources for people with disabilities* (2nd ed.). Alameda, CA: Hunter House.

Armstrong, M. & Lauzen, S. (1994). *Community integration program* (2nd ed.). Ravensdale, WA: Idyll Arbor, Inc.

Brooks, S. (1998.) Year of the database. *Contemporary Long Term Care, 21*(2), 39-45.

Congress of the United States, General Accounting Office. (1993). *Managed health care: Effects on employer's costs difficult to measure*, GAO/HRD-94-3. Washington, DC: US Government Printing Office.

Congress of the United States, Office of Technology Assessment. (1994). International comparisons of administrative costs in health care, OTA-BP-H-135, Washington DC: US Government Printing Office.

Congress of the United States, Office of Technology Assessment. (1995). *Bringing health care online: The role of information technologies*. Washington, DC: US Government Printing Office.

Gostin, L., Turek-Brezina, J., Powers, M., Kozloff, R., Faden, R. & Steinauer, D. D. (1993). Privacy and security of personal information in a new health care system. *The Journal of the American Medical Association, 270*(20), 2487-2493.

Harpool, J. & Yancy, E. (1997). Using technology to simplify your processes. *Contemporary Long Term Care, 20*(8), 73.

Hawver, C. (1997). More than just a bureaucratic chore. *Contemporary Long Term Care, 20*(10), 100.

Jackson, E. (1993). Recognizing patterns of leisure constraints: Results from alternative analyses. *Journal of Leisure Research, 25*(2), 129-149.

Mohan, S. (1996). Microsoft MAPI spec wins universal support. *Computerworld, 30*(7), 16.

Moore, J. (1997). Benchmarking deserves a chance. *Contemporary Long Term Care, 20*(12), 33-34.

National Committee for Quality Assurance. (1997). *NCQA releases HEDIS®3.0/1998; Improvements will clarify and standardized health plan performance measurement.* http://www.ncqa.org/news/98rel.htm 7/11/98 5:51 p.m.

NovaCare. (1998). Rehab forum: PPS checklist — What to do and when to do it. *Special advertising section in Contemporary Long Term Care, Spring, 6-8.*

Oatway, D. (1997). Getting the most out of your information system. *Contemporary Long Term Care, 20*(12), 67.

Ralston, A., Reilly, E. D. & Dahlin, C. A. (Eds.). (1993). *Encyclopedia of computer science.* New York: Van Nostrand Reinhold.

Issues for the Future

Chapter 26

Impacts of Global Trends

Miriam P. Lahey

Professions come into being in response to specific needs of society. This concern for the common good is precisely what sets the professions apart from the entrepreneurial orientation of other occupational groups. To the extent that a profession has a clear view of its mission within society, it will be able to perform its role and continue to define itself through periods of societal change. Indeed, within the last two decades, questions of societal role and obligations have become increasingly central in the discussion of professional ethics, especially within the therapeutic and health-related fields (Jennings, Callahan & Wolf, 1987). Recreational therapy, a profession which lacks philosophical consensus, and whose members often define themselves as "aphilosophical," if not downright "anti-philosophical," thus runs the risk of losing its way in times of global upheaval such as we are now experiencing.

In this chapter we will look at the major trends which are sweeping global society and the American health care system to see how they may affect the practice of recreational therapy in the next millennium.

Effects of Globalization

The sweeping changes in society today amount to a globalization of such scope and intensity as to upset old institutions and give rise to new sets of social problems. Globalization is a many-stranded development, involving interlocking relationships among ecological, social, economic, political and cultural systems. As many environmental problems become global in scope, the need for coordinated actions by the world's peoples has become crucial. Economic activity, too, has become increasingly global in scope. Indeed, some transnational corporations have budgets which dwarf those of many national governments. Newly integrated financial markets circulate as much as a trillion dollars a day, undermining the ability of national governments to determine their own social and economic policies. When this degree of change is occurring at the level of national governments, it is certain to bring radical changes within specific professions.

The simultaneous need for coordinated action and the erosion of national sovereignty has spawned new institutions and organizations, both "above" the nation state and "below" the nation state. Further, significant shifts in human populations have led to tensions and changes in the idea of national identity. In the cultural area, the integrative forces of "modernization" are sweeping the globe at the same time as increasing fragmentation is manifest in the form of national, regional, ethnic and religious movements. This tendency towards globalization is not a simple evolution in the direction of integration of the world's peoples. Rather, the emerging world is a complex mosaic of junctions and disjunctions, yielding new questions and new uncertainties and demanding a creative, flexible response at all levels.

Scholars of international relations point to the growing interconnectedness of national economies and expanding global trading patterns. While these experts may argue over any number of issues, they generally agree that three broad areas of global change will have enormous impact on all of our lives: (a) the continuing technology explosion; (b) global population changes; (c) the transformation of the global labor force (Kennedy, 1993).

The first of these, the impact of *technology* upon our lives and professional service is so pervasive, profound and obvious that it needs little discussion. The pace of today's technological changes, together with the liberation of investment capital and the information revolution, results in an outpouring of new devices, techniques, instruments and products — items which we swiftly take for granted but which hardly existed ten years earlier (cellular phones, advancing computer technology and applications, the growth of Internet communications). We must ask ourselves how this technological explosion affects our profession and how our profession responds to it — both in terms of adaptation and contribution to the new technology. The simple change from a pen-and-paper method of record keeping to a national computerized data set for Medicare and Medicaid reimbursement is one example of the impact of technology on the health care professions. Far from adapting to such changes, many have resisted them. The nature of coming global changes is such that the professions need to be in the forefront of designing the new technologies. Where are recreational therapy professionals when it comes to developing new computer games for rehabilitation clients? When it is a question of designing software applications which will expedite the record keeping system so that it can be integrated with the information needed by other professions?

A second major global trend is the vast increase in the human *population* of the planet (Aronowitz & DiFazio, 1994). There were two billion people living in

1925 and that had doubled to four billion by 1975. Today there are almost six billion people alive and we are adding to that total by about ninety-five million each year. These increases are not uniform across the globe — 95% of the forecast doubling of the world's overall population in the next half-century will take place in the poorer societies (Kennedy, 1993). This major change will have enormous impact on all human service professions, including our own. For example, the population explosion projected to occur in poorer societies will not remain there. Massive shifts in human populations through migrations will continue to bring about tensions and value conflicts related to cultural differences. Human service professionals in the new global economy will ideally be multilingual, and able to deal with cultural diversity. Migration patterns can mean changes in urban housing, life-style and health needs. Building community in the face of such changes will call for flexible thinking and creativity and professionals prepared to function on the cutting edge of policy making.

The third major force for global change, which results from the combination of the other two, is the vast expansion of people predicted to enter the *workforce* over the next generation. There are an estimated 250 million workers in North America and Europe. These workers enjoy relatively high wages internationally. Over the last twenty years we have seen many of these workers come under pressure from the emergence of 90 million further workers in the far East who can produce the same goods at considerably lower cost (our Nike sneakers, for example). In the industries affected, this change has already led to considerable downsizing and relocation of factories to lower labor cost regions (Aronowitz & DiFazio, 1994). But, it is estimated that over the next 20 years a further 1.2 billion workers will enter into the global workforce in South Asia, East Asia and Latin America, with an average wage of merely three US dollars a day compared with the average wage in the US and Europe of 85 US dollars a day (Kennedy, 1993).

The consequences of this process are staggering. Predictions are that wages in the affected industries will fall by 50% over the next two decades. The struggle for survival will reach monumental proportions. The question, simply put, is this: can 1.2 billion people enter the global workforce within one generation without damaging the ecosystem — or are those numbers simply so large, and is the pace of change going to be so fast that it will overwhelm existing social and political structures, both in the developed world and the developing world (Aronowitz & DiFazio, 1994)?

Effects on the West

The explosion within the global workforce has already begun. Most of us have already seen the effects of down-sizing in this country in production of goods, and in middle management levels of goods and services. As an illustration of this trend, Kapstein (1996) cites frightening unemployment figures.

> Manufacturing employment fell by 1.4 million between 1978 and 1990. Those who lost their jobs were, in general, the unskilled, and when they found new work it was usually at lower pay. The experience has now become familiar to middle managers as well, as evidenced by the recent spate of major corporate layoffs. The failure of the industrial sector to generate new jobs has been a major cause of labor's economic problems, and perhaps some of America's social problems more generally. Fully two percent of all working-age American men are behind bars. (Kapstein, 1996, p. 23)

Lest we should think the US is alone in this alarming situation, Kapstein, (1996) cites similar, and in some cases even darker, unemployment figures from Canada and Western Europe. In fact, he believes that the Europeans have created a lost generation of workers and are now suffering for it in terms of increased crime, drug abuse, violence against immigrants and the increasing popularity of extremist political groups. Judy and D'Amico (1997) note that while automation and globalization will bring continued loss of manufacturing jobs in the US, the manufacturing jobs that remain will be more highly skilled and more highly paid. These authors predict that most employment growth will remain concentrated in the service sector. Aronowitz and DiFazio (1994), too, predict continued extensive losses of well-paid jobs across the board as a result of coming global workforce changes. On top of the lower pay, there is another concern with the new jobs. Many of them do not have health care benefits. This trend in the job market is another force which will reduce the number of dollars available for health care. These authors do have one prediction that is heartening, namely, that those service sector jobs which are focused on *caring* will be more likely candidates for growth.

Effects on Health Care

Unfortunately the trend in health care seems to be away from caring as more and more energy is put into the business side of the health care industry. Our efforts are put into trying to be more productive, more closely aligned with the new global model of a successful business. Just as business has seldom cared about its workers beyond contractual requirements, the health care industry is traveling the path of not caring about its patients. The concern is for cheaper, faster, better, but not for patients, only for profits. Because of this, critics of the American medical system have faulted it for its relationship to big business. Kass (1985), a physician himself, believes that American medicine is in real trouble. He finds that it has forsaken the relationship between doctor and patient. Citing the lack of funding for palliative care within the American health care system, Kass argues that the business approach has permitted the profit motive to thwart the real goals of medical care. Thus, a patient whose disease is not responsive to curative treatment is not eligible for most funded health care services. Others, too, have described medical situations illustrating the fact that business and medicine are ethically incompatible (Veatch, 1983; Fins, 1992). They would claim that the very thing that makes business successful in a populous land of consumers — mass production — is essentially incompatible with the aspect of medical care most Americans treasure, namely competent personal care clearly in the interest of the patient, a fiduciary relationship, a sense of professional trust.

Treatises on the art of medicine point this out as critically important to healing people in contrast to treating disease. Unfortunately, medicine has caught the eye of those who look to its profitability and not to its purpose, of which profits are only a spin-off. Health care in the US exists within a complex marketplace, and within this setting it seems to be becoming a commodity — "like beer or pantyhose" as Veatch (1983) puts it.

Implications for Recreational Therapy

Where is recreational therapy in the midst of such overwhelming global and system change? The temptation for recreational therapy, as for many human service professions, is not to look at the wider world changing around it, but to concentrate instead on its own immediate sphere of experience. With cutbacks in social service funding, restrictive pressures from managed care and reduced funding for the health care system, human service professions can see themselves facing hard times, even as the US economy crests toward the millennium. In this context, Callahan (1981) warns that hard times can bring a shrinking moral perspective, one that loses sight of the community and the common good, and seeks rather to compete as successfully as possible for a share of the dwindling resources. For the helping professions, then, the risk of hard times is the adoption of a self-protective "survival mode" that nurtures a self-interested approach to the service sector, tough competition with other professions and little concern for the larger moral issues.

At this point in the history of the service professions, such a minimalist view would be woefully retrogressive. We face constant warnings about the short-sightedness of "me-first-ism," especially as practiced by large interest groups. If recreational therapy is to shape its future with a keen sense of moral issues and socioeconomic realities, it must get beyond the blinkered perspective of a survival mode. We exist in an emerging global economy which ranges beyond local concerns and the seemingly fixed patterns of the past. Our corresponding moral perspective requires an ethical sensitivity that is communal in a breathtaking way. In this perspective, we are called to have moral concerns that stretch from the rain-forests of Central America to the urban blight of Detroit and Calcutta, from the Asian child labor that produces our sneakers to the multi-national corporate takeovers that can destabilize labor forces worldwide (Aronowitz & DiFazio, 1994).

While a minimalist ethical approach would simply confine itself to concern about the threats these global changes might bring to our personal lives and our profession, experts suggest that global survival is only going to be possible if we can get beyond local, self-interested concerns and adopt a world-view approach (Judy & D'Amico, 1997).

Even in the midst of potential economic threats, the profession may be able to move beyond an ethic of survival and invest its energies in the caring side of service but there are no guarantees. If there is any question about this being a real concern, we need only look at the recent history of the profession.

The unabashedly commercial aspects of the health care business model can be discerned in some of our recent developments. For example at recent annual ATRA and NTRS conferences, special sessions have been offered on managed care, and ATRA itself has contracted with a Washington law firm to help it monitor reimbursement and managed care issues. NTRS also is involved in such monitoring. Similarly, a recent text in recreational therapy discusses implications of the rapidly changing and reform-conscious health care market, and explains how insurance companies want to be able to predict the length and course of hospitalization for specific diagnoses, to be able to evaluate the hospital's cost efficiency in the delivery of accepted and appropriate quality care (Grote, Hasl, Krider & Mortensen, 1995). In short, the health care business model brings not only a clinical framework to our profession; it also brings the framework of the medical marketplace.

Because the commercial sector tends toward the minimalist ethical position, a number of moral risks and challenges arise when only the commercial model is applied in professions which are essentially dedicated to caring. It is indeed difficult for caring professions to exist in the commercial sector without compromising their service to individuals and to society. It is interesting, if not alarming to note, for example, that two out of five Florida physicians have an interest in a medical business venture to which they self-refer patients and that 93% of imaging centers in that state are owned by physicians (Brammer, 1992). Medical journals are replete with articles on the conflict of interest between good medical practice and medical cost containment. One case describes a New Jersey hospital where a thoracic surgeon's privileges were withdrawn because he was compared with another surgeon who screened his patients carefully, rejecting smokers, overweight people and other risks. The surgeon who lost privileges accepted sicker patients who had to stay in the hospital an average of five days longer. There is no information given about whether the costlier surgeon's patients were less happy to be alive or less worthy contributors to society. It seems he was punished simply because his work cost the hospital more than insurers were willing to pay (Begley, 1993). Indicating the same concerns, Morreim (1988) warns that financial incentives to reduce cost represent a profound challenge to physicians' fiduciary commitment to honor patients' interests above their own.

It is clear from these and other examples that the commercial model can be used to deconstruct professional values and goals, to the point that long cherished notions of professionalism can disappear. This can happen in our profession, too. A report from the ATRA Reimbursement Committee (1994) urges practitioners "to prioritize the patients we know we can obtain an outcome with and market ourselves as a cost-effective, reimbursable service." We might ask — is the profession here looking to see how it can serve the needs of the community or how the community can serve its needs? A speaker at the 1995 NRPA conference in San Antonio, urged rather sternly, that it was time to get beyond fun and games and realize that we are a business. The point is that when professional self-interest drives decisions about service, the professional/client relationship inevitably erodes and society eventually begins to lose trust in the profession. This is increasingly apparent in managed care, where the patient is seen more and more as product. Is this really the route we, as a profession, want to take?

Suggested Solutions

Having said all this, I have to add that I do believe that there is much that we can learn from business, from the commercial approach. We do not necessarily have to fixate on the bottom line, nor on prestige and power and position; neither do we have to shift into minimalist ethics and the competitive quality of the marketplace. Peter Drucker, one of the acknowledged business experts in this country, tells us that the first requirement for good business is excellence of product or service (Drucker, 1993). He insists further that good business looks to both long term and short term goals. Third, he tells us that good business is creative.

Provocatively, Drucker insists that the era in which we are living is a time of transition from a post-capitalist society to a knowledge society. In the emerging post-capitalist world, the educated person must function in terms of global knowledge. This means, first of all, that the educated person must be universally educated, not simply grounded in the Western, Judeo-Christian tradition. The coming global knowledge society will need people educated to appreciate a wide diversity of cultures and traditions. Education of this sort means training in perception as much as in analysis. The educated person must be a citizen of the world, a person of wide-ranging vision, horizon and information. S/he will have to be prepared to live and work simultaneously in two cultures — that of the "intellectual" who focuses on words and ideas and that of the "manager" who focuses on the interaction of people and the processes of work.

In Drucker's view this special sort of expertise calls for an integration of *techne* with knowledge. For too long, he insists, *techne* (professional knowledge, particularly in its practice-based application) was not considered genuine knowledge and, as a result, a kind of mutual antagonism has developed between the two. We see this in the university setting where some academics do not consider professional knowledge to involve real scholarship and, conversely, we find professionals looking down upon the liberal arts as useless knowledge. This point has direct implications for the recreational therapy professional. Too frequently s/he is focused exclusively on *techne* issues, those directly pertaining to delivery of recreational therapy service. That is not enough, Drucker is telling us. It has not been enough in the past, and it certainly will not be enough in the global knowledge society where the world of ideas will have to be included in the recreational therapy practitioner's service.

The educated person in the knowledge society, says Drucker, may indeed become more specialized, but s/he will understand the various other knowledges. What is each one about? What does each one do? What are its central concerns and theories? What major new insights has it produced? How are they connected with our special knowledge? The specialists, he insists, have to take responsibility for making both themselves and their specialty understood, and the specialties must be understood for what they are — serious, rigorous, demanding disciplines, keenly interested in, open to and aware of what is going on in every other specialty. If we do this we will be able to move a long way toward fighting the global trends which tend to make health care less caring and move into the next millennium with the understanding that the profession has of its mission to provide caring services. Not much has been done in recreational therapy yet, but one of the early steps can be found in this book in Chapter 13, *Customer Service*.

Summary

The discourse of recreational therapy does not generally connect these larger political, economic and social issues with its service. Yet, our profession has much to contribute to public policy in every area, but especially in this vital area that guarantees that caring remains in health care. If we fail to become involved in shaping public policy, we run the risk of simply perpetuating (for our own advantage) the ills of the system we are supposed to be serving. Such a minimalist ethics approach might have sufficed in the past. The global transformation which is now taking place, however, is of such magnitude that only a serious concern for the common good will enable us to survive.

Learning Activities

1. Collect five days worth of the daily newspaper. Make an inventory of all the articles which relate to each of the three broad areas of global change listed by Kennedy (1993). Summarize each article in two to six sentences. Then summarize all the contents of each area. Write a short summary of how the information in each area may affect future practice in recreational therapy.
2. Find three health care journal articles which discuss cost containment or managed care. What services were lost due to cost containment/managed care? Were any added? What were the reasons and justifications given/implied in the articles for the cost containment measures? How would you justify (or would you justify?) restoration of the lost services to your facility's board of directors?
3. Compare journal articles from the 1960's and 1970's to journal articles from the 1980's and 1990's. (Preferably these articles are related to recreational therapy or activity therapy services.) Is there a difference in scope and number of articles discussing cultural issues? What are the differences and what kind of trends do you see?
4. Review at least five web sites of different health care professional groups. What information can you find which would fit into the three broad areas of global change as discussed by Kennedy? What trends do you find (or not find)? Discuss your findings related to how well the professional groups are addressing global change. Are they being pro-active or survivalist? Why do you feel this way?
5. Obtain a copy of the want ads in the Sunday newspaper. Go to the library and find a copy of the same paper's want ads from 15 years earlier (same month). Compare the difference in the number and type of health care, recreational therapy/activity professional and technology jobs being listed. What are the differences and the similarities you find when you compare the two sets of want ads?

Study Questions

1. What are Kennedy's three broad areas of global change which will have enormous impact on all of our lives?
2. Why might a rugged professional individualism and adopting a survivalist mode weaken the field's well-being in the emerging global economy?

3. How must an educated person function in the emerging post-capitalistic world?
4. Why is *techne* not enough?
5. What are the effects of managed care on the fiduciary relationship between the health care professional and his/her patient?

References

Aronowitz, S. & DiFazio, W. (1994). *The jobless future*. Minneapolis: University of Minnesota Press.

ATRA Reimbursement Committee. (1994). Reimbursement for partial hospitalization. *American Therapeutic Recreation Association Newsletter, 9*(7), 3.

Begley, C. (1993). Cost containment and conflicts of interest. In G. Winslow & J. Walters (Eds.). *Facing limits*. Boulder, CO: Westview Press.

Brammer, R. (1992, March 30). Dubious practice: Radiation is at the center of the storm over self-referrals. *Barron's*, pp. 10-11, 37-39.

Callahan, D. (1981). Minimalist ethics: On the pacification of morality. In A. Caplan & D. Callahan (Eds.). *Ethics in hard times*. New York: Plenum Press.

Drucker, P. (1993). *Post-capitalist society*. New York: HarperCollins.

Fins, J. (1992). The hidden costs of market-based health care reform. *Hastings Center Report, 22*(3), 6.

Grote, K., Hasl, M., Krider, R. & Mortensen, D. (1995). *Behavioral health protocols for recreational therapy*. Ravensdale, WA: Idyll Arbor.

Jennings, B., Callahan, D. & Wolf, S. (1987). The professions: Public interest and common good. *Hastings Center Report, 17*, 1-20.

Judy, R. & D'Amico, C. (1997). *Workforce 2020: Work and workers in the 21st century*. Indianapolis, IN: Hudson Institute Press.

Kapstein, E. (1996, May/June). Workers and the world economy. *Foreign Affairs*, (16-37).

Kass, L. (1985). *Towards a more natural science*. New York: Free Press.

Kennedy, P. (1993). *Preparing for the twenty-first century*. New York: Random House.

Morreim, E. (1988). Cost containment: Challenging fidelity and justice. *Hastings Center Report, 18*, 20-25.

Veatch, R. (1983). The case for contract in medical ethics. In E. Shelp (Ed.). *The clinical encounter: The moral fabric of the patient physician relationship*. Boston: Reidel.

Chapter 27

Future of the Profession

Thomas K. Skalko

We must respect the past, and mistrust the present, if we wish to provide the safety of the future.

— Joseph Joubert

Successful speculation about the future of the profession is contingent upon our abilities as a collective to be proactive in an ever-changing health care environment. The activities of the whole, including efficacy research, continued resolutions of philosophical differences and public policy activities, will propel the profession forward into the 21st century. To fully appreciate the complexity of the issue and to establish an understanding of the potential future of the profession, one must begin by comprehending the past and our evolution to the present.

Historically, recreational therapy has its roots in hospital recreation. The provision of hospital recreation services was advanced as a result of World Wars I and II. However, as indicated by O'Morrow (1989), the growth of hospital recreation was slow until the Second World War. Since the 1940's, recreational therapy (therapeutic recreation) has experienced a steady period of growth. This growth has been a result of shifting concepts in health care, expanded provision of recreational therapy services, the improved practice of recreational therapy and the development of professional organizations representing the profession (Reynolds & O'Morrow, 1985).

The future of every allied health profession will be defined by the evolving health care and social systems and the professional activities of the discipline. For recreational therapy, such activities as continued debate regarding our philosophical foundations, public policy activities, professional preparation, research and moves toward the standardization of professional practice will all play a significant role in mapping the future.

Progress in the Rights of Persons with Disabilities

Significant progress was made with regard to the rights of persons with disabilities during the decades of the seventies, eighties and nineties. The passage of the Architectural and Transportation Barriers Act of 1968 (PL 90-480), the Rehabilitation Act of 1973 (PL 93-112) and subsequent amendments, and the passage of the Education for All Handicapped Children Act of 1975 (PL 94-142) and subsequent amendments including the Individuals with Disabilities Education Act of 1992 (IDEA, PL 101-476) have all transformed access to services for persons with disabilities. These efforts have been monumental in setting the groundwork for today's system of services.

Although the principles of these legislative efforts are rarely fully implemented in our imperfect system, progress has been realized. In 1992, the passage of the Americans with Disabilities Act (ADA, PL 101-336) served as a true advancement in the rights of persons with disabilities to accessible opportunities and services. The application of the principles of the ADA alone has significant implications for all public service fields and will affect the mission of our discipline.

Demographic Influences

Demographic trends have impacted and will continue to influence service delivery in recreational therapy. As the percentage of our population comprised of older adults, individuals with chronic disabilities, persons who are frail or at-risk and persons with severe and diverse disabilities increases, the demands for professional service providers will also escalate. Currently, persons 65 years of age or older represent nearly 13% of our population. In the first quarter of the next century, this segment of the population will represent 25% of the population in the US (Riley & Skalko, 1998). Currently, the physical therapy and occupational therapy professions hold dominant positions in projections for allied health professionals. Recreational therapy has also been identified among the fastest growing of all professions (US Department of Labor, 1994). Ultimately, however, the most marketable service provider will be the multi-skilled *health care* practitioner with professional training founded in strong clinical practice and the support of a unified professional body. Without reform within professional preparation, the prognosis for recreational therapy is evident.

Another trend is the increasing diversity of the cultural composition of our social system. In the year 2000, it is estimated that one-third of the North American population will be comprised of ethnic minorities. This percentage will grow to 52% by the year 2010 (Atkinson, Morten & Sue, 1993). Such changes will require professionals with the multi-cultural sensitivity necessary to respond to the needs of the consumer.

Continuing Health Care Reform

Coupled with the advancement of social rights for all persons, including persons with disabilities, and the changing demographics of our social system, has been the rapidly transforming health care industry. Since the inception of the Social Security Act of 1935 and the subsequent amendments, the health care industry has evolved into a system that requires responsible practice, cost-effective service delivery, accountability and outcome-focused care (Reitter, 1989; Skalko & Malkin, 1992). Practices of the retrospective payment systems are non-existent and the prospective payment system is rapidly becoming obsolete. Capitated systems of health care delivery are emerging as ways to stem the upward spiral in health care costs (Zimmerman & Skalko, 1994) and health care rationing is being examined as a viable alternative. Only those services that are deemed medically necessary to the treatment and/or rehabilitation of the individual will be included in the bundle of services provided to the consumer. These will be the services perceived to possess value.

As our health care system struggles with ways to keep costs down, more emphasis will be placed on preventative services. For example, behavioral medicine approaches are emerging as a possible option to the strict medical model to treating disease and illness and focus will be on personal health and preventative practices. Recreational therapy service providers possess a unique opportunity to refine their skills through professional preparation and continuing education to develop the competencies and credentials to secure a place in the preventative market. As with all of allied health, such alternatives will be required in order to meet the demands of accountability, cost-effectiveness and health outcome production.

Disciplines that do not respond to the rapidly charging environment will not survive the revolution. Again, it will be the charge of the profession and the individual practitioner to assume the responsibilities for facilitating progress that is responsive to the shifting health care environment. The transformations essential for recreational therapy to position itself as a viable service alternative are obvious. The discipline must seriously evaluate the incompatible practices in professional preparation and professional affiliations that do not translate well to the health care system. The lack of consistency in recreational therapy professional practice for addressing patient health outcomes and increased attention to the demonstration of meaningful health care value must be a priority. Finally, the activities of the professional associations (American Therapeutic Recreation Association and National Therapeutic Recreation Society) must either focus on unified activities that promote the discipline as a viable health care service option, or the organizations must choose to defend the separate yet parallel missions of treatment and recreation based upon the philosophical orientation of each organization.

Given the past and current trends, the future of recreational therapy will be contingent upon resolution of several issues. It will be the successful resolution of these issues that will propel recreational therapy into the twenty-first century.

Philosophy and the Future

Although there exist differing philosophical positions within the field as a whole, the ultimate mission, as practiced, has been the provision of health oriented services whether that be in the form of active treatment services within the medical system or the provision of recreation services and opportunities in a community setting. The outcomes of our services have focused on the facilitation of the individual consumer's functional skills and abilities and the provision of opportunities so that the individual may access the highest possible quality of life.

The differences that have existed in our philosophical orientations may become less obvious. On a more pragmatic and perhaps optimistic note, the passage of the Americans with Disabilities Act of 1992 (PL 101-336) should bring about some resolution to the philosophical position discussion. If all persons are entitled to the provision of a full range of integrated services and opportunities as a legal right, then the provision of recreation services is the charge of all providers of the broader recreation and leisure service industry. The provision of recreation services for individuals with disabilities cannot and should not therefore be entitled "therapeutic recreation," "recreational therapy," special recreation or any other vernacular denoting an exception to standard services. Since this landmark legislation embraces the concept of human dignity, to relegate persons to "specialized" services is contradictory to the intent of the law and appropriate practice. The mission of the field, consequently, may move to that of providing services that address the preventative, treatment or health promotion needs of the consumer. This mission, however, does not abrogate our profession's responsibility to advocate for the provision of recreation services for all persons (including persons with disabilities) or to provide recreation services if it is perceived that the qualified provider best suited for these endeavors is the Certified Therapeutic Recreation Specialists (CTRS). In fact, the concept of illness prevention and treatment and health promotion is consistent with these advocacy activities. The CTRS employed as a health care practitioner may make opportunities available for health care consumers to engage in recreation services as an aspect of their service delivery system. The primary mission of the health care agency and service department, however, will remain that of treatment and health promotion/illness prevention. In turn, the primary mission of our discipline must be consistent with the treatment and health promotion/illness prevention focus of the health care delivery system of the present and future (Skalko, 1997). To compete within this market, however, we must be recognized as an allied health discipline versus a recreation and park service.

It is important to note that the terms recreational therapy and therapeutic recreation have been used interchangeably. Perhaps it is time to define these terms and to adopt language to differentiate these services. The philosophical orientation that emerges in the future will dictate the most appropriate nomenclature. If, indeed, our discipline is a treatment modality, then perhaps the appropriate and accepted taxonomy is "recreational therapy." If we perceive ourselves as a recreation and park discipline, then the historically agreed upon vernacular is "recreation," "therapeutic recreation," or "hospital recreation." (For a discussion on terminology, see Reynolds & O'Morrow, 1985, pp. 17-18).

Health Care Public Policy, Accreditation, Regulatory Standards and the Future

Activities to influence public policy and health care regulatory and accreditation standards are among the most salient endeavors in which recreational therapy must engage. It is through lobbying and education efforts that policy makers, administrative managers, health care regulatory agencies, health care accreditation agencies and consumers are informed about our services and the role recreational therapy plays in the rehabilitation/habilitation, treatment and prevention process. Until we educate policy and standard makers at all levels, recreational therapy will not realize its goal of full integration into the health care delivery system as a recognized allied health discipline (Hamilton & Austin, 1992).

Traditionally, recreational therapy has not demonstrated itself to be a politically active lobby for the inclusion of recreational therapy as a treatment modality within the health care system. Unless recreational therapists, as individuals, accept personal responsibility for participating in the political process, the future will require continuous energy reacting to the evolving health care system instead of engaging in proactive enterprises.

Public Policy Efforts

The 1990's have represented a significant shift and have increased attention to public policy activities for recreational therapy service providers. Due to the efforts of both professional organizations, the public policy arena has been partially transformed. Through the leadership of ATRA's 1993-94 Health Care Reform Task Force, the 1994 ATRA Committee on Public Policy, the NTRS

Legislative Action Committee and the Boards of Directors of the American Therapeutic Recreation Association and the National Therapeutic Recreation Society, pivotal progress was made. In addition, collaborative activities of both the NTRS and the ATRA Board of Directors and public policy representatives served to increase awareness across the discipline and among policy representatives. Among the activities of consequence for the profession have been

- The development of four documents by the ATRA Task Force on Health Care Reform. *Recreational Therapy: A Comprehensive Aspect of Health Care, Recreational Therapy: A Cost-Beneficial Option, Recreational Therapy: A Summary of Health Outcomes* and *Therapeutic Recreation's Role in Health Care Reform* were developed to educate and promote the inclusion of recreational therapy as a standard benefit within the health care reform initiative.
- The National Therapeutic Recreation Society's Legislative Action Committee developed and disseminated a separate document, *Therapeutic Recreation and Health Care Reform*, also urging the inclusion of recreational therapy in any standard medical plan developed as a part of the health care reform initiative.
- In February, 1994, a joint statement was developed and adopted by the American Therapeutic Recreation Association and the National Therapeutic Recreation Society called *Therapeutic Recreation: Responding to the Challenges of Health Care Reform*.
- The dissemination of the health care reform documents and materials to every member of the United States Congress (House of Representatives and Senate) via mass mailings and individual visitations by representatives of ATRA, NTRS and the profession.
- The hosting of several congressional receptions for members of both the Unites States House of Representatives and Senate to promote the health outcomes of recreational therapy services. ATRA alone sponsored five congressional receptions between July 1993 and June 1994 and continued annually through the Annual Summit on Legislative Advocacy. In addition, the National Recreation and Park Association and the National Therapeutic Recreation Society host a congressional reception and legislative day during the annual mid-year meetings.
- The provision of representation by both ATRA and NTRS on national health care coalitions and offering input into the language in health care legislation.
- The submission of reports by ATRA to private actuary firms collecting information for Congress on health care benefits and costs.

- The implementation of a national effort to gather data on the cost-utilization of recreational therapy services in health care by the ATRA Committee on Public Policy.

Through these efforts, every member of Congress and related public policy players received materials promoting the provision of recreational therapy services as a viable treatment option within the rehabilitation process. These activities were significant in educating public policy interests on the role and benefits of recreational therapy services.

It is important to note, however, that unprecedented work continues to be required. Due to professional affiliations and service priorities, we as a professional collective have neglected the health care public policy realm for decades. The legislative council representing recreational therapy since the 1960's, for example, has ignored the Social Security Act and subsequent amendments. Current efforts must make up for past digressions and disregard for the inclusion of recreational therapy within health care public policy. In addition, collaborative efforts between the national organizations will continue to be a must in the public policy arena.

Health Care Accreditation and
Regulatory Agency Interactions

Other advancements that will shape the future of recreational therapy include activities of our professional organizations and individuals with regard to health care accreditation and regulatory agencies, particularly the Joint Commission on Accreditation of Healthcare Organizations (JCAHO), CARF: The Rehabilitation Accreditation Commission and the Health Care Financing Administration (HCFA) (Smith & Land, 1989). Within the past decade, the profession has significantly increased activity in this realm (Donovan, 1987).

The early work of individual professionals from the National Therapeutic Recreation Society served as the beginning point in the incorporation of recreational therapy into contemporary health care accreditation standards. The recent efforts of both the American Therapeutic Recreation Association and the National Therapeutic Recreation Society have produced further progress in promoting the recognition of recreational therapy services within the standards of the Joint Commission on Accreditation of Healthcare Organizations (JCAHO). As part of the restructuring of the JCAHO standards review process, related allied health interests were consolidated into the Coalition of Rehabilitation Therapy Organizations. The Coalition of Rehabilitation Therapy Organizations (CRTO) was comprised of representatives (primarily the presidents and executive directors) from the American Occupational Therapy Association (AOTA), the American Physical Therapy Association (APTA), the American Speech, Language and Hearing Association (ASHA), the American Therapeutic Recreation Association (ATRA), the National Coalition of Arts Therapies Association (NCATA) and the National Therapeutic Recreation Society (NTRS). The CRTO, as part of the input loop of the Joint Commission, collectively holds one seat on each of five Professional and Technical Advisory Committees (PTACs) with the opportunity to send observers from each of the participating organizations. The five PTACs represent diverse health care service settings and include the Hospital PTAC, the Long Term Care PTAC, the Ambulatory Care PTAC, the Home Health PTAC and the Behavioral Health PTAC. These PTACs review and respond to proposed modifications in the standards of each service area. Since the inception of the CRTO in 1991, ATRA and NTRS have provided sound leadership and involvement in the standards process by financially supporting the representation and participation of highly qualified recreational therapy professionals in the standards review process of the five Professional and Technical Advisory Committees (PTACs). This involvement represents meaningful progress and promise for the future of recreational therapy within the health care accreditation standards of JCAHO. These activities must be maintained as a priority of both of our national organizations if the progress is to continue.

A second significant accomplishment securing the future of recreational therapy as a viable player in the health care arena is the long term involvement of the American Therapeutic Recreation Association and the National Therapeutic Recreation Society with CARF: The Rehabilitation Accreditation Commission. Recreational therapy consumers and professionals, in concert with ATRA's and NTRS's CARF liaisons were instrumental in promoting the inclusion of recreational therapy within the CARF standards. ATRA became an Associate Member of CARF in 1988 thus enabling the profession to have input into the CARF standards review process. In 1992, ATRA advanced to a Sponsoring Member of CARF, thereby earning a seat on the CARF Board of Trustees. In addition, NTRS became an Associate Member of CARF providing representation and input from both professional organizations. Through this participation, recreational therapy has secured an avenue to educate health care accreditation interests on the role of recreational therapy within physical rehabilitation. Again, these efforts, paired with support from consumers, will help to secure an ongoing position for our profession in the health care industry of the future.

Within the structure of the federal government, the Health Care Financing Administration (HCFA) oversees regulations and guidelines as they relate to the federal Medicaid and Medicare programs. The profession has been involved in a series of sporadic activities and communications with HCFA representatives on the inclusion of recreational therapy as a reimbursable treatment modality under

Medicare and Medicaid. In the past, with the National Therapeutic Recreation Society and, more recently, with the ATRA Third-Party Reimbursement Committee and NTRS's HCFA liaison, communication between the profession and HCFA representatives has advanced support for the inclusion of recreational therapy (treatment services) as potentially reimbursable under Medicare and Medicaid. The service must, however, be medically necessary and address the medical and health care needs of the consumer (Thompson & Wagner, 1993; Wagner, 1994). The implications for the future are significant. In turn, our discipline must continue to differentiate between treatment and diversional activity. To date and for the foreseeable future, the provision of recreation and leisure services is seen as diversional activity and is not and will not be accepted as "active treatment." Furthermore, the expression of an "appropriate leisure lifestyle" has not been considered a medically necessary outcome and does not serve us well professionally or in the broader health care market place (Shank & Kinney, 1987). This is not to say that HCFA does not recognize the need for recreation and leisure opportunities as a routine service. The provision of recreation and leisure opportunities to the consumer is indeed identified in the guidelines. The question is whether our profession has considerably more to offer and whether focusing on the provision of diversional activity as our gift to the consumer fulfills our mission.

Activities of the future must focus on demonstrating the cost-effectiveness of recreational therapy services and the promotion of recreational therapy as a treatment service to public policy makers, third party intermediaries and the health care industry. The profession must continue to focus on our role in the prevention of illness and disability, the treatment of conditions and the promotion of health for the consumer through active, efficacious therapeutic approaches.

Professional Preparation and the Future

Professional preparation of qualified clinicians for the delivery of recreational therapy services ranks prominent among the needs of the field (Austin, 1989; Compton, 1989; Hamilton & Austin, 1992; Skalko, 1992; Skalko & Goldenberg, 1994). Educational reform may well serve as a pivotal factor in designing the future of our profession. This issue must be addressed on several fronts: first, the need for general educational reform in entry level preparation; second, the need for refinement of clinical skills for practicing professionals; finally, the critical shortage of doctoral personnel for higher education with clinical experience in recreational therapy practice.

At the entry level of preparation, questions are repeatedly asked about the role of the recreation core within the curriculum structure for recreational therapy professional preparation and the appropriateness of the educational accreditation standards set by the National Recreation and Park Association's Council on Accreditation in responding to recreational therapy curricular needs (Austin, 1989; Brasile, 1992; Compton, 1989; Skalko, 1992; Skalko & Goldenberg, 1994). The need exists for the establishment of a more unified set of curriculum standards specific to recreational therapy and the adoption of a more uniform professional preparation curricula across the nation. (See Chapter 19, *The Recreational Therapy Degree Program: Trends in Education* for more on this topic.) Currently, the diversity of curriculum offerings and the lack of consistency from university to university present a real dilemma (Hamilton & Austin, 1992). This quandary has implications that permeate recreational therapy practice itself. These standards should increasingly address the necessary core competencies for practice in the field.

In the area of professional continuing education, the issue remains consistent with that of pre-professional preparation (i.e., preparation or refinement of clinical competencies). Without ongoing involvement in well-planned continuing education activities the individual practitioner runs the risk of becoming obsolete (MacNeil, Teague, Cipriano, 1989). This holds true for direct service providers, managers and educators. It is essential that we maintain an emphasis on continuing education and begin to focus our efforts on practice competencies.

Finally, what of the future of the discipline? If there is a scarcity of doctoral personnel and a shortage of doctoral programs for the professional preparation of highly qualified educators and researchers, the future is in jeopardy. As presented by Compton (1989), "One of the major threats to the existence of professional preparation programs in therapeutic recreation is the diminishing number of quality doctoral programs and students" (p. 493). This concern was further reinforced in a study commissioned by the American Therapeutic Recreation Association and conducted by Compton in 1992. The study, designed to determine the status of therapeutic recreation in higher education, reinforced the realization that there is a crisis in professional preparation in content, accreditation and doctoral preparation (ATRA, 1992). Our professionals must begin to evaluate their potential for graduate and doctoral preparation in order to supply the depth of highly qualified personnel needed to support both entry level preparation and continuing education efforts. Again, the issue is not only a problem of higher education; it is also a problem of future vision on the part of the individual practitioner.

Professionals, both collectively and individually, must begin to understand the past, look to the future and demand reform within the system of higher education. This reform must embrace professional preparation that is responsive to recreational therapy practice competencies of today and tomorrow. Given the resistance to change at the university level, it will be the individual practitioners and the alumni of universities that must facilitate/demand professional preparation reform.

Professional Practice and the Future

Consistent with and contingent upon the issues of philosophy, public policy and professional preparation is the issue of professional practice. Currently, the field is challenged to continue productive discussion on these essential issues. However, significant progress has been made.

The field does possess documents regarding standards of practice to assist in establishing some semblance of consolidated practice. Although the application of modalities may vary, the standards of practice must remain constant (Reynolds & O'Morrow, 1985).

The National Therapeutic Recreation Society published, in 1982, the *Guidelines for Administration of Therapeutic Recreation Service in Clinical and Residential Facilities* and revised these standards in 1994. In 1993, the American Therapeutic Recreation Association published its most current set of professional practice standards entitled, *Standards for the Practice of Therapeutic Recreation & Self Assessment Guide*. These latter standards include contemporary health care practice concepts of structure, process and outcome criteria as they relate to the application of standards of practice for the field. In addition, the ATRA publication includes a *Self Assessment Guide* for use by the practitioner to better evaluate compliance with professional practice standards. Although these documents exist, it appears that some practitioners have not fully integrated the established standards of practice into everyday service delivery and there is extreme variability in practice. As we look to the future, it is incumbent upon our professional preparation programs and continuing education opportunities to educate the practitioner on the application of our professional standards of practice in every day service delivery.

Research and the Future

A final issue of critical concern with regard to the future of recreational therapy service delivery is the empirical validation of the efficacy of our services. This call has been voiced repeatedly across decades and authors (Compton, 1984; Coyle, Kinney, Riley & Shank, 1991; Hamilton & Austin, 1992; Linford & Kennedy, 1971; Reynolds & O'Morrow, 1985) and continues to dominate the literature. As with all allied health disciplines, we must begin to validate the efficacy of our services. It is through the demonstrated outcomes of our interventions (prevention through active treatment) that recreational therapy will secure its position as an effective health care service provider.

In examining this issue, the interrelated nature of most of the issues discussed in this chapter becomes evident. For instance, the professional preparation of highly qualified graduate and doctoral personnel as researchers, as well as administrators and educators, significantly affects the quality and quantity of research produced (Compton, 1989; Hamilton & Austin, 1992). The interrelatedness of outcomes research can also been seen within the public policy and regulatory domain. The demonstrated efficacy of recreational therapy interventions will have a profound impact upon the competitiveness of our discipline in efforts to include recreational therapy within public policy and regulatory domains. Research initiatives will also affect the marketability of recreational therapy services and the recognition of qualified professionals within the health care industry.

The most notable achievement for our field in recent times has been the research project conducted by Temple University and supported by the National Institute for Disability and Rehabilitation Research. The project was designed to demonstrate efficacy of therapeutic recreation as treatment modality. The outcomes of the project offer a pool of research on the benefits of interventions used in the practice of therapeutic recreation across diagnostic categories (Coyle, Kinney, Riley & Shank, 1991). The final report, however, identified the anemic status of research in the field and the reliance of the field on a base of research from a host of disciplines.

Outcome research will continue to be among the highest priorities for the field. It is, however, a long-term project and must be integrated into the strategic plans of the professional organizations. In 1992, ATRA through the American Therapeutic Recreation Foundation established a separate efficacy research fund to support efficacy research. This prompted the establishment of a similar fund within the NTRS in 1994. It will be through such efforts that a portion of the long term research needs of the field can be accomplished. These initiatives will not substitute for the inclusion of research within the strategic planning for our profession.

Within the longitudinal picture, research efforts are essential for long term health and prosperity. Faculty, practitioners and students of today will determine the progress of our research agenda for tomorrow. As with all issues, research does not belong to the academicians but to the collective. The collaborative efforts of educators, practitioners, students, consumers, health care agencies and professional organizations will define the research needs of the future.

The Future of Recreational Therapy

Next to being what we ought to be, the most desirable thing is that we should become what we ought to be as fast as possible.

— *Herbert Spencer*

The actions of the individual recreational therapist in concert with efforts of the composite will determine the future of the profession. Despite the reality of the issues and challenges of our current scenario, the progress of the past decade has been significant. Because of the efforts of individuals and organizations, recreational therapy practitioners have benefited from a number of advances including:

- expanded representation within public policy initiatives,
- representation within the health care accreditation process,
- increased communication with regulatory agencies,
- the evolution of the National Council for Therapeutic Recreation Certification as an accredited national professional credentialing organization,
- the continued advancement of professional preparation programs,
- a growing body of research, and
- an expanding program of education on the values of recreational therapy as a treatment modality to the health care industry.

Although issues must be addressed, we should always keep in mind the progress that has been made and the positive potential for the future. The changing health care environment, the altering demographics of our society and the potential contributions of our discipline through the individual practitioner will all interact to create the future.

The future of recreational therapy services is ultimately dependent upon the actions of the individual practitioner in concert with the whole. Should you express your discouragement in not being able to reach your vision, ask yourself what you have done to bring about that vision. Perhaps the first steps are to begin by adopting the first three of Covey's (1990) seven habits of highly effective people:

Habit #1: Be Proactive
As presented by Covey, proactivity is more than taking initiative but also responsibility for making things happen. Positive action is always better than reaction.

Habit #2: Begin with the End in Mind

Begin today with a picture or vision in your mind of who you will be at the end of your life as the criterion from which everything else can be examined. If you translate this to your profession and professional career, you can establish a vision for who you will be in relation to your professional endeavor. In being proactive, you can create the product.

Habit #3: Put First Things First

Habit 3 is the "day-in, day-out, moment-by-moment doing it" (Covey, 1990, p. 147). It is the implementation of Habits 1 and 2 while implementing principles of personal management and prioritizing activities.

If we can begin with these simple habits, perhaps the four remaining habits of Think Win/Win; Seek First to Understand, Then to Be Understood; Synergize; and Sharpen the Saw will come easier.

Habit #4: Think Win/Win

Effective relations seek to establish win/win scenarios. It is through win/win outcomes that all parties can continue to work in a collective and collaborative manner.

Habit #5: Seek First to Understand, Then to be Understood

The concept is to retrain yourself to listen to the other person's message without compromising the understanding by your own frame of reference. Through understanding the other person, you offer him/her an opportunity to meet his/her need to be understood, affirmed, validated and appreciated. After this occurs, you are able to focus on influencing and problem solving.

Habit #6: Synergize

To synergize is to put the parts into a whole. All the facets are put into an interdependent whole that works toward creative, productive outcomes. As practitioners we are all challenged to be proactive, establish visions and to work to integrate the parts into a collective whole.

Habit #7: Sharpen the Saw

Throughout the process of becoming, you must always take care of you. Find time for renewal and, with renewal, continue the process of reaching the vision.

To progress, we must begin by taking proactive, responsible action. The future will be what you envision if you are willing to accept the challenge.

Take charge of your life!...To act intelligently and effectively, we still must have a plan. To the proverb which says, "a journey of a thousand miles begins with a single step," I would add the words "and a road map."

— Cecile M. Springer

Learning Activities

1.   Divide the class into two groups. Have each group take the position of recreational therapy/therapeutic recreation being a member of either the recreation and parks profession or an allied health profession. Each group should defend its position.
2.   Identify the barriers to the advancement of the profession. Have groups offer solutions to the dilemmas that confront the discipline.
3.   Have each member of the class close their eyes and to envision what they would like the profession to be in the future. Have each member write a brief statement of his/her vision.
4.   Have the class divide into two or three groups. Have each group project what skills they think a recreational therapist should have when they graduate from college.

Study Questions

1.   Identify at least three implications of the current philosophical dilemma and discuss the importance of establishing a philosophical position for the field.
2.   Discuss at least three successes with regard to establishing recreational therapy as a viable health care discipline.
3.   Discuss your thoughts on professional preparation for recreational therapy and provide justification for your position.
4.   Identify at least three barriers to the advancement of recreational therapy as a viable health care discipline.

References

American Therapeutic Recreation Association. (1992). Status of therapeutic recreation in higher education. Study conducted by D. Compton. Unpublished report.

American Therapeutic Recreation Association. (1993). *Standards for the practice of therapeutic recreation & self assessment guide.* Hattiesburg, MS: American Therapeutic Recreation Association.

Atkinson, D. R., Morten, G. & Sue, D. W. (1993). *Counseling American minorities: A cross cultural perspective.* Dubuque, IA: Brown and Benchmark.

Austin, D. M. (1989). Therapeutic recreation education: A call for reform. In David Compton (Ed.). *Issues in therapeutic recreation: A profession in transition* (pp. 145-156). Champaign, IL: Sagamore Publishing.

Brasile, F. M. (1992). Professional preparation: Reported needs for a profession in transition. *Annual in Therapeutic Recreation, 3*, 58-71.

Compton, D. M. (1984). Research priorities in recreation for special populations. *Therapeutic Recreation Journal, 18*(1), 9-17.

Compton, D. M. (1989). Epilogue: On shaping the future of therapeutic recreation. In D. Compton (Ed.). *Issues in therapeutic recreation: A profession in transition* (pp. 483-500). Champaign, IL: Sagamore Publishing.

Covey, S. R. (1990). *The 7 habits of highly effective people: Powerful lessons in personal change.* New York: Fireside.

Coyle, C. P., Kinney, W. B., Riley, B. & Shank, J. W. (1991). *Benefits of therapeutic recreation: A consensus view.* Ravensdale, WA: Idyll Arbor, Inc.

Donovan, G. (1987). You want me to do what? Regulatory standards in therapeutic recreation. In B. Riley (Ed.). *Evaluation of therapeutic recreation through quality assurance* (pp. 25-35). State College, PA: Venture Publishing.

Hamilton, E. J. & Austin, D. R. (1992). Future perspectives of therapeutic recreation. *Annual in Therapeutic Recreation, 3*, 72-70.

Linford, A. G. & Kennedy, D. W. (1971). Research: The state of the art in therapeutic recreation. *Therapeutic Recreation Journal, 5*(4), 168-169, 190.

MacNeil, R. D., Teague, M. L. & Cipriano, R. E. (1989). The discontinuity of continuing education. In David Compton (Ed.). *Issues in therapeutic recreation: A profession in transition* (pp. 155-181). Champaign, IL: Sagamore Publishing.

National Therapeutic Recreation Society. (1980). *Standards of practice for therapeutic recreation service.* Ashburn, VA: National Recreation and Park Association.

National Therapeutic Recreation Society. (1982). *Guidelines for administration of therapeutic recreation service in clinical and residential facilities.* Ashburn, VA: National Recreation and Park Association.

National Therapeutic Recreation Society. (1992, May). *Philosophical statement of the National Therapeutic Recreation Society.* Ashburn, VA: National Recreation and Parks Association.

O'Morrow, G. S. & Reynolds, R. P. (1989). *Therapeutic recreation: A helping profession.* Englewood Cliffs, NJ: Prentice Hall.

Peterson, C. A. (1989). The dilemma of philosophy. In D. Compton (Ed.). *Issues in therapeutic recreation: A profession in transition* (pp. 20-33). Champaign, IL: Sagamore Publishing.

Reitter, M. S. (1989). Third-party payers: Are we getting our share? In D. Compton (Ed.). *Issues in therapeutic recreation: A profession in transition* (pp. 239-256). Champaign, IL: Sagamore Publishing.

Reynolds, R. P. & O'Morrow, G. S. (1985). *Problems, issues, and concepts in therapeutic recreation.* Englewood Cliffs, NJ: Prentice-Hall, Inc.

Riley, B. & Skalko, T. K. (1998, May). The evolution of therapeutic recreation. *Parks and Recreation, 33*(5), 65-71.

Shank, J. & Kinney, T. (1987). On the neglect of clinical practice. In C. Sylvester (Ed.). *Philosophy of therapeutic recreation: Ideas and issues. Vol. 1* (pp. 65-75). Ashburn, VA: National Recreation and Park Association.

Skalko, T. K. (1992, May/June). Recreational therapy: Clearing the confusion. *ATRA Newsletter,* *8*(3), 3-4.

Skalko, T. K. (1997). Therapeutic recreation: At pragmatic crossroads. *Virginia Recreation and Park Society Magazine, 21*(3), 8-9,13.

Skalko, T. K. & Goldenberg, R. (1994, September). Practitioners' perspective on educational preparation: A national survey. Poster Session conducted at the American Therapeutic Recreation Association Annual Conference, Orlando, FL.

Skalko, T. K. & Malkin, M. J. (1992). Current status of third-party reimbursement for therapeutic recreation services: Where do we go from here? *Annual in Therapeutic Recreation, 3*, 80-89.

Smith, S. H. & Land, C. (1989). Playing the standards game: Considerations for the 1990s. In D. Compton (Ed.). *Issues in therapeutic recreation: A profession in transition* (pp. 271-288). Champaign, IL: Sagamore Publishing.

Thompson, G. T. & Wagner, D. (1993, November/December). Reimbursement committee Q & A. *ATRA Newsletter, 9*(6), 3-4.

US Department of Labor. (1994). *Occupational outlook handbook*, 1994 Edition. Washington, DC: US Department of Labor.

Wagner, D. (1994, January/February). HCFA reaffirms position in rehabilitation. *ATRA Newsletter, 9*, 7.

Zimmerman, D. & Skalko, J. J. (1994). *Reengineering health care: A vision for the future.* Franklin, WI: Eagle Press.

Appendices

Appendix A

Definitions

American Therapeutic Recreation Association

Therapeutic Recreation is the provision of treatment services and the provision of recreation services to person with illnesses or disabling conditions. The primary purposes of treatment services, often referred to as Recreational Therapy, are to restore, remediate or rehabilitate in order to improve functioning and independence, as well as reduce or eliminate the effects of illness or disability. The primary purposes of recreation services are to provide recreation resources and opportunities in order to improve health and well-being. Therapeutic Recreation is provided by professionals who are trained and certified, registered and/or licensed to provide Therapeutic Recreation.

(Adopted by the ATRA Board of Directors, 1987)

National Therapeutic Recreation Society

Practiced in clinical, residential and community settings, the profession of therapeutic recreation uses treatment, education and recreation services to help people with illnesses, disabilities and other conditions to develop and use their leisure in ways that enhance their health, independence and well-being.

(Approved by the NTRS Board of Directors, February, 1994)

Appendix B

Standards of Practice

American Therapeutic Recreation Association Standards for the Practice of Therapeutic Recreation[5]

Developed by the American Therapeutic Recreation Association, the Standards reflect levels of service provision for therapeutic recreation professionals to implement in a variety of settings. The following twelve Standards are further described by structure, process and outcome criteria in the original document, providing clarity and directions to the individual therapeutic recreation professional. The Standards will assist the therapeutic recreation professional in assuring the systematic provision of quality therapeutic recreation services.

Standard 1: The therapeutic recreation specialist conducts an individualized assessment to collect systematic, comprehensive and accurate data necessary to determine a course of action and subsequent individualized treatment plan.

Standard 2: The therapeutic recreation specialist plans and develops the individualized treatment plan that identifies goals, objectives and treatment intervention strategies.

Standard 3: The therapeutic recreation specialist implements the individualized treatment plan using appropriate intervention strategies to restore, remediate or rehabilitate in order to improve functioning and independence as well as reduce or eliminate the effects of

[5] ATRA Standards of Practice Task Force
American Therapeutic Recreation Association, 1991.
For further information see: American Therapeutic Recreation Association, *Standards for the Practice of Therapeutic Recreation & Self Assessment Guide.* Hattiesburg, MS: American Therapeutic Recreation Association.

illness or disability. Implementation of the treatment plan by the therapeutic recreation specialist is consistent with the overall patient/client treatment program.

Standard 4: The therapeutic recreation specialist systematically evaluates and compares the client's response to the individualized treatment plan. The treatment plan is revised based upon changes in the interventions, diagnosis and patient/client responses.

Standard 5: The therapeutic recreation specialist develops a discharge plan in collaboration with the patient/client, family, and other treatment team members in order to continue treatment, as appropriate.

Standard 6: Recreation opportunities are available to patients/clients to promote or improve their general health and well-being.

Standard 7: The therapeutic recreation specialist adheres to the ATRA Code of Ethics.

Standard 8: The therapeutic recreation department is governed by a written plan of operation that is based upon *ATRA Standards of the Practice of Therapeutic Recreation* and standards of other accrediting/regulatory agencies, as appropriate.

Standard 9: The therapeutic recreation department has established provisions for assuring that therapeutic recreation staff maintain appropriate credentials and have opportunities for professional development.

Standard 10: Within the therapeutic recreation department, there exists an objective and systematic quality improvement program for the purposes of monitoring and evaluating the quality and appropriateness of care, and to identify and resolve problems in order to improve therapeutic recreation services.

Standard 11: Therapeutic recreation services are provided in an effective and efficient manner that reflects the reasonable and appropriate use of resources.

Standard 12: The therapeutic recreation department engages in routine, systematic program evaluation and research for the purpose of determining appropriateness and efficacy.

National Therapeutic Recreation Society
Standards of Practice
for Therapeutic Recreation Services[6]

Standard 1: Scope of Service

Treatment services are available which are goal-oriented and directed toward rehabilitation, amelioration and/or modification of specific physical, emotional, cognitive, and/or social functional behaviors. Therapeutic recreation intervention targeting these functional behaviors is warranted when the behaviors impede or otherwise inhibit participation in reasonable and customary leisure participation. (Note: This may not apply to all therapeutic recreation settings for all clients.)

Leisure education services are available which are goal-oriented and directed toward the development of knowledge, attitudes, values, behaviors, skills, and resources related to socialization and leisure involvement. (Note: This may not apply for all clients.)

Recreation services are available that provide a variety of activities designed to meet client needs, competencies, aptitudes, capabilities and interest. These services are directed toward optimizing client leisure involvement and are designed to promote health and well-being, and improve the quality of life.

Standard 2: Mission and Purpose, Goals and Objectives

Mission, purpose, goals and specific objectives are formulated and stated for each type of therapeutic recreation service based upon the philosophy and goals of the agency. These are then translated into operational procedures and serve as a blueprint for program evaluation.

Standard 3: Individual Treatment/Program Plan

The therapeutic recreation specialist develops an individualized treatment/program plan for each client referred to the agency for therapeutic recreation services.

---

[6] These are the major headings from the Standards of Practice. For further information see: National Therapeutic Recreation Society, *Standards of Practice for Therapeutic Recreation Services and Annotated Bibliography.* Ashburn, VA: National Recreation and Park Association.

Standard 4: Documentation
The therapeutic recreation specialist records specific information based on client assessment, involvement, and progress. Information pertaining to the client is recorded on a regular basis as determined by the agency policy and procedures, and accrediting body standards.

Standard 5: Plan of Operation
Therapeutic recreation services are considered a viable aspect of treatment, rehabilitation, normalization and development. Appropriate and fair scheduling of services, facilities, personnel and resources is vital to client progress and the operation of therapeutic recreation services. See the *NTRS Guidelines for the Administration of Therapeutic Recreation Services* (1990)[7] for additional reference information.

Standard 6: Personnel Qualifications
Therapeutic recreation services are conducted by therapeutic recreation specialists whose training and experiences have prepared them to be effective at the functions they perform. Therapeutic recreation specialists have opportunities for involvement in professional development and life-long learning.

Standard 7: Ethical Responsibilities
Professionals are committed to advancing the use of therapeutic recreation services in order to ensure quality, protection, and to promote the rights of persons receiving services.

Standard 8: Evaluation and Research
Therapeutic recreation specialists implement client and service-related evaluation and research functions to maintain and improve the quality, effectiveness, and integrity of therapeutic recreation services.

---

[7] National Therapeutic Recreation Society. (1990). *Guidelines for the Administration of Therapeutic Recreation Services.* Ashburn, VA: National Recreation and Park Association.

Appendix C

Codes of Ethics

American Therapeutic Recreation Association Code of Ethics[8]

The American Therapeutic Recreation Association acts as an advocate for members of the Therapeutic Recreation profession and consumers. ATRA's objectives include:

- to promote and advance public awareness and understanding of Therapeutic Recreation.
- to develop and promote professional standards for Therapeutic Recreation services with education, habilitation, rehabilitation, and medical treatment of individuals in need of services.
- to support and conduct research and demonstration efforts to improve service.
- to support and conduct educational opportunities for Therapeutic Recreation professionals.

The American Therapeutic Recreation Association's Code of Ethics is intended to be used as a guide for promoting and maintaining the highest standards of ethical behavior. The code applies to all therapeutic recreation personnel. The term therapeutic recreation personnel includes certified therapeutic recreation specialists (CTRS). certified therapeutic recreation assistants (CTRA) and therapeutic recreation students. Acceptance of membership in the American Therapeutic Recreation Association commits a member to adherence to these principles.

---

[8] ATRA Ethics Committee, March 1990.

Principle 1: Beneficence/Non-Maleficence

Therapeutic recreation personnel shall treat persons in an ethical manner not only by respecting their decisions and protecting them from harm but also by actively making efforts to secure their well-being. Personnel strive to maximize possible benefits, and minimize possible harms. This serves as the guiding principle for the profession. The term "persons" includes not only persons served but colleagues, agencies and the profession.

Principal 2: Autonomy

Therapeutic recreation personnel have a duty to preserve and protect the right of each individual to make his/her own choices. Each individual is to be given the opportunity to determine his/her own course of action in accordance with a plan freely chosen.

Principal 3: Justice

Therapeutic recreation personnel are responsible for ensuring that individuals are served fairly and that there is equity in the distribution of services. Individuals receive service without regard to race, color, creed, gender, sexual orientation, age, disability/disease, social and financial status.

Principal 4: Fidelity

Therapeutic recreation personnel have an obligation to be truthful, faithful and meet commitments made to persons receiving services, colleagues, agencies and the profession.

Principal 5: Veracity/Informed Consent

Therapeutic recreation personnel are responsible for providing each individual receiving service with information regarding the service and the professional's training and credentials, benefits, outcomes, length of treatment, expected activities, risks, and limitations. Each individual receiving service has the right to know what is likely to take place during and as a result of professional intervention. Informed consent is obtained when information is provided by the professional.

Principal 6: Confidentiality and Privacy

Therapeutic recreation personnel are responsible for safeguarding information about individuals served. Individuals served have the right to control information about themselves. When a situation arises that requires disclosure of confidential information about an individual to protect the individual's welfare or the interest of others, the therapeutic recreation professional has the responsibility/obligation to inform the individual served of the circumstances in which confidentiality was broken.

Principal 7: Competence
Therapeutic recreation personnel have the responsibility to continually seek to expand one's knowledge base related to therapeutic recreation practice. The professional is responsible for keeping a record of participation in training activities. The professional has the responsibility for contributing to changes in the profession through activities such as research, dissemination of information through publications and professional presentations, and through active involvement in professional organizations.

Principal 8: Compliance with Laws & Regulations
Therapeutic recreation personnel are responsible for complying with local, state and federal laws and ATRA policies governing the profession of therapeutic recreation.

National Therapeutic Recreation Society
Code of Ethics[9]

Preamble

Leisure, recreation, and play are inherent aspects of the human experience, and are essential to health and well-being. All people, therefore, have an inalienable right to leisure and the opportunities it affords for play and recreation. Some human beings have disabilities, illnesses or social conditions which may limit their participation in the normative structure of society. These persons have the same need for and right to leisure, recreation, and play.

Accordingly, the purpose of therapeutic recreation is to facilitate leisure, recreation, and play for persons with physical, mental, emotional or social limitations in order to promote their health and well-being. This goal is accomplished through professional services delivered in clinical and community settings. Services are intended to develop skills and knowledge, to foster values and attitudes, and to maximize independence by decreasing barriers and by increasing ability and opportunity.

The National Therapeutic Recreation Society exists to promote the development of therapeutic recreation in order to ensure quality services and protect and promote the rights of persons receiving services. The National Therapeutic Recreation Society and its members are morally obligated to contribute to the health and well-being of the people they serve. In order to meet this important social responsibility, the National Therapeutic Recreation Society and its members endorse and practice the following ethical principles.

I. The Obligation of Professional Virtue

Professionals possess and practice the virtues of integrity, honesty, fairness, competence, diligence, and self-awareness.

A. Integrity: Professionals act in ways that protect, preserve and promote the soundness and completeness of their commitment to service. Professionals do not forsake nor arbitrarily compromise their principles. They strive for unity,

---

[9] Approved by the NTRS Board of Directors, 1990.

fairness, and consistency of character. Professionals exhibit personal and professional qualities conducive to the highest ideals of human service.

B. Honesty: Professionals are truthful. They do not misrepresent themselves, their knowledge, their abilities, or their profession. Their communications are sufficiently complete, accurate, and clear in order for individuals to understand the intent and implications of services.

C. Fairness: Professionals are just. They do not place individuals at unwarranted advantage or disadvantage. They distribute resources and services according to principles of equity.

D. Competence: Professionals function to the best of their knowledge and skill. They only render services and employ techniques of which they are qualified by training and experience. They recognize their limitations and seek to reduce them by expanding their expertise. Professionals continually enhance their knowledge and skills through education and by remaining informed of professional and social trends, issues and developments.

E. Diligence: Professionals are earnest and conscientious. Their time, energy, and professional resources are efficiently used to meet the needs of the persons they serve.

F. Awareness: Professional are aware of how their personal needs, desires, values, and interests may influence their professional actions. They are especially cognizant of where their personal needs may interfere with the needs of the persons they serve.

II. The Obligation of the Professional to the Individual

A. Well-Being: Professionals' foremost concern is the well-being of the people they serve. They do everything reasonable in their power and within the scope of professional practice to benefit them. Above all, professionals cause no harm.

B. Loyalty: Professionals' first loyalty is to the well-being of the individuals they serve. In instances of multiple loyalties, professionals make the nature and the priority of their loyalties explicit to everyone concerned, especially where they may be in question or in conflict.

C. Respect: Professionals respect the people they serve. They show regard for their intrinsic worth and for their potential to grow and change. The following areas of respect merit special attention:

1. Freedom, Autonomy, and Self-Determination: Professionals respect the ability of people to make, execute, and take responsibility for their own choices. Individuals are given adequate opportunity for self-determination in the least restrictive environment possible. Individuals have the right of informed consent. They may refuse participation in any program except where their welfare is clearly and immediately threatened and where they are unable to make rational decisions on their own due to temporary or permanent incapacity. Professionals promote independence and avoid fostering dependence. In particular, sexual relations and other manipulative behaviors intended to control individuals for the personal needs of the professional are expressly unethical.

2. Privacy: Professionals respect the privacy of individuals. Communications are kept confidential except with the explicit consent of the individual or where the welfare of the individual or others is clearly imperiled. Individuals are informed of the nature and the scope of confidentiality.

D. Professional Practices: Professionals provide quality services based on the highest professional standards. Professional abide by standards set by the profession, deviating only when justified by the needs of the individual. Care is used in administering tests and other measurement instruments. They are used only for their express purposes. Instruments should conform to accepted psychometric standards. The nature of all practices, including tests and measurements, are explained to individuals. Individuals are also debriefed on the results and the implications of professional practices. All professional practices are conducted with the safety and well-being of the individual in mind.

III. The Obligation of the Professional to Other Individuals and to Society

A. General Welfare: Professionals make certain that their actions do not harm others. They also seek to promote the general welfare of society by advocating the importance of leisure, recreation and play.

B. Fairness: Professionals are fair to other individuals and to the general public. They seek to balance the needs of the individuals they serve with the needs of other persons according to principles of equity.

IV. The Obligation of the Professional to Colleagues

A. Respect: Professionals show respect for colleagues and their respective professions. They take no action that undermines the integrity of their colleagues.

B. Cooperation and Support: Professionals cooperate with and support their colleagues for the benefit of the persons they serve. Professionals demand the highest professional and moral conduct of each other. They approach and offer help to colleagues who require assistance with an ethical problem. Professionals take appropriate action toward colleagues who behave unethically.

V. The Obligation of the Professional to the Profession

A. Knowledge: Professionals work to increase and improve the profession's body of knowledge by supporting and/or by conducting research. Research is practiced according to accepted canons and ethics of scientific inquiry. Where subjects are involved, their welfare is paramount. Prior permission is gained from subjects to participate in research. They are informed of the general nature of the research and any specific risks that may be involved. Subjects are de-briefed at the conclusion of the research, and are provided with results of the study on request.

B. Respect: Professionals treat the profession with critical respect. They strive to protect, preserve, and promote the integrity of the profession and its commit-ment to public service.

C. Reform: Professionals are committed to regular and continuous evaluation of the profession. Changes are implemented that improve the profession's ability to serve society.

VI. The Obligation of the Profession to Society

A. Service: The profession exists to serve society. All of its activities and re-sources are devoted to the principle of service.

B. Equality: The profession is committed to equality of opportunity. No person shall be refused service because of race, gender, religion, social status, ethnic background, sexual orientation, or inability to pay. The profession neither con-ducts nor condones discriminatory practices. It actively seeks to correct inequi-ties that unjustly discriminate.

C. Advocacy: The profession advocates for the people it is entrusted to serve. It protects and promotes their health and well-being and their inalienable right to leisure, recreation, and play in clinical and community settings.

Contributors

Leandra A. Bedini, PhD, CTRS Associate Professor in the Department of Recreation, Parks and Tourism, University of North Caroline at Greensboro. Dr. Bedini is currently the Project Director of a federal grant titled, "Training of Minority Students in Therapeutic Recreation" and is interested in research related to the study of leisure and caregivers of older adults, attitudes toward people with disabilities and leisure education. In 1997 she was awarded the National Therapeutic Recreation Society's Professional Research Award.

Thomas M. Blaschko, MA Editor-In-Chief, Idyll Arbor, Inc.

Frank Brasile, PhD, CTRS Professor of Recreational Therapy in the School of HPER at the University of Nebraska, Omaha. Dr. Brasile has served as a board member and President of the American Therapeutic Recreation Association and coach of the USA Women's Wheelchair Basketball Team.

Charles C. Bullock, PhD, Chair, Department of Health Ecology, University of Nevada at Reno. During his professional career Dr. Bullock has written, presented and consulted extensively in the area of therapeutic recreation as a related service in special education.

joan burlingame, CTRS, ABDA, HTR Ms. burlingame is the President of Idyll Arbor, Inc. and works as an on-call therapist at Harborview Medical Center in Seattle, WA. In addition to her twenty years of clinical experience, she has also worked as a consultant and as a state surveyor for the State of Washington.

Cynthia Carruthers, PhD, CTRS Associate Professor, Leisure Studies Program at the University of Nevada, Las Vegas. Dr. Carruthers has done the majority of her of research in the areas of addiction and mental health.

Peg Connolly, PhD, CTRS Executive Director of NCTRC since 1986.

Catherine P. Coyle, PhD, CTRS Associate Professor, Department of Health Studies, Temple University. Dr. Coyle teaches in the undergraduate and graduate program in Therapeutic Recreation and has an active research agenda examining leisure and quality of life issues among individuals with physical disabilities. She is currently the principle investigator on a three year research grant funded by NCMRR on health promotion among women with physical disabilities.

Patti Gorham Ms. Gorham is the administrator of the Great Plains Paralyzed Veterans of America Education Center. In that capacity she also provides training and consultation relative to ADA compliance strategies.

Alice Gustafson Shareholder in the law firm of Graham & Dunn. Ms. Gustafson has been practicing law for twenty-two years specializing in a variety of practice areas including copyright.

Ann James, PhD, CTRS Recreational therapy historian, Dr. James, coordinates the recreation therapy program at Clemson University. She is a former president of NTRS and former member of the Board of Directors of ATRA.

Danny E. Johnson, PhD, CTRS Assistant Professor, Department of Health, Physical Education and Recreation at the University of North Carolina, Wilmington. Dr. Johnson is currently doing research on the development of friendship in children with disabilities and on the impact of including families in leisure education.

René P. Katsinas, RhD, CTRS Assistant Professor, Sport Management, Recreation and Tourism Division, School of Human Movement, Sport, and Leisure Studies at Bowling Green State University. Dr. Katsinas has helped draw attention to the issue of excess disability and the role of the recreational therapist in remediating the conditions that create excess disability.

Betsy S. Kennedy, MEd, CTRS Instructor, Department of Exercise Science, Physical Education and Recreation, Old Dominion University. Prior to joining the faculty at Old Dominion, Ms. Kennedy worked in physical rehabilitation specializing in brain injury and neurological disorders.

Miriam P. Lahey, EdD Associate Professor, Department of Health Services, Chair, Core Curriculum, Lehman College, City University of New York. Dr. Lahey is a past chair of NTRS's Ethics Committee and has special interests in the areas of professional ethics, cognitive rehabilitation and philosophy of leisure.

Marjorie J. Malkin, EdD, CTRS Associate Professor in the Department of Health, Education and Recreation at Southern Illinois University, Carbondale. She has presented and published nationally and internationally on recreation therapy interventions in psychiatric and substance abuse treatment and on research methods in recreational therapy.

Nancy D. Montgomery, MA, CTRS Instructor of Recreation and Leisure Studies, Virginia Wesleyan College. Ms. Montgomery started the Virginia Beach Parks and Recreation Therapeutic Recreation Program in 1975, and has continued to support the use of therapeutic recreation in the community since that time.

Linda O. Niemeyer, PhD, OTR Research Coordinator at Rehabilitation Technology Works in San Bernardino, CA and also an Adjunct Instructor of Clinical Occupational Therapy at the University of Southern California, Department of Occupational Science and Occupational Therapy. Dr. Niemeyer specializes in promoting outcome research in clinical practice using state-of-the-art information technologies.

Michael Rhodes, MA, CTRS Program Manager, Inpatient Rehabilitation Unit at Crittenton Hospital, Rochester, MI. Mr. Rhodes is a past president of the American Therapeutic Recreation Association.

Nancy Rickerson, OTR/L Supervisor of Psychiatric Occupational Therapy, Physical Therapy and Therapeutic Recreation. Ms. Rickerson has been a practitioner for eighteen years with the majority of her experience in psychiatry. She is a member of Harbor Medical Center's (Seattle, WA) clinical pathway committee.

Carmen V. Russoniello, EdD, CTRS Dr. Russoniello is a past president of the American Therapeutic Recreation Association.

Judi Singley, MEd, ACC Ms. Singley is the Coordinator of the Recreation and Leisure Services Program at Greenfield Community College, Greenfield, MA. She is actively involved in the National Certification Council for Activity Professionals (NCCAP) and currently serves on NCCAP's committees related to the education and training of activity professionals.

Thomas K. Skalko, PhD, TRS/CTRS Professor and Chair of Recreation and
Leisure Studies, School of Health and Human Performance, East Carolina University. Dr. Skalko has been actively involved in professional
preparation and public policy issues.

Melany Bailey Spielman, PhD, CTRS, RTC Associate Professor, Coordinator
of Recreation Therapy, Department of Recreation and Community
Service, California State University, Hayward. After twenty years as a
recreational therapist in rehabilitation, mental health, chronic pain and
cancer, Dr. Bailey returned to the University of Oregon for her graduate work.

Index

D

E